The Reading and Preaching
of the Scriptures
in the
Worship of the Christian Church

Volume 4

THE AGE OF THE REFORMATION

The Reading and Preaching
of the Scriptures
in the
Worship of the Christian Church

Volume 4

THE AGE OF THE REFORMATION

Hughes Oliphant Old

WILLIAM B. EERDMANS PUBLISHING COMPANY
GRAND RAPIDS, MICHIGAN / CAMBRIDGE, U.K.

Wm. B. Eerdmans Publishing Co.

255 Jefferson Ave. S.E., Grand Rapids, Michigan 49503 /
P.O. Box 163, Cambridge CB3 9PU U.K.

Printed in the United States of America

07 06 05 04 03 02   7 6 5 4 3 2 1

Library of Congress Cataloging-in-Publication Data

Old, Hughes Oliphant.
The reading and preaching of the Scriptures in the worship of the Christian church /
Hughes Oliphant Old.
p.   cm.
Includes bibliographical references and index.
Contents: v. 4. The age of the Reformation.
ISBN 0-8028-4775-7 (alk. paper)
1. Preaching — History.   2. Public worship — History.
3. Bible — Homiletical use.   4. Bible — Liturgical use.
I. Title.
BV4207.043   2002

264'.34 — dc21   97-30624
                                                      CIP

www.eerdmans.com

Contents

CHAPTER II
The Counter-Reformation   158

CHAPTER III

The Puritans

CHAPTER VI

The Flowering of Protestant Orthodoxy in France

CHAPTER VII

The Flowering of Protestant Orthodoxy in the Netherlands

Preface

Having gotten to volume IV of the planned seven volumes of this work, I find myself feeling rather relieved. More than half of it has appeared. Most of the remaining three volumes is written. It is coming out *Deo volente!* Even more, I find myself very thankful. A large part of the work has been done. With the thanksgiving there are certain debts of gratitude.

There have been some big changes in my life since the first two volumes have come out. A particularly significant change has been my taking up teaching responsibilities at Princeton Theological Seminary. It was in 1955 that I first stepped onto this campus. The last half of the twentieth century has passed by since then. It is not as though I have been here all the time. For longer or shorter periods of time I have been to plenty of other places, but this is the place to which I always return. Here is where I mark the highs and lows of the ever changing theological tide.

As I look around myself in the closing months of the twentieth century, I find myself lecturing to students who are at home in a completely different world than I once knew here in this idyllic green town. In just a few months now they will be going out into the third Christian millennium. It is a world which I, too, hope to enter, but I will enter it as an old man. And yet I am determined to go with my students. In fact, they seem to be pulling me with them, and I am really rather excited about going along. If for no other reason, I want to be able to cheer them along. Maybe I should just get out of the way and let them start their own new century. But then, too, maybe I can be of help just telling them they are doing a good job.

Holy history is in their favor. God has a way of pouring out his Spirit new in every age.

". . . I will pour out my spirit on all flesh;
your sons and your daughters shall prophesy,
    your old men shall dream dreams,
    and your young men shall see visions."

(Joel 2:28 RSV)

When I started this study in the mid-eighties, the song seemed to be "Where have all the preachers gone?" The Great American School had apparently run its course. But now, when I go to chapel and hear my students, I hear a different song. I think a new school of American preaching is already on the horizon.

But another change has been getting to know Robb Redman and Chuck Fromm. Robb was directing the Doctor of Ministries program at Fuller Seminary at the time, and was working with pastors who had little interest in the liturgical renewal movement but were interested in contemporary Christian worship. It was Robb who hooked me up with Chuck Fromm and Maranatha! Music. What a surprise! That the editor of *Worship Leader* would be interested in the sort of thing I was writing amazed me. When I discovered that he was passing out copies of the first two volumes of my work on preaching to Calvary Chapel pastors, he disarmed me completely. I thank Chuck Fromm for drawing me into the discussion he is so vigorously pursuing.

Slowly it was beginning to dawn on me that I was talking to a bunch of people I had never envisioned. Then came the invitations to lecture at Reformed Theological Seminary in Charlotte, North Carolina. In talking to the students there, I realized I was coming into contact with a completely new generation of young Christians who were asking very different questions about worship than their grandparents. What was coming into focus was an audience I could hardly have imagined.

As all this was going on I kept being invited to Korea. I taught a course on the history of Protestant worship at the Asian Center for Theological Studies in Seoul. The course was translated by Professor Jung Kyu-Nam, and much of the credit for the success of the course is surely due to him. To him I am particularly grateful! Then there was Dr. Song Tse-Gun, who served as my guide around that exciting land. I will never forget the train ride from Seoul down to Kyung-Ju, the ancient capital of Korea, and looking out the window at night and seeing all the illuminated crosses in every town and village. As the third Christian millennium begins, the Christian faith is now firmly planted on the mainland of East Asia.

Each time I have taught in Korea, several students from Young Nak Presbyterian Church have been so generous in taking the time to translate the services I have attended in their church and have helped me understand what was happening in those inspiring worship assemblies. It is an amazingly healthy church that I found there. It is so different! I give the remarkable pastor of the Hallelujah Church, Dr. Kim Sang-Bok, credit for giving me a glimpse of what the Church of the future is going to be. Each of the three times I have been to Korea I have had the opportunity to worship in the Hallelujah Church. Most recently I was able to participate in the beautiful new house of prayer they are building in the mountains south of Seoul. Nothing encourages me about the future of the Church quite so much as my visits to Korea! To my Korean friends I want to express my very special appreciation.

One of the big advantages in teaching is having enthusiastic students who have aided me in one way or another. Joshua Wait has served as a special theological computer "techie." Christian Andrews and Roger McDaniel have acted as research assistants, digging up material I would never have found otherwise. To them I am especially appreciative.

With these remarks I lay down the pen for volume IV.

3 September 1999

CHAPTER I

The Reformation

I. Introduction — the Reformation of Preaching

The classical Protestant Reformation produced a distinct school of preaching. It was a preaching of reform, to be sure, but it was also a reform of preaching. Our concern in this work is primarily with the Reformation as a reform of preaching, although we can hardly ignore the reform that was preached.

One thing we want to be very clear about in our study is the continuity between the preaching of the classical Protestant Reformation and the preaching which had gone before it. One will never get a clear appreciation of Reformation preaching without an appreciation for the preaching of the Middle Ages. There was a tremendous amount of preaching in the Middle Ages, and much of it was of a high quality. It was done with both learning and devotion. We would be terribly misled if we imagined that the Protestant Reformers rediscovered preaching. The Church in which the Reformers were born and brought up loved preaching. It was highly cultivated and richly endowed. If anything was wrong with it, it was too richly endowed, too institutionalized. It was a bit like the churches in which it took place: flamboyant and gothic. What happened was that with the Reformation came a refocusing of preaching, a rethinking of its purpose and a reevaluation of its relation to the worship of the Church.[1] In this chapter we hope to discover exactly what that reform was.

1. Cf. Alfred Niebergall, "Die Geschichte der christlichen Predigt," in *Leiturgia,*

1

As we have seen, there had been reforms of preaching before. The Antiochene School of preaching was an attempt at the reform of preaching. Both Caesarius of Arles and Gregory the Great aimed at a reform of preaching. The Dominicans made significant preaching reforms, Humbert of Romans taking it in a pastoral direction and Thomas Aquinas showing its potential for the theological education of the faithful. The Franciscan reform was a preaching reform of the most thorough sort. Begun by Saint Francis, this school of reform was developed in different ways by Anthony of Padua, Bonaventure, and others, although certain aspects of the Franciscan reform were constant among them all.

The point we want to make in this chapter is that the Reformation produced a school of preaching. Luther sparked a movement, and surely he is to be regarded as its initiator, but what he began others developed in ways that gave the movement increasing power and depth.[2] Zwingli, the Reformer of Zürich, initially inspired by Luther, was also inspired by the preaching ministry of John Chrysostom. Zwingli carried the prophetic zeal of the great patriarch of Constantinople into the social and political spheres of Swiss society. In the same way Oecolampadius, the Reformer of Basel, studied the sermons of the Fathers and modeled his preaching on their work. In 1523 he published a Latin translation of Chrysostom's sermons on Genesis and demonstrated the value of preaching a grammatical-historical interpretation of the Old Testament. His historical work encouraged the Reformers to turn from the allegorical exegesis of the Alexandrian School to the more sober exegesis of Antioch. The Reformers of Strasbourg developed a number of the pastoral and liturgical dimensions of this reform. They rendered particular service in developing the liturgical setting of preaching in the context of prayer, praise, the celebration of the sacraments, and the giving of alms, which emphasized that the reading and preaching of Scripture is above all the worship of God. Cal-

---

Handbuch des Evangelischen Gottesdienstes, ed. Karl Ferdinand Müller and Walter Blankenburg, 5 vols. (Kassel: Johannes Stauda Verlag, 1955), 2:25ff.

2. While there are clear similarities between the reform of preaching led by Luther and that led by Francis of Assisi on one hand and Dominic on the other, there are also a number of differences. One is clearly the fact that the reforms of Francis and Dominic developed independently of each other. Therefore, in the previous volume, one chapter was given to the Franciscans and another to the Dominicans. The situation was very different in regard to Luther, Zwingli, and the south German Reformers. Zwingli, Oecolampadius, Bucer, and Calvin were clearly dependent on Luther while Dominic was not dependent on Francis, nor Francis on Dominic.

vin, the supreme exegete of the Reformation, worked his way through the bulk of Holy Scripture, setting a high standard for expository preaching. In many ways Calvin was the Jerome of his day, picking up the unfinished work of the *vir trilinguis* and bringing it a thousand years forward. A number of preachers took the reform to England and Scotland. Of these, John Knox is by far the best known.[3] Hugh Latimer, on the other hand, preached the Reformation using the approach of the old Scholastic *ars predicandi*. There are many more whose contributions we will want to study, yet the inspiring figure of Martin Luther will always be pivotal to this reform.

II. Martin Luther (1483-1546)

Luther had the best academic credentials the medieval German church could confer.[4] He began his university studies in 1501 and earned his

3. While John Knox should be treated in this chapter, we will reserve consideration of his ministry for a subsequent volume, where we will treat him as one who shaped the Scottish School of preaching.

4. From the tremendous amount of literature available on the life and thought of Luther, the following have been found especially helpful: Paul Althaus, *Die Theologie Martin Luthers*, 2nd ed. (Gütersloh: Gerd Mohn, 1963); James Atkinson, *Martin Luther and the Birth of Protestantism* (Harmondsworth: Penguin Books, 1968); Roland H. Bainton, *Here I Stand: A Life of Martin Luther* (New York: New American Library, 1955); Ernst Bizer, *Fides ex auditu*, 3rd ed. (Neukirchen-Vluyn: Neukirchener Verlag, 1966); Heinrich Bornkamm, *Luther's World of Thought*, trans. Martin H. Bertram (St. Louis: Concordia Publishing House, 1958); Heinrich Bornkamm, *Martin Luther in der Mitte seines Lebens* (Göttingen: Vandenhoeck und Ruprecht, 1979); Martin Brecht, *Martin Luther*, 3 vols. (Minneapolis: Fortress Press, 1985-93); Gerhard Brendler, *Martin Luther, Theology and Revolution*, trans. Claude R. Foster, Jr. (New York and Oxford: Oxford University Press, 1991); Helmut Diwald, *Luther, Eine Biographie* (Bergisch Gladbach: Gustav Lübbe Verlag, 1982); Gerhard Ebeling, *Luther: An Introduction to His Thought*, trans. R. A. Wilson (Philadelphia: Fortress Press, 1970); Mark U. Edwards, *Luther and the False Brethren* (Stanford: Stanford University Press, 1975); Brian A. Gerrish, *Grace and Reason: A Study in the Theology of Luther* (Oxford: Clarendon Press, 1962); Emanuel Hirsch, *Lutherstudien*, 2 vols. (Gütersloh: C. Bertelsmann, 1954); Karl Holl, *Gesammelte Aufsätze zur Kirchengeschichte*, 6th ed., 3 vols. (Tübingen: J. C. B. Mohr [Paul Siebeck], 1932); Heiko A. Oberman, *Luther: Man between God and the Devil* (New Haven: Yale University Press, 1989); Heiko A. Oberman, *Die Reformation von Wittenberg nach Genf* (Göttingen: Vandenhoeck und Ruprecht, 1986); Steven Ozment, *The Age of Reform (1250-1550): An Intellectual and Religious History of Late Medieval and Reformation Europe* (New Haven and London: Yale University Press, 1980); Ernest G. Schwiebert, *The Reformation*, 2 vols. (Minneapolis: Fortress

bachelor of arts and master of arts degrees at the University of Erfurt, one of the largest and best-attended universities in Germany. During those years he studied the Latin classics and even attained a basic knowledge of Greek. He had at least an introduction to the methods of Renaissance humanism and its approach to literary criticism. His studies continued for years. In 1509 he earned his bachelor of theology degree in biblical studies at the University of Wittenberg. Then he turned to systematic theology, lecturing at Erfurt on the *Sentences* of Peter Lombard. This was the fundamental discipline of the medieval universities for the formation of its leading theologians. Finally, in 1512 he received his doctor of theology, returning then to the University of Wittenberg to become professor of biblical studies, a position he occupied to the end of his life. Luther was as well trained in the academic disciplines of theology as anyone in Germany, or for that matter, in Christendom.

Luther's spiritual training was of an equally high order. As a boy he spent a year at the cathedral school of Magdeburg, which at the time was under the leadership of the Brethren of the Common Life. This school gave him a thorough grounding in the pietism of late medieval nominalism. Only after earning his master of arts degree at the University of Erfurt did he enter the monastic life, choosing the Augustinian cloister in Erfurt, which was considered the strictest religious community in that vigorously devout university town. As he advanced in his theological studies, he increasingly came under the influence of the more classical sort of Scholasticism advocated by Thomas Aquinas. His sensitive and learned spiritual director, Johann von Staupitz, was a *via antiqua* theologian. But at the same time, Luther studied the works of Augustine, the patron of his order. By the time he had received his doctorate, the future Reformer had been thoroughly initiated into the intellectual and devotional world of late medieval Christianity.

It was Staupitz who laid the yoke of the preaching ministry on Luther's shoulders. He recognized Luther's thirst for the things of God, the sincerity of his wrestling with the questions of faith and doubt, and his keen insight into spiritual matters. Luther understood this call to preach as a call from God himself.

Once Luther had received his doctorate, he was assigned the chair of biblical studies at the University of Wittenberg. He began to lecture on

---

Press, 1993); and David C. Steinmetz, *Luther and Staupitz: An Essay in the Intellectual Origins of the Protestant Reformation* (Durham, N.C.: Duke University Press, 1980).

the Psalms, then the apostle Paul's Epistle to the Romans, followed by Galatians and Hebrews. These five years were crucial to him. His study of the Scriptures was very thorough and very profound. It was out of this study that his new appreciation of the gospel began to open up.

Luther may have had all the theological credentials, but he was no mere academic. Luther was a passionate thinker. He did theology with his heart. The sheer awesomeness of God brought him to his knees. He was determined to win God's favor. As he worked on his lectures for his students and preached several times every week at the town church in Wittenberg, he began to realize that the whole point of the gospel is that God out of his love for us has given us his Son that we might be saved through faith in him. As he found it in the Gospel of John, "For God so loved the world that he gave his only Son, that whoever believes in him should not perish but have eternal life" (John 3:16 RSV). We don't have to win God's favor. Christ has done that for us. His sacrifice on the cross has atoned for all our sins. It is sufficient for our salvation. This gracious saving act proves God's righteousness. When we recognize this and put our faith in God's righteousness, then God receives us as righteous. When we come to believe in the grace of God, the whole relationship changes. We begin to trust God and follow God's ways. All this was summed up in the words of the apostle Paul, who said concerning the gospel, "It is the power of God for salvation to every one who has faith. . . . For in it the righteousness of God is revealed through faith for faith; as it is written, 'He who through faith is righteous shall live'" (Rom. 1:16-17 RSV).

Paul's teaching on justification by faith took the anxiety out of religion for Luther. Luther had for years submitted himself to the disciplines of medieval spirituality. They had not given him the peace they promised, but in his study of the Bible he rediscovered the gospel and began to preach it in the pulpit of the town church of Wittenberg. Preaching for Luther was above all the preaching of the gospel.

Luther is a many-faceted Reformer. It can hardly surprise us that his preaching has many facets, too. As we shall see, his preaching ministry covered in one way or another most of the preaching genres we have already discussed. He had much to say on how the ministry of the Word should be exercised, and much to say on the theology of preaching. His sermons were taken down by stenographers, so that the collection of his sermons is extensive. In his *postils* he provided other preachers with an abundance of preaching material. And yet with all his popularity, Luther made no attempt to be a great orator. He had none of the rhetorical cul-

5

ture that Basil, Chrysostom, or Augustine had. Luther was a popular preacher with a natural mastery of language. He taught the preachers of the Reformation to preach in the language of the people. The effect of all this was to make German a literate language which could convey the most profound devotion and the most refined theology. He was a reformer of the language of preaching as well as its content.[5]

Luther did have the standard training in rhetoric which was part of a university education in the late Middle Ages. Ulrich Nembach has shown that Luther had learned from the literary studies of the Renaissance to look at the traditional textbooks on rhetoric with a certain objectivity. Luther was critical of both Aristotle and Augustine. Quintilian, on the other hand, was very popular with Luther,[6] and a good teacher for him to follow. He taught Luther a rhetoric appropriate for a teacher who aimed at showing his listeners how to live a good life.[7] Among the Roman orators, Quintilian was relatively free of the affectations one usually associates with classical rhetoric, and, as Luther well understood, a preacher of the gospel has to get beyond rhetoric, as helpful as it may be.

Let us turn now to Luther's sermons.[8] The legacy of sermons Luther

---

5. On the preaching ministry of Luther, see the following: Ragnar Bring, *Luthers Anschauung von der Bibel* (Berlin: Lutherisches Verlaghaus, 1951); Gerhard Ebeling, *Evangelische Evangelienauslegung: Eine Untersuchung zu Luthers Hermeneutik,* 3rd ed. (Tübingen: J. C. B. Mohr [Paul Siebeck], 1991); Robert Frick, "Luther als Prediger, dargestellt auf Grund der Predigten über 1. Kor. 15 (1532/33)," *Lutherjahrbuch* 21 (1939): 28ff.; John O'Malley, "Lutheran Preachers," *Michigan Germanic Studies* 10 (1984): 3-16, reprinted in John O'Malley, *Religious Culture in the Sixteenth Century: Preaching, Rhetoric, Spirituality, and Reform* (Brookfield, Vt.: Variorum, 1993); Ulrich Nembach, *Predigt des Evangeliums, Luther als Prediger, Pädagoge und Rhetor* (Neukirchen-Vluyn: Neukirchener Verlag, 1972); Niebergall, "Die Geschichte der christlichen Predigt," 2:182-352; and Vilmos Vajta, *Die Theologie des Gottesdienstes bei Luther* (Göttingen: Vandenhoeck und Ruprecht, 1952).

6. Nembach, *Predigt,* pp. 124ff.

7. Nembach, *Predigt,* pp. 127-72.

8. For the text of Luther's sermons, see the following: Martin Luther, *Ausgewählte Werke,* ed. H. H. Borcherdt and Georg Merz, 3rd ed., 7 vols. (Munich: Chr. Kaiser Verlag, 1953-63), hereafter Luther, *Ausgewählte Werke* (Munich edition); Martin Luther, *D. Martin Luthers Werke kritische Gesamtausgabe,* ed. J. C. F. Knaakel et al., 67 vols. (Weimar: Hermann Bohlaus, 1883ff.), hereafter Luther, *Luthers Werke, Gesamtausgabe* (Weimar edition); and *Luther's Works,* ed. Jaroslav Pelikan and Helmut T. Lehmann, 55 vols. (St. Louis: Concordia Publishing House; Philadelphia: Fortress Press, 1955-76), hereafter Luther, *Works* (American edition).

has left us is enormous, and so we shall choose carefully in order to give an impression of the breadth of his preaching ministry.

A. Sermon Preached at Erfurt on the Journey to Worms, 7 April 1521

The whole preaching ministry of Martin Luther could well be regarded as prophetic. When he preached his series of expository sermons, when he preached the Gospels and Epistles of the lectionary, even when he preached his catechetical sermons, he spoke as a prophet who had a very distinct message for a very definite time. In all of his preaching he assails the abuses of the Church of his day and the culture and society in which he lived. Just as we shall see that Luther is always an expository preacher, so it is equally true that he was always a prophetic preacher.

There were a number of times, however, when Luther preached sermons which from the standpoint of literary form clearly belonged to the prophetic genre, the essence of which is that it is a creative word spoken at a critical time. Whether it was Isaiah meeting King Ahaz when he went out to inspect the fortifications of Jerusalem or Jean Gerson's sermon to the Council of Constance after the departure of John XXIII, timing plays an important role in prophetic preaching. Prophetic preaching is the right word for the right time. It is by nature occasional. Luther often preached on great occasions. One such sermon he preached was at Erfurt on his way to the Diet of Worms.[9]

Luther's journey to Worms was almost a triumphal procession. He had become to all levels of German society not only a prophetic voice, but a heroic figure. He had spoken a powerful word against ecclesiastical abuses which had remained uncorrected for centuries. Some of these were profoundly theological; some were matters of an antiquated church polity and discipline; others were matters of the complicated power politics of the German nation. It had been only a bit more than three years before that he had tacked his ninety-five theses on the church door at Wittenberg. Intended only as a challenge to the theologians and students of that peaceful university town, the document caught fire, igniting the

---

9. For the German text, see Luther, *Ausgewählte Werke* (Munich edition), 6:254-58; Luther, *Luthers Werke, Gesamtausgabe* (Weimar edition), 7:808-13; for an English translation, see Luther, *Works* (American edition), 51:60-61.

whole of Germany. Luther's challenge was taken up all over Germany. It was debated not only by theologians and university students but by shopkeepers, poets, peasants, and princes. And now Luther had been summoned to the imperial diet of Worms, where he and all Germany expected that he would have the chance to lay his prophetic word before the highest authority of the German nation. The anticipation was great as Luther started his long journey, going by foot across Germany from Wittenberg to Worms. Every city he passed through greeted him with excitement. Could something be done about the Roman hegemony over the German church? Could the corrupt financial system of the Church be reformed? Did Germans have to keep on sending all this money to Rome so that the papal court could live in such opulence? Was Luther's teaching on grace really the teaching of Scripture, or was he just one more heretic? Had Germans been cheated by the sale of indulgences? What about the monastic orders? Had their effectiveness come to an end? Should they be disbanded? Everyone was troubled by these questions, and they wanted to hear for themselves what Luther had to say.

Luther was no stranger in Erfurt. Erfurt was home to the university where he himself had studied, and as an Augustinian monk, he naturally stayed at the Augustinian cloister. Of course he had to preach in the chapel, prepared or not. He was their student, this doctor of theology about whom all Germany was talking. The appointed Gospel for the day was John 20:19-31, the story of Jesus appearing in the Upper Room on the evening of the resurrection. Luther might have chosen a better text had he been given a choice or the time to prepare a proper sermon, but there was plenty in the text about which he was glad to preach. He announced a three-point sermon. First he would treat the words "Peace be with you" (John 20:19), then "Behold my hands and side" (20:20), and finally "As the Father has sent me, even so I send you" (20:21).[10] What he intends to draw from this passage is how we attain salvation and how we are to exercise true Christian piety.[11] Luther tells us that genuine piety consists of

10. "Ihr lieben Freunde, die Historie vom heligen Thomas will ich jetzt stehen lassen und beruhen auf eine auedere Zeit, sondern will ansehen das Wörtlein von Christo gesagt: 'Habt Friede' und 'sehet meine Hände und Seiten' und 'wie mich mein Vater gesandt hat, also sende ich euch.'" Luther, *Ausgewählte Werke* (Munich edition), 6:254. As a general rule, if biblical quotations in this book do not identify an established translation of the Bible, say the KJV or RSV, they emanate from the sermons themselves.

11. This sermon, which apparently was preached extemporaneously or nearly so, has come down to us through the notes of an unknown man who simply describes himself

two kinds of works: those we do for others and those we do for ourselves. Those things we do for others are essential and fundamental. For Luther works of Christian love and charity are always of the greatest value. The problem comes with religious works which are directed to ourselves. The chapels we build to earn our own merit, the pilgrimage we make to Saint Peter's in Rome or to Santiago de Compostela in Spain, the prolonged fasts and proliferated prayers by which we try to impress God — it is these works which are a problem.[12] They do not represent true piety, nor do they bring us salvation. Such works give us no standing with God at all. They have no power to destroy sin. On the other hand, "God has chosen a man, the Lord Christ Jesus, to crush death, destroy sin, and shatter hell."[13] For Luther it is obviously in beholding the pierced hands and side of the risen Christ, mentioned in this text, that one finds the source of our salvation.

Luther goes on to explain this from Paul's Epistle to the Romans. Apparently he had in mind chapter 5, which makes particularly clear the vicarious nature of Christ's sacrifice on the cross. He explains Paul's idea that just as Adam's sin entangled us all in sin, so Christ's death releases us from that sin. It is not our works which release us from our sin, but Christ's work. This is not what the papal authorities are teaching us.[14] They tell us that in order to be saved we have to keep all their rules about fasting, praying, and butter eating. They have deluded us into thinking

---

as "a layman." Apparently he was not a trained stenographer, and we can well imagine that much in the sermon escaped the pen of this amateur. In fact, we often lose the train of thought in this report of this sermon. The interpretation of the sermon offered here takes the liberty of trying to figure out what Luther must have actually said. At certain points it seemed advisable to quote the German text in the footnote.

12. "Nun steht die rechte und wahrhaftige Frömmigkeit in zweierlei Werken: in fremden Werken, das sind die rechten, und in eigenen Werken, das sind geringe. Also, dass ihr des einen Grund habt: einer bauet Kirchen, der andre wallet zu Sankt Jakob oder Sankt Peter, der dritte fastet oder betet, trägt Kappen, geht barfuss oder tut sonst, was des sein mag. Solche Werke sind ganz nichts und müssen in Grund zerstört werden." Luther, *Ausgewählte Werke* (Munich edition), 6:254.

13. "Denn Gott, der hat auserwählt einen Menchen, den Herrn Christum Jesum, dass der soll den Tod zerknirschen, die Sünde zerstören und de Hölle zerbrechen." Luther, *Ausgewählte Werke* (Munich edition), 6:254.

14. "Christus aber hat den Tod zerbrochen um unsertwillen, also durch seine Werke, die uns fremd sind, und nicht mit unsern Werken selig werden. Aber die päpstliche Gewalt, die tut uns vil anders." Luther, *Ausgewählte Werke* (Munich edition), 6:254.

that our salvation lies in our own good works. "But I say that none of the saints, no matter how holy they were, attained salvation by their works. Even the holy mother of God did not become good, was not saved, by her virginity or her motherhood, but rather by the will of faith and the works of God, and not by her purity, or her own works."[15] Salvation does not lie in our works; it can be brought about only by faith. The text makes this very clear. Jesus says, "Peace be with you," and then tells the disciples to behold his hands and side. Luther obviously is still thinking of Romans 5, where peace with God is shown to come from Christ's vicarious sacrifice: "Therefore, since we are justified by faith, we have peace with God through our Lord Jesus Christ" (Rom. 5:1). Luther makes it clear that our peace comes from Christ's redemptive work. Christ is the only one who has taken away our sin and redeemed us. Therefore we have peace. Once more he returns to Romans 5. Just as we all inherited sin from Adam, sin which we did not commit, so by God's grace we have received salvation through the work of Christ. We are free from death by what Christ did, not by what we did. Luther calls on several other passages to make the point that Christ is our Redeemer, and then in a flash of irony tells us that this teaching of Scripture is quite different from what the teachers of the Church are telling us today. They would tell us, yes, Christ is our Redeemer, that is true, but it is not enough.[16]

Luther continues to explain the doctrine of justification by faith, and then takes up his third point: "As the Father has sent me, even so I send you" (John 20:21). (His transition is again not very clear. This may be because of the extemporaneous nature of this sermon or because the stenographer did not get it down.) Those who have been sent out to preach today have done a poor job of preaching, Luther complains. The preacher runs through the gospel superficially and then follows it up with a fable about Attila the Hun or a story about Dietrich of Bern, or he

15. ". . . Ich sag aber, dass alle Heiligen, sie seien gewesen so helig sie wollen, so haben sie die Seligkeit nicht erlanget mit ihren Werken. Auch die heilige Mutter Gottes mit ihrer Jungfrauschaft oder Mutterkeit nicht fromm oder selig worden ist, sondern durch den Willen des Glaubens und durch die Werk Gottes und nicht mit ihrer Reinigkeit oder eigenen Werken." Luther, *Ausgewählte Werke* (Munich edition), 6:255.

16. "Darum spricht Gott: Siehe, Mensch, ich bin deine Erlösung, wie auch Paulus sagt ad Corinth. 'Christus est justificatio, redemptio,' etc. Christus ist unsre Rechtfertigung und Erlösung, wie er denn sagt an dem Ort. Da sagen unser Herrn: Ja, redemptor oder Erlöser, es ist wohl wahr, es ist aber zu wenig." Luther, *Ausgewählte Werke* (Munich edition), 6:255.

mixes in something from Plato, Aristotle, or Socrates.[17] For Luther the problem with the preaching of his day was that it aimed at teaching people to do good works rather than at preaching the gospel. He brings in the words of Jesus to Peter, "Simon, . . . do you love me? . . . Feed my lambs" (21:15-17). He comments that feeding the flock is a matter of preaching the Word of God, not of making laws and regulations. Again Luther turns this irony against the papacy: "Indeed the clergy of our day feed the sheep in their pastures as butchers do before the slaughter."[18] But he does not stop with criticizing the pope for not feeding the flock by regularly preaching the Word. He has the same criticism of his fellow monks. Instead of preaching out in the world as true ministers of Christ, they stay in their cloisters and pray the canonical hours and say the Mass.[19]

Luther concludes his sermon in a positive vein, exhorting his hearers to put their faith in God for their salvation and then they will have the peace of God.[20] Putting their faith in God, they will do those good works toward their neighbors which are in truth well pleasing to him.

The sermon was received enthusiastically. Eoban Hess, a professor of the University of Erfurt, reported that "By the power of his mouth hearts were melted like snow by the breath of spring as he showed the way to heaven's goods which had been closed for centuries."[21] The sermon was published by a local printer, and it was so popular it was reprinted

17. ". . . so sagt man das Evangelium überhin, und darnach eine Fabel von dem alten Esel oder eine Historie vom Dietrich von Bern; oder mischt ein die heidnischen Meister, Aristotelem, Platonem, Socratem, etc. . . ." Luther, *Ausgewählte Werke* (Munich edition), 6:256. Here we follow the suggested emendation of the text by the editors of *Luther's Works* in the American edition.

18. "Ja, es ist wohl geweidet! Sie werden die Schafe, wie die Fleischhauer am Osterabend tun." Luther, *Ausgewählte Werke* (Munich edition), 6:257.

19. "Wenn du verlässt deinen Nächsten und siest ihn irren und hilfst ihn nicht, predigst ihm nicht, so will ich Rechenschaft von dir haben seiner Seele. Den Spruch liest man nicht. Aber ich sage: du wirst ein Pfaffe, ein Mönch, darum, das du deine sieben Zeiten betest, hältst Messe und meinst, du wollst fromm sein. Au weh ja, du bist ein feiner Gesell! Es wird dir fehlen. Du betest den Psalter, du betest Rosenkränze, du hast mancherlei anderlei andere Gebete und machst viele Worte, du willst Messe halten. . . ." Luther, *Ausgewählte Werke* (Munich edition), 6:257.

20. "Auf dass ich beschliess: So soll ein jeglicher Mensch sich besinnen und denken, dass wir nicht helfen können, sondern Gott, auch dass unsre Werke gar gering sind, so haben wir den Frieden Gottes; und ein jeglicher Mensch soll sein Werk also beschicken, dass es ihm nicht allein nütz sei, sondern auch einem andern, seinem Nächsten." Luther, *Ausgewählte Werke* (Munich edition), 6:258.

21. Quoted in Luther, *Works* (American edition), 51:61.

seven times in that same year. The text of the sermon as reported is not remarkable. One can easily ask why it was so popular and why it made such a great impression. To be sure, one often asks the same questions about the written sermons one knows to have been tremendously effective when they were preached. It is not the words of the preacher which really make the difference, but that these words were spoken at the right time. And yet, it is not in the end even this. If Professor Hess attributed the effect to the power of Luther's mouth, Luther himself would have sought a very different explanation. This was the Word God sent him to preach. In fact, he tells us this quite explicitly in the course of the sermon. There he stood; he could do no other. That was the message God sent him to deliver, and through the work of the Holy Spirit, the message bore fruit.

B. The Christmas Postil of 1522

The story is well known of how Luther, after his dramatic appearance at the Diet of Worms in October 1521, was kidnapped by his friends and hidden in a secluded castle deep in the Thuringian Forest. That castle, called the Wartburg, was the Mount Sinai of Protestantism. It was there that the Word of God was etched on the German heart. For a year or more the Reformer was kept safely in the Wartburg lest he be assassinated by the soldiers of the emperor. During this time Luther produced his translation of the New Testament, which made it possible to put the Bible in the hands of every German burgher. But it was not just a translation; it was a great translation. As with Jerome's Vulgate, it was in a style that was both popular and literary. This translation, as has so often been pointed out, made Germany biblically literate in a way it had not been before.

But Luther produced another important work while in the Wartburg. This work was aimed at the preachers of Germany, who had the responsibility of coming up with a sermon each Sunday. In 1522 there had been no reorganization of the service of worship, no division made between Catholic priests and evangelical ministers. There were simply two kinds of priests: those who liked what Luther had to say and supported his proposed reforms, and those who didn't. For those who were interested, Luther produced his *Postil,* a series of sermon helps for preachers who were expected to preach a sermon on the Gospels and Epistles of the official lectionary. Most were obligated to preach the lectionary selections, and Luther wanted to show them that they could preach the Gospel quite effectively despite this obligation.

The *Postil* came out in installments, of which the *Christmas Postil* was the first. This was followed shortly thereafter by the *Advent Postil.* The *Lenten Postil* was published in 1525, and in 1527 the *Summer Postil* and the *Festival Postil* appeared. Then in 1531 and 1535 Luther added a second series. In the meantime, Luther's approach to the job of interpreting Scripture had developed considerably.

The exciting thing about Luther's *Postil* is the way it is filled with insights into the question of hermeneutics. In it he intends to show the preacher how the appointed lesson for the day is to be preached to the glory of God and the salvation of the faithful. He wants to show how each text can be preached so that it builds up faith, awakens hope, and inspires brotherly love. It is when this is done that the ministry of the Word fulfills its purpose. The lectionary had of course been put together over the centuries under certain theological presuppositions. Into it were built certain emphases. Luther at one point expressly said that whoever had put together the lectionary had put a much stronger emphasis on the moralistic aspects of the Christian life than was appropriate. In fact, he looked forward to the day when the lectionary could be put aside and one could preach through the text in its own order. The grace of God, as Luther saw it, did not always come through as clearly in some of the selections of the lectionary as it should. One could accuse Luther of using his *Postil* as a way of showing how his favorite emphasis could be drawn out of the lectionary selections, but that would miss the point. Luther, as Augustine before him, had understood that there are in Scripture certain overarching themes in light of which the whole of Scripture should be understood. The preacher should stress these themes, which should then lead him to put the passage before him into the perspective of the whole of Scripture. Let us look at several of the sermons, or perhaps more correctly, sermon notes, to see how he advised that the lections be preached.

First we take Luther's treatment for the Christmas Eve Gospel, Luke 2:1-14. Luther's main point here is that it is not enough to preach merely the historical event of Christ's birth. The point to be made is that Christ was born for our salvation. This is very clear from the words of the angel who announced Christ's birth to the shepherds. "*For you* is born this day in the city of David a Savior, who is Christ the Lord." Faith believes not that Jesus was born but that he was born for us. Christ's birth is for our salvation. He was born that we might experience a new birth. He was born into our world that we might be born anew into his world, as we find it in the Gospel of John (John 3:3-6).[22] We find this made very clear by the words of the prophet Isaiah, "For to us a child is born, to us a son is given" (Isa. 9:6) (p. 16). Luther was very clear even in the beginning of the Reformation that faith is far more than accepting the truth of certain historical statements. Faith is receiving the gospel. In this case it is the gospel of the incarnation as proclaimed by the angel to the shepherds, and as should be proclaimed even today by the Christian preacher on Christmas Eve.

Next we look at how Luther believes the Gospel selection appointed for the early service on Christmas Day is to be preached. This Gospel is Luke 2:15-20, which tells of the shepherds going to Bethlehem to see the Christ child. As Luther reads it, we have in this Gospel a picture of the life of faith because it begins with faith and flows from faith. The shepherds believed the Word of the Lord as they heard it from the angels. If they had not believed it, they would not have gone to Bethlehem. Luther makes the point that the faith of the shepherds was in the Word of God they heard from the angels rather than in the angels themselves. The text specifically says it was the Lord who made this marvelous occurrence known to them. Luther then makes a number of other points from the text about the life of faith. This life is single-minded, for we read, "Let us go . . . and see this thing." Those who hear the Word of God and believe it are united together in one Spirit. The life of faith is a life of humility. The shepherds remained shepherds even though they had been the recipients of a most marvelous revelation. They did not imagine that the ministry they performed entitled them to a more exalted station in life (p. 34). The life of faith renounces the self and loves the neighbor. We read that the shepherds left their sheep and went to the stable in Bethlehem. They did this not because they were told to, but voluntarily out of love. Love is always like that. It is not constrained, but it naturally and voluntarily forgets its own concerns and turns toward the neighbor, in this case Mary, Joseph, and the baby (pp. 35ff.). The life of faith follows through with action. The shepherds actually go to find the child. Then we discover that when they found the baby Jesus, they told everyone about what had been told them of the child. The life of faith does not keep silent but freely confesses and publicly proclaims what God has made known. Finally the life

---

22. Luther, *Works* (American edition), 52:15. The page references that appear in this section of the text are from volume 52 of the American edition of Luther's works.

of faith is filled with praise and thanksgiving to God for his saving grace (p. 38), for we read, "The shepherds returned, glorifying and praising God for all they had heard and seen, as it had been told them" (Luke 2:20). What is interesting about this sermon is the way Luther makes clear how the preaching of the gospel inspires good works. While it is faith alone which saves, the faith which saves is not alone. It bears the fruit of good works, as the apostle Paul himself taught in Galatians 5:22. There we read that love, joy, and peace are the fruit of the Spirit. Such fruit grows naturally from faith, as was demonstrated by the shepherds.

The Gospel lesson for the main service of Christmas Day is John 1:1-14. Luther understands this as a key passage of the New Testament (p. 41), and in it the gospel of the incarnation is made particularly clear. Care should be taken, however, that this passage be preached directly and simply as gospel. One should avoid bringing into it all the sublimities of philosophy which the Scholastic theologians like to read out of the passage. The passage is really very easily understood, Luther assures his readers (p. 43). When taken simply and straightforwardly, it tells that the incarnation is, as the words of the Nicene Creed put it, "for us men and for our salvation." The passage was never intended to be the basis of a metaphysical system. It does not speak about philosophy but proclaims an act of divine grace. Because man by his own nature cannot save himself, God had to enter into human nature to save him. For Luther many of the philosophical interpretations of John 1:1-14 added up to a Pelagian misunderstanding of the passage (p. 75). The Scholasticism of the late Middle Ages, particularly the nominalist school, tried to find some kind of natural theology in the passage, but the whole passage underlines grace again and again. If natural theology was of the sort the nominalists advocated, the incarnation would hardly have been necessary. The passage makes clear, as does the Gospel of John as a whole, that Jesus is true God and true man, and it is this which the preacher should make clear when preaching this passage (p. 88).

One thing is clear from Luther's *Postil.* All preaching is for him evangelistic, in the sense that it should aim at the proclamation of the gospel. To be sure, not all Luther's sermons are evangelistic in that they are addressed to those outside the community of faith; Luther was certainly preaching inside the Church to men, women, and children who had made a Christian commitment. His sermons are clearly to Christians, not to pagans. He did not even have unbaptized pagans in his congregation, as Gregory of Nazianzus or John Chrysostom did. His sermons are not evangelistic from the standpoint of genre, but they are evangelistic from the standpoint of content.

The sermons for Christmas we have just discussed are a good example of Luther's approach to the preaching of the Christian feasts. For Luther it is not enough simply to preach a sermon treating in a general way the theme of the feast. All these sermons are expositions of the passage of Scripture appointed for the feast day, but it is not the feast day which interests Luther so much as the Scripture read on the feast day. In fact, Luther sometimes complains that the selection of Scripture appointed for the day is not really appropriate, but that is not important. It makes no difference at what time a passage is preached (p. 102). Obviously for Luther, what is important is that the Word of God be preached and that it be preached faithfully. His emphasis is clearly on the Word of God, not the theme of the church calendar.

For Luther the celebration of the Christian feasts served to bring before the Church in a regular order the cardinal points of the Christian gospel. The regular celebration of Christmas gives the preacher an opportunity to preach the gospel of the incarnation. The celebration of Holy Week and Good Friday provided the opportunity to preach the gospel of the cross. Easter was a time to proclaim the gospel of the resurrection, and Pentecost the gospel of Christ's abiding presence through the Holy Spirit. For Luther the value of celebrating the feasts was this regular reemphasis of the central acts of God's grace.

C. Catechetical Sermons of 1528

The Reformation brought a revival of catechetical preaching. In fact, this was one of the first liturgical reforms actually to be instituted. This was true not only in Wittenberg but in the Upper Rhineland as well. In south Germany the project had been discussed by the Christian humanists in the generation before the Reformation. Johann Geiler von Kaysersberg had preached series of sermons on the catechetical pieces in Strasbourg, and in Basel the reforming bishop Christoph von Utenheim had encouraged such preaching in the first two decades of the sixteenth century. When Erasmus published his paraphrase of the Gospel of Matthew in 1521, he wrote into the preface an appeal for the revival of catechetical preaching. As a Christian humanist, he was always interested in the revival of the practices of Christian antiquity, and he was quite familiar

16

with the catechetical preaching of the fourth-century Church Fathers.[23] This appeal suggested that since baptism was in the sixteenth century normally administered to infants and since catechetical instruction was pointless before the baptism of infants, it be revived before young people were admitted to their first Communion. Erasmus went on to suggest that after they had this catechetical instruction they be asked to make a solemn and public profession of faith before the congregation, and that the bishop then confirm them with the laying on of hands. Within a year of the publication of this suggested program, we find parts of it being implemented both in Wittenberg and Zürich. The churches of Basel, Strasbourg, and Constance followed. While Erasmus's suggestion about confirmation was not adopted immediately, the suggestion about catechetical preaching was adopted with enthusiasm.

Wherever the Reformation was received, catechetical preaching was revived.[24] It was not just a matter of reviving catechetical preaching, to be sure; it was the adoption of a whole program. From its inception this program was a serious attempt at the Christian education of children. Although as time went on the Reformers began to see the value of extending the scope of the program to include adults, the concern for children was never lost. Catechisms were published so that the young people could learn them by heart. Catechetical instruction was given in the schools, and in some places catechetical hymns were provided to be sung at the catechetical services. What had been merely attempts and suggestions among the Christian humanists became a solid plank in the program of the Reformers.

Luther's catechetical sermons of 1528 are of interest not because they are the first such series recorded for us from the Reformation, but rather because they show us what catechetical preaching had become after it had been going on for a few years.[25] Catechetical preaching was held

---

23. Cf. John Payne, *Erasmus: His Theology of the Sacraments* (Richmond: John Knox Press, 1970).

24. For more detailed information on the reestablishment of catechetical instruction at the time of the Reformation, see my work *The Shaping of the Reformed Baptismal Rite in the Sixteenth Century* (Grand Rapids: Wm. B. Eerdmans Publishing Co., 1992), pp. 179-200.

25. This study is based on the English translation of the ten catechetical sermons preached between 30 November and 18 December 1528, as found in Luther, *Works* (American edition), 51:135-93; the page references in the text are from volume 51 of this work. For the German text, see Luther, *Luthers Werke, Gesamtausgabe* (Weimar edition), 30:1-122.

17

four times a year in Wittenberg at this point. Ten sermons total would be given during the two-week instruction, each at two o'clock in the afternoon five days a week. As the editor of *Luther's Works* points out, these sermons are the groundwork for both the *Shorter Catechism* and the *Larger Catechism* which Luther published the following year. By 1528 the Reformers had essentially settled on the fourfold makeup of the catechism: namely, the Ten Commandments, the Apostles' Creed, the Lord's Prayer, and an explanation of baptism and the Lord's Supper. That catechetical instruction should include an explanation of the sacraments was suggested by such fourth-century classics as the catechetical sermons of Ambrose of Milan and Cyril of Jerusalem. The explanations of the creed and the Lord's Prayer probably go back even further. The sermons on the Ten Commandments, however, are another matter. It was no doubt during the Middle Ages that the Ten Commandments first was linked with the creed and the Lord's Prayer as one of the basic documents every Christian should know and understand. One thing is clear: by the time of the Reformation there was no question but that a Christian explanation of the Ten Commandments was an essential part of basic, introductory Christian instruction (p. 138).

The ten catechetical sermons Luther preached at the end of 1528 covered the following subjects:

1. Introduction and first commandment
2. Second and third commandments
3. Third commandment
4. Fourth, fifth, and sixth commandments
5. Seventh, eighth, ninth, and tenth commandments
6. The creed
7. The Lord's Prayer: first, second, and third petitions
8. The Lord's Prayer: fourth, fifth, and sixth petitions
9. Baptism
10. Communion

One notices that half the sermons treat the Ten Commandments while only one is devoted to the creed. This is probably explained by the fact that Luther is indeed directing his sermons to children (p. 164). Generally speaking, there is very little development of the theological themes one might expect. Very little is said in the discussion of the Ten Commandments about law and gospel, which ordinarily is a favorite theme of the Reformer. It is Luther's purpose simply to explain what a Christian must do and not do (p. 169). The single sermon on the creed also avoids a theological discussion of the doctrines mentioned therein and emphasizes but three points, that from the Father we receive our creation, from the Son our redemption, and from the Holy Spirit our sanctification. In the same way, the two sermons on the Lord's Prayer avoid the theological themes found in the prayer and aim at establishing the practice of daily prayer. Luther tells us, "In the first place necessity itself requires that we admonish you to pray but also teach you to pray" (p. 169). The Reformation implied a radical reform of the practice of prayer. For Luther the beginning of this reform is found in the Lord's Prayer, which teaches us for what things we are to pray (p. 171). On the other hand, the sermons on baptism and Communion do get involved in the polemics of the day, but then the simplicity at which Luther aimed is not always achieved with the first attempts (pp. 188ff.). Preaching to children was hardly a cultivated homiletical form at the beginning of the sixteenth century. It is to the credit of Luther that he even made an attempt.

D. Sermons on the Gospel of John, 1537

Luther began to preach through the Gospel of John in 1537 while his colleague Johann Bugenhagen of Pomerania was in Denmark reorganizing the church at the invitation of King Christian III. Bugenhagen, one of the most faithful of Luther's lieutenants, was pastor of the church of Wittenberg. In his absence others had to fill the pulpit. Luther still had his usual lectures at the university, but in Bugenhagen's absence he took over the preaching on Saturday, which had by this time been designated as the day for preaching through the Gospel of John. Luther begins with the comment, "I neither know nor can I ascertain from anyone where our pastor, Dr. Pomeranus, broke off his sermons on the evangelist St. John, which he preached to us on Saturdays. Therefore I make bold to go back to the beginning with my commentary on the evangelist."[26] We suspect this was said with a twinkle in the eye, for Bugenhagen had a reputation

26. This study is based on the English translation of Luther's sermons on the Gospel of John found in Luther, *Works* (American edition), vols. 22ff. For the original text, see Luther, *Luthers Werke, Gesamtausgabe* (Weimar edition), vols. 46ff. The quotation above is found in Luther, *Works* (American edition), 22:5; the page references in the text are from volume 22 of this edition of Luther's works.

for being a bit tedious. Luther probably had other reasons for wanting to begin at the beginning. Surely, more than anything else, it was because he himself wanted to make a fresh and systematic restudy of the Gospel.

Furthermore, Luther remarks, we

> must remain conversant with this evangelist; to this end we must familiarize ourselves with his way of speaking. Therefore we propose to consider his Gospel in the name of the Lord, discuss it, and preach it as long as we are able, to the glory of our Lord Christ and to our own welfare, comfort, and salvation, without worrying whether the world shows much interest in it. Nonetheless, there will always be a few who will hear God's precious Word with delight; and for their sakes, too, we must preach it. For since God provides people whom He orders to preach, He will surely also supply and send listeners who will take this instruction to heart. (p. 5)

These introductory sentences are of tremendous importance for our study. They tell us that the purpose of preaching is, above all, to glorify Christ and, second, to serve the welfare of God's people. For Luther, preaching was worship because it was doxological. As we find it here, the Gospel is preached "to the glory of our Lord Christ." God called and sent preachers to proclaim his Word in his name, that he might be glorified. Preaching, to be sure, builds up the Church, because that is the means God has provided for the building up of the Church. We do not preach because it is popular or because it effectively draws people, but because God has sent us to preach. The Church in her worship hears sermons because God has called us to hear sermons in order that we might be transformed into his image by his Word and thereby reflect his glory. These introductory remarks give us a good insight into Luther's theological understanding of the ministry of the Word.

Having made these introductory remarks, Luther quotes the first three verses of the Gospel and tells us that these words document the traditional Christian doctrine of the Trinity, "according to which we believe and confess the one true, almighty, and eternal God. But [John] states expressly that three distinct Persons dwell in that same single divine essence, namely, God the Father, God the Son, and God the Holy Spirit. The Father begets the Son from eternity, the Holy Spirit proceeds from the Father and the Son, etc. Therefore there are three distinct Persons, equal in glory and majesty; yet there is only one divine essence" (pp. 5ff.). Luther continues to recount the affirmations of Nicene orthodoxy and then offers an illustration, which he labels rather crude: "As a human son derives his flesh, blood, and being from his father, so the Son of God, born of the Father, received his divine essence from the Father from eternity. But this illustration, as well as any other, is far from adequate; it fails to portray fully the importation of the divine majesty. The Father bestows his entire divine nature on the Son. But the human father cannot impart his entire nature to his son; he can give only a part of it. This is where the analogy breaks down" (p. 6). Surely Luther is not the first to make this illustration; it is the obvious commonsense illustration. But then he follows it with another homely but effective illustration. In this Luther is following the well-worn paths of many preachers before him. One notices that Luther takes great pains to explain this text, surely one of the richest doctrinal passages of the New Testament, as traditional orthodoxy had always explained it. For him the orthodox tradition of the Church had understood the text and explained it well.

Luther goes on to explain what John means by Word. Again he reaches into the storehouse of ecclesiastical tradition and tells us that far more is meant here than my word or yours. "For we, too, have a word, especially a 'word of the heart,' as the holy fathers call it. When, for example, we think about something and fully investigate it, we have words; we carry on a conversation with ourselves. Its content is unknown to all but ourselves until such words of the heart are translated into oral words and speech, which we now utter after we have resolved them in our heart and have reflected on them for a long time" (pp. 8ff.). Our preacher develops this at some length. He then relates these ideas to John 1:18, "The only Son, who is in the bosom of the Father, he has made him known." Again we see Luther's ability to make the classic teachings of the Church clear and interesting. It is not that he is so orthodox or so learned, but that he is so clear. He has obviously studied the historic doctrines of the Church so carefully that he can make them simple and cogent to this congregation.

This is a long sermon. Luther goes through the text word by word. He treats the doctrine of the true divinity and true humanity of Christ, the errors of Arius, the trinitarian doctrine of Augustine, all with interesting and engaging profundity. For Luther the history of Christian doctrine is edifying and intelligible once it is understood not from human reason but from divine revelation. In Luther's preaching the most profound doctrines become meaningful when they are used to explain the text of Scripture. One is amazed at Luther's ability to make what so many preachers

21

have turned into a jungle of verbiage into a beautiful and well-ordered garden of surpassing beauty.

The second sermon takes up again with verse 3, "All things were made through him, and without him was not anything made that was made." He had treated this verse in the previous sermon, but he has more to say. This verse means, to be sure, that "The Son of God is co-creator of heaven and earth with the Father." But Christ, as cocreator, is not like a carpenter or architect who, after completing a house, a ship, or the like, turns over the house to its owner for his residence or the ship to the boatman or mariners for sailing, and then goes his way. "Craftsmen are wont to do this; after doing a job or finishing a task, they leave without any concern for their work and enterprise and without any regard for its maintenance. God proceeds differently. God the Father initiated and executed the creation of all things through the Word; and now He continues to preserve His creation through the Word, and that forever and ever" (p. 26). Luther is making a bold departure from the Scholastic theology of the Middle Ages. In developing the concept of *potencia absoluta* and *potencia ordinata,* the late Middle Ages had driven a sharp wedge between creation and providence. God was not viewed as immediately directing the lives and actions of all his creatures. For the Reformers the elaborate explanations of the distinction between primary and secondary causes which late medieval Scholasticism had developed rendered God remote and abstract, and the Reformers saw in the biblical and patristic doctrine of providence a much more immediate way of relating to God. God was indeed directing the lives of his people immediately and individually. This insight of the Reformation was closely connected to its insight into the biblical doctrine of grace. The Reformation reacted strongly against the Pelagianism of late medieval nominalism. One of the places where this reaction is seen most clearly is in the doctrine of providence.

We see here in the way Luther develops his doctrine of providence one of the most admirable qualities of Luther's preaching. Luther was a master at putting profound ideas in a simple way. This is a gift only the most brilliant seem to have, but Luther had it to a high degree. One could have expected Dr. Martin Luther, professor of theology at the University of Wittenberg, to have mastered the discussion of the Schoolmen on the distinction between creation and providence. That was his job. That he had a criticism of it, one would also expect. That was after all his job, too. But what is surprising here is that he puts the whole thing in terms of carpenters and shipyards. His simple illustration from common life makes his point. The whole discussion of providence, which takes up about a third of the sermon, is a skillful presentation of a very complicated theological concept. To be sure, Luther takes his time developing the idea, but he does it with the most admirable simplicity. What is interesting in this sermon is Luther's teaching on providence. It has strength and vitality. It is not interesting because of any literary ornamentation. His illustrations are not particularly colorful or interesting in themselves. What is interesting above all is the way Luther shows us that Christ is our Creator, that he is working still (John 5:17), and that he who began a good work in us will bring it to completion (Phil. 1:6).

This sermon has more than one powerful idea. Luther's exposition of "the life was the light of men" (John 1:4) is equally profound and equally clear. It is the Word who is the light of God's people. Luther speaks first of the light of nature, then of the light of reason, and finally of the light of the gospel.

> It is amazing that the evangelist St. John is able to discuss such sublime and weighty matters in such plain and simple language. He wants to say that the Son of God draws so close to men that He is their Light. And this Light is far different from that which all the irrational animals perceive. The cows and the pigs, to be sure, also enjoy the universal light of the sun by day and the light of the moon by night. But man alone is endowed with the glorious light of reason and intellect. Man's ability to devise so many noble arts and skills, his wisdom, dexterity, and ingenuity, all are derived from this Light, or from the Word, who was the Light of men. . . . But in addition to this light, which all men, both the good and the bad, enjoy in common, there is a particular light which God grants only to His own. To this applies everything that John later writes about the Word, namely, that He reveals Himself to His elect through the Holy Spirit and the oral Word, and that He wants to be the Light of His people. (p. 30)

One would have to search for some time to find such a lucid exposition of this text.

Another attractive feature of Luther's preaching is his lively imagination. Taking up the text "The light shines in the darkness" (1:5), Luther tells how the light of the gospel was revealed even to Adam and Eve and how the antediluvian patriarchs preached the gospel in their age. With what sparkling imagination Luther portrays both Adam and Noah as preachers of the gospel (p. 33). He speaks of how the light shone in the preaching of the prophets of the Old Testament and finally is revealed in all its fullness in Christ. All along the way there were those who resisted the preaching of the gospel. All along the way there was darkness, there were those who would not believe, but the light continued to shine in spite of the darkness. This highly imaginative portrayal of the history of the preaching of the gospel from Adam to Christ is far from pure fantasy. Even the New Testament speaks of Noah as a preacher of righteousness (II Pet. 2:5). Yet the fertile imagination of Luther has put it all together in a way that makes the text magnificently pictorial and richly meaningful.

The third and fourth sermons have to do with John the Baptist. "There was a man sent from God, whose name was John. He came for testimony, to bear witness to the light, that all might believe through him. He was not the light, but came to bear witness to the light" (John 1:6-8). Luther with his expansive imagination provides us with all the information Scripture gives on John the Baptist. One is amazed at how much material he heaps up. Luther must have had an extraordinary faculty for recalling this kind of information. Having reminded us of all that Scripture says about John, our preacher makes the point that John's ministry was to bear witness to Christ. Luther is aware that John is often called on to justify asceticism and the monastic way of life, but Luther points out that John's ministry was not to call all peoples to asceticism but to faith in Christ. John the Baptist preached Christ, that all might believe through him. It is not through asceticism that we are saved but through faith in Christ. With this Luther develops his criticism of the monastic orders.

The fifth sermon is of particular interest because we see Luther treating one of the political problems of the day, the threat of Turkish invasion. Treating the text "yet the world knew him not" (1:10), Luther remarks that there were those in Germany in his day who would ignore the spiritual revival which was taking place and organize the whole nation to fight off the Turks, who by that time were threatening the gates of Vienna. Not only would these people ignore the spiritual revival, they even persecute it. They are a worse threat than the Turks, according to Luther. He recalls the Crusades of the Middle Ages, which, he tells us, God did not bless (p. 83). As Luther sees it, God will save us if we have faith in him and first concern ourselves with the spiritual problems of our day. As is well known, Luther was not a pacifist, but he was also not one for sending Christians off on every crusade which presented itself.

The sixth sermon takes up the text "But to all who received him, who believed in his name, he gave power to become children of God"

(1:12). The sermon begins as abruptly as a trumpet blast, with an exposition of the doctrine of justification by faith, a doctrine Luther finds as clearly in the Gospel of John as in the epistles of Paul.

> Here you learn what a great glory and what an ineffable eternal treasure the advent of God's Son brought to those who accept Him, believe in Him, and regard Him as the Man sent by God to help the world. . . . If we believe that He is the eternal Word of the Father through whom all things were made (John 1:3), if we believe that He is the eternal life and light of man (John 1:4) and the Lamb of God who bears the sins of the world (John 1:29) and removes these sins and casts them into the depths of the sea, . . . if we call upon Him in every need and thank Him for His inexpressible grace and benefits — then we shall have the singular privilege, liberty, and right to be the dear children of a gracious Father in heaven, to be heirs of His eternal and heavenly goods, to be, as Paul declares in Rom. 8:17, the brethren and fellow heirs of Christ, and to have salvation and life eternal. (p. 87)

This outpouring of evangelical joy is surely one of the things that made Luther's preaching most effective. One finds this again and again in the preaching of Luther. It has a power to kindle the faith of the congregation. It is this evangelical joy, which we hear in Luther's hymns as well, that is the mainspring of praise and thanksgiving. It is this joy in the saving grace of God that makes worship true worship. After reading a sermon like this, one hardly needs to ask how preaching is related to worship.

With the seventh sermon Luther begins his exposition of John 1:14, "And the Word became flesh and dwelt among us." He begins by setting this verse in relation to the foregoing verses and briefly summarizing its meaning. Then he remarks at some length about the great respect the Church has always maintained for this verse. He quotes Bernard of Clairvaux, for whom the Reformers had the highest regard, on the centrality of the doctrine of the incarnation (p. 104). Even under the papacy the importance of this doctrine was clearly recognized. Our preacher spends some time discussing the meaning of the word "flesh" (p. 111). The text tells us that Christ became a complete human being in both body and soul. By using this word the Evangelist wants to make clear the full extent of Christ's humanity. Taking up the phrase "and dwelt among us," Luther criticizes the Manichaeans, who did not accept the full humanity of Christ (pp. 112ff.).

The sermon continues with a consideration of the phrase "the only Son from the Father." Here our preacher distinguishes the sonship of Christ from the sonship of Christians. Luther speaks of the uniqueness of Christ's sonship but then tells us, "God has many sons and daughters besides; but He has only one only-begotten Son, of whom it is said that all was created through Him. The other sons are not the Word, through which all things were made; but they themselves were created through this only-begotten Son." Luther postpones this subject for the following sermon, when he will discuss it at greater length and finally tell us that Christ is Son of God by nature while Christians are children of God by grace.

He concludes this sermon by telling us about the beauty of the doctrine of the incarnation. "We must treasure this text and take comfort from it in hours of sadness and temptation. Whoever lays hold of it in faith is lifted out of his distress, for he is a child of eternal bliss" (p. 115). Somehow one senses in this a personal witness. Here, as so often in the sermons of Luther, one becomes aware that Luther is speaking from his heart. He himself knows the comfort and consolation of Scripture, and those who hear him preach are assured that they themselves will find the same salvation in the same Word.

In the tenth sermon our preacher turns to the text "For the law was given through Moses; grace and truth came through Jesus Christ" (1:17). The distinction between law and grace is a favorite subject of Luther's, and the Gospel of John gives him ample opportunity to discuss it at length. Luther's remarks here are particularly interesting because he is commenting on a Johannine, rather than a Pauline, text. First he gives us an exposition of what is meant by grace, and then what is meant by law (pp. 139ff.). One is surprised at how positively he understands law. These sermons were preached in 1537, after the controversy with the antinomians, which obviously deepened Luther's thought on the subject. As Christians, our preacher tells us, we should not attempt to be saved by law, for that was brought by Moses. The salvation that Christ brought was by grace. The law teaches us and even brings us to Christ, but it does not save us. When God supplies grace and truth, then one can keep the first tablet of the law. Then one can love God and hallow his name. This love for God comes through the illumination of the Holy Spirit, from regeneration by the Word, and from faith in Christ (p. 144). This love does not come from keeping the law. Before one has faith, one has no delight in the law, but when one does have faith, then one can keep the law with delight.

With the eleventh sermon Luther finishes his exposition of the prologue of the Gospel of John. "No one has ever seen God; the only Son, who is in the bosom of the Father, he has made him known" (1:18). First Luther takes up a problem of translation. In German one cannot speak of a father having a bosom, Luther tells us. One might convey it in German by saying that Christ is enfolded in the embrace of the Father or that Christ clings to the Father and rests snugly in his arms (p. 149). Then Luther turns to the difference between the Christian and the non-Christian knowledge of God. He compares this passage to the first chapter of Romans, which speaks of the knowledge of God which pagans have. There is an analogy, according to Luther, between the knowledge of God the pagans have through their philosophy and the knowledge of God one has through the law. The law, just as pagan philosophy, can tell us of the difference between right and wrong. Luther takes off at the doctors of Scholasticism and the subtle disputations between the Franciscans and Dominicans. He sees all this as nothing more than a philosophical attempt to know God. Luther dwells on this subject at some length and then returns to the picture of Christ embraced by the Father which he had so beautifully drawn at the beginning of the sermon (p. 156). It is this Christ who is now incarnate in human flesh who is our doctor. Moses saw the back of God, but in Christ we see the face of God. It is in the Word become flesh that the truth is known (p. 157). Here we have a vivid and moving conclusion to what could easily have been a very dry and abstract doctrinal discussion. Luther's ability to teach Christian doctrine in a pictorial and imaginative way is one of his greatest assets as a preacher.

Luther preached on through the Gospel of John every Saturday for years. We have something like a hundred or two hundred sermons in this series. These sermons on the prologue of the Gospel give us a good impression of Luther's preaching at its most mature. Luther is at his best as an expository preacher, and here we see Luther's expository preaching at its best.

E. Preaching and the Reform of the Calendar

Luther could be quite ambiguous on the subject of the lectionary. While he vacillated between favoring the *lectio continua* and the Gospels and Epistles of the liturgical calendar, he preached both. One of the most interesting things about studying Luther is that almost everything he said got written down. While this may at times make him look inconsistent, if not contradictory, it does let us in on some of the tensions in his thought. The fact that he had these tensions is for us today an especially attractive characteristic of the Reformer. In the end, these intellectual tensions have a way of producing deeper, more profound thought. It belongs to the essence of Luther's wisdom that not only did he have a brilliant vision of reform, but at the same time he had a great love for the old ways.

It is often said that Luther had to be pushed into making any specific changes in the service of worship. This is true, but it is also true that he had a vision of changes that needed to be made even though the piety of his congregation was not yet deep enough to support them. Luther was very sensitive to the danger of the shepherd going on so far ahead of the sheep that the flock loses sight of its supposed leader. The liturgical reforms Luther actually implemented were very realistic in that they kept in view the capacity of the Christians of Wittenberg. Luther needs to be taken quite seriously in his protestation that the plans he drew up for the service of worship were not intended to be definitive and that in time one would need to go further in reforming worship than he was at that time able to go with the church of Wittenberg. Any pastor who has ever tried to reform the worship of a particular congregation can appreciate Luther's wisdom at this point.

It was a bit over a year after the intemperate efforts of Dr. Andreas Carlstadt to bring the liturgy of Wittenberg up to date that Luther first put down on paper his ideas for the reform of worship. *On the Ordering of Worship in the Congregation* appeared in the spring of 1523.[27] This work reflects the changes which either had just been made or were being contemplated by the church of Wittenberg. In substance they involved the establishing of daily preaching services to take the place of a daily celebration of Mass.

Luther begins with a few remarks on the nature of the reforms he is making. He tells us that the service of worship as a whole, just as the preaching ministry in particular, has a legitimate origin, and so there is no question of simply dropping it. It needs to be reestablished as it was originally so it can serve the purpose for which it was set up.[28] As Luther sees

27. See Martin Luther, *Von der Ordnung des Gottesdienstes in der Gemeinde*, in Luther, *Ausgewählte Werke* (Munich edition), 3:107-10; Luther, *Luthers Werke, Gesamtausgabe* (Weimar edition), 12:35-37.

28. "Wie wir nun das Predigtamt nicht abtun, sondern wieder in seinen rechten

it, three abuses stand out. First, the Word of God is no longer proclaimed in churches but is rather read and sung. By this he meant that the reading and chanting of the sacred text had taken the place of preaching it. Second, mixed in with the Word of God are many fables and fabrications. By this Luther had in mind not only the legends of the saints that were read at the daily office, often side by side with the canonical Scriptures, but, perhaps even more, the exempla which had become part of the late medieval preacher's stock-in-trade. These exempla about which so many Reformers complained were in many ways similar to the sermon illustrations to which modern American preaching is so addicted. Third, one performed worship as a work to earn one's salvation. For Luther this last abuse was particularly serious because it had to do with inward inclination of the heart. For Luther this was the seat of genuine worship. It was the inward experience of worship that was the first concern of the Reformation. All the Reformers, Luther, Zwingli, Calvin, were clear about this from the very beginning.

When it came to the outward, objective ordering of the service of worship, Luther wanted to lay down as a primary principle that whenever the Church came together there be the preaching of the Word of God. In fact, he went so far as to say that the Church should never gather without preaching and without prayer.[29] To make this point he refers to two passages. The first is I Corinthians 14, in which the apostle Paul tells his followers about the nature of Christian preaching and teaching in the service of worship. In addition to this he quotes Psalm 103:21-22, which in Luther's translation reads, "When the kings and the people come together to serve God they are to proclaim God's name and his praise."[30] Surely, Luther figures, it should be clear from these passages that when the Christian congregation gathers together, there should be prophecy, teaching, and admonition. Our Reformer finds that the practice of the ancient

---

Stand begehren zu bringen, so ist auch nicht unser Meinung, den Gottesdienst aufzuheben, sondern wieder in rechten Schwang zu bringen." Luther, *Ausgewählte Werke* (Munich edition), 3:107; and Luther, *Luthers Werke, Gesamtausgabe* (Weimar edition), 12:35.

29. "Nun, diese Missbräuch abzutun, ist aufs erst zu wissen, dass die christliche Gemeine nimmer soll zusammenkommen, es werde denn daselbst Gottes Wort gepredigt und gebetet." Luther, *Ausgewählte Werke* (Munich edition), 3:107; and Luther, *Luthers Werke, Gesamtausgabe* (Weimar edition), 12:35.

30. "'Wenn die Könige und das Volk zusammenkommen Gott zu dienen, sollen sie Gottes Namen und Lob verkündigen.'" Luther, *Ausgewählte Werke* (Munich edition), 3:107; and Luther, *Luthers Werke, Gesamtausgabe* (Weimar edition), 12:35.

Church was to gather together each morning and read a portion of Scripture and that, following this, someone interpreted this passage in order that everyone understood it, learned it, and was admonished from it. As Luther sees it, I Corinthians 14 makes very clear that there is no point for people to speak in tongues in a public service of worship if there is no interpretation and if no one understands what is being said. It was much the same thing with liturgical reading and chanting of lessons and psalms in the late medieval service of worship. Not only was there the problem that the reading and chanting was in a language most people did not understand, but it is the very nature of sacred Scripture that it needs to be interpreted. The Reformers generally seemed to have a good feel for this dimension of sacred Scripture. As we have often noticed in earlier volumes of this study, Scripture was written to be meditated upon, interpreted, and preached upon. The style in which Scripture is formulated demands that it be unpacked. This is particularly clear with the sayings of Jesus and the oracles of the prophets. Jesus fully intended to give his apostles texts to preach upon. These sayings come to us in a concentrated, pungent form. They were put this way with the full expectation that the preacher would interpret them and apply them.

As well as Luther apparently perceived this dimension of the relation between text and sermon, there was another dimension of this problem which he probably did not perceive. Luther does not seem to have thought about what happens when the members of the congregation have a printed Bible at home in their own language. By 1523, printed books were becoming increasingly common. Luther's German translation of the Bible must have already been in the hands of many of the faithful Christians in Wittenberg. The appearance of the printing press was bound to have its effect on corporate worship. And once people had Bibles in their own hands, the public reading of Scripture was sure to lose some of its importance. The preaching was another matter. If anything, the reading of the Bible in every Protestant home would only increase the interest of the people in hearing the Scriptures interpreted by a learned preacher. This will be an important factor in the shaping of public worship for a number of generations yet to come.

Today Luther's dictum that if there is public worship there must be preaching sounds a bit extreme. The idea is nevertheless often repeated in Protestant circles. The problem, which would become more and more obvious, is that if small groups of Christians are to gather for worship, they might not have someone trained in the interpretation of Scripture.

In Reformed circles this would become a particularly vexing problem. Classical Protestantism, unlike the Anabaptist movement, always put a strong emphasis on a learned ministry. In the seventeenth century daily family prayer became an important spiritual discipline. While family prayer had psalm singing, Scripture reading, and prayer, it did not have preaching. Family prayer, and even daily prayer at school, was normally observed without preaching.

The specific problem Luther is dealing with here is the discipline of daily prayer. The reciting of the daily office had no doubt been maintained for generations in the town church at Wittenberg. Wittenberg was not a large city, and so only one church was involved. There were surely in Wittenberg a number of other religious communities for different religious orders, and they would have had their own ways of maintaining the discipline of daily prayer. Mass must have been said in a number of private chapels each day, and in the town church there would have been several dozen altars and at each one a Mass would have been said. What Luther either intends to do or already has done is to bring a greater order to this lush profusion of religious rites. What he seems to envision, for the town church at least, is one celebration of the Mass on Sundays and holy days, and daily prayer services through the week. He suggests in regard to daily prayer that there be a service at four or five in the morning and another at five or six in the evening. He leaves open the possibility of a service after supper, but he essentially comes down to morning prayer and evening prayer. At each service a passage of Scripture is to be read and then interpreted. This is to be followed by the praying of the psalms and other prayers.

It is the preaching of the *lectio continua* which Luther has in mind for these daily services. For the reading, "One is to take one particular book and read a chapter or two or a half a chapter, until one has completed the book. Then another book is to be taken until one has read through the whole Bible."[31] At one point Luther talks about reading the Old Testament historical books in the morning and the prophetic books in the evening. At another point he speaks of Old Testament in the morning and New Testament in the evening, or he says it could be the other

---

31. "Die Lektion soll aber sein aus dem Alten Testament, nämlich dass man ein Buch für sich nehme und ein Kapitel oder zwei oder ein halbes lese, bis es aus sei; darnach ein anderes fürnehmen und so fortan, bis die ganze Biblia ausgelesen werde. . . ." Luther, *Ausgewählte Werke* (Munich edition), 3:108; Luther, *Luthers Werke, Gesamtausgabe* (Weimar edition), 12:36.

way around. Whatever Luther has to say about law and gospel, he certainly intends to get the reading of the Old Testament back into the liturgy. This kind of conscientious expository preaching, Luther is confident, will go far in building the faith of the congregation.

Luther has a different approach to the Sunday service. The Sunday service is for the whole Christian community of Wittenberg, both the intelligent and the simple. At Mass the usual Gospels are to be preached, and at vespers the usual Epistles. On the other hand, if the pastor prefers, he may preach through a particular book on Sundays as well.[32]

After the preaching, the whole congregation is to respond with thanksgiving, praise, and prayer that the Word bear its fruit. This approach to worship is characteristic of Luther. He very often speaks of worship as our response to the Word. It can be put very strikingly in German: worship is our *Antwort* to God's *Wort*. This approach to worship is expressed very naturally in the arrangement he proposes here of beginning the service with the reading and preaching of the Word and following that with the prayers and psalms. One notices here that this praise and thanksgiving is to be expressed by the congregation singing the psalms. Luther was particularly fond of using psalm prayer. It apparently was an important component of his own devotional life.

The great importance of psalmody and hymnody to Protestant worship hardly needs to be insisted upon. It is just as essential to our worship as other forms of prayer. To understand it as some sort of audience participation gimmick would be to misunderstand Protestant worship seriously. In singing the psalms and hymns of the Church, the congregation responds to God in praise and thanksgiving. In time Protestantism will develop a rich understanding of the liturgical function of church music. This initial insight of Luther's, however, remains a valuable way of regarding the relation of preaching to the rest of the service of worship. In preaching, God speaks to us; in psalmody and hymnody, we respond. Worship is communion with God, and communion involves dialogue; it involves listening to God's word as well as pouring out our prayers to him.

32. "Des Sonntags aber soll solche Versammlung für die ganze Gemeine geschehen, über das tägliche Versammeln des kleinern Hausens, und daselbst, wie bisher gewohnet, Mess und Vesper singen; also, dass man zu beider Zeit predige der ganzen Gemeine, des Morgens das gewöhnlich Evangelion, des Abends die Epistel; oder es stehe bei dem Prediger, ob er auch ein Buch für sich nehme oder zwei, ihm das nützest dünkt." Luther, *Ausgewählte Werke* (Munich edition), 3:109.

One subject Luther takes up with particular interest at this point is the reform of the church calendar, where his chief concern seems to be to get rid of the saints' days. As he saw it, the legends of the saints were all too often of questionable historical value. The legends of the holy cross would better be left aside, simply because there is a great amount of just plain foolishness in them. Even the readings for the apostles' days had much apocryphal material. The Marian feasts are just as bad, but one had probably better leave them alone until one could find a suitable substitute. As we have already noticed, it was back in the sixth and seventh centuries that the growth of the saints' days had begun to confuse the order of Scripture readings on weekdays. Luther was actually restoring the ancient practice at this point.

If the liturgical calendar had up to this point dictated the choice of prayers, psalms, antiphons, and other musical responses, the pastor would now have the responsibility to choose such material.[33] This is an important juncture in the reform of worship. Once more the pastor is being given considerable responsibility in the conduct of the service. The lectionary and the liturgical calendar had in effect taken such responsibility out of the pastor's hands. Once the calendar was established, then appropriate lessons were selected for the calendar and, after that, appropriate psalms, prayers, and antiphons. Once the *lectio continua* was adopted, the whole system of a prescribed liturgy became unglued. Luther was ready to do this with the weekday services, but not yet with the Sunday services. That is the point Luther had reached in the spring of 1523. He contemplated doing this for the Sunday services, but in the months that followed he drew back from the idea.

Only a few months later Luther was again pressed into putting his ideas on liturgical reform into print. This time it was in response to Nicolaus Hausmann, pastor in Zwickau. *Formula missae* appeared in December 1523, and was obviously intended for a much broader distribution. While the earlier work focused on the reform of the daily office, this work narrows in on the reform of the Mass. Much of it is beyond our field of interest, but some definite points are made about the reading and preaching of the Scriptures, particularly as they were done in the celebra-

33. "Aber das Gesänge und die Psalmen täglich des Morgens und Abends zu stellen, soll des Pfarrers und Predigers Amt sein, dass sie auf einen jeglichen Morgen einen Psalmen, ein fein Responsorium oder Antiphon mit einer Kollekten orden." Luther, *Ausgewählte Werke* (Munich edition), 3:109.

tion of Mass. One of the most interesting things in this document is Luther's remarks on the reading of the Epistles of the lectionary. He figures the time has not yet come to rework this list of readings, but, he insists, they do need to be revised. The selections rarely treat the essential matters of faith. They treat instead matters of conduct.[34] About this Luther was quite correct. We have spoken about this before. The Epistles were, in fact, selected by someone who was primarily concerned with moral catechism. It is somewhat better, as Luther sees it, with the Gospels; nevertheless, a new selection of Scripture passages should be made eventually. What should be in the Scripture readings of the main Sunday services, Luther tells us, are the most weighty passages in the whole Bible.[35] Regrettably, Luther never pressed on to this point.

The *Formula missae* had a wide circulation and influenced the reform of worship all over Germany. Several churches went ahead and began to celebrate a German Mass. The suggestions of Luther's two works we have studied so far on the reform of the liturgy were often followed, but other Reformers sometimes had other ideas. And of course, Luther had envisioned just exactly that. He never saw any reason for all of Germany to follow the orders that were being developed in Wittenberg. He was not always too pleased with what other Reformers developed, but he never insisted on liturgical uniformity. That was part of Luther's genius; he suggested more things than anyone could ever put into practice. He himself never realized some of his most brilliant visions. It has always been that way with the most profound of theologians. His beloved Augustine was another case in point.

But something else needs to be said about the *Formula missae*. As the title makes clear, it was Luther's suggestion for a reform of the Mass. As yet, the old Latin Mass was still being said in Wittenberg as it had al-

---

34. "Post hanc lectio Epistolae. Verum nondum tempus est et hic novandi, quando nulla impia legitur. Alioqui cum raro eae partes ex Epistolis Pauli legantur, in quibus fides docetur, sed potissimum morales et exhortatoriae, ut ordinator ille Epistolarum videatur fuisse insigniter indoctus et superstitiosus operum ponderator, officium requirebat eas potius pro maiore parte ordinare, quibus fides in Christum docetur." Luther, *Luthers Werke, Gesamtausgabe* (Weimar edition), 12:209.

35. "Idem certe in Euangeliis spectavit sepius, quisquis fuerit lectionum istarum autor. Sed interim supplebit hoc vernacula Concio. Alioqui si futurum est, ut vernacula missa habeatur (quod Christus faveat), danda est opera, ut Epistolae et Euangelia suis optimis et potioribus locis legantur in missa." Luther, *Luthers Werke, Gesamtausgabe* (Weimar edition), 12:209-10.

ways been said. In Wittenberg the method of preaching had changed, but the liturgy in which it took place was essentially unchanged. All over Germany liturgical reform was taking place, but Luther held back. Among the churches which had begun to celebrate a service of worship in which there were distinct liturgical reforms were those in Nördlingen, Strasbourg, Nuremberg, and Zürich.[36]

At last, in October 1525, Luther came up with a new liturgy for Wittenberg, the *Deutsche Messe*. The liturgy was tried on the feast of All Saints and then, starting with Christmas, was put in general use. In January 1526 it was published. Even more expressly than in the two previous documents, Luther makes quite explicit that he has no intention of drawing up any canons of evangelical worship. This service he drew up for Wittenberg is not to be treated legalistically; he drew it up for a particular church at a particular time. There is a distinct recognition of the authority of other local churches to order their own worship. This was a dearly held principle in Germany at the time, and had been for several centuries. In a land filled with hundreds of individual principalities and free imperial cities, the idea of local authority was highly developed. Before the Reformation began, each bishop in Germany published the ritual of his own church. The church of Constance, the church of Basel, the church of Mainz all published their own liturgical books. Yes, there was a clear liturgical unity at the time, but there was also a flamboyant gothic variety. Luther put it quite succinctly: "For it is not my intention that all Germany should have to follow the liturgical forms of Wittenberg."[37]

Luther sees the Sunday morning service as intended for the average Christian. He uses the phrase "simple laymen," which was probably appropriate then, but under the influence of the recently instituted catechetical training, this was beginning to change. Luther figures that even in Christendom much of the population is not really Christian even if everyone packed into church on Sunday morning. And so it is not surprising that for Luther the main service on Sundays and feast days is directed toward men and women who still need to hear the essentials of the gospel.[38] That is, worship should have a definite evangelistic dimension.

---

36. See Julius Smend, *Die evangelischen deutschen Messen bis zu Luthers Deutsche Messe* (Göttingen: Vandenhoeck und Ruprecht, 1896).

37. "Denn es nicht meine Meinung ist, das ganze deutsche Land so eben musste unser wittenbergische Ordnung annehmen." Luther, *Ausgewählte Werke* (Munich edition), 3:128ff.; Luther, *Luthers Werke, Gesamtausgabe* (Weimar edition), 19:73.

38. "Denn Summa, wir stellen solche Ordnung gar nicht um deren willen, die

Having made these preliminary remarks, Luther begins his description of the German Mass of Wittenberg with a strong statement of the primacy of the Word. "Because the largest and most important part of our worship service is the preaching and teaching of God's Word, we hold fast to the traditional reading and preaching. On holy days and Sundays therefore we read the usual Gospels and Epistles and in the course of the day we have three sermons."[39] There was an early service at five or six in the morning, at which the appointed Epistle from the lectionary was read and preached. The main service was at eight or nine, and there the Gospel from the old lectionary was preached. Finally at vespers, late in the afternoon, a lesson from the Old Testament was selected on the basis of the *lectio continua* and a sermon preached on it.[40] At this point Luther gets a bit defensive about still using the old lectionary. A number of other churches, particularly in south Germany along the Rhine and in Switzerland, had already begun to celebrate an evangelical liturgy and had come out very strongly for the *lectio continua*. The *lectio continua* preaching of Capito, first in Basel and then in Strasbourg, of Zwingli in Zürich, of Oecolampadius in Basel, and of Bucer in Strasbourg had been received with enthusiasm. The Reformers of Strasbourg were, of course, the most important example. The church of Strasbourg had a distinguished college of pastors which included several well-known Christian humanist scholars and several of Germany's most well known preachers. The fact that they had taken such a strong lead in this direction was, we can be sure, overlooked neither by Luther nor his readers.[41] From the spring of 1523,

---

bereits Christen sind. Denn die bedürfen der Dinge nicht, um welcher willen man auch nicht lebt; sondern sie leben um unsert willen, die noch nicht Christen sind, dass sie uns zu Christen machen; sie haben ihren Gottesdienst im Geist." Luther, *Ausgewählte Werke* (Munich edition), 3:129.

39. "Weil alles Gottesdiensts das grösste und vornehmste Stück ist Gottes Wort predigen und lehren, halten wirs mit dem Predigen und lesen also: Des heiligen Tags oder Sonntags lassen wir bleiben die gewöhnlichen Epistl und Evangelia und haben drei Predigt. . . ." Luther, *Ausgewählte Werke* (Munich edition), 3:133-34; Luther, *Luthers Werke, Gesamtausgabe* (Weimar edition), 19:78.

40. "Nach Mittag unter der Vesper, vor dem Magnificat, predigt man das Alte Testament, ordentlich nacheinander." Luther, *Ausgewählte Werke* (Munich edition), 3:134; Luther, *Luthers Werke, Gesamtausgabe* (Weimar edition), 19:79.

41. "Dass wir aber die Episteln und Evangelia nach der Zeit des Jahres geteilet, wie bisher gewohnt, halten, ist die Ursach: wir wissen nichts sonderlichs in solcher Weise zu tadeln. So ists mit Wittenberg so getan zu dieser Zeit, dass viel da sind, die predigen lernen sollen an den Orten, da solche Teilung der Episteln und Evangelia noch geht und

when Luther first began to think of changing the order of preaching in Wittenberg, until the liturgical reforms were finally established in 1526, three years later, there must have been considerable discussion of the relative merits of following either the lectionary or the *lectio continua,* and a compromise was finally reached. The lectionary Gospels and Epistles would be preached in their traditional form on Sunday mornings. There would be a *lectio continua* of the Old Testament at Sunday vespers and a *lectio continua* of other biblical books at morning and evening prayer during the week.[42]

Luther at this point is very sensitive to the fact that there are not enough preachers who can do expository preaching to expect all of Germany to change over to regular expository preaching simply by the inspiration of the Reformers. There probably were not more than a couple dozen preachers in all of Germany who could preach through a whole book of the Bible doing genuine expository preaching. That being the case, Luther had several expedients. There was his *Postil,* which we have already spoken of at length. Luther had not yet written the whole of this collection of model sermons on the customary Gospels and Epistles of the lectionary, but he intended to. If a pastor could not preach, he could at least read his congregation an appropriate passage from the *Postil.* Another expedient was that by sticking to the lectionary one could more easily help beginners to do genuine expository preaching. In 1526 there were many preachers who were sympathetic to the teaching of the Reformation and to the approach to preaching which was developing but were required to do their preaching in the context of the usual Latin liturgy, and Luther wanted to show them how they could preach the gospel in their situation. He had made this clear with his *Postil,* and many priests were doing just what Luther had suggested. In the context of the Catholic liturgy, they were preaching the Protestant gospel. That possibility would

---

vielleicht bleibt. Weil man denn mag denselbigen damit nütze sein und dienen ohn unser Nachteil, lassen wirs so geschehen; damit wir aber nicht die tadeln wollen, so die ganzen Bücher der Evangelisten für sich nehmen. Hiemit, glauben wir, habe der Laie Predigt und Lehre genug; wer aber mehr begehrt, der findet auf andere Tage genug." Luther, *Ausgewählte Werke* (Munich edition), 3:134.

42. At the time the *Deutsche Messe* was written, the daily services in the town church of Wittenberg were as follows: Monday and Tuesday, catechetical preaching; Wednesday, *lectio continua* on Matthew; Thursday and Friday, *lectio continua* on the New Testament Epistles; Saturday, *lectio continua* on the Gospel of John. How long this arrangement lasted I cannot, at this point in my research, say with certainty.

not last long, but when Luther wrote his *Deutsche Messe* it was still open. In actual fact, it was not long before the Reformation did produce enough learned preachers to supply every village in Germany, but in 1526 Luther had to think in terms of liturgical reforms which could be realized by the preachers who were then available.

F. Luther's Theology of the Word

Luther's theology of the Word is the bedrock on which his preaching was based. In fact, that was the secret of its effectiveness. For Luther, to preach was to preach the Word of God, and that meant nothing less than to teach the Scriptures and exhort the congregation to live by them. It was as simple as that and yet as profound as that.

The first thing that needs to be noticed is that for Luther, Scripture and Scripture alone has ultimate authority in the Church. *Sola Scriptura,* "Scripture alone," was one of the watchwords of the Protestant Reformation. Scripture, as the Reformers understood it, has authority because it is God's Word. Paul Althaus, one of the foremost interpreters of Luther in the twentieth century, tells us that for Luther the authority of Scripture is the underlying presupposition of all of Luther's theological thought. His theology has no other purpose than the interpretation of Scripture. Basically Luther's theology takes the form of exegesis.[43]

Quite naturally, then, preaching is fundamentally an interpretation and application of Holy Scripture. Preaching is a matter of reading the Bible, explaining its meaning for the life of the congregation, and urging God's people to live by God's Word.[44] This, of course, is what we find Luther doing. Normally he lectured to his students at the university each day and then preached three times a week at the Castle Church in Wittenberg. As Gerhard Ebeling points out, that was the way he understood his calling as doctor of theology. It was his job to interpret the Scriptures to the congregation.[45] As we saw in the previous volume, the

43. "Zuerst also: die Authorität der Schrift ist allem theologischen Denken bei Luther vorgegeben. Seine Theologie will nicht mehr tun als die Schrift auslegen. Sie hat wesentlich die Gestalt der Exegese." Althaus, *Die Theologie Martin Luthers,* p. 17.

44. Ulrich Nembach, in his most helpful study of Luther's preaching, finds that for Luther the purpose of preaching can be summed up by the two Latin terms *doctrina* and *exhortatio.* Nembach, *Predigt,* pp. 25-29.

45. Ebeling, *Evangelische Evangelienauslegung,* pp. 14-16.

best of theological training in the Middle Ages had as its aim the training of preachers. Quite legitimately, then, for Luther the call to teach the interpretation of Scripture as professor of Scripture at the University of Wittenberg was to teach preachers what to preach. What he taught them was to preach the Word of God. As professor of Scripture Luther was training preachers, and as preacher in the Castle Church he was giving an example to his students. Luther's whole point was that if the preaching of his day was to be revived, it had to be brought back to its true purpose, the proclamation of the Word of God. Only this gave preaching authority; only this could demand the attention of the world.

It is from Scripture that the authority of the preacher comes, and yet the tradition of the Church did have its place for Luther. The creeds of the ancient Church as well as the Fathers of Christian antiquity have a certain authority because they witness to the teachings of Scripture. This is particularly the case in regard to the classic doctrines of the Trinity and the true humanity and true divinity of Christ.[46] For Luther, as for the Reformers generally, the tradition of the Church had authority to the extent that it witnessed to the authority of Scripture.

It is because of the authority of the Word of God that the reading and preaching of Scripture has a definite centrality in the well-ordered service of worship. It is not merely preparation for worship, as the English High Church movement of the nineteenth century would have it. Vilmos Vajta has made this particularly clear in his groundbreaking study on Luther's theology of worship.[47] The preaching of Scripture is in itself an act of worship. In fact, it is one of the central acts of Christian worship.

For Luther the most important reform needed in the worship of the Church of his day was to reestablish the centrality of the reading and preaching of the Word in public worship. To make this point he reminds us of the story of Mary and Martha in Luke 10. One thing is needed, that text tells us, namely, that Mary sit at the feet of Christ and hear his word daily. That is the best thing Mary could ever do, and that will never be taken away from her. Anything else will with time pass away, but the Word of God is an eternal Word.[48]

For Luther, "To hear God's Word and to believe it is worship at its

46. Althaus, *Die Theologie Martin Luthers,* p. 20.
47. Vajta, *Gottesdienstes bei Luther,* pp. 118-22.
48. Vajta, *Gottesdienstes bei Luther,* p. 118.

highest."[49] This was particularly clear to Luther from the story of the transfiguration in Matthew 17. Peter, John, and James went up on the mountain with Jesus, and there a voice from heaven told them that this Jesus was the Son of God and that they, therefore, were to hear him. Jesus, as Luther understood it, had been sent to preach; it is then the responsibility of his disciples to hear him. This is to be their service, their service of worship.

The second thing needing our notice is that in Luther we have a sense of what we have elsewhere called the kerygmatic presence of Christ. Christ is present to the congregation through the preaching of his Word. Where the Word of Christ is preached, there is Christ present, as we found it in the *Didache*. For Luther this doctrine of the kerygmatic presence of Christ has a particular twist. It is the saving presence of Christ which Luther emphasizes.

The preached Word has authority because it is the Word of Christ. This christological focus of Scripture is an important dimension of Luther's understanding of the ministry of the Word. For Luther the heart of Scripture is the gospel, the good news about Christ's victory over sin and death. To preach the Bible aright is to bring all the parts of the sacred book together into this central message of salvation in Christ. Gerhard Ebeling has brought this hermeneutical principle of Luther's to our attention.[50] Luther indeed had a strong sense of hermeneutic. It is when the gospel is proclaimed in such a way that it brings new life to the people of God and thereby honors God that we recognize its authority and understand best its place in worship. It is this gospel, this authoritative, saving Word of Christ, which is the focus of the sermon.

The point of Luther's doctrine of the kerygmatic presence is that when the gospel of Christ is presented in all its saving power for God's people to receive for their salvation, then Christ is present to those who receive him by faith.

Having said this, we must go on to say that the sermon not only teaches the Word of God, it actually presents it to us; it brings it to us. At this point Ebeling speaks of the sacramental power of preaching. What it says to us it brings to us.[51] For Luther the Word is a means of grace, just as the Lord's Supper is. Luther insisted on the eucharistic real presence, and in the same way he insisted that Christ is truly present in the reading

49. Vajta, *Gottesdienstes bei Luther,* p. 119.
50. Ebeling, *Evangelische Evangelienauslegung,* pp. 359-454.
51. Ebeling, *Evangelische Evangelienauslegung,* pp. 371ff.

and preaching of the Word. The eucharistic real presence is balanced by a kerygmatic real presence.

For Luther, what the Bible contains, namely, the gospel, is nothing less than a sermon which is continued in the sermon we hear today in the Church. In fact, Heinrich Bornkamm goes so far as to say, "The word of the preacher is an incarnation of the Word of God."[52]

The third thing we need to notice about Luther's theology of the Word is what he says about the Word in relation to the Spirit. If Luther had a strong sense of Christ being present through his Word, he also emphasized that this presence is through the Holy Spirit. It is through the work of the Holy Spirit in our hearts that Christ is present to us in his Word.

Without the work of the Holy Spirit, the word we preach is merely an "outward word," which is also the case with the word that is read. This terminology had been developed in the nominalist pietism of the late Middle Ages, and was a popular theme with the Anabaptists of Luther's day. Luther, however, was careful to guard the objectivity of God's Word in Holy Scripture. He had no interest in a spiritualistic doctrine of the Word of God. For Luther God's Word is not merely an "outward word" spoken by human lips and heard by human ears, for, as he understands it, it is with these outward words that God speaks his truth to our inward hearts.[53] God uses the ordinary means of the reading and preaching of the Word by the ministers of the gospel. These ordinary means must not be despised by vainly demanding that God come into my little prayer closet and speak to me privately. Luther warned against the spiritual enthusiasts of his day who sought an immediate mystical experience of God. He insisted that God uses means to bestow his grace upon us. The work of the Holy Spirit in our hearts always begins with our hearing the reading and preaching of this "outward word."[54] The word may start out being outward, but it becomes inward when inwardly it is received and believed. This is the work of the Holy Spirit. It is through the Word that the Holy Spirit works.[55]

---

52. Heinrich Bornkamm, "Das Wort Gottes bei Luther," in *Luthergesellschaft,* 7:37.

53. Cf. Althaus, *Die Theologie Martin Luthers,* p. 43.

54. " 'Wir müssen nicht wie die Rottengeister uns vornehmen, dass Gott ohne Mittel und ohn sein Wort im Herzen tröste.' So ist also das Wirken des Geistes im Herzen auf alle Fälle an das vorherige Hören des 'äusserlichen Wortes' gebunden." Althaus, *Die Theologie Martin Luthers,* pp. 43-44.

55. Althaus, *Die Theologie Martin Luthers,* p. 44.

As Luther understands it, the Holy Spirit convinces us that the outward word which is read in the Bible and preached from the pulpit is indeed that inner Word which God speaks in our hearts. The Holy Spirit is the Spirit of Truth. As the Spirit of Truth, then, he convinces us of the truth of the Word. Far from giving us other revelations, the Holy Spirit witnesses to the revelation which has already been given to us in Scripture. This revelation came to us through the inspiration of both the prophets and apostles, and even beyond that through Jesus, whom the Holy Spirit anointed at the beginning of his ministry. God's revelation in Scripture is "Spirit filled" from beginning to end.

Finally we need to notice what Luther has to say about the relation of faith to the Word of God. For Luther faith is always based on God's Word. In fact, one cannot even speak of faith without speaking of God's Word. The two belong to each other, because faith depends on God's Word, and because the Word of God is basically a call to faith and faith is basically an answer to the Word. The Word produces faith. Faith is not some sort of human quality. It is not the same thing as faithfulness. It is rather a response to the Word of God. It is a matter of saying yes to God when he calls us, of believing the promises of the Word of God. Faith receives the gospel. For Luther the apostle Paul's dictum was important, "So faith comes from what is heard, and what is heard comes by the preaching of Christ" (Rom. 10:17 RSV). For the Reformer of Wittenberg, faith is nothing less than taking to one's heart the promises of the gospel and building one's life on them.[56]

This relationship of Word and faith is especially significant for Luther's understanding of the place of the ministry of the Word in Christian worship. As Luther sees it, to believe God's Word is central to our worship. When we hear God's Word and take it for the truth, when we believe the good news of the gospel and understand that God is just and merciful, a faithful and loving Father to his children, then we honor God. To hear God's Word and believe it is the essence of worship. Althaus gives us a quotation from Luther which puts it precisely: "When we staunchly believe God's Word, we believe him to be true, devout, and right. It is in this way that we give him the very highest honor that we can give him. When we do this we confess him to be true and faithful and in doing that

---

56. "Den Glauben gibt es nur im Gegenüber zum Wort Gottes. Dieses allein gibt ihm den Grund und den Inhalt. Genauer gesagt handelt es sich um das Wort der 'Verheissung,' also das Evangelium." Althaus, *Die Theologie Martin Luthers,* p. 48.

we honor him."[57] By preaching, hearing, believing, and following the Word of God, we worship him in the most profound sense possible.

III. Ulrich Zwingli (1484-1531)

In the last few years Reformation scholars have begun to develop an increasingly favorable opinion of the Reformer of Zürich.[58] Although we have only a few of his sermons at which to look, the impression we get from other sources is that he was one of the outstanding preachers of the Reformation period. Even at that, one is tempted to skip over Zwingli in this study, simply because we have so few of his sermons. Generally speaking we have, in this work, passed by preachers whose sermons have not been recorded. We have made some exceptions, as with Francis of Assisi, which had to be made because he had such a great influence on preaching. Zwingli will be excepted for the same reason. From the earliest years of the Reformation he set an example of preaching that was both scholarly and prophetic, both systematic and popular.[59] It was Zwingli who first popularized the preaching of the *lectio continua* in the Protestant pulpit, and it was Zwingli who taught the Reformation its prophetic responsibility toward the civil government.[60]

All too often Zwingli has been treated as some sort of extremist to whom the blame must be attached for dividing Protestantism almost at its inception. Particularly in English circles he has traditionally been the whipping boy of the "High Church" movement. It was Zwingli, they figure, who was the antithesis of liturgical refinement.

---

57. "Wenn die Seele Gottes Wort festiglich glaubt, so hält sie ihn für wahrhaftig, fromm und gerecht. Damit tut sie ihm die allergrösste Ehre, die sie ihm tun kann, denn da gibt sie ihm recht, da lässt sie ihm recht, da ehrt sie seinen Namen." Luther, quoted in Althaus, *Die Theologie Martin Luthers,* p. 49.

58. Particularly noteworthy are the following: Oskar Farner, *Hüldrych Zwingli,* 4 vols. (Zürich: Zwingli Verlag, 1943-60); Gottfried Locher, *Die Zwinglische Reformation in Rahmen der europäische Kirchengeschichte* (Göttingen: Vandenhoeck und Ruprecht, 1979); and George R. Potter, *Zwingli* (Cambridge and New York: Cambridge University Press, 1976).

59. Thanks to the prodigious research of Oskar Farner, it is possible to get a clear picture of Zwingli as a preacher even if we have few sermons from him. Cf. Farner, *Hüldrych Zwingli,* vol. 3, *Seine Verkündigung und ihre ersten Früchte.*

60. Capito started to preach a *lectio continua* of Romans in Lent of 1518, but he did not popularize it the way Zwingli did. See below.

This evaluation of the situation, if nothing else, fails to take account of the variety of problems the Church faced at the beginning of the sixteenth century. Those who study the Reformation are more and more beginning to find considerable value in the concept of a constellation of Reformers rather than simply one star who sets the course. Many of us see far more value in the way the Reformers supplemented each other. Calvin's systematic approach complements Luther's flashes of insight, and Luther's earthiness is a good balance to Calvin's classic austerity. Zwingli, more than either of them, was a man of wit and practical wisdom. He had an appreciation for human nature.

Zwingli's contribution to the team is his recognition of the value of the political community and his practical appreciation for Swiss democracy. In our day we can appreciate his prophetic criticism of mercenary soldiering. More than anyone else, he was responsible for transforming Switzerland from a land that made its living by providing soldiers for the battlefields of Europe into a land famous for its neutrality. And this he did primarily from the pulpit. Zwingli might be regarded as one of the prophets of the peace movement, although he was very realistic in his vision.

One of the greatest errors of the popular, traditional portrait of Zwingli was that it ignored his impressive scholarly accomplishments. He was at the center of the intellectual life of his day. He was on intimate terms with the Christian humanists of Basel, a circle which at that time was presided over by Erasmus of Rotterdam.

Christian humanism was an important intellectual movement at the beginning of the sixteenth century. One must be careful to distinguish it from philosophical humanism, which understands man as the center of the universe. While philosophical humanism is the antithesis of theism, Christian humanism is an approach to theology which advocates an intensive study of the humanities, that is, Latin, Greek, and Hebrew. It is a very literary approach to theology which studies the Scriptures and the writings of the ancient Christian Fathers in their literary context. The motto of Christian humanism was *ad fontes,* "back to the sources." It was in this Christian humanism that Zwingli was educated.

By the time the Reformation began, Basel had become one of the centers of Christian humanism. In Basel Erasmus, the *Gelehrtenfürst,* "the prince of scholars," held court over an impressive group of intellectuals. The universities of Oxford, Paris, and Louvain would all have loved to have had him in their company. Cardinal Ximénes did his best to attract him to Spain for his newly founded University of Alcalá, but the printers of Basel finally won him for their city, making it the seat of an impressive intellectual empire. Before Erasmus arrived in Basel, the city was already a center of learning. It was to Basel that young Zwingli was sent off to school. With the arrival of Erasmus, many of Zwingli's old school friends became the chamberlains of that exalted intellectual court. For ten years, high in the canton of Glarus, where the alpine snows shut him in all winter, he studied all the latest books that had come off the printing presses of his friends down in Basel. He knew his Greek and Hebrew, and when the Erasmus edition of the complete works of Saint Jerome was published, for which the scholarly world had waited for a generation, Zwingli was one of the first to study it. In those days Jerome was regarded as the ideal biblical scholar, the prototype of Christian humanism. As *vir trilinguis,* proficient in the three ancient languages, he was the master of biblical studies. But the further Zwingli went into those nine big folio volumes, the more convinced he was that he would have to turn to the text of Scripture itself. Zwingli wrote out the Greek text of the New Testament in his own hand and then committed it to memory. This personal manuscript has been preserved, and in its margins Zwingli wrote the textual variations he found in the commentaries of the Fathers. He had clearly studied the works of Ambrose, John Chrysostom, Gregory of Nazianzus, and Augustine very closely. Zwingli built up an extensive private library while up in Glarus. His devotion to the study of the Scriptures was remarkable, but even more remarkable is that this study was done with all the technical precocity of the new literary sciences of the Renaissance.[61]

61. Walther Köhler began to appreciate the importance of Zwingli's background in Christian humanism and realized this was what made the difference between him and Luther. Walther Köhler, *Zwingli und Luther. Ihr Streit über das Abendmahl nach seinen politischen und religiösen Beziehungen,* 2 vols. (Leipzig: M. Heinsius Nachfolger, 1924). Köhler, in his work *Huldrych Zwinglis Bibliothek* (Zürich: Kommissionsverlag Beer, 1921), was able to recover Zwingli's amazing library from a number of libraries in Switzerland which still preserve his personal copies of something over three hundred books, many of which he has marked with his own name and are filled with marginal notations in his own hand. It was left to more recent research to demonstrate that in the last analysis Zwingli belongs with Luther and Calvin to classical Protestantism rather than to Renaissance rationalism.

A. The Lectio Continua

When Zwingli began his ministry as preacher in the Great Minster of Zürich in January 1519, he was determined to do serious expository preaching. He wanted to begin with the first chapter of the Gospel of Matthew and preach through it just as Chrysostom had done in Antioch in the fourth century. Zwingli's friend Johann Froeben, who at that time was Basel's leading publisher, had sent him a copy of Chrysostom's *lectio continua* sermons on Matthew shortly after they were off his presses. This was a little more than a year after Luther posted his theses on the church door of Wittenberg, but it was, nevertheless, the first liturgical reform of Protestantism.

Elsewhere I have shown at considerable length how Zwingli was inspired by the *lectio continua* preaching of Chrysostom.[62] He followed the system throughout his entire ministry, covering in succession Matthew, which took a whole year's worth of daily preaching, the Acts of the Apostles, I Timothy, the two epistles of Peter, and Hebrews.[63] In 1524 he is known to have preached through the Gospel of John and then to have finished up the rest of the Pauline Epistles. After seven years of daily preaching he had treated most of the New Testament. He then turned to the Old Testament, preaching first the Psalms. Then he began the Pentateuch in the middle of July 1526. He seems to have continued through the Historical Books until March 1528, when he began Isaiah. Then he continued through the Prophets for some time — how long we do not know.[64] This systematic interpretation of Scripture was received with considerable enthusiasm in Zürich, and his colleagues observed it with great interest. One by one the Christian humanist preachers of the Upper Rhineland began to follow his example. In southern Germany it was this kind of systematic biblical preaching which won the people to the Reformation.

Zwingli did not always keep to his *lectio continua*. Oskar Farner has listed the occasional sermons he is known to have preached both in Zürich and elsewhere. Some of these, such as "On the Shepherd's Office,"

---

62. Hughes Oliphant Old, *The Patristic Roots of Reformed Worship* (Zürich: Theologischer Verlag Zürich, 1975), pp. 195ff.

63. Gottfried Locher, *Zwingli's Thought: New Perspectives* (Leiden: E. J. Brill, 1981), p. 27. This was the way Zwingli explained it to the bishop of Constance in 1522 after four years of following the *lectio continua*.

64. Cf. Farner, *Hüldrych Zwingli*, 3:42-43.

preached at the Second Zürich Disputation, and "The Clarity and the Certainty of the Word of God," preached to the Dominican Sisters at Oetenbach, were recorded and published.[65] It is generally agreed that Zwingli edited and emended them quite heavily for publication, but they do, if nothing else, show us that he did preach occasional sermons. Besides this he is known to have preached sermons for the major feasts, but it is not known whether he followed the traditional Gospels or Epistles for these sermons. Zwingli's sermons at the Disputation of Bern in 1528 and at the Marburg Colloquy have been preserved. In addition, we know that at the height of the controversy over Lenten fasting he broke his *lectio continua* to preach on the question. This was a sensitive question, and it needed a thorough explanation. It was the same way with his campaign against mercenary soldiering. He seems to have done this sort of thing every so often.[66] But these were exceptions; the great bulk of his preaching consisted in systematically preaching through one book of the Bible after another.

While we do not have a very large collection of Zwingli's sermons as the basis for a thorough study of his ministry of preaching, we do nevertheless have other kinds of documentation which show that he was an outstanding expository preacher.[67] Expository preaching was the foundation of his ministry. Building on this foundation, he had, in addition, a notable prophetic ministry. This also the record makes clear, even if the absence of sermon texts precludes us from seeing just how he exercised this ministry. About Zwingli's prophetic ministry we will have more to say a bit further on in our study. Whether he himself entered into the catechetical ministry of the church of Zürich is not clear. It is clear that this church did institute catechetical preaching early in the Reformation, but Zwingli seems to have turned over this responsibility to Leo Jud. As we have shown elsewhere, Leo Jud did a superb job of directing the catechetical ministry.[68]

---

65. For "Of the Clarity and the Certainty of the Word of God," see below. For "On the Shepherd's Office," see vol. 3 of *Huldreich Zwinglis sämtliche Werke*, Corpus Reformatorum 90 (Berlin: Verlag von C. A. Schwetschke und Sohn, 1905), pp. 1-68; hereafter Corpus Reformatorum 90.

66. Cf. Farner, *Hüldrych Zwingli*, 3:45-53.

67. Oskar Farner has given us a detailed study of all the available documents. Cf. Farner, *Hüldrych Zwingli*, vol. 3, *Seine Verkündigung und ihre ersten Früchte.*

68. Cf. Old, *Reformed Baptismal Rite,* pp. 182-94.

B. A Theology of Proclamation

One of the sermons which has come down to us, the one Zwingli preached to the Dominican Sisters of Oetenbach, "Of the Clarity and Certainty of the Word of God,"[69] deserves our attention not because it is an example of Reformation preaching but because of what it says about the ministry of the Word. With prophetic fervor the sermon — albeit more a treatise than a sermon in its published form — calls for a fresh, fearless, unfettered study of Scripture. The Bible is not some sort of sacred preserve to be studied only by Church Fathers, councils of bishops, and faculties of Schoolmen (p. 79). It is the common property of the whole people of God. It is to be read by all of us to nourish our faith and direct our lives (pp. 93-95). All too often this sermon has been discounted as enthusiastic but naive biblicism. When one realizes, however, the high level of Zwingli's biblical scholarship, one can hardly look at it this way. Zwingli was an accomplished scholar who knew the Scriptures in the original languages and had studied deeply in the Fathers. When such a man tells us that the Scriptures have a self-authenticating authority which outstrips the recommendation of the Fathers, the councils, or any other human authority simply because it is the Word of God, that cannot be tossed off as naive enthusiasm (p. 78).

Zwingli's point is a good one. The authority of the Word of God is self-authenticating (pp. 76ff.). How could we imagine that this authority should be dependent on the authority of the Church (p. 89)? The Church may indeed commend the Bible to us, but the authority of the Bible cannot be based on that recommendation. Christian parents commend the Bible to their children, and we may, experientially speaking, believe what the Bible teaches because of that recommendation, but none of us would imagine that the authority of Scripture is based on the authority of our parents. The Word of God has authority because it is God's Word. Zwingli, far from being the rationalist he is often portrayed as, is insistent that the authority of the Word of God is not to be established philosophically any more than it is ecclesiastically (p. 86). One of Zwingli's biggest

69. For an English translation of this sermon, see Ulrich Zwingli, "Of the Clarity and Certainty of the Word of God," in *Zwingli and Bullinger,* ed. G. W. Bromiley, Library of Christian Classics, vol. 24 (Philadelphia: Westminster Press, 1953), pp. 59-95; the page references in the text are to this work. For the original German text, see vol. 1 of *Huldreich Zwingli's sämtliche Werke,* Corpus Reformatorum 88 (Berlin: Verlag von C. A. Schwetschke und Sohn, 1905), pp. 160-75; hereafter Corpus Reformatorum 88.

problems with Scholasticism was its claim to continue the heritage of the philosophy of the ancient world. We may have reasons for accepting the authority of Scripture, but that authority is not based on reason any more than on the authority of the Church.

Interestingly enough, Zwingli puts his strong doctrine of biblical authority in terms of personal experience (pp. 90ff.). He has himself experienced this ability of Scripture to speak with authority. One hears the Word and one recognizes that it is true. This had been his experience during all those years he spent tucked away in his alpine parsonage. He had poured over the pages of the authorities like Jerome and Ambrose, and still the pages of the apostles and prophets spoke more convincingly than those of their commentators (p. 91). Zwingli has put his finger on something here. Authority may not be proved by this insight, but it is certainly demonstrated by it. The Scriptures do have an ability to speak to us century after century, in one culture after another. The authority of Scripture transcends our ages and our cultures (p. 92). While today one gives a great deal of attention to the cultural relativity of the biblical writers, one needs to recognize that Scripture manages to transcend this cultural relativity. This is something Zwingli experienced, and something many others in every age and every kind of culture have experienced in much the same way (p. 90). The fact that this happens again and again demonstrates that Scripture does indeed have authority. The truth of what Zwingli experienced is demonstrated today even more as we discover that the Word of God is transforming the lives of black Africans and South American Indians at the turn of the third Christian millennium every bit as much as it did northern European whites in the sixteenth century or the Hellenistic world in the fourth century. This may be a pragmatic way of looking at it, but the gospel has the power to transform people's lives. The apostle Paul put it very clearly: the gospel "is the power of God to salvation" (Rom. 1:16). What else is authority than just that?

Zwingli spoke of the Word of God being alive (pp. 70ff.). This is a very good way of putting it. The Word of God, whether understood as the incarnate Christ, the preaching of the gospel, or the written Scriptures, does have a vitality about it. It indeed convinces, corrects, overthrows, and brings to light (p. 75). It nourishes, sustains, and supports our faith, and ultimately it is the Word by which we are born again unto eternal life. All Scripture, Zwingli reminds us, can be described as *theopneuston,* to use the word of the apostle Paul (II Tim. 3:16). It has the breath of life breathed into it; it is indeed inspired (p. 93).

As an heir to the heritage of late medieval Rhenish pietism, Zwingli, not surprisingly, has quite a bit to say about the role of the Holy Spirit in the ministry of the Word (pp. 76, 82, 85, 91). This is another way, it would seem, of saying that the Word of God is alive, or at least, of pointing at this same experience of the ability of the Scripture, both written and preached, to transform our lives. It is the Holy Spirit who opens our hearts to receiving the Word (p. 78), who enlightens our minds to understand the Word, and who makes the reading and preaching of Scripture a means of grace (p. 82).

Another insight we value in this sermon is the way Zwingli never lets his doctrine of the Word slip into a static conception of Scripture (pp. 74-76). We would expect one who had been so well schooled by the Christian humanists to have a rather sophisticated understanding of the Word. And in fact, Zwingli does have a rather good grasp of rhetoric and grammar, the various qualities and functions of language, the relation of word to event and of the spoken word to the written word. He was enough of a Renaissance philologist to appreciate the difference between the original text and the translation of that text on one hand and the interpretation of it on the other. No, one can hardly accuse Zwingli of a naive biblicism. Quite to the contrary, he has a very refined understanding of the place of the Bible in the ministry of the Word.

C. A Prophetic Ministry

Zwingli's preaching ministry had many facets to it, but the most interesting for our day is its prophetic facet. There is no question but that Gottfried Locher, in his recent studies of Zwingli's life and thought, is quite correct in emphasizing that the key to the Reformer of Zürich is his Christology. Zwingli above all preached Christ and the saving power of his death and resurrection. According to Locher, the eminent Swiss Reformation historian, Zwingli's soteriology had a strong Anselmian character, and that soteriology was at the center of Zwingli's ministry. That was generally true, however, of the preachers of the Reformation. They were all, above everything else, preachers of the gospel, and people came to hear them because of the good news they preached. It was not the relevance of their critique which turned people on, to put it in the clichés of our day; it was the clarity of their gospel.

Having said this, however, we must also remember Zwingli especially for his prophetic word on such subjects as idolatry, mercenary soldiering, and asceticism. As Neoplatonism came to have greater and greater influence on Christianity, asceticism began to gain an ever stronger grip on Christianity. This was particularly evident in the matters of fasting and celibacy. Fasting had come to be the touchstone of a serious devotional life. It was at the heart of the liturgical calendar. There were two long fasting seasons of the year, Advent and Lent; then there were Friday fasts. Celibacy had come to have such great importance that it was considered a prerequisite for any kind of ministerial vocation. This was the ideal; in actual fact, the typical parish priest in Switzerland was a married man, but for this failing he had to pay a penalty to the bishop. As Zwingli saw it, asceticism was foreign to the Christian gospel, and he forthrightly preached against it.

Dispensing with the traditional liturgical calendar was, of course, only consistent when one dispensed with asceticism. One can hardly be said to observe either Advent or Lent if one does not fast during these seasons. Two sermons have come down to us in which Zwingli broke into his *lectio continua* to preach against Lenten fasting, "Von Erkiessen oder Underscheid der Spysen" and "Ob man Gewalt hab, die Spysen zuo etlichen Zyten verbieten."[70] Apparently the revolt against the fasting laws arose spontaneously among the citizens of Zürich. It was not a planned program of reform. During Lent of 1522 several prominent citizens of Zürich, including the distinguished publisher Christophel Froschauer, publicly broke the Lenten fast. There was a hearing over the matter, and the defendants appealed to Zwingli's preaching to justify themselves. There was consideration of the matter throughout the town, and Zwingli took to the pulpit to assure his congregation that Christians living under grace were not bound by laws regarding which foods were permitted and which were not permitted. That had been characteristic of the Law of Moses, not the gospel of Christ. Since Froschauer had been particularly involved, it is not surprising that he published Zwingli's sermon.

Idolatry was another matter against which Zwingli exercised his prophetic ministry.[71] The canonical prophets had been specially con-

70. Ulrich Zwingli, "Von Erkiessen oder Underscheid der Spysen" and "Ob man Gewalt hab, die Spysen zuo etlichen Zyten verbieten," in Corpus Reformatorum 88:77-136.

71. See Locher, *Die Zwinglische Reformation,* pp. 130ff., and Carlos M. N. Eire, *War against the Idols: The Reformation of Worship from Erasmus to Calvin* (Cambridge: Cambridge University Press, 1986).

cerned with the constant tendency of Israel to fall into idolatry again and again. Zwingli was not an enemy of art nor was he an iconoclast. For him it was a matter of convincing the civil authority and having the town council remove the offending pictures and statues decently and in order. Zwingli was able to carry his point, and finally in June 1524 the city council had the churches cleared of all traces of idolatry.

Zwingli's greatest prophetic concern was mercenary soldiering. While in Glarus he had served as chaplain to a group of soldiers employed by one Italian prince or another. He was appalled by the carnage, the useless waste of life. Not only was he disgusted by the savagery of war, but he saw what it did to the quality of life at home. It was hard work wresting crops from the soil of the Swiss valleys, but when all the young men were off at war, the crops were never even planted. Agriculture disappeared when fast money from the princes of Italy and France was offered. Finally, at the Battle of Pavia, the small-town pastor had seen enough. Zwingli returned from Italy resolved that Swiss young men should never become the pawns of foreign princes. That the flower of Swiss youth should be sold to the pope to wage his petty wars seemed an incredible irony. Back in Switzerland, he began to preach against mercenary soldiering. This was not very popular in Glarus, where a number of the town fathers received handsome pensions from the agents of various Italian princes for the right to recruit soldiers from their small town. These agents bribed their way into town, and when Zwingli set his pulpit squarely against the system, no one thought it amusing. He soon became persona non grata. This, of course, had happened to prophets before him.

With the opposition he encountered in Glarus, Zwingli might well have dropped the issue when he went to Zürich, but he did not. Gottfried Locher recounts a particularly courageous occasion when one of the pope's cardinals arrived in Zürich to arrange for the recruitment of mercenary soldiers.

> In 1521, when the all-powerful Cardinal Schinner was staying in Zürich in connection with the renewal of the alliance with the Pope (Schinner was a humanist, who sought to win Zwingli's friendship) the Reformer preached a memorable sermon, as the papal nuncio was sitting in full vestments below the pulpit: "He also spoke against treaties with princes and noblemen which, if they had been made, were closely watched by every good man to see that what had been promised should be done. Therefore one should not conclude any military treaties, and

if God helped a people to get out of treaties, they should take care and not enter into them again, for they cost a lot of blood. And I wish, said Zwingli, that someone would punch a hole through the Pope's treaty and stick it on his messenger's back so that he could carry it back home. He also said: they sound the alarm for a wolf that eats animals, but nobody wants to restrain the wolf that destroys people. They do right to wear red hats and cloaks: for if you shake them, ducats and crowns will fall out; and if you wring them, the blood of your son, your brother, your cousin, your good friend will run out."[72]

For centuries, even down to our own, the Catholic cantons of Switzerland provided the pope with his Swiss Guard, but generally speaking Zwingli's preaching has shaped the national policy of Switzerland. Swiss soldiers do not fight on foreign soil. Zwingli's opposition to mercenary soldiering has become a national policy in Switzerland. It is from Zwingli's pulpit that Swiss neutrality stems. Ever since, the Protestant pulpit has understood itself to have a prophetic ministry.

IV. John Oecolampadius (1482-1531)[73]

John Oecolampadius, the Reformer of Basel, was one of the anchormen of the Reformation.[74] Along with Ulrich Zwingli, Martin Bucer, and Wolfgang Capito, he was a leading Reformer of the Upper Rhineland. His prodigious scholarship won respect for the Reformation among the intellectuals of his day. Above all, he was an outstanding patristic scholar, who translated for the first time an impressive amount of the writings of the Greek Fathers. He deserves to be recognized among those who have done the most to make Greek Christian

72. Locher, *Zwingli's Thought,* p. 16.

73. Much of the information in this section was previously printed as Hughes Oliphant Old, "The Homiletics of John Oecolampadius and the Sermons of the Greek Fathers," in *Communio Sanctorum: Mélanges offerts à Jean-Jacques von Allmen* (Geneva: Labor et Fides, 1982), pp. 239-50.

74. The definitive work on Oecolampadius is that of Ernst Staehelin, *Das theologische Lebenswerk Johannes Oekolampads,* Quellen und Forschungen zur Reformationsgeschichte, vol. 21 (Leipzig: M. Heinsius Nachfolger, 1939). Professor Staehelin has also supplied us with two volumes of documentary material: *Briefe und Akten zum Leben Oekolampads,* vols. 1 and 2, Quellen und Forschungen zur Reformationsgeschichte, vols. 10 and 19 (Leipzig: M. Heinsius Nachfolger, 1927 and 1934).

thought known in the West.[75] Many of his translations were sermons, which he translated to demonstrate what preaching ought to be. Oecolampadius was a highly respected preacher himself.[76] What is interesting for our study is that he was one of those chiefly responsible for fashioning the homiletical practice of the Rhenish Reformation.

On the eve of the Reformation, Oecolampadius had already won a reputation as a preacher. He followed closely in the footsteps of such great preachers as Strasbourg's Johann Geiler von Kaysersberg and Basel's Johann Heynlin von Stein.[77] He was well schooled in the tradition of Johann Ulrich Surgant's *Manuale curatorum.*[78] These preachers were all leaders in the Christian humanist movement, having given themselves to a careful study of the classical patristic preaching manuals such as Augustine's *De doctrina christiana,* Ambrose's *De officiis,* and Gregory the Great's *Regula pastoralis.* Preaching played an important role in the inner-church reform program of these Christian humanists, and it had been to them that the Church had turned for a preaching ministry in those opening years of the sixteenth century just before the Reformation.[79] Endowed pulpits had been established in most of the cities of the Upper Rhineland, and were supported not only by cathedral chapters and monastery churches but by guilds and city councils as well. Christians of the day loved good preaching and made generous provision for its support.

Oecolampadius occupied three pulpits before he began his work as a

75. On the patristic studies of Oecolampadius, see Old, *Patristic Roots,* pp. 111-18.

76. For an indication of the extent of his reputation as a preacher, see Staehelin, *Lebenswerk,* p. 103, and Staehelin, *Briefe und Akten,* 1:89.

77. On the work of these two great preachers, see Rudolf Cruel, *Geschichte der deutschen Predigt im Mittelalter* (Detmold: Meyer'sche Hofbuchhandlung, 1879); Jane Dempsey Douglass, *Justification in Late Medieval Preaching: A Study of John Geiler of Keisersberg* (Leiden: E. J. Brill, 1966). See as well the study of Johann Geiler which appeared in the previous volume of this work, pp. 530-43.

78. Johann Ulrich Surgant, *Manuale curatorum predicandi prebens modum; tam latino quam vulgari sermone; practice illuminatum: cum certis aliis ad curam animarum pertinentibus: omnibus curatis tam conducibilis quam salubris* (Basel: Michael Furter, 1503). See further, Dorothea Roth, *Die Mittelalterliche Predigttheorie und das Manuale curatorum des Johannes Ulrich Surgant* (Basel, 1956).

79. On Christian humanism in the south German cities, see Otto Herding, "Probleme des frühen Humanismus in Deutschland," *Archiv für Kulturgeschichte* 38 (1956): 344-89; Bernd Moeller, "Die deutschen Humanisten und die Anfänge der Reformation," *Zeitschrift für Kirchengeschichte* 70 (1959), and Bernd Moeller, *Reichsstadt und Reformation* (Gütersloh: Verlaghaus Gerd Mohn, 1962); Lewis W. Spitz, *The Religious Renaissance of the German Humanists* (Cambridge: Harvard University Press, 1963).

Reformer.[80] The first of these, from 1516 to 1518, was in Weinsberg, his native city. In 1518 he was called to the cathedral of Augsburg, one of the leading pulpits of Germany. It was only a few months before this that Luther posted the ninety-five theses on the door of the church in Wittenberg. Oecolampadius observed the events which followed with growing interest. Four years later he left this prestigious post, presumably because of his support of Luther. One would imagine that the bishop would not have been too happy about having an advocate of the Reformation occupying his cathedral pulpit. From Augsburg he went to preach in the monastery of Altomünster, a post he held for only a short time. This position offered him a retreat to think over the issues facing the Church of the time. His preaching evidently was well received not only by the members of the order, but by the people served by the monastery church.

For these early years we have a good amount of source material. There is a collection of twenty manuscript sermons from his Weinsberg ministry.[81] Only two sermons have survived from his Augsburg ministry, although from this period we have a number of Latin translations of the sermons of Gregory of Nazianzus.[82] Six sermons from his ministry at Altomünster have been preserved.[83] We also have a short treatise on

80. On the preaching ministry of Oecolampadius at Weinsberg, Augsburg, and Altomünster, see Staehelin, *Lebenswerk,* pp. 71ff., 97ff., 135ff.

81. The twenty-two sermons from Oecolampadius's Weinsberg ministry have been preserved in manuscript. A photographic reproduction of this manuscript is found in the University Library of Basel. Staehelin, *Lebenswerk,* pp. 72ff.

82. The only sermon preserved from the sermons Oecolampadius preached in the cathedral at Augsburg is "Von den fruchtbarlichen, auch von den schödlichen winden des gartens der seele; ain nutzlicher sermon von den weysen junckfrawen, dero sancta Katherina aine gewesen ist. . . ." See Staehelin, *Lebenswerk,* pp. 97ff. The translations of Gregory of Nazianzus appeared in two collections: John Oecolampadius, *De amandis pauperibus Gregorii Nazanzeni episcopi et theologi sermo, eiusdem ad virginem admonitorius, eiusdem laudes Maccabaeorum, interprete Joanne Oecolampadio, concionatore Augustensi* (Augsburg: Grimm und Wirsung, 1519); a second selection of three sermons appeared two months later: John Oecolampadius, *Divi Gregorii Nazanzeni eruditi aliquot et mirae frugis sermones: In Pascha; In dictum Mattaei . . . , cap. XIX; Laudes Cypriani Martyris, Oecolampadio interprete . . .* (Augsburg: Grimm und Wirsung, 1519). Oecolampadius planned to publish translations of all the sermons of the Cappadocian Father until he discovered that Peter Mosellanus had already undertaken the work. Staehelin, *Lebenswerk,* pp. 103 and 118.

83. Ernst Staehelin, *Oekolampad-Bibliographie, Verzeichnis der im 16. Jahrhundert erschienenen Oekolampaddrucke* (Basel: Verlag der historischen und antiquarischen Gesellschaft, 1918), pp. 39-40, 45-47, 54, 55, 56-60.

preaching which he wrote as a letter to his friend Capito, the renowned preacher of the cathedral of Basel.[84] These documents give us a fairly good picture of the future Reformer's early preaching ministry.

The typical preaching program of the endowed preacher included the following: weekly Sunday preaching, preaching on feast days and saints' days, and daily preaching during Advent and Lent. Among these early sermons of our Reformer, we have two sermons for Easter Sunday, a sermon for the second Sunday after Easter, and a sermon for the third Sunday after Easter. Each is preached on the Gospel lesson for the day. There is a sermon for Ascension Day and a Pentecost series of eight sermons on the seven gifts of the Holy Spirit which began the Sunday before Pentecost and lasted until the fourth Sunday after Trinity. It developed the text from Isaiah 11:2: ". . . and the Spirit of the Lord shall rest upon him, the spirit of wisdom and understanding, the spirit of counsel and might, the spirit of knowledge and the fear of the Lord." Series of this sort were quite characteristic of later medieval preaching. There are three sermons preached on saints' days, as well as a series of seven sermons on the Canticle of Mary (Luke 1:46-55) preached on the Marian feasts. The impression we have here is that the preaching program of Oecolampadius was largely inspired by the feasts of the Christian year and that, to a large extent, the feasts provided the subject matter of the sermons. A text was chosen to develop the general subject. It was the feast, however, which inspired the sermons. On Sundays Oecolampadius preached from the Gospel pericope for the day. While only two examples of this have survived, he must have preached this sort of sermon frequently. His earlier sermons show him to be a typical late medieval preacher.

During this early period the influence of Gregory of Nazianzus is nevertheless clearly discerned.[85] Among the forty-five sermons of Gregory are a number for the Christian feasts, and they are among his most memorable sermons.[86] There are a sermon for Christmas Day, two ser-

---

84. John Oecolampadius, *De risu paschali Oecolampadii ad V. Capitonem theologum epistola apologetica* (Basel: J. Froben, 1518). A modern edition of the text is found in Staehelin, *Briefe und Akten,* 1:44-59.

85. Oecolampadius quotes Gregory three times in *De risu paschali:* Staehelin, *Briefe und Akten,* 1:50, 53, and 56.

86. On the preaching of Gregory of Nazianzus, see A. Donders, *Der heilige Kirchenlehrer Gregor von Nazianz als Homilet* (Münster, 1909); Jaul Gallag, *Langue et style de S. Grégoire de Nazianze dans sa correspondance* (Paris, 1943); M. Guignet, *S. Grégoire de Nazianze orateur et épistolier* (Paris, 1911); Jean Plagnieux, *Saint Grégoire de Nazianze*

mons for Epiphany, two sermons for Easter, and a sermon for Pentecost. There are also several hagiographical sermons preached on various saints' days. His sermon on Saint Athanasius is still considered a model of the hagiographical sermon. Given the sort of preaching program Oecolampadius was expected to fulfill, one can see that the sermons of Gregory of Nazianzus would be particularly helpful to him.

Gregory was not an expository preacher. That, at least, is the picture we get from the collection which has come down to us. He left us no series of sermons on the biblical books, and only one of his surviving sermons is based on a text. The great Cappadocian was a biblical preacher in a rather indirect sense. While his sermons are filled with brilliant biblical allusions and polished scriptural similes, they are focused on some religious theme or subject rather than on the text of Scripture itself. Gregory used the Bible as a source of illustrative material. He is a master of the scriptural example. How effectively he uses biblical characters to dramatize and personify the virtues he extols! Most often this biblical material is focused on some point, principle, or doctrine. The feast of the Epiphany, the life of Saint Cyprian, or the orthodox doctrine of the Trinity is chosen as the subject, and then a wealth of biblical material is gathered around it to support and develop the theme.

As we pointed out in the second volume of this work, Gregory may well have preached series of sermons on different books of the Bible as well. The collection of sermons that has come down to us is designed to show that Gregory was the Christian Demosthenes. Panegyrics and doctrinal sermons, therefore, tended to predominate in this collection. Gregory would probably have preached expository sermons like those of his friends Basil and John Chrysostom.

The Protestant approach to the observance of Christian feasts seems to have been significantly influenced by the Reformers' study of the festal sermons of Gregory of Nazianzus. The Reformation Act of 1529 tells us that the major feasts of the Christian year were to be observed in the Church with prayer, preaching, the celebration of Communion, and the giving of alms.[87] Oecolampadius's concern for the reform of religious hol-

---

Théologien (Paris: Éditions Franciscaines, 1951); Johannes Quasten, *Patrology,* 3 vols. (Utrecht and Antwerp: Spectrum, 1966), 3:236-54; and Rosemary Radford Ruether, *Gregory of Nazianzus, Rhetor and Philosopher* (Oxford: Clarendon Press, 1969).

87. ". . . ettliche fyrtag, vff die man sich in den kilchen zu horung des Gottlichen worts, vmb gemeynen gebets, vnnd bezugung Christlicher liebe. . . ." *Ordnung so ein Ersame Statt Basel den ersten tag Apprilis in jrer Statt vnd Landschafft fürohn zehalten*

idays was largely inspired by the great doctor of the Eastern Church. Gregory tells us in his sermon for Christmas Day that Christians should celebrate their feasts not in the way the heathen festivals are celebrated, not with dancing and decorating the streets, not with luxurious food and clothing, perfume and incense, nor with the glittering of gold and changes of color. The Christian feast should be a feast of the Word. If there be luxury in the Christian feast, it should be found in the passages of Scripture which celebrate the sacred events.[88] It is precisely this concern to reform the feast days which we find in the Reformation Act of 1529.[89] Even beyond this, one notices that the calendar reflected by the festal sermons of Gregory is quite similar to that which the Reformed Church of Basel finally adopted. Gregory's calendar was dominated by a few major feast days rather than being divided into the seasons of the Christian year. That was typical of the fourth and fifth centuries. The great feasts are, above all, Easter, Ascension, Pentecost, Christmas, and Epiphany. The Basel Reformation Act established four major feasts, Christmas, Easter, Ascension, and Pentecost.[90] Other factors helped form the new liturgical calendar of Basel, of course, but the fact that the Continental Reformed churches emphasized the celebration of the major Christian feasts is surely to some extent due to the influence of Gregory of Nazianzus.

The Reformer of Basel, as the other Reformers, thought the cult of the saints had been elaborated to the point of obscuring the centrality of God's revelation in Christ; nevertheless, for Oecolampadius the passing on of the witness of great Christians from the past was a legitimate part of preaching. He never lost his interest in the hagiographical sermon, and this is surely due in large measure to his admiration for the sermons of Gregory of Nazianzus. In the Reformation Act of 1529 we read, "But the good works, great piety and blessedness of the holy and ever blessed Virgin Mary, the holy Apostles, St. John the Baptist, and the martyrs of Christ . . . should be earnestly remembered in those churches where daily

---

erkant. Darinnen, wie die verworffene myssbruch, mit waren Gottes dienst ersetzt . . . , MDXXIX. Quoted from the edition of Aemilius Ludwig Richter, *Die evangelischen Kirchenordnungen des sechzehnten Jahrhunderts,* ed. Aemilius Ludwig Richter, 2 vols. (Weimar: Landes-Industriecomptoirs, 1846), p. 126.

88. Gregory of Nazianzus, *Oration XXXVIII* 5.

89. Ernst Staehelin, *Das Buch der Basler Reformation* (Basel: Helbing und Lichtenhahn, 1929), p. 211.

90. Richter, *Kirchenordnungen,* p. 126.

morning prayer and sermon are held, . . . and their feast days should remain on the calendar."[91] Although the saints' days were not to be regarded as public holidays, the saints were to be remembered in the regular course of daily preaching. This was to be done by using the lives of saints as sermon illustrations. In the first article of the Reformation Act, "How the Word of God Is to Be Proclaimed," we find a number of very specific ways in which the preacher is to expound upon the text of Scripture. One is to illustrate the teaching of Scripture through stories from the lives of the saints. "When it is appropriate to celebrate the memorial of the Blessed Virgin Mary, the Mother of Jesus Christ, and the other elect saints of God, who now live in eternal blessedness, then the preacher ought to celebrate such feast days in such a way that God is praised in his saints."[92] Here is a clear allusion to Gregory's sermon on Saint Athanasius, where the great patristic orator begins by saying, "In praising Athanasius I shall be praising God."[93] What Oecolampadius seems to have in mind is not so much a hagiographical sermon, but rather an expository sermon preached in regular course that, when appropriate, uses hagiographical illustrations. This, of course, was quite consistent with the Reformer's understanding of the relation of Scripture and tradition. For Oecolampadius, Scripture alone had divine authority. The Fathers, the church councils, and the saints of the past were *testes veritatis,* witnesses to the truth. They witnessed to Scripture, expounded Scripture, and in their lives illustrated the truth of Scripture.

Leaving the monastery at Altomünster in January 1522, Oecolampadius was well on his way to becoming an open supporter of the Refor-

91. "Aber die verdienst, hohe tugenden vnd seligkeit, der heyligen ewigen junckfrawen Marie, der heyligen Apostelen, sant Johansen des Touffers, vnnd der lieben Marterer Christi, diewyl man taglich frubet vnd tag predig haben wurt, Sollen mit ernstlicher (wie davor in Verkundigung des Gottlichen worts bevolhen ist) begangen werden, vnd die tag jrer gedechtnuss im kalender unverruckt bliben." Richter, *Kirchenordnungen,* p. 126.

92. "Vnd ob sich zun zyten zutragen, das man der gebenedieten junckfrawen Marie, der muter Jesu Christi, oder anderer usserwelten Gottes heyligen, so yetzt in ewiger seligkeit sind, gedechtnuss begon, do sollen die Predicanten solche fest der massen halten, damit Gott in synen heyligen gebrysst, die Gottliche ehr nit den creaturen." Richter, *Kirchenordnungen,* p. 121.

93. Gregory of Nazianzus, *Oration XXI* 1. Oecolampadius entitled one of his Marian sermons, "De laudando in Maria Deo," once again inspired by the same passage of Gregory. The sermon was published both in Augsburg and Basel. Staehelin, *Lebenswerk,* p. 138.

mation. Almost two years passed before he continued his public preaching ministry. In the meantime he devoted himself to translating the works of John Chrysostom. Soon after Oecolampadius returned to Basel, Andreas Cratander, one of the leading publishers of the city, set him to making a Latin translation of the sixty-six sermons of Chrysostom on the book of Genesis.[94] These sermons represent an entirely different approach to preaching than the sermons of Gregory of Nazianzus.[95] They are based on the *lectio continua,* and are basically a verse-by-verse exposition of the text. As we saw in volume II of this work, the major portion of Chrysostom's sermons are preached via the *lectio continua.*[96]

In the fall of 1523 Oecolampadius was asked to preach the Advent sermons at Saint Martin's Church in the center of Basel.[97] The regular preacher was in poor health, and so Oecolampadius took up the responsibility of preaching each workday during Advent. He chose to preach through the First Epistle of John in much the same way Chrysostom had preached through Genesis.[98] The sermons had been carefully composed

94. John Oecolampadius, *Divi Ioannis Chrysostomi, Archiepiscopi Constantinopolitani, in totum Geneseos librum Homiliae sexaginta sex, a Ioanne Oecolampadio hoc anno uersae* . . . (Basel: Cratander, 1523).

95. On the preaching of John Chrysostom, see Leopold Ackerman, *Die Beredsamkeit des heiligen Johannes Chrysostomus* (Würtzburg, 1889); Thomas Ameringer, "The Stylistic Influences of the Second Sophistic on the Panegyrical Sermons of St. John Chrysostom: A Study in Greek Rhetoric" (Ph.D. diss., Catholic University of America, 1921); Paul Albert, *St. Jean Chrysostome considéré comme orateur populaire* (Paris, 1858); Chrysostomus Baur, *John Chrysostom and His Time,* trans. M. Gonzaga, 2 vols. (Westminster, Md.: Newman Press, 1959); Mary Albania Burns, "Saint John Chrysostom's Homilies on the Statues: A Study of Their Rhetorical Qualities and Form" (Ph.D. diss., Catholic University of America, 1930); H. M. Hubbel, "Chrysostom and Rhetoric," *Classical Philology* 19 (1924): 261-76; and Quasten, *Patrology,* 3:424-82.

96. See my section on John Chrysostom in Hughes Oliphant Old, *The Reading and Preaching of the Scriptures in the Worship of the Christian Church,* vol. 2, *The Patristic Age* (Grand Rapids: Wm. B. Eerdmans Publishing Co., 1997), pp. 171-222.

97. Staehelin, *Lebenswerk,* pp. 220ff.

98. As we have seen, Oecolampadius was not the first Reformer to be attracted to the *lectio continua* through the sermons of John Chrysostom. In 1519 Zwingli began his ministry in Zürich with a series of sermons on the Gospel of Matthew, following closely the pattern of Chrysostom. He continued following the sermons of Chrysostom for a number of years. Influenced by Zwingli, Capito began the same practice in Basel shortly thereafter. Cf. Old, *Patristic Roots,* pp. 191-97. Equally important was the fact that Wolfgang Capito had begun to preach a series of *lectio continua* sermons on the Epistle to the Romans at the cathedral of Basel just a few years before. We will have more to say about this in the section on Capito. One should not overlook a second patristic influence.

and a short time afterwards were published.[99] Like the sermons of Chrysostom, they aim primarily at explaining the text of Scripture; that is, they are expository sermons. The series of twenty-one sermons proceeds through the five chapters of the book taking three to six verses for each sermon. The exposition is very sober, relying chiefly on the principle that Scripture is best explained by Scripture. Passages from the Law, the Psalms, the Prophets, and the Gospels are all called on to explain the text of John's epistle. There is almost no use of what today we would call the sermon illustration, the human interest story, or the literary allusion. There are references to Christian history, quotations from the Fathers, and biblical illustrations, but they are very lean and sober. The more elaborate rhetoric of Gregory of Nazianzus has been replaced by the more chaste rhetoric of John Chrysostom. There is nothing which attempts to display erudition or literary prowess. The example of Chrysostom has disciplined and purified Oecolampadius's style. Again, it is following the example of Chrysostom that we find a good balance in these sermons between exposition and application. These sermons show confidence in the ability of the text to interest the congregation. Oecolampadius evidently feels no need to capture the ears of his hearers by storm.

The preaching of Oecolampadius was well received, and in March 1525 he became the regular preacher at Saint Martin's. A number of his sermons have been preserved from this period.[100] Six of these were preached on the Sunday lectionary. One was preached on the feast of Saint Matthew and one on the feast of Pentecost. The Pentecost sermon, taking the Gospel of the day, John 14:23-29, develops the subject of the Holy Spirit as Comforter. It begins by telling us all the names by which the Holy Spirit is identified. The preacher alludes to the medieval hymn

---

Augustine had preached a similar series on I John. See Augustine of Hippo, *Saint Augustin, Commentaire de la première épître de S. Jean,* ed. Paul Agaësse (Paris: Éditions du Cerf, 1961).

99. John Oecolampadius, *In epistolam Joannis apostoli catholicam primam Joannis Oecolampadii demegoriae, hoc est: homiliae una et XX* (Basel: Cratander, 1524). These sermons went through several editions in Latin, German, and French. Staehelin, *Lebenswerk,* p. 232 n. 1.

100. These were published in 1536 by Oswald Myconius as an appendix to Oecolampadius's commentary on the Gospel of Matthew: *Enarratio in evangelium Matthaei d. Jo. Oecolampadio auctore et alia nonnulla, quae sequens pagella indicabit,* ed. Oswald Myconius (Basel: Cratander, 1536). Several of these sermons are reprinted in Karl Rudolf Hagenbach, *Johann Oekolampad und Oswald Myconius, die Reformatoren Basels, Leben und ausgewählte Schriften* (Elberfeld: R. L. Friderichs, 1859).

"Veni creator spiritus," which gives to the Holy Spirit so many marvelous names. Still other names are given by David, the prophets, and the apostles. In this text Jesus makes a special point of calling the Holy Spirit the Comforter because he is about to begin the events of his passion. For his first point Oecolampadius develops the meaning of the word "comforter." In his second point he speaks of the uselessness of seeking comfort in the things of this world. This is developed by means of a number of verses from the Psalms, Moses, and Isaiah. He explains the passage from Jeremiah concerning the two baskets of figs. One can have spiritual fruit or the fruit of this world. He quotes Gregory to show that those who cultivate the comforts of the flesh resist the comforts of the Spirit. He quotes several passages from the Gospels in which Jesus speaks about serving two masters or seeking one's comfort in riches. The Reformer tells of the thoughts of Augustine on how Jesus was strengthened by the Holy Spirit in his passion. For his third point he speaks of God as the source of true comfort in time of need, developing it with the aid of the psalm text, "I thought on thy judgments and was comforted." We receive comfort, the Reformer tells us, from meditating on the gracious acts of God. He concludes the sermon by urging the congregation to seek true comfort in God alone. Here is a good example of Antiochene exegesis. The word "comforter" is explained in its literary context, that is, in relation to the story of Christ's passion. Here we see Scripture interpreted by Scripture and the passing on of the patristic witness to Scripture. Exposition and application are well balanced. This sermon is a good example of how effective a very simple and unadorned explanation of Scripture can be.

On Sundays and feast days Oecolampadius was obliged to follow the lectionary. He was likewise required to preach Lenten and Advent sermons. While he indeed preached in Advent, his sermons on I John were not in any significant sense Advent sermons. That is, they did not develop the traditional themes of Advent, but focused on the biblical text itself. During Lent of 1527, he preached a series of thirty-seven sermons on Lamentations.[101] The appropriateness of the book for Lent was obvious, but with the Turks already threatening the gates of Vienna the book had a special relevance. Oecolampadius was not always so fortunate. His most significant preaching during this period had to be preached outside the

---

101. John Oecolampadius, *Inn die clag Hieremie, des heligen propheten, eine schöne uszlegung durch Johanem Oecolampadium in der Kirchen zu Basel geprediget, vorhin nie im truck uszangen* (Basel: Ruprecht Winter, 1545).

traditions of the Christian year. Beginning in the summer of 1525, he did a *lectio continua* series on the Psalms.[102] These sermons were delivered on weekday mornings at eight o'clock, and the series lasted well over a year. We also hear of series on Daniel, Ezekiel, and Paul's two letters to the Corinthians, although the text of these sermons has not come down to us.[103] Until the liturgical reforms proposed by the south German Reformers were officially adopted in 1529, Oecolampadius honored to some extent the traditions of the lectionary and the Christian year. He worked as best he could within these traditional structures, but the sermons of John Chrysostom had led him to desire to make the center of his preaching ministry a systematic preaching through of one biblical book after another.

With adoption of the Reformation Act of 1529, Oecolampadius became pastor of the cathedral of Basel. The liturgical reforms advocated by the south German Reformation were adopted. The preaching of the *lectio continua* became one of these reforms in Basel, just as it had been in Strasbourg and Zürich. Oecolampadius was the preacher at the principal service of worship each Sunday. He began his ministry at the cathedral by preaching through the Gospel of Mark.[104] This was, of course, a tacit recognition that he was the successor of his friend Wolfgang Capito, who as cathedral preacher in 1515-19 had begun the Reformed preaching ministry in Basel cathedral by preaching through the Gospel of Matthew.[105] Oecolampadius continued this series on Mark until his death in November 1531. One hundred thirty-one of these sermons have been preserved. Two other sermons were preached at the cathedral each Sunday, in services at noon and at four in the afternoon. In all probability the sermons at these services treated Old Testament books or New Testament epistles.[106] There was also daily preaching each morning. How these sermons were divided up among the other ministers assigned to the cathedral, we do not know. We do have a series of sermons on Colossians which Oeco-

102. Staehelin, *Lebenswerk*, pp. 411-18.

103. Staehelin, *Lebenswerk*, pp. 232 and 428.

104. These sermons were recorded by Balthasar Vögelin. Staehelin, *Lebenswerk*, p. 490 n. 1. The diary of Bonifacius Amerbach also frequently gives brief indications of the contents of these sermons. Staehelin, *Lebenswerk*, p. 490.

105. Much new light has been shed on this fascinating figure by Beate Stierle, *Capito als Humanist*, Quellen und Forschungen zur Reformationsgeschichte, vol. 42 (Gütersloh: Gerd Mohn, 1974).

106. Staehelin, *Lebenswerk*, pp. 489-92.

lampadius was preaching at the time of his death.[107] These sermons were preached at the daily services rather than on Sunday. Perhaps upon beginning his ministry at the cathedral, Oecolampadius started preaching a *lectio continua* series on the Pauline letters.

For Oecolampadius the reform of preaching was at the heart of the reform of worship. This is very clear from the first article of the Reformation Act of 1529, where we find some of the homiletical principles which shaped the Reformer's preaching ministry. "From now on nothing is to be preached but the holy Word of God, the Gospel of Jesus Christ. The glad tidings is to be preached to the faithful, pure, clear and simple, to the glory of God and the building up of brotherly love."[108] God is glorified in the preaching of his Word. The preaching of the Word of God is an act of worship, one of the principal acts of Christian worship. The Reformation Act continues: "In order that the Word of God be preached with purity and clarity the ministers of the Word are to preach only the books of the Old and New Testament Scriptures."[109] As the Reformers of Basel understood it, the text of Scripture itself was to be the subject matter of the true sermon. The Scriptures are to be interpreted out of faith and love and are to serve the glory of God and the increase of Christian love. To be sure, the preacher may in the service of his exposition of the biblical text use parables, comparisons and parallels from history and nature, popular proverbs, and other such things, provided they are consistent with Christian faith and virtue. This is to be done with moderation according to the example of Christ, the prophets, and the apostles.[110] Oecolampadius has nothing against a chaste use of rhetoric, provided it draws attention to the text rather than obscuring it. He advocated expository preaching, but it was a very sober sort of expository preaching. A sermon must give primary attention to the Holy Writings themselves. It is here that the influ-

---

107. John Oecolampadius, *In epistolam d. Pauli ad Colossenses conciones aliquot piae ac doctae, ad tempora nostra valde accomodae, nunc primum in lucem editae, authore Joanne Oecolampadio* (Bern: Mathias Apiarius, 1546). Cf. Staehelin, *Lebenswerk,* pp. 492-96.

108. ". . . nutzit anders, dann allein das heilig Gottlich wort, das Evangelion Jesu Christi, die froliche bottschafft der gloubigen, pur, klar unnd heyter, zu der ehren Gottes vnd pflantzung bruderlicher liebe truwlicher verkunden." Richter, *Kirchenordnungen,* p. 120.

109. "Damit aber das Gottlich wort klar vnd rein geprediget, sollen die diener des worts sich allein der Biblischen bucher, das ist der Nuwen vnd Alten Testamenten gebruchen." Richter, *Kirchenordnungen,* p. 121.

110. Richter, *Kirchenordnungen,* p. 121.

ence of John Chrysostom is most evident. The doxological nature of preaching is best served by purity, clarity, and faithfulness to the Word of God.

Another thing to be noticed in the Reformation Act is the way the doxological and didactic aspects of preaching are to balance each other. Preaching is doxological; it is to glorify God. It is the doxological aspect of preaching which makes it legitimately a part of worship. Ever since his treatise *De risu paschali,* Oecolampadius had a horror of sermons which tried to entertain the congregation. Nevertheless, sermons also had a didactic function. Preaching is also to build up the Church and edify the neighbor. "The Word of God is food for the soul and the guideline for the Christian life."[111] It is to promote Christian fellowship and virtue. It should teach; it should instruct. Indeed, all this is found quite clearly, both by example and precept, in Gregory of Nazianzus and John Chrysostom. If some today disdain the didactic preaching of the Reformation, they are deploring an aspect of the Reformation most clearly inspired by the Fathers.[112]

V. Strasbourg

No city in Germany was blessed with so many extraordinary preachers during the first generation of the Reformation as Strasbourg.[113] For several generations Strasbourg had known an intense spiritual life. It was a

---

111. "Diewyl das heylig Gottlich Wort, die ware spyss der seelen, vnd richtschyt eins Christenlichen lebens ist. . . ." Richter, *Kirchenordnungen,* p. 120.

112. Gregory of Nazianzus, *Oration II* 35-39 and 45-49. John Chrysostom, *De sacerdote* 4.3-8; 5.1-8.

113. On the city of Strasbourg at the beginning of the sixteenth century, see Lorna Jane Abray, *The People's Reformation: Magistrates, Clergy, and Commons in Strasbourg, 1500-1598* (Ithaca, N.Y.: Cornell University Press, 1985); Johann Adam, *Evangelische Kirchengeschichte der Stadt Strasbourg bis zur französische Revolution* (Strasbourg: Heitz, 1922); Miriam Usher Chrisman, *Lay Culture, Learned Culture: Books and Social Change in Strasbourg, 1480-1599* (New Haven: Yale University Press, 1982); Miriam Usher Chrisman, *Strasbourg and the Reform* (New Haven: Yale University Press, 1967); Andreas Jung, *Geschichte der Reformation der Kirche im Strassburg und der Ausbreitung derselben in den Gemeinden des Elsasses* (Strasbourg: F. G. Leyrault, 1830); Moeller, "Die deutschen Humanisten und die Anfänge der Reformation"; Moeller, *Reichsstadt und Reformation;* Steven E. Ozment, *The Reformation in the Cities* (New Haven: Yale University Press, 1975); and Spitz, *The Religious Renaissance of the German Humanists.*

city accustomed to good preaching. In fact, the city had taken an impressive lead in the cultural life of Germany. It was one of the centers of Alsatian Christian humanism.[114] Sebastian Brandt, one of the leading poets of Germany, lived and wrote in Strasbourg. Johann Gutenberg, usually credited with inventing printing, had spent many years in Strasbourg, and the city still had an impressive printing industry at the beginning of the Reformation. Jakob Wimpfeling, one of the pacesetting educational reformers of the Renaissance, had founded his famous Latin school in nearby Sélestat and was constantly in Strasbourg encouraging the budding literati who had been his students. Strasbourg could even claim the honor of having Johann Geiler von Kaysersberg as the preacher of their magnificent cathedral.[115] Geiler was surely one of the greatest preachers of the Middle Ages, perhaps the last great preacher of medieval Germany. He preached there from 1478 to 1516, and in that time taught the prosperous merchants and gifted artisans of that very prosperous city to value good preaching.

A. Matthäus Zell (1477-1548)

It was Matthäus Zell who first preached the Reformation in Strasbourg. Zell had succeeded to the elaborately carved stone pulpit of Johann Geiler in 1518, just a few months after Luther first sounded the trumpet of reform.[116] When called to Strasbourg he was a mature man in his early for-

114. Christian humanism refers to a particular approach to the Church which developed in northern Europe a generation before the Reformation. It should not be confused with philosophical humanism. It was called humanism not in opposition to theism but because it emphasized the humanities, that is, the recovery of Latin, Greek, and Hebrew. Its motto was "Back to the sources of Christian antiquity." By this was meant a renewed study of Scripture in the original languages as well as a study of patristic literature. For the Christian humanists this was an alternative to medieval Scholasticism. See Herding, "Probleme des frühen Humanismus in Deutschland"; Moeller, "Die deutschen Humanisten und die Anfänge der Reformation"; and Spitz, *The Religious Renaissance of the German Humanists*.

115. See Hughes Oliphant Old, *The Reading and Preaching of the Scriptures in the Worship of the Christian Church*, vol. 3, *The Medieval Church* (Grand Rapids: Wm. B. Eerdmans Publishing Co., 1999).

116. On Matthäus Zell, see Robert Stupperich, "Zell, Matthäus," in *Religion in Gegenwart und Geschichte*, 3rd ed., 7 vols. (Tübingen: J. C. B. Mohr [Paul Siebeck], 1957), 6:1891ff.; A. Erichson, *Matthäus Zell* (1879); Johannes Fider, "Matthäus Zell," in

ties who had lectured in theology at the University of Freiburg and eventually become rector of the university. He, as Johann Geiler, had come from the Alsatian town of Kaysersberg, the same town, incidentally, where Albert Schweitzer was born. The call to the pulpit at Strasbourg was an honor. It was in itself recognition that he was an accomplished preacher. Almost immediately Zell was attracted by Luther's call for reform. By 1521 he openly embraced the Reformation and began to preach, we are told, "as Luther preached." We wish we knew more exactly what that meant. More than likely it meant that Zell began to preach justification by faith in Christ. No doubt when Luther's *Postil* appeared the following year, Zell would have been one of the first to use it in shaping his own preaching ministry. It was for preachers like Zell that Luther intended his *Postil.*

Matthäus Zell was a very popular preacher. He had quickly won the support of the people of Strasbourg, and when he began to preach the Reformation they supported him enthusiastically. Apparently none of his sermons have been preserved for us. As much as he followed the example of Luther in his preaching, he also seems to have retained the popular style of preaching he learned from his predecessor Johann Geiler. Zell, too, had a reputation for preaching practical sermons for the common people in a vivid and simple style. However much he may have embraced the Reformation, he still continued the tradition of Alsatian Christian humanism which had, since the end of the fifteenth century, cultivated an intense inward devotion and a practical piety among the common people.

B. Wolfgang Capito (1478-1541)

In 1523 Zell was joined by another of the leading preachers of the Rhineland, Dr. Wolfgang Capito.[117] Born in Hagenau, a small city just

---

Realencyklopädie für protestantische Theologie und Kirche, 3rd ed., 22 vols. (Leipzig: J. C. Hinrichs'sche Buchhandlung, 1896-1906), 21:650-52; Timotheus W. Röhrich, "Matthäus und Katherina Zell," in *Mitteilungen aus der Geschichte der evangelischen Kirche des Elsasses,* 3 vols. (Paris: Treuttel und Wurtz, 1855), 3:84-179; and William H. Klaustermeyer, "The Role of Matthew and Catherine Zell in the Strassburg Reformation" (Ph.D. diss., Stanford University, 1965).

117. On Capito, see Stierle, *Capito als Humanist;* James M. Kittelson, *Wolfgang Capito, from Humanist to Reformer* (Leiden: E. J. Brill, 1975); and Otto Erich Strasser, *La pensée théologique de Wolfgang Capiton* (Neuchâtel: Secrétariat de l'Université, 1938).

north of Strasbourg, Capito was a native Alsatian and had strong family connections in Strasbourg. The Köpffel family were leading printers at the time, "Capito" being the Latin form of the family name. After a successful ministry as cathedral preacher in Basel, he was called to Mainz as cathedral preacher. Not only was this call an opportunity to occupy a prestigious pulpit, it was also an opportunity to influence one of the leading princes of the German church.[118] For three years Capito was able to encourage Archbishop Albrecht von Brandenburg to at least give Luther and his supporters a fair hearing during those early, critical years.[119] But after three years of the intrigues of court life, Capito became disenchanted with the politics of reform.[120] In Mainz he had taken the role of compromise, as one would expect from a disciple of Erasmus. He knew he would not be able to make an overt and public commitment to the Reformation without losing his influence at the court of Germany's most powerful archbishop. The move to Strasbourg would make it possible to make an open witness and take an active role in the reform by preaching the gospel; it freed him from the ambiguities of his ministry in Mainz. If in Mainz he could only be a crypto-Protestant, in Strasbourg he would be free to begin the work of reform. So it was that, encouraged by Zell, Capito became provost of the collegiate Church of Saint Thomas. It was an influential post in a prosperous city.[121] It would give him an opportunity both to preach and to continue his biblical studies.

Capito had already made a significant contribution to the reform of Christian worship. During his Basel pastorate he had initiated a reform of preaching, beginning in the spring of 1518 a series of expository sermons on the Epistle to the Romans following the *lectio continua*. This might well be regarded as the first liturgical reform of the Protestant Reformation. It was a reform, however, rooted not in Wittenberg but in the Christian humanism of the Rhineland, and flowed naturally from the concerns of Jakob Wimpfeling, Johann Geiler, and the Alsatian Christian humanists who wanted to restore the Church of their day by a recovery of both biblical and patristic theology. But it was also a reform shaped by the concerns of Erasmus and his very literary approach to Christian humanism.

118. We remember that it was to buy this eminent post, the archbishopric of Mainz, that the family of Albrecht von Brandenburg paid the papacy too lavishly, so lavishly that the money had to be raised by the sale of indulgences.

119. Kittelson, *Wolfgang Capito*, pp. 52-82.

120. Kittelson, *Wolfgang Capito*, pp. 88ff.

121. Kittelson, *Wolfgang Capito*, pp. 91ff.

Capito was a highly respected member of the more international Erasmian circle of Christian humanism. He belonged to that elite circle of Renaissance scholars who knew all three of the ancient languages: Latin, Greek, and Hebrew. When Capito was cathedral preacher in Basel he drew great crowds, and those crowds included the aristocracy of the scholarly world: Johann Froeben, Bonifacius Amerbach, John Oecolampadius, and even Erasmus, who never missed a sermon of Capito's.

At the beginning of Lent in 1518, Capito began the required Lenten series of sermons by taking up Romans and preaching through it every day, verse by verse, until he finished the first chapter.[122] (Until Beate Stierle's recent discovery of a transcript of this series of sermons, it was believed that no sermons from Capito had come down to us.) Then in Advent of the same year he took up where he had left off and continued through to chapter 4. In Lent of 1519 he returned to the book, preaching through the fourth and fifth chapters. And before leaving Basel he evidently took up the series again, getting at least as far as the seventh chapter.[123] About this time Capito also began a *lectio continua* series of sermons on the Gospel of Matthew, apparently following the lead of Zwingli. The series on Romans, however, seems to have been Capito's own idea as much as it may have been inspired by John Chrysostom. As cathedral preacher, his contract required that he preach for Sundays and feast days of the year, but also daily during Advent and Lent. The Advent and Lenten series had become traditional in the late Middle Ages, but unlike the tradition of the Gospels and Epistles of the lectionary for Sundays and holidays, there were no required Scripture lessons for these sermons.

Preaching through Romans on a *lectio continua* was nevertheless a surprising thing for Capito to do, even if it did not break any rules. Capito was very intentionally returning to what he knew was the practice of the patristic age. Long before the lectionary of the Christian year had developed, the Fathers had preached the *lectio continua*. Capito was a good enough patristic scholar to have gathered this from a number of sources. On the other hand, one source of this information must have been especially significant. Only a few months prior to this Capito's good friend, Johann Froeben, the distinguished publisher, had given the scholarly world five folio volumes of the sermons of Chrysostom, most of

122. On the theological significance of these sermons, see Kittelson, *Wolfgang Capito,* pp. 43ff.

123. Stierle, *Capito als Humanist,* pp. 55 and 63.

which were *lectio continua* sermons on various New Testament books. As we have shown, this edition of Chrysostom's sermons inspired Zwingli's series of *lectio continua* sermons on Matthew less than a year later when he began his ministry in Zürich.

According to Stierle, these sermons are based on a very careful philological study of the Greek text of Romans. In making this study Capito used all the new methods of Renaissance literary analysis. He obviously used the paraphrase of Romans Erasmus had published just a short time before.[124] This work intended to help the preacher of the day get behind the Latin Vulgate, by providing in Latin a fresh interpretation of the Greek. Erasmus had hoped, by paraphrasing the text, to bring out nuances of meaning which a more straightforward translation would not be able to convey. Besides the paraphrase of Erasmus and his own knowledge of Greek and the general literature of antiquity, Capito had also studied the patristic commentaries. He used Origen's commentary on Romans, although he more likely than not disagreed with him.[125] He used Ambrosiaster and Theodoret of Cyrus, as well as Theophylactus of Bulgaria, who had made a learned anthology of Antiochene commentators on various books of the Bible.[126] What is unusual in these sermons is that the preacher lets his congregation see his work of interpretation. He lets his hearers see him at work with his tools. It is fascinating to watch, but it also demonstrates the integrity of the preacher's work.

What is most interesting about this series of sermons by one of the leading preachers of Germany is that it was in progress when the preacher began to hear about the teachings of Martin Luther. The first part of the series was begun only four months after the appearance of Luther's ninety-five theses and shows no acquaintance with Luther's teaching on justification by faith.[127] But in between the first part and the second part, preached in December 1518, Capito had begun to read the works of Luther. According to Stierle, this study of Luther inspired Capito to become more rigorous in his study of Scripture and to develop a Pauline doctrine of justification by faith very similar to Luther's.[128]

We wish we knew more about the preaching ministry of Capito after he came to Strasbourg. Unfortunately we do not have any of his

124. Stierle, *Capito als Humanist,* p. 57.
125. Stierle, *Capito als Humanist,* p. 66.
126. Stierle, *Capito als Humanist,* p. 67.
127. Stierle, *Capito als Humanist,* pp. 102ff.
128. Stierle, *Capito als Humanist,* pp. 174-77.

Strasbourg sermons. We imagine, however, that he made a significant contribution to the liturgical shaping of the ministry of the Word in Strasbourg, and about this we will speak a bit further along. There is one thing we can be fairly certain about in regard to Capito's preaching ministry at Strasbourg. He was very much concerned to restore the reading and preaching of the Old Testament to its rightful place in Christian worship. He was one of the pioneers in the recovery of biblical Hebrew. In 1516 he published a Hebrew grammar.[129] In fact, it was the first Hebrew grammar published by a Christian. While in Strasbourg he published three commentaries on Old Testament books: on Habakkuk in 1526, on Hosea in 1528, and finally on the creation narrative in Genesis. To this commentary he gave the name *Hexaemeron,* showing his intention to continue the long tradition of preaching a series of sermons on the six days of creation.[130] We also know that he edited commentaries on Isaiah and Jeremiah by his friend Oecolampadius while in the city. While these publications are not sermons but rather commentaries, they probably can be taken as an indication that Capito gave considerable time to preaching through these books of the Old Testament.

C. Kaspar Hedio (1494-1552)

Often called the first Protestant church historian, Kaspar Hedio was born in Baden and studied in the famous Latin school of Pforzheim, one of the seedbeds of Christian humanism in the German Rhineland. He did his university studies at Freiburg and Basel. While in Basel he was inspired by the interpretation of Scripture Wolfgang Capito was preaching at the Basel cathedral. His own mastery of Greek made it possible for him to do original expository preaching of the New Testament. For several years he preached at Saint Theodore's Church in a suburb of Basel, and then in 1523, through Capito's influence, he was called to Strasbourg. Although the terms of the call stipulated that he not preach in a Lutheran tendency, he seems to have ignored the restriction.

While Hedio was not a theologian of wide reputation as were Zell,

---

129. On Capito's Hebrew grammar in particular and his Old Testament studies in general, see Old, *Patristic Roots,* pp. 135-36.

130. On the *Hexaemeron* of Basil the Great, see vol. II of this work; on the *Hexaemeron* of Bonaventure, see vol. III.

Capito, and Bucer, he was a greatly beloved pastor in the city of Strasbourg. He was particularly concerned with the support of charitable institutions, schools, nursing homes, and orphanages. Another of his concerns was foreign missions. While we do not have a collection of Hedio's sermons, we know that he published two large folio volumes of the sermons of John Chrysostom, one on the Gospel of Matthew and the other on the Gospel of John. We imagine the purpose of this was to give German preachers a good example of expository preaching.[131] It was above all from Chrysostom that the Rhenish Reformers learned their approach to preaching. He was the patristic model of their reform.

D. Martin Bucer (1491-1551)

Among the Protestant Reformers of the sixteenth century, Martin Bucer had the most penetrating insight into the questions of the reform of worship.[132] Bucer was first of all a biblical scholar. He was, sad to say, a classic case of a child from a large family who was placed in a monastery at an early age to ensure his receiving the sort of education he could otherwise never have afforded. At the age of fifteen he entered the Dominican cloister at Sélestat. The Dominicans gave him an excellent education, sending him ten years later to the University of Heidelberg, a recognized center for the new learning of Christian humanism. There he steeped himself in the knowledge of Greek and biblical Hebrew.

Already in Sélestat he had been introduced to the Christian humanism of Jakob Wimpfeling, the renowned Alsatian Latinist whose famous Latin school had trained so many of the best scholars of the day. Bucer was an especially gifted student. It was there that he picked up his strong

131. See my study of Hedio in Old, *Patristic Roots*, pp. 131-34.

132. On Bucer and his significance for Protestant worship, see the following: Heinrich Bornkamm, *Martin Bucers Bedeutung* (Gütersloh: C. Bertelsmann, 1952); Hastings Eells, *Martin Bucer* (New Haven: Yale University Press, 1931); Constantin Hopf, *Martin Bucer and the English Reformation* (Oxford: B. Blackwell, 1946); Friedhelm Krüger, *Bucer und Erasmus, Eine Untersuchung zum Einfluss des Erasmus auf die Theologie Martin Bucers* (Wiesbaden: Steiner Verlag, 1970); Johannes Müller, *Martin Bucers Hermeneutik* (Gütersloh: Gerd Mohn, 1965); Peter Stephens, *The Holy Spirit in the Theology of Martin Bucer* (Cambridge: University Press, 1970); G. J. van de Poll, *Martin Bucer's Liturgical Ideas* (Assen: Van Gorcum, 1954); and Edward Charles Whitaker, *Martin Bucer and the Book of Common Prayer*, Alcuin Club Collection, vol. 55 (Great Wakering: Mayhew-McCrimmon, 1974).

72

Augustinian theology and his love not only for Scripture but for patristic literature as well.

When young Bucer arrived at Heidelberg, Erasmus was the bright light of Christian humanism. True to the program of Christian humanism, he steeped himself in Greek and Hebrew, the biblical languages. He studied the biblical commentaries of the rabbis, something few Christian scholars had done up to that time. Heidelberg was one of the few universities where such a course of study was possible. Bucer was fascinated by the Erasmus publication of the complete works of Jerome, and eagerly learned all he could from Erasmus. But then in April 1518, a few months after he had come out with his ninety-five theses, Luther arrived in Heidelberg for his famous debates with several of the distinguished theologians of the Dominican Order. Luther may not have won over the leaders of the Dominican Order, but he did win young Bucer.

Within a short time, that is, in 1521, Bucer obtained a release from his monastic vows and began to exercise a pastoral ministry, vigorously preaching the Reformation. Shortly after, he married Elizabeth Silbereisen, becoming one of the first priests to marry. For some time he preached at the invitation of the local priest in Wissembourg, a small city north of Strasbourg, and soon won the people to the cause of reform. From the beginning he did expository preaching, going through the Gospel of Matthew and the First Epistle of Peter. In 1523 he was excommunicated by the bishop of Speyer, and because his parents were by this time citizens of Strasbourg, he sought refuge in that city, which was rapidly moving in a Protestant direction. He was a popular preacher in Strasbourg, being called on frequently to preach in the larger churches.

Bucer is another important preacher for whom we have few sermons.[133] We do however have the commentaries which give us the biblical studies on which his pulpit ministry was based. As we have seen, this often has been the case down through the history of the Church. What we read in the commentaries was first preached in the pulpit.

Bucer's sermons on the Psalms must have been especially rich, as his commentary was a breakthrough in biblical interpretation. He commented on the Hebrew text, something all but unknown to the medieval

133. One series of sermons we do have are those with which he tried to introduce the Reformation into Benfield, a small town in the neighborhood of Strasbourg. For the text, see *Martin Bucers deutsche Schriften,* ed. Robert Stupperich, 7 vols. (Gütersloh: Gerd Mohn, 1960-78), 7:13-66.

preacher,[134] and even went so far as to compare it with the different Greek versions of antiquity. Bucer was a master of the literary arts so brilliantly developed by the Christian humanists of the Renaissance. This commentary was regarded as something of a wonder at the time; it inspired the superb metrical psalms of the French lyrical poet Clément Marot. One wonders, of course, whether it might be his profound study of the Psalms so early in his ministry which gave him his deep insights into the nature of worship.

Even though Bucer was one of the best biblical scholars of his day, his greatest contribution is in another field, namely, the field of worship. His gifts were not in systematic theology so much as in practical theology. He did much for the development of a type of church polity which was able to avoid the pitfalls of the old monarchical episcopacy and yet give the church a strong enough organizational unity to stand on its own, without having to be dependent on the state. Beyond this, Bucer made an outstanding contribution to the catechetical ministry of the Church. I spoke of this at length in my book on baptism.[135] Even with all this, Bucer's work on the development of Protestant worship was without doubt his primary achievement.

Let us turn now to the liturgical shaping of the ministry of the Word as it was worked out in Strasbourg during Bucer's ministry. We must take care, however, to recognize that this was not the work of Bucer alone. Much more correctly, it is to be regarded as the work of a college of pastors. Zell, Hedio, Capito, and a number of others all contributed to this work.

E. The Liturgical Shaping of the Ministry of the Word at Strasbourg

The most thorough attempt to rethink the forms of Christian worship and to reshape them according to Scripture occurred in Strasbourg.[136] In

---

134. The exception was Nicholas of Lyra. The Reformers were very interested in Nicholas of Lyra. See Old, *Patristic Roots,* p. 320. See as well, the chapter in vol. III of this work on the schools.

135. Old, *Reformed Baptismal Rite,* pp. 209ff.

136. On the liturgical reforms of Strasbourg, see Friedrich Hubert, *Die Strassburger liturgischen Ordnungen im Zeitalter der Reformation* (Göttingen: Vandenhoeck und Ruprecht, 1900); Markus Jenny, *Die Einheit des Abendmahls gottesdienstes bei den*

the Upper Rhineland there had been considerable talk of church reform for more than a generation, but with Luther's criticism of the sacramental system in his *Babylonian Captivity of the Church* in 1520, and with his *Formula missae* of 1523 with its suggestions for the reform of the Mass, the demand for liturgical reform began to crystallize. Luther's works struck a particularly resonant chord in the Rhineland because of the concerns for liturgical reform which had already been voiced there. By 1523 Zell, Capito, and Bucer began to preach against liturgical abuses with particular vigor, and by the end of 1524 a number of very concrete changes in the service of worship had been instituted. These first attempts at the reform of worship were discussed in *Grund und Ursach,* a work Bucer wrote in the name of his colleagues.[137] Over the next decade the Reformers of Strasbourg developed a form of worship which would in the course of time have a considerable influence on Protestant worship.[138] The *Strasbourg Psalter* of 1537 gives us the mature expression of the liturgical ideas of this remarkable college of pastors, and so we will look at this document to see how the pastors of Strasbourg related the ministry of the Word to the whole worship of the Church.[139]

For the Reformers of Strasbourg, the restoration of the reading and preaching of the Word of God to its proper place in Christian worship demanded a reshaping of worship. Throughout the Middle Ages, despite the best efforts of the Franciscans and the Dominicans, preaching was at

Elsässischen und Schweizerischen Reformatoren (Zürich and Stuttgart: Zwingli Verlag, 1968); and Smend, *Die evangelischen deutschen Messen bis zu Luthers Deutsche Messe.* For an analysis of these texts, see Old, *Patristic Roots,* especially pp. 18-42 and 80-87.

137. Martin Bucer, *Grund und ursach auss gottlicher schrift der neüwerungen an dem nachtmal des herren, so man die Mess nennet, Tauf, Feyrtagen, bildern und gesang in der gemein Christi, wann die zusamenkompt, durch und auf das wort gottes zu Strassburg fürgenomen,* in *Martin Bucers deutsche Schriften,* vol. 1, *Frühschriften 1520-1524,* ed. Robert Stupperich (Gütersloh: Gerd Mohn, 1960), hereafter Bucer, *Grund und Ursach.*

138. There are several recent studies of the reform of worship in Strasbourg, including Old, *The Patristic Roots of Reformed Worship,* and René Bornert, *La réforme protestante du culte à Strasbourg au XVIe siècle (1523-1598)* (Leiden: E. J. Brill, 1981).

139. Martin Bucer, *Psalmen und geystliche Lieder, die man zu Strassburg, und auch die man inn anderen Kirchen pflegt zu singen. Form und gebett zum eynsegen de Ee, den heiligen Tauff, Abentmal, besuchung der Krancken, und begrebnüss der abgestorbnen. Alles gemert und gebessert. Auch mit seinem Register* (Strasbourg: Hans Preüssen, 1537). For further bibliographical information, see Hubert, *Strassburger liturgischen Ordnungen,* pp. xxii-xxvii; for the text, see pp. 88-114. For an English translation, see Bard Thompson, *Liturgies of the Western Church* (Cleveland and New York: World Publishing Co., 1961), pp. 159-81.

best an accompaniment to worship. That, at least, is the impression one frequently gets. Real worship was understood as the celebration of Mass or the saying of the daily office. The sacramental system was central to the life of the medieval Church, and preaching was an optional accompaniment. It had the function of bringing people to the sacramental system, particularly the sacrament of penance, which was so crucial to the worship of the medieval Church. It instructed the people on how to live the Christian life so that they could worthily offer the sacrifice of the Mass and receive the grace of the Sacrament. On the other hand, it was not a channel of grace, as the seven sacraments were. This was particularly the case with the more Pelagian forms of nominalism. Preaching functioned as a means of bringing about the proper disposition of the heart and discipline of life that made the sacraments effective. The more one understood worship as sacrifice, the less preaching was understood as worship. Preaching might prepare one to make the sacrifice, but it was not the sacrifice itself. The eucharistic sacrifice was the ultimate act of worship. Even in relationship to the doctrine of Christ's presence in Christian worship, there was in the nominalist understanding of things very little sense of Christ's presence through the reading and preaching of the Scriptures. Christ's presence was understood in terms of transubstantiation. If the *Didache* could say that Christ was present where his word was proclaimed, or if many of the Church Fathers could speak of Christ being present through the ministry of preaching, there was no strong sense of this by the end of the Middle Ages.

For the Reformers, however, preaching was worship. When the congregation came together and the Word of God was read and preached, God was worshiped. This did not mean that the minister of the Word worshiped while the congregation listened or that the act of preaching was an act of worship; it meant that the hearing and believing of the Word of God was worship. The more Augustinian theology of the Reformers brought them to understand worship not as a human work but as a divine work. The reading, the preaching, and the hearing of the Word was the work not of the minister or of the congregation or even of the Church as a whole, as it was the work of the Holy Spirit. That being the case, then, the minister of the Word was a listener just as much as the believing congregation. Together they serve God by bearing witness to the eternal truth.

In his *Grund und Ursach* of 1524, Bucer suggested that Acts 2:42 gives us the essential elements of Christian worship. "And they devoted themselves to the apostles' teaching and fellowship, to the breaking of bread and the prayers."[140] He understood this to mean that Christian worship should include the ministry of the Word, the giving of alms, the celebration of the Lord's Supper, and the ministry of prayer. The Reformers had no intention of replacing the eucharistic service with a preaching service. All four elements were necessary. They much more intended to bring preaching back into the worship of the Church and to give it the prominence it once had. Even more, they wanted to relate preaching to the reading of the Scriptures, to prayer, to praise, and to the sacraments.

Let us first look at how the Reformers of Strasbourg related preaching to the reading of the Scriptures. Of first importance here is that preaching was to be an exposition of Scripture. In the regular worship of the Church, the Scriptures were to be read and preached. Preaching was worship to the extent that it was God's Word. It was when God's Word was read and preached that God was present in the congregation. The ministers of the Word had authority to the extent that what they preached was the Word of God rather than simply their own word. For this reason the ministers of Strasbourg returned to the ancient Christian form of expository preaching, that is, commenting on the Scripture lesson passage by passage. They found this approach in the sermons of Origen, John Chrysostom, Ambrose, Augustine, Cyril of Alexandria, and Gregory the Great, and they used these ancient preachers as their example. Each preacher took a different book of the Bible and preached through it chapter by chapter.[141] At different times we know that Matthäus Zell preached through the Gospel of Matthew, Bucer preached through the Psalms and Romans, and Capito through the Old Testament prophets. We do not know on what Hedio preached except that he published a German translation of Chrysostom's sermons on Matthew and a volume of his sermons on John. This made abundantly clear that for him and for the other pastors of Strasbourg the *lectio continua* preaching of Chrysostom was the example they intended to follow.

Expository preaching became the backbone of the preaching of Strasbourg. There was also some festal preaching. The *Strasbourg Psalter* of 1537 indicates that in addition to the weekly celebration of the Lord's Day, Christmas; Holy Week, and particularly Good Friday; Easter; As-

---

140. Bucer, *Grund und Ursach,* pp. 211, 246, and 247.
141. Hubert, *Strassburger liturgischen Ordnungen,* p. 97.

cension; and Pentecost were observed.[142] On these feast days the sermons were to treat the appropriate saving work of Christ. Since we do not have any of these sermons from Strasbourg, we do not know what Scripture passages were preached, but presumably the obvious passages from the Gospels, the Acts of the Apostles, or other parts of the Bible were commented upon. One imagines that festal preaching was also expository preaching. This was no doubt worked out by the pastors of Strasbourg much as it had been by Luther.

The Roman lectionary was not used.[143] In his *Formula missae* of 1523, Luther envisaged the eventual setting aside of the lectionary. He recognized that it imposed a certain theological interpretation on the Scriptures. For the time being, however, he felt it was better to keep the lectionary. There were not enough trained preachers to do expository preaching, and until such a time as there were, he provided his *Postil* to show how one could preach the lectionary without being led astray by the theological presuppositions which had shaped it. This was one of the liturgical reforms Luther never made, but the Reformers of Strasbourg did make it. Zwingli, Capito, Hedio, and Bucer were all committed to the *lectio continua* before Luther published his *Formula missae*. Surely Luther's suggestion strengthened their resolve even if it was not its primary inspiration.

The church of Strasbourg provided daily preaching.[144] There was, however, special preaching on the Lord's Day. At the main Sunday service, the service at which the sacrament of the Lord's Supper was celebrated, the Gospels were read and preached. At the Sunday evening service the Epistles were normally heard.[145] During the week any book might be preached, but often it was then that one preached the books of the Old Testament.[146] It was also understood that certain services at certain churches directed the preaching at a more popular congregation while, for instance, the preaching at Saint Thomas on Sunday afternoon was directed to a learned congregation.

The liturgical shaping of the ministry of the Word gave particular attention to its relation to prayer and praise.[147] At the daily services the

---

142. Hubert, *Strassburger liturgischen Ordnungen*, p. 91.
143. Hubert, *Strassburger liturgischen Ordnungen*, p. 97.
144. Hubert, *Strassburger liturgischen Ordnungen*, p. 88.
145. Hubert, *Strassburger liturgischen Ordnungen*, p. 97.
146. For a study of the weekday prayer services, see Hughes Oliphant Old, "Daily Prayer in the Reformed Church of Strasbourg, 1525-1530," *Worship* 52 (1978): 121-38.
147. Bucer, *Grund und Ursach*, pp. 246-47.

form of morning and evening prayer was preserved.[148] The service was begun with the Prayer of Confession followed by the Assurance of Pardon.[149] The Prayer of Confession had a major liturgical function in the Strasbourg service. As Bucer saw it, just as the preaching ministry of Jesus was prefaced with John the Baptist's ministry of repentance, so Christians should approach the preaching of the Word with humility and a due acknowledgment of our need and our unworthiness.

The Prayer of Confession was followed by Christian psalmody.[150] The church of Strasbourg worked very hard at producing a collection of psalms and hymns which could be sung in the language of the people, and the psalmody it produced was an outstanding liturgical achievement. It gave the ordinary congregation a chance to participate in the ministry of prayer and praise which for centuries only the *scola cantorum,* or cloistered monks and nuns, had known. To dismiss the psalmody of Strasbourg as nothing more than a liturgical framing or setting of the preaching is to be insensitive to what was in fact going on. The singing of Christian psalmody was an affirmation of faith.[151] It was the sacrifice of praise and thanksgiving. It was the recognition that God is truly present in his Word and therefore claims the acclamation of his presence. Praise is, in its essence, the recognition of God's presence. Thanksgiving, on the other hand, is the recognition of God's claim on our lives. Having received God's gifts, we owe God the dedication of our lives. It is with praise that we enter God's presence and with thanksgiving that we go forth from worship into the world. The psalmody of the Strasbourg service bore great theological weight.

Of particular importance to the liturgical shaping of the ministry of the Word was the Prayer for Illumination.[152] This prayer took the place of the old calendar collects of the Roman Mass. Before the Scriptures were read and preached, the minister was to offer a prayer asking that God grant a true understanding of his Word so that we might with faith recognize both his will and his love and then live accordingly, all to his praise and glory.

The Scripture lesson was read and the sermon preached.[153] After

148. See Old, "Daily Prayer in the Reformed Church of Strasbourg, 1525-1530."
149. Hubert, *Strassburger liturgischen Ordnungen,* p. 88.
150. Hubert, *Strassburger liturgischen Ordnungen,* p. 89.
151. Bucer, *Grund und Ursach,* p. 247.
152. Hubert, *Strassburger liturgischen Ordnungen,* p. 96.
153. Hubert, *Strassburger liturgischen Ordnungen,* p. 97.

the sermon another psalm or hymn was sung. There were prayers following this.[154] For the weekday services of morning and evening prayer, the
minister might pray about those things he had treated in the sermon and
conclude the prayer with the reciting of the Lord's Prayer. For the Sunday
service the prayer following the sermon was to be a rather full series of intercessions for the needs of the Church, the leaders of both Church and
state, and support of the faithful. As time went along, these prayers of intercession became an increasingly important part of the service both in
the Lord's Day service and in the daily services. More and more they were
understood as a response to the command of Christ.[155] The New Testament contained a number of specific commands or admonitions to prayer
such as I Timothy 2:1-8, Ephesians 6:18, and Matthew 9:36-38. These
biblical admonitions to prayer shaped the prayers of intercession. Not
only did one approach the reading and preaching of the Word with
prayer, one followed it with prayer. The Word gave rise to prayer. It awakened the congregation to the needs both of their own souls and of the
community as a whole, and therefore the Word brought the congregation
to prayer.

The Lord's Supper followed, at the end of which was another hymn
or psalm and a benediction.[156] Perhaps the most important feature of the
liturgical shaping of the ministry of the Word was the way the Word was
related to the Sacrament.[157] What the Reformers of Strasbourg envisioned was a single Lord's Day service at the cathedral which the whole
Christian community of Strasbourg would attend.[158] The theological intention was that the whole Body of Christ be united together each Lord's
Day by the proclamation of the Gospel and the celebration of Communion. This single Communion service they were not able to achieve. It involved too many practical inconveniences. Too many people found it difficult to walk all the way downtown for church. Others wanted to send
their servants to an early service so dinner would be ready when they got
home from the later service. Alas, it was not the first time in the history of
the Church that liturgical reform was shouted down by corporeal comfort. Auxiliary Communion services had to be arranged in the neighborhood churches at least once each month in addition to the weekly Lord's

154. Hubert, *Strassburger liturgischen Ordnungen,* pp. 100-109.
155. Hubert, *Strassburger liturgischen Ordnungen,* pp. 110, 103, and 105.
156. Hubert, *Strassburger liturgischen Ordnungen,* p. 113.
157. Hubert, *Strassburger liturgischen Ordnungen,* pp. 111-13.
158. Bucer, *Grund und Ursach,* pp. 243-45.

Day service at the cathedral.[159] Nevertheless, neither at the cathedral nor at the parish churches was the Lord's Supper to be celebrated without the preaching of the Gospel, the prayers, or the giving of alms. The Lord's Day service was to include all four elements. If the Reformers allowed for Sunday morning services which did not include the Lord's Supper at the neighborhood churches and for the full Lord's Day service in these other churches once a month, it was by way of compromise. Basically they still held to the hope that the whole church of Strasbourg be gathered together each Lord's Day to hear the Gospel and celebrate the Lord's Supper.[160] The Lord's Supper was to be unique to the Lord's Day.[161] On other days there were to be services of prayer, praise, and the reading and preaching of the Scriptures, but the service of the Lord's Day was to be a service of Word and Sacrament celebrating the death and resurrection of Christ. The Lord's Supper and the Lord's Day went together.

The theology behind this Lord's Day service was a covenantal understanding of Word, prayer, sacraments, and alms. In the reading and preaching of the Word the new covenant was proclaimed; in prayer and alms the covenantal fellowship or communion was experienced. In the prayers of lamentation and confession God's people brought their sorrows and needs before their God and acknowledged the debt they owed their God for having heard their cries.[162] In confessing their need and witnessing to God's saving help they renewed the covenant.[163] In the Sacrament of the Lord's Supper the covenant was sealed by uniting the Church together in the one Body of Christ.

The Strasbourg Reformers developed a profound understanding of the Lord's Day.[164] It was an important biblical sign for them. Their study of the Scriptures led them to see a special tie between the Lord's Day and the Lord's Supper.[165] For Christians to remember the Sabbath to keep it holy meant to hold the Lord's Supper in remembrance of Christ. It meant

---

159. Hubert, *Strassburger liturgischen Ordnungen,* p. 99.

160. Bucer, *Grund und Ursach,* p. 242.

161. Bucer, *Grund und Ursach,* pp. 242-46.

162. Bucer, *Grund und Ursach,* p. 215.

163. On the covenantal dimension of Christian worship, see Hughes Oliphant Old, *Themes and Variations for a Christian Doxology* (Grand Rapids: Wm. B. Eerdmans Publishing Co., 1992), pp. 111-37.

164. An important contribution to this was Capito's research on the origins of the Christian Sabbath.

165. Bucer, *Grund und Ursach,* p. 243.

to proclaim the Lord's death until he comes. It was upon the first day of the week, the weekly memorial of the resurrection, the Lord's Day, that this proclamation and this memorial were to be held. The commandment to remember the Sabbath was fulfilled when on the Lord's Day the Christian congregation came together and did this "in remembrance of me" (I Cor. 11:24). The theology of the Lord's Day was part and parcel of the theology of the Lord's Supper.

The Reformers of Strasbourg did not limit worship to the Lord's Day. The service of the Lord's Day was unique, but there were services of worship every day in Strasbourg.[166] Each day there was preaching; each day there was morning and evening prayer. They found that in the Temple there had been daily prayer and daily teaching, and they were convinced that the earliest Christians continued the same tradition. They knew that the apostle Paul taught daily in Ephesus, and that many of the Church Fathers taught daily as well. As the Reformers of Strasbourg understood it, the service of daily prayer and the service of daily preaching and teaching was integral to the life of a well-ordered Church. It was worship every bit as much as the Lord's Day service.

The Strasbourg Reformers were also concerned to relate the ministry of the Word to baptism.[167] The restoration of catechetical preaching had been one of the most cherished projects of Rhenish Christian humanism for some time. Christoph von Utenheim, the reform-minded bishop of Basel, had tried to establish catechetical preaching shortly after the beginning of the century, but very little came of it. We have already spoken of how Erasmus had developed a program for the implementation of this project, and how almost immediately many of his proposals were put into practice in both Wittenberg and Zürich. The Reformers of Strasbourg were only a little behind their colleagues elsewhere. Whereas series of catechetical sermons were held daily at certain times of the year in Wittenberg, the practice in Strasbourg was to hold *Kinderbericht* each Sunday afternoon. Evidently all the pastors took their turn at preaching these catechetical sermons. Zell, Capito, and Bucer all published catechisms which we imagine reflected their preaching.

Just as the ministers of Strasbourg were careful to relate the ministry of the Word to the sacrament of the Lord's Supper within the context of the service for the Lord's Day, so they tried to insist that baptism was to

---

166. Hubert, *Strassburger liturgischen Ordnungen,* p. 88.
167. Hubert, *Strassburger liturgischen Ordnungen,* p. 114.

have its place in the Lord's Day service as well.[168] Again this was done on the basis of a covenantal theology of Word and Sacrament.[169] The Strasbourg Reformers developed a strong covenantal theology of baptism, particularly as they defended infant baptism against the Anabaptists. When baptism was administered to children, the parents did not take the baptismal vows for the children but were asked rather to promise that their children would receive the catechetical instruction which the Church now provided. After receiving this, the children were to make their own profession of faith and be admitted to Communion. The Reformers felt that this discipline answered the more legitimate concerns of the Anabaptists, but even more it responded to the institution of Jesus, who in the last chapter of Matthew had commissioned the apostles to make disciples by baptizing them and teaching them to observe all that he had commanded them.

VI. Johann Brenz (1499-1570)

For those of us who have a special place in our hearts for Schwabenland, Johann Brenz, the Reformer of Württemberg, calls forth considerable admiration.[170] Brenz was first of all a biblical scholar, then a pastor. He fulfilled the Protestant ideal of the pastor-scholar. At the center of his piety were an intense study of the Bible and a strong doctrine of providence. In his preaching he interpreted the Scriptures with pastoral purpose; it was both scholarly and pious. It was simple, chaste, and unadorned, and yet thorough and profound. Brenz somehow set the character of Swabian Protestantism. One recognizes the same character in his lineal descendant, Johannes Albrecht Bengel, the great eighteenth-century New Testament scholar. Karl Heim and Otto Michel have carried the tradition down to our own day.

Born the son of the mayor of Weil, a small city south of Stuttgart, Brenz was sent to Heidelberg to study. Heidelberg was an exciting place to study on the eve of the Reformation, one of the few universities in Europe where one could learn both Greek and the newly recovered biblical

---

168. Hubert, *Strassburger liturgischen Ordnungen*, p. 99.

169. On the relation of baptism to the Lord's Supper in the worship of the Reformed Church of Strasbourg, see Old, *Reformed Baptismal Rite*, pp. 167ff.

170. For a contemporary study of Brenz, see Martin Brecht, *Johannes Brenz, Neugestalter von Kirche, Staat und Gesellschaft* (Stuttgart: Calwer Verlag, 1971).

Hebrew. While there he studied under Oecolampadius and became a friend of Bucer. In 1518 Luther appeared in Heidelberg for his famous disputation, and from that point on Brenz was a stout supporter of the Reformation. A few years later, in 1522, at age twenty-three, he was called to the pastorate of Saint Michael's Church in Swäbish Hall because he was a recognized advocate of reform. There he remained for twenty-six years and, through his preaching, won the city to the Reformation. In 1523, at the annual fair of Saint James, he preached a series of sermons against some of what he regarded to be the more patent abuses of the day: prayers to the saints, monastic orders, and the sacrificing of the consecrated bread and wine of the Mass.[171] His preaching was successful, and in 1526 the town council passed a new church order. During his pastorate at Hall he preached through over thirty books of the Old and New Testaments. Many of these sermons he revised and published in the form of commentaries, but some were published as sermons. In 1528 he published a series of 134 sermons on the Gospel of John, and in 1534 he published 122 sermons on the Acts of the Apostles. This was followed by a series on the Gospel of Luke published in two volumes, the first in 1537, the second in 1540. Brenz was also interested in the revival of catechetical instruction. He published his own catechism in 1528, a year before Luther's catechism. Each year Brenz did a series of sermons on the *Larger Catechism.*

It was in the controversy over the Lord's Supper that the young Brenz first came to the attention of the theological world. In 1525 he published his *syngramma suevicum,* in which he attacked the eucharistic theology of Zwingli and his former teacher Oecolampadius. This work was published with the subscription of thirteen other Swabian theologians. It did much to win the allegiance of south German Protestants to the Lutheran rather than the Zwinglian position in the controversy over the Lord's Supper. Having expressed his position so well, he was naturally invited to the Marburg Colloquy in 1529. At Marburg he won the admiration of his prince, Duke Ulrich of Württemberg, who more and more looked to Brenz for leadership in the reformation of his principality.

With the Interim the emperor set a price on his head, and in June 1548 he had to flee Swäbish Hall. Christoph, who had in the meantime succeeded Ulrich as duke of Württemberg, kept him hidden, and with

---

171. Julius Hartmann, *Johannes Brenz, Leben und ausgewählte Schriften* (Elberfeld: R. L. Friderichs, 1862), pp. 7-14.

the end of the Interim established him in Stuttgart as *probst* of the Stiftskirche, that is, senior pastor of the major church in the duchy of Württemberg, general superintendent of the church of Württemberg, and member of the governing council.

Even with his new honors and greater responsibilities, Brenz remained a regular preacher. It was in this capacity that he chose to put the heavy weight of his reforming ministry. Brenz was not at heart a controversialist. Although he did not shrink from the responsibility of theological criticism on the one hand or doctrinal apologetic on the other, he preferred to guide the Church Sunday by Sunday, day by day through the systematic interpretation of the Scriptures. In 1550 he published a *Postil* on the lectionary readings for Sundays and feast days. Here we find Brenz, as Luther before him, providing the less gifted preachers of Württemberg with practical sermon helps. Brenz knew that few preachers in Schwabenland had his knowledge of the original languages or of the history and culture of the ancient world. Without this knowledge his fellow pastors could not realistically be expected to rethink the interpretation of Scriptures which they had heard from childhood. On the other hand, Brenz published his collections of sermons on whole books of the Bible as well as commentaries. He wanted the preachers of Württemberg to do *lectio continua* preaching, too. This was why, even during his twenty years in Stuttgart, his steady flow of published sermons and commentaries never ceased.

For Brenz the *Postil* and the published sermons were only a temporary measure. He knew that training a ministry which could preach with both piety and learning was needed even more. A major step in that direction was taken in the reforming of the University of Tübingen, a school which depended heavily on the patronage of the duke of Württemberg.

Yet even more significant was the establishing of a series of preparatory schools for boys who wanted to enter the ministry. For this purpose Brenz converted the monasteries of Blaubeuron, Malbronn, Urach, and Bebenhausen into preparatory schools for those who intended to enter the university to study theology. There boys received without cost an education in the tradition of Christian humanism.[172] Great attention was

172. Perhaps it would not be out of place to explain once more the meaning of the term "Christian humanism." At the beginning of the sixteenth century Christian humanism meant very specifically an emphasis on the study of the humanities, that is, the literature of antiquity, biblical Hebrew, the Greek and Roman classics, the Scriptures and the

given to the development of language skills. The literature, philosophy, and culture of antiquity, and above all the biblical languages, were carefully studied. Having that kind of foundation, then, students were sent to Tübingen to study theology. There they were given room and board at the Tübingen Stift, a former cloister converted at the time of the Reformation. This system of theological education has produced even down to our own day a steady supply of learned preachers in Württemberg.

Brenz's sermons make good devotional reading. The leader of German Pietism, August Hermann Francke, regarded them highly. One is tempted to study them here at length simply because they are edifying. We have, however, chosen to study his sermons on the book of Daniel, simply because there is a modern edition available. The eight folio volumes of the sermons and commentaries of Brenz, collected and published by his son, contain only a portion of the seven hundred works published during his lifetime. These sermons are not like those of Luther — stenographic recordings of actual sermons — but rather formulations of what the preacher intended to say which he himself wrote before preaching the actual sermon. These preparatory formulations were written in Latin, according to the practice of the day, but were then preached in German. They tend to be much shorter than either the stenographic reports of sermons or finished-up sermons which preachers sometimes prepared for publication after their preaching.

The twelve chapters of Daniel are covered in thirty-three sermons. In the first sermon Brenz speaks of the message of the book as a whole. The book does pertain to Christians of our time, he says, because it speaks of the reign of Christ and shows us that before his kingdom the kingdoms of this world are but shadows, vanities, and dreams.[173] From the very beginning of the world it was necessary to preach the coming of Christ and his reign because there is no other name by which we may be saved. Even Adam and Eve were given the promise of the coming of a Savior, and by faith in that promise they were saved. Neither the Law, nor good works, nor suffering, nor sacrifices save anyone from sin. Only faith

---

writings of the Fathers in the original languages. One should not confuse Christian humanism with philosophical humanism, a philosophy which puts man rather than God at the center of existence.

173. For the modern edition of these sermons, see Johann Brenz, *Homiliae vel Sermones nonnulli in Prophetam Danielem,* ed. Martin Brecht, W. Willy Göltenboth, and Gerhard Schäfer (Tübingen: J. C. B. Mohr, 1972), p. 1; hereafter Brenz, *Sermones in Danielem.* The page references in the text are from this work.

in Christ frees us from sin. So it is, then, that even in earliest times Christ's reign was preached by the prophets. Daniel is particularly interesting because he made the reign of Christ known to the Gentiles. He made clear before such powerful monarchs as Nebuchadnezzar, Darius, and Cyrus that God was even more powerful than they, and that before the kingdom of God their kingdoms would pass away (p. 2). The book of Daniel teaches us to be steadfast in adversity, just as we find in the stories of Joseph, Job, David, and Christ himself. The stories about Daniel show us that God never allows us to suffer evil unless he brings far greater good from it. They teach us patiently to bear the hand of God in our suffering and faithfully await the relief he will surely send (p. 3). As Brenz sees it, to preach on Daniel is to preach faith in Christ and the coming of his kingdom. Luther himself could not have put it more eloquently.

The second sermon is on the story of Daniel, Shadrach, Meshach, and Abednego and their training at the court of Nebuchadnezzar. Our preacher particularly focuses on the way these four Jewish youths maintained the Jewish dietary laws despite the temptations to enjoy the delicacies of the king's table. The sermon begins with a brief statement of the significance of the story (p. 4). It shows us an example of God's goodness to those who, in spite of danger, obey the teaching of the Word of God, so that we too may imitate that kind of obedience. Brenz is quite clear that for Daniel and his friends faith in God entailed the keeping of the Law. God had been good to those young men. They had found favor in the eyes of their captors and had been given amazing opportunities, and they in turn recognized that the favor they received was a gift from God. They were obedient to the Word of God and they kept the Law. When God finds those who fear him and obey him, he adorns them with the surpassing gifts of wisdom and intelligence and even bestows upon them great honors (p. 5). The interesting thing is that there was no one those young men should detest more than Nebuchadnezzar, that Gentile king who had devastated their homeland. Yet it was through that detestable king that God sent relief to those young men. Our preacher then enumerates several other examples, all taken from Scripture, of God's doing the same thing. God even gave Daniel and his friends the advantages which Babylon enjoyed. They were given the education of the court school. God did the same thing for many of the Church Fathers, such as Chrysostom, Cyril of Alexandria, and Jerome, who profited from the best schooling the Gentile world had to offer (p. 6). So it is that by the grace of God even one's enemies can become one's friends. Brenz then takes up the text "But

Daniel resolved that he would not defile himself with the king's rich food . . ." (Dan. 1:8 RSV). He broaches the question of whether this does not imply that the devout should abstain from certain kinds of food. Our preacher assures his congregation that Daniel knew that no food defiles us. It was not superstition that guided Daniel, but rather a confession of faith. It was the proving of his constant faith before the Gentiles. The sermon then concludes with the assurance that the Lord honors those who are obedient to him (p. 7). Obviously for Brenz faith leads to obedience.

Let us look at Brenz's sermons on the seventh chapter of Daniel. This is one of those passages in Daniel which has so often inspired chiliast speculations. We find none of this in the three sermons Brenz devotes to this chapter. Our preacher does, on the other hand, apply the teachings of Daniel to his own day, when the newly established reforms were threatened with suppression from the emperor and all Germany was terrified by Turkish invasion.

Brenz begins by explaining the four beasts which appeared to Daniel in his dream.[174] The first beast is the Babylonian Empire, the second the Persian Empire, the third the Greek empire of Alexander the Great, and the fourth the Roman Empire. The sermon, in effect, unfolds as a synopsis of ancient history as the preacher tells us how one empire rose, fell, and was succeeded by another.[175] Brenz uses the Greek and Roman historians Herodotus, Livy, Pompeius Trogus (in Justin), Valerius Maximus, and Flavius Josephus to explain why these symbolic descriptions of the four empires were appropriate. These colorful descriptions of ancient times were no doubt fascinating to the congregation. People usually find antiquity most interesting. That history is boring is something we first learn in school. There is nothing particularly novel in Brenz's interpretation; indeed, this is the way the writers of the Church have usually interpreted the four visions, he says (p. 92). He seems to have studied Jerome's commentary on Daniel, and no doubt other patristic commentaries, but faithful student of Oecolampadius that he was, he had little interest in the allegorical interpretation in which so many of these commentaries were engrossed. He preferred to approach the text in the Antiochene tradition of grammatical-historical interpretation. He was, therefore, much more

---

174. Brenz's interpretation of Dan. 7 is found in Sermons XXIII, XXIV, and XXV.

175. Unfortunately, someone at this point got confused and mixed the sequence of these descriptions of the second and third beasts. Cf. Brenz, *Sermones in Danielem,* pp. 90 and 91.

interested in elucidating the text with the help of the classical historians. This was fundamental to the Reformation's approach to preaching.

Sermon XXIV has to do with the interpretation of the ten horns and the establishment of the judgment throne of the Ancient of Days.[176] In this passage the crucial point is the identity of the blasphemous king who will wear out the saints (7:24-25). Our preacher tells us that this symbolizes Antiochus Epiphanes, the arch-persecutor of the Jews in the second century before Christ. Here Brenz is very close to what biblical historians would say today. What Brenz says next, however, is much more interesting. He says Antiochus was a foreshadowing of the rulers of the sixteenth century who were threatening to wear out the endurance of the faithful Christians in the land (p. 93). Brenz has in mind first the papacy and second the Turks. He then proceeds to show how the papacy is guilty of the same sins as the blasphemous king mentioned in the text. Then he follows the same procedure with the Turks (p. 94).

This is particularly interesting because this approach recognizes that the visions of Daniel speak to many ages. It would be quite different if Brenz had simply identified the blasphemous king with the Roman pope or the Turkish sultan. Then the significance of Daniel 7 would be over. It would no longer speak to the twentieth century and tell us about Adolf Hitler, Joseph Stalin, and a number of other Antichrists. It would no longer tell us what it originally told the Jews about Antiochus Epiphanes. Brenz has his finger on a very important principle of preaching. The events of Scripture foreshadow the events of our own lives and our own times, and this is true not only in regard to the sins and sufferings of God's people but even more so in regard to the hopes and the victories of God's people. Antiochus Epiphanes may have foreshadowed a whole host of persecutors who would come and go down through the centuries, but the "one like a son of man" (7:13) remains the transcendent figure of justice and power, and it is to him that the kingdom and the power and the glory are given (7:14). Brenz had a good sense of hermeneutics; that is, he knew how to move from the text to the congregation. This was true of Luther and Zwingli as well. The Reformers generally had a good sense of hermeneutic.

It is here that Sermon XXV takes up. This sermon undertakes to in-

---

176. This sermon treats the whole rest of the chapter, not simply 7:8-10. Likewise, Sermon XXV treats the chapter as a whole. What we really have here is three sermons on one chapter.

terpret the figure of the Son of Man to whom power and dominion are given. When the power of Antiochus Epiphanes passes away, just as the Babylonian Empire, the Persian Empire, and the empire of Alexander perished before him, then will come the Son of Man who is Jesus Christ (p. 96). He will establish an eternal reign. Our preacher brings out a number of New Testament passages to show that Christ will be given the name that is above all names and that before him every knee shall bow and every tongue confess that Christ is Lord. Christ will enter into an eternal kingdom, and with him those who believe in his name. They, too, reign above all kings and dominions, and their rule is perpetual. This is important for us to know. It confirms our faith when we experience the repressions of the papacy and the threat of Turkish invasion. We will not have to consent to their religion. Through faith in Christ we will be able to stand firm, and in the end we will reign with Christ (p. 97).

This is great Christian preaching. It gives a Christian interpretation of an Old Testament book which respects the original intention of the author. Preaching the book of Daniel has always been somewhat tricky. It is one of those books on which millenarians of various sorts have based their theories. Only the book of Revelation and the Song of Solomon can claim more bizarre treatment than Daniel. The historical criticism of the nineteenth century found Daniel an embarrassment, insisting that it had only the loosest connection with history. Yet it is a wonderful book even with all the unique problems it presents to the modern biblical scholar. The book is still there in all its vivid imagery. It is still fascinating in its steadfast and heroic faith. It still demands being preached, and one could do much worse than taking a few hints from Johann Brenz on how to go about it.

VII. John Calvin (1509-64)

The Reformers were a team, and they are best understood as a team. Luther had the spark of insight; he was the most imaginative, the Reformer of penetrating genius. Cranmer was the courtier among the Reformers. He knew how to manage the king and bring about reforms from the top. Melanchthon and Capito were more academic Reformers. They gave intellectual fiber to the Reformation. The quintessential scholar of the Reformation was undoubtedly Oecolampadius. Zwingli was the most politically astute, the Reformer who had a sense of the social implications of the Reformation. John Knox was the most daring, pitting himself against the House of Stuart and winning the whole of Scotland. Knox was an inspiring preacher as well as a man of action. But of all the Reformers, Calvin was the theologian.[177] He was, like Luther, a creative genius, but his genius was not to be found in imaginative flashes of insight, but in the systematic working out of the basic theology of the Reformation. It was Calvin who in his *Institutes of the Christian Religion* produced the systematic theology of the Reformation. Several of the Reformers had written learned volumes of theology, but none produced such a complete and thorough explanation of the whole of Christian theology. It is much the same way with the preaching of Calvin. He followed the other Reformers in doing expository preaching, but he was able to preach through almost the whole Bible. The thoroughness and completeness, the systematic nature, of his expository preaching is truly remarkable.

When Calvin arrived in Paris to begin the study of theology, he was only a teenager, a precocious teenager, to be sure, but hardly old enough to realize the magnitude of the theological earthquake which was just beginning to topple the theological establishment of medieval Christianity. For centuries, ever since Peter Abelard, Thomas Aquinas, and Bonaventure, Paris had been the center of the theological discussion. Paris was the capital of Scholasticism, and Scholasticism was now being challenged as never before. At the Collège de Montague, famous as a citadel of theological orthodoxy and rigorous piety, Calvin learned the old theology. He got his bachelor's degree, but then his father redirected him toward the study of the law.

His father may or may not have realized that he was pulling his son out of the old learning and planting him in the new learning. But that is what it really amounted to. Calvin studied law both at Orléans and at Bourges, where the new learning of the Renaissance was being taught. Pierre de l'Etoil and the great Andrea Alciati introduced him to the histori-

---

177. For the most recent work on Calvin's life and work, see the following: William J. Bouwsma, *John Calvin: A Sixteenth-Century Portrait* (New York: Oxford University Press, 1988); Jean Cadier, *Calvin: L'homme que Dieu a dompté* (Geneva: Labor et Fides, 1958); Bernard Cottret, *Calvin, Biographie* (Paris: Éditions Jean-Claude Lattès, 1995); H. Jackson Forstman, *Word and Spirit: Calvin's Doctrine of Biblical Authority* (Stanford: Stanford University Press, 1962); Alister McGrath, *A Life of John Calvin* (Oxford: Blackwell, 1990); T. H. L. Parker, *John Calvin: A Biography* (London: J. M. Dent & Sons, 1975); and Richard Stauffer, *L'humanité de Calvin* (Neuchâtel: Delachaux et Niestlé, 1964).

cal-critical method of studying the law. At the same time, Melchior Wolmar introduced him to Greek as well as to the ideas of the Reformation.

In 1531, one year after the Augsburg Confession had signaled the final break between Catholics and Protestants, Calvin's father died. Calvin was at last free to devote his attention to the historical and literary studies of the Christian humanists such as Erasmus and Jacques Lefèvre d'Étaples. He returned to Paris and entered the newly founded Collège de France, where, under royal patronage, the new learning held sway. In Paris Calvin continued his study of Greek under Pierre Danès and began to study Hebrew under François Vatables. These two men were far and away the leading scholars in their fields.

Calvin's mastery of this new learning, especially classical Greek and Hebrew, brought him into an elite circle of intellectuals who were committed to church reform. In November 1533 a member of this circle, Nicholas Cop, professor of medicine and personal physician to the king, was chosen as rector of the University of Paris. In his rectoral address Cop espoused the reforms not only of the Christian humanists but of Protestantism as well. The court was scandalized. Calvin may have been the ghostwriter of the speech. At any rate, both he and Cop were obliged to flee. Finding refuge in Basel, Cop's hometown, Calvin settled down to a life of study. In 1536 he published the first edition of his *Institutes of the Christian Religion.* A few months later William Farel, the Reformer of Geneva, called Calvin to begin a ministry of teaching and preaching in that rowdy crossroad town.

Let us focus in on Calvin as preacher.[178] Again, he is best understood as part of the team. He certainly did not originate the Protestant approach to preaching, but followed the older Reformers in emphasizing

---

178. On the preaching of Calvin, see the following: John H. Leith, "Calvin's Doctrine of the Proclamation of the Word and Its Significance for Today," in *John Calvin and the Church, a Prism of Reform,* ed. Timothy George (Louisville: Westminster/John Knox Press, 1990), pp. 206-29; Pierre Marcel, "L'Actualité de la prédication," *La Revue Réformée* 7 (1951); Pierre Marcel, "Une lecture non-Calviniste de Calvin," *Supplément à la Revue Réformée* 4 (1979); Olivier Millet, *Calvin et la dynamique de la Parole. Essai de rhétorique réformée* (Paris: H. Champion, 1992); T. H. L. Parker, *Calvin's Preaching* (Edinburgh: T. & T. Clark, 1992); Rodolphe Peter, "Jean Calvin Prédicateur," *Revue d'histoire et de philosophie religieuses* 52 (1972): 111-17; Rodolphe Peter, "Rhétorique et prédication selon Calvin," *Revue d'histoire et de philosophie religieuses* 55 (1975): 249-72; Richard Stauffer, *Dieu, la création et la providence dans la prédication de Calvin* (Bern: P. Lang, 1978); and Richard Stauffer, "Un Calvin méconnu; le prédicateur de Genève," *Bulletin de la Société de l'histoire de Protestantisme français* 123 (1977): 184-203.

expository preaching. He followed them very closely by studying the text of Scripture in the original languages. Capito and Oecolampadius had pioneered the study of biblical Hebrew and had begun to catch sight of the veins of gold to be mined in the Old Testament. Many of the Reformers had brought out glistening nuggets from their study of the Hebrew Scriptures. Luther had produced a marvelous translation of the Hebrew Old Testament. Bucer had done a brilliant commentary on the Psalms in which he both held to a grammatical-historical interpretation of the Hebrew text and maintained the legitimacy of the Christian interpretation of the Psalms. Brenz did a remarkable commentary on Ecclesiastes, one of the most difficult books in the Bible. It was Calvin who most consistently and most profoundly worked the whole vein.

Again Calvin followed the older Reformers in rejecting the allegorical interpretations of the Alexandrians and adopting the grammatical-historical exegesis of Antioch. The other Reformers had made tremendous progress in setting the Scriptures in their historical context, but Calvin had a mastery of the culture of classical antiquity which was more extensive than that of his older colleagues. He knew the Greek and Roman classics far better than did Luther, Bucer, Brenz, or even Zwingli. He had mastered Renaissance historical criticism, as well as the literary arts of the new learning. He drank in all that Erasmus had to offer on the grammar and rhetoric of antiquity. In fact, he could even show Erasmus a few tricks. Calvin, and much the same can be said of Bullinger, did not have to discover the value of grammatical-historical exegesis before beginning to master it — the older Reformers had done that for him. Essentially Calvin had the same tools for a rereading of the Bible which the older Reformers had; it was just that Calvin's tools were a bit sharper.

Calvin was primarily an expository preacher. From the standpoint of homiletical genre, all his sermons are expository sermons. He was a strong supporter of catechetical instruction, and we can assume that, at least in his earlier days, he preached catechetical sermons. If he did, these sermons have not been preserved, and so we cannot be sure what they were like. We can only assume that they were rather like those of the older Reformers. From the standpoint of homiletical form, we have neither prophetic sermons nor evangelistic sermons from Calvin.[179] However, we

179. One exception may be his four sermons on fleeing idolatry. Cf. T. H. L. Parker, *The Oracles of God: An Introduction to the Preaching of John Calvin* (London and Redhill: Lutterworth Press, 1947), pp. 162 and 166.

must add that the prophetic word constantly resounds in his sermons, just as the gospel is constantly proclaimed in his preaching. Besides that, Calvin had a way, as we shall show below, of pointing his expositions to an evangelistic purpose whenever the Lord's Supper was to be celebrated.

A. Lord's Day Sermons

The restoration of the Lord's Day was a primary liturgical concern of the Reformation. This was particularly the case in the Rhineland, in the Swiss cities, and eventually in the kingdoms of England and Scotland. As with much of the best liturgical thinking of early Protestantism, this concern seems to go back to Strasbourg. All the Reformers were concerned about the reform of the calendar. The number of feasts and saints' days had grown unchecked for years. The need to do a thorough trimming job was generally admitted.

Early in the Reformation a group of Anabaptists advocated a return to the Sabbath observance, insisting that Sunday worship was the invention of Constantine. They wanted to celebrate worship on Saturday rather than Sunday. The Reformers of Strasbourg gave Wolfgang Capito, their most respected scholar, the responsibility of thinking out the implications of this challenge. Capito was well suited for this task since he was an Old Testament scholar and, besides, had a doctorate in law. He studied the question not only from the biblical perspective but also from the standpoint of Roman imperial law. His study resulted in a strong affirmation of the liturgical importance of the Lord's Day.[180]

The Reformed Church of Strasbourg saw in the weekly celebration of the Lord's Day an important foundation of Christian worship. We spoke of this in our section on the liturgical reforms of Strasbourg. The Lord's Day was an occasion for all the Christians of the city to come together for the preaching of the gospel and the celebration of the sacraments of the Lord's Supper and baptism. At this dominical service the sermon was to be an exposition of a passage from one of the Gospels, preached according to the *lectio continua*. The Lord's Word and the Lord's Supper were at the center of the Lord's Day. The Strasbourg Reformers

---

180. Capito's work on this subject is found in a series of notes reprinted in *Quellen zur Geschichte der Täufer,* vol. 7, ed. Manfred Krebs and Hans Georg Rott (Gütersloh: Gerd Mohn, 1959), pp. 363-93.

tried to reserve the celebration of both Communion and baptism to the Lord's Day. That was the ideal, at least. The custom of baptizing children immediately after birth was thoroughly ingrained, and many parents were reluctant to wait until the Lord's Day. One eucharistic service each Lord's Day was even harder to implement. Getting all the Christians of Strasbourg together for one Lord's Day service proved impractical, but the theological significance of the Lord's Day had been caught sight of and many of the earliest Christian insights regarding the biblical concept of the Lord's Day were rediscovered. The Reformers of Strasbourg were well aware that the early patristic sources all give great importance to the observance of the Lord's Day.

Just how much of this thinking was taken up by Calvin is not, at this point in our research, completely clear. We do know that he wanted a celebration of the Lord's Supper each Lord's Day, and that he preached from the Gospels at the Sunday morning service. This would certainly indicate that he did follow the thinking of Strasbourg in this regard. Disappointingly, the *Institutes* is not too clear on whether he followed the Strasbourg theology of the Lord's Day.[181] What we get is the suggestion that the Sabbath rest is a sign of the graciousness of our salvation. By turning away from human works, we make it clear that it is not by such works that we are saved. This is an exciting idea, and it would seem to be one of those seminal thoughts which Calvin often supplies. But that Calvin had no other thoughts on the subject is unlikely. Surely he admitted a typological relation between Sabbath and Lord's Day. We imagine, at least at this point in our research, that he followed his older colleagues in Strasbourg in his understanding of the Lord's Day and the Christian Sabbath. Surely one thing would have been evident for Calvin, whose mother tongue, after all, was French: the true name for the day of worship was *Dimanche*, "Jour du Seigneur," the day of the Lord. For Calvin as a Latinist, the term was *dies dominicus*, the Lord's Day. Calvin would not have been deceived by a word like "Sunday."

There is no question that the worship of the Lord's Day was unique among the many other services held during the week in Geneva. The

---

181. John Calvin, *Institutes of the Christian Religion,* ed. John T. McNeill, trans. Ford Lewis Battles, 2 vols., Library of Christian Classics, vols. 20 and 21 (Philadelphia: Westminster Press, 1960), 2.8.28-34; hereafter Calvin, *Institutes.* For a Latin text, see *Joannis Calvini, Opera Selecta,* vols. 3-5, ed. Petrus Barth and Guilelmus Niesel (Munich: Christoph Kaiser, 1957), hereafter Calvin, *Opera Selecta.*

dominical service on the morning of the Lord's Day was the main service. Let us look at some of these Lord's Day sermons.

A particularly good example of Calvin's typical Lord's Day sermons is his four sermons on the Beatitudes.[182] They were preached as part of his *lectio continua* sermons on the Gospel of Matthew held at Saint Pierre in Geneva between 1560 and 1561.[183] Here we find Calvin in all his directness and all his depth.

The first thing we notice in these sermons is that Calvin's interpretation of the Beatitudes implies an important reform in Christian spirituality. Our preacher makes clear several of the basic principles of what has become the Protestant understanding of the Christian way of life. The ascetic way of life is not at all what Calvin finds in the Beatitudes. That approach had been essential to the spirituality of the Middle Ages. One begins to find it as early as Origen, who often interpreted the Scriptures in a Platonic or Neoplatonic sense. Origen and other Christians who held on to these various forms of Greek philosophy were usually led to follow an ascetic approach to life.

Right from the beginning our preacher recognizes that what Jesus tells us in the Beatitudes has to do with a subject often discussed in the philosophical schools of the pagans of antiquity: the perfection of goodness, *la fin de tout bien* (p. 773). What the philosophers meant by this was human happiness, *la félicité des hommes*. At this point Calvin discusses the ideas of the pagan philosophers, something he does not often do. The more materialistic philosophers claim that only those who are free from pain are happy. As they see it, the good life is one in which there is no suffering. Then there are those who think the good life is the life filled with pleasures and luxuries, and those who identify happiness with virtue — they look at things in a much more refined way. When all this discussion is over, the philosophers still end up figuring that those who are poor,

---

182. One of the preeminent French Calvin scholars of a generation ago published these four sermons as a particularly fine example of the Reformer's preaching. Pierre Marcel, "Jean Calvin: Les Béatitudes, quatre prédications," *La Revue Réformée* 120 (1979).

183. The original text, entitled "Sermons sur l'Harmonie des trois evangelists: S. Matthieu, S. Luc et S. Marc," is found in *Joannis Calvini Opera Quae Supersunt Omnia*, ed. William Baum, Eduard Cunitz, and Eduard Reuss, 59 vols., Corpus Reformatorum 29-87 (Brunswick and Berlin, 1863-1900), 46:1-826. The sermons specifically on the Beatitudes are found in 46:771-826; the page references in the text are to these pages. Quotations are taken from this edition. It was Calvin's custom to preach through the Gospel of Matthew but to add the passages of the other Gospels where appropriate.

who are afflicted with poverty or illness, or who are rejected by society or are simply ignored have missed out on life. Their lives have never been fulfilled. They are simply miserable. Calvin admits that the common wisdom of his day looked at things in much the same way. The poor, the hungry, the sick, the afflicted, and the dispossessed will never know happiness (p. 774).

The school to which our Lord Jesus has called us teaches us something quite different, according to Calvin. In this school we learn to take up our cross and follow our teacher. We notice how simple and yet how effective this metaphor is. Jesus is the teacher of a school very different from those of classical philosophy. He fulfilled his life by bearing his cross, taking up the sufferings of the world, and dying for them. God has given to each of us a burden to bear. "We need to sense this and valiantly to bear our burden, that burden which has been put on our backs" (p. 774).[184] From Jesus we learn how to live under the threat of death, with the knife at our throats. We learn to rejoice even if in carrying our cross we have to endure every kind of suffering. In the school of Christ we learn to serve God and to find our happiness in performing this service. "These are the ABC's which we learn in the school of our Lord Jesus Christ" (p. 775).[185]

Taking up the first of the Beatitudes as they are given in Matthew, "Blessed are the poor in spirit," our preacher points out that in the Gospel of Luke we are told simply, "Blessed are the poor." Some would tell us that Jesus was really teaching that we should be humble, for that is what is meant by poverty of spirit. As Calvin sees it, this is a bit too subtle. We should take quite seriously the more straightforward version we find in Luke. Jesus really does promise his blessing to those who endure poverty for the sake of his kingdom (pp. 775ff.). To suffer poverty in the most literal sense of the word does have a way of proving the genuineness of our devotion. For those who are wise, poverty makes it very clear that in ourselves we are nothing but poor wretched creatures. Poverty, as any kind of adversity, teaches us modesty. It teaches us to bow our heads, and not to stiffen our necks and carry our heads too high (p. 776).

Wealth can be very deceiving. No wonder those who enjoy the

184. "Il faut que nous sentions cela, et que nous le portions vaillamment comme un fardeau qui nous sera mis sur le dos, comme si un homme avoit à cheminer, il portera son pacquet sur son dos."

185. "C'est l'a, b, c, qui nous est appris en l'eschole de nostre Seigneur Iesus Christ."

riches of this world are led astray by them. The crowds applaud them. They are served everything their desires would have. They are pampered with the luxuries of the table. They bathe themselves in delicacies and delights (p. 778). They are at ease on the lap of luxury. Who can be surprised if they glorify themselves and become swollen with pride? It is only natural that the rich become rigid and stiff-necked in their arrogance. To be sure, many poor people are filled with pride. They may be outwardly poor, but inwardly they are proud and envious. They resist God at every opportunity. Jesus makes it very clear when he speaks of being poor in spirit that our poverty must enter into our hearts and purge our souls of presumption and pride (p. 777). One cannot help but notice here the power of Calvin's language. Our pale paraphrase hardly does it justice. One easily notices the metaphors and similes, but the flow of his sentences and the variety of his vocabulary elude translation. Calvin's use of the language has vitality!

As Calvin so often does, he calls on another passage of Scripture to interpret his text. The Song of Mary, "The Magnificat," found in the Gospel of Luke, makes the same point when it speaks of how God

> "has scattered the proud in the imaginations of their hearts,
> he has put down the mighty from their thrones,
> and exalted those of low degree;
> he has filled the hungry with good things,
> and the rich he has sent empty away."

> (Luke 1:51-53 RSV)

As Mary well understood, it is those who recognize their need and look to God for their salvation who discover the greatest blessings of life. Certainly this passage of Scripture does not suggest that God is arbitrary in his providence. To suggest that God capriciously directs our lives like someone playing tennis or pool would make the universe an absurdity. What we learn from the virgin Mary is that those who abuse the blessings of God will eventually lose them; those who stuff themselves in vain will finally burst. On the other hand, those who hunger and come to one who is in a position to relieve their necessity are truly "poor in spirit." It is when we come to God because we know that in him we have security that we have true happiness (p. 778).

Having spoken at some length of poverty of spirit, our preacher turns to how the poor in spirit inherit the kingdom of heaven. For Calvin it is our humility, our hunger and thirst, our mourning, our suffering persecution, and our steadfast faith in the face of every affliction which give us happiness. It is the Christian hope which, even in the worst of circumstances, gives us joy. God has promised us the kingdom of heaven, and we rejoice because we are confident that God keeps his promises. It is a very different matter with the philosophers of pagan antiquity. Calvin, never one to display his vast knowledge of classical literature, no doubt has in mind the Stoics, who taught a stern resignation in the face of misfortune. Even today we speak of the Stoic approach to the reverses of life. As Calvin well knew, the Stoics firmly believed in fatalism, and he will have nothing to do with this philosophy. Evidently Calvin saw predestination as something quite different. He rejects the Stoic philosophy with one of his perceptive similes. As he sees it, these philosophers demand that we be like anvils which no hammer is able to soften.

As for the speculations of the philosophers, they are nothing but a minor confusion. Our Lord teaches us that such speculation is of no help. Quite in a different way, he gives us a solid foundation on which to build our lives. He teaches us that in all our tribulations we should lift our eyes and meditate on the kingdom that is to come. For it is there rather than here that our felicity is to be found (p. 779).

Having made this point, our preacher develops at some length the themes of faith and hope. The Christian lives by faith in the faithfulness of God. Fate is blind and chance is arbitrary, but God is faithful to his own. Calvin puts succinctly the foundation of the Christian life. God has given us his promise, and if indeed we are saved through hope, it stands to reason that our hope is hidden. Alluding to words of the apostle Paul (Rom. 8:24), Calvin reminds us that we do not hope in what we see but in what we do not see. And yet faith assures us that there is an invincible certitude in the truth of God.

Just to make sure that his congregation understands the practical application of what he has said, our preacher tells us that if we are to live the Christian life in happiness, we need to learn to meditate on the promises of divine salvation contained in the Word of God (p. 780). Living on the promises of God exercises our faith, and to live by faith is the essence of the Christian life.

The sermon moves on to the second beatitude, "Blessed are those who weep and who in the end rejoice and will be consoled." The text on which Calvin preaches is the Greek text, and the translation he offers his congregation is often a free translation, as we find here. From the stand-point of homiletical form, one may wonder why the second beatitude is brought into the sermon so close to the end. The traditional preacher's hour is almost up. Would Calvin not have had a much better sermon out-line if he had divided his remarks up a bit more evenly or left the second beatitude for the following day? The homiletical taste of our day would certainly insist on this. Concerns for a proper outline had been important to the Scholastic preachers of the High Middle Ages as well. The preach-ers Calvin would have heard as a young man growing up in Paris would have been careful to maintain a balanced sermon outline, but the exposi-tory preachers of the Reformation had other concerns. To them the text itself and the message within it demanded its own literary form. It was much looser and freer than the literary form of the Scholastic sermon, ei-ther as understood in the late Middle Ages or in more recent times.

As regards this particular sermon, our preacher maintains his unity of theme by telling us that the second beatitude has much the same to say as the first. If we are poor of spirit, then it only follows that from time to time we weep, that is, we are in distress and anguish. For we are not insen-sible like the philosophers we spoke of earlier. We do not pretend to be the oblivious anvils on which the hammers of fate beat away. That is just not the way our human nature is. We are weak and fallible creatures and we have to recognize our misery. It is unrealistic for us not to sense the transience of our nature (p. 781). To make his point Calvin uses one of his favorite rhetorical techniques: he paraphrases the message of the text. It is as if Jesus had said:

> When I tell you that your happiness is not lessened, even though you have been oppressed by many afflictions, it is not that I think you have met all this stunned like stones or trunks of trees that have no feeling; no, not at all. You have wept, you have suffered diseases, oppositions, rejections, and all the trials one can suffer in this world. All of this you have felt and have been wounded to the heart so that indeed you have wept. But be that as it may that does not keep you from having a pro-found happiness. And why is that? One cannot do other than come to this conclusion: await the consolation that comes from above. (p. 782)[186]

186. "Voyla donc pourquoy nostre Seigneur Iesus-Christ conioint yci le pleur avec la pauvrete d'esprit. Comme s'il disoit: Quand ie di que vostre felicite n'est point amoindrie, combien que vous soyez opprimez de beaucoup d'afflictions, ce n'est pas que

Again, to make his point clear, the Reformer of Geneva uses another favorite rhetorical device. He tells us what the text does not say. Jesus does not say that in weeping we will be happy, as though this in some way proves our virtue. Calvin is of course well aware that the spirituality of the Middle Ages put a high value on "spiritual tears." The most sincere of saints contemplated the sufferings of Christ and the sins of the world to the point where they fell into weeping. These spiritual tears proved the profundity of their contemplation. Here is an ascetic practice which Calvin simply does not find taught by Jesus here or anywhere else in the New Testament. What Jesus teaches us is that God has promised to console us when we weep before him in humility. We need never doubt, Calvin assures us, that God will have pity on us, that all our affliction will turn to our blessing, for in the end we have sought our happiness in God rather than in ourselves (p. 782).

Calvin does not often end his sermons with a stirring conclusion. Here, however, he does. Again he paraphrases the words of Jesus. He expands the text in such a way as to suggest how it is that God speaks to us in Scripture:

> Here then is how each one of us should appropriate this teaching. One should know that our Lord Jesus Christ speaks to us secretly in our hearts and that what he says here is, "If you are poor then be poor in spirit. Be truly humble. If you are ruined or rejected, carry it in your heart. And yet know that even if the world thinks you are most miserable and even if your human nature tells you otherwise, still you can firmly answer, Amen, so be it! and accept the blessing I propose to you. And you will see in the end, that you were not fooled but that you have entered into the heritage of the kingdom of God. You will discover how God blesses those of his children who have had to suffer the sadnesses of this life and how he fills with good things those who have hungered and thirsted for righteousness." (p. 784)[187]

---

i'entende que vous resistiez avec une telle stupidite que vous ne sentiez rien, que vous soyez là comme troncs de bois sans estre esmeus de rien; non, Vous pleurerez (dit-il), vous sentirez les disettes, les opprobres, les maladies, et tout ce qui vous fera languir au monde. Vous le sentirez, et en serez navrez jusqu'au coeur, en sorte que vous en pleurerez. Mais quoy qu'il en soit, cela n'empeschera point que vous ne soyez touiours bien-heureux. Et pourquoy? Il faut venir à cette conclusion: Attendez la consolation d'en haut."

187. "Voyla donc comme il faut que chacum approprie a soy la doctrine, et qu'il sçache que nostre Seigneur Iesus-Christ parle à luy comme en secret: et qu'il luy dit, Il faut

To grasp the full effect this sermon must have had on its hearers at Saint Pierre in Geneva at the beginning of the 1560s, one must remember that this very congregation was filled with exiles. Calvin himself was an exile from France. In the pews before him were the widows and orphans of those who had been martyred because they had preached reform. Then there were the exiles from England whose colleagues Queen Mary had burned at the stake. The congregation at Saint Pierre that morning knew all about those who had suffered everything for the joy that was set before them.

Let us turn now to the second sermon on the Beatitudes. If the first sermon treated but two of the Beatitudes, the second sermon treats three. Without any sort of overall introduction, the sermon jumps right into the first of the three, namely, "'Blessed are the meek, for they shall inherit the earth'" (Matt. 5:5 RSV). Calvin does not discuss his translation, "Bienheureux les debonnaires: car ils heriteront la terre," but he obviously understands that this beatitude commends to us being good-natured, simple, and gentle. For Calvin this beatitude teaches us to have a trusting and open spirit, an accepting attitude toward other people. As the Reformer of Geneva sees it, God created us in his image, and if we keep this in mind we will trust other people because they were created in the image of God just as we were (p. 784). Sad to say, we don't keep this in mind and we treat each other with suspicion, always worried we will lose control of the situation. In pride and envy we fear, lest our honor be compromised. To be sure, we would rather be nice, gentle people, but we figure that the world is a rough, unfriendly place. To justify our rough and suspicious behavior we quote the familiar saying, "You had better howl with the wolves or you'll be eaten with the sheep." As we shall see, our preacher makes good use of this proverb throughout his explanation of this beatitude. Again we find Calvin contrasting the common wisdom of the day with the teaching of Jesus. It is an effective rhetorical device, and Calvin uses it skillfully. Experience shows us that those who are the most aggressive get ahead in life. Those who are meek, peaceful, and good-natured only ex-

---

que si tu es povre, que tu le sois d'Esprit, que tu sois vrayement humilié, que tu portes un aneantissement en toy et en ton coeur. Et alors, cognoy que combien que le monde te repute miserable, et que ton sens naturel t'en dise autant, toutesfois tu me peux hardiment repondre Amen, et accepter la beatitude que ie te propose. Et tu verras en la fin que tu n'as point este trompé, mais que tu parviendras à l'heritage, auquel tu cognoistras comment Dieu resiouit ses enfans apres qu'il les a contristez au monde: et comme il les remplit, qu'il les a affamez!"

pose themselves to one sort of injury after another. It hardly makes sense to behave like a lamb when one finds oneself in the midst of a pack of wolves (p. 785).

Even though the profane will never understand this teaching, it should be obvious to all that those who are in a frenzy to get ahead in life, those constantly scrapping with others, pillaging and plundering for all they can get, may have their triumphs, and yet they have made a wreck of their lives. Making full use of his vast vocabulary, Calvin examines the wretchedness of those who have given ambition full rein. They have made the world into their enemy. Our preacher helps himself to several brilliant figures of biblical speech. Isaiah put it very well in one of his similes. They are like the waves of the sea in the midst of a tempest. They are under the judgment of God and troubled by their own consciences. Nowhere can they find rest. They are like Cain, fugitives and wanderers on the earth (Gen. 4:14) (p. 786).

On the other hand, those who go through life in simplicity and patience, enduring the oppressions of their more ambitious neighbors, will indeed possess the land. In a very profound sense, as Calvin sees it, this world will be theirs, because God has given it to them for their use. Even though they may not own so much as a square foot of land, not so much as a vineyard or a field or a house, nevertheless, if they know that God has put them on this earth, then they know they have a right to it. They can be as content as birds sitting on a branch. If they know that God governs their lives, they can be sure that the earth will yield up to them its fruit, for God himself ordained it to that end. If God created me and put me on this earth, then I am his guest. When we know God and trust that he supports us and always will support us, then we possess something far greater than all those who have grabbed for themselves kingdoms and duchies and lands and cities. Surely here is a passage as eloquent as any in the whole of homiletical literature.

After the sheer beauty and inspiration of this passage, Calvin, artist that he is, changes his pace completely. Taking up again the popular proverb that so many would use to contradict this beatitude, Calvin introduces a bit of sarcasm. He assures us that our Lord Jesus is not at all interested in being a pastor of wolves. If we would receive the pastoral care of Christ, we must be as gentle and trusting as lambs (p. 787).

The sermon now turns to another beatitude, "'Blessed are those who hunger and thirst for righteousness, for they shall be satisfied'" (Matt. 5:6 RSV). Calvin points out that the Gospel of Luke puts it a bit more simply: "Blessed are you that hunger . . ." (Luke 6:21). Take either version, Calvin insists; the teaching is the same. It is those who learn to live by faith who are truly happy (pp. 789ff.). Hunger and thirst, just as poverty and illness, have their function in life. They teach us how fallible and transient human life really is. Those who are realistic about this will in the end be much happier than those who try to ignore it. God often keeps us in a state of privation to exercise us in patience and faith. In the end, however, God provides for our needs and, even more, fulfills our lives.

An ascetic interpretation of the Christian life would surely latch onto this beatitude and suggest that those who fast regularly can expect to be blessed. But interestingly, Calvin says nothing about fasting in his interpretation of this beatitude.

The third beatitude he takes up is, "'Blessed are the merciful, for they shall obtain mercy'" (Matt. 5:7 RSV). Calvin's discussion of mercy is especially perceptive (pp. 791ff.). He begins by contrasting mercy with the hardness of heart that so many develop toward the suffering of others. The wisdom of the world develops a thick skin to protect itself from the suffering of others. Christ would teach quite a different approach in this beatitude. As Christians, we should learn to embrace the poverty of our neighbors. We find the same attitude in the apostle Paul, who teaches us to weep with those who weep (Rom. 12:15). As Calvin sees it, we should join ourselves to those who are afflicted and tormented. We should have compassion toward them and search out ways to support them in their need. It is to this point that we must take our belief in the unity of the Body of Christ (p. 792).

As Calvin defines it, mercy is nothing less than taking to ourselves the sadness of another. Even if one has enough to eat or drink and has to face no threat or peril, the Christian is moved within, so as to be miserable along with one's neighbor and to help bear the neighbor's burden. Mercy, to be sure, has to do with a formal giving of alms, but more than that it is a recognition of the Body of Christ. It is a participation in the unity of our human nature. It recognizes that we are by nature creatures of need. When we recognize this, then we are open to God's mercy toward us in our need. To be human toward others is to recognize the true nature of our humanity (p. 796). What is particularly clear in Calvin's interpretation of the Beatitudes is that the Christian life should not be motivated by asceticism but by a recognition of our true human nature. God has made us to live in faith toward him, and we are happiest when we live just that way. This is the inner logic of what might be called a Christian humanitarianism. It recognizes human nature for what it is. Again we see that Calvin's interpretation of the Beatitudes suggests Christian alternatives to the asceticism taught during the Middle Ages.

The third sermon also takes up three beatitudes, namely, "Blessed are the pure in heart. . . . Blessed are the peacemakers. . . . Blessed are those who are persecuted . . ." (Matt. 5:8-10). The sermon begins rather abruptly without any sort of general introduction by saying that everyone agrees that the principal virtue which should be maintained among us is purity of heart. Without it everything is a jumble of confusion. Integrity is essential for any kind of human communication, commerce, or community. "Purity of heart," strictly speaking, is a metaphor which implies many things, and our preacher heaps up a generous supply of synonyms to convey the fullness of this teaching. An ample vocabulary is one of Calvin's most helpful tools as a public speaker. To read this sermon in sixteenth-century French is pure delight for a lexicographer. The pure in heart are those "qui sont nets de coeur." The pure in heart are those who have "rondeur" and "intégrité." They are "sans feintise." They are free from "astuces et des cachettes, et ne soit déguisé." The pure in heart have a wonderful "simplicité." For the pure in heart it is important to "cheminer rondement" (p. 798).

Again we find Calvin defining the meaning of purity of heart by contrasting it with its opposite. Purity of heart is opposed to deviousness. If the worldly wise know every trick for taking a profit from their neighbors, if they selfishly use their neighbors again and again to their own advantage regardless of the harm it brings them, the pure in heart may seem a bit simple and a bit foolish. If the pure in heart are not sharp enough to see the profits of this world, if they are not clever enough to know how to gather the commodities, the pleasures, the delicacies, and the honors of this world, there is something much more important which comes their way. This beatitude promises that they will see God. As the Reformer of Geneva understands it, this means they will enjoy the presence of God, in which they will find their happiness, their joy, and their glory.

Calvin asks just how literally we are to understand the blessing of this beatitude, that is, seeing God. The Protestant polemic against idolatry had stimulated an active discussion of texts which in one way or another speak of seeing God. Calvin's remarks are quite nuanced. He says it is really superfluous to dispute the subject. Because God's essence is spiritual, we cannot contemplate him with our corporeal eyes. Properly speaking, spiritual beings do not really see, although certainly they do perceive. Certainly angels, who are spiritual beings, contemplate God. Several passages are quoted to make the point (p. 799). As Calvin understands it, we can know God only to the extent that we are like him. To inquire too exactly into what God might look like, or how it is that angels see him, or how we will see him on the Last Day is more a matter of curiosity than wisdom (p. 800). As Calvin so often says, the important thing for us now is to know his will in terms of both his commandments and his promises.

The sermon now turns to the verse which follows, "'Blessed are the peacemakers, for they shall be called sons of God'" (5:9 RSV). According to Calvin, it was common in his day to mistake this beatitude for an admonition for Christians to be tranquil or passive. But the Greek text implies that Jesus teaches us to be active in bringing about peace (pp. 801ff.). Jesus was no quietist, as Calvin understands him.

We have several times spoken of the variety of Calvin's vocabulary. Here we might point out the variety of his sentence structure. This, too, is a good way for an orator to keep the interest of his auditors. In telling us what it means to be called children of God, Calvin uses a series of rhetorical questions. Could anything be more desirable than to be recognized and accepted as children of God? Could anything be more helpful to us than to be able to call on God as our Father? For without such a privilege, what would be our situation? If God were to reject us, what would be left for us? What sorts of curses, what sorts of confusions would we be liable to if God were not propitious to us? There you are, Calvin concludes. Nothing can be the source of more prosperity, of more blessing, than to sense the favor and the love of God toward us. There is nothing greater to which we can aspire than the assurance that God is indeed our Father and that we are indeed his children.

It is because this is true that Jesus follows this beatitude with the next, "Blessed are those who are persecuted for righteousness' sake, for theirs is the kingdom of heaven" (5:10). The text of this beatitude, in both Matthew and Luke, is much more fully developed than any of the others. Its exposition takes up not only the last half of the third sermon, but the whole of the fourth sermon as well.

Calvin begins by telling us to observe two things. The first is that although we who receive the gospel are rejected in place after place, excommunicated for being troublers and traitors, we should nevertheless be calm and peaceable, patiently bearing our injuries and refusing to nourish

106

our quarrels. Second, we must be careful to seek peace, even though we know full well that we always have to do war against the devil, who, we must remember, is the father of contention (p. 804).

The problem is that God has not only called us to be peacemakers, he has also called us to be advocates of justice and witnesses to the truth (p. 805). It is here where the difficulties begin. Too often, being zealous for the truth or taking a strong stand for justice incites the anger of the wicked. As a result, faithfulness can expect to be persecuted (p. 807). One cannot be silent when the truth of God is suppressed or corrupted. Silence may keep the peace, but it is not a true peace. One can hear behind our preacher's remarks all the controversies of the turbulent times in which he lived. Obviously there were no easy answers then, any more than there are any easy answers today.

The fourth and last sermon on the Beatitudes begins with Calvin observing that the previous Sunday his congregation learned how difficult it is for a faithful Christian to live peacefully here on earth and at the same time fulfill his duties both to God and to his neighbor. This remark, incidentally, makes it evident that these sermons were preached on Sundays rather than on weekday mornings. But beyond that, we learn from this sentence how important Calvin finds this contrast between the Christian duties of being a peacemaker and being an advocate of justice. Here is the problem of the Christian life once it leaves the monastery. It is very clear here that, as Calvin sees it, the Christian often has to enter into combat to support good and just causes and to support the innocent. It is not enough simply to abstain from evil (p. 811). For many in Calvin's congregation, all this was of very great interest. Many, as we have said, had fled their homeland for the sake of the evangelical faith. Calvin himself was an exile. Many had experienced persecution, and their colleagues or members of their own families had experienced martyrdom. There was a whole congregation of Englishmen in Geneva who had fled the reign of Bloody Mary. No subject could have gripped Calvin's congregation more than this. We are hardly surprised that our preacher developed the subject at such length. He wanted to make it clear that persecution is not a condemnation of those who suffer it. It is only inevitable that in a world which so resists the will of God, so many saints will suffer (p. 812).

Much more could be pointed out about these sermons. They are important to us because they show us the vitality of Calvin's pulpit ministry. From these sermons we get a good picture of Calvin as an orator. We get a taste of the directness of his interpretation of Scripture. We see how he refuses to force a passage of Scripture into neat sermon outlines and yet seems to have a full command of the arts of language.

Calvin would be the last to want us to be more interested in his rhetoric than in his message. What is most interesting about these four sermons is the way he sums them up by asking a big question. This question has to do with the nature of the Christian life. So much has been said in the last two of these four sermons about the witness of those whom God has called to endure martyrdom. What about those who are called to lives of ease and comfort? Can such a life ever receive God's blessing (p. 821)?

For Calvin it is quite clear that God does call many Christians to live quiet, peaceful lives. God has given to many ease and even prosperity. The point is that the faithful must use such blessings soberly. They should receive them with thanksgiving as God's blessings (p. 821).[188] If someone receives a gift from God, it would be hypocrisy to deny it or to hide it. If some are rich, if some have good health, if some have received excellent gifts of the Holy Spirit, they should recognize them as the evidence of God's grace toward us. They should praise God for them and enjoy them. "It is like this, then, that the faithful should use all the good things of the present life" (p. 822).[189]

One easily recognizes that this interpretation of the Beatitudes points the Protestant understanding of the Christian life in a very different direction from the direction taken during the Catholic Middle Ages. For Calvin there is a very important place for sacrifice, for suffering, and for self-denial, just as there had been in the spirituality of the Middle Ages. But there is more to the Christian life than suffering. There is the whole dimension of living by faith as Luther had so well understood it. Then there is the dimension of living from the promises of God. From the Beatitudes we learn of the happiness that comes from the Christian life. We learn to rejoice in the hope that is set before us. But then from

---

188. "Pour mieux comprendre cela, regardons comme les fideles se portent en leurs aises. Il est vray que si Dieu leur envoye prosperite et repos, ils rapporteront le tout à sa louange, car ils useront sobrement de ce qui leur est donné, voire à telle fin que touiours ils tascheront de bien vivre. Eh bien, Ils ne voudront pas que ces biens-là soyent perdus: mais ils les recognoissent comme benedictions de Dieu."

189. "S'ils sont riches, s'ils ont santé corporelle, et mesme (comme i'ai dit) qu'ils soyent douez de quelques dons excellents du sainct Esprit, ils recognoistront les graces de Dieu en tout cela, et s'y esiouiront, et luy en rendront louange.

"Voyla donc comme les fideles useront de tous les biens de la vie presente."

God's gifts to us we learn of the love of God, whose providence is so generous to us. For Calvin stewardship is such an important dimension of the Christian life! We are stewards of God's gifts, to use them with sobriety and to relieve the needs of our neighbors. Calvin has not so much worked out a new spirituality program in these four sermons as he has begun to see a crucial passage of Scripture in a significantly new way.

In the context of contemporary American Protestantism, Calvin's sermons on the Beatitudes do not seem particularly remarkable, but if we compare them to the sermons of Gregory of Nyssa, they take on a very different light. Gregory's sermons on the Beatitudes, studied in the second volume of this work, are brilliant philosophical essays, but as beautiful as they are, they do not really explain what Jesus taught. Calvin makes a serious attempt to understand what Jesus really did teach in the Sermon on the Mount. What should be clear from these sermons for the Lord's Day is that Calvin believed it very important that the preaching of the Lord's Day pass on Christ's teaching. To the observance of the Lord's Day belonged the hearing of the Lord's Word.

B. Weekday Sermons

Let us next look at Calvin's sermons on the prophet Micah. These twenty-eight sermons were given Monday through Saturday at the morning service,[190] beginning Wednesday, 12 November 1550, and continuing through Saturday, 10 January 1551. Calvin preached without manuscript or notes, and the sermons were taken down by professional stenographers.[191]

In the first sermon Calvin introduces the book. He begins by assuring his congregation that the prophetic message has as much meaning to the Church of their day as it did to ancient Israel. To make his point he cites several passages from the New Testament. While the prophets spoke appropriately to their own day, they speak to our times as well (pp. 1-2). He then comments on the introductory words of the text: "The word of the LORD

---

190. Calvin preached at the weekday morning services only every other week. Other preachers preached in the intervening weeks, treating the New Testament books.

191. For a good introduction as well as the original text, see John Calvin, *Sermons sur le Livre de Michée,* ed. Jean Daniel Benoît, Supplementa Calviniana, vol. 5 (Neukirchen-Vluyn: Verlag des Erziehungsvereins, 1964), pp. vii-ix; page references in the text are from this volume.

that came to Micah of Moresheth in the days of Jotham, Ahaz, and Heze-kiah, kings of Judah . . ." (Mic. 1:1 RSV). Our preacher proceeds to put Micah in his historical context, telling us that Micah exercised his ministry at the same time as Isaiah and Amos. Essentially these three prophets have the same message, speaking as if by one mouth. Calvin tells us that much of what Micah has to say is hard to listen to, because he speaks about God's wrath against the ungodly. He speaks of the sin of Jerusalem and Samaria in order to bring the people to repentance, but he does this that in the end they might learn of God's love and infinite goodness (p. 4). Calvin notes that the message of Micah is particularly directed to "Samaria and Jerusa-lem" (1:1). The prophet preached particularly against the sin of the large cities. This is because at that time they had become the source of idolatry, and yet Jerusalem was supposed to be the center of true worship. Jerusa-lem's sin was especially grievous because of that city's high calling. From this we in Geneva, Calvin admonishes his congregation, should take special warning. Geneva has received the gospel and therefore has the responsibil-ity to produce the fruit of the gospel (p. 7). We have a high calling to honor God and to serve him, but if we fail and lead others astray, then we stand under the same judgment as Jerusalem.

The sermon proceeds to the second verse:

> Hear, you peoples, all of you;
> hearken, O earth, and all that is in it;
> and let the Lord GOD be a witness against you,
> the Lord from his holy temple.

> (1:2 RSV)

These words show that these prophetic oracles do not come from Micah's own thoughts; they come from God himself. So it is with all godly teach-ing. It comes to us with divine authority. When God's Word is preached, then it becomes the foundation of our faith. It is by his Word that he would govern us. God's Word does not fail, and if we build our lives on it we will stand fast. God reveals himself for our salvation, but if we refuse this revelation it turns to our judgment (p. 9). When God's Word is pro-claimed, it is never in vain. God's Word has power! It raises up those who receive it in faith; it condemns those who reject it. If God's Word reveals to us today our sin, let us be well assured that it reveals even more the sur-passing mercy of our Lord Jesus Christ, who wishes us to receive all the graces of his Father. Let us therefore bow down before God in prayer and ask from him true repentance and that he receive us in mercy and give us the grace to serve him to his glory and the profit of our neighbors, and that this grace not only be to us but to all peoples and nations of the earth (p. 10). This call to prayer, which in very similar words usually concludes his sermons, is one of the most notable features of Calvin's preaching. For Calvin the Word again and again brings the Church to prayer.

The second sermon in the series begins by reviewing what had been said the day before. Then it takes up the next verse: "For behold, the LORD is coming forth out of his place . . ." (1:3 RSV). To be sure, comments Calvin, God is present over all and does not need to come and go in order to accomplish his will. To say that he comes forth out of his place is simply to make clear his relationship to us. Those who think God is far away from them and cares not whether they do good or evil need to hear that God is coming toward them in judgment. This language is necessary only because of our infidelity. Those who have a strong faith in God's providential care are aware that God is always with them (pp. 11-13). What a profound twist Calvin gives to the problem of anthropomorphism which so many philosophers, both ancient and modern, have leveled against the Bible. The problem, as Calvin sees it, is not that the writers of Scripture are naive, but that infidelity is shortsighted. Faith has a wisdom which surpasses the understanding of infidelity, whether that infidelity is of the lawless or of the philosopher.

Passing on to the next part of verse 3, "and will come down and tread upon the high places of the earth," Calvin comments that this is a figure of speech which tells us God will humiliate the proud of the earth. Micah's message is a warning against the princes and governors of this world who have been unfaithful to the trust committed to them by God. Ignoring God, they have stolen from the poor, corrupted the courts, and murdered the defenseless. They have particularly blasphemed the honor of God, because God is the ultimate governor of the affairs of men. When there is bad government God is insulted (p. 13). Calvin takes up the next verse:

> And the mountains will melt under him
> > and the valleys will be cleft,
> like wax before the fire,
> > like waters poured down a steep place.

(1:4 RSV)

Our preacher carefully draws out the meaning of the literary imagery the prophet uses. The point is that when God's judgment finally comes to the proud, they will have no power to stand against God. They will melt like wax. They will, like falling water, be dashed on the rocks (pp. 14-15). One notices again and again that Calvin has a great sensitivity to the literary images of Scripture, and is careful to explain them.

Calvin goes on to comment on this verse. It is true that God in his judgment takes into account our human frailties. We find this with particular clarity in Psalm 103:

As for man, his days are like grass;
  he flourishes like a flower of the field;
for the wind passes over it, and it is gone,
  and its place knows it no more.

(vv. 15-16 RSV)

It is because God knows the frailty of human nature that he has pity on us. When we humble ourselves under his hand, then he has no need to humiliate us by his judgments. When we are humble and obedient toward God, then there is no need for him to manifest his judgment. It is to those who are too proud to hear his Word that God brings hard times and confusion. This, Calvin tells his congregation, is as true today as it was in Micah's time (pp. 15-16).

Calvin now turns to the text:

What is the transgression of Jacob?
  Is it not Samaria?
And what is the sin of the house of Judah?
  Is it not Jerusalem?

(Mic. 1:5 RSV)

Again our preacher takes up Micah's theme, that the infidelity of Israel comes from her cities. Those two cities were veritable gates of hell, filled with all manner of crimes, pollution, and wickedness. Country people should not become too indignant about urban sins, because there are sins among the rural population as well, but here Micah is primarily concerned about urban sin and above all about idolatry. It is really the idolatry which started first in Samaria and then in Jerusalem which is the root

112

of the evil. Here Calvin interprets the words of the prophet with the help of the historical books of the Old Testament, which give an account of the introduction of idolatry into Samaria and Jerusalem. If the Jews had not corrupted true worship, Calvin comments, then all the other sins would not have followed.

Finally, as a conclusion to his exposition, Calvin applies Micah's warning to Samaria and Jerusalem to the city of Geneva. It is important for Geneva to maintain a purified worship, a godly common life, and sound teaching in order that the city give no occasion for the weak to stumble. Again our preacher calls his congregation to pray about the matters raised in the sermon, particularly that the Holy Spirit give them humble hearts so that they might do homage to his majesty, that their lives be so reformed by God's grace that others might be drawn to the way of salvation, and that they all together might arrive in his kingdom.

With the third sermon Calvin continues to speak of the sin of Jerusalem. He presents some historical material from II Chronicles. He explains that in the reign of the good king Hezekiah there was neither public corruption nor religious superstition in the city of Jerusalem, but with Ahaz, who was king at the time of Micah, many things contrary to the true service of God were introduced. By this Calvin has in mind making images, burning incense, setting up altars on every high hill and under every green tree, and the proliferation of sacrifices even to the point of offering children on the altar of Moloch (cf. II Chron. 28:1-4). It must be pointed out, Calvin tells his congregation, that God's judgment against such idolatry makes no exception of person, time, or place. Idolatry is just as wrong in Jerusalem as it is in Samaria. It is just as wrong today as it was in ancient times. As Calvin sees it, the papacy had in his day introduced similar forms of idolatry and superstition into the worship of the Christian Church (p. 19). Rome, Calvin charges, just as Jerusalem, claims great piety and lofty authority while introducing into the service of God all kinds of fantasies of its own invention. In so doing, the papacy has provoked the judgment of God (pp. 20-21). What Micah promised Jerusalem applies equally well to Rome: "All her images shall be beaten to pieces" (1:7 RSV).

Calvin goes on to the remainder of verse 7:

> all her hires shall be burned with fire,
> and all her idols I will lay waste;
> for from the hire of a harlot she gathered them,
> and to the hire of a harlot they shall return.

Our preacher comments that here Micah is using a figure of speech common to Scripture (p. 23). Idolatry is pictured as a form of spiritual adultery by Jeremiah. We find the same idea put in a positive way by the apostle Paul, who pictures faithfulness to Christ in terms of a marriage contract (II Cor. 11:2-3). Idolatry is a spiritual adultery which God finds so detestable that he threatens destruction to the city which practices it. Samaria could hardly plead ignorance as an excuse for her idolatry. Jeroboam knew the Law when he introduced idols into the worship of Samaria. His idolatry was a rebellion against God, and Samaria was destroyed (p. 24). How thankful we should be here in Geneva, Calvin tells his congregation, that God has been gracious to us. This church in which we are gathered was until quite recently filled with altars and idols, but it has pleased God to restore pure worship here.[192] As it is now, we assemble here in his name to hear his Word. In common accord we call on his name; he is in the midst of us with his angels (p. 26). All this he has done most graciously in spite of our faithlessness in times past. For this we have good reason to give thanks to God. Let us pray to him that we might continue to reap the blessings of the gospel which calls us away from sin and makes us the servants of his glory.

In the fourth sermon Calvin interprets one of Micah's most powerful oracles (Mic. 1:10-16). In this oracle the prophet addresses one city of Judah after another, proclaiming the ruin each is to experience. Micah makes a play on words with the name of each city, and our preacher explains each of these in turn. Each of these cities will come to ruin because it has not allowed itself to be governed by God and his Word. Geneva should learn from this passage, Calvin tells his congregation. A city which submits itself to the will of God will be secure (pp. 33-34). Geneva, being an independent city-state, was sensitive to the perils of maintaining its freedoms. In the sixteenth century it was surrounded by neighbors who would gladly have made it submit to their rule. This sermon, therefore, spoke quite directly to the hopes and fears of his congregation. Calvin

192. Carlos Eire, in *War against the Idols,* demonstrates the cardinal importance of the rejection of idolatry to the liturgical reforms of the sixteenth century and to Calvin in particular. As informative as this book is at many points, it mistakenly tries to explain Calvin's opposition to idolatry by his transcendentalism, his exaggerated dichotomy between the physical and the spiritual. We find it hard to agree. It was neither philosophical nor theological considerations which account for Calvin's strong opposition to the use of idols, but rather the clear prohibition of the use of idols in Scripture. See Eire, pp. 195-233.

concluded his sermon by exhorting his congregation to put their faith in God, who in the end raises up his people (p. 34).

With the fifth sermon in the series Calvin begins his interpretation of chapter 2, in which Micah preaches against the social tyranny of the rulers of the land. They have not respected the property rights of the peasants. They have corrupted the courts of justice, charged exorbitant usury, and exacted high taxes. Through all these methods they have amassed for themselves vast landed estates and have left the peasants impoverished.

> Woe to those who devise wickedness
>> and work evil upon their beds!
> When the morning dawns, they perform it,
>> because it is in the power of their hand.
> They covet fields, and seize them;
>> and houses, and take them away;
> they oppress a man and his house,
>> a man and his inheritance.
>
> (2:1-2 RSV)

Calvin tells us that when worship is corrupted, it naturally follows that the social order will be corrupted as well. There are two tablets of the Law. The first and more important has to do with the service we owe to God. The second, which follows from the first, has to do with our service to the neighbor (p. 36).

In this sermon Calvin develops his doctrine of stewardship in regard to what God expects from both those who have been given the power to govern and those who have been given wealth and property to supply the needs of the people (pp. 38-39). God has given wealth to us that we might do good, but the wealthy of Jerusalem used it for their own ends. They used their political and economic power to do evil (p. 38). It is because of the avarice of the rich and powerful that Micah preaches against them. It is just as the apostle Paul put it, "The love of money is the root of all evils" (I Tim. 6:10). Wealth in itself, Calvin continues, is not evil. In fact, it is one of God's blessings. Commerce is a necessary part of human society, but when merchants are corrupted by greed, then it becomes evil. Greed comes when we lose faith in God's providence. Saint Peter and Saint Paul both tell us to put our trust in God for the material things of life (p. 39). If we trust God to supply our needs, then we do not have to hoard the material necessities of life and store them away against an un-

115

certain future. Obviously Calvin's doctrine of providence and his doctrine of stewardship go hand in hand.

Calvin takes up Micah's charge that the city people have stolen the patrimony of the country people:

> They oppress a man and his house,
>   a man and his inheritance.
>
> (2:2 RSV)

Family homes and family farms have been stolen away in order to build the large estates of the government bureaucrats of Jerusalem. For Micah, as for the Old Testament in general, the passing on of the patrimony is a sacred right. Calvin, too, is sensitive to the concern of the members of his congregation, city people as they may be, to pass on a patrimony to their children (pp. 40-42). He speaks at some length of the father's legitimate concern to provide for his family, but that does not give him an excuse to steal from others. It is far wiser to put oneself in God's care and to commend one's children to God. If one relies on the favor of God, one will find that God will provide for all our needs and that his care will last from generation to generation (p. 42). Here we see a good example of how Calvin made the themes of the Old Testament relevant to Christians of his own time. After preaching Micah's prophecies against cities, he led his congregation of city people in one of the budding mercantile centers of Europe to pray that God so reform them that they no longer live for the luxuries and vanities of this world, but be content with what God provides; that they use the material wealth God has so abundantly given them for the fraternal care of their neighbors and thereby enter into the patrimony of an eternal kingdom.

Having looked at a number of Calvin's sermons in their order, and having thereby gotten a sense of how the sermons build on one another, we pass over a number of sermons and take up the series again in the middle, where Calvin is commenting on one of the classic messianic passages of the Old Testament. Sermons 13, 14, and 15 treat Micah 3:11–4:7, in which Micah envisions the final establishment of the kingdom of God. This will show us that Calvin's concern to maintain grammatical-historical exegesis is balanced by a recognition of the established Christian interpretation of the Old Testament.

Sermon 13 begins by contrasting the prophecy of destruction which concludes the third chapter and the prophecy of hope which begins the fourth (pp. 104-6). Calvin comments that here Micah, as indeed all the other prophets, never threatens the unfaithful Jews with judgment without giving a consolation to the faithful Jews who have put their hope in God and will therefore be delivered from their affliction. As Calvin reads the Old Testament, justification by faith is to be found there just as in the New Testament. Therefore we read,

> It shall come to pass in the latter days
>> that the mountain of the house of the LORD
> shall be established as the highest of the mountains.

(4:1 RSV)

This passage tells us of the coming of Christ, when he will be revealed to the whole world and will pour out his Holy Spirit on all flesh, as Saint Peter preached on the Day of Pentecost (p. 106). We should note, however, that this passage tells us nothing about the rebuilding of a material temple more splendid than Solomon's Temple. It is not the Temple of Zerubbabel which the prophet envisioned (p. 107). Obviously Calvin has in mind the teaching of Jesus that the time will come when the true worshiper will worship God in spirit and truth (John 4:23).

Next Calvin takes up the second verse:

> "Come, let us go up to the mountain of the LORD, . . .
> that he may teach us his ways
>> and we may walk in his paths."

(4:2 RSV)

Our preacher comments that when Christ comes, all peoples of a common accord and a common faith will come to Christ to hear the Word of God. Although at one time the teaching of God's Word was limited to the land of Judah, now it is to be published to the ends of the earth. This same prophecy, that the gospel is to be preached to all nations, is found throughout the Old Testament. The very fact that it is also found word for word in Isaiah 2:2-3 indicates how important this teaching is (p. 107).

Calvin returns to the question of how the prophecy of hope is related to the prophecy of destruction. Here we see our preacher at his best as an orator. Solomon's Temple was abused by the hypocrites of the day.

They used it as armor to protect themselves against the judgments of God and as a cape to cover their iniquity. It is therefore that Solomon's Temple would be destroyed. Truly Jeremiah reproached them, "Speak no more of the Temple of God for you have made it a den of thieves" (Jer. 7:11). Micah perceives the folly of their presumption and tells them that as much as Mount Zion may be called the house of God and the Temple may have been built for the invocation of God's name, none of that will save it from destruction. But now Micah speaks of a mountain of God that will be lifted up above all others, so that its glory and excellence shall flow forth over the whole world, and there God shall be glorified. And how is this to be? It is to be in spirit and truth (John 4:23). Such a temple can never be abused by hypocrites. This temple will be a true house of God where God will dwell in the midst of his people. And God will dwell there in truth, for there is the temple truly dedicated to God.

It is of course the Church, the Body of Christ, that is the temple where the true worshiper will serve God in spirit and truth. Calvin asks how this spiritual temple is raised up. It is through our Lord Jesus Christ. It is he who raises up what has been cast down. That is the office of Christ, to bring the dead to life. It is that way with our experience today as well, Calvin says. As much as the Church may be despoiled, Christ still exercises his office, repairing what has been ruined, revitalizing what has lost its force, so that the Church might remain what God intended it to be. Here we see God's love for the Church (p. 108).

Calvin goes on to say that the glory and dignity of the Church is to be found in God's love for the Church. It is this dignity which raises it above all the mountains of the earth. It is not that one finds in the Church an earthly pomp and splendor, for the kingdom of Christ is very different from the kingdoms of this world. They have their glory of outward splendor, their financial resources and their political power, but the glory of the Church is that she is precious to God, because she is ordered by his Word and worships him alone in spirit and truth (p. 109). Here is a passage of surpassing eloquence, and the essence of that eloquence is found in its Christian interpretation of the Old Testament Scriptures.

Returning to the text, "'that he may teach us his ways / and we may walk in his paths'" (4:2 RSV), Calvin asks what the purpose is in our going to the house of God. Clearly the purpose in our gathering into the Church is to be taught the ways of God. We are joined together to hear God's Word. This is why preaching must be the preaching of God's Word, not the fanciful proclamations of the preacher (p. 121).

Sermon 14 begins with a few remarks about the teaching ministry of the Church. Calvin calls attention to the fact that Micah's vision of the Church shows it to have a strong teaching ministry. It is to learn God's Law and God's ways that the faithful came to Zion from all the peoples of the earth. Our preacher levels vigorous polemic against the papacy for neglecting the teaching ministry of the Church. The rule of Christ in the Church is not exercised by political force but by the preaching of the Word (pp. 114-17). Calvin also points out that those who go up to Mount Zion admonish one another, and from this we should learn that Christians have the responsibility of witnessing to their neighbors.

Finally Calvin comes to the text:

> And they shall beat their swords into plowshares,
>   and their spears into pruning hooks;
> nation shall not lift up sword against nation,
>   neither shall they learn war any more;
> but they shall sit every man under his vine and under his fig tree,
>   and none shall make them afraid;
>   for the mouth of the LORD of hosts has spoken.
>
> (4:3-4 RSV)

Three things are to be noted in this prophecy, according to Calvin. First, when men do not submit to the lordship of Christ, they fight with each other with swords and spears. Second, when men do accept the reign of Christ, they devote themselves to the prosperity of their neighbors. Third, it is not enough that we abstain from evil; we must devote ourselves to aiding and protecting one another (p. 118). Peace, Calvin goes on to say, comes from submitting ourselves to God and working for the common good. Here again we see Calvin speaking to the concerns of a Christian city in the midst of this world. Calvin sees his congregation neither as a monastery in flight from the world nor as a ghetto defending itself against the world. The work that Christians do is of the greatest importance to society. It is important that we be useful to our neighbors. The text speaks specifically of agricultural work, but other professions are just as useful. The important thing is that the work we do be done with regard to the benefits it has for society as a whole (p. 119). As he always does, Calvin ends the sermon with an admonition to prayer. Let us bow down before our good God, he says, praying that he open our eyes in the recognition of his Son, that we show ourselves to be his people, and that our profession of the gospel bear its fruit, not only for ourselves but for all peoples and nations (p. 120).

The next sermon, Sermon 15, deals with the promise of prosperity which Micah proclaims and how this promise is fulfilled to the faithful. As Calvin so often does, he begins by reviewing the sermon of the previous day. Yesterday, he says, we heard about the blessing we receive from the gospel. It is when our Savior reconciles us with himself that we have peace with him. Peace with him entails living with each other in fraternal peace, aiding one another and devoting ourselves to the service of our brethren. This is how we are to be the Church of God (p. 121). This does not come of our own power; it is a divine gift. It comes when Christ reforms our hearts and gives us a new love for one another and strengthens our courage. In the Scripture we are treating today, Calvin tells his congregation, we learn that when the reign of Christ is established among us, God will pour out upon us an abundance of good things and we will enjoy these good things in peace and tranquillity.

> But they shall sit every man under his vine and under his fig tree,
> and none shall make them afraid.

> (4:4 RSV)

Yet it should be noted, Calvin cautions, that those blessings of Christ's reign will never be completely realized in this world. As much as the reign of Christ has indeed begun and advances and grows in us, and as much as the blessings of the kingdom may already be experienced in this world, they are never completely fulfilled on earth. It should also be noted that the reign of Christ is above all spiritual and is not the same thing as the peace and prosperity of a merely secular society. God does not want us to be misled into thinking that our paradise is here below, or that our happiness is to be found in worldly vanities. Nevertheless, it is also true, as Saint Paul teaches us, that when we serve God with a pure conscience, the blessings of God will belong to us not only in the world to come but in this world as well (I Tim. 4:8). In this world also, to be sure, God supplies all the needs of the faithful. God is even now helping us, establishing us in all his blessings, and encouraging us with his generosity and grace (pp. 121-22).

Our preacher goes on to the end of this verse and points to the fact that after the prophet has given us this oracle of promise, he confirms it with these words, "For the mouth of the LORD of hosts has spoken" (Mic. 4:4 RSV). Calvin comments that when God promises something, we can be sure it will come to pass. To be sure, this promise must have appeared to be broken when a few years later the Jews lost their kingdom, the Temple was destroyed, and the people were taken into captivity. How could the vision of Micah ever come to pass? But we should never judge the promises of God by outward appearances. God has the power to bring about his purposes far beyond our highest hopes. God has promised that the reign of Christ will be for all time, and that Zion will be established in spirit and truth. This, Calvin concludes, can be understood in regard to the restoration of the Church today (p. 125).

Calvin goes on to the next verse,

> For all the peoples walk
>   each in the name of its god,
> but we will walk in the name of the LORD our God
>   for ever and ever.

(4:5 RSV)

Then he raises the obvious objection. Is this not a contradiction of what Micah had just prophesied? Not at all, Calvin says. Even though the promise was made to all peoples, not all receive it. Until the end of this world there will be those who will follow after their own gods, but this should not be a stumbling block to Christians. Even if others turn aside, we must persevere to the end (pp. 127-28). The sermon is concluded with the prayer that our eyes be opened more and more to find all our highest joys in Christ, that we advance and grow in him, and that, fortified by the Holy Spirit, we arrive at the fullness and perfection to which God has called us and all the peoples of the earth (p. 129).

In these sermons on Micah, we see very clearly one important way in which Calvin understood the purpose of preaching. It was to present to the people of God both the promises of God and the warnings of God, that they might be received by faith. If the people receive the Word, then it is a Word of life which brings to them true blessing and thereby magnifies God's eternal glory.

C. Sermons for Holy Week

The church of Geneva did observe, during Calvin's pastorate, the evangelical feast days.[193] The cardinal points in Christ's saving work, that is, his nativity, his passion and resurrection, and his giving of the Holy Spirit at Pentecost, were observed by appropriate preaching and the celebration of Communion. Several sermons preached on these evangelical feast days have been preserved. We have, for example, sermons for the celebration of Christmas at which the Lord's Supper was celebrated. It seems that Christmas was usually observed on a Lord's Day in Geneva rather than on 25 December.

There were two reasons for this, quite aside from the "Puritan fanaticism" to which it is usually ascribed. The working people of Geneva were not too happy about stopping their work every few days for religious holidays. Holidays for the artisans of the late Middle Ages were a hardship, particularly when it became obvious that many of their apprentices found the holiday a good excuse for spending the day in the tavern. The middle class had good reason for objecting to frequent holidays. A Christmas observance which included Christmas, the feast of Saint Stephen, the feast of the Circumcision, the feast of the Holy Innocents, Epiphany, and the feast of the Purification made for six holidays in a bit more than a month. This could also be a problem for a day laborer during the middle of the winter, when there were extra expenses for fuel. The middle of the winter was no time to lose six days' wages. But there was also a theological problem. It was well known in the sixteenth century that Christmas was originally a pagan feast day and that it was not until the fourth century that one began to celebrate the birth of Christ on the old birthday of the sun god. It was also well known that the Christian Church had been careful to celebrate the Christian Passover on a Sunday in order to make it clear that they were not simply celebrating the old Jewish feast. The Christians of the second century celebrated Easter on a Lord's Day for the same reason the church of Geneva insisted on celebrating Christmas on the Lord's Day.

There are also a number of special sermons for Pentecost in which the celebration of Communion is mentioned. So, already we notice that festal preaching tends to be sacramental preaching in the Reformed tradi-

---

193. On Calvin and the observance of feast days, there are a number of unanswered questions which we hope at some time to address. For the present, see Leith, "Calvin's Doctrine," pp. 206-29. See particularly p. 214 n. 36.

tion. Where this is particularly in evidence is in the series of sermons preached on the passion narrative of the Gospels. Let us look at one of these series which apparently was preached at Easter in 1558 and published shortly thereafter by Conrad Badius.

Nine sermons have been preserved.[194] The first was preached on the Sunday morning before Easter, the second at vespers later that day, and then one each day through the whole of Holy Week, the ninth sermon being preached on Easter Sunday morning at the celebration of Communion. The Scripture lessons were taken from the Gospel of Matthew as follows:

1. Sunday Morning	Matthew 26:36-39
Garden of Gethsemane	
2. Sunday Vespers	Matthew 26:40-50
The Arrest	
3. Monday	Matthew 26:51-66
Trial before the High Priest	
4. Tuesday	Matthew 26:67–27:11
The Denial of Peter and the Despair of Judas	
5. Wednesday	Matthew 27:11-26
Jesus before Pilate	
6. Thursday	Matthew 27:27-44
Jesus Mocked	
7. Friday	Matthew 27:45-54
Jesus on the Cross	
8. Saturday	Matthew 27:55-60
The Burial	
9. Sunday Morning	Matthew 28:1-10
The Resurrection	

In 1548 the city council specifically indicated that the pastors were to preach on the passion narrative during Holy Week, although nothing is said about these days being holidays, that is, about closing one's workshop or not going out into one's fields. Easter Sunday or Pentecost Sunday was another matter. Those feasts were always celebrated on a Sunday.

194. These sermons, entitled "Sermons sur la Passion de Nostre Seigner Iesus Christ," are found in Calvin, Corpus Reformatorum 46:833-954. The page references in the text refer to vol. 46 of the Corpus Reformatorum.

Several things should be pointed out about this series of sermons. First we notice that, as they stand, there is a definite pastoral integrity to the nine sermons. The first announces that on the Lord's Day following, that is, on Easter Sunday, the Lord's Supper is to be celebrated. The whole series of sermons, then, becomes a preparation for that celebration. The conclusion of the series is the invitation to participate in the covenant meal, and thereby make a faith commitment. The pastoral thrust of the series is obviously evangelistic. What we have here is the beginning of the Reformed Communion season, that practice which flowered in eighteenth-century Scotland and eventually gave rise to the camp meetings of the American frontier. In this series of sermons we have the prototype of the traditional Reformed preparatory service. Here, very clearly, we see Calvin as evangelist.

This is particularly clear in how Calvin presents the religious experience of those who surrounded the cross. Throughout the series he gives careful attention to the disciples who could not stay awake in the Garden of Gethsemane, Peter's failure of faith, the despair of Judas, Pilate's agnosticism, the blindness of the scribes, the repentance of the thief on the cross, Joseph of Arimathea's piety, the final faithfulness of Nicodemus, and the devotion of the women. As Calvin preached, he was aware that each of them was sitting in his congregation. Before him sat those whose faith had failed just as Peter's had; those who, as Nicodemus, had come to Jesus by night but might now be ready to come to him in broad daylight; and those whose lives had been changed by Christ, as had Mary Magdalene's, and would come to Christ faithfully wherever he might be and do his bidding wherever he might send her. There were those who had betrayed Jesus as had Judas, and to such Calvin wanted to make clear that the way of repentance was open, just as it had been to Peter. There were those who, like the thief on the cross, would in the preaching of Christ's passion come to see Jesus as the Lamb of God and pray that he would remember them when he came into his kingdom (p. 912).

In fact, when one reads Calvin's treatment of the repentant thief, one realizes that this was just how Calvin understood his preaching ministry during Holy Week. It was his job to present the passion so that those in the congregation would recognize Christ as their Savior and so come to the Lord's Table and pledge their faith in him by participating in the covenant meal. For Calvin, to preach the cross meant to present Christ's sacrifice as the revelation of God's atoning love for the humanity he had created, and to present it so clearly that those who heard it would come to faith.

124

Second, we notice that for Calvin it was very important to present the cross as vicarious atonement. Christ suffered for us and for our salvation. The preaching of the cross is, after all, gospel. It is good news. The cross is far more than an example, far more than something for us to do; it is something that has been done for us, something we could not do for ourselves (p. 858). Apparently it was Calvin's regular practice to preach on the passion narrative during Holy Week. One year, however, he apparently preached on the fifty-third chapter of Isaiah. This is the most important and most extended passage of all of Scripture on the subject of the vicarious atonement. The New Testament quoted verses from the chapter to explain the meaning of Christ's passion. It is one of the passages of the Old Testament Scriptures most constantly alluded to in the New (p. 866). The fact that Calvin should preach through this chapter during Holy Week surely makes evident the importance he gave to the vicarious nature of Christ's suffering for us. The burden of preaching the cross for Calvin is not to exhort his congregation to take up their cross and follow Christ; although that theme is not absent from Calvin's preaching, it is not primary (pp. 858 and 906). That had been the primary message of the late Middle Ages. It was thoroughly consistent with the Pelagian tendencies of the more pietistic nominalists such as the Brethren of the Common Life. The primary theme in Calvin's preaching is that God was in Christ reconciling the world unto himself. Christ's declaration on the cross, "It is finished," is the key word for understanding the passion. It means the sacrifice has been accomplished, the atonement has been made.

Several different dimensions of the vicarious atonement are brought out with particular clarity in this series of sermons. That the sacrifice of Christ was a vicarious atonement rather than simply a heroic example was made clear for Calvin when Jesus stood trial before both Caiaphas and Pilate. Jesus made no defense because he willingly offered himself as sacrifice for those who were guilty, that he might suffer in their place (pp. 870 and 899). Pilate recognized the innocence of Jesus and sent him to death just the same. As Calvin sees it, Jesus could have established his innocence, just as he could have escaped, except that he knew the Father had sent him to offer the expiatory sacrifice which could be offered only by one who was innocent. For Calvin, all this is implied in Christ's being called the Lamb of God.

From the very beginning of the series, Calvin wants to make clear that the suffering of the passion was the experiencing of God's rejection of sin. "Christ's love for us was so great that he forgot himself and let the whole storm fall on his head, so that we would be delivered from the anger of God" (p. 840).[195] This becomes clear when we hear Jesus praying the Twenty-second Psalm, "'My God, my God, why hast thou forsaken me?'" (Matt. 27:46 RSV, referring to Ps. 22:1). As Calvin sees it, this shows that Jesus bore the full weight of God's rejection of sin. The agony was quite real. It was the agony of knowing that God had turned away. And yet Jesus never lost faith. He still claimed God as his God. He knew he would be faithful (pp. 920ff.). The suffering was the experiencing of God's anger at sin, the experiencing of God's wrath at injustice and unrighteousness in all forms. Christ died, Calvin tells us, "that he might sense the curse of God" (p. 920),[196] that is, the divine curse which rests upon sin. But he experienced it for us, that experiencing it he might atone for sin. The imagery here comes from the sacrificial system of the Old Testament. As the Lamb of God, he took the curse for us (p. 900). In another of these Holy Week sermons, Calvin tells us that Jesus took upon himself the ignominy we merited and, as the scapegoat, bore it away (p. 903). The rite of the scapegoat was a distinctly different image from that of the Passover lamb. Both are figures of vicarious sacrifice. While the Passover lamb is a figure of the redemptive power of innocent suffering, particularly as we find it in Isaiah 53, the figure of the scapegoat emphasizes the bearing away of the sin. These are two important dimensions of the concept of vicarious sacrifice.

There is a third dimension of this concept, and that is the concept of ransom. When a prisoner was captured by an enemy, that prisoner could be recovered by the payment of a ransom. This is another biblical figure for Christ's sacrifice (Mark 10:45) which Calvin uses to convey the urgency of the demand for the offering of a sacrifice (p. 905). The figure of paying a ransom also conveys another dimension of this complex mystery of vicarious sacrifice: that the captive is powerless to save himself. He is in the power of the enemy and must be saved by someone who has not been overpowered by the enemy.

A fourth biblical figure of vicarious sacrifice Calvin uses is that

195. ". . . mais quand il a fallu que nostre Seigneur Iesus Christ endurast telles angoisses, c'est signe qu'il nous aimoit, tellement qu'il s'est oublié soy-mesme, et a souffert que tout l'orage tombat sur sa teste, afin que nous fussions delivrez de l'ire de Dieu."

196. "Iesus Christ n'a iamais este reietté de Dieu son Pere, c'est chose certaine: mais il a falu neatmoins qu'il sousteinst ces douleurs-la et qu'il combatist vaillamment . . . c'est d'autant qu'il estoit là en nostre personne, soustenant la malediction de nos pechez. . . ."

Christ's obedience on the cross paid back to God the debt man owes for his disobedience. Man's disobedience is an offense to God, and reparation needs to be made. The obedience of Christ, an obedience even unto death, pays the debt that is owed and repairs the ruptured relationship between God and his creation. That this member of the human race who suffered the cross was the incarnate Son of God makes his obedient suffering so exceedingly precious to his Father that it abundantly covers the whole debt of human sin (p. 858).

For Calvin the preaching of the cross witnesses to the supreme revelation of God's love. This is both the first point and the last point that Calvin makes in this series of sermons. "As Scripture explains, three things are to be recognized in regard to our salvation. The first is the inestimable love which God has for us . . ." (p. 833).[197] God's love for his fallen creatures is so great that he sends out his unique Son, his beloved Son, to make the ultimate sacrifice, that they be restored to fellowship with him (p. 881). So precious are the souls of men to God (pp. 840 and 895)! In the final sermon of the series, the invitation to the Lord's Supper is presented as a call to the children of God to gather around the table of their Father, for it is at this table that they experience the fraternity of the household of faith and the infinite goodness of God (pp. 952ff.). We are well aware, of course, that there are those who tell us that Calvin has nothing to say of the love of God, or that the love of God does not seem to have any function in Calvin's theology. We will let others worry about whether this rather harsh judgment is justified elsewhere in Calvin's writings. One thing is clear when Calvin enters the pulpit to preach the cross, however: at the heart of his ministry we hear quite a bit about the love of God. For Calvin there is no understanding of the cross without seeing it in terms of the relation of the Father to the Son and the Son to the Father. This is a relationship of love, and it is the type, or pattern, of our relationship to God; through faith in Christ we are brought into this relationship of love. Faith, for Calvin, is the means of entering into communion with God, and that communion is nothing other than a love relationship. Faith is the means; love is the end.

Finally, we notice a third characteristic of these Holy Week sermons. For Calvin the preaching of Holy Week is the preaching of the Christian Passover (p. 953). It is not two celebrations, a celebration of Christ's

197. "Quand il nous est parlé de nostre salut, l'Ecriture nous propose trois fin. L'ume c'est que nous cognoissions l'amour inestimable que Dieu nous a porté."

death on Good Friday and a celebration of his resurrection on Easter Sunday, but one, the celebration of the Christian Passover. It presents to us the story of how Christ made the passage from this life to the life to come. The Gospels are of course already permeated with this thought. That Calvin should preach nine sermons during Holy Week and devote only one to the resurrection seems a bit unbalanced. It can only be explained by the fact that the Gospels themselves are written that way. They give much more space to the passion than to the resurrection. There is something else, however, and that is that Calvin aims in his preaching to show the way for each of us to make the same passage. The good news of the resurrection announces to us that the way to fellowship with God is open. The risen Christ has made the passage to the Father, to his Father and our Father, and this good news is addressed to the whole multitude of the faithful. It is because Christ is risen that we have communion with the Father (pp. 951-53). The resurrection appearances as Calvin presents them have the function of assuring us that indeed the passage was made. In this sense these sermons reflect the Gospels themselves.

The sermon concludes with an invitation to the Lord's Supper. The table has been prepared for us, that we be united to Christ as he is united to the Father. It is for this reason that we are called his brethren. He would have us participate in the sacrifice which he has once and for all made for our salvation. He would bring us from death to resurrection. The gate of heaven is open so that we may come before our Father, presenting ourselves to him, knowing that he always receives us as his children (p. 954).

D. Calvin's Homiletics

After looking at three very different series of Calvin's sermons, let us make some observations.[198] First, let us ask why Calvin was regarded so highly as a preacher. Why did people listen to him? Calvin did not have the warm personality of Luther. One does not find in Calvin the oratorical elegance of Gregory of Nazianzus nor the lively imagination of Origen. He was hardly the dramatic public speaker that John Chrysostom was, nor

198. The recent essay of John Leith, "Calvin's Doctrine of the Proclamation of the Word and Its Significance for Today," is a particularly perceptive study of Calvin as preacher.

did he have the magnetic personality of Bernard of Clairvaux. Gregory the Great was a natural-born leader, as was Ambrose of Milan, but that was not a gift Calvin had. Yet, few preachers have affected such a tremendous reform in the lives of their congregations as did the Reformer of Geneva.

Although Calvin is never thought of as a great orator, he did have some important gifts of public speaking. He seems to have had an intensity which he focused on the text of Scripture which was so powerful that he drew his hearers into the sacred text along with him. This intensity comes from his tremendous power of concentration. It is this same sort of concentration, of course, which enabled him to preach without notes or manuscript. One can be sure that he carefully studied the text beforehand and consulted the commentaries of others on the passage. His commentaries show how thoroughly he had studied the text. Yet the sermon itself was put together before the congregation. This was, of course, the way the great preachers of the patristic age had worked. Calvin followed the same method. Concentrating both on the passage at hand and on the congregation before him, he drew out of his well-stocked memory the meaning of the Holy Scriptures for his people.

Another gift of public speaking Calvin had in the highest degree was clarity of thought and expression. He knew how to use the language. Even more than that, he was a pioneer in developing the French language as a suitable means for expressing religious insights.[199] Those who specialize in such matters tell us that his vocabulary was brilliant. Words are used with the greatest precision. His vocabulary is rich but never obscure or esoteric. It is never vain or contrived. Calvin never had to work at giving the impression of being learned. He often presents us with marvelous similes and metaphors such as the one we noticed in his sermons on Micah, where he says the hypocrites used the Temple as armor against God's judgment and as a cape to cover their wickedness. Although it is hard to speak of this on the basis of a written text, Calvin seems to have spoken with considerable variety of pace and mood. The cool of literary analysis was balanced by both prophetic indignation and mystic rapture. Calvin can speak of God's love for his Church with as much fervor as he can about God's judgment upon the wicked. We noticed this in the sermons on the passion.

---

199. On Calvin's part in shaping the French language, see McGrath, *Life of John Calvin,* pp. 133-36, and Francis Higman, *The Style of John Calvin in His French Polemical Treatises* (Oxford: Oxford University Press, 1967).

One of the strong points of Calvin's preaching was his constant concern for application. If Micah had preached about the responsibilities and failures of ancient Israel, Calvin was quick to draw attention to the vocation of Geneva on one hand and its failure to fulfill it on the other. If Micah had fulminated against the idolatry of Samaria, Calvin applied the warnings of the prophet against the superstitious rites purveyed by Rome. The gracious promises which God made to his people through the mouth of Micah, Calvin proclaimed to the people of God in his own time. As the Reformer of Geneva understood it, the prophetic promises of the prophets are to be claimed by the Church both now and to the end of the world.

We have asked why people listened to Calvin's sermons with such interest. Surely the fundamental answer is not to be found in their oratorical form but rather in their religious content. Calvin drew out of the Scriptures aspects of Christian teaching which the Church had not heard for centuries. This was above all the case with the doctrine of grace. The promise of salvation was presented to all who would believe it. Calvin preached justification by faith, as all the Reformers did. More than some, perhaps, he also preached sanctification by faith. The lives of those who believed the Word of God would be transformed by that Word. Holiness was the fruit of faith. To believe the Word was to live by the Word, and that life lived according to the Word of God was blessed, both in this world and in the world to come.

The preaching of grace by the sixteenth-century Reformers was received with joy and enthusiasm by those who heard them, because for generations they had been oppressed by the preaching of Pelagianism. The preachers of the late Middle Ages had put the emphasis on outward forms of religious devotion, the disciplines of penance, the sacramental system, the correct performance of rites, and the techniques of mystical ascent. The elaborate homiletical forms of the late Middle Ages had become worn and tired. The Christians of western Europe longed for something more than the routine piety they had been preached. Those attracted to Calvin's preaching prized not its outward form but its content.

One is puzzled today that Calvin preached such long series on Deuteronomy, on Job, and on the Major and Minor Prophets. It seems that these sermons on Old Testament books were of particular interest to Calvin's congregation, and there was a good reason for it. Christians had not heard the Old Testament preached in centuries, at least not in the way the Reformers were preaching it. Occasionally Old Testament books were preached during the Middle Ages, but for the most part the interpretation was highly allegorical. There were exceptions, as has been noted in earlier chapters, but generally speaking few Christians knew Hebrew and not very many preachers ever attempted to dig beneath the highly artificial Christian interpretation of Origen. When the Reformers began to interpret the Hebrew text of the Old Testament, equipped with their knowledge of Hebrew and dedicated to a historical-grammatical interpretation, they were providing the Church of their day with fresh and very exciting material.

Much of the excitement the rediscovery of the Old Testament generated was because it helped the Reformers break the grip Hellenistic asceticism had gotten on Christian piety. The piety taught by the Old Testament was one to be practiced by men and women who lived in this world. It was concerned with the morality of farmers, merchants, and politicians, and addressed itself to the aspirations and frustrations of family and community. The prophets very particularly preached against the formalism and ceremonialism of the religious institutions of their day. For the Reformers the prophetic message was clearly applicable to their own day. It did not take the Reformers long to discover that it was out of the context of the Old Testament that the piety of the New Testament Church had developed. Jesus and the apostles were as critical of a formalized piety and a ceremonial worship as were the prophets. The New Testament was as concerned with the morality of family and business as was the Old Testament. The rediscovery of the Old Testament enriched the Reformers' understanding of the New Testament. If the Reformers gave much attention to the preaching of the Old Testament, it was because they discovered its prophetic value to the Church of their day. If their congregations heard their preaching of the Old Testament with enthusiasm, it was because that preaching did in fact speak to the same needs and concerns to which it had originally spoken.

Another reason people listened to Calvin's sermons was that the sermons had a high sense of the authority of Scripture. The preacher himself believed he was preaching the Word of God. He saw himself to be the servant of the Word. God had called him to be such a servant, and he devoted all his energies to be faithful in that service. That sort of wholehearted devotion can be sensed in a preacher. Surely it was one of the things that made the preaching of John Chrysostom so compelling. John Calvin had such a strong sense of standing under the authority of Scripture that it kindled the devotion of a whole generation of preachers.

One of the most amazing things about Calvin's handling of Scripture is that his high regard for the authority of Scripture goes hand in hand with his willingness to regard it as a completely historical document. Calvin studied the Scriptures with all the means of Renaissance historical criticism and literary analysis that were available to him. His reverence for Scripture did not suggest that there was anything to be feared from studying it too carefully. He was confident that the most careful historical study of the text would only make its meaning clearer and its authority more obvious. His hearers rejoiced in this fearless intellectual who was at the same time confidently devout.

For Calvin, the very fact that his ministry was to expound the Word of God filled him with a profound reverence for the task before him. Classical rhetoric had emphasized that great oratory must have a sense of serving a great cause. That Calvin had and in generous measure. To preach was to be the minister of the oracles of God (I Pet. 4:11). What greater cause could an orator serve?

E. Preaching as Worship

Let us turn now to how Calvin understood the reading and preaching of Scripture to be worship. We can start with the axiom that, for Calvin, worship is to serve God's glory.[200] When God's Word is heard, God is glorified. Just as "the heavens are telling the glory of God; and the firmament proclaims his handiwork"; just as "day to day pours forth speech, and night to night declares knowledge"; so God is glorified when the Word of God revives the soul, makes wise the simple, rejoices the heart, and enlightens the eyes (Ps. 19:1-8). Preaching displays the treasures of God's Wisdom, that we might rejoice in them. Calvin's understanding of the place of the Word in worship has deep foundations in the Wisdom theology of both the Old and New Testaments. God is glorified when his Word is heard by his people and they are transformed into his image. Through the preaching of the gospel God's people are transformed into the image of Christ. Calvin's Wisdom theology, like that of Augustine, is thoroughly Johannine.[201] When God's people hear the Word and receive

200. "Comme c'est une chose bien requise en la Chrestienté, et des plus necessaires, que chascun fidele observe et entretienne la communion de l'Eglise en son endroit, frequentant les assemblees, qui se font, tant le Dimanche que les aultres iours, pour honnorer et servir Dieu. . . ." Calvin, *Opera Selecta* 2.12.

201. On Augustine's Wisdom theology, see Old, *Reading and Preaching*, 2:346-58 and 397ff.

it by faith, they are saved from their sins and born into a new and eternal life, and being born from above and renewed by the Holy Spirit, they now worship God in spirit and truth (John 1:12; 3:5; 4:23). God is glorified simply in the proclamation of the Word, to be sure, but the Word has power to bring about what it says. The Word bears fruit, and this fruit magnifies God's glory.

We have seen in Calvin's sermons on Micah how the Reformer understood the worship of the transformed Jerusalem. All the peoples of the earth go up to Jerusalem to learn of God's Law. As Calvin understands it, this means that the reading and preaching of Scripture is to have a central place in the worship of the Church; it is its primary responsibility. This kind of worship, centered around the reading and preaching of the Word, is what God demands of us in the first tablet of the Law.[202] For Calvin the four commandments of this tablet should order Christian worship even to this day.[203] They should order it in its Christian form, to be sure, and that form is the summary of the Law Jesus gave: The first and greatest commandment is, thou shalt love the Lord thy God with all thy heart, with all thy mind, and with all thy soul (Matt. 22:37-38). It is in worship, above all, that we fulfill the first and greatest commandment.

In the sermons on Micah we find a very clear statement of what we have called the doctrine of the kerygmatic real presence. According to this doctrine, Christ is present in the reading and preaching of his Word. We spoke of it in regard to the *Didache,* that most ancient and venerable of Christian documents, and in regard to Jerome. And we find a very similar thought in Calvin's sermons on Micah.[204] There we read that the presence of God among his people is through his Word, by which he declares his will and exercises his rule.

For Calvin, however, we must give special attention to a covenantal theology of worship, which understands worship in terms of the covenantal relationship between God and his people. It is in worship that the covenant is established, maintained, nourished, and renewed. In worship we experience God as our God and ourselves as his people. In baptism we are introduced into the covenant community. In the reading and preaching of the Scriptures as well as in the Lord's Supper, we are nour-

---

202. Calvin, *Institutes* 2.8.16.

203. Calvin, *Institutes* 2.8.11.

204. "Or quelle est la presence de Dieu, sinon ceste parolle par laquelle il nous declare sa volunté." Calvin, *Sermons sur le Livre de Michée,* p. 130.

ished in the covenant relationship. In the sermon the Word is proclaimed; in the Supper it is signed and sealed. In prayer and the giving of alms, again and again we exercise the bond of covenant love. Especially in the praises of the Church, in the hymns and psalms, we experience the awe and the joy of the sacred relationship. We enter into his gates with thanksgiving and into his courts with praise (Ps. 100:4). By entering into the covenant and living according to the covenant, we both glorify God and enjoy him forever.

VIII. England

Reformation had been budding in England for some time.[205] It was like a springtime which had tarried long. Well before Luther, the English fields had been plowed and the seed sown for a profound revival of Christian faith. One would have expected the Reformation to have come to England long before it came to Germany. That it was a Saxon rather than an Anglo-Saxon, a Martin Luther rather than a John Wycliffe, whose sickle first brought in that harvest is a bit surprising. But then, for some of us the Reformation is not to be explained in terms of national culture. There are those who like to explain far too many things by *Volkgeist,* some sort of national genius or racial uniqueness. For others of us national culture is not the essence of life. We would be slow to say that the Reformation is somehow peculiarly German or in some way an expression of the German national character. The Reformation in England was long overdue, but its coming was complicated by a situation very much unlike the situation in Saxony, and again, very much unlike the situation in the Rhineland.

While the Reformation on the continent of Europe had outstanding theologians and, even more, outstanding biblical scholars, the English

---

205. On the Reformation in England, see John E. Booty, *The Godly Kingdom of Tudor England* (Wilton, Conn.: Morehouse-Barlow, 1981); Horton Davies, *Worship and Theology in England, from Cranmer to Hooper, 1534-1603* (Princeton: Princeton University Press, 1970); James Gairdner, *The English Church in the Sixteenth Century from the Accession of Henry VIII to the Death of Mary* (London and New York: Macmillan, 1902); Philip Hughes, *The Reformation in England,* 2 vols. (London: Hollis & Carter, 1950-54); John R. H. Moorman, *A History of the Church in England,* 3rd ed. (1973; reprint, London: A. & C. Black, 1980); Stephen C. Neill, *Anglicanism,* rev. ed. (London: Mowbrays, 1977); and Harry C. Porter, *Reformation and Reaction in Tudor Cambridge* (Cambridge: At the University Press, 1958).

Reformation had adept politicians. Again, this is not to be explained by any kind of national character, any kind of genetic weakness or strength. In another generation the situation could have been completely reversed. Cranmer, Latimer, and Ridley, the three bishops who led the Reformation in its first phase, were men of deep faith and firmly committed to the reform of the Church. They intended to carry through this reform without schism. This intention seemed quite realistic considering the fact that they all attained leading positions in the organizational structure of the English church. Thomas Cranmer was archbishop of Canterbury and primate of England for over twenty years. He was in the ideal position to reform the Church from within its traditional structure. The leading English Reformers made their compromises, compromises they felt they needed to make in order to achieve their end, but the fact that they finally paid the price of martyrdom for their Protestant faith eloquently reveals their ultimate sincerity.

The story of how King Henry VIII, a determined Catholic, a defender of the faith, unwittingly opened the door to the Reformation in order to get a divorce has been told many a time, to the embarrassment of all concerned. What irony! The king who would be a defender of the Catholic faith became the patron of Protestantism. And what a reluctant patron he was! Every concession to reform had to be pried out of His Royal Highness, and no sooner was it granted than it was revoked. As one reads the story, one wonders what it was that made England Protestant. The king was set against Protestantism. The hands of the Reformers were repeatedly tied. For years at a time Hugh Latimer, by far England's best preacher, either had to refrain from preaching or do his preaching in obscure pulpits. When wondering how England became Protestant, one can only invoke the maxim of the apostle Paul. It was not so much he who planted or he who watered as it was that God gave the increase (cf. I Cor. 3:7).

Thomas Cranmer was a man remarkably suited for the unique role he was to play.[206] He was not a great theologian, but he did understand great theology. He had studied in Germany and had caught the vision of

---

206. On Thomas Cranmer, see Geoffrey W. Bromiley, *Thomas Cranmer, Archbishop and Martyr* (London: Church Book Room Press, 1956); Geoffrey W. Bromiley, *Thomas Cranmer, Theologian* (New York: Oxford University Press, 1956); Albert F. Pollard, *Thomas Cranmer and the English Reformation, 1489-1556* (London: G. P. Putnam's Sons, 1905); Edward C. Ratcliff, "The Liturgical Work of Archbishop Cranmer," *Journal of Ecclesiastical History* 7 (1956): 189-203; and Jasper G. Ridley, *Thomas Cranmer* (Oxford: Clarendon Press, 1962).

justification by faith. That was in fact the center of his theology, as it was for the other Reformers. Justification by faith was the unifying theme of the Reformation, and Cranmer realized that it was the theological key to reform, the passkey that would unlock the whole labyrinth of interrelated chambers of abuse which had defied reform for so many centuries. Cranmer was the sort of man who had the tact and discretion, even more, the humility, that made it possible to deal with King Henry VIII. He had a good sense of when he could press reform and when he would have to wait. He had that sort of humility in the face of providence which makes it possible for men of faith to wait for the moving of the Spirit. And for a Christian leader, that is a great virtue.

One thing one has to reckon with in the English Reformation is that it stems as much from Wycliffe as from Luther.[207] Many partisans of the English Reformation have been loath to admit this, but it is hard to deny. One notices the influence of Wycliffe as one reads through the sermons of Latimer. The great concerns of Latimer had for the most part been those of Wycliffe a century and a half before. Wycliffe had insisted that the English church had no need to recognize the Roman pope. When Latimer discounts "that Italian bishop yonder," the conciliarist protests of the fourteenth century are transparent. The Act of Supremacy, which gave the king rather than the pope control of the Church of England, was thought out along much the same lines as Wycliffe had developed. Wycliffe's denial of the Scholastic doctrine of transubstantiation foreshadowed the discussion of the matter in England. In fact, when one reads the English on the subject, one often gets the feeling that they rarely penetrated to the heart of the discussion as it developed on the Continent. This may well be explained by positing that the discussion went back to Wycliffe rather than to Luther or Zwingli. Above all, and particularly for our discussion, Wycliffe had raised the issue of the sole authority of Scripture and had pressed for an English Bible and vernacular preaching. Even though Wycliffe died at the end of the fourteenth century, the Lollards had kept the tradition alive. They circulated their English Bible and preached wherever they could. The demand for reform did not necessarily have a German accent.

A significant dimension of the English Reformation for our study is the tremendous struggle the English Reformers had to go through to get

---

207. James Gairdner, *Lollardy and the Reformation in England: An Historical Survey,* 3 vols. (London: Macmillan, 1908-11).

the English Bible. As with so much in the English Reformation, it was a political struggle. Ever since Wycliffe the Catholic hierarchy had opposed a vernacular Bible. As early as 1522 William Tyndale saw the need of a fresh translation along the lines of Christian humanist scholarship.[208] Tyndale's vision was broader and more profound than Wycliffe's; the Wycliffe Bible had not been a fresh translation from the Greek and Hebrew, but rather a translation of the Latin Vulgate. Thanks to Christian humanism, Tyndale had a much better appreciation of what an English translation of the Greek and Hebrew involved. While a student at Cambridge, Tyndale had been won to the cause of Christian humanist biblical studies but had not yet been won to the Reformation. Approaching Cuthbert Tunstall, the bishop of London, he found no support for his project. Henry VIII, still a determined defender of the faith, was not at all amenable to an English Bible. In fact, those who promoted a vernacular Bible were persecuted by the government with discouraging regularity. So, understandably, Tyndale went to pursue his project in Germany, where the leaders of Christian humanist biblical scholarship were to be found. There he came into contact with Continental Protestantism. Apparently it was while in Europe that he first committed himself to the Reformation. He visited Wittenberg, but then moved on to Cologne because of its flourishing printing industry, and there began producing his translation. Johann Cochlaeus, one of Germany's most influential Catholic apologists, got wind of the project and had the authorities of Cologne close down the operation. Not content with that, he alerted Henry VIII and the English hierarchy of the danger of a new English Bible. The English government responded with a vengeance, and many who attempted to distribute Tyndale's translation were punished with imprisonment or burned at the stake. Tyndale, constantly on the wing, continued his work. During his lifetime he was able to publish both the complete New Testament and the Old Testament Pentateuch. It was a very good, solid translation, a fresh attempt to render the text from the original tongues. From a scholarly standpoint it was a translation of high quality. It was, as one would expect, done from the standpoint of the new biblical scholarship of

208. On William Tyndale, see Stanley L. Greenslade, *The Works of William Tyndale* (London: Blackie and Son, 1938); James Frederic Mozley, *William Tyndale* (New York: Macmillan, 1937); *The Work of William Tyndale,* ed. G. E. Duffield, Courtenay Library of Reformation Classics, vol. 1 (Appleford, Eng.: Sutton-Courtenay Press, 1964); and Charles Harold Williams, *William Tyndale* (London: Nelson, 1969).

the Christian humanists. Tyndale had learned quite a bit from Erasmus, but also he had learned much from Luther.

In order to continue his work, Tyndale took up residence among the English merchants in Antwerp. But before he finished his translation, he was apprehended by the authorities of Charles V and executed as a heretic. Happily, Miles Coverdale had been working on a very similar project at about the same time and was able to complete Tyndale's work. He, too, had found it prudent to flee England. His translation was not a fresh rendering of the Greek and Hebrew, as Tyndale's had been. He depended rather heavily on other attempts, among them Luther's Bible and the Zürich Bible. Coverdale's translation was nevertheless a good translation because he used his sources judiciously and possessed a literary facility which made his work good reading. Although not a particularly outstanding biblical scholar, he was a competent one, and even more, he was a good writer. Finally in 1537 Archbishop Cranmer was able to convince Henry VIII to permit the publication of an English Bible. Although it was not recognized at the time, this Bible was the work of Tyndale completed by Coverdale. It was called Matthew's Bible because the editor, John Rogers, published it under an assumed name, Thomas Matthew. Rogers had been chaplain to the English merchants in Antwerp, and while there he had worked with Tyndale. One might say Rogers was Tyndale's heir in regard to that most important work of Christian scholarship. Rogers was able to provide a manuscript of the remainder of Tyndale's translation of the Old Testament historical books, that is, from Joshua through Chronicles. Interestingly enough, Rogers was the first martyr to die under Queen Mary, so he was Tyndale's heir in martyrdom as well. This Bible combined Tyndale's New Testament and the historical books of the Old Testament and Coverdale's Psalms, Prophets, and the Wisdom Books. It became the foundation of the Authorized Version finally completed in the reign of King James.[209] This English Bible, produced at such great cost of life and labor, has ever since been the treasure of English-speaking Christianity. It is this Bible which has been read and preached in the worship of the Church in which most of us have been brought up.

209. Charles C. Butterworth, *The Literary Lineage of the King James Bible, 1340-1611* (Philadelphia: University of Pennsylvania Press, 1941).

A. Hugh Latimer (ca. 1485-1555): The Prophet of Reform

The son of an English yeoman, Hugh Latimer was sent off to study at Cambridge.[210] It was only slowly that he was won to the Reformation. He prolonged his studies for years, but they were of the traditional Scholastic sort. The new learning of Christian humanism, so influential for the Rhenish Reformers, did not seem to have influenced him. He did nevertheless develop into a fine preacher in those years, but he developed his preaching in the lines of the late medieval preaching techniques the preaching orders had fashioned.

Preaching in England on the eve of the Reformation was not nearly so impressive as it was in Italy or in the Rhineland. There was at the beginning of the fifteenth century no English Savonarola, no Johann Geiler von Kaysersberg. While in Germany the Reformation was a reform of preaching, in England one of the chief reforms that was needed was simply to supply preaching. Preachers had to be developed before the Reformation could come into its own. Latimer makes the point again and again: England was spiritually starved for lack of preachers, and it would be a few generations before that lack would be supplied. If on the Continent the Reformation was brought in by preachers, the problem in England was to find enough preachers to fill her idle pulpits. The clergy of the old order did not have a very strong preaching ministry. There were exceptions, and of course Latimer was the most notable, but the leaders of the English Reformation were not preachers. Latimer's famous taunt that preachers were like strawberries — they came but once a year and then only for a short time — could never have been made in the Rhineland, but it did hit home in England.[211]

Reading Latimer's sermons, one notices that he is a master of the late medieval homiletical forms.[212] One finds again and again the typical

210. On Hugh Latimer, see Allan G. Chester, *Hugh Latimer, Apostle to the English* (Philadelphia: University of Pennsylvania Press, 1954); and Robert Demaus, *Hugh Latimer, a Biography* (London and Dallas: Lamar & Barton, n.d.).

211. We are indebted to Allan G. Chester for a particularly fine edition of Latimer's sermons. Hugh Latimer, *Selected Sermons*, ed. Allan G. Chester (Charlottesville: University Press of Virginia, 1968). It is this edition on which the following study is based. The above comment was taken from Latimer, "Sermon on the Plough," in *Selected Sermons*, p. 32.

212. In addition to Latimer, *Selected Sermons*, see also Hugh Latimer, *Sermons*, 2 vols., Parker Society edition (Cambridge: University Press, 1844).

medieval introduction, the *prothema*.[213] One finds the rich *exempla* of the medieval sermon. His famous "Sermon on the Cards," in which he pulled a deck of cards out of his preaching gown and used it to make his points, was the sort of thing late medieval preachers would have done often but Continental Reformers would never have done.[214] Latimer's sermons are even today a joy to read. They have a literary charm one rarely finds in the sermons of the Continental Reformers. As Allan Chester has pointed out, Latimer knew all the tricks of rhetoric and used them with skill. His use of irony, ridicule, personal reminiscence, epithet, simile, metaphor, and alliteration is especially strong.

Latimer was not at all averse to accommodating his text to his message, as we find particularly in the early sermons that have been preserved, but in his later sermons he becomes much more expository. It was inevitable that he should move in this direction. One would expect that as his doctrine of Scripture became stronger, he would be more willing to let the Scriptures lead him rather than simply employing Scripture to make his point. But when he employs the accommodated sense, he does it very well. For example, in his "Convocation Sermon" of 1536 he takes as his text Luke 16:8, "The children of this world be much more prudent and politic than the children of light in their generation,"[215] and spins out from it his whole critique of the medieval Church and his program for reform. Neither his critique nor his reforms are even suggested by his text. The sermons he preached before Edward VI, on the other hand, show a much greater penetration into the meaning of the text. The text for the first of these, Deuteronomy 17:14-17, speaks of God's choosing a king for Israel. It makes the point that the king of God's choosing is not a foreigner and is clear that he is not to be a big spender. He is to maintain neither a large stable of horses nor a harem of many wives.[216] It is on these

213. Allan Chester, whose biography of Latimer is particularly helpful for the attention it gives to Latimer's preaching, tells us that the texts we have of Latimer's sermons are considerably abridged. It may well be that the *prothema* was not as fully reported as the body of the sermon. On the other hand, one finds highly developed *prothemas* in the "Convocation Sermon" of 1536 and the "First Sermon before Edward VI." See Latimer, *Selected Sermons*, pp. 1-9 and 50-54.

214. Latimer's famous "Sermon on the Cards" has come down to us in a report found in Foxe's *Book of Martyrs*. We do not have a text. For a critical study of Foxe's report, see Chester, *Hugh Latimer*, pp. 38ff.

215. Latimer, *Selected Sermons*, p. 2. It is, of course, the Latin text which Latimer used.

216. Latimer, *Selected Sermons*, pp. 53ff.

ideas, found in the text, that the main points of the sermon are developed. Latimer selected the text for the occasion rather than following something prescribed by a lectionary, but then, having selected the text, he follows it fairly consistently. Latimer well understands that the secret of prophetic preaching is to select the right text for the right occasion.

Latimer was often called upon to preach at critical moments in the history of the English church. One such was the opening of convocation in 1536, at the moment when Henry VIII was most open to having the Church of England move toward reform. He was called upon because it was recognized that he was the best preacher in England and because his preaching had for some time advocated reform. He had been consecrated bishop of Worcester in 1535 and was therefore an accepted leader of the Church of England. His friend Thomas Cranmer would be presiding, and he carefully directed Latimer as to what needed to be said at this time. Even at that, Latimer's preaching was bold. Not long before, he had been tried for heresy by this same convocation of English prelates. He understood full well that many of them resented his being selected to preach. What Latimer knew he had to do was confront them with their failings. Many of them were the prelates who never preached, the divines who dined so daintily. It was the prelates themselves who were the children of this world who were so much more prudent and politic than the children of light.[217] Elaborating on the words of Jesus, our preacher charges his listeners: "I commanded you that with all industry and labor ye should feed My sheep; ye earnestly feed yourselves from day to day, wallowing in delights and idleness. I commanded you to teach My commandments and not your fancies, and that ye should seek My glory and My vantage; you teach your own traditions and seek your own glory and profit. You preach very seldom, and when ye do preach ye do nothing but cumber them that preach truly, as much as lieth in you. . . ." Even though Latimer knew he was for the moment supported by the king — however, it must be remembered, when Henry VIII might change his mind one could never tell — it still must have taken courage to preach that message to that group of churchmen. Latimer preached with prophetic abandon, knowing well that it might cost him his life. And, to be sure, it did.

Much of Latimer's prophetic burden was to restore the ministry of the Word to the Church of England. To do this three things needed to be

---

217. Latimer, "Convocation Sermon," in *Selected Sermons,* p. 7.

done.[218] First, a new translation of the Bible into English was needed. We have already spoken of the long and complicated struggle to get an English Bible, of how William Tyndale and Miles Coverdale produced such a translation and how its publication and distribution had been for some time forbidden in England. Second, Latimer made an appeal for preaching prelates. By prelates he meant the leadership of the Church, above all the bishops. Preaching was the first responsibility of the bishops, the essential apostolic ministry, as Latimer understood it. The English government was happy to employ the bishops of the Church of England as civil servants, for then it could pay them out of church revenues. Latimer was ruthless in his exposure of benefices. This system had for centuries made it possible for absentee clergymen to collect the revenue of endowments intended to support the ministry of the local church and then, leaving the local church in the charge of a curate, spend their time as they pleased. The clergyman who held the benefice might well have had the education to care for his congregation, but the curates were far less capable. This financial system tended to weaken the preaching ministry, if not totally destroy it. The financial structure of the Church was complained of rather generally throughout Europe.

Another matter the prophetic ministry of Latimer focused on was idolatry. That the money which should have gone for the support of the poor was spent in gilding and bejeweling idols brought the constant outcry of many Reformers. It is certainly clear from Latimer's sermons that the cult of images was opposed because of its expense on one hand and its callousness to the needs of the poor on the other.[219] The wealth of the Church, whether expressed in rich vestments or the cult of images or rich church decorations, had been a grievance of the poor for some time. This was not, however, the primary concern in the Reformation's attack on idolatry. The primary concern was that the biblical tradition was fundamentally opposed to it. This is clear from the way Latimer quotes the good example of Hezekiah, the wise king of Israel, who took a strong initiative in ridding Israel of idols.[220] Idolatry corrupts our understanding of God. Far from revealing God, idols obscure God. They betray God's nature rather than intimate it. Idolatry is a perversion of the truth. Latimer

218. Latimer, "Convocation Sermon," p. 7; Latimer, "Sixth Sermon before Edward VI," in *Selected Sermons,* pp. 98ff.; and Latimer, "Sermon on the Plough," pp. 31, 36, 38, and 48.

219. Latimer, "First Sermon before Edward VI," in *Selected Sermons,* pp. 66ff.

220. Latimer, "Sermon on the Plough," p. 48.

ridicules the burning of candles before idols of Christ, the Virgin, and the saints. At midday, no less, one still burns candles before them. This pouring out of luxury is not only idolatrous, it is bad stewardship.

Latimer's attack on enclosures and high rents is interesting in light of the fact that his father was a yeoman. He tells us in one of his sermons how much rent his father paid and how much more the man who now farms it must pay for that same property.[221] Enclosures were complained of in England for several generations. Landlords were beginning to discover that they could turn the farmland into sheep pastures and make much more money producing wool than they could farming it. It saved labor costs. All that was needed was a shepherd and his dog on a piece of land that used to take a whole village to farm. The Reformation in England obviously pressed for a variety of changes that affected the whole life of the nation.

Some forty of Latimer's sermons have come down to us, including several that he preached on important occasions. These are indeed great prophetic utterances, and they deserve to be regarded as among the most significant sermons preached in England. On the other hand, his catechetical sermons preached in the chapel of the duchess of Suffolk were directed to her household and are beautifully simple and pastoral. It is the same way with a number of sermons, following the lectionary of *The Book of Common Prayer,* for Sundays and feast days, including the Sundays of Advent, Christmas Day, the feast of Saint Stephen, the feast of Saint John, Epiphany, and the Sundays after Epiphany. They, too, were preached in the same chapel or perhaps in village churches nearby. What one does not find are sermons of a primarily expository nature. There are no systematic attempts to interpret major portions of Scripture such as we find in Luther's sermons on the Gospel of John, Zwingli's sermons on Matthew, or Calvin's sermons on the prophets.

The preaching ministry of Hugh Latimer is in several ways typical of the English Reformation both in its strengths and in its weaknesses, but it was not typical of the Reformation as a whole. In the preaching of Latimer we find an excessive dependence on the state. One preached at the pleasure of the government. If one's preaching did not please the government, then one had better be silent. This, no doubt, was all quite consistent with the Act of Supremacy and the whole concept of a national church, but today it seems terribly subservient. The most important sermons were the sermons preached at court.

221. Latimer, "First Sermon," pp. 66ff.

Under Elizabeth this became a disaster. If under her long and prosperous reign a number of other literary forms flourished, the pulpit did not. During this time there was no great preacher who even began to have the reputation of Latimer, no Elizabethan preacher who did for the pulpit what Shakespeare did for the Elizabethan stage. There was good reason for this. Elizabeth figured the less preaching the better. One thing she did not want was another John Knox. She intended to rule England herself, and she wanted no interference from the pulpit. A dozen preachers for her realm would be about enough, as she saw it. The typical Protestant emphasis on the pulpit was not to her liking. With the English pulpit so dependent on government support, it is not surprising that when the government was indifferent, English preaching was indifferent as well. The time would come, however, when the English pulpit would be able to withstand this political domination, but that is the subject of another chapter. First we must look at another English preacher of a different sort.

B. John Hooper (ca. 1495-1555)

The early life of John Hooper is obscure.[222] He was born in Somerset, probably to a family of some means. He received his degree from Oxford in 1519 and, after completing his studies, is supposed to have entered a Cistercian monastery. With the dissolution of the monasteries in 1538, he began to study the works of the Continental Reformers. For a time he was employed in the household of Sir Thomas Arundel. This brought him into close contact with the court. His primary interests, however, were still theological. He became particularly interested in Henry Bullinger's commentaries on the Pauline Epistles. Both in London and Oxford he entered into the current discussion of church reform which was such an important part of the intellectual culture of the day. He had an important disputation with Stephen Gardiner, the bishop of Winchester, one of the leaders of the Catholic opposition, and as a result had to flee England. Visiting several of the best-known centers of the Reformation, he was able to get a firsthand knowledge of the reform as it had been

---

222. For works on the life of Hooper, see E. W. Hunt, *The Life and Times of John Hooper (c. 1500-1555), Bishop of Gloucester* (Lewiston, N.Y.: E. Mellen Press, ca. 1992); and John Charles Ryle, "Life of John Hooper," in *Five English Reformers* (London: Banner of Truth Trust, 1965).

developing in Europe. After an adventurous journey he arrived in Zürich, where he settled for several years, studying and writing a number of significant works, including a thorough and well-thought-out refutation of Gardiner's attack on Protestant eucharistic theology. By the time Hooper had reached Zürich, he must have been close to fifty years old and was surely Bullinger's senior in age. Very wisely the leader of the church of Zürich took considerable interest in Hooper.

When Hooper returned to England in 1549, he was able to speak with authority on the reforms of Rhenish Protestantism. By this time he was allowed to preach freely in his native land, and the duke of Somerset made him his personal chaplain. His preaching was well received, and he was invited to preach the traditional series of Lenten sermons before King Edward VI. The series was evidently successful in stirring up support for the Reformation at court, and as a result Hooper was appointed bishop of Gloucester. Evidently he had scruples against his appointment. The ordination oath required calling upon the saints and using medieval episcopal vestments. He seems to have had doubts about the whole concept of episcopacy. Finding bishops who could preach was a major problem for the leaders of the English Reformation, and eventually they prevailed on Hooper to accept the position.

Arriving in Gloucester, the new bishop found the condition of the church in decline. The ignorance of the clergy was a scandal, and Hooper vigorously set himself to reform his diocese. The system of benefices had left the preaching and teaching ministry of the church of Gloucester in the hands of vicars, many of whom could scarcely recite the Lord's Prayer, the Ten Commandments, and the Apostles' Creed, let alone teach their congregations the basic rudiments of the faith. Hooper published simple English explanations of all three of these catechetical pieces. From this it would appear that Hooper's program of reform was directed primarily at the general population. He was concerned to teach the people the basic verities of the faith and the fundamentals of the Christian way of life. His approach to reformation was primarily pastoral. If nothing else, his own preaching in the diocese of Gloucester did much to bring about the reform.

The voice of this preaching bishop was soon to be silenced. Not long after Mary came to the throne, Stephen Gardiner, with whom Hooper had debated, became one of the principal agents of the Catholic restoration. As Gardiner saw it, Hooper was one of the most dangerous of the Reformers and was therefore quickly put in prison. He shared his imprisonment with Cranmer for a time, but he was martyred before the archbishop, being sent to his cathedral city of Gloucester to give his final witness. He was burned at the stake 9 February 1555.

We assume from the fact that Hooper published popular works on the three aforementioned catechetical pieces that he gave ample attention to catechetical preaching.[223] The only sustained picture we get of Hooper's pulpit ministry, however, is the seven Lenten sermons he preached at the court of Edward VI.[224] The sermons printed several months afterward seem for the most part to be précis of the sermons that were actually preached. On the other hand, there is a long digression on the Lord's Supper in the fifth and sixth sermons which appears to have been an addition for the reading public. Aside from this supplementary material, the sermons are remarkably simple and direct. The preacher seems not at all interested in impressing the court. His main concern is to call his hearers to repentance. To this end he took the book of Jonah to show how the king of Nineveh led the Ninevites to repent of their wickedness in response to the preaching of Jonah. The whole series is developed in the manner of the typical patristic exegetical sermon as taken up and developed by the Continental Reformers. While Latimer may have learned to preach from the traditions of the late medieval Church, Hooper learned to preach from the Reformation. His decision to preach on Jonah is significant. For Hooper the program of reform needed to be an act of national repentance. It is in this penitential light that he gives us his whole program of reform.[225] His concerns sometimes lead him to stretch the text, particularly since the nature of Nineveh's sin is never elaborated in the book of Jonah. On the other hand, his application of Jonah's reluctance to preach to the clergy of his day is surely to the point.[226] One never gets the impression from these sermons that Hooper was a great preacher. One never sees the flashes of homiletical brilliance that one so often finds in the published sermons of Latimer. We find here neither great oratory nor great exposition. We find nothing of the exciting exposi-

223. For the text of Hooper's works, see the following: John Hooper, *Early Writings*, ed. Samuel Carr, 2 vols., Parker Society edition (Cambridge: University Press, 1843); and *Later Writings of Bishop Hooper*, ed. C. Nevinson (Cambridge: University Press, 1852).

224. John Hooper, *An oversight and deliberacion uppon the holy prophet Jonas* (London: John Tisdale, 1550), hereafter Hooper, *Sermons upon Jonah.*

225. Hooper, *Sermons upon Jonah*, p. 445.

226. Hooper, *Sermons upon Jonah*, p. 511.

tion of the biblical text which was so typical of the Continental Reformers. It is, however, competent preaching on the part of a man who had a good sense of what needed most to be preached to his generation. He understood well the need to preach against superstitious practices, the system of benefices, and a clergy which showed little interest in the ministry of the Word. His critique is well balanced and appropriate to the situation in England at this time. One notices with relief that the sermons are relatively free of the fawning deference so often found in sermons preached at court. Hooper succeeds in a dignified and yet firm manner at presenting his program of church reform to those people who were interested in his ideas and were in a position to implement his reforms.

John Hooper has often been pictured as an extremist who tried to impose a foreign program of reform on the Church of England. Whether this view is fair or not needs to be considered. English historians have a way of preferring to look at their country in isolation. The fact is that Europe, from one end to the other, was filled with thoughts of reform in the first half of the sixteenth century. England was not isolated from these ideas. England had an active commerce in those days as well as today, and it exported and imported ideas as well as goods. Hooper imported foreign theology no less than Cranmer, Cardinal Pole, or the brilliant Counter-Reformation theologian Thomas Stapleton. On the other hand, Hooper saw himself as continuing in the tradition of John Wycliffe.[227] Wycliffe was, of course, quite English, and one finds many of his ideas surfacing again in the English Reformation: the rejection of the papacy, the criticism of monasticism, the scruples over transubstantiation, and above all, the commitment to the ministry of the Word in the English language. While one might regard Hooper as one who rashly imported foreign ideas, one might just as easily regard him as a Reformer who saw the problems of the Church of England in a larger context, both historically and geographically. He was, after all, one of the older Reformers. He seems to have come to the Reformation as a mature man who had both learned and digested the older theology. His work indicates that his position was solidly developed and steadfastly maintained right up to his martyrdom.

227. Hooper, *Sermons upon Jonah*, p. 527. As time went on, those who opposed the concerns of the Puritans happily connected them with Wycliffe and his followers and rather hastily denied any connection between the reforms advocated by the fourteenth-century "heretic" and the *via media* of the Church of England.

C. The Prayer Book Lectionary

In England the reshaping of the lectionary found in *The Book of Common Prayer* was a genuine reformation of the ministry of the Word.[228] This dimension of the English Reformation has received nothing like the attention it deserves, but it needs to be pointed out that the lectionary of the first prayer book of Edward VI opened up the whole of Scripture to the great mass of Englishmen in a way it had never been opened before. There were several reasons for this. As we have already pointed out, England had nothing like the number of preachers who were available on the continent of Europe to proclaim the evangelical faith. The new learning of the Christian humanists had appeared in only a few circles in England; it had not produced an elite corps of biblical scholars all eagerly studying the original languages as it had, for example, in the Upper Rhineland.[229] Even in the reign of Edward VI we hear only occasionally of preachers who were able to do the kind of expository preaching that so many of the Continental Reformers did. Before liturgical reforms could be made, the people had to be taught why these reforms were necessary. England did not have the preachers to do this. Latimer seems to have understood this, and this is surely why so much of his preaching stressed the importance of developing a preaching ministry. Cranmer surely understood it all very well. In England the Reformation could not depend on preachers to preach the reform, as it had on the Continent.

---

228. On *The Book of Common Prayer*, see the following: John E. Booty, "Book of Common Prayer," in *Oxford Encyclopedia of the Reformation*, 4 vols. (New York: Oxford University Press, 1996), 1:189-93; Frank Edward Brightman, ed., *The English Rite*, 2 vols. (London: Rivingtons, 1915); William Kemp Lowther Clarke and C. Harris, eds., *Liturgy and Worship: A Companion to the Prayer Books of the Anglican Communion* (New York: Macmillan, 1932); Gregory Dix, *The Shape of the Liturgy*, 2nd ed. (Westminster, Eng.: Dacre Press, 1949); Francis A. Gasquet and E. Bishop, *Edward VI and the Book of Common Prayer* (London: John Hodges, 1890); Francis Procter and W. H. Frere, *A History of the Book of Common Prayer* (London: Macmillan, 1949); Bard Thompson, "The First and Second Prayer Books of King Edward VI," in *Liturgies of the Western Church*, pp. 225-84; and Frederick Edward Warren, "Prayer, Book of Common," in *Encyclopedia Britannica*, 11th ed., 32 vols. (New York: Encyclopedia Britannica, 1910), 22:258-62. It should probably be noted that the literature on *The Book of Common Prayer* is so vast that the card catalogue of the library I most often use lists over four thousand works on this subject.

229. One would not want to overdraw the picture in this regard. John Colet, for example, had managed to interest English scholars in New Testament Greek and William Tyndale did get his inspiration while still in England.

Another reason for the importance of *The Book of Common Prayer's* lectionary to the reform of the ministry of the Word in England was what today we would call the Erastian nature of the English Reformation. While on the Continent the new liturgies developed as a result of the Reformation, in England *The Book of Common Prayer* became the chief means of bringing about the Reformation. Cranmer's gifts were quite different from Luther's, and the lands in which these two Reformers worked were indeed very different lands. While in Germany the Reformation almost exploded into existence, in England it was slowly maneuvered into place. Cranmer was a convinced Erastian, not surprising for a man of his time, and as such he set about to reform the Church of England.[230] *The Book of Common Prayer* became for the Reformed Church of England what the Nicene Creed had been for the Church of the Constantinian empire. If the king of England was to be the defender of the faith, the divinely anointed sponsor of the Church as Constantine had once been, then he needed a standard for that faith, and *The Book of Common Prayer* became that standard.

An infinite amount of ink has been spread over countless pages on the subject of the sources of *The Book of Common Prayer.*[231] Some scholars have been determined to show its undoubted Catholic sources, while others have wanted to show its basic Protestant sources. Perhaps a less tendentious way to put it is as follows. It is a well-thought-out and beautifully written adaptation of the traditional forms of worship done under the influence of the Christian humanist ideals of the reform of worship. Cranmer, in other words, stands rather close to Bucer. That Bucer generally approved of Cranmer's prayer book is not at all surprising. Bucer, too, was a student of Christian humanism.

There were, however, differences. Cranmer did not always follow the Christian humanist approach. Nationalism was becoming an increas-

---

230. It might be a bit of an anachronism to call Cranmer an Erastian. Thomas Erastus (1524-83) did not begin to teach until 1558, three years after Cranmer's martyrdom. Erastianism taught that in the Christian state the civil government had authority in ecclesiastical as well as secular matters. Whatever name this teaching may bear, it had clearly been taken up by a number of church leaders well before Erastus appeared on the scene. One might say that caesaropapism was common in the sixteenth century, but that word is not quite right for England. Be that as it may, it all amounted to the same thing: state control of religion.

231. For a well-balanced survey of this literature, see Davies, *Worship and Theology,* pp. 165-226.

ingly strong force in the sixteenth century, and it tended to work against the universalism of Christian humanism. The traditional liturgical rites Cranmer intended to reform were those of the diocese of Salisbury. Elsewhere we have gone at length into the various diocesan rites of Germany and how they affected the evangelical baptismal rites in Wittenberg, Strasbourg, and Zürich.[232] England had various diocesan rites as well; York, Hereford, Lincoln, and Salisbury all had their own, a fact mentioned in the preface to the Prayer Book of 1549.[233] The rite of Salisbury was the most widespread of these, and Cranmer decided to make it the basis of his reform. In this, Cranmer's work does show a decided concern for continuity with the Middle Ages. On the other hand, there was something quite characteristic of the Renaissance in this decision. While the late Middle Ages would have gloried in the diversity of local rites, the spirit of Christian humanism cultivated the more universal interests. It was therefore that Christian humanism pressed its motto: *ad fontes,* "back to the sources." These sources were understood as the practice of the ancient Church and especially Scripture itself. That Cranmer focused on the English rites and then chose but one of them as the basis of the reform was not really consistent with the more universal concerns of Christian humanism.

One Catholic on whom this Christian humanist reform had an effect was Cardinal Francisco de Quinones, a Spanish Franciscan who was asked by Pope Clement VII to prepare a new breviary.[234] Deeply influenced by the Christian humanist approach to reform, he prepared a breviary which gave respect to the integrity of the psalms as well as individual books of the Bible.[235] This, of course, was an important principle of the new learning. Scripture was to be treated as literature. It was divinely inspired literature, to be sure, but it was literature, and as such was to be read in its historical and literary context. There were many representing

---

232. Cf. Old, *Reformed Baptismal Rite,* pp. 4-6.

233. For the preface of the Prayer Book of 1549, see Joseph Ketley, ed., *The Two Liturgies, A.D. 1549 and A.D. 1552 with Other Documents Set Forth by Authority in the Reign of King Edward VI,* Parker Society edition (Cambridge: At the University Press, 1846), pp. 17-19; hereafter Ketley, *Liturgies of Edward VI.*

234. For a modern edition of Quinones' breviary, see J. Wickham Legg, ed., *A Second Recension of the Quignon Breviary,* 2 vols. (London: Henry Bradshaw Society, 1908-12).

235. Cf. J. M. Lenhart, "Quinones' Breviary," *Franciscan Studies,* n.s., 6 (1946): 468.

the old learning who attacked Quinones' breviary, and in the Catholic Church it was finally discarded, but Cranmer, as many other Christian humanists, saw its value.

Another document which influenced Cranmer was the Reformed liturgy worked out for the proposed reform of the diocese of Cologne. This liturgy was the joint effort of Bucer, Melanchthon, and several of their colleagues. To be sure, both Bucer and Melanchthon were as thoroughly influenced by Christian humanist ideals as was Cardinal Quinones. Christian humanist ideals of liturgical reform were perhaps the strongest single influence on *The Book of Common Prayer*. This observation will, of course, satisfy neither those who want to prove the prayer book's Protestantism nor those who want to prove its Catholicism.

But beyond this, the influence of the Protestant liturgical reforms on the Continent is rather hard to discount. The fact that Cranmer married the niece of Osiander, the Lutheran Reformer of Nuremberg, should be evidence enough that Archbishop Cranmer was sympathetic to the liturgical reforms of Germany. Protestantism went beyond the reforms of Christian humanism, as similar as they were at many points.

Much more could be said about the prayer book and its sources, but our concern here is primarily to illuminate its lectionary, especially the lectionary for daily prayer, which so obviously had its sources in the sort of Christian humanism which influenced the Rhenish Reformers as well as Catholic Reformers such as Cardinal Quinones. This lectionary was much more important to the framers of the prayer book than one usually recognizes. All the English Reformers — including Cranmer, Latimer, Ridley, and of course, Tyndale — were very much concerned with the translation, publication, and distribution of an English Bible. As we mentioned above, the difficulty in printing an English Bible can probably be explained by the long struggle of the Catholic hierarchy of England to stamp out the influence of John Wycliffe and his vernacular Bible. The Wycliffe translation came into existence many years before the printing press was invented, but by the time the presses had begun to operate in England, official opposition to Wycliffe, and therefore to a vernacular Bible, was sufficiently strong to prevent its being printed.

If the English Reformers wanted an English Bible, they had to overcome considerable opposition to get it, much more than did their peers on the Continent, where a number of vernacular Bibles were in print before the Reformation. It was only in 1537 that an authorized vernacular Bible was finally in print and, with the prayer book lectionary of 1549, a system was available for the daily public reading of that Bible throughout England. Daily church attendance was significant in England, especially in schools where morning and evening prayer were part of the regular schedule. Apparently it was not private reading of the vernacular Bible which would first teach the Scriptures to Englishmen, but its public reading in the ordinary worship of the Church. The family Bible would come, but for the first generation or two it would be the pulpit Bible from which the average Englishman would hear the Word of God.

Simply hearing the Bible read by the clergy was all the framers of the Prayer Book could count on. They could not count on the preaching of Scripture. The quality of their clergy precluded that.[236] But with the Prayer Book lectionary they could count on an appreciable number of Englishmen hearing four chapters of Scripture a day.[237] And it was the daily Christian humanist lectionary read at morning and evening prayer which most people most often heard, not the more traditional lectionary of the Communion liturgy based on the Christian year. In the preface of the 1549 prayer book, Cranmer sounds like Martin Bucer or any other Reformer, Catholic or Protestant, who had been deeply influenced by Christian humanism when he says: "But these many years passed, this godly and decent order of the ancient Fathers hath bee(n) so altered, broken, and neglected, by planting in uncertain stories, Legends, Responds, Verses, vain repetitions, Commemorations, and synodals, that commonly when any book of the Bible was begun, before three or four chapters were read out, all the rest were unread."[238] Very specifically Cranmer is complaining about the way the traditional *lectio continua* of Scripture, which had always been followed, on weekdays at least, from the very earliest times, was now interrupted for all kinds of special feast days and saints'

236. It is well known that Archbishop Cranmer asked Bucer to write an evaluation of the first Prayer Book. In the conclusion of this evaluation Bucer made the observation that no matter how good the reforms proposed by the Prayer Book might be, they would not accomplish very much unless the churches were provided with an educated ministry. Too many parish churches lacked ministers who were trained to preach the Word of God. Too many parish churches had nothing more than readers. Cf. Whitaker, *Martin Bucer,* p. 150.

237. This, at least, seems to be the assumption of those who drew up the preface to the Prayer Book. It was "that the people (by daily hearing of holy Scripture read in the Church) should continually profit more and more. . . ." Ketley, *Liturgies of Edward VI,* p. 17.

238. Ketley, *Liturgies of Edward VI,* p. 17.

days. Sometimes these special readings were not taken from Scripture but from other sources, frequently the acts of martyrs which were of questionable authenticity. The special feasts and therefore the special readings multiplied during the course of the Middle Ages, and this squeezed out the orderly reading of the Bible. What a Cranmer, a Quinones, or a Bucer wanted was a reading through of Scripture in course which respected the literary integrity of the sacred Word and from which the corruptions of the text, the glosses, and the accretions of centuries of inaccurate and uncritical copying had been removed. This was a concern dear to the heart of Christian humanism. The Christian humanists regarded the lectionary somewhat the same way they regarded the *Sentences* of Peter Lombard or the *Decretals* of Gratian, a collection of short excerpts gleaned from the tradition to serve the needs of days long past. Just as the Christian humanist canon lawyer wanted to read the ancient legal codes in their literary and historical context, and just as the systematic theologian of the early sixteenth century wanted to read Augustine, Basil, and Chrysostom in the *omnia opera* of each author so that the context was clear, so the Christian humanists wanted to read the Scripture not in a *lectio selecta* but in the *lectio continua*. This is all quite plain in Cranmer's preface. The old lectionary was all right for Sundays and holidays, but for day-to-day worship he wanted to read through the whole of the Bible, one book at a time, in course. It was in this way that Cranmer intended to acquaint England with the Scriptures.

Let us look at the characteristics of the lectionary that was set up for the first Prayer Book of Edward VI and would continue in use with but few changes for the next century.[239] This lectionary has two parts: the daily reading through in *lectio continua* of the complete Bible designed for use at morning and evening prayer,[240] and the *lectio selecta,* the lectionary used for the Communion service on Sundays and holy days.[241] There is nothing of particular interest about the lectionary for the Communion service. It is nothing more than the traditional Gospels and Epistles as they had developed in the sixth and seventh centuries in Rome and were then imposed on the Western Church by Charlemagne two centuries later. For our purposes the lectionary for the daily prayer services is of par-

239. For the text of the 1549 *Book of Common Prayer,* see Ketley, *Liturgies of Edward VI,* pp. 9-158.
240. Ketley, *Liturgies of Edward VI,* pp. 22-28.
241. Ketley, *Liturgies of Edward VI,* pp. 41-75.

ticular interest. Two lessons at morning prayer and two lessons at evening prayer are to be read each day, one at each service from the Old Testament and one from the New.[242] The idea is that the Old Testament is to be read through once in the course of the year.

The apocryphal books of Tobit, Judith, Wisdom, Ecclesiasticus, and Baruch are included in these Old Testament lessons. This may be surprising to us, but in the sixteenth century Protestants were often of mixed mind on this issue. Jerome had argued strongly against the Apocrypha, and many Christian humanists, especially those who had studied Hebrew, agreed with him. How one decided this issue did not necessarily follow how one decided on the Reformation.

Several sizable portions of the canonical Old Testament were omitted. The tenth chapter of Genesis is missing, probably because it is mostly genealogy. The legal and ceremonial codes of Exodus, Leviticus, and Numbers are omitted as well. The Song of Solomon is omitted, probably for the same reason that it was not read in the synagogue. Most of Ezekiel was omitted. Again Cranmer is no doubt following the wisdom of the rabbis. Chronicles does not appear, doubtless because it repeats material found in Kings.[243] These omissions show a practical wisdom with which, for the most part, few would argue.[244] This arrangement gives a whole chapter of the Old Testament for both morning and evening prayer for each day of the year. The obvious renewed interest in the reading of the Old Testament is no doubt a reflection of the recovery of biblical Hebrew by the Christian humanists.[245] This was a major concern of the Continental Reformation, particularly in the Rhineland.

At each service a chapter from the New Testament was read as

242. Ketley, *Liturgies of Edward VI,* p. 22.

243. Several of the apocryphal books, such as I and II Maccabees and the Septuagint's additions to Daniel, are omitted as well.

244. For those interested in worship, Chronicles has rich passages. One hates to have omitted the important passages in Ezekiel and Revelation, but Cranmer was aiming at beginners.

245. The Christian humanists, whether Bucer, Quinones, or Cranmer, believed that the ancient Church regularly read through the Scriptures of both Testaments. The "High Church" movement questioned this assumption, insisting that the reading of the Bible in course originated only with the monastic office. As we have shown in earlier volumes of this work, there is abundant evidence that the regular reading through of Scripture has always been a prominent feature of Christian worship, just as it had been of Jewish worship. For the "High Church" position, see Clarke, "The Lectionary," in *Liturgy and Worship,* p. 296.

well.[246] In the morning it was taken from the Gospels and Acts, in the evening from the Epistles. The book of Revelation was not read through, although at the feast of Saint John the first and last chapters were read. The English Reformers were terribly worried about apocalyptic sects, and this no doubt explains the omission of Revelation as well as a good part of Ezekiel.[247] This was hardly an innovation, however; in the history of Christian worship, one often finds that Revelation was avoided. All things considered, the important thing is that virtually the whole New Testament was read. The New Testament is much shorter than the Old Testament, which meant that while the Old Testament was read through once each year, the New Testament was read through three times.

An interesting feature of this lectionary is how little affected it is by the old liturgical calendar.[248] Only about fifty lessons break the *lectio continua*. When one considers that fourteen hundred lessons are read in the year, these fifty special lessons appear very infrequent. This means that while the prayer book allowed for a limited observance of traditional feast days and for the observance of saints mentioned in the New Testament, the *lectio continua* was not frequently interrupted for these observances. In some cases there was one special lesson, or perhaps two. Only for a few major feast days were there special readings for both Old and New Testament lessons at both morning and evening prayer.[249] The special lessons are as follows:

FEAST DAYS	morning	evening
Christmas Day		
Old Testament	Isaiah 9	Isaiah 7:10-25
New Testament	Matthew 1	Titus 3:4-9
Saint Stephen's Day		
New Testament	Acts 6:8–7:23	Acts 7:23-55
Saint John the Evangelist		
New Testament	Revelation 1	Revelation 22

246. Ketley, *Liturgies of Edward VI,* p. 22.

247. Cranmer hoped to develop a biblically literate ministry which could interpret these difficult works.

248. It was not until the "High Church" movement of the nineteenth century that the medieval liturgical calendar reasserted its influence. See Clarke, "The Lectionary," pp. 296-301.

249. Ketley, *Liturgies of Edward VI,* pp. 23-28.

Innocents' Day
    Old Testament   Jeremiah 31:1-18
Circumcision
    Old Testament   Genesis 17   Deuteronomy 10
    New Testament   Romans 2   Colossians 2
Epiphany
    Old Testament   Isaiah 60   Isaiah 49
    New Testament   Luke 3   John 2
Wednesday before Easter
    Old Testament   Lamentations 1
Thursday before Easter
    Old Testament   Lamentations 2   Lamentations 3
Good Friday
    Old Testament   Genesis 22   Isaiah 53
Easter Even
    Old Testament   Lamentations 4 and 5
Easter Day
    Old Testament   Exodus 12
    New Testament   Romans 6   Acts 2
Monday after Easter
    New Testament   Matthew 28   Acts 3
Tuesday after Easter
    New Testament   Luke 24   I Corinthians 15
Ascension Day
    New Testament   John 14   John 4
Whit-Sunday
    New Testament   Acts 10:34-48   Acts 19:1-20
Trinity Sunday
    Old Testament   Genesis 18
    New Testament   Matthew 3

SAINTS' DAYS

Conversion of Saint Paul
    New Testament   Acts 22   Acts 26
Saints Philip and James
    New Testament   Acts 8
Saint Barnabas
    New Testament   Acts 14   Acts 15

Saint John the Baptist
Old Testament	Malachi 3	Malachi 4
New Testament	Matthew 3	Matthew 4

Saint Peter's Day
New Testament	Acts 3	Acts 4

All Saints
Old Testament	Wisdom 3	Wisdom 5
New Testament	Hebrews 11 and 12	Revelation 19

A number of these selections can undoubtedly be explained by the desire to offer a reading different from the Gospel and Epistle selections read for the Communion service. One notices this particularly for Christmas Day. The saints' days with special lessons are restrained in number. While Mary Magdalene, James the Apostle, Saint Andrew, Saint Matthew, the Annunciation of the Virgin Mary, the Purification of the Virgin Mary, Saint Michael and All Angels, Saint Luke the Evangelist, and several others are recognized on the calendar, they do not have special readings at either morning or evening prayer. Why some saints are so specially favored and others are not is perhaps a matter of logistics. When one finishes up, one has to have exactly 730 lessons from the Old Testament and 730 lessons from the New Testament. It was inevitable that something was going to be either spread out or squeezed out. It seems easier to explain things this way than to explain why Saint Barnabas got special lessons and Saint Andrew did not.[250] All this, however, we leave to specialists in the lectionary of the Church of England.

The main drift of the lectionary is clear. It is a serious attempt to guarantee the reading of the whole Bible through in the course of a year in such a way that the literary integrity of the different books is respected and the context of each passage is evident.[251] It put a high value on the public reading of Scripture in a day when printed Bibles were only beginning to appear, and it allowed for the fact that many services were conducted by vicars and curates who had little knowledge of the Scriptures and therefore needed to have explicit instructions as to what was to be read and what was not.

250. When *The Book of Common Prayer* was reestablished by Queen Elizabeth I, the special lessons for saints' days were augmented. One notices particularly that special Old Testament lessons from Ecclesiasticus, or the Wisdom of Jesus ben Sirach, were given to New Testament saints.

251. Ketley, *Liturgies of Edward VI*, pp. 17-19.

CHAPTER II

The Counter-Reformation

There is no question that the Counter-Reformation had its glory.[1] In fact, magnificence was of its essence. One need only look at the architecture with which Bernini filled the city of Rome for it all to become quite clear. To understand the Counter-Reformation, we must look at Bernini's colonnade around the Piazza di San Pietro, his altar inside that sumptuous basilica, with its serpentine-columned baldachino, and finally the throne of Saint Peter emblazoned in the golden rays of the Holy Spirit. Perhaps even more explicit is the Jesuit church, the Church of the Gesu, with that dramatic sculpture of the Church triumphant over all heresies, with the sarcophagus of Ignatius Loyola and the altar of Francis Xavier.[2] The

1. One often discusses the justification of the term "Counter-Reformation." Some have preferred the term "Catholic Reformation." This title seems particularly appropriate in the case of Spain, and maybe even of Italy, but it is less appropriate in France and Germany. Some have preferred the term "Catholic Revival," but more was involved than a revival. The Council of Trent made Catholicism something it had never been before. For a brief discussion of the problem, see Eric W. Cochrane, "Counter-Reformation or Tridentine Reformation? Italy in the Age of Carlo Borromeo," in *San Carlo Borromeo: Catholic Reform and Ecclesiastical Politics in the Second Half of the Sixteenth Century,* ed. John M. Headley and John B. Tomaro (Washington, D.C.: Folger Books, 1988), pp. 31-46; and Elmer Lewis Lampe, "Counter-Reformation," in *New Catholic Encyclopedia,* 17 vols. (Washington, D.C.: Catholic University of America Press, 1968), 4:384-89. For a more thorough discussion, see Hubert Jedin, *Katholische Reformation oder Gegenreformation?* (Lucerne: Stocker, 1946).

2. For general works on the Counter-Reformation, see H. Outram Evenett, *The Spirit of the Counter Reformation,* ed. John Bossy (Cambridge: University Press, 1968);

158

church is filled with columns of porphyry, paved with marble, encrusted with lapis lazuli, and framed in gilded bronze. Above it all Baciccio's illusionistic ceiling carries the worshiper into the very heavens. Here is a splendor that even surpasses the grandeur of ancient Rome.

For an American Protestant to look at the Counter-Reformation with sympathy is, admittedly, rather difficult. Its absolutism is so foreign to us; its pomp seems so excessive; its luxury so needless. It all seems much more Roman than Catholic. To be sure, we Protestants cannot help seeing the Counter-Reformation as a time when many turned away from the Word of God and insisted on traditions which had developed over the centuries but were of neither dominical nor apostolic authority. In fact, they were traditions which to us seem so contrary to the clear Word of God. Even worse, they had been used to support abuses which compromised the gospel itself and hampered the preaching of the Word of God. As much as we would like to be ecumenical, the Counter-Reformation makes it difficult. Ecumenism and absolutism are hard to mix.

Even at that, we must try to understand the Counter-Reformation. A large part of the Church did not receive the preaching of the Reformers anymore than it had received the prophetic ministry of Wycliffe, or Hus, or Savonarola. That is the way it always is with prophetic preaching. Still, Luther and Calvin succeeded in a way their predecessors had not. The success of the Reformation was a great blow to the ecclesiastical establishment. The Church as it had been institutionalized in western Europe by the beginning of the sixteenth century was shaken up quite thoroughly.

The sheer shock of the Reformation, however, enabled the institution of the papacy to make reforms it had not been able to make up to this point. The Reformation had denied the whole authoritarian system on which the institution of the Western Church had been built up for so many centuries. For centuries the Roman pope had claimed a sort of imperial authority over the whole of Christendom which many simply could not recognize. That was the shock. The Reformers attacked this authority. It was supposed to be by divine appointment that the Roman Church

---

Philip Hughes, *Rome and the Counter-Reformation in England* (London: Burns and Oates, 1942); Pierre Janelle, *The Catholic Reformation* (Milwaukee: Bruce Publishing, 1941); Werner Kaegi, *Humanische Kontinuität im konfessionellen Zeitalter,* Schriften der "Freunde der Universität Basel," vol. 8 (Basel, 1954); Beresford James Kidd, *The Counter-Reformation, 1550-1600* (London: SPCK, 1933); and Henri Daniel-Rops, *The Catholic Reformation,* trans. J. Warrington, History of the Church, vol. 5 (London: Dent; New York: Dutton, 1962).

exercised this authority, and the Reformers were able to convince many that it simply did not have that authority.

The Counter-Reformation was an attempt to reimpose that authority where it had been denied, and in many areas it was successful. It transformed the whole nature of preaching. Catholic preaching went a very different direction from the preaching of the Reformation. In fact, it is probably in regard to preaching more than anything else that the term "Counter-Reformation" is especially appropriate. Its preachers simply refused to move in the direction the Reformers moved in their reform of preaching. As we will see, there were some exceptions, but for the most part Counter-Reformation preaching quite intentionally moved in the opposite direction.

As difficult as it inevitably is to be completely sympathetic with the preachers of the Counter-Reformation, let us at least recognize that this era produced some noteworthy preachers and let us admire the spiritual treasures they indeed produced. Even after making all the criticisms we feel obliged to make, we still want to recognize that Christ was preached and, through the preaching of the Counter-Reformation, many came to faith. For that we must recognize these preachers as brothers in the service of the gospel.

I. Spanish Preaching in the Golden Age

For centuries Spain had played only a minor role in the affairs of Christian Europe, but with the marriage of Queen Isabella of Castile and King Ferdinand of Aragon in 1474 things began to change. This union brought together almost the entire nation. Only Granada was left under Moorish rule, and during their reign, in 1492, even these last vestiges of Islamic rule would finally be pushed out of the Iberian Peninsula. In that year Columbus, backed by these two Spanish sovereigns, would open up the Americas and win for Spain that tremendous empire with all its wealth. This, of course, presented the Church with an unparalleled opportunity for missionary preaching, and at this we will certainly want to look. But before we can do this, we must consider the religious reform these sovereigns instituted during their forty-year reign, for this was the basis of the golden age of Spanish Christianity.[3]

3. See Hilary Dansey Smith, *Preaching in the Spanish Golden Age: A Study of Some*

The church reform that Ferdinand and Isabella led aimed first at finding church leaders of true learning and genuine piety. At the end of the fifteenth century the papacy could not be looked to for this kind of leadership. Happily, Ferdinand and Isabella had the ability to recognize genius when they saw it. Just as they recognized the genius of Christopher Columbus, so they recognized the genius of Francisco Ximénes de Cisneros. Queen Isabella appointed the future cardinal as her confessor in 1492. He was given increasingly important positions until he eventually became the archbishop of Toledo and therefore primate of Spain. Ferdinand and Isabella had also been blessed in his predecessor, Pedro González de Mendoza, an enlightened Renaissance prelate who supported the Spanish sovereigns generously, but Ximénes, in addition to being endowed with the learning of the Renaissance, was a man of passionate devotion. In this, of course, he was very much like Columbus. It was this sort of person who gained the support of the Spanish throne, and one therefore cannot underestimate the importance of the king and queen in this religious reform.

In Spain the sovereign still had significant privileges in the appointment of bishops and other religious leaders, and Ferdinand and Isabella were determined to use these powers to ensure that men of learning and piety were appointed, and that these positions be filled with Spaniards who would themselves fill their benefices and live in their dioceses.

Cardinal Ximénes gave a most enlightened leadership to the Spanish church. Typical of the Christian humanists of the Renaissance, he supported research on the text of Scripture, publishing the Complutensian Polyglot Bible in 1514-17. This aimed at providing the new Christian humanist scholars with the texts of Scripture in the original languages. European Christians were beginning to learn the biblical languages, but finding good, accurate texts was difficult. At the beginning of the sixteenth century, those biblical scholars who could read the Scriptures in the original languages had to depend on handwritten manuscripts. The Complutensian Polyglot Bible provided them with a printed text for the first time.

Another scholarly interest of Ximénes was the Mozarabic liturgy.[4]

Preachers of the Reign of Philip III (Oxford: University Press, 1978). This very helpful book is primarily a study of Spanish language and literature. It focuses on the preaching of the early seventeenth century, while the present study focuses on the mid–sixteenth century. Even at that, it offers many useful insights into the earlier period of Spanish preaching. If nothing else, Smith's work demonstrates the riches of Spanish preaching.

4. For more on this liturgy, see Hughes Oliphant Old, *The Reading and Preaching of*

Interest in the various Mozarabic liturgical texts was quite consistent with the great love of Christian antiquity so characteristic of Christian Renaissance scholars. Having seen to the publishing of a good number of Mozarabic texts, he endowed a chapel of his cathedral to maintain the use of the ancient Spanish liturgy as it had been celebrated before the Arab invasion.

To promote the learning of the Christian humanists, Ximénes founded and richly endowed the University of Alcalá. There had been various schools of higher learning in this small but ancient city for some time, but only when Ximénes founded his school there did Alcalá take on its character as the foremost center of Renaissance learning. In this respect it differed significantly from Salamanca, which remained the citadel of Spanish Scholasticism. At its zenith, the University of Alcalá had over twelve thousand students. Typical of an institution of higher learning sponsored by the Christian humanists, it featured instruction in both biblical languages, Greek and Hebrew. Its intellectual flavor was heavily spiced by Erasmus, and in fact, Ximénes tried for many years to win the great Dutch scholar-prince for the university. Many of the leaders of Spanish Christianity, and several of her best preachers, studied or taught there during the following two centuries, the most notable being Juan of Ávila, Thomas of Villanova, Ignatius Loyola, Luis de Molina, and Francisco Suárez.

The impression one has of the church in Spain at the end of the fifteenth century is that no church in Christendom was in a better position to back the missionary enterprise which was rapidly being opened up both to the West and to the East. One senses a purity and an integrity in the leadership of the Spanish church which is in refreshing contrast to the leadership of the church in Italy, or Germany, or England, or France. In reading the Spanish preachers of the sixteenth century, one finds the spiritual energy and enthusiasm needed to produce one of the major missionary advances in the history of the Church. Let us look at three of the great Spanish preachers of the golden age, Thomas of Villanova, Juan of Ávila, and Luis of Granada.

the Scriptures in the Worship of the Christian Church, vol. 3, *The Medieval Church* (Grand Rapids: Wm. B. Eerdmans Publishing Co., 1999), pp. 99-109.

A. Thomas of Villanova (1486-1555): Scripture and Tradition in the Pulpit

A fascinating preacher who treats us even today with erudite meditations on the traditional feasts, Thomas of Villanova is remembered as one of the outstanding preachers of Spain's great century. He was born three years after Luther's birth, but he outlived Luther by almost a decade.

Thomas of Villanova had the privilege of studying at the University of Alcalá when it was at its zenith as the center of Spanish Christian humanism.[5] In time he ascended the academic ladder, lecturing in the university. Then in 1516 he became an Augustinian monk. Again we mark the parallel to Luther. In the same year Luther posted his ninety-five theses on the door of the town church of Wittenberg, Thomas became prior of the Augustinian community at Salamanca. In 1519 he was appointed director of the Augustinian province at Andalusia, which brought him in close contact with the work of the missionaries in Mexico, Cuba, and Peru. In 1542 he was named archbishop of Valencia. In that ancient city on the shores of the Mediterranean, he was a model prelate who devoted himself to preaching and the pastoral care of his congregation.

Thomas was an outstanding preacher.[6] He presents us with a good example of the preaching of Christian humanism come to full flower and yet maintaining a continuity with the best of the Middle Ages. It was a Christian humanism that carefully avoided crossing the line into Protestantism. In fact, Thomas can even be critical of Erasmus for being reckless in his reading of the Greek New Testament (p. 51). The Christian humanism of Villanova is a very conservative Christian humanism.

The most obvious way we recognize the Christian humanism of this preacher is in the reappearance of the sermonic forms of the patristic

5. On the life of Thomas of Villanova, see Pierre Jobit, *L'évêque des pauvres, saint Thomas de Villeneuve*, Bibliothèque Ecclesia, vol. 63 (Paris: Montréal, 1961).

6. For his Spanish sermons, see Thomas of Villanova, *Obras: Sermones de la Virgen y Obras castellanas* (Madrid). I have not been able to trace this volume further. There is also supposed to be an edition of Latin translations of his sermons together with other works that was printed in six volumes in Manila, Philippines, between 1894 and 1897. I have not had access to this publication either. Happily, a marvelous collection of sermons in English translation has very recently appeared: *The Works of Saint Thomas of Villanova: Sermons, Part 2: Christmas,* trans. Maria Boulding, ed. John E. Rotelle, Augustinian Series, vol. 20 (Villanova, Pa.: Augustinian Press, 1994); the page references in the text are to this volume.

preachers. Admittedly, the thematic sermon of the Schools leaves a few traces in Villanova's preaching. We find a good Scholastic *prothema* from time to time (pp. 7-8, 45-46, 182-84). Generally, however, he moves through the passage appointed for the day, giving attention to each subject as it comes up. In this his sermons are much like those of Oecolampadius, or Brenz, or even Calvin, all of whom had been nourished on the patristic sermons by their Christian humanist teachers. Even more we find a real similarity to Luther, because it is a very conservative use of Christian humanism. Fairly consistently Villanova's preaching is expository rather than thematic. He has for the most part pulled away from the Scholastic sermon forms.

Another way the influence of Christian humanism shows up in these sermons is in his use of the patristic sources. Villanova's knowledge of the Fathers comes from the printed editions the Christian humanists produced during the years he was a student in Alcalá. It does not appear to be culled from florilegia or from Lombard and Gratian. He knows whole works such as Augustine's work on the Trinity (pp. 67, 91, 194). The question one has to ask is to what extent he used biblical Greek and Hebrew. One would have expected a student of the Christian humanists to have learned the original languages, but one does not get the impression he really used them even if he probably studied them. On the other hand, he may have had scruples about trying to get behind the Vulgate. The Counter-Reformation took a strong stand on the authority of the Vulgate. Also, he may have used his Greek and Hebrew but was careful not to let it show. Whether in sixteenth-century Spain or in early twenty-first-century America, one can get into quite a bit of trouble by knowing something not everyone else knows.

As much as Villanova may have studied under the Christian humanists of the University of Alcalá, he carefully maintains a continuity with the theology and especially the spirituality of the Middle Ages. One does not find the polemic against the Scholastic doctors that one finds in the Christian humanists. There were plenty of Christian humanists like Erasmus who were very critical of Scholasticism even though they never became Protestants. Villanova is not critical of medieval Catholic tradition. It is part of the spiritual heritage which had come down to him.

Villanova's continuity with the medieval tradition is especially recognized in his development of the sermon cycles based on the liturgical Gospels and Epistles. These cycles were very popular beginning with Gregory the Great, the Venerable Bede, Rabanus Maurus, Bernard of Clairvaux and continuing even to the end of the Middle Ages. We find at several places that Villanova has studied the Gospel homilies of Gregory (pp. 26, 103, 166); he even used the festal sermons of Leo the Great (p. 198). Bernard's cycle of festal sermons is so frequently quoted that one gets the impression that Villanova must have had a copy of this classic open before him (pp. 100ff.). The cycle of festal sermons based on the lectionary of the liturgical year had become an important tradition in the medieval pulpit, and Villanova continued this tradition, leaving us a masterpiece.

When we read Villanova's interpretation, we realize what the decrees of the Council of Trent on Scripture and tradition meant for Catholic preaching. The sermons are indeed interpretations of Scripture, but they are interpretations of those passages the liturgical tradition of the Church over the centuries has picked out as central. Not only that, the way they are arranged in the church calendar assumes their fundamental interpretation. One reads the lessons and then the sermons such preachers as Leo, Gregory, Bede, and Bernard have worked out. Having thoroughly meditated on the tradition of interpretation, then Villanova offers his understanding of the tradition. There is a definite continuity of tradition here. No one could deny that, but just the same one wonders. By the time this tradition gets down to the sixteenth century, it seems rather remote from the gospel Jesus and his disciples preached.

Perhaps this approach is inevitable to those steeped in the spirituality of Neoplatonism. How easy it is for the Neoplatonist to understand the preaching of the Gospel in terms of the emanations of divine truth. For the first disciples these emanations were in full force. They were still very strong when preached by Leo and Gregory, but by the sixteenth century they were of necessity a bit like the light of the setting sun on a hazy day (p. 45). For the spirituality of the Council of Trent, intermediaries were essential. No one can look directly at the noonday sun, but when it is all red just before sunset, that is another matter. As the Council of Trent understood it, we must approach divine truth through mediators, through the hierarchy. Truth has to be mediated by the saints and the holy hierarchs like Leo and Gregory and Isidore. That was clearly the case with preaching. Ideally the preacher should be the bishop, like Thomas of Villanova, Charles Borromeo, or Robert Bellarmine. Ideally preaching should stand in continuity with a tradition like that of the cycle of festal sermons so richly elaborated by the homilies of Gregory the Great and Bernard of Clairvaux.

Another place where we notice the continuity of Villanova's sermons with the Middle Ages is in the continual influence of the sort of Neoplatonic mysticism we found in the sermons of Meister Eckhart and John Tauler. Villanova's sermons are rich in theological speculation. In the fourth sermon for Christmas, for example, we find an inspiring meditation on the text "The Word was made flesh and dwelt among us" (John 1:14). In the introduction our preacher reminds his congregation that in years past he had preached to them on the history of Christ's birth, but this year he intends to preach about the mystery of his eternal generation and his incarnation (p. 45). The sermon is a long one, loaded up with Greek philosophy. At one point our preacher goes into some detail about the significance of the concept of the Word for Aristotle (p. 51). We hear a long discussion of the divine intelligence (p. 52). The text of the Gospel of John is fully explained from the concepts of Greek philosophy, but then a text is brought in from the Epistle to the Hebrews which demonstrates that the apostle Paul understands things in much the same way. "He is the splendor of the Father's glory, the very imprint of his nature" (Heb. 1:3) (p. 53). With this a thoroughly Neoplatonic explanation is given. "The Word of God is not made out of nothing, but overflows from the heart and womb of God." The Word proceeds from the Father by way of the intellect (p. 54). This is the manner of his generation. This was a wonderful truth for our preacher because it shows him how consistent the various strands of biblical teaching are with each other and asks how consistent they are with reason. In this context it is clear that what Villanova meant by reason here is reason as understood by Greek philosophy (p. 57).

More and more this sermon turns to Neoplatonic philosophy to explain the Gospel. Alas, Villanova, as so many in the Middle Ages, was led astray by Dionysius. The text from Hebrews is now explained by the supposed Areopagite. The Word descends to this world and then ascends by "a kind of purgation, as Dionysius remarks" (p. 57). Interestingly enough, our preacher justifies his heavy use of Greek philosophy by an appeal to Augustine, who said he learned all the truths about the incarnation first from Plato. The Counter-Reformation was intent on bringing the classical philosophy of ancient Greece and Rome into concord with the teaching of Christ and the apostles, and here is an obvious example. An appeal to Augustine sounds quite orthodox, but the sermon finally ends with an explanation of salvation in terms of deification (pp. 59-62). For many of us this will seem a far piece from what the Gospel teaches.

If Villanova was inspired by the rationality of the Christian faith, he was equally inspired by its mystery. We find this especially in the second sermon for Christmas, where our preacher takes a text from the Song of Solomon:

> Go forth, daughters of Zion, and behold
> King Solomon wearing the crown his mother
>   set upon him on his wedding day,
> the day when his heart rejoiced.

(Song of Sol. 3:11)

The sermon follows along in the tradition of the mystical interpretation of this erotic masterpiece. All the mystery of the incarnation is put before us. Our preacher calls us to bring our tambours and run out to meet the king. "His high majesty deserves to be welcomed with the respect and honor of which we are capable." We must put aside everything else "and devote ourselves to this high mystery. . . . We should present ourselves before the holy mystery with minds and affections fully at liberty, allowing nothing to distract us from the contemplation of it." In a beautiful piece of rhetoric, the text is turned into a very practical exhortation: "*Go forth, daughters of Zion* . . . from the secular cares which entangle you; *go forth* from the racking, tumultuous business of the market-place of this world; *go forth* from the alluring suggestions of the flesh and all transient pleasures; *go forth* from the insatiable desires aroused by deceitful wealth; *go forth* from depraved moral habits . . . so that you may take part in these mysteries" (p. 27). In good patristic form the sermon develops each phrase of the text as it comes along, making appropriate applications.

When our preacher gets to the reference to King Solomon, we are given a very tasteful meditation on the meaning of the name Solomon. Nothing is said about the meaning of the Hebrew name. The good archbishop feels no need to display his knowledge of Hebrew. "*And behold King Solomon,* Solomon the peaceful, the exceedingly wise king. Behold him who is the wisdom of God and the true peace of all humankind, who was born for this and sent for this: to spread peace throughout the world and bring peace to all" (p. 29). The homiletical good taste of this play on names is exemplary.

The shepherds were the first to heed this admonition to go forth and behold the Christ, the fulfillment of Solomon (p. 30). We should follow their example. "So, then, maidens, this is the spectacle to which your fond mother, the Church, today invites you. It is a noble and glorious

167

sight, a display greater than any other and most worthy of your gaze, a wonder beyond all wonders, none other than our great Solomon. *Go forth and behold* God in a baby boy, the eternal in a tender little body, the divine majesty in a crying child" (p. 31). Here we see this beautiful sermon as a magnificent piece of baroque art with all its love of the dramatic paradox, the mysterious, and the majestic.

Baroque art was fascinated by ecstasy, and in this sermon we catch something of this delight in the transporting experiences of religious devotion. So much of the religious exercises of the Counter-Reformation were designed to bring the fervent Christian into ecstatic experiences. In this sermon Villanova speaks of such a religious experience. He mentions the transport of Saint Paula, a religious woman under the pastoral care of Saint Jerome (p. 34). She had the mystical experience of being present when the Virgin gave birth to the Christ child. Saint Bernard had a similar experience, according to the archbishop of Valencia (p. 34). With an admonition to dedicate oneself during the Christmas season to a meditation on these mysteries, the sermon is then concluded (p. 35).

Villanova has left us some very beautiful sermons. Somehow the naiveté of his allegorical exegesis, the extremes of his devotion to the Virgin, and his almost superstitious approach to the intercession of the saints are a bit disturbing to an American Protestant, but even at that they are beautiful examples of Christian preaching.

B. Juan of Ávila (1500-1569)

Among the classic preachers of Spain, Juan of Ávila has always had a preeminent place. He was an evangelist who aimed at converting his hearers to the higher forms of the Christian life. He wanted nominal Christians to become dedicated Christians. His rigorism was often resented, but he won the admiration of such leaders of the Spanish church as Ignatius Loyola, Teresa of Ávila, and Luis of Granada. Through his preaching he did much to deepen the faith of his fellow countrymen.

Born in Almodóvar del Campo in New Castile, he was the son of a wealthy Jewish family which had accepted baptism not long before.[7] In

---

7. For biographical material on Juan of Ávila, see the introduction to Juan of Ávila, *Obras completas del B. Mtro. Juan de Ávila: Edición crítica,* edited and introduction by Luis Sala Balust, 2 vols. (Madrid: La Editorial Católica, 1953), 1:1-221.

his early years his Jewish roots were often held against him. Apparently he received a good basic education in Almodóvar, but in time he went off to Salamanca, where the old theology still held sway. There he studied arts and letters as well as theology in the usual Scholastic way. Passing to Alcalá, the university which was more open to the new learning, Juan devoted himself more and more to theological interests, developing an admiration for Erasmus and the learning of Christian humanism. Loyola also arrived at Alcalá about this time, but apparently the two never met.

In 1526, about the time the first missionaries were beginning their work in Mexico, he went to Seville, whose archbishop governed ecclesiastical affairs in Mexico, with the hope of going to the New World to help in the evangelism of the Indians. Juan's Jewish roots disqualified him from this mission, however, and the archbishop sent him instead to Ecija, a small city in Andalusia. There he quickly won a reputation as a sincere preacher. He challenged his parishioners to the most serious sort of devotion, encouraging laymen to practice mental prayer, which traditionally had been the preserve of those living in monastic communities. To many this seemed excessively devout. Juan honored the women of his parish by making a special effort to develop their religious potential, something that was not common at the time. His preaching was in no way limited to the churches. He often took to the plaza, attacking the vices of the day. His personal life was simple and blameless, which, as always, gave authority to his message. In time, however, this earnestness was understood as a Judaistic influence or perhaps a Protestant tendency. He was therefore called before the Inquisition. In time he was cleared of the charges brought against him and was sent back to Ecija.

In 1534 Juan was called to Córdoba. There he became even more popular as a preacher and won a reputation for preaching Christ crucified. His preaching in Córdoba resulted in several notable conversions. In 1543 he preached a remarkable series of Lenten sermons at which several members of the high nobility were converted to a religious life.

Juan prepared his sermons carefully.[8] He studied the text intently, but as he saw it, a sermon must be prayed before it is preached, and he is supposed to have spent two hours each morning and two hours each evening praying through his text. As the story goes, he never slept the night before preaching because he was so absorbed in formulating his thoughts

---

8. On the preaching methods of Juan of Ávila, see the introduction by Luis Sala Balust in Juan of Ávila, *Obras completas del B. Mtro. Juan de Ávila: Edición crítica,* 1:1-32.

and developing his expressions. His sermons often lasted more than two hours. The faithful filled the churches, listening intently. Often he brought his congregation to tears. His sermons were not written out, but were preached from notes. Sometimes he dictated them after they had been preached, but often all we have are his sermon notes. His disciples edited his sermons, and often with a heavy hand. Only recently, in 1948, has a collection of these unedited sermons been found.

The sermons of Juan of Ávila are true oratory in the same way as those of Augustine or John Chrysostom or, for that matter, George Whitefield. They are not written sermons but preached sermons. The written documents which have come down to us are far less exciting than the sermons which were actually preached. Even at that, Juan is considered one of the masters of the Spanish language, and the fragments of his sermons which have been preserved are held in high honor.

C. Luis of Granada (1504-88)

When the beautiful capital of the Moorish caliphate of Granada finally came back under Christian rule, the family of Luis, originally from the little Galician town of Sarria in the northwest of the Iberian Peninsula, came to seek a share in the future of a city which had all the promises of prosperity. Things did not go too well for the family. Luis's father died when he was five years old, and to support her children his mother did laundry for the Dominican convent of Santa Cruz. When Luis was twenty years old, he entered the same convent and there received a thorough education. Having done well, he was sent to the Dominican convent in Valladolid, where he received what in those days amounted to a graduate education. There he had the privilege of studying under both Melchior Cano and Bartolomé Carranza, the leading conservative and leading liberal theologians of Spain. His education consisted of studying the Christian classics such as Augustine, Gregory the Great, Bernard of Clairvaux, Thomas Aquinas, and Bonaventure, but it also included the classics of pagan antiquity which had always been part of the Dominican education. He read widely in Plato, Aristotle, Seneca, Cicero, and the Stoics. Finishing these studies, he returned to Granada and took up the responsibilities of preaching and teaching for which his education had prepared him.

Almost immediately Fray Luis won a reputation as a preacher, which he maintained throughout his long life. The picture we get is that of a classic preacher in the Dominican tradition. One could always depend on Fray Luis for clear, simple, and sincere sermons on the fundamental affirmations of the Christian faith. His preaching maintained a good balance between doctrine, ethics, and devotion. He spoke to the concerns of both the cloister and the world in his day.

These gifts were recognized rather early in his life. Sometime around 1540 he was sent to reorganize Scala Coeli, a Dominican monastery in the mountains surrounding Granada. There he came to know Juan of Ávila, another outstanding Spanish preacher. In fact, Juan impressed him so much that eventually he became his biographer. Fray Luis must have been quite successful as a monastic administrator, because ten years later he was named to organize a new monastery at Badajoz on the Portuguese border. This brought him into ever closer contact with Portugal. The royal family, inspired by his preaching, extended him particular favor. He was offered the archbishopric of Braga but turned it down in favor of a life of preaching. His preaching put him in a position of leadership in the Portuguese church, and between 1556 and 1560 he was named provincial of the Dominican Order in Portugal. All the while he was winning an ever greater reputation as a writer of devotional literature. Sad to relate, the very fervor of this literature made it suspect in certain quarters. It seemed to smack of Protestantism and consequently was condemned by the Inquisition. Aside from its being dangerously devout, his Spanish translation of rather sizable portions of the Sermon on the Mount was also viewed by the Inquisition as a dangerous threat to Catholic unity. Humbly he went over his works and revised them so that they would be acceptable to the ecclesiastical authorities of the day.

Today the Spanish-speaking world looks back on Luis of Granada as one of the creators of the Spanish language. Certainly one can say of preachers, as one often says of poets, that they are the creators of the language. How the language sounds when it is shaped from the pulpit will always define its beauty. We have spoken about this with a number of preachers. Slowly students of literature are beginning to realize how preachers create the language every bit as much as do poets, or novelists, or songwriters.

A good number of Luis's sermons have come down to us. As early as 1576 four volumes of his *Conciones de tempore* were published in Lisbon. We will turn our attention, however, to a small collection of thirteen festal sermons which appear in the Biblioteca de Autores Españoles, published in Madrid in 1945.[9] The collection is of particular interest because it shows us in very brief summary form what the faith of the Counter-Reformation sounded like once one had decided to hear the Word of God as the tradition of the Church heard it. The Council of Trent taught Catholic preachers to preach the Scriptures as they had been taught in church tradition. Surely nowhere was it quite so clear how specifically Roman Catholic tradition interpreted the Scriptures as in the lectionary. The lectionary had over the centuries sifted the Scriptures and picked out the most important passages to be read and then assigned them a place in the liturgical calendar. Cycles of festal sermons had been used ever since Gregory the Great to epitomize or summarize the Gospel. We have looked at a number of such cycles.

Of all these cycles, that of Bernard of Clairvaux is perhaps the most thorough, the most complete. As we said in the previous volume, it is a recapitulation of the Gospel as tradition had understood it up to his time, the twelfth century. It is in fact the real summa of early medieval theology. Quite clearly the sermons of Fray Luis to which we now turn are built on the foundations of Saint Bernard. Fray Luis quotes no other author quite so often as Bernard. Bernard's collection must have been open before our preacher as he prepared his interpretation of this venerable tradition.[10]

The first thing we notice is the selection of feast days which make up this cycle:

3. Sermon for the Feast of the Birth of Our Lord
4. Sermon for the Feast of the Circumcision
5. Sermon for the Feast of the Kings
6. Sermon for the Sunday after Epiphany
7. Sermon for the Feast of the Purification of Our Lady
8. Sermon for the Feast of the Annunciation of Our Lady
9. Sermon for the Feast of the Resurrection of Our Lord
10. Sermon for the Feast of the Ascension of Our Lord
11. Sermon for the Feast of Pentecost
12. Sermon for the Feast of the Most Holy Sacrament
13. Sermon for the Feast of the Assumption of Our Lady

9. Luis of Granada, *Obras*, vol. 3, Biblioteca de Autores Españoles, vol. 11 (Madrid: Ediciones Atlas, 1945). We will be looking at his *Trece Sermones* in this volume; hereafter Luis of Granada, *Sermones*.

10. Luis of Granada, *Sermones*, sermons 1, 2, 3, 5, 7, 10, and 13.

14. Sermon for the Feast of All Saints
15. Sermon for the Feast of the Conception of Our Lady

This is indeed a cycle of feast day sermons. There are no sermons for fast days, no sermon for Good Friday, nor a sermon for the beginning of Lent or the first Sunday in Advent.

A second thing we notice is that this cycle gives special importance to the Marian feasts. The feast of the purification, the feast of the annunciation, the feast of the assumption, and the feast of the conception are all given careful attention. In fact, several of the other feast days give devout attention to the Virgin. Surely this would be appropriate for the feast of the nativity, but it seems a bit forced in the sermon for the ascension, where we learn at length how Mary wanted to ascend into heaven with Christ but in all humility remained behind and gave him her blessing (sermon 7). For an American Protestant this seems a rather curious concern, but if tradition is to have equal authority with Scripture, as the Council of Trent defined, this is what one is inevitably going to come up with.

We also notice that these sermons are very moralistic. Even the central acts of redemption are moralized. The sermon for the feast of the Epiphany, for instance, emphasizes presenting to God the gold of perfect charity, the incense of devotion, and the myrrh of mortification (sermon 2). This is, to be sure, one very traditional way of developing this text. We have heard this interpretation a number of times as we have read through the history of preaching. There are, however, other, more theological ways of developing the text, as we find in many a patristic sermon. The moralism of the sermon on the boy Jesus in the Temple is particularly strong (sermon 2). Jesus gives us an example by his willing submission to authority. He was submissive to his mother. The Virgin, too, was submissive — to her husband. Submission to legitimately constituted authority was a heroic virtue in the Counter-Reformation, and it was perfectly exemplified by the holy family. The sermon for the feast of the purification again takes up the theme of submission, although it is not the point of the whole sermon (sermon 4). At the beginning of the sermon we are told that just as Jesus, who was pure and innocent, submitted to circumcision, so now Mary submits to the Law of Moses by going through the Jewish rites of purification.

Finally, regarding the eloquence of these sermons, the preacher makes a conscious attempt to be eloquent which the reader notices immediately. Luis of Granada is remembered in Spanish literature as one who introduced a greater eloquence to the language. In fact, his essay on pulpit eloquence, *Ecclesiastica rhetórica,* gained a broad readership throughout the Catholic world.[11] We will find a bit further on that Cardinal Borromeo commended it in the most enthusiastic terms.

These sermons give us an example of the sort of language that appealed to the taste of the day. It is very easy to close one's eyes and imagine these sermons being preached in a Spanish baroque church. Here, for example, is a passage from the sermon for the feast of the three kings:

Acerca de la adoracion y ofrenda de los reyes, considera primeramente cuán grande fué la devocion destos sanctos varones; pues vinieron de tan léjas tierras, y se pusieron á un tan largo y tan peligroso camino, y á tantos trabajos como en él pasaron, por ver con sus ojos corporales al que ya habian visto con los del alma, teniéndose por bienaventurados con esta vista. Lo cual sin duda es para grande confusion nuestra, que tan mal acudimos á la casa de Dios á oir su palabra y los divinos oficios, adonde á tan poca costa y trabajo podriamos ver y adorar al mismo Señor que ellos con tanto trabajo buscaron y adoraron.[12]

Another equally elegant passage is found at the conclusion of this sermon:

Y no sé por cierto, hermanos mios, por qué nos han de agradar mas los caminos ásperos de los vicios, que los llanos de las virtudes. En la humildad se halla el descanso, la tranquilidad y paz. Porque como ella sea de su natural pacífica y llana, aunque se levanten contra ella los vientos y tempestades del mundo, no hallan adonde quebrar las fuerzas

---

11. Luis of Granada, *Ecclesiastica rhetoricae, sive De Ratione Concionandi* (Lisbon: A. Riberius, 1576). The Spanish title is *Los seis Libros de la Retórica Eclesiastica, o De la Manera de Predicar.* See Biblioteca de Autores Españoles, vol. 11, for a modern Spanish edition.

12. Luis of Granada, *Sermones,* sermon 2, p. 3. Appreciation is expressed to Michael Riley, who has provided English translations for these passages from Luis of Granada. "Concerning the worship and offering of the kings, consider first how great the devotion of these saintly men; after all they came from such distant lands, and placed themselves on such a long and dangerous path and submitted themselves to the travail it offered, to see with their physical eyes what they had already seen with the eyes of their souls, considering themselves blessed for having seen this sight. Which without a doubt is a great confusion for us, who so poorly attend the house of God to listen to His Word and the divine positions, where with such little cost and effort we would be able to see and worship the same Lord that they, with so much effort, searched for and adored."

de sus ímpetus furiosos. Blandamente se allanan las grandes ondas de la mar en la arena, que con grande ruido suenan y baten las altas peñas; cualquiera encuentro que venga á dar sobre el humilde, como no le resiste, ántes baja la cabeza, despídele de sí, dándole lugar, y dejándole pasar. Toda la braveza de la mar es contra las altas rocas y peñascos, y pierde su furia en la blandura de las llanas y blandas arenas. En los altos montes andan recios los vientos, que no se sienten en los valles bajos y humildes. Los caminos de los soberbios son quebrados, llenos de barrancos y peñascos; porque adonde está la soberbia, está la indignacion, allí la ferocidad, allí la inquietud y desasosiego; porque aun acá padezca el soberbio esta justa condenacion, y acá comience el malo su infierno: como al alma del bueno denda acá tiene ya principio de su gloria en la quietud de su conciencia.[13]

We notice here the moralism so typical of Counter-Reformation preaching, and yet the beauty of the language makes this moralism poetic. The rhetoric lifts up these moralistic thoughts so that they have a certain sort of beauty.

Again in the sermon for the Sunday after Epiphany, which treats the story of the boy Jesus in the Temple, we find an eloquent passage: "Pues vuestro Hijo es Dios, buscadle en el templo, que es el lugar de Dios. El templo es casa de oracion; ahí hallaréis á vuestro Hijo Dios. Cuando tú, hermano, te hallares triste y desconsolado, tibio, seco, sin centella alguna de devocion, y juzgares que has perdido á Dios, búscale en su casa, en el templo: esto es, en el lugar de la oracion, que sin duda le hallarás, si fiel y

---

13. Luis of Granada, *Sermones,* sermon 2, p. 5. "And I do not know for certain, my brethren, why we enjoy most the uninviting paths of vices when we can enjoy the most virtuous, smooth paths. In humility one finds rest, tranquility and peace. Because she is naturally peaceful and smooth, even though the winds and storms of the world will rise against her, they do not find where to break the strength of her furious power. Softly, the same waves of the sea flatten on the sand, who also with great noise strike the tall cliffs; I find that anyone who meets a humble man and is not resisted, lowers his head, greeting him, giving him space, and allowing him to pass by. All the courage of the sea is against the tall rocks and cliffs, but the fury is lost in the softness of the smooth and flat sand. In the tall mountains the winds are strong, but they are not felt in the low and humble valleys. The paths of proud men are uneven, filled with cliffs and peaks; because where pride is, indignation is also there, ferocity is also there, nervousness and lack of calmness are also there; because even here does the proud man carry out their condemnation, and here begins hell for the evil man: just as the soul of the good man has begun his time of glory in the quietness of his conscience."

humildemente perseverares; y conocerás haberle hallado, cuando allí hallares alivio, devocion, esfuerzo, alegría."[14]

Not surprisingly, Luis fills his sermon for the feast of the resurrection with several splendid passages. The introduction is a play on the 118th Psalm. "Este es el dia que hizo el Señor, gocémonos y alegrémonos en él. Todos los dias hizo el Señor que hizo el tiempo; mas este se dice particularmente ser obra del Señor, porque en él acabó la mas excelente de todas sus obras, que fué la obra de nuestra redempcion. Pues así como esta se llama por excelencia obra de Dios, por la ventaja que hace á todas las obras, así tambien este se llama dia de Dios, porque en él se acabó esta mas excelente obra de Dios."[15] A bit further on in the same sermon our preacher gives us a superb piece of high rhetoric. He reports Christ's victory over death as perceived by the souls imprisoned in the underworld. He gives us a monologue of one of these souls:

Y todos en medio de sus tinieblas comenzaron entre sí á murmurar, y decir: ¿Quién es este tan fuerte, tan resplandesciente, tan poderoso? ¡Nunca tal hombre como este se vió en nuestro infierno! ¡Nunca á estas cuevas tal persona nos envió el mundo, nuestro tributario! Acreedor es este, no deudor; quebrantador nuestro, no pecador; juez parece, no culpado; á pelear viene, y no á penar. Decid: ¿adónde estaban nuestras guardas y porteros cuando este conquistador rompió nuestras puertas y cerraduras? ¿Cómo ha entrado por fuerza? ¿Quién será este que tanto puede? Si este fuera culpado, no sería tan osado. Si tuviera alguna escuridad de pecado, no resplandescieran nuestras tinieblas con su luz. Mas si es Dios, ¿qué hace en el infierno? Si es hombre, ¿cómo tiene tanto atrevimiento? Si es Dios, ¿qué hace en el sepulcro? Y si es hombre,

14. Luis of Granada, *Sermones,* sermon 3, p. 6. "For your Son is God, search for Him in the temple. The temple is a house of prayer, there you will find your Son God. When you, brother, find yourself sad and inconsolable, fragile, dry, without any spark of devotion, and you judge that you have lost God, look for Him in His house, in the temple: this is, in the place of prayer, where without doubt you will find Him if you faithfully and humbly persevere: and you will know you have found Him when you find relief, devotion, strength, happiness."

15. Luis of Granada, *Sermones,* sermon 6, p. 13. "This is the day that the Lord has made, let us rejoice and be glad in it. Every day was made by God, who makes time itself; but today is particularly the work of God because in it He completed the most excellent of all His works, which was the work of our redemption. Just as this is called, for reason of excellence, the work of God, because of the advantage it has on all other works, it is also called day of God, because in it was completed this most excellent work of God."

¿cómo despoja nuestro limbo? ¡Oh cruz, cómo tienes burladas nuestras esperanzas, y causada nuestra perdicion! En un árbol alcanzamos todas nuestras riquezas, y agora en el de la cruz las perdimos."[16]

For our taste this might be a bit too melodramatic, but for a Spanish baroque pulpit it is magnificent. The same can be said for the apostrophe which concludes the sermon. "¡Oh Virgen bienaventurada! Básteos, Señora, solo este bien; básteos que vuestro Hijo sea vivo, y que le tengais delante, y le veais ántes que salgais desta vida, para que no os quede mas que desear. ¡Oh Señor, y cómo sabeis consolar á los desconsolados por vuestra causa! Ya no le parece grande aquella primera pena en comparacion desta alegría. Si así consolais á los que por vos padecen, bienaventuradas y dichosas todas sus pasiones; pues así por vos han de ser remuneradas."[17] Here is the spirit of the Counter-Reformation in all its dramatic art.

D. Spanish Missionary Preaching in Mexico

On 8 November 1519, scarcely two years after Luther posted his ninety-five theses, Hernán Cortés entered the magnificent capital of the vast Aztec empire, Tenochtitlán.[18] He marveled at the beauty of the city built of

16. Luis of Granada, *Sermones,* sermon 6, p. 14. "And all the souls in the middle of their darkness began to murmur between them and say: "Who is this who is so strong, so shining, so powerful? Never has a man like this been seen in our hell! Never has the world, our tributary, sent such a man to these caves! He is a creditor, not the debtor; our punisher, not the sinner; he appears to be the judge, not the accused; he comes to fight, not to mourn. Tell me: Where were our guards and door keepers when this conqueror broke the doors and locks? How has he powered his way in? Who is he who can do so? If he was an accused, he would not be so bold. If he had some darkening sin, he would not shine through our darkness with his light. But if he is God, What is he doing in the grave? And if he is man how has he thrown off our limbo state? Oh cross, how you have mocked our hopes and caused our perdition! In a tree we reached for all our riches and now in the tree of the cross we have lost them."

17. Luis of Granada, *Sermones,* sermon 6, p. 16. "Oh blessed Virgin! May it be enough for you, Lady, only this good; may it be enough for you that your Son is alive and that you have Him before you and that you see Him before you leave this life so that you have nothing more to desire. Oh Lord, how you know to console the inconsolable for your cause! The initial sorrow no longer seems great in comparison to the present happiness. If that is how you console those who suffer for you, blessed and fortunate is all their passion because they will be repaid by thee."

18. For sources on the history of Mexico, see *Coleccion de Incunables Americanos,*

white stone, with its majestic pyramids, its splendid temples, and its luxurious palaces, floating as it were on the lake of Texcoco. With elaborate ceremony he was received as an emissary of the god Quetzalcóatl. Suspecting treachery, Cortés audaciously entered the audience chamber of Montezuma, took him hostage, and demanded that he submit to the authority of the king of Spain and convert to the Christian Church. Submit to the king of Spain he did, but convert to Christianity he would not. Deterred not in the least, Cortés demanded the destruction of idols and the cessation of human sacrifice. He himself climbed to the top of the principal pyramid of the city and smashed the Aztec idols.[19] Mass was celebrated on the tops of the pyramids, and crosses as well as images of the Virgin were erected. He even had his priest, Father Olmedo, preach sermons to the Aztecs. Presumably they were translated by Marina, an Indian princess whom Cortés had taken as his concubine. Cortés did everything he could to bring about the conversion of the Aztecs, but more was needed than political evangelism.

Hernán Cortés was a loyal subject of the king of Spain, and to about the same degree a staunch supporter of the Church, but the religious and moral teachings of the Church were beyond his perception. He was a notorious womanizer, a reckless gambler, and a cruel warrior. How he could present himself as a supporter of the Church is beyond our comprehension. We wince at the naive methods he used to evangelize the pre-Columbian Indians. In all fairness, it should be reported that Father Olmedo had reservations about the type of evangelism the great conquistador was promoting.

Things changed in 1524 when a group of Franciscan friars arrived. These friars had a true apostolic motivation for their missionary work.[20] They applied themselves to learning the languages of the various Indian nations.[21] Aside from the Aztec language, a dialect of the language

---

Siglo XVI, prologo Don Ramon Menendez Pidal (Madrid: Ediciones cultura Hispanica, 1944), hereafter Pidal, *Incunables;* Bernal Diaz del Castillo, *The Discovery and Conquest of Mexico,* trans. A. P. Maudslay, introduction to the American edition by Irving A. Leonard (New York: Noonday Press, 1956); Henry Bamford Parkes, *A History of Mexico* (Boston: Houghton Mifflin, 1969); and Gordon R. Willey, William T. Sanders, and John V. Murra, "Pre-Columbian Civilizations," in *The New Encyclopedia Britannica,* 15th ed., 32 vols. (Chicago: Encyclopedia Britannica, 1994), 26:1-44.

19. Parkes, *A History of Mexico,* p. 52.

20. Parkes, *A History of Mexico,* p. 62.

21. Apparently Cortés himself realized the need to develop Spanish preachers who

Nahuatl, there was Michoacán, which was spoken by a nation to the west of Mexico City. This was an important language for the missionaries because this nation had rather early allied itself with Cortés in his attack on the Aztecs. Then there was the language of the Otomis, who were north and east of the city of Mexico. The Mayan language was spoken in the Yucatán peninsula. Totenac was the language of the central Gulf coast, and Huastec was the language of the north Gulf coast. In the valley of Oaxaca, Mixtec and Zapotec were the most important languages. Learning all these languages was a formidable task for the missionaries, but they well understood how crucial it was for their work.

Those who had little gift for languages or little skill in preaching had plenty they could do to support the missionary enterprise. They built Christian churches on the foundations of the old temples. They rid the land of pagan idols and erected images of the Virgin and crucifixes in their place. They constructed convents and set up schools. They tried their best to end polygamy, a practice which was strong among the nobles.

The success of their evangelistic work was great, especially in the central plateau, which was the center of the Aztec empire. Hundreds of thousands of Indians were baptized. The population was eager to embrace the religion of their conquerors, but the teaching of the converts was necessarily slow. It took time to develop preachers who could present the gospel in the indigenous language. Often those who had been baptized simply honored the same old gods under different names. Too often the priests made this easy, hoping that by good preaching and teaching they could move their converts to more solidly Christian beliefs and practices.

The efforts of the Spanish missionaries to translate teaching materials into the native languages were impressive. As early as 1538 the bishop of Seville, Vasco de Guieroga, published a catechism in Michoacán.[22] His assistant Fray Juan de Zumárraga got royal permission to set up a press in Mexico. This produced a series of publications designed to support the catechetical ministry of the missionaries. In 1539 there appeared a manual of Christian doctrine both in brief form and in a more thorough form. Much of this was the work of Alonzo de Molina and his son Alonsito. In 1540 a manual for adult baptism appeared, and in the next decade more than twenty publications, including catechisms and homili-

could preach in the indigenous languages. He sent Alonzo de Molina and his mestizo son Alonsito back to Spain to develop the linguistic tools for the priests.

22. Pidal, *Incunables,* p. vii.

aries, were published. Some of these were in the Aztec language, while others were in the language of the Huastecanos and the Chucona.[23]

The Franciscan Juan de Gaona was one of the first priests to become proficient in the language of the Aztecs. His mastery of the language did much to raise the level of Christian preaching in Mexico. In addition to catechetical sermons, he produced translations of devotional works by Luis of Granada as well as a treatise of his own on the peace and tranquillity of the Christian and a work on the passion of Christ.

Even the briefest sketch of the conversion of Mexico must recount the story of Our Lady of Guadalupe. In 1531 a recently baptized Indian, Juan Diego, had a vision of the Virgin. As the story goes, the Virgin revealed her desire to have a church built for her at that spot, a hill a short distance north of the city of Mexico. This simple peasant went to the bishop and told him about it, but the bishop was skeptical and sent the peasant on his way. Again the Virgin appeared to Juan Diego. She sent him back to the bishop with a sign. Juan Diego was to go and gather a bouquet of roses, which miraculously appeared where they would never have grown naturally. He was to wrap them in his cloak and present them to the bishop. This Juan Diego did, but when he opened his cloak it was not roses which the bishop saw, but a picture of the Virgin imprinted on the cloth. This, for the Indians, was a sign that the Virgin had taken the Indians into her special care and protection, but for the Spanish it was a sign that indeed the Indians were to be received into the household of faith.[24]

Often historians have been very cynical about the conversion of the Mexicans, but there was more to it than one usually admits. Anyone who has taken more than a passing glance at the archaeological monuments of the pre-Columbian Indians of Mesoamerica has seen the evidence of the appalling practice of human sacrifice. The images of the angry gods who demanded these bloody rites are terrifying! That the general population should have turned away from these fearful deities on the least provocation needs little explanation. That the virgin Mary should have so easily displaced Tlaloc is quite understandable.

One readily admits that one of the reasons Cortés was so successful was that the rule of the Aztecs was so despotic. The taxes Montezuma imposed were already leading to widespread revolts. He poured wealth into

23. Pidal, *Incunables,* p. x.
24. Parkes, *A History of Mexico,* pp. 107ff.

his temples and supported costly ceremonials, all paid for by taxation of his vassal states. Even more resented was the taking of their men for the rites of human sacrifice. At one point Montezuma erected a new altar and consecrated it with a thousand human sacrifices. The sacrifice of the Mass was a welcome relief.

The conversion of the Otomis was particularly enthusiastic. They had long resented Aztec rule. So many of them who had been taken captive in battle had been sacrificed on Aztec altars. No wonder they supported Cortés, claimed the protection of the Virgin, and flocked to the unbloody sacrifice of the Mass.

Only very rarely do missionaries leave any record of their missionary preaching. We have a few very brief reports of the missionary preaching of the apostles in the New Testament, as we noted in our first volume. Neither Patrick nor Columba left us any sermons. Columbanus did leave us sermons, but they are very sketchy. So there are exceptions. However, for the most part missionaries are too busy to get their preaching down on paper, even though it is often of tremendous importance. Happily we do have a collection of missionary sermons for the catechetical teaching of the Aztecs. The purpose of the book is apparently the training of Spanish priests to preach in the Mexican language, that is, the Aztec dialect of Nahuatl. The book has appropriate sermons with the Aztec text on one side of the page and the Spanish text on the other. The book, *Doctrina Christiana en Lengua Española y Mexicana por los Religiosos de la Orden de Santo Domingo,*[25] was printed in Mexico in 1548. An edition may have been published in Mexico as early as 1535 and again in 1537, but no copy has survived.

This collection contains forty sermons. Sermons 1 through 17 teach the creed, starting with the articles on the divinity of Christ followed by the articles on the humanity of Christ. Sermons 18 through 26 explain the Ten Commandments. The seven sacraments are treated in sermon 27, while sermons 28 and 29 give special treatment to the sacrament of confession. This is followed by sermons on heaven and hell, virginity and chastity, the unity of the Catholic Church, the sign of the cross, the creation of the world, the Lord's Prayer, and the Ave Maria.

This collection is the most important document which has come down to us, but there is evidence that much the same thing was done in

---

25. For a photolithographic edition of this work, see Pidal, *Incunables,* folio 10-151.

other native languages. A catechism in Huastec was published in 1571, as well as one for the Otomis in 1576. The Dominican Fray Juan de Córdoba published a dictionary and grammar of the Zapotec language in 1578, but no catechism has survived. A whole series of dictionaries and grammars appeared before the end of the sixteenth century in most of the major pre-Columbian languages. The missionaries, to put it simply, performed an amazing work in translating Christian teaching into the pre-Columbian languages. Curiously, however, with all this translating of catechisms, liturgical books, devotional literature, and even sermons, nothing is said about the translation of the Bible.

We notice that these missionaries did not engage in what we would call evangelistic preaching but rather catechetical preaching. We will notice the same thing in the preaching of Francis Xavier. What we do not find here is the preaching of the gospel in such a way that the hearer responds in faith. Instead we have the teaching of Christian doctrine and instruction in Christian piety.

II. The Jesuits

In volume 3 of this work, we found it helpful to speak of Benedictine preaching, Cistercian preaching, Franciscan preaching, and Dominican preaching. Several times in the history of preaching a particular religious order has given rise to a definite school of preaching. We find the same to be true of the Jesuits. Their distinctive spirituality gave a unique quality to much of the preaching of the Counter-Reformation.[26]

Although we can probably say that Ignatius of Loyola was the one

26. From the extensive literature on the history of the Jesuits, see the following: William V. Bangert, *A History of the Society of Jesus* (St. Louis: Institute of Jesuit Sources, 1972); John Francis Broderick, "Jesuits," in *New Catholic Encyclopedia,* 7:898-909; Joseph de Guibert, *The Jesuits: Their Spiritual Doctrine and Practice,* trans. William J. Young (Chicago: Loyola University Press, 1964); Martin Patrick Harney, *The Jesuits in History: The Society of Jesus through Four Centuries* (New York: American Press, 1941); Richard Littledale and Ethelred Taunton, "Jesuits," in *Encyclopedia Britannica,* 11th ed., 32 vols. (New York: Encyclopedia Britannica, 1910), 15:337-47; Theodore Maynard, *St. Ignatius and the Jesuits* (New York: P. J. Kennedy, 1956); and John O'Malley, "Early Jesuit Spirituality," originally in *Christian Spirituality: Post-Reformation and Modern,* ed. Louis Dupré and Don Saliers (New York: Crossroad Publishing, 1982), pp. 3-27, reprinted in John O'Malley, *Religious Culture in the Sixteenth Century: Preaching, Rhetoric, Spirituality, and Reform* (Brookfield, Vt.: Variorum, 1993).

personality more than any other which crystallized the Counter-Reformation, he was not a preacher, and therefore does not really have a place in the history of preaching. Still, he and the religious order he founded had a tremendous effect on preaching. With Loyola we have a personality who shaped a whole age.[27]

Born the youngest son of a noble Spanish family, he was brought up to be a soldier. He was hardly more than a boy when he was sent off to be a page in the service of a relative at the court of the kingdom of Castile. In his midtwenties he was knighted, serving another relative, the duke of Nájera. He tells us in his autobiography that he took great delight in military exercises. Chivalry was his ideal. When he was thirty, however, his military career was brought to an end. Defending Pamplona from the French, he was seriously wounded by a cannon blast. One leg was broken and the other seriously wounded. During his long convalescence he more and more gave himself to devotional reading. To occupy his mind he recounted the heroic deeds of the saintly soldiers who drove the Moors from Spain. Holiness and chivalry went hand in hand. Finally, when he was well enough to travel, he started out on a pilgrimage to Montserrat and there abjured the life of worldly ambition, handing over his sword to the Virgin.

For the next few months he lived as a beggar and devoted himself to prayer, fasting, and flagellation. Daily he attended Mass, and at night he slept in a cave. During this time he had an experience of illumination which made clear to him the direction his life was to take. Apparently he understood this in terms of a spiritual reconquest of the Holy Land. Such a vision might seem quite feasible to a young Spanish knight only a generation after the Moslems had been driven out of Iberia. In 1523 he started out on a pilgrimage to the Holy Land. Within two weeks of his arrival in Jerusalem, his excessive zeal had so offended the Moslem rulers of the city that the Franciscans in charge of the Latin Christians of the city insisted that he leave.

Back in Spain a year after he set out, he decided to change tack. Already thirty-three years old, he began to prepare himself for the university

27. For the ministry of Loyola see the following: James Brodrick, S.J., *St. Ignatius of Loyola: The Pilgrim Years* (New York: Farrer, Stans and Cudahy, 1956); Cándido de Dalmases, "Ignatius of Loyola, St.," in *New Catholic Encyclopedia,* 7:354-56; Paul Dudon, *St. Ignatius of Loyola,* trans. W. J. Young (Milwaukee: Bruce Publishing, 1949); Hugo Rahner, *The Spirituality of St. Ignatius Loyola,* trans. F. J. Smith (Chicago: Loyola University Press, 1953); and Ethelred Taunton, "Loyola, St. Ignatius of," in *Encyclopedia Britannica,* 11th ed., 17:80-84.

by learning Latin. He seems to have made rapid progress, and two years later he was on his way to the University of Alcalá. Devoting himself to his theological studies, he made rapid progress, but he still had time to give to various kinds of ministry. Apparently he did what today we would call spiritual counseling. Again his intense zeal got him in trouble, this time with the Spanish Inquisition. Although able to clear himself, he was advised not to perform any pastoral functions until he had finished his theological training. He finally decided to pursue his studies at Salamanca. Again he found himself in prison because of his zeal, and again he was able to clear himself. Finally he set out for Paris. By this time he had gathered a group of companions, but as yet there was no thought of founding a religious order.

His plans to study theology had been frustrated in Spain, but this did not stem his fervor. The capital of the theological world at that time was still Paris, and determined soldier of the cross that he was, he set his sights on the spiritual prizes to be won there. He arrived in Paris in 1528, beginning his studies at the famous Collège de Montaigu, the same institution where Calvin had studied less than five years before. This introduced him to the study of the arts as it was understood in more conservative Scholastic circles. It was during his days of study at Paris that the challenges of the Protestant Reformation were starting to rock the theology of the university establishment, and it was apparently while in Paris that Loyola began to regard Protestantism rather than Islam as the primary threat to Catholic Christianity. He continued his studies in Paris and at one point took his master of arts degree. Again he gathered a group of like-minded men about himself, but this time they moved toward organizing themselves into a formal religious community. Several of these men were fellow Spaniards. Prominent among them was Francis Xavier, who later took Catholic Christianity to India, Ceylon, and Japan. More and more these men understood the theological discussion provoked by the Reformation in terms of spiritual warfare. They understood themselves as the company of Jesus, a military company, a task force of knights with special skills of battle. They saw themselves as men called to accomplish heroic deeds. To put it in contemporary terms, they saw themselves as the Catholic marines, the religious Green Berets.

Having studied in Paris for seven years, Loyola once more took up his pilgrimage, spending time in Spain and Venice. He still had his sights set on Jerusalem, but the opportunities did not present themselves, so more and more he turned his attention to Rome. Then he had another vision in which Christ smiled on his ventures and promised him success. Arriving in Rome in the fall of 1537, two of his company were given important teaching positions at the Sapienza. Faber was given the chair of Holy Scripture and Laynez the chair of Scholastic theology. The men worked hard at gaining the approval of church authorities in Rome. They occupied themselves with services to the needy and leading people through their spiritual exercises. In 1540 Pope Paul III gave official recognition to their order. From that point on Loyola directed the activities of his society from Rome. The Jesuit interpretation of the Reformation as a sort of foreign invasion caught the imagination of many devout Catholics. Enthusiastically they enlisted and armed themselves for the spiritual warfare. They developed a strong doctrine of authority. The general of the order demanded absolute obedience and justified this because the Church was in a state of siege. The Jesuits grew rapidly. At the time of the founder's death in 1556, the society numbered over a thousand members.

Much of the character of the Jesuits was set by the *Spiritual Exercises* which Loyola started to develop in Spain, at the outset of his pilgrimage. These exercises are meditation, ideally to be used at a retreat made under the guidance of a director and lasting four weeks. They instruct one to imagine a series of sacred images of eternal realities. One is to imagine every detail of these scenes. Whether it is the image of the crucifixion or the image of the Last Judgment, one is encouraged to imagine the sweat on Christ's brow, the blood of his wounds, and the pain of the nails in his hands. One is to smell the sulfur fumes of hell and feel the heat of eternal fire. The whole point is to convince one of the seriousness of human sin and the terror of divine judgment. But then one is directed to meditate on Christ's call to enlist in the military service of the kingdom of God and to imagine the rewards given to those who serve under the standard of Christ. These exercises aimed at producing obedient soldiers in the army of the Catholic Church.

Modern experts in the theory of communication marvel at the holistic approach of these exercises. By playing on the full range of senses, the oral, the visual, and the tactile, these exercises were most effective in motivating the religious energies of Catholics. The imagery and the drama and the heroism of Ignatian spirituality could not help but have its influence on the Jesuit pulpit. These spiritual exercises produced a very distinctive spirituality, a spirituality that would, more than any other, animate the preaching of the Counter-Reformation.

A. Francis Xavier (1506-52): Missionary to the Far East

The Spanish and the Portuguese had amazing success as missionaries in the sixteenth century, and Francis Xavier was only the most successful and well known of them.[28] He was born in the Xavier Castle, in the same part of Spain where Ignatius Loyola had been born, and also like Loyola, he was the youngest child of a large noble family. Before he was twenty years old he was sent off to Paris to prepare for theological studies. He began at the Collège de Sainte-Barbe, just across the street from the Collège de Montaigu, where Loyola would begin his studies three years later. There were a number of Spaniards in these two schools, and eventually several of them formed a fast friendship. Loyola was older than the other young men and was the natural leader. In 1534 this group formalized their friendship and, as we have said, joined themselves together in the Company of Jesus.

For the next few years this company set its sights on a spiritual crusade to rescue the Holy Land from the Moslems, but the way never seemed to open up. In 1540 the king of Portugal called Xavier to serve the Christian community in South India. Thirty years earlier the Portuguese had established a port at Goa on the western coast of India. It flourished, and in fact became a major base in the trade route the Portuguese navigators had opened up around the Cape of Good Hope to the Far East. In April 1541 Xavier set sail for Goa. The voyage was long and exhausting, and much time was lost in the Doldrums. Xavier suffered from seasickness and the sailors from scurvy. Then the ship was blown off course along the coast of Brazil. Five months later they had gotten no farther than Mozambique, where the captain decided to winter. Xavier fell ill with a fever while attending the sick in the hospital. Finally the voyage was resumed, arriving in Goa in May 1542, more than a year after it had begun.

Xavier presented his papers to the bishop of Goa and devoted himself to learning the Tamil language. In the meantime he cared for the sick and gave catechetical instruction to the children and slaves of the Portu-

28. For works on the life of Francis Xavier, see James Brodrick, S.J., *Saint Francis Xavier (1506-1552)* (New York: Wicklow Press, 1952); Kingsley Garland Jayne, "Xavier, Francisco de," in *Encyclopedia Britannica,* 11th ed., 28:882-83; Georg Schurhammer, *Francis Xavier: His Life, His Times,* trans. Joseph Costellac, 4 vols. (Rome: Jesuit Historical Institutes, 1973-82); and Josef Wicki, "Xavier, Francis, St.," in *New Catholic Encyclopedia,* 14:1059-60.

guese colonists. The colony was a generation old when Xavier arrived. Many of the Portuguese had taken wives or concubines from the native population and had raised families, and thus plenty of people in the colony were bilingual. Besides that, there were a good number of black slaves. When the Portuguese had arrived on the east coast of Africa, they found that the Arabs depended on black slaves for any kind of heavy labor or menial household tasks. The Arabs maintained the slave trade all along the shores of the Indian Ocean, and in a short time the Portuguese became slave owners themselves. Apparently a good portion of the population of Goa was made up of these black slaves. As in the Americas, especially in the Caribbean, the slaves very quickly developed a sort of Creole version of Portuguese. At first it was in this language that Xavier did his catechetical preaching.

Several churches had already been organized in Goa. Church buildings had been constructed and regular services were held. Something like two dozen Catholic priests served the Portuguese colonists, but there had also been definite attempts to evangelize the native population. It has to be admitted that the methods of evangelism were for the most part rather naive, if not crude, but that went with the nature of the colony. It was nothing like what transpired in Mexico, however. In Goa we are dealing with a much smaller number of people. We hear nothing of evangelistic preaching, although converts from the native population had been made and a few villages had accepted baptism. These new converts, however, had received little in the way of Christian teaching. In fact, for the most part they had not even been given basic catechetical instruction.

The reports that have come down to us give a fairly clear picture of the catechetical teaching of Francis Xavier.[29] Each evening he would go about the town with a little bell announcing catechetical services and with a loud voice urging people to send their children and their slaves to learn about the faith. He might gather as many as a couple hundred students this way. They would follow him to a church, where he would begin the lesson by singing the Gospel. He had two boys sing it after him, and then all present were asked to sing it. This was followed by several prayers. After that he sang the creed, and again the two boys who were helping him would sing the text, and then the congregation. It was done this way, we are told, so that the text would become more thoroughly impressed on the memory. Then Xavier would go over each article of the creed, giving a

29. Schurhammer, *Francis Xavier*, 2:218-24.

few explanatory comments and then asking if his catechumens believed this teaching. They would then profess that indeed they did. With all this repetition the creed, as well as Xavier's interpretation of it, was learned by rote.

After the creed had been rehearsed, the Lord's Prayer and the Ave Maria were repeated. The Ten Commandments were then gone through in a similar manner. To this was added the seven deadly sins, the seven virtues, and a number of other catechetical texts which had become popular in Europe during the Middle Ages. One gets the impression that this was moral catechism at its most moralistic. This becomes clear when we learn that after reciting the Ten Commandments Xavier was in the habit of admonishing his catechumens, "God says: 'Whoever keeps these Ten Commandments will go into paradise.' God says: 'Whoever does not keep these Ten Commandments will go to hell.'"[30]

Having led his catechumens in the recitation of the catechetical pieces, Xavier then preached a catechetical sermon on one of the articles of the creed, one of the commandments, or some other Christian precept. The whole thing took an hour and a half or perhaps two hours. We should point out that one of the reasons for the success of this program was the work of the two boys, who were no doubt sons of interracial marriages and therefore bilingual. It was they who could make the preacher understandable in the street language of the colony. Although Xavier was credited with having the gift of tongues, we do know that he gave much energy to learning Tamil, the language of South India, as well as Japanese a few years later. He clearly used translators, although he appears to have made every effort to learn the local language himself. In this we find the famous missionary already developing the concept of accommodation which in years to come will play a significant part in Christian evangelism.

Xavier in no way limited his catechetical ministry to slaves, those of mixed race, and children. On Saturdays and Sundays he did catechetical preaching for adults. Very little of this sort of thing had been done in the colony up to this time, and this ministry was very well received.

Xavier had ministered in the colony less than a year when he heard about the Paravas, a people who had accepted baptism a few years before but had received no ministerial attention since that time. The Paravas

---

30. Schurhammer, *Francis Xavier*, 2:220.

were pearl fishers living along the South Indian coast facing Ceylon on the other side of Cape Comorin.

For almost two years Xavier went from village to village ministering to the spiritual needs of the people, baptizing the newborn children, calling on people in their homes, praying for the sick, and comforting the dying. This gave him an opportunity to teach the people the Christian hope of everlasting life. In the evenings he would preach on the verandas of people's homes. Here, again, he used young men who were bilingual, and yet his ability to preach in Tamil was apparently improving. Much of this preaching was catechetical in nature, and to support this he had developed a Tamil catechism.

On Sundays he gathered the people for Mass, but he also held extended catechetical services similar to those he had developed in Goa.[31] As with most missionaries, he had to devote much of his preaching to admonishing the people to leave the superstitions of the old religions behind. The Paravas had been baptized, but like new Christians on many mission fields, they found it hard to recognize the borders between idolatry and faith. Xavier found that he had to preach against pagan beliefs, against drunkenness and adultery constantly. We remember that the missionary monks of the early Middle Ages had to do the same thing.

The fascinating story of the evangelistic travels of Francis Xavier tempts us to follow along in great detail as he preached his way through Ceylon, back to Travancore, and then to the Strait of Malacca on the Malay Peninsula. In Japan he had to learn still another language. He evidently learned it well enough to discuss philosophy with Buddhist scholars. He did in fact establish a church in Japan which has remained ever since. As fascinating as the story is, we will have to leave it here. We have seen enough, however, to get an idea of how Xavier preached the Christian faith to those outside the bonds of Christendom.

As far as we can discover, Xavier emphasized catechetical preaching rather than evangelistic preaching. Perhaps we would get a different impression if we had his sermons. Perhaps the records which have come down to us were not sufficiently sensitive to what our preacher was saying. For whatever reason, one misses true evangelistic preaching. Xavier does not seem to win converts by proclaiming the gospel. He teaches the Christian faith and the Christian way of life. As we will see again and again, this was typical of Jesuit preaching.

31. Schurhammer, *Francis Xavier*, 2:335.

B. Peter Canisius (1521-97)

The outstanding Counter-Reformation preacher in Germany, Peter Canisius, is best known for his catechetical ministry. Following the lead of the Protestant Reformers, he revived this whole dimension of the ministry of the Word. As we pointed out in the previous chapter, Luther, Zwingli, and Bucer had made great strides in reviving the catechetical ministry. Here was one reform which the Counter-Reformation emulated with vigor. Apparently this was especially the case with the Jesuits. We noticed this with Francis Xavier, and now we find the same characteristic with Peter Canisius. The fullness of his vision is remarkable. Not only did he develop the major Catholic catechism, but he taught Catholics the value of a catechetical ministry. Even more, he trained a whole army of Jesuit priests to teach and preach the catechism he produced. It is because of this, more than anything else, that German Catholics honor him with the title, the Second Apostle of Germany.[32]

Canisius was born in the Netherlands, where his father served for many years as mayor of the city of Nijmegen. His childhood was comfortable, secure, and devout. It was in the meticulous piety of the *Devotio Moderna* that he was nurtured. As a young man he was sent to the University of Cologne, where he became active in the first attempts to establish the Jesuit Order in Germany. In 1543, at only twenty-two years of age, he went through his first Jesuit retreat following the *Spiritual Exercises* of Ignatius Loyola. When he finally made his solemn profession, he became the first Jesuit recruit from Germany.

Already in Cologne it became obvious that he had a natural gift for oratory, and it was there that he began his preaching ministry.[33] This was when the archbishop of Cologne, Hermann von Wied, was trying to bring his important archdiocese into the Reformation. Canisius, therefore, studied theology in one of the theological storm centers of Germany. It is quite understandable that his approach to preaching was so polemi-

32. On the ministry of Peter Canisius, see James Brodrick, S.J., *Saint Peter Canisius* (Chicago: Loyola University Press, 1962); John Patrick Donnelly, "Canisius, Peter," in *Oxford Encyclopedia of the Reformation*, 4 vols. (New York and Oxford: Oxford University Press, 1996), 1:253; and Julius Oswald and Peter Rummel, eds., *Petrus Canisius — Reformer der Kirche, Festschrift zum 400. Todestag des zweiten Apostels Deutschlands* (Augsburg: Sankt Ulrich Verlag, 1996).

33. See Philipp Überbacher, "Petrus Canisius als Hofprediger," in *Petrus Canisius — Reformer der Kirche*, pp. 202-20.

cal. With all the enthusiasm of youth, he devoted his life to checking the influence of Protestantism.

In 1545 Canisius's singular devotion to the Catholic cause came to the attention of the bishop of Augsburg, Otto Truchsess von Waldburg, who took him to the Council of Trent as his theological consultant. Canisius became a zealous promoter of the teaching of the council, and settled into his preaching ministry in Augsburg, Germany's largest Protestant city. Being appointed preacher at the Cathedral of Augsburg in 1559, he set himself to a vigorous schedule. Besides the usual sermons on Sundays and holy days, he preached four times a week during Advent and Lent. In addition, he delivered three discourses on Christian doctrine each week at the cathedral and at the Church of Saint John the Baptist. Church attendance increased dramatically.

Almost forty years had passed since Oecolampadius had exercised his short ministry in Augsburg. Although the city had achieved a Protestant majority from an early date, a number of its wealthier citizens, such as the Fuggars, the famous banking family, had remained firmly Catholic. The cathedral was still under the control of the archbishop. The Protestants had never been able to hold a strong preacher in any of the leading pulpits, although several leaders had served in Augsburg for shorter periods of time. In choosing Augsburg, Canisius had used good strategy.

For seventeen years he continued his ministry in Augsburg. His sermons were filled with content and had a simple, direct quality. He knew how to communicate. Particularly evident is the careful preparation he gave to his preaching. Some twelve thousand pages of his sermon notes have come down to us.[34] Apparently these notes were not for the catechetical sermons he delivered three times a week, but rather for his Sunday and feast day sermons on the liturgical Gospels.

As far as I have been able to discover, his catechetical sermons have not been preserved. What has been preserved are the catechisms themselves. The first one he published was the *Summa doctrinae christianae,* which appeared in Vienna in 1555. For the most part it follows the pattern of Luther's catechism, adding certain elements which would be essential for Catholics.[35] In something more than two hundred questions it

---

34. These have been published in Peter Canisius, *S. Petri Canisii doctoris Ecclesiae Meditationes seu notae in evangeliae lectiones,* 3 vols. (Freiburg and Munich, 1939-61).

35. See my work on baptism: Hughes Oliphant Old, *The Shaping of the Reformed Baptismal Rite in the Sixteenth Century* (Grand Rapids: Wm. B. Eerdmans Publishing Co., 1992).

treats the traditional catechetical pieces: the Ten Commandments, the Lord's Prayer, the Hail Mary, the Apostles' Creed, and the seven sacraments. It was intended for the training of those who would give catechetical instruction.

The following year the shorter catechism appeared, *Summa doctrinae christianae per questiones tradita et ad captum rudiorum accomodata.* This was designed for children and went over the same material as the larger catechism, but at a much simpler level. A third catechism appeared in Vienna in 1558, *Catechismus minor seu parvus catechismus catholicorum,* designed for the instruction of young people in secondary schools.

The enormous success of his catechetical ministry was largely due to his rigorous training of catechists. All over southern Germany he established Jesuit colleges, and to these training schools he entrusted the teaching of his catechisms. The Jesuits developed a system of education which gave a high value to memorization. They developed a whole philosophy of education which rapidly gained a monopoly in the Catholic world. In strongly Catholic lands, wherever the Jesuits were influential, the doctrines of the Counter-Reformation were learned by rote by all who had any claim to a formal education.

C. Robert Bellarmine (1542-1621)

It is with considerable respect that Protestants have always regarded Robert Bellarmine. He was the obvious champion of the Counter-Reformation, the Catholic theologian, above all others, with whom one must deal if one is to defend the Protestant faith against the Catholicism of the Council of Trent. Bellarmine made an honest attempt to understand what Protestantism was about. He knew the basic writings of the Reformers and drew up his vision of baroque Catholicism in antithesis to their teachings rather than in blind reaction against any challenge to the establishment. Bellarmine in no way compromised with Protestantism. True to the Jesuit vision, he made the distinction very clear. What was not clear at the time, and what is now only beginning to become clear, is that Bellarmine's baroque Catholicism is a very distinct approach to being Catholic, but an approach which hardly exhausts the possibilities.[36] His vision of Catholic

---

36. One of the problems in writing this chapter is that a considerable amount of literature is currently being produced by a number of scholars who feel the need to reeval-

Christianity is clear, and certainly impressive; it is just that others have visions of Catholicity which are quite different.

Everything about Robert Bellarmine fitted him to be the champion of the Counter-Reformation.[37] He was born in one of the hill towns of central Italy, Montepulciano, south of Florence, not too far from Assisi. It was not a very important town, but the Bellarmines were one of its patrician families. They qualified as what we in America might call county seat gentility. This great scholar-prince of the Church was mined from the rock ribs of Italy.

There was nothing fancy about Montepulciano, and certainly nothing pretentious about the Bellarmine family, but Robert's uncle was pope. Marcello Cervini had been born in Montepulciano and was the brother of Robert's mother. He had been in the papal administration for many years when he was elevated to the papacy in 1555, when Robert was a teenager. Regrettably his pontificate lasted only a short time, but he held the honor long enough for Palestrina to dedicate the *Pope Marcellus Mass* to him. Pope Marcellus was one of the most respected of the reform popes of the sixteenth century, and one regrets that he did not live long enough to institute the reforms he had always supported as a member of the papal court.

Very early in life Robert came under the influence of the Jesuits. The order maintained a college in Montepulciano, and from there he went to Rome, where again he studied under the Jesuits. Pope Marcellus had been a supporter of the Jesuits. He, as many sincere Catholics in that day, was attracted to the Jesuit vision of a purified and disciplined Catholicism. It was hardly surprising that a young man with this kind of background would decide for a career in the Church, nor is it surprising that he would seek it for the highest motives and seek to develop those aspects

---

uate the contribution of the late sixteenth and early seventeenth centuries. An interesting contribution to this discussion is that of John O'Malley, "Was Ignatius Loyola a Church Reformer? How to Look at Early Modern Catholicism," in O'Malley's collection of essays, *Religious Culture in the Sixteenth Century*, pp. 177-93.

37. For biographical material on Bellarmine, see James Brodrick, S.J., *Robert Bellarmine, Saint and Scholar* (Westminster, Md.: Newman Press, 1961); John Patrick Donnelly, "Bellarmino, Roberto," in *Oxford Encyclopedia of the Reformation*, 1:139ff.; Joseph Peter Friske, "Bellarmine, Robert, St.," in *New Catholic Encyclopedia* 2:250-52; and Gustavo Galeota, ed., *Roberto Bellarmino: Archivescovo de Capua, teologo e pastore della Riforma Cattolica* (Capua, Italy: Archidiocesi de Capua, Istituto superiore di scienze religiose, 1990).

of the ministry which were of its essence. It was at exactly this that the Jesuits aimed, and so it was completely appropriate that young Robert should join the Jesuit Order in 1560 before he was twenty years old.

Having finished his studies in Rome, he was sent to teach in a Jesuit school at Mondovì in the Piedmont. There he gave attention to studying and teaching Greek, a combination that was already part of the Jesuit educational system; one learns best what one must teach. Apparently the future orator gave special attention to the Greek orators and rhetoricians such as Demosthenes and Isocrates. The Jesuits were enthusiastic supporters of the humanistic studies of the Renaissance, and the study of the Greek orators would be almost as important as the Latin orators Cicero and Quintilian. Quite naturally this kind of study bore fruit in Bellarmine's own preaching. Already in Mondovì he had begun to preach and was beginning to build a reputation as a preacher. As one would expect, the preaching of this young Jesuit became pulpit oratory.

In 1569 the Jesuit Order sent him to the University of Louvain in Flanders. Louvain had become the center of Counter-Reformation thought in northern Europe. Here Protestantism was in much closer range than in Rome, and a Catholic theologian had to be more realistic about the challenge of the Reformation. Bellarmine spent seven years in Louvain, being the first Jesuit appointed to a chair of theology, during which time he began to appreciate the importance of the Augustinian revival to the Reformation. And of course, this revival was in no way limited to Protestantism; a good number of Catholics had come to rediscover Augustine and began to turn away from the Pelagian tendencies in late medieval Scholasticism. For the humanism of the Italian Renaissance, the Augustinian ideas of original sin, irresistible grace, and predestination were very hard to appreciate, and from the beginning Bellarmine was suspicious of this Augustinian revival. It was only in years to come, however, that this would become a major theological concern of this great theologian.

In 1576 he was called back to Rome and entrusted with the chair of controversial theology at the newly founded Gregorian University. It was here that Bellarmine did his most creative work, work which grew naturally out of his position as professor of controversial theology. In substance, what he did was systematize baroque Catholicism. The Council of Trent, which had ended a bit more than ten years before, had defined Counter-Reformation theology, but the apologetic which was such an important dimension of baroque Catholicism still had to be organized. The definitions of Trent needed theologians who could work out a theological system from them. Bellarmine was one of those who realized the aims of Trent with particular brilliance. His three-volume work, *Disputationes de controversiis Christianae fidei adversus hujus temporis haereticos,* appearing between 1586 and 1593, is, in effect, the summa of Counter-Reformation theology.

1. The Baroque Synthesis

Bellarmine is a theologian in whom we find the baroque synthesis in a particularly clear form.[38] Although we cannot go into his theology at length, a quick sketch will give us a better understanding of his preaching.

Baroque Catholicism is a synthesis of many elements. One part is the heritage of Greek and Roman antiquity. The ancient literature of the Greeks and the Romans which the Renaissance had recovered had been cherished for well over a century, particularly in Italy. Being an Italian, born in Tuscany and educated in Rome, Bellarmine came to this heritage only too naturally. Another part of this synthesis was biblical revelation. While in Louvain, Bellarmine was exposed to the advances in biblical studies which the Christian humanists of northern Europe had made. Protestants particularly had opened up new approaches to the study of Scripture. Bellarmine realized that a conscientious theologian had to deal with these matters, and in an effort to become conversant with the new biblical scholarship, he even went so far as to teach himself Hebrew.

The Council of Trent, in its zeal to press the ideal of *Romitas,* had insisted that the Latin Vulgate of Saint Jerome be received as the authoritative version of Scripture. This made problems for Catholic biblical scholars who had discovered the insights which the original Hebrew and Greek texts shed on the meaning of Scripture. Not the least of these problems was establishing the original text of Jerome's Vulgate. Trent left the matter to be solved by the pope, but it was not until Sixtus V that it was taken in hand. Bellarmine, equipped for such work because of his studies in northern Europe, was called upon to help with the project. Sad to say, the baroque understanding of papal authority and the newer understanding of biblical scholarship came into sharp conflict. Sixtus was very unhappy with the results of the committee's work and decided that he himself would produce the authoritative text. The text he produced was a

38. The classic work on the theology of Bellarmine is that of Joseph de la Servière, *La théologie de Bellarmin* (Paris: Beauchesne, 1909).

catastrophe, one of the classic blunders of ecclesiastical bureaucracy, but happily not many copies had been released when Pope Sixtus died. This very embarrassing problem was not solved to the satisfaction of the papal court until the pontificate of Clement VIII. While one can certainly be very sympathetic to all the problems Bellarmine had with the irascible pontiff, and while one can admire his gentlemanly insistence that the memory of Sixtus V not be tarnished, the whole affair does demonstrate some of the problems under which Counter-Reformation biblical scholarship labored.

Another part of the synthesis of baroque Catholicism is its acceptance of a certain analogy between an ultramontane approach to papal authority and the rapidly developing absolute monarchies of the various nations of Europe.[39] Here, too, there was a tension, between the secular humanism of Machiavelli and the political theory of Thomas Aquinas. Being the leading theologian of the city of Rome, Bellarmine, as a matter of course, became involved in the discussion. His approach to the question was unique. At one point it called down the wrath of Pope Sixtus V and for centuries prevented Bellarmine's canonization as a saint. As Bellarmine saw it, the pope had an indirect authority over secular rulers rather than direct authority. This did not go along too well with the absolutism of the Council of Trent, but Bellarmine was trying his best to reconcile Thomistic political thought with the Machiavellian maneuvers of Italian politicians at the end of the sixteenth century. Bellarmine could apply his principle one way in dealing with the Republic of Venice and quite a different way in dealing with King James I of England. The amazing thing is that he struggled to explain the whole thing within his great synthesis, but then that was the nature of baroque Catholicism.

Perhaps one of the most telling perceptions into the system of Bellarmine is his dealing with Galileo.[40] Here the tension was between the absolutist approach to scientific truth and the more empirical approach. Bellarmine was fascinated by the innovative scientific discoveries of Galileo, and when Galileo first came to Rome the distinguished cardinal received him warmly. The discussions wore on and Bellarmine maintained his courtesy through it all, but Galileo and his understanding of

39. Franz Xaver Arnold, *Die Staatslehre des Kardinals Bellarmin* (Munich: M. Heuber, 1934); J. C. Murray, "St. Robert Bellarmine on the Indirect Power," *Theological Studies* 9 (1948): 491-535.

40. Richard J. Blackwell, *Galileo, Bellarmine, and the Bible* (Notre Dame, Ind.: University of Notre Dame Press, 1991).

the solar system just did not fit into the baroque synthesis. Happily for Bellarmine Galileo recanted.

Finally we have to return to Bellarmine's work on the theology of grace.[41] An important part of the baroque synthesis is a compromise between the Augustinian theology of salvation by grace and the insistence of humanism that man can save himself. This was fundamental to the difference between the Reformation and the Counter-Reformation. Bellarmine and the Jesuits saw this very clearly. At Louvain Bellarmine had encountered the Augustinian revival with its attempt to recover the biblical concept of grace, so central to the theology of Augustine, and being a faithful student of the Renaissance, he almost immediately suspected this movement in both its Protestant and Catholic forms. In fact, the whole Jesuit Order found the Augustinian concept of grace repugnant, and for several generations waged an unrelenting battle against it. It was while Bellarmine was so influential at Rome that the Jesuits and the Dominicans in Spain became embroiled in a discussion of this problem. The Dominicans, led by Baenez, so well known as the adviser to Saint Theresa of Ávila, had insisted that grace is indeed irresistible and that God by his sovereign grace converts the elect and brings them to salvation. The Jesuits under the leadership of Molina taught that God gives grace to those he knows beforehand will choose him. His somewhat younger contemporary, the Dutch Protestant theologian Arminius, was beginning to teach much the same thing at about the same time. Protestants, of course, know this discussion very well; it was, however, carried on a bit differently in sixteenth-century Spain. There, of course, it centered on what Thomas Aquinas taught. The Jesuits tried their best to make Thomas a supporter of free will, but understandably they were not able to convince the Dominicans.

The controversy came to the Vatican, and Bellarmine prepared a long brief defending the Jesuit position. The Jesuits pleaded that to support the position of Baenez would give too much support to the Protestants. To be sure, the Jesuits had a point, because many humanists such as Erasmus had finally stayed with the Catholic Church and given up their Protestant leanings on just this point. It was, of course, on this issue that Erasmus finally broke with Luther. A salvation achieved by a decision of the free will followed by a life of virtue and good works was much more

41. N. Hens, *Die Augustinusinterpretation des heiligen Robert Bellarmine* (Rome, 1939).

consistent with philosophical humanism than the idea that one is saved by grace through faith.[42] After a long debate, no decision was made. For all practical purposes, however, the Jesuits won, and Baenezianism came to be regarded as a curious Spanish interpretation of Thomistic thought, a sort of sixteenth-century Spanish precursor of Jansenism.

As much as we may want to disagree with Bellarmine, he was a serious theologian who with earnestness and energy addressed himself to the great issues of his day.

2. Preaching Lent in Rome in 1600

As an example of Bellarmine's preaching, let us look at a series of seven sermons he preached in Rome from the first Sunday in Lent to Easter Sunday in 1600.[43] Bellarmine was almost sixty years old when he preached this series. He had already attained the position of premier theologian of the Roman court, and his preaching was received with great respect.

These sermons, never intended for publication, and accordingly only published recently, had been preserved in manuscript form in the hand of the preacher. They obviously were written by Bellarmine as part of his own sermon preparation. This being the case, we cannot expect to gather too much about his technique as a public speaker, except that his primary effort was expended on sermon content rather than oratorical techniques. His eye was always on what he wanted to say rather than on how he was going to say it. This fact alone is no doubt largely responsible for his effectiveness in the pulpit.

The sermons as we have them have no introductions except a simple and very brief statement of the *scopus* of the sermon. This is surely one of the principles of classical literary composition which Bellarmine had learned well. Surely it is one of his work habits which helps explain his unfailing clarity. There are also no carefully worked out conclusions in the manuscripts. This does not mean, of course, that once in the pulpit our cardinal preacher, led by the natural gifts of an orator, did not improvise appropriate introductions or inspiring perorations. As any experi-

---

42. Here, once again, we must be careful to distinguish between philosophical humanism and Christian humanism. See chap. I above.

43. For the text of these sermons, see Robert Bellarmine, *Opera oratoria postuma,* ed. Sebastian Tromp, 9 vols. (Rome: Gregorian University Press, 1945). The references in the text for Bellarmine's sermons in this section and the next two are to this work; the volume number is cited first, followed by the page reference.

enced public speaker knows, the most appropriate introductions are often suggested by the immediate circumstances of arriving in the pulpit. In the same way, the interaction between the preacher and the congregation which develops as the message unfolds often inspires a conclusion far exceeding anything which could have been thought up in the study. But since the evidence we have does not allow us to make too many speculations, let us turn our attention to those things we can discover from the sermon manuscripts themselves.

The first thing which draws our attention is how much this series of Lenten sermons differs from those of Bernardino da Siena we found so interesting at the end of the Middle Ages. That series formed a whole evangelistic campaign as that idea had grown from the founding of the preaching orders. Bernardino's evangelistic preaching had profited from more than two hundred years of preaching experience; while his series may have been preached in the full noonday of the Renaissance, it was the flowering of late medieval preaching. It is a very different matter with Bellarmine's Lenten sermons in Rome in the first year of the seventeenth century. The Italian Renaissance had already spent its force. The age of the Renaissance was now rapidly melding into the age of the baroque. Yet Bellarmine's sermons still have a Renaissance classicism about them. They have learned much from the Renaissance, particularly from the standpoint of literary form. The literary form is clear, direct, and simple.

But one notices something else, something equally characteristic of the Renaissance, and that is the obvious disciplining of these sermons by an appeal to the classics of antiquity. These sermons have been strongly influenced by the Lenten sermons of Leo the Great. What could have been more appropriate for a preacher in Rome at the height of the Counter-Reformation than to return to the sermons of that great pope who had preached Lent more than a thousand years before in that same city? Bellarmine has patently returned to the sermons of Leo and drawn out from them his basic message, namely, that Lent is a time to devote oneself to fasting, prayer, hearing the Word of God, and giving alms. In doing this one prepares oneself to receive the blessings of Christ's saving death and resurrection. Leo normally preached only one sermon at the beginning of Lent, but twelve of these sermons have been preserved. As we saw in our second volume, they all say much the same thing. Bellarmine has spread that message out into the first four sermons of his series. His first sermon is devoted to fasting, his second to prayer, his third to the hearing of God's Word, and his fourth to giving alms.

The last three sermons in the series have a different orientation from the first four. The fifth sermon is for Passion Sunday and takes as its subject the suffering of the Savior. The sixth sermon is for Palm Sunday and focuses on the royalty of Christ which demands the praise of his people. The seventh, for Easter Sunday, treats the meaning of the resurrection. The rather awkward arrangement of Passion Sunday, Palm Sunday, and Easter is demanded by the lectionary. One wonders why there were no sermons for Maundy Thursday or Good Friday, or why the pattern of Leo had not been followed at this point. Leo preached on the passion of Christ twice during Holy Week, the Sunday before Easter and then on Wednesday. No doubt Bellarmine was not completely responsible for the preaching schedule any more than most preachers. On Good Friday the passion narrative was simply read, or at least large portions of it, and this by itself would take a considerable amount of time. A good number of other devotional rites were observed, such as the veneration of the cross, and perhaps it was felt that the heavy ceremonial demands of the occasion precluded a genuine sermon. We have run into this problem before.[44] Be that as it may, the seven sermons taken together make up a festal series of the most important of feasts, the Christian celebration of Passover. Here we have an important example of the genre of festal preaching.

As we have often noticed, it is characteristic of festal preaching that it easily slips away from the exposition of a specific passage of Scripture and gives a more general development of the feast and the themes traditionally associated with it. This is certainly true here. The Gospel selections offered by the lectionary seem almost incidental to the sermons. Centuries before Bellarmine the lectionary selections were probably chosen to reinforce the sorts of Lenten penitential disciplines about which our preacher has spoken. In other words, Bellarmine has probably done a rather good job of discovering the original intention of those who put together the lectionary. This is particularly the case in regard to Leo the Great, as we have noted. But that is something quite different from discovering the original intention of the texts themselves. Bellarmine has been eminently faithful to the teaching of the Council of Trent. He has understood Scripture as the tradition of the Church has understood it, particularly as that traditional understanding has been embodied in the lectionary.

As it happens, one of the devotional disciplines Bellarmine preaches

44. See Old, *Reading and Preaching,* 2:153-60; 2:433; 3:210; and 3:217.

about is listening to the Word of God. The third sermon in the series has for its title *Dominica tertia quadragesima, de verbo Dei.* It takes its text from the Gospel of the day, "Blessed are those who hear the word of God and keep it" (1:211). The preacher announces in his introduction that he intends to take up two aspects of the subject: the excellence and the utility of the Word of God. Its excellence, our preacher tells us, is recognized from the fact that the office of preaching is recognized as the first and most excellent office in the Church.

Here Bellarmine with great care echoes the decrees of the Council of Trent. Christ was the supreme prince of the world and the head not only of all men but of angels as well. This most noble of persons had as his principle — in fact, as his unique office — to preach the Word of God (1:212). It was the same way with all the great leaders of the Church: John the Baptist was above all a voice, a voice crying in the wilderness (Matt. 3:3); the apostle Peter understood that it was the office of the apostle to be set apart "for prayer and the ministry of the Word" (Acts 6:4); the apostle Paul made the point that he was not called to baptize but to preach (I Cor. 1:17). Having made the point that preaching is the primary apostolic ministry, Bellarmine goes on to tell us that it is then the primary office of the bishops since they are the successors of the apostles. Calling our attention to the ancient practice of the preacher to give his sermon while seated in his cathedra while the congregation stood, Bellarmine says this recognizes that it is the responsibility of servants to hear their master. When the bishop preaches from his cathedra, he speaks in the place of Christ (1:212). The congregation in those days used to stand to receive the instructions of their Master. We today, then, ought at least to hear preaching with the greatest reverence, for it is the most excellent of ministries.

In speaking about the utility of the Word of God, Bellarmine draws our attention to three images Scripture uses for the preaching of the Word. The Word of God is the seed from which we are born again, the bread by which we are nourished, and the sword by which we are defended. Referring to several New Testament texts, Luke 8:11, James 1:21, and I Peter 1:23, Bellarmine concludes that it is from hearing the preaching of the Word that faith arises in the hearts of unbelievers and that conversion from sin is brought about in the hearts of believers. Bellarmine is particularly interested in the idea that we are reborn from the Word of God. This plucks a familiar chord for evangelical Protestants, to be sure. Uppermost in his mind is certainly I Peter 1:23, "You have been born anew, not of perishable seed but of imperishable, through the living and abiding word of God." No less important is Luther's favorite text, Romans 10:14-17, "Faith comes from what is heard, and what is heard comes by the preaching of Christ" (v. 17). Obviously the Reformers were not the only ones to have understood the principle.

This champion of the Counter-Reformation goes on to tell us that in the faithful faith and hope are made alive by the Word, while for sinners both faith and hope are dead. Never very far from his polemic against the Reformation, he quickly evokes the text from James that was often used against Luther: "Faith apart from works is dead" (James 2:26), and sets it next to I Peter 1:3, "We have been born anew to a living hope." He draws the conclusion that faith and hope are dead when they do not move toward accomplishing what we believe and hope. With this, to be sure, the Reformers would hardly have disagreed. In fact, they often made exactly the same point. What one finds so beautiful in Bellarmine's words is the clarity and precision with which he puts this important idea. Such clarity only comes with long and concentrated thought, and it is quite obvious that this is what Bellarmine has given this subject which had so embroiled the sixteenth century. If Bellarmine's preaching exemplifies anything, it is the power of clear thinking in the pulpit. What one finds so disappointing is that he seems unaware that Protestant thinkers were capable of an equal refinement in this matter.

Bellarmine has more to say on the seminal quality of preaching. He reminds us of the parable of the mustard seed (Matt. 13:31), which although in outward appearance is the smallest of seeds, produces nevertheless a great tree. This should teach us, Bellarmine says, that simple preaching, without ornament, without subtlety, but yet with warmth and love, has tremendous power. It is in the end love which produces the greatest eloquence.

Bellarmine's manuscript does not provide many sermon illustrations, but here he briefly sketches the story of the simple bishop at the Council of Nicaea who converted the philosopher simply by his obvious love. That is all Bellarmine's manuscript leaves us of a story he surely told at greater length in the pulpit. The editor of the *Opera oratoria* has identified the story as coming from the *Ecclesiastical History* of Rufinus. There are many examples of this in the sermons we have studied. Bellarmine never unfolds his illustrations in his manuscript. His focus is always on his doctrinal and moral teaching. He really believes that it is the Word of God spoken in love which brings salvation to the listener. For the preacher this is the ultimate sincerity.

It is because of the love of the preacher, Bellarmine continues, that even those most knowledgeable in the study of Scripture should go to the sermons of much less scholarly preachers. Even the most learned can profit by the warmth of a loving witness! The preaching of the Word by a devout and loving minister makes the written Word glow (1:215).

Not only does the Word bring us to a new life, but having done so it nourishes us in this new life. It is therefore that Scripture speaks of the Word as bread or sometimes as milk. The prophet Habakkuk spoke about this when he said that the just shall live by faith, and Paul took up the same idea in Romans 1:17, which, as we all know, was the text which was so crucial to Luther. What this text means, Bellarmine tells us, is that the people of God are sustained in their exile by the truths of the faith, which one learns about from the Word of God.[45] Hearing about God's love for us, hearing about the suffering love of God in Christ, kindles in us love for God (1:215). It is in this way that the Word nourishes the Christian life. But then Bellarmine asks why so few preachers actually come up with this kind of nourishing fare for their congregations. The reason is that they are much too concerned with cooking up delicacies of eloquence and learning. They want to appear to be theologians, philosophers, or historians. The true bread of life, as Bellarmine sees it, is the knowledge of salvation, which teaches humility, patience, and charity (1:220). The good preacher is able to feed his congregation with this bread only by the sweat of his brow, only by imploring God for it with tears, prayers, and meditations. But of course, not only must the preacher give this kind of labor to his preaching the Word; it is just as much the responsibility of the hearers of the Word to chew it and digest it. It is appropriate that after feasting on the Word one sleep on it, that is, appropriate it through prayer and meditation. One needs to ask oneself, are these things not true which I have heard? Certainly, they are most true! Then why do I not do them? It is in this way that one grows strong and healthy through the preaching and hearing of the Word.

Finally Bellarmine considers the Word as a sword. He takes up Ephesians 6:17, which tells us that the Word of God is the sword of the Spirit. To this he adds the words of Hebrews 4:12, "For the word of God is living and active, sharper than any two-edged sword." The two edges,

---

45. Bellarmine's understanding of the text is quite different from Luther's. For Luther faith is a personal relation of trust toward Christ. It is much closer to what Bellarmine means by love. For Bellarmine faith is obviously understood as correct doctrine.

our cardinal preacher tells us, are the threats of God on one side and the promises of God on the other. These threats and promises marvelously defend us from all temptations. Not only do they repel the thrusts as a shield, but they even kill the adversary. For the adversaries are either inordinate fears or inordinate loves. A thorough consideration of both the threats and promises of God effectively removes these adversaries. The promises of God are far richer than all our temporal loves; temporal fears are nothing compared to the threats of God (1:221).

This sermon on the spiritual discipline of hearing the Word of God shows how much the champion of the Counter-Reformation had learned from the Reformation. It helped him understand his own Catholicism in a much more profound way. And the graciousness of the man is discerned in the fact that he seems to have no hesitation in letting it show.

But despite the many excellent qualities of Bellarmine's Lenten preaching, one thing is troubling, and that is its unmistakable Pelagian tendency. The late Middle Ages had more and more gone in the direction of an understanding of salvation in terms of an *imitatio Christi* rather than as a vicarious atonement. There is a tremendous difference between these Lenten sermons and the series of Holy Week sermons of John Calvin which we studied in the previous chapter. Bellarmine's doctrine of vicarious atonement is nowhere near as well developed as Calvin's. Apparently for Bellarmine it was not a matter of Christ's doing for us what we could not do for ourselves, but rather a matter of Christ's leading the way and our following in his footsteps. Christ was Savior not so much because he bore our sins and suffered in our place but because he set an example of redemption through suffering. In Bellarmine's sermon for Passion Sunday, he treats fully his understanding of how Christ's passion brings about our salvation (1:229-37). He quotes John 14:6, "I am the way, and the truth, and the life," and then explains that those who consider this and are illumined and inspired by it enter into a life of imitating Christ, and therefore achieve eternal life with Christ (1:237).

However much one might regret the Pelagian tendency of these sermons, one must admit that these outstanding sermons are an example of how a preacher who has something to say has a way of getting our attention. Bellarmine's basic earnestness always comes through, and this earnestness compels us to listen.

3. Preaching Ministry in Capua

Shortly after Bellarmine preached these sermons in Rome, he was appointed archbishop of Capua, one of the most important sees of southern Italy. This gave him the opportunity to preach from the cathedral pulpit Sunday by Sunday and exercise the preaching ministry as he understood it should be exercised. He had always taught that preaching was the primary ministry of the bishop. In practice very few bishops of that age preached, even though the Council of Trent had acknowledged that this was indeed the bishop's first responsibility. One often gets the impression that what the theologians of Trent really had in mind was that true preaching had to be licensed by a bishop. Only the bishop really had the authority to preach, but he could delegate that authority. The important thing was that there be episcopal authority behind the preacher. However others might have honored this principle in the breach, Bellarmine now had a chance to preach with full episcopal authority and show by example how the bishop should exercise his ministry.

During his first year in Capua, Bellarmine preached through the Epistles of the Roman lectionary. That he should have known anything of the ancient Capuan Epistles is highly unlikely.[46] The second year he preached the Gospels of the lectionary. The third year he preached through the Sermon on the Mount in a *lectio continua*. He began the series on All Saints' Day and continued each Sunday, and also on several feast days and saints' days, until Quinquagesima Sunday, 20 February 1605. The following Sunday being the first Sunday in Lent, a special Lenten preacher took over. A few days later Pope Clement VIII died and Bellarmine left for Rome, never to return. Twenty sermons had been preached in the series, but the preacher had not yet completed the fifth chapter of Matthew. That he should have done this, which so many of the Reformers had done, even following them in the selection of the Sermon on the Mount, is particularly interesting.

One wonders what led him to make this departure. Had he so often preached on the traditional pericopes that they had become stale to him and he was eager to try something new? Had he felt that as bishop he had the necessary authority to depart from the lectionary? Perhaps he was aware that many of the Fathers had preached a *lectio continua* and he wanted to try his hand at it. As we shall see, when Bellarmine wrote down

46. See Old, *Reading and Preaching*, 3:149-50.

a list of the great sermons of the past, an amazing proportion of them were *lectio continua* sermons. If he was favorably impressed by the sermons, he was probably favorable toward their method. Or perhaps he knew that the Reformers had done this with particular success and he wanted to see if the same thing would work in Capua. One can only speculate as to his reason, or reasons. Surely the least one can draw from it is that he recognized the liturgical integrity of preaching the *lectio continua*.

Our cardinal preacher went through his *lectio continua* very slowly, as the following schedule indicates (6:13).

1.	Introductory sermon	1 Nov.	All Saints' Day
2.	Blessed are the poor	7 Nov.	22nd Sunday after Pentecost
3.	Blessed are the meek	14 Nov.	23rd Sunday after Pentecost
4.	Blessed are those who mourn	21 Nov.	24th Sunday after Pentecost
5.	Blessed are those who hunger	28 Nov.	1st Sunday in Advent
6.	Same text applied to Saint Andrew	30 Nov.	Feast of Saint Andrew
7.	Blessed are the merciful	5 Dec.	2nd Sunday in Advent
8.	Blessed are the pure in heart	8 Dec.	Feast of the Immaculate Conception
9.	Blessed are the peacemakers	12 Dec.	3rd Sunday in Advent
10.	Blessed are the persecuted	19 Dec.	4th Sunday in Advent
11.	The salt of the earth	27 Dec.	Feast of Saint John
12.	Not to abolish the law	1 Jan.	Feast of the Circumcision
13.	Unless your righteousness	6 Jan.	Feast of the Epiphany
14.	You shall not kill	9 Jan.	1st Sunday after Epiphany
15.	You shall not kill (continued)	16 Jan.	2nd Sunday after Epiphany
16.	You shall not kill (continued)	23 Jan.	3rd Sunday after Epiphany
17.	You shall not commit adultery	30 Jan.	4th Sunday after Epiphany
18.	A bill of divorce	6 Feb.	Septuagesima
19.	You shall not bear false witness	13 Feb.	Sexagesima
20.	An eye for an eye	20 Feb.	Quinquagesima

Several interesting things appear in this list. Apparently, only on one occasion did he not follow his *lectio continua,* and that was Christmas. There is no sermon for Christmas Eve or for Christmas Day. Nor are there sermons for the two Sundays following Christmas, 26 December and 2 January. One would surely expect that the archbishop of Capua would preach on Christmas, but if he did he must have chosen another text. He did preach from his *lectio continua* on the feast of Saint John, although it fell on a Monday, and the feast of the Circumcision, although it fell on a Saturday. One can well imagine that he would have been more than eager to preach the kind of festal sermon at Christmas for which Leo the Great was so famous. On the other hand, one notices here, as elsewhere, that Bellarmine does not often preach more than once a week. A second very interesting point is that Bellarmine often preached his *lectio continua* on some major feasts. For the feast of the Epiphany (6 Jan.), the feast of the Immaculate Conception (8 Dec.), and the feast of Saint Andrew (30 Nov.), he preached his *lectio continua.* On these occasions he read the usual Epistles and Gospels of the lectionary, as he sometimes notes in his sermons. In several cases, such as the feast of Saint Andrew when he preached on Andrew as an example of the blessedness of those who hunger and thirst for righteousness, and the feast of the Immaculate Conception when he preached on "Blessed are the pure in heart," Bellarmine finds the text offered by the *lectio continua* particularly appropriate to the occasion. Those who have followed a *lectio continua* know how this often happens.

In a careful reading of the sermons themselves, one is very favorably impressed. They are among the most edifying that I have read! The manuscripts he left behind indicate that he was a serious preacher who intended to interpret the Scriptures for the faithful Christian of his time. Let us look at some of the characteristics of his pulpit ministry as we find it in this series.

Above all, one notices that these sermons are marked by a lucid exegesis. At some points it is better than at others, but we must remember that this is not a published collection of sermons but rather the private manuscripts of a preacher who preached at least once a week and at the same time was presiding over a large and important archbishopric. Given the kind of documents we have, we should not expect brilliant exegesis in every sermon. When he is at his best, however, he is excellent! One of the exegetical methods he uses particularly well is the elaboration of a biblical concept by the use of parallel passages. Bellarmine often cultivates a biblical idea such as mercy by digging into other passages of Scripture. Preaching on the text "Blessed are the merciful," he discusses those great affirmations on mercy found in Psalm 103. The mercy of God is the pattern of Christian mercy, and our cardinal preacher sets out the nature of that mercy in its height and depth, in its patience and long-suffering, in all its breadth and width (6:105). After quoting Psalm 103:17, "The steadfast love of the LORD is from everlasting to everlasting," he comments that God's mercy begins before all time with our predestination and ends in the last everlasting day with our glorification. God's steadfast love leads us in a long journey which begins with nothingness and finally arrives at the *summum bonum,* the highest good (6:106). God is long-suffering; as the psalmist says, "The LORD is merciful and gracious, slow to anger and abounding in steadfast love" (Ps. 103:8). God's mercy is such that he not only forgives our sins but keeps us from returning to our sin, for as we find in Psalm 103:12, "As far as the East is from the West, so far does he remove our transgressions from us" (6:107). Then Bellarmine tells us that God's mercy by its very nature is directed toward us: "As a father pities his children, so the LORD pities those who fear him" (Ps. 103:13). God's mercy is full and abundant (6:109). God's mercy has consequences; that is, it is effective in our lives, as we find in Psalm 103:3-5, "Who heals all your diseases, . . . who crowns you with steadfast love and mercy, . . . who satisfies you with good as long as you live." The mercy of God is far more than a divine virtue, it is a divine force of blessing in the lives of his people.

Another place where Bellarmine is at his best in his exegesis is his sermon on "Blessed are the peacemakers, for they shall be called sons of God." In trying to explain why peacemakers should be called the sons of God, our preacher collects an array of parallel passages which throw a most interesting light on the subject. First he calls on that curious text from Psalm 82:6, "I say, 'You are gods, sons of the Most High, all of you.'" The passage, according to Bellarmine, refers to princes who participate in the power of rulership. This rulership puts them in the place of divinity, as if they were God. Now, since the principal end of rulership is the peace of the peoples, the first responsibility of princes is to be peacemakers. It is peacemakers, Bellarmine suggests, who are the real princes (6:126). In the end, it is to these peacemakers that God subjects all other powers, whether they be demonic powers, natural powers, or heavenly powers. Next our preacher calls on two texts from Job (Job 1:6 and 33:7) and that marvelous line, "Where were you . . . when all the morning stars sang together, and all the sons of God shouted for joy?" (Job 38:7). These texts suggest that peacemakers are called the sons of God because they are like angels, perfect in their obedience to the will of God (6:127). Thirdly, Bellarmine suggests that the peacemakers are called sons of God because they are like Christ, for the apostle Paul tells us that Christ is a peacemaker. He has made peace through the blood of his cross (Col. 1:20) (6:128). Finally, peacemakers are called sons of God because they are like God himself. As we so often find it in Scripture, God is a God of peace (Rom. 15:33 and 16:20), or again, God brings about peace (II Cor. 5:19). Many sons are not similar to their fathers, Bellarmine admits, but other sons truly reflect their father's image and are quickly recognized. That is the way it is with peacemakers (6:128-29). It is therefore that they are called the sons of God.

Another exegetical method Bellarmine frequently uses is to show the text in its context. In his sermon on the first beatitude, "Blessed are the poor in spirit, for theirs is the kingdom of heaven," he discusses exactly what is meant by the poor in spirit. He notes that certain heretics who despise evangelical poverty claim that this really means those who are afflicted. This cannot be so because that is the subject of the last beatitude; that is, the context does not support this meaning. Many understand it to mean those who are lowly in spirit, that is, the humble, those who are free of pride, but according to Bellarmine, that cannot be so for that is too close to the meaning of the second beatitude. Besides, when Luke gives his version of the Beatitudes, he contrasts the poor with the rich rather than with the proud (6:52). A careful and thoughtful reading of the text is the best exegesis, and Bellarmine often does this most effectively.

This simple reading of the text can be very effective even if one is only reading one of the standard translations, be it the Revised Standard Version or the Latin Vulgate, and it is the Latin Vulgate on which Bellarmine prepares his sermons. That, of course, was consistent with the decrees of the Council of Trent, as we have had several occasions to remark. The Latin Vulgate for Catholics was to be the authoritative text of Scripture. That the Scriptures were authoritative in their original languages, on the other hand, had been maintained by the Reformation. This was of the essence of the new approach to the study of sacred Scripture which had set the foundations of the Reformation. Bellarmine was no doubt well aware of the importance of studying the Scriptures in their original languages to the Protestants, and he had, to be sure, given careful attention to the study of both Greek and Hebrew. In spite of all this, he does not seem to prepare his sermons on the basis of the original Greek text, much less the original Hebrew. Only on rare occasions does he refer to the insights given by the biblical languages.

In his sermon on the first beatitude we have one of those rare occasions. He tells us that the word πτωχός means beggar (6:53; another passage is found on 6:68). Here, as elsewhere, one gets the impression that Bellarmine uses his Greek on occasion to settle an argument or make clear a fine point, but he is not inspired by being face-to-face, as it were, with the original Greek or Hebrew text. There is no question that the Vulgate is one of the great translations of Scripture, but it is a translation, not the original text. The sixteenth century had a passion for the pure, original text. Sixteenth-century scholars wanted to read the text in the original language, and this, of course, is what made the expositions of the Reformers so luminous. Reading the Scriptures in the original languages gave the Reformers a sense of freshness and immediacy in the study of Scripture which had the effect of breathing life into their preaching. Bellarmine preached on the Latin Vulgate text, and although he very conscientiously studied the Latin text, and undoubtedly got much of the original meaning from it, he still was working with a translation.

If his exegesis missed the urgency of studying the text in the original languages which had been so essential to the Reformers, he did get a sense for the value of the literal meaning of the text. That was another fundamental principle of Reformation preaching. Bellarmine is quite willing to speak of the four senses of the text as were the preachers of the Middle Ages, but the heavy weight of his exegesis is literal. In fact, he seems particularly well balanced in this matter. He obviously knows the more elaborate allegorical interpretations of such masters as Gregory of Nyssa, but he does not seem to be interested in pursuing this kind of interpretation, at least not in this series of sermons.

Bellarmine gives much attention to the history of exegesis. To be sure, the great Counter-Reformation cardinal, devoted as he was to upholding the decrees of the Council of Trent, understood this not so much as the history of exegesis as he understood it as tradition. Revelation, for Trent, was to be found both in Scripture and in tradition. In fact, for Bellarmine Scripture needed to be completed by tradition; Scripture alone was not sufficient for a complete knowledge of divine truth. Not all Catholic theologians today would agree with this understanding of the relation of Scripture and tradition. Bellarmine stands at one end of the discussion of the matter, even among Catholic theologians. His preaching reflects the tremendous authority he gives to tradition.

We notice that Bellarmine gave special attention to the way tradition had interpreted the Scriptures. One often gets the impression that in his preparation of the text he has consulted six or eight Church Fathers. In his sermon on "Blessed are those who hunger and thirst after righteousness," he begins by telling us of the interpretation of Hilary, Jerome, Augustine, Ambrose, Leo, and Bernard (6:82). Both Hilary and Jerome had done commentaries on the Gospel of Matthew, and so it seems more than likely that Bellarmine would have consulted their commentaries. Augustine had done a series of sermons on the Sermon on the Mount. Ambrose had done sermons on Luke and had of course treated the version of the Sermon on the Mount found in that Gospel. Any conscientious interpreter of Scripture in those days would have consulted these same sources. The Protestants had done the same thing, of course. They were more critical in their use of the Fathers, but they recognized many of them as faithful interpreters of Scripture. Bellarmine was not as critical, but he does recognize that the Fathers often had opposing interpretations of particular passages of Scripture. A bit further on in the same sermon he tells us of a different interpretation by Rupert of Deutz (6:83). In the sermon on "Blessed are the pure in heart," Bellarmine tells us that some of the Greeks such as John Chrysostom and Theophylactus understand by the pure in heart those who are chaste (6:111). Others such as Augustine understand them to be the simple, the straightforward. Still others such as Jerome, Hilary, and Bernard understand them to be those who are free from all sin (6:112). As Bellarmine sees it, all three opinions are correct. Even at that, they do not fully explain the text, and Bellarmine goes on to give us his interpretation. As one finds Bellarmine seeking out the interpretation of Scripture developed by the Fathers and even the medieval Schoolmen, it really seems very well balanced.

One notices that Bellarmine, no less than the Protestants, had a definite group of Church Fathers which he preferred. Augustine and John Chrysostom are among his favorites. Gregory of Nyssa, on the other hand, had published a very fine series of sermons on the Beatitudes, and from one reference it is clear that our cardinal preacher was familiar with the work. The work is very much under the influence of Neoplatonic philosophy, and Bellarmine seems to have been little influenced by it. The Reformers would have agreed with him. As they saw it, Neoplatonism had influenced all too many of the Fathers and had often misled them, even the best of them. We

211

shall have occasion to say more of this, but for the moment we want to point out that Bellarmine made a definite selection of the Fathers, and, no less than the Reformers, tended to move away from those who were most heavily influenced by Neoplatonism, although he would never have agreed that those Fathers had been misled by Neoplatonism.

Let us look briefly at the works Bellarmine seems to have understood to mediate the tradition, particularly the tradition of interpretation as it related to the Sermon on the Mount. First of all, Augustine preached a series of sermons on the Sermon that in fact may well be regarded as Bellarmine's inspiration. He mentions it at the beginning of his first sermon and frequently throughout the whole series (6:43 and passim). He mentions Jerome's commentary on the Gospel of Matthew a few paragraphs later, and refers to it frequently from then on (6:44). He apparently values Ambrose as one of the most reliable sources of tradition, because he frequently consults his commentary on Luke to see what he says about that Gospel's version of the Sermon (6:44). Chromatius, the late-fourth-century bishop of Aquileia, left a series of sermons on the Beatitudes which Bellarmine knows but refers to only once (6:45). Chrysostom's sermons on Matthew are referred to frequently. They were greatly admired throughout the sixteenth century by Protestant and Catholic alike. In the second sermon Bellarmine lists the opinion of several Fathers: Basil, Jerome, Ambrose, Anselm, Bede, and Bernard (6:53). One notices that three medieval Christian writers are mentioned right along with the Fathers of the ancient Church. In fact, Bernard's sermon for All Saints' Day is often quoted in regard to the Beatitudes. Bernard was one of Bellarmine's favorite sources for acquainting himself with the tradition, and his admiration for Bernard was typical of almost everyone in the sixteenth and seventeenth centuries. No one represented the "traditional" interpretation of the liturgical Gospels and Epistles quite so thoroughly as Bernard. And as we mentioned above, Gregory of Nyssa's sermons on the Beatitudes are mentioned once but otherwise seem to have been ignored by our preacher (6:69).

The sermon for the feast of Saint Andrew is particularly interesting in regard to the question of tradition. In the early third century there had been an apocryphal work on the ministry and martyrdom of Saint Andrew, and in later centuries other works had been spun out of it. A rather fully developed account of the apostle's trial before the Roman governor in Patras and his martyrdom by crucifixion is recounted. The actual historical value of the work is not known, since the original version has been lost. Bellarmine got the text of one of these secondary versions, and in his sermon comments on it almost as though it were Scripture (6:91ff.). In addition to this, he has studied sermons by Peter Damian and Bernard of Clairvaux to acquaint himself with the tradition on the subject of Saint Andrew (6:92 and 94). It is this sort of thing that Protestants objected to most strongly. They were perfectly happy to hear how the different Fathers interpreted Scripture, but when third-century traditions were treated as having the same authority, or even almost the same authority, as Scripture itself, then the Reformers were very unhappy.

Bellarmine's series on the Sermon on the Mount shows how much medieval Scholasticism survived in the Counter-Reformation pulpit. This was true in relation both to what was taught and to the homiletical form in which these teachings were conveyed. The whole effect of these sermons is to systematize the teaching of Jesus found in the Sermon on the Mount along the lines of Scholastic theology. The preaching orders of the Middle Ages had produced several manuals on moral theology. In volume 3 we spoke of Guillaume Peraldus and his *Summa* on moral theology, an important preaching tool from the thirteenth century on down through the Renaissance. It represented a particularly Scholastic approach to preaching and served to center preaching on moral catechism. It was the same way with the treatment Thomas Aquinas gave moral virtues in his *Summa theologica*. What finally has to be said is that Bellarmine's sermons on the Beatitudes end up being a series of sermons on the virtues of evangelical poverty, humility, long-suffering, justice, mercy, purity, tranquillity, and patience.

From the introductory sermon on, we find the assumption that the essence of beatitude is the vision of God, and the vision of God is the *summum bonum* of the philosopher (6:49).[47] Neither Aristotle nor Thomas Aquinas is mentioned here, but the whole work is permeated with the Scholastic attempt to use classical philosophy to support Christian moral theology. At times Thomas is quoted, but his influence is much more pervasive than these quotations would suggest (6:56, 75, 86, 107). The whole method is Scholastic, particularly the method of gleaning proof texts from the Fathers. To be sure, a study of the appropriate commentaries from the Fathers was much more consistent with the Renaissance use of patristic studies, but to gather sayings here and there

---

47. "Visio enim Dei est essentia beatitudinis, ad quam consequuntur omnia bona iam dicta. Visio Dei est summum bonum. . . ."

from one classic after another in the manner of Peter Lombard's *Sentences* or Gratian's *Decretals* was thoroughly Scholastic. A great part of these classics of medieval theology is devoted to the lining up of authorities. Scripture comes first, then the Fathers, and then the most enlightened of the pagan philosophers. That is what we find Bellarmine doing. The way he uses the Fathers and even the pagan philosophers or the saints and scholars of the Middle Ages is amazingly reminiscent of Scholasticism.

The way he delineates his thoughts in these sermons is thoroughly Scholastic. A central theme is taken, such as evangelical poverty, mercy, or peacemaking, and divided into two, three, four, or even six or seven points. Then these points are divided further into subpoints. Each point brings out a particular dimension of the main theme. Here we have once again the thematic preaching developed by Scholasticism. Anyone who has read much from the philosophical or theological treatises of the Middle Ages is aware of how skillfully those scholars could pursue a subject in this method. This method is still very much in use today. Every time we set down an outline, we are using a tool bequeathed to us by the Middle Ages. Neither in the biblical nor the patristic period were people nearly that systematic, and consequently when one applies this method to biblical or patristic material it often mangles it. It often fails to get the point of the sacred text it tries to interpret. The Christian humanists and the Reformers who followed their lead were, on the other hand, becoming more sensitive to the way the biblical writers had used the language. Sometimes we find Bellarmine following the new learning, but at other times he falls back into the old Scholastic habits.

If Bellarmine's sermons are filled with references to both biblical and patristic authorities and thus continue the practice of the Schoolmen, they also continue the Middle Ages' practice of giving exempla. Never had Christian preaching used anything like the examples, the illustrative stories, and anecdotes that became so popular with the sermons of the preaching orders during the late Middle Ages. Thomas Aquinas and other preachers of Scholasticism may have used effective exempla, but by the end of the Middle Ages the practice had been abused considerably. Luther's famous ridicule of sermons about blue ducks was far from unjustified. Bellarmine's exempla, on the other hand, are disciplined, one might even say chaste. They are not stories to entertain; they are not spicy tales to make drab material palatable. They are exempla in a very profound sense. We have already noticed that when Bellarmine preaches the passion, he understands it as the pattern of the Christian life. The Christian life is for Bellarmine an *imitatio Christi*. Christ's death on the cross is the ultimate exemplum. But in the same way, the lives of the saints are exempla as well. The setting forth of the exempla becomes one of the preacher's major tasks. When Bellarmine preaches on the crucifixion of Saint Andrew, he is giving an example of how one follows the way of the cross. One is crucified just as Jesus was. When one tells the story of Saint Elizabeth of Hungary, the queen who embraced evangelical poverty, one is giving an example of how one follows in the way of the cross. She was an example of self-denial, and that is the essence of the cross.

The Middle Ages had developed a very rich hagiographical literature, and this was quite natural the more that age emphasized an *imitatio Christi* soteriology. We have already spoken of the Christology of Abelard which tried to understand the death of Christ as a moral example, and of Thomas à Kempis and his understanding of the imitation of Christ. This approach to understanding the cross had strong implications for preaching. The frequent use of exempla had a sort of ideological integrity in the Counter-Reformation pulpit, just as it had in the medieval pulpit. In fact, the exempla were so important that sometimes one gets the impression that a sermon was made up of three parts: the quotation of authorities, the giving of reasons, and the recounting of examples (cf. 6:69).

In the sermon on purity of heart, Bellarmine mentions several passages from Bonaventure's life of Saint Francis which speak of how he was an example of the purity of heart of which Jesus spoke in the Sermon on the Mount (6:118-19). Here, as always in Bellarmine's manuscript sermons, the exempla are merely noted, but they were no doubt recounted in the pulpit in considerably more detail. One can well imagine that when the sermon was actually preached, it was told with all the charm with which Bonaventure himself told of the sanctity of the *Poverello*. Then another story occurs to Bellarmine, one Jerome tells of Paul the Hermit that would not recommend itself to a contemporary congregation unless it were told with tongue in cheek. In fact, the story suggests that both Bellarmine and his congregation may have regarded it as a bit of humor. But then after a bit of humor our preacher turns to the sublime exemplum of purity, the Blessed Virgin Mary. It happens that this sermon on "Blessed are the pure in heart" was prepared to be preached on the feast of the Immaculate Conception (6:119-20).

Not all of Bellarmine's exempla were hagiographical. He comes up with some beautiful specimens of mendicant sermon exempla as well. One of the best is in his sermon on the blessedness of those who are persecuted. His point is that when persecution comes, then it becomes clear who God's people really are. It is like walking along a road, Bellarmine tells us, and seeing a dog following along. It is not always clear who the master of the dog is. When a fork in the road comes, however, and one of the travelers turns off to the right and the dog follows off in the same direction, then it is clear to which master the dog belongs. So it is with those who follow the way of the cross.

One more thing needs to be said about these sermons, and that has to do with how the baroque spirit interpreted medieval asceticism. The asceticism of the Hellenistic world allied itself with Christianity quite early, even if it is clear that Jesus himself was not an ascetic and that the New Testament does not teach asceticism. Among early Christians, however, there were a number of devoted ascetics. Origen is one of the most striking examples. With him it was accentuated by the influence of Neoplatonism. In fact, asceticism is far more legitimately the child of Neoplatonism than of either Christianity or Judaism. One might well say that the Hellenistic world was infatuated with asceticism, and many Christians, even very early in the history of the Church, came under its influence. As classical civilization crumbled, its heirs quite commonly adopted a *contemptus mundi* approach to life. They fled the decaying world, entered the monastery, and meditated on the city of God. As the barbarians more and more took over, asceticism became increasingly the Christian stance.

Some Christians, on the other hand, began to find more positive dimensions of worldly life as civilization began to rebound in the High Middle Ages. The Franciscans are supposed to have led the way in this, and yet they retained much of the old asceticism. Then the Renaissance began to revel in the delights of this world. With the Reformation asceticism was repudiated, but its approach was quite different from that of the Renaissance. There was never any question of reveling in sensuous pleasures, no matter how refined they might be. As the Reformers saw it, asceticism was not the only way to a sober and serious Christian life. Since it was not taught in Scripture, the Reformers denied its claims on the Christian. Marriage and family life, the business world, scientific inquiry, and the affairs of state were increasingly regarded as legitimate spheres of the Christian life. The Reformation found a very different approach to the Christian life in its study of the Scriptures.[48]

---

48. See above in this volume, Calvin's sermons on Micah, as well as his sermons on the Beatitudes, pp. 94-121.

The Reformers admitted that many of the most ancient Fathers had taught asceticism, but this was one place where they had been more influenced by their Hellenistic culture than by the teaching of Christ and the apostles. In short, asceticism, as the Reformers looked at it, may well have found its way into tradition, but it was not taught by Scripture.

The Sermon on the Mount would obviously be one place in Scripture where one could test out this Protestant theory. Perhaps that is one reason why Bellarmine wanted to study the Sermon with his congregation. What is interesting about these sermons is that in his exposition of the Sermon Bellarmine seems to recognize that a thoroughgoing ascetic interpretation does not really do justice to the text. On the other hand, when he calls on the tradition, he comes out teaching an ascetic approach to life. One notices this tension in his sermons on "Blessed are the poor in spirit" and "Blessed are those who mourn."

In actual fact, the Counter-Reformation was anything but ascetic. The papal court in those days was noted for its sumptuousness. A conscientious prelate such as Bellarmine had qualms of conscience about arriving at great ecclesiastical affairs with the customary retinue. He is supposed to have had hesitations about maintaining his household in princely style. Yet, in spite of their hesitations, typical Counter-Reformation prelates supported this lifestyle because it went along with the absolutism that was the key to the whole age. Bellarmine preached asceticism, but Caravaggio, Titian, Palladio, Rubens, and above all Bernini expressed the spirit of the Counter-Reformation in the luxuries of baroque art. The Jesuits built splendid monumental churches, of which the Church of the Gesu in Rome is only the first example. Filled with sculpture, covered with marble, and crowned with an illusionistic ceiling, this church tries to speak of the glories of heaven in terms of the wealth of this world. It is surprising that in such a building an ascetic type of Christianity should be taught.

Surely one of the most ambiguous works in the history of art is Bernini's sculpture of the ecstasy of Saint Theresa. Theresa was an ascetic, and yet her spiritual glory is depicted in the most sensuous of artistic expressions. This is typical of that age. The baroque spirit dramatized asceticism. It was a very dramatic age, as we have said, and it took great delight in making heroes and heroines of the saints. The asceticism of the saints made them spiritual champions worthy of firing the zeal and charging the emotion of a very worldly culture.

Bellarmine's interpretation of the Sermon on the Mount was an honest attempt to do systematic expository preaching. The preacher had the purest of intentions as he worked away at his series of sermons, but the tradition he so dearly loved was so ponderous that the message just never got out.

4. Essay on Preaching

It was after a long and honored preaching ministry that Cardinal Bellarmine put down on paper a short essay on preaching, *De ratione formandae concionis.* The essay was not published until recently, and the editor of *Opera oratoria,* Sebastian Tromp, makes no suggestion as to why it might have been written (cf. 1:140ff.). According to Tromp, it had to have been written after 1613; that is, Bellarmine was over seventy years old when he wrote it. Although it is very brief, it gives us some insights into the rationale behind the ministry of the Word as it was understood by the Counter-Reformation.

With his appreciation for order and purpose, Cardinal Bellarmine begins his essay by telling us that there are two reasons for preaching. He usually began his sermons by defining the *scopus* of the sermon, and he begins this essay by giving us the *scopus* of preaching in general. First, preaching should teach what people ought to know of divine teaching concerning the virtues which ought to be cultivated and the vices which should be avoided. Second, preaching should move people to follow the virtues they have been taught (1:145).[49] No doubt behind this statement is the well-known Franciscan maxim that preaching is to deal with "vices and virtues, punishment and glory." As we will see, the Council of Trent made this dictum its own.[50] In other words, the preaching of the Counter-Reformation is geared toward teaching Christian morals and doctrine and persuading people to live according to it (1:145). In reading through Bellarmine's sermons, it is clear that while he is concerned about teaching correct doctrine, he is more concerned about instilling pious practices. When he gets into the pulpit, Bellarmine is above all a moral catechist.

We should notice here that he tells us a sermon should not only teach but also persuade. The Counter-Reformation gave high billing to

49. "Finis christiani concianatoris esse debet docere fideliter, quae populum oporteat vel deceat scire ex doctrina divina, et simul, movere ad virtutes consequendas et vitia fugienda."

50. Frederick J. McGinness, *Right Thinking and Sacred Oratory in Counter-Reformation Rome* (Princeton: Princeton University Press, 1995), pp. 29-61.

persuasion. The art of preaching was the art of persuasion. It was therefore that Christian preachers turned especially to Cicero to learn that art which the teachers of rhetoric had so carefully cultivated.

The literary form of the panegyric had, at least in certain circles, influenced Christian preaching in late antiquity. When those such as Gregory of Nazianzus sought to bring literary culture to the Christian pulpit surveyed the literary forms of Hellenistic culture, they chose the panegyric. If one had to borrow one of the pagan literary forms, it was surely the most well suited. Its purpose was to celebrate. But when the Counter-Reformation turned to the literary culture of the ancient world to borrow elegance for the pulpit, it found a very different literary model. It turned not to the panegyric of the feast day but to the orations of the law court.[51] Cicero, the lawyer, the master persuader, taught the Counter-Reformation its pulpit artistry. Sermons became orations. By the derivation of the word, an oration is an appeal. The oration of antiquity took shape in the court of law, where the object was to convince the jurors. The Reformation had made the Counter-Reformation preacher keenly interested in the pulpit as a place where one could persuade the Christian people of Europe to remain faithful to the old ways.

Regarding the actual preparation of a sermon, Bellarmine tells us, the first thing a preacher needs to do is figure out the scope his sermon should have as a whole and then how its different parts fit in (1:145).[52] Having decided that, he needs to gather together the reasons, applications, and examples which are helpful in achieving his purpose (1:145).[53] When it comes to teaching, it is not enough to repeat the words of the Gospel, nor to use the text as a pretext to discuss whatever one wishes, but rather one must search out the genuine and the literal sense of the passage. From there one needs to speak of the dogmas of the faith and the rules for living that have been developed by the Church. "What one must do as a preacher is to preach what the Holy Spirit through these words

---

51. John O'Malley, who has written so many important works on the preaching of the Counter-Reformation, has come up with a somewhat different view in his *Praise and Blame in Renaissance Rome: Rhetoric, Doctrine, and Reform in the Sacred Orators of the Papal Courts, c. 1450-1521* (Durham, N.C.: Duke University Press, 1979).

52. "Quare necesse est, ut qui est concionaturus, primum omnium sibi praefigat scopum quo dirigat totam sciam actionem et singulas partes."

53. "Ac propterea colligam rationes, utilitates, exempla et alia quae ad hunc finem obtinendum juvabunt."

54. ". . . docere quod Spiritus Sanctus per ea verba doceri voluit."

wishes to be taught" (1:146).[54] Bellarmine, the great theologian, has given us here an intriguing formulation. It certainly has something to recommend it. One assumes that he is trying to get around a sort of literalistic misunderstanding of Scripture all too often found among those who insist too narrowly on the literal sense of Scripture. One can hardly overlook the fact that this appears to be a deliberate challenge to the often repeated formula, "to preach what the original author intended to preach." Bellarmine evidently wants to allow for something more than the literal sense. He is definitely leaving the door open for a spiritual sense, but then he does not encourage us to use the four senses of Scripture as they have traditionally been developed. One can only regret that he did not develop his thoughts more fully at this point.

When it comes to moving the people to seek after virtue, which is the second end of preaching, it is not enough, according to Bellarmine, to rail at sinners and lash them with the tongue. Vain harangues sometimes terrify the simple, but they are laughed at by the wise. What one needs to do in a sermon is to give solid reasons which the preacher has deduced from divine revelation and personal meditation and experience. To get this message across with power so that people are genuinely moved, nothing is more helpful than examples, illustrations, and appropriate similes.

Bellarmine goes on to say that three things are required for those who would have a fruitful pulpit ministry: zeal, wisdom, and eloquence. Our cardinal preacher gives us a marvelous biblical figure for this. He tells us that this was symbolized by the tongues of fire which appeared above the apostles on the Day of Pentecost. It was then that they were created preachers. The heat of this Pentecostal fire points to zeal, the splendor to wisdom, and the form of tongues to eloquence (1:146ff.).[55]

As children of the twenty-first century, we might well pause and admire this bit of medieval symbolism. It may be quite foreign to our way of thinking, but when one contemplates it, one begins to realize what a high doctrine of preaching it assumes. It shows preaching to be a divine anointing, a charisma conferred by the pouring out of the Holy Spirit. Not only are the spiritual gifts of love and zeal the gifts of the Holy Spirit,

---

55. "Tria sunt necessaria ei qui utiliter concionari velit: zelus Dei sive spiritus et fervor caritatis, sapientia, et eloquentia, quae tria significabant linguae igneae, quae super Apostolos apparuerunt, cum a Deo crearentur concionatores primi evangelici; ardor ignis zelum, splendor sapientam, forma linguae eloquentiam designabat."

but wisdom and eloquence are as well. What is particularly interesting is that wisdom is understood as a charisma, a divinely given gift.

From this Bellarmine goes on to insist on a strong relation between preaching and prayer and between preaching and the devotional study of Scripture. Nothing, he tells us, develops zeal in a preacher more than earnest prayer and serious thought (1:147).[56] He recommends, to the clergy at least, daily study of Scripture; this is how the preacher cultivates wisdom. This wisdom is a very pietistic sort of wisdom, and yet it is worldly at the same time, for Bellarmine tells us that a preacher must add to this sacred wisdom all kinds of erudition in order to have a copious supply of reasons and examples. There is obviously nothing contradictory between understanding wisdom as a divine gift and understanding it as a scholarly discipline. As pietistic as Bellarmine may have been, he was devoted to formal education.

Characteristically our preacher leaves the development of eloquence until last. It is in this, of course, that he is least baroque. Christian eloquence, he tells us, insists that while art may emend and polish, it has no right to destroy or corrupt nature (1:147).[57] Bellarmine sees no value in a highly dramatic or ornamental style of preaching with an emphasis on poetic phrases and theatrical gestures. A sermon should be more conversational in tone. It should be the sort of honest conversation with a friend that seriously attempts to persuade, rather than a public display of the art of public speaking. Here, once again, one notices the emphasis on persuasion. It is to the end of persuasion that eloquence is justified.

Having presented us with this thumbnail essay on preaching, he concludes with what we might call a short bibliography. First, he gives us some examples of what he regards as the classics of the patristic pulpit. He tells us there are three kinds of sermons. There is what we have called the expository sermon, the purpose of which is explaining Scripture. Such sermons are teaching sermons, and the classic examples of this type are Augustine's sermons on John,[58] Basil's sermons on the Hexaemeron, and Chrysostom's sermons on Genesis. The second kind of sermon treats a particular subject or theme, and the classics here are Chrysostom's ser-

56. "Ad zelum seu spiritum hauriendum, cui potissimum studere debet christianus concianator, nihil magis prodest quam oratio ad Deum assidua et rerum collestium continua."

57. "Ad eloquentiam christianam, imo ad omnem veram eloquentiam requiritur ut ars emendet et polat, sed non destruat aut corrumpat naturam."

58. Presumably Bellarmine has in mind the long series on the Gospel of John.

mons to the people of Antioch, Basil's topical sermons, and many sermons of Augustine, Leo, and other Fathers.[59] Third are sermons which partly explain Scripture and partly exhort people to virtue and living a good Christian life. Chrysostom's sermons on the Pauline Epistles are a good example of this, as are Augustine's sermons on the Psalms.[60] In addition to these exemplary sermons from the Fathers of the ancient Church, Bellarmine recommends several distinguished works on ecclesiastical rhetoric that were written in his own day. He mentions a work by Augustine Valerius, cardinal archbishop of Verona; one by Diego de Estella; the work we mentioned above by Luis of Granada; and finally a work by Alphonse Zorilla (1:149). As we will notice, Cardinal Borromeo recommended a similar list of books on ecclesiastical rhetoric.[61]

D. Conclusion — Jesuit Preaching at Its Best

For an American Protestant, the preaching of Cardinal Bellarmine is much more accessible than the typical Counter-Reformation preaching. Catholic scholars may look at it differently, but for a Protestant Bellarmine seems to have held himself back from the worst excesses of the baroque age. Perhaps he took the Reformers seriously enough to recognize elements of true catholicity in the Protestant approach to preaching. He seems to have been influenced by it, something we noticed especially in his sermon for the third Sunday in Lent on the subject of the Word of God. We also noticed that he made a serious attempt to do systematic expository preaching in his series on the Sermon on the Mount. None of this, of course, meant that he was soft on Protestantism or that he compromised his Catholicism. It was much more a case that his engagement with Protestantism helped him discover dimensions of Catholicism which had been forgotten. It is sometimes that way: the ecumenical discussion often helps us discover riches in our own tradition which we ourselves had too long forgotten.

59. Bellarmine no doubt has in mind Chrysostom's sermons on the statues, Basil's sermons for feast days, as well as the festal sermons of Augustine and Leo.

60. In both Chrysostom's sermons on the Pauline Epistles and Augustine's sermons on the Psalms we formally have expository sermons, but Bellarmine is right in saying that they do lean heavily to moral catechism.

61. On these works see John W. O'Malley, "Saint Charles Borromeo and His Preaching," in Headley and Tomaro, eds., *San Carlo Borromeo*, p. 140 n. 10 and pp. 146-48.

III. Charles Borromeo (1538-84)

One of the most admirable leaders of the Counter-Reformation, Charles Borromeo did much to reshape Catholic preaching. Because of both his influential position as archbishop of Milan and his family connections — he was cardinal nephew of Pope Pius IV — he was in a position to direct the preaching practice of the post-Tridentine Catholic Church. This he did very effectively, but he was not so much a great preacher as a popularizer of a particular school of preaching. The Counter-Reformation loved heroes, and Charles Borromeo was the hero of Counter-Reformation preaching.

Born in the family castle on the shores of Lago Maggiore, he was the second son of Count Gilberto Borromeo and Margherita de' Medici, sister of the future pope.[62] At an early age he was sent off to Pavia to study law. As was so often done in those days, he studied law rather than theology because he had been destined by his family for a position in the leadership of the Church. Moreover, he studied law in the manner of the Renaissance humanists rather than the Scholasticism of earlier times. He therefore learned canon law and civil law side by side. He earned his doctorate in both laws, as the expression was, and the education he received was thoroughly under the influence of the new learning of the time. About the time he finished his degree, his mother's brother, Giovanni Angelo de' Medici, became pope, on 31 March 1560. Young Carlo was called to Rome immediately and rapidly rose in his uncle's service. Throughout the papacy of Pius IV he was his uncle's most trusted adviser. His uncle made him cardinal when he was only twenty-two years old, but despite his age he proved a most able supporter. This was especially so in the third and final session of the Council of Trent.

Among the honors Borromeo received from his uncle was the archepiscopal see of Milan, one of the most powerful offices in the Italian church. As long as his uncle lived, however, young Charles administered the archdiocese from Rome, leaving him free to assist his uncle in his deli-

---

62. Borromeo has been the subject of numerous biographies and monographs. Of special interest are the following: André Deroo, *Saint Charles Borromée: Cardinal réformateur, docteur de la pastoral* (Paris: Éditions Saint-Paul, 1963); Headley and Tomaro, *San Carlo Borromeo;* Cesare Orsenigo, *Vita di S. Carlo Borromeo,* 2 vols. (Milan: Casa Editrice S. Lega Eucaristica, 1929); Cesare Orsenigo, *Life of St. Charles Borromeo,* trans. Rudolph Kraus (St. Louis and London: B. Herder Book Co., 1943); and Agostino Valiero, *Vita Caroli Borromaei* (Verona: apud Hieronymum Discipulum, 1586).

cate dealings with the Council of Trent. Such matters of high ecclesiastical diplomacy were not his only concern, however. While in Rome he was instrumental in establishing what today is called the Confraternity of Christian Doctrine. This organization, which exercised a catechetical ministry, was an attempt to bring basic elementary Christian teaching to the common people of the city of Rome. The cardinal obviously had a broad understanding of the ministry of the Word.

In 1565, after his uncle's death, Cardinal Borromeo took up residence in Milan. The Council of Trent had discussed at length the problem of too many bishops and other ecclesiastical functionaries who were absentee administrators, and once Borromeo took up residence in Milan, he set himself to being a model bishop as the Council had envisioned the office. This was especially the case in regard to the preaching office, which is, to be sure, our particular interest.[63]

Borromeo was not a great preacher, and only in the eighteenth century were his sermons published.[64] He was a competent preacher and he preached frequently, sometimes as many as three or four times a day. His sermons were usually homilies in the patristic sense. He moved away from the thematic sermons of Scholasticism.[65] His sermons do, on the other hand, have elements of high oratory in the sense of classical rhetoric. The important thing was that he set the example. He actually became a preaching archbishop, as Ambrose of Milan, his ancient predecessor, had been. In fact, the parallels between the two men are remarkable.

Borromeo was above all the popularizer of the Tridentine vision of the preacher. The Council issued its decree on preaching on 17 June 1546,[66] and two things stand out in this decree. First, the council recog-

---

63. John W. O'Malley, S.J., has given us an especially fine study, "Saint Charles Borromeo and the *Praecipuum Episcoporum Munus:* His Place in the History of Preaching," in *San Carlo Borromeo,* pp. 139-57, reprinted in O'Malley, *Religious Culture,* pp. 139-57.

64. Charles Borromeo, *Homiliae nunc primum e mss. Codicibus Bibliotecae Ambrosianae in lucem productae,* ed. Giuseppe Antonio Sassi (Milan: Bibliotheca Ambrosiana, 1747-48). This work was not available for this study.

65. O'Malley, "Saint Charles Borromeo and the *Praecipuum Episcoporum Munus,*" p. 145.

66. On the Council of Trent and its approach to the reform of preaching, see Giuseppe Albergio, "Carlo Borromeo come modello di vescovo nella chiesa post-tridentina," *Revista Storica Italiana* 79 (1967): 1031-52; Marc Fumaroti, *L'âge de l'éloquence: Rhetoric et "res literaria" de la Renaissance au seuil de l'époque classique* (Geneva: Droz, 1980); Hubert Jedin, *A History of the Council of Trent,* 2 vols. (London: Thomas

nized preaching as *praecipuum episcoporum munus,* "the principal office of bishops." With this, of course, Protestants heartily agreed. Preaching is the first responsibility of the Christian ministry. It had been a deformation for centuries that bishops had become feudal lords, even princes, who managed the affairs of a solidly institutionalized Church. All too many bishops handed over the responsibility of preaching to others while they ran the Church. Some simply neglected that essential task. Borromeo, consummate administrator that he was, gave high priority to preaching and fulfilled this sacred responsibility himself.

Another aspect of this definition which is particularly characteristic of the Counter-Reformation is that preaching is carefully tied into the hierarchical structure of the Tridentine Church. It was the bishops, in whom ecclesiastical authority was vested, who were to exercise, lead, and control the preaching ministry. It was they who had the authority to preach. Others might preach only insofar as they were commissioned by the bishop or had his permission, but it was the office of the bishop to preach. For the Council, authority was the fundamental concept. No longer were preachers to take up the prophetic mantle and criticize those in authority. Preaching must confirm the institution and those who ran it.[67]

Second, the Council defined preaching in terms of the Franciscan dictum, that the preacher is to preach virtues and vices, punishments and rewards.[68] As contemporary scholars have often suggested, this pointed the preaching of the Counter-Reformation in a decidedly moralistic direction. Much Catholic preaching from this point on is centered on extolling the virtues of the Christian life and warning against the vices which so easily assail the human condition. The Counter-Reformation pulpit constantly threatened the punishments which would fall on sinners and heretics and pointed to the glories which would be the reward of the faithful and the virtuous. As one constantly sees in the painting and sculpture of the Counter-Reformation, the heroic glories of the saintly are ever and again celebrated. Just as the spiritual exercises of Ignatius Loyola meditated on the triumphs of godliness, so the Counter-Reformation preacher extolled them from his pulpit.

Borromeo popularized this highly moralistic approach to preaching.

Nelson and Sons, 1957-61), 2:99-124; and A. Larios, "La reforma de la predicatión en Trento," *Communio* 6 (1973): 223-83.

67. See McGinness, *Right Thinking,* p. 36.

68. See the chapter of McGinness, "Vices and Virtues, Punishment and Glory," in his *Right Thinking,* pp. 29-61.

Excoriating sin and heresy and glorifying holiness and devotion, this approach sought to win back those who because of the Reformation had wandered away from the one, holy, catholic, and apostolic Church.

An important aspect of Borromeo's popularizing of the Council's decree on preaching was the establishment of seminaries which taught this new approach to preaching. He wanted his seminarians to get beyond the old Scholastic method of preaching and to adopt a more humanistic and patristic approach. The Christian humanists had by this time provided the preacher with editions of the sermons of Origen, Ambrose, Leo, John Chrysostom, Augustine, and Gregory the Great, and these were the examples Borromeo encouraged his seminarians to follow. Strangely enough, he was encouraging them to do just what Zwingli, Oecolampadius, Capito, and Bucer had done forty years before.[69] Borromeo entrusted his seminaries to the Jesuits, and in a generation provided northern Italy with a new breed of preacher, thoroughly committed to the preaching program of the Council and expertly trained to carry it out.

Finally, Borromeo encouraged a whole series of preaching manuals which took a very different approach than those of the Middle Ages.[70] Instead of basing preaching on the literary methods of Scholasticism, these new manuals were much more thoroughly influenced by the literary concerns of Christian humanism. Augustine's *De doctrina christiana* was studied very carefully, as were Aristotle, Cicero, and Quintilian. According to O'Malley, the most popular manuals were those of the cardinal archbishop of Verona, Augustine Valerius, *De rhetorica ecclesiastica,* published in 1574; Luis of Granada, *Ecclesiastica rhetoricae, sive de Ratione concionandi,* published in Lisbon in 1576; and Diego de Estella, *Modo de Predicar,* published in Salamanca in 1576.[71] These manuals brought to the pulpit of the Counter-Reformation a new eloquence, the sort which fit right in with the baroque churches that Bernini and his followers were building all over Rome.

If Scholasticism showed the preacher how to teach the people

---

69. O'Malley traces this concern to the influence of Erasmus and his *Ecclesiastes* of 1535. As we pointed out in the previous chapter, Capito had taken this approach to his sermons on Romans and Matthew in Basel as early as 1518. Zwingli did the same thing in Zürich in 1519. Erasmus, who was living in Basel at this time, is said to have never missed one of Capito's sermons.

70. For a brief study of these manuals, see McGinness, *Right Thinking,* pp. 49-61.

71. O'Malley, "Saint Charles Borromeo and His Preaching," p. 147.

Christian morality and if the Protestant Reformers showed preachers how to expound the Word of God, the Counter-Reformation showed preachers how to move the wills of their congregations. This was the direction in which the new spirituality of the Jesuits was pointing the Catholic Church. The problem was the will, as the Jesuits saw it, and it was the will which had to be moved.

Charles Borromeo epitomized this whole shift. He was the nephew of a Medici pope, a lawyer trained in Renaissance humanism. He understood the power politics of his day and how preaching could play a role in it. He knew that as a successor of Ambrose of Milan he was in the position to shape Christian society, and with single-hearted devotion he gave his life to doing just that.

IV. French Catholic Humanism

The Counter-Reformation in France was rather slow to organize itself. A good portion of the population had found Protestantism very attractive, and from the middle of the sixteenth century there was much Protestant preaching throughout the land. This sparked a vigorous controversy, as plenty of preachers in France defended the old ways. Paris was, after all, the capital of Scholastic theology. The pope may have been in Rome, but the theologians of the Catholic Church were in Paris. To attack Scholastic theology, which was, after all, one of the central targets of the Reformation, was to attack the "Doctors of the Sorbonne." The theology of Paris may have lost its creativity, but it was not about to surrender its prerogatives to the new theology.

The pulpits of Paris were quick to defend Catholicism as it had been preached in those same pulpits for the last four centuries. As the lines of defense were drawn up for the Wars of Religion, preaching became more and more controversial. It was the preachers of the Catholic League who held Paris against the siege of the Protestant forces under Henry of Navarre. Their preaching fired the Parisian resistance. They denied every affirmation of Protestantism, vilified her leaders, and consigned her followers to damnation. Calvin was made to bear every conceivable insult. The Bible, the Fathers, and reason were all made to witness against the innovators. This kind of preaching may not convey the gospel, nor nourish the Church, but it did win the day.

In 1593, when Henry of Navarre decided that "Paris was worth a mass," Counter-Reformation preaching began a new phase.[72] French Catholic preaching was transformed during the reign of Henry IV, and it is this new approach to preaching which interests us. Henry's decision may have made him king of France, but it also made very clear that from now on the function of Catholicism was to support the throne. It was to supply the religious sanctions of the French monarchy. For the kingdom of France the political realities were to have precedence over all other considerations. It would continue to be that way for the next two hundred years, until finally with the Revolution France ceased entirely to be a Christian nation. The Catholic Church, in the end, paid dearly for the royal chapel of the House of Bourbon. Henry IV, the first of the Bourbon kings, wanted a compliant, humanistic religion that would support his absolute monarchy. Unwittingly as it may have been, that is what Counter-Reformation Catholicism gave him.

Henry IV was a charming man, the most likable man who ever sat upon the throne of France. He had a tremendous sense of the authority he possessed as king, and he seemed devoted to bringing prosperity to his people. Besides this, he seemed to have real sympathy for the common people. He was a capable military leader, whose bravery and daring had already been proven in many a battle. He was a good hunter, a man's man, but, alas, also a woman's man. His family life was unfortunately complicated by a number of mistresses, but he seems to have been devoted to his children. He was a patron of the arts, and under him French literature began its golden age. He made significant contributions in the support of commerce and industry. That he was called Henry the Great is understandable. Henry was a good king, as kings go, and there is no denying he improved the life of France enormously. But one thing has to be said: he was a firm believer in absolute monarchy and he recognized in Catholicism its most logical religious complement. That, for many of us, is a significant fault.

French Catholic humanism of the seventeenth century produced a remarkable literature. It was however heir to the literary tradition of the French Renaissance, and could never have existed without it. The earthy humor of Rabelais had consigned Scholasticism to oblivion, and with it the old Catholicism. He was not a Protestant, although he had obviously been influenced by Luther and supported a good number of Protestant

---

72. The classic study on this subject is that of Arien Lezat, *De la prédication sous Henri IV* (Geneva: Slatkin Reprints, 1970).

positions. His work was nourished by a thorough knowledge of the Greek and Roman classics. That, of course, was what the Renaissance was all about. Clément Marot, on the other hand, had developed a French lyrical poetry which was very earnest about life and deeply Christian. He was a devout Protestant. Calvin had made an important contribution to literature by demonstrating that French could be used in serious theological discussion. Then Montaigne had opened up the common language to a more urbane, worldly wisdom. His pragmatic attitude toward Catholicism was influential for the next two centuries. He saw traditional religion as necessary to hold society together, but he was himself something of a skeptic. He outwardly conformed, but his deepest thoughts were elsewhere. He was the obvious precursor of Henry IV's attitude toward Catholicism. Ronsard and the Pléiade had attempted to invigorate French poetry with the forms of the Greek and Roman classics, and they were quite successful. Their work was gallant. The poetry of love, heroism, and the affairs of the court was idealized. And yet Ronsard, particularly, regarded himself as a good Catholic. The epic poetry of pagan Greece and Rome and the salvation history of the Bible went hand in hand. As we see in the paintings of Nicolas Poussin, Moses and Ulysses, Christ and Plato are all painted in the same colors.

With the reign of Henry IV the literary culture of France began to revolve more and more around the court. Courtly manners and courtly ideals were honored. Malherbe's ode to Marie de' Medici, welcoming her to the court of France, is emblematic of the new age of French literature. At the same time, literary disciplines of classical antiquity were brought more strictly to bear on French literature. Greek and Roman mythology, as well as classical history, became the subject matter of much French literature. This classical tradition was usually Christianized in some sort of way. Biblical stories were rewritten in the literary forms of ancient Greece and Rome, as in Malherbe's *Larmes de Saint Pierre*.

Cardinal du Perron (1556-1618) is a good example of the spirit of this French Catholic humanism established by Henry IV. Born in Bern, one of the German-speaking Protestant cantons of Switzerland, he came to Paris as a young man to study. He shed his Protestantism rather quickly upon arrival and soon became a very popular controversialist. In fact, he became one of the most popular preachers of Paris. When Henry of Navarre decided to embrace Catholicism, du Perron was there to show him how. A convert from Protestantism himself, he was very sympathetic toward the future king's conversion. It was he who instructed Henry IV in

Catholic doctrine and then went to Rome to arrange his reception into the Catholic Church. The king understandably appointed him royal chaplain. He was made a cardinal in 1604. For the history of French pulpit eloquence, Cardinal du Perron's funeral sermon for the poet Ronsard is of the greatest interest. Far from following the sermon models of Scripture, it is a perfect Greek panegyric. All the forms of Greek and Roman oratory are followed with utmost faithfulness.

Pierre Charron (1541-1603) is another good example of this new approach to Catholicism. A native of Paris, he entered the priesthood as a young man but then went to study law at Bourges, Orléans, and Montpellier. Returning to Paris, he began to practice law but soon gave it up in favor of theology. His reading focused on systematic theology and the Fathers of the ancient Church. Although he began his preaching ministry in Paris, he was soon called to Bordeaux, and for the next seventeen years preached in the southwest of France. In 1595 he was again called to Paris. In Lent of the following year he filled the pulpit of Saint Eustache. During all this time he achieved a reputation as a doctrinal preacher, and consequently he was appointed theological adviser to several bishops. Eventually he himself became bishop of Auxerre. Henry IV had a great admiration for him. Charron even won the friendship of Montaigne. The famous essayist, skeptic though he was, found his preaching both interesting and edifying. After a while Charron published a popular philosophical work, written in a fine French style, to which he gave the name *La sagesse*. The work is best described as a good Catholic version of Montaigne. Typical of the age, it binds everything into a very neat Catholic humanism. Politics, the arts, philosophy, and theology all go together into a cultural synthesis in which for a worldly wise society the golden mean is attained.

One should also mention the father confessor of Henry IV, Pierre Coton, whose ability in the pulpit evidently endeared him to the king. Father Coton, typical of the Jesuit Order to which he belonged, had a prodigious knowledge of many subjects and was sincerely convinced that his sovereign was the divinely appointed savior of France, so much so that he maintained in one sermon that it was more blessed to pay taxes than to give alms. In return for this kind of clerical support, the king would escort his preacher to and from the pulpit. The obvious appreciation of the court for this kind of preaching encouraged many preachers to follow suit.

A. Francis de Sales (1567-1622)

Francis de Sales is the most important of the French Counter-Reformation preachers.[73] He was the son of a country gentleman of Savoy, born in the family château not far from Geneva only three years after Calvin's death. For centuries there had been a struggle between the city of Geneva and the House of Savoy. Geneva had understood itself as a free city, and yet, at the time Francis was born, the duke of Savoy was aggressively pressing his claims on both Geneva and the surrounding territory. Very important for our story is this: Francis's father was a strong supporter of the duke of Savoy. In 1534, when the Genevans exiled their bishop, Pierre de la Baum, he took refuge in the Savoyard city of Annecy, where he set up his exiled episcopal administration. Young Francis was sent to school in that city. In 1580 he was sent off to a Jesuit college in Paris where he continued for eight years, receiving the best training the Counter-Reformation could offer. This would, as a matter of course, include a thorough grounding in the classics of Greek and Roman literature. The teaching of the classics, especially the Latin classics, was always a major component of a Jesuit education. In 1588 he went to Padua where, as he put it, he studied law to please his father and theology to please himself. Returning to Savoy in 1591, having earned a doctorate in both civil and canon law, he pressed his family to support his entering the priesthood. They finally consented when he was given an important office by the exiled bishop of Geneva. In 1593 the duke of Savoy finally won military control of the Chablais and asked the exiled bishop to give him some priests to reconvert the area to Catholicism. Francis was one of those sent to drive Protestantism from Savoy.

Francis de Sales was a man of great personal charm who understood well how to win people's hearts to his vision of French Catholic humanism. He worked effectively through both personal conversation and preaching. He was determined to outdo the Protestants in their pulpit

---

73. For information on Francis de Sales, see Edward John Carney, "Francis de Sales, St." in *New Catholic Encyclopedia,* 6:34-36; André Jean Marie Hamon, *Life of St. Francis de Sales,* trans. Harold Burton, 2 vols. (London: Burns, Oates & Washbourne, 1925-29); Ruth Kleinman, *Saint François de Sales and the Protestants,* Travaux d'Humanisme et Renaissance, vol. 52 (Geneva: Droz, 1962); Etienne-Jean Lajeunie, O.P., *Saint François de Sales, l'homme, la pensée, l'action,* 2 vols. (Paris: Éditions Guy Victor, 1967); and H. B. Mackey, "Francis of Sales," in *Encyclopedia Britannica,* 11th ed., 10:940ff.

ability, and to do so attempted to develop a completely different approach to preaching. For the next few years he waged a vigorous evangelistic campaign, particularly in the Chablais, east of Geneva along the southern shore of the lake, which by this time was thoroughly under the military control of the duke of Savoy. Although he won some converts, the duke finally decided to take control and force the conversion of those de Sales had not convinced. Protestant ministers were exiled, Protestant books confiscated, and all who supported the Reformation were denied public office.

In 1602, by papal appointment, de Sales was made bishop of Geneva, and only a few days later the duke of Savoy tried to take over the city of Geneva with a very impressive army, thus opening to his new bishop the Cathedral of Sainte-Pierre. This military attack on Geneva, the famous Escalade, was successfully resisted by the people of the city, who wanted neither the monarchy of the duke of Savoy nor the episcopacy of de Sales.

For the next twenty years, still insisting he was bishop of Geneva, de Sales maintained his episcopal court at Annecy. He exercised his pastoral ministry in those parts of the former diocese of Geneva in which the duke of Savoy had reestablished Catholicism and devoted himself to cultivating the disciplines of the Christian life. It was then that he wrote his classic *Introduction to a Devout Life* (1609), followed a few years later by his *Treatise on the Love of God*. In the two works he developed a type of religious stance that for generations would attract the courtiers of Europe. He set out to show that one could be a devout Catholic and still be active in the affairs of the world. Protestantism had made a strong point of Christian involvement in the world, and de Sales maintained that Catholics could do the same thing. The piety he sought to cultivate was above all urbane and genteel. It made its appeal to those who wanted to appear educated and cultured. His rather delicate spirituality was in obvious contrast to the more virile approach to the Christian life in Protestant Geneva.

Realizing that Protestantism won its success primarily through preaching, de Sales was determined to reclaim the pulpit for Catholicism. It is interesting, however, that he did not use the typically Protestant sermon form. Protestant preaching was preeminently biblical expository preaching. De Sales, however, used the literary forms of Greek and Roman oratory. Sometimes he used the panegyric and sometimes the oration as developed by Cicero, but even more often he used the discourse as de-

veloped by the Stoic moralists. His sermons tended to be moral discourses. This was apparently true for the homilies delivered during the
celebration of the Mass as well as for the more formal sermons delivered
on Sunday afternoons, the latter being given most attention by French
Catholics at the time. Here the contrast with Protestantism was especially
evident. For Protestants the main sermon was delivered on Sunday morning in the course of the regular service of worship. In Catholic churches,
however, the Sunday morning homily tended to be short and simple, and
was rarely published, while Sunday afternoon sermons tended to be much
more carefully prepared. Regrettably, few of de Sales's sermons have come
down to us. The only sustained example of his preaching we have is his
Spiritual Conferences, which seem to have been taken down quite faithfully and which, apparently, best exemplify the preaching of this very creative pulpit orator. However, to see these *Spiritual Conferences* in perspective, we must first study a short essay on preaching written in 1604 in the
form of a letter to the newly appointed archbishop of Bourges, André
Frémont.[74]

1. Letter to André Frémont

What we have here is a formal essay on the ministry of preaching.[75] Although the literary form of the letter is used, this is a short, well-balanced,
and carefully composed treatise. It conveys a relaxed geniality, a quality
which is the secret of de Sales's appeal. Surprising to say, the work is amazingly similar to a number of the well-known *ars predicandi* written in the
Middle Ages. What is striking about this essay is that although it was
written at the beginning of the seventeenth century, it advocates an approach to preaching which is thoroughly Scholastic. This is obvious from
the outset. When de Sales tells us that he intends to discuss preaching according to its four causes, the efficient cause, the final cause, the material
cause, and the formal cause, it becomes clear that the thought forms in
which he thinks are still quite medieval (p. 21). In fact, the further we
read, the clearer it becomes: the homiletical approach of de Sales is a
restoking of the homiletics of the thirteenth-century preaching orders.

74. Sometimes written Frémyot or Frémiot.
75. The text used for this study is that of John K. Ryan: Francis de Sales, *On the
Preacher and Preaching,* translation of a letter to André Frémont, introduction and notes
by John K. Ryan (Chicago: Henry Regnery, 1964); the page references in the text are to
this translation.

Having announced his intention to study the preaching ministry from the standpoint of the Scholastic concept of causality, he begins with the efficient cause. Who, then, must preach? The bishop is the basic preacher, according to de Sales (p. 23). Not only is preaching primary to his ministry, it is primarily the bishop who is responsible for performing this ministry. Here, of course, de Sales comes strangely close to Calvin. In fact, all the Reformers insisted that the ministry is essentially the gospel ministry. If the bishops of Geneva, whom de Sales claimed as his predecessors, had actually been preachers, they might never have lost their cathedral city. As we pointed out, the Council of Trent tried to reinterest its bishops in the preaching ministry, but, outside of a few brilliant exceptions, and de Sales would be one of them, it failed to bring this reform about. Leaders of the Counter-Reformation such as de Sales tried their best, as this letter to André Frémont, the newly appointed archbishop of Bourges, indicates. It is easy to understand why this problem had become so serious. There was a good reason why bishops rarely preached. Frémont's appointment exemplifies the problem.

Frémont, in spite of his excellent family connections and his good intentions, was not trained as either a theologian or a preacher. Typical of the higher clergy of his day, he had been trained for leadership in public affairs. How often we have noticed that the leaders of the Counter-Reformation got their university degrees in law rather than theology. Frémont had neither training for nor experience in the ministry. Being the son of an important political figure who had distinguished himself by his loyalty to both the Catholic cause and the French crown, he was awarded a series of church offices and given the necessary ordination to the priesthood and consecration to the episcopacy. None of this was at all shocking in a society that understood a bishop as primarily a prince of the Church.

Valiantly, de Sales struggled to encourage Frémont to be a preaching prelate. De Sales pleads with him: it is not necessary that one be eloquent to be a faithful preacher. All one needs to do is say with conviction and simplicity what one knows to be true. One does not have to understand the systematic theology behind it in order to affirm one's trinitarian faith, for example. The preacher should never pretend to be a learned theologian when he is not; there is plenty a simple, believing Christian can preach. The very fact that the bishop affirms the faith is of great importance to his congregation. Here de Sales is at his best!

Secondly, de Sales takes up the final cause, or the purpose of preaching. To make his point he calls on a text from the Gospel of John, "I am come that you might have life and have it more abundantly." As the great baroque homiletician understands it, Jesus came preaching that we might have a better life. Preaching is supposed to change people's lives, and change them for the better. "To sum it all up, the preacher must bring light to the intellect and warmth to the will" (p. 32). For his hearers to have a more abundant life, a preacher must do two things, namely, instruct and motivate. He must teach about virtues and vices: about virtues so as to make men love, desire, and practice these virtues, about vices so as to make them detest, struggle against, and fly from them. There are those, de Sales tells us, who advance a third purpose for preaching, namely, to delight. At this point de Sales insists that any preacher who opens up a better way of life gives a far greater delight to his hearers than even the most skillful speaker who tickles the ears with rhetorical artistry. It is quite obvious here, as throughout his works, that de Sales looks at preaching primarily in terms of moral catechism. The sermon is supposed to teach us what the good life is, then admonish us to live it. Even doctrinal catechism is apparently secondary to moral catechism. Expository preaching, it would appear from this, holds little interest for him. He hardly seems to be aware that many in his day understood it to be the primary homiletical genre. That the proclamation of the Word of God is worship, or that it glorifies God, does not even come into consideration.

Thirdly, there is the material cause, that is, what we must preach. The apostle Paul, de Sales reminds us, says we are to preach the Word. Indeed we are, but unfortunately de Sales does not elaborate on what the apostle might have meant by this. Jesus taught us to preach the gospel, and de Sales does explain what Jesus meant. He meant the same thing Saint Francis of Assisi meant when he commanded his friars to preach on virtues and vices and on hell and paradise. After this statement one wonders how profoundly de Sales understands the New Testament concept of gospel. He goes on to say, "There is sufficient matter in Scripture for all of this; nothing further is needed" (p. 37). Again de Sales is very brief, and we should not speculate too much on what he might have meant, but more than likely he meant little more than that the Bible is a sourcebook for Christian moral teaching. As we shall have occasion to observe, de Sales never impresses us with being a diligent student of the Bible.

After this apparent statement of the sufficiency of Scripture, de Sales turns right around and demands, "Is there no need then to make use of Christian doctors and the writings of the saints? Is it indeed necessary to do so?" (p. 37). To explain the necessity of tradition de Sales uses a simile. Understanding the Scriptures is like eating a nut. It cannot be eaten simply as it is because of the shell. Tradition cracks open the nut and disposes of the shell so that the meat can be eaten. It is plain that de Sales has a very different understanding of revelation than the Reformers did, but then the Council of Trent had been quite explicit on the difference between Protestant and Catholic doctrines of revelation. This difference becomes even more evident when he tells us how profane history and natural history take their place in the matter of preaching. Saint Anthony, he informs us, since he had no Bible, heard the Word of God by meditating on nature. The dynamic conception of the Word of God found in the logos Christology of the early Church is totally absent!

Still under the heading of the matter of the sermon, de Sales addresses the arrangement of a sermon. The first part of the sermon is made up of Scripture and its interpretation. It deals with the authorities. Interpretation is essential to the nature of the sermon. This part is first because it is the foundation of the whole structure of the sermon (p. 40). All the way through this essay the theme of authority is to be heard. Indeed, this is one of the most important concerns of baroque culture. Here, de Sales tells us, "In the last analysis we preach the word, and our doctrine rests on authority. *'Ipse dixit.' Haec dicit Dominus,* the prophets say. Our Lord himself states, *'Doctrina mea non est mea, sed ejus qui misit me*" (p. 40).[76] The sermon should start out with the authoritative statements of Scripture, which then need to be interpreted. One is struck by the fact that de Sales introduces here a long section on the four senses of Scripture as they were developed in the Middle Ages. The thoroughly medieval nature of this essay is once again patent. As one reads, one gets the impression that biblical exegesis is still a matter of sifting the patristic and Scholastic commentaries. De Sales did use some commentaries from his own time, but they are for the most part from Spanish scholars, who were still strongly under the influence of Scholasticism.

With the interpretation being largely a matter of appealing to tradition, de Sales hardly needs to mention tradition any further, but he does. "After scriptural pronouncements those taken from the Fathers and councils hold second rank" (p. 46). He recommends that pronouncements be

---

76. As we so often find with the Counter-Reformation authors, Scripture is always quoted in Latin. The three Latin quotations found here are translated as follows: *Ipse dixit,* "He himself has said it"; *Haec dicit Dominus,* "Thus says the Lord"; and *Doctrina mea non est mea, sed ejus qui misit me,* "My doctrine is not mine but his who sent me."

taken from such authorities as Augustine and Bernard, and that they be short and pithy. Long quotations are not nearly as effective. One gets the impression that the Fathers, the councils, and the doctors are to be quoted in Latin and then translated into French. Evidently de Sales has in mind doing this with Scripture as well, for he always quotes Scripture by the Latin text in his writings, even though the works themselves are in French. In fact, for de Sales, as for the Counter-Reformation generally, it is the Latin Vulgate which is authoritative. The Council of Trent had made this clear. We have already remarked in regard to several Counter-Reformation preachers that neither the Greek nor the Hebrew seems to have soaked into their theological deliberations, let alone their actual sermons. As much as the Jesuits may have taught de Sales Greek, one never gets the impression that the Greek text of the New Testament had much of an impression on him.

Having dealt with Scripture and then made one's appeal to tradition, the preacher should apply reason to the subject. The Schoolmen were particularly good at supporting Christian virtue with what they understood as sound reason. As de Sales puts it, "With regard to such arguments, they are more easily found among the doctors and especially St. Thomas" (p. 47).

Still treating the material cause, our preacher turns to the subject of illustration. De Sales, as the Franciscans and Dominicans before him, was a profuse illustrator. He does, however, thoroughly criticize the excesses which mendicant preaching developed. For example, he strongly criticizes the introduction of dialogue into sermons. We found this sort of thing done by Bernardino da Siena in his sermon on Christ's appearance to Mary Magdalene in the garden. As Bernardino did it, it seemed quite masterful, but he must have been copied for generations. This sort of thing, of course, happens in every school of preaching; certain techniques are developed which at first are quite fresh and effective, but when used too frequently by those who are not too skilled, they quite rapidly lose their effectiveness. It is to de Sales's credit that he trimmed up the luxuriant growth of late medieval preaching with considerable skill, but his strong dependence on illustration is still quite clear. One notices again, as we noticed with Bellarmine, that a sermon is made up of three parts, authorities, reasons, and illustrations.

Under the subject of homiletical method de Sales suggests several models. First he recognizes that different types of composition are required by different kinds of texts. One kind of text is the biblical narrative, that is, biblical stories such as the nativity or the resurrection. Another kind is the short maxim, such as "He who humbles himself will be exalted" (Luke 14:11). Another is a liturgical pericope, that is, one of the Sunday Epistles or Gospels. Still another is a group of texts on a particular subject such as hope or patience. Finally, another kind might be a text chosen as the basis for a sermon on the life of a saint. Some methods are more appropriate to certain types of texts than others. The first method he suggests is to consider how many persons are mentioned in the story and then draw some reflection from each of them. Another method is to take up the principal event in the story and then point out what led to it and resulted from it. Another would be to study a story by asking, Who was involved? Why did it occur? and How did it come to pass? A particularly effective method is to begin by giving a brief paraphrase of the story and drawing two or three observations or lessons from it. When one is preaching on a text, a method that works very well is to decide what virtue is taught by the text and then consider in what this virtue consists, its true marks, its effects, and the means of acquiring it. Again, one could take the approach of showing how the virtue is to be honored, how it is useful, and why it is delightful. Finally, when one is discussing an entire Sunday Gospel, the method usually followed is to make a running commentary on the passage. Selection is of the essence of this method, because so many things could be developed and only a few can be treated. Strangely enough, de Sales, not recognizing the antiquity of this method, tells us that it is not very fruitful. One wonders if he intends with this rebuff to make clear his distaste of Protestant preaching.

Seven methods are suggested, and one gets the impression when reading them that our homiletician is in reality hammering the biblical text into the sorts of literary forms which appealed to the baroque spirit. With all its admiration for Roman literature, the baroque world had a very particular perception of classical antiquity, a perception quite different from that of the Renaissance. Biblical antiquity, on the other hand, it understood not in the least. These "methods," as de Sales calls them, are not very sensitive to the literary forms of Scripture. The one exception is the last, the running commentary on a passage of Scripture, and that, as we have remarked, actually goes back to the biblical literary world. It is tailored to dealing with biblical literature. As we shall see, by the time de Sales gets through with the Gospel, it has a distinctly different sound from what it had in the New Testament.

The fourth subject our homiletician takes up is the formal cause, that is, how we must preach. True Scholastic that he is, de Sales begins with a quotation from "the philosopher," that is, Aristotle, to the effect that it is form which gives a thing being. De Sales goes on, "Say marvelous things but do not say them well, and they are nothing. Say a little but say it well and it is very much" (p. 63). Preaching must be spontaneous, dignified, courageous, natural, sturdy, devout, serious, and a little slow. One must speak with affection and devotion, with simplicity and candor. One must speak with confidence and be convinced of the doctrine that is preached. Finally de Sales comes back to the subject of love, the subject which, for him at least, explains everything. In the end he wants to understand preaching in terms of love. "I like preaching that issues from love of neighbor rather than from indignation at them, even in the case of the Huguenots, whom we must treat with great compassion, not flattering them but lamenting over them" (p. 66).

By way of conclusion de Sales offers us this short definition: "Preaching is the publication and declaration of God's will, made to men by one lawfully commissioned to that task, to the end of instructing and moving them to serve his divine majesty in this world so as to be saved in the next" (p. 67). Preaching for de Sales is clearly a matter of moral catechism. It teaches us how we must live if we are to attain salvation. That preaching be done only by those who have the authority to do it was of the greatest possible importance to the Counter-Reformation. The doxological nature of preaching, on the other hand, does not appear.

2. Conferences to the Sisters of the Visitation

Like other famous preachers, Francis de Sales has left us little in the way of recorded sermons. Apparently, only a handful of the sermons he preached in Paris have survived, although he is supposed to have revolutionized French Catholic preaching at the end of the sixteenth century. As we have said, the best sustained look we get at de Sales's preaching is in some twenty spiritual conferences he held for the Sisters of the Visitation at various times toward the end of his life.[77] For the most part these conferences were held at the sisters' convent at Annecy. The sisters are supposed to have taken down these sermons very carefully and to have gone

---

77. In the introduction to his translation of the *Spiritual Conferences,* Dom Mackey tells us that most of the conferences were given in 1612 or shortly thereafter but that a few were given as late as 1617 or 1619.

over them to see if anything had been left out.[78] In his later years de Sales was regarded as a living saint, particularly by the Sisters of the Visitation, the religious order he had founded. This would lead one to imagine that they did indeed take the greatest possible care in collecting the words of their revered founder.

The monastic conference is a special type of sermon. A number of great examples have come down to us. So far we have looked at the *Catechism* of Philoxenus of Mabbug, the *Moralia on Job* by Gregory the Great, the *Catechism* of Symeon the New Theologian, and the famous sermons on the Song of Solomon by Bernard of Clairvaux. De Sales, who knew the monastic tradition very well, is supposed to have been inspired by the practice of Pachomius. He must have been well aware of the role played by conferences in monastic communities. He is known to have studied the conferences of John Cassian at some length, for example. Generally the monastic conference was held at some time other than either the celebration of the Eucharist or one of the daily offices such as lauds or vespers. One should probably not make too much of this distinction. The whole daily routine of the monastery was a sort of liturgy in itself, and the fact that sermons were preached at another time or place certainly does not imply that they were any less liturgical. On the other hand, the fact that the sermon was not at the Eucharist or at vespers gave the monastic conference the opportunity to be a bit more informal, an informality de Sales took full advantage of. It seems to be of the nature of the man that he relished the more informal situation. While some of these conferences are sermons in the chapel, others were apparently delivered in the garden. Sometimes they treat the Scripture passages appointed by the lectionary; sometimes they seem to address questions raised by the sisters.

The monastic conference, in terms of sermon genre, is a very specific type of catechetical preaching. In fact, a number of classics in the field bear the name catechism, as we have already noted. It is also an advanced type of catechetical preaching; it is not really intended for beginners but rather for those who have made substantial advances in the Christian life. It is very specifically moral catechism, as opposed to doctrinal catechism. The point of the monastic conference is to deepen the religious devotion of the monastic community as a whole, and of each

---

78. This study is based on *The Spiritual Conferences of St. Francis de Sales,* trans. H. B. Mackey (Westminster, Md.: Newman Bookshop, 1943). The page references in the text are to this volume.

member of that community as an individual. It is to guide the religious in the road to perfection. It aims at a sort of heroic Christian morality.

In the hands of Francis de Sales, so obviously a disciple of the French Renaissance, these conferences bear a distinct resemblance to the moral essays of Montaigne. To be sure, the view of life de Sales advanced is quite different from that of Montaigne. Although Montaigne always professed to be a Catholic, his approach to life was entirely humanistic. He was more Epicurean than Christian. In the end, he was primarily concerned with human life and how it should be lived. Theistic concerns were beyond his field of vision. His essays, however, had a strong influence on the development of French Catholic humanism. De Sales is also interested in human behavior, but in a very different sort of human behavior. A simple look at the titles of his *Conferences* makes this very clear.

     I. Obligation of the Constitutions
    II. On Confidence
   III. On Constancy
   IV. On Cordiality and the Spirit of Humility
    V. On Generosity
   VI. On Hope
  VII. Three Spiritual Laws
 VIII. On Self-Renouncement
   IX. On Religious Modesty
    X. On Obedience
   XI. The Virtue of Obedience
  XII. On Simplicity and Religious Prudence
 XIII. On the Rules and the Spirit of the Visitation
 XIV. On Private Judgment
  XV. The Will of God
 XVI. The Antipathies
XVII. On Voting in a Community
XVIII. The Sacraments and Divine Office
 XIX. On the Virtues of Saint Joseph
  XX. Why We Should Become Religious
 XXI. On Asking for Nothing

Some of these are occasional sermons. Conference XX, for example, was preached in Paris at the consecration of several new members of the order, while Conference VI was preached on the occasion of sending out a group of nuns to establish a new convent. But the greatest number of conferences are what might be called discourses or pulpit essays on various moral virtues.

Several themes appear again and again in these sermons. A number of sermons take up the question of how we are to love one another in a religious community where the love should be inclusive and without discrimination or partiality. De Sales makes the point that the Christian community is bound together by love, but it is a well-moderated sort of love which comes from obedience to God rather than the passions. The true religious, according to de Sales, offers to God the perfume of a holy submission (p. 24). In fact, these conferences return again and again to this surpassing virtue of self-renunciation and resignation. Self-renunciation is exemplified by Jesus on the cross when he prayed, "Father, into thy hands I commend my spirit," but it is also exemplified by the pagan philosopher Epictetus, who, being a slave, was offered his freedom but in an extreme act of renunciation refused to accept his liberty (pp. 20-23). The third conference, "On Constancy," is on the flight of the holy family to Egypt. Here the biblical story is interpreted to show how we must be submissive to God's providence and therefore constant in faith. De Sales tells us that we should be like Saint Joseph and "embark on the sea of divine Providence without store of biscuit, without oars or sculls, without sails, in a word without preparing anything at all, leaving to Our Lord all the care of ourselves and the result of our affairs, without doubts or questionings or fears as to what may happen" (pp. 46ff.). For us today, the emphasis on renunciation seems a bit more Stoic than Christian, but de Sales has a strong doctrine of providence, a theme strangely absent from modern spirituality.

Humility is another important theme in these conferences. In the fifth conference, "On Generosity," we learn that "Humility is the recognition that we are absolute nothingness" (p. 74). Generosity, on the other hand, is confident that by God's strength within us we can do all things (pp. 75ff.). The perfect example of humility is the response of the virgin Mary to the archangel Gabriel, "Behold the handmaid of the Lord," and the perfect example of generosity is, "Be it done to me according to thy word." Both humility and generosity, as well as all the other virtues de Sales discusses in these conferences, are seen in the perspective of submission to authority. One is submissive to God, to the revealed will of God in the commandments, and to the religious authority under which one lives. This is taken up particularly in Conference XV, "The Will of God" (pp. 284-85). It is a matter of religious modesty that each sister do the bidding of the mother superior without complaint or criticism. One should never imagine oneself more devout than the rules of the order or one's religious superior. One should set aside one's private judgment and live in the flow of the religious order if one is ever to arrive at perfection.

One is impressed by the religious heroism of these moral teachings. The stoic resignation is clearly the legacy of classical antiquity, while the self-renunciation and humility are so very medieval. The heroism of de Sales's quest for spiritual perfection, nevertheless, is the essence of the baroque. On the one hand the true nun seeks humility, and on the other she tries to be heroic in the attainment of perfection. This is the drama of baroque spirituality.

Francis de Sales was the Harry Emerson Fosdick of the Catholic pulpit. He changed the whole course of the homiletical craft. His pulpit ministry introduced a different kind of preaching from that of the Reformation, in both method and message. That the message was so different was bound to have its effect on the more external aspects of sermon craft. His sermons, unlike those of the Protestant Reformers, abound with illustrations. These illustrations have a certain character which we need to study in some detail.

De Sales's sermon illustrations might well be understood as simply a continuation of the exempla of medieval preaching. Surely they can be seen in terms of continuity with the sermons of the mendicant orders. Some had no doubt been used for centuries. A case in point is the story of the father who had an older son and a younger son. The older son was a mature, capable young man of whom the father was very proud. The younger son was still a child who liked to crawl up on his father's lap and play. The father loved both sons, and yet in very different ways. This story, as our preacher in fact remarks, was customarily used to show the difference between affective love and effective love (p. 266). No doubt the literary critic could show that a number of these sermon illustrations go back to traditional exempla. In addition to these, de Sales uses a number of biblical stories such as the sacrifice of Abraham, the request of Israel for a king, and the annunciation to illustrate the points of the sermon. One notices, however, that these biblical illustrations lack freshness. One does not get the impression that our preacher has cut them from the cloth of Scripture himself. De Sales's study of Scripture gives the impression of being secondhand or perhaps picked up more from the tradition rather than from an intensive study on his own part. In fact, it is sometimes difficult to distinguish Scripture from tradition in these sermons. As we find in his sermon on Saint Joseph, for example, our preacher often passes on apocryphal material or invents material which one cannot readily infer from Scripture.

It is another matter with the legends and sayings of the saints he uses so frequently, and with such freshness. One gets the impression that our preacher has gathered these quotations and anecdotes from his own reading rather than from the oral tradition of the monastery. Saint Bernard of Clairvaux is frequently quoted on the virtues of the monastic life, and is in fact often referred to as "our own St. Bernard." This is, to be sure, quite natural, because Bernard had lived and worked in much the same part of France as de Sales, and the French have always regarded him as their own particular saint. De Sales seems to have studied the works of Bernard frequently. It is the same way with Saint Pachomius, who represented a distinctly Oriental type of monasticism. In the sermon "On Religious Modesty," de Sales tells us that recently he had read a story about Pachomius. When the famous saint at first retired into the desert to follow the monastic life, he was frequently tempted by evil spirits. They at first ridiculed him in order to make him depressed, but the saint found this amusing. Foiled in their first attempt, they tried to entangle him by levity and so constructed an elaborate folly that the saint be distracted from his meditation. This folly, described at length, is really quite amusing, but Pachomius, even in this ridiculous folly, found something to remind him of Christ's passion, and when the spirits saw this they fled this very holy man (p. 148). The story adds humor to the sermon, but it also makes the point that humor may be useful in the devout life.

Pachomius is the subject of another illustration in the sermon "The Will of God" (p. 285). According to this story, the saint was making straw mats one day and a child was watching him. The child objected to the way he was making the mats and told him how it ought more properly to be done. The saint did as the child told him. Later, one of the monks observing what had happened upbraided Pachomius for letting the child instruct him. The saint answered that if God would grant him the humility to follow the child, then perhaps he in return could impart that same humility to the child. Monastic tradition is filled with stories like these which for centuries have been used to instill monastic ideals in the hearts of the newly religious. These stories are surprising, probably because this monastic modesty, this self-effacing humility, is so exotic to our understanding of the Christian life.

Another of these edifying monastic stories concerns Saint Anselm. He was a man who was always willing to follow the will of others. If one of his monks bid him drink a bit of broth for his good health, he immediately did so; if another told him the broth would not be good for him, he immediately gave up drinking it. This characteristic of the beloved saint was not looked upon too kindly by some of his monks, and finally they remonstrated with him that he ought not bend to everyone's will, but should insist that they bend to his since he had authority over them. He replied that if he did the will of others, then perhaps the time would come when God would in return do his will (pp. 282ff.). The story is told elaborately and with a great deal of charm. In fact, it is because these stories are so exotic that we find them so charming. Another example is a story about Arsenius, the famous classical scholar of Christian antiquity. After many years at court where he lived a virtuous Christian life, Arsenius entered a monastery. After a while the monks noticed that when he sat down he crossed his legs. The monks considered this a worldly affectation. They did not want to offend him, but at last it was brought to his attention and he received the correction with consummate meekness (p. 140). De Sales fills his sermons with stories like these which impress us with the heroic virtues of the monks and nuns and their celestial life here on earth.

Another kind of sermon illustration de Sales uses with particular brilliance is the fable. A well-known literary device of classical antiquity, the fable was revived by La Fontaine during the French literary renaissance a generation after de Sales. The art of the fable is to tell a story about plants or animals which is really aimed at making certain traits of human behavior appear with greater clarity. The whole of Conference VII, "Three Spiritual Laws," is built on three characteristics of the dove, which de Sales used because the appointed Gospel lesson for the day tells of the baptism of Jesus and the descent of the dove. Our preacher's use of Scripture is rather stretched here, but he goes on to tell us that all souls dedicated to the service of the divine majesty are bound to be like pure and loving doves. This is why the bride in the Song of Solomon is often called a dove (pp. 105ff.). In another sermon the qualities of the palm tree become the framework for discussing the virtues of saintliness. Our preacher's excuse for using this literary device is that the liturgy provides Psalm 92:13 for the feasts of confessors, and this psalm tells us that the just shall flourish like the palm tree (pp. 364ff.). Our preacher often uses the life of bees in their well-ordered hive as a sermon illustration for the monastic life. It is particularly important to notice how the bees are completely dependent upon their king. Without their king they are nervous and without direction, but with him they are content. The same characteristic is to be observed in those living under the discipline of the religious life (pp. 104 and 144). These fables are a charming literary device with great popular appeal, and they were particularly characteristic of the literature of the time. Our preacher was well aware of the fashion of his age and was intent on using any effective means he could to get his message across.

De Sales's sermons are remarkable in their use of personal reminiscences. This sort of thing one encounters almost never in the history of preaching up to his time. Let us look at two examples. In Conference IX, for example, our preacher, in the course of warning his nuns of the danger of curiosity about different methods of arriving at perfection, tells of a nun he once knew who had an immoderate devotion to Mother Teresa of Ávila. She had even learned to speak like her, so that one might have fancied her a little Mother Teresa, and had taken her devotion so far that she seemed to enter into the sorts of trances the Spanish mystic is supposed to have experienced. Unfortunately, de Sales tells us, this dear woman was agitated by all these attempts to copy Saint Teresa. She was constantly seeking unusual ways of finding perfection other than those recommended by her order (p. 146). Our preacher is very kindly in his telling of the story, yet one gets the point nevertheless.

In another sermon he tells of speaking to a nun who had asked if she might receive Communion more frequently than was customary in her order. His reply was that one should not try to be any more religious than one's order expected. One should not seek extraordinary fasts, unusual disciplines or hardships, such as hair shirts or iron corsets, but simply bear those imposed by the order. If he had it to do over again, our preacher confides, he would simply take hardships as they came (p. 399). This very personal note is most effective. Surely other preachers had done this sort of thing before! It may simply have been regarded as inappropriate in that day to record such personal touches. The more personal and intimate preaching style of de Sales, however, seems to allow, even encourage, such familiar touches.

Francis de Sales used a brilliant palette of literary forms to make his sermons charming. In fact, charm is surely one of their most obvious qualities. Unlike Ignatius Loyola, the founder of the Jesuits, and unlike John Calvin, the man whose work he was determined to undo, de Sales was above all *charmant.* He was a man who had *les sentiments raffinés.* He was a man of good taste and courtly manners. One might almost say that for Francis de Sales holiness was a sort of spiritual gallantry. Many who listened to his sermons were won by their sparkle and wit. They were always quite sincere, to be sure, but they did have charm.

B. Gaspar de Seguiran (1569-1644)

While Francis de Sales and Vincent de Paul are probably thought of as the most important preachers of seventeenth-century France, Gaspar de Seguiran is perhaps the most representative. Sad to say, for de Sales we have only the Sunday afternoon sermons he preached to the Sisters of the Visitation. For Vincent we have nothing.[79] On the other hand, de Seguiran published a tremendous number of sermons which were used widely in French Catholic circles. These sermons were apparently published to help other preachers prepare their sermons. A number of the collections of his sermons were published and republished.[80]

De Seguiran was born in Aix-en-Provence and at an early age enlisted in the Jesuit Order. He received the typical Jesuit education with its emphasis on memorization and the study of the classics of ancient Greece and Rome. He rose to prominence in his order while gaining popularity as a preacher in Paris. Between 1626 and 1630 he served as preacher to the court of Louis XIII. As Peter Bayley puts it, Catholic preaching of the day felt a need to appear highly educated, and de Seguiran was happy to gratify this concern.[81] The title of his first collection belies this desire for erudition, *Sermons doctes et admirables.*

Let us look at de Seguiran's sermon for Easter Day. The text is taken from the appointed Gospel and recited in Latin. In fact, de Seguiran always recites his sermon texts in Latin. "Iesum quaeritis Nazarenum,

79. Peter Bayley, *French Pulpit Oratory, 1598-1650* (Cambridge and New York: Cambridge University Press, 1980), p. 304.

80. Gaspar de Seguiran, *Sermons doctes et admirables sur le Evangilles des Dimanches et Fests de l'année* (Paris: Nicolas de Fossé, 1612). Bayley lists seven more editions of this work published over the next thirty years. At about the same time there appeared Gaspar de Seguiran, *Sermons sur la parabole de l'enfant prodigue* (Paris: Nicolas de Fossé, 1612). The following year still another collection appeared: Gaspar de Seguiran, *Sermons doctes et admirables sur tous les jours de Caresme* (Paris: Nicolas de Fossé, 1613).

81. Bayley, *French Pulpit Oratory,* p. 78.

crucifixum, non est hic, ecce locus ubi posuerunt eum" (Mark 16:6). You seek Jesus of Nazareth who was crucified; he is not here; behold the place where he was laid. The text, however, does not play much of a role in the sermon. Rather than developing the text, the sermon is a meditation on the traditional themes of Easter. It begins with a short reference to the parallel between the deliverance of Joseph from prison and the resurrection of Christ.[82] In good Scholastic tradition this brings the preacher to invite his congregation to pray for the Virgin's help in a devout consideration of the mystery to be celebrated.

Our preacher gives us another biblical illustration of the resurrection of Christ, the story of Samson breaking out of the city of the Philistines where he had slept the first half of the night. It was the same way with Jesus, who had slept in hell but has now come forth breaking through the gates of death. We are assured that there are a number of parallels between Samson and Christ. Samson was a Nazarite while Christ was from Nazareth (p. 34). Then, too, there is a similarity between the way the Philistines betrayed Samson and how the scribes and Pharisees betrayed Jesus (p. 36).

With this our preacher brings up a theological point he learned from John of Damascus. While the spirit of Christ was offered up to the Father at his death and while his soul descended to hell and his body rested in the tomb, both the body and the soul were still united with the eternal Word (p. 38). This truth, our preacher tells us, is illustrated by the rainbow mentioned in Habakkuk, as well as by the stretched arms of the crucified Christ. The body and soul of Christ are never really separated because they are united by the eternal Word (p. 39).

After this rather abstruse observation, the sermon turns to one of the most often quoted Easter texts, "O mors ero mors tua, O inferna ero morsus tuus, ubi est inferna victoria tua? ubi est, O mors stimulus tuus" (I Cor. 15:54-55). O death, where is your sting? O hell, where is your bite? Again the Bible is quoted in Latin. With an exhaustive display of erudition, our preacher goes through a long catalogue of natural parallels to the text. For example, he embarks on a long discussion about the sting of bees and how bees, by their sting, bring death to themselves (pp. 42ff.).

There are two ways this text can be understood. It can be under-

---

82. De Seguiran, "Jour de Pasque," in *Sermons doctes et admirables sur le Evangilles des Dimanches et Fests de l'année*, p. 31. Page references in the following text are to this volume.

stood passively, "O death, you have bitten me," or actively, "O death, I shall bite you." This reminds our preacher of a story from ancient Greece, told by an Italian Renaissance historian, Nicolaus Leonicus, that involved a dragon who kept menacing the population. An oracle, consulted as to how to get rid of the dragon, recommended sacrificing a man to appease its appetite. The man, however, was dressed in armor that would make the dragon choke to death. It was the same way, our preacher assures us, with the death of Christ (p. 45). His death conquered death.

Next, our ingenious preacher turns to the bite of the serpent. Having again consulted the natural histories on the subject, he gives us a generous helping of his erudition, all of which he figures will help us understand the mystery of the resurrection (pp. 48ff.). The bites of panthers and lions are discussed to the same purpose (pp. 56-58). Our preacher also gives us a generous helping of biblical illustrations; the resurrection of the widow's son by Elisha, the resurrection of Samuel by the witch of Endor, and the resurrection of Lazarus are all brought to bear on the subject (pp. 59 and 64). Again the relevant passages of Scripture are quoted in Latin, giving an air of learning to the whole sermon. In each case he points out the contrast between these stories of resurrection and the resurrection of Christ to everlasting life.

The sermon has a dramatic conclusion in which the preacher appeals to Christ as his sacred phoenix, his heavenly bird, who died on an aromatic scaffold of cedar and olive wood. It was Christ, the true phoenix, who was immolated in the flames of divine love and thereby reborn and transformed. Then, addressing his congregation, our preacher urges them to submit to the disciplines of penance that their vices and pleasures might be reduced to ashes, that the world be crucified to them and they to the world, that in the end they be reborn and raised up in grace and immortality (p. 66).

Here is the perfect baroque sermon. It is long, erudite, and dramatic. It is the sort of sermon cultivated by a Jesuit education. It is a thorough blend of the culture of classical antiquity and the piety of the Catholic Church.

V. Conclusion

We said when we started that this would be a difficult chapter. On the other hand, the material we have gone over has been fascinating.

Bellarmine and Borromeo are about as interesting as any figures in the history of the Church. I spent hours following Francis Xavier through the Far East, and even more time trying to put in context the missionary work of the friars who went to Mexico with the conquistadors. Missionaries have always had my highest admiration. One of the surprises of this study has been the discovery that, from the Catholic side, Spain probably produced the best preaching of the sixteenth century. Certainly a good number of the Counter-Reformation preachers were true Reformers. Borromeo, when one considers that he was a descendant of the Medici family, really did make tremendous strides toward true reform. Bellarmine did indeed present the tradition of Trent in the most favorable light possible. But none of these preachers was a pulpit star of first magnitude. The Counter-Reformation produced no Bernard of Clairvaux, no John Chrysostom, no Bernardino da Siena.

One searches in vain for a preacher who sums up that very important age and who was in that day recognized as a great preacher. Borromeo and Bellarmine were certainly good preachers, but apparently neither of them ever drew great crowds. No one in their day saw to the publication of their sermons as examples of what preaching should be. It is only in retrospect that we recognize their quality. The problem was that with the Counter-Reformation, preaching was no longer where the action was, to use the jargon of our day. Borromeo was a competent preacher, but his first attention went to other things. He was from beginning to end an ecclesiastical statesman. Bellarmine, too, was a competent preacher, but it was to systematic theology that he gave his first energies. The Council of Trent may have defined preaching as the first responsibility of the bishop, but in actual fact not many bishops really devoted themselves to it. When it came to preaching, the Counter-Reformation just never pulled it off. And the reason is plain. In the final analysis, preaching was not central to the ministry of Counter-Reformation Catholicism. In this respect the Counter-Reformation had wandered far from Dominic and Francis of Assisi and from the Fathers of the ancient Church, let alone the apostles or Jesus himself. Hopefully, the Counter-Reformation is not the last word on Catholicism.

CHAPTER III

The Puritans

I. Introduction

Puritanism produced profound preaching.[1] It engendered a popular revival of preaching, especially of biblical preaching. From its begin-

---

1. On Puritanism in general, the following works have been most helpful: William Barker, *Puritan Profiles, Fifty-four Puritans: Personalities Drawn Together by the Westminster Assembly* (Fearn, Ross-shire, Scotland: Christian Focus Publications, 1996); Patrick Collinson, *The Elizabethan Puritan Movement* (Berkeley: University of California Press, 1967); Patrick Collinson, *English Puritanism* (London: Historical Association, 1983); J. S. Coolidge, *The Pauline Renaissance in England: Puritanism and the Bible* (Oxford, 1970); Gerald Robertson Cragg, *Puritanism in the Period of the Great Persecution, 1660-1688* (Cambridge: University Press, 1957); Horton Davies, *Worship and Theology in England*, 6 vols. (Princeton: Princeton University Press, 1961-75); Everett H. Emerson, *English Puritanism from John Hooper to John Milton* (Durham, N.C.: Duke University Press, 1968); Michael George Finlayson, *Historians, Puritanism, and the English Revolution* (Toronto and Buffalo: University of Toronto Press, 1983); William Haller, *The Rise of Puritanism; or, The Way to the New Jerusalem as Set Forth in Pulpit and Press from Thomas Cartwright to John Lilburne and John Milton, 1570-1643* (New York: Columbia University Press, 1938); Marshall M. Knappen, *Tudor Puritanism: A Chapter in the History of Idealism* (Chicago and London: University of Chicago Press, 1939); William M. Lamont, *Puritanism and the English Revolution* (Aldershot, Hampshire: Gregg Revivals; Brookfield, Vt.: Distributed by Ashgate Publishing, 1991); David Martyn Lloyd-Jones, *From Puritanism to Nonconformity*, 2nd ed. (Bridgend: Evangelical Press of Wales, 1991); Daniel Neal, *History of the Puritans*, 2 vols. (New York: Harper, 1848-49); John F. H. New, *Anglican and Puritan: The Basis of Their Opposition, 1558-1640* (Stanford: Stanford University Press, 1964); Leonard J. Trinterud, *Elizabethan Puritanism* (New York: Oxford University Press, 1971); and Owen C. Watkins, *The Puritan Experience* (New York: Schocken Books, 1972).

ning it was a movement for the reform of worship. This reform embraced the public prayer of the Church, the administration of the sacraments, and the preaching of the Word. While the actual controversies that were raised often seemed to center on such ceremonial details as vestments, the serving of Communion from a table rather than an altar, or refusal to use the sign of the cross at baptism, the real concern of the Puritans was the deepening of the experience of worship. For them the reformation of the rite was only a means of reforming the inner life of the Christian. It was the reforming of the heart that really interested them, and yet they recognized that outward reforming of the institution of the Church and the forms of public worship was an important means to that end.

If the Reformation institutionalized in the sixteenth century was to have its full effect, it needed to be carried into the hearts and minds of Christians and transform the life of the whole congregation. Preaching, as the Puritans understood it, was to have an important part in this, for the preaching of the Word of God was the means God had given for the reforming of the heart. It was not the only means, to be sure, nor was it so much the most important means. It was much more a case of preaching being the most obviously neglected means. Whereas the Continental Reformation was led by a host of competent preachers, the English Reformation suffered from a scarcity of ministers who could preach the reform. Yes, there were a few preachers of outstanding ability, Hugh Latimer, Nicholas Ridley, and John Jewel, but that was hardly enough to serve the whole kingdom.

Even by the end of the sixteenth century, many English parish churches lacked ministers who were capable of preaching any kind of sermon, let alone a learned exposition of Scripture. It was this kind of preaching that was essential to Protestantism, and England did not have it until several generations after the Reformation had been instituted. The leadership of the Church of England was very slow both to recognize and to remedy the problem. Queen Elizabeth felt that perhaps a dozen good preachers were enough for her kingdom. She was quite content to have ministers read from the official book of homilies. They were politically quite safe. One thing was sure: she wanted no John Knox in England! Unfortunately, the more the devout of the land cried out for real preachers, the more defensive the bishops became. Archbishop Laud tried his best to assure everyone that what went on at the altar was more important than what went on in the pulpit, but Englishmen were not convinced; they longed for intelligent and edifying preaching. And they wanted it in every parish church. If the reform of preaching was a major concern of the Puritans, it was because the English church had failed to produce in sufficient quantity the kind of preaching that would make the Reformation more than a mere institutional reform.

To get a deeper appreciation of Puritan preaching, we must look more thoroughly at the theological aspects of Puritanism. First, Puritanism had a high sense of the sovereignty of God. The Puritans were, after all, Calvinists. At first the Anglicans were Calvinists too — at least a good number of them were — particularly during the reign of Elizabeth. But they simply were not as consistent in their Calvinism. A really consistent Calvinist had one very big problem with the Church of England. It was a state-dominated church. Henry VIII replaced Roman rule with royal rule. When Elizabeth I came to the throne, she was determined to keep the Church under control. For anyone with a Calvinistic vision of the sovereignty of God, a church controlled by the state is hard to accept. This was what was really involved in the Vestiarian Controversy at the beginning of Elizabeth's reign. The Puritans did not feel the queen had the right to insist that ministers wear a stole and surplice. They attacked it as being "popery." That the Puritans could safely do. What they could not safely say was that it was "tyranny." Elizabeth would have considered that treason. For her it was obvious that she had the right to rule the Church of England as well as anything else that was English.

Thomas Cartwright's presbyterianism was designed to free the Church of England from state control. What Cartwright did was rethink the doctrine of the ministry and the church polity developed by Bucer, Calvin, and Beza, and adapt it to a much larger national church than any of the Continental churches. Bucer and Calvin had worked out their polity for the churches of independent city-states such as Strasbourg and Geneva. The congregationalists a few generations later may have taken a different approach, but they shared a common concern to make the Church independent of state control. Both Puritans and Anglicans wanted a state church, but not a state-controlled church. As long as the Church was ruled by bishops who were appointed by the throne, the Church would be controlled by the throne. Elizabeth understood very well what the Cambridge presbyterians were up to, and she was not about to let them get even so much as a foot in the door. Her successor, James I, considered episcopacy an essential support to monarchy. He had not been able to control the presbyterians of Scotland, and he had no intentions of letting anything like presbyterianism develop in England. As James saw it, all quite piously to be sure, he as king of England had by divine right control over the Church of England. The Puritans wanted to be loyal subjects of their king, and they wanted to be good Englishmen, but, as they saw it, God had the ultimate sovereignty over the world and the sovereignty of the state had its limitations. The Puritan doctrine of the sovereignty of God could not help but have its political implications.

If "Man's chief end is to glorify God and enjoy him forever," as the Westminster Catechism put it, then matters of worship are not merely questions of religious etiquette or ecclesiastical protocol. The practice of religion is central to life. It is not merely a private hobby, but a primary concern of human society. When one has a strong sense of the sovereignty of God, not even society, much less culture, is an end in itself. In every age there are those who feel it is the responsibility of religion to keep to the dark corners of life. There was secularism in the sixteenth and seventeenth centuries, just as there is today. The secularist is usually willing to give a place to religion, provided the place is not too conspicuous. If religion is polite and discrete, and stays out of court and marketplace, the secularist is willing to tolerate it. The Puritans were not willing to do this, and consequently they were not to be tolerated. They insisted that religion is an ultimate concern of the whole of society, and the secularists of the seventeenth century resisted this vigorously. They lost no opportunity to defame the Puritans, and even today the secular humanist feels obliged to make the Puritans look ridiculous. But then, what else would one expect? To the secular humanist nothing could be more ridiculous than that man's chief end is to glorify God.

For those to whom religion is a central concern of life, a good sermon an hour or two long could be fascinating. When Puritans were free to celebrate Communion as they wanted to, it must have taken the better part of the week to prepare for it and most of the Lord's Day morning to celebrate it. Speedy and perfunctory celebrations were annoying to the Puritans. If the sermons spoke to the central issues of faith and life, why not listen through the second turn of the hourglass? The congregations who came to hear the Puritans preach were intensely interested in what they had to say. Not only did they come to listen twice on Sunday and once during the middle of the week, they even found the resources to endow special "lectureships" in those parishes where the officially appointed minister was unable or unwilling to preach. In London alone there were over a hundred of these lectureships supported by special funds during the first three decades of the seventeenth century.[2] The Puritan sermon was addressed to congregations of men and women who had made God and the things of God the central passion of their lives. Thomas Watson, in his sermon on the first question of the *Westminster Shorter Catechism*, speaks at considerable length about enjoying God in Word, prayer, and sacrament. As hard as it may be for us to imagine, these two-hour sermons were "enjoyed" by those who heard them.

Another matter touching the Puritan understanding of the sovereignty of God is that they saw no reason why their worship should be English in any significant way. To be sure, they wanted their worship to be in the English language, but aside from that they saw no reason why it should express any particular national or ethnic character. They saw themselves as part of an international fellowship. When worshiping in Frankfurt, they had no problem following the usual patterns of Protestant worship followed in that city. They read German Lutheran theologians with appreciation. They felt a particularly strong kinship with the Huguenots of southern France. They were quick to come to the aid of the Italian Waldensians. In North America they immediately took the gospel to the Indians. They greatly admired the church of the Netherlands, and when some of them had to flee England, they knew they would be welcomed in Holland. The fever of nationalism was on the rise in the sixteenth and seventeenth centuries, but the Puritans resisted it. For them the kingdom of God transcended the concerns of nationalism.

All this had its effect on Puritan preaching. It was through his Word that God exercised his rule in the Church. The sovereignty of God was exercised by the preaching of his Word. If God was to reform, guide, and build up the Church, the Word of God had to be heard by the Church. It was the preacher of the Word, as a preacher, through whom God ruled. Neither ministers nor even bishops who did not preach had any authority to rule the Church. The authority was in the Word rather than in the person. Even kings had authority only to the extent that their rule was in accordance with God's Word. The Christian monarch was to be ruled by the law of Christ. It was from the Word of God that the good order of the Christian state must come. Samuel Rutherford had put it very well in his Latin motto *Lex rex:* the law is king. It was the Word preached which gave

2. For further information on the Puritan lectureships, see Paul S. Seaver, *Puritan Lectureships: The Politics of Religious Dissent, 1560-1662* (Stanford: Stanford University Press, 1970).

255

life to the Church, and if the Church was to be a living reality, if it was to have vitality and good order, then the Scriptures had to be studied intently and preached vividly.

If the sovereignty of God was an overriding concern for the Puritans, the sanctification of Christians was an undergirding concern. If for the first generation of Reformers justification by faith was the primary concern, for the second generation sanctification by faith began to assume an equal importance. The Puritans were preachers of holiness. It was a distinct kind of holiness, to be sure; it was a holiness to be lived in this world. The Puritans were concerned that holiness be worked out in the life of the family, in the affairs of business, in the way one did one's work, and in the common life of the community. It was to be experienced in the life of the congregation and in the affairs of state. It was not a privatistic understanding of holiness, but a vitally social kind of holiness.

It was therefore natural that Puritan preaching tended to become more evangelistic. It aimed at conversion. The Puritan understanding of conversion was not what the contemporary Protestant most usually understands by the term. The Puritan understanding answered to the problems of the English church of that day. Most Englishmen were already Christians to some degree or another. They had been baptized and had even made some sort of profession of faith. The problem was that they had not gone very far beyond that. They had the beginnings of faith, but the faith they had, had not matured. The conversion at which the Puritans aimed was not one from paganism to Christianity, but from an initial faith to a more profound faith. They wanted to move their congregations from faith to faith. Their evangelistic preaching was aimed not so much at justifying faith as at sanctifying faith. They did not mean by conversion a single, totally transforming experience at the beginning of life which, if genuine, never needed to be repeated, but rather a lifelong process by which they more and more died unto sin and lived unto righteousness.[3]

The traditional Puritan hagiography counts Edward Dering as the first truly popular Puritan preacher.[4] Dering was educated at Cambridge during the reign of Queen Mary. On receiving his degree he became a fellow and won distinction for his mastery of Greek. That is, he had the traditional ministerial education of the English church. His very effective

3. Cf. *Westminster Shorter Catechism*, Q. 35.
4. This, at least, is the way Leonard Trinterud puts it. See his *Elizabethan Puritanism*, pp. 132-36.

ministry in the pulpit of Saint Paul's Cathedral in London was short. It cannot be dated exactly, but it fell between 1570 and 1575. It is presumably during his ministry there that he preached his famous series of *lectio continua* sermons on the Epistle to the Hebrews. Sometime around 1575 he was forbidden by Queen Elizabeth I to preach further. The ministry which had such promising beginnings had but a short duration.

One is hardly surprised that the queen suppressed his preaching ministry. What is surprising is that she allowed him to preach that long. Dering had preached before the queen in 1570, and his sermon, published afterward, surely deserves to be remembered as one of the most daring pieces of prophetic preaching which has come down to us. It is moderate and well tempered, and yet it is a tacit denial of the Erastianism of the Elizabethan settlement. It very simply makes clear that the biggest problem of the Church of England, namely, its inability to provide a learned ministry of the Word, is to be blamed on the government and its tight control of religious affairs. As long as the Church of England was run by government-appointed bishops, one could not expect an end to such abuses as benefices and pluralism. Dering made it clear that the court itself could reform the greatest abuses still found in the Church of England. It was because the government had perpetuated instead of reformed these abuses that the Church of England was still only half reformed. When Leonard Trinterud calls this sermon the prototype of Puritan preaching, he had this above all in mind.[5] This was the central concern of the Puritan movement. The Church must maintain a learned and regular ministry of the Word throughout the entire land.

There is nothing new about the message of Edward Dering. Hugh Latimer preached this same message at convocation in the reign of Henry VIII and John Hooper preached it at the court of Edward VI, but it still needed to be preached ten years into the reign of Elizabeth. A whole generation had passed, and still the pulpits of England were filled with "dumb dogs" — vicars and curates who either could not or would not preach. The abuses we spoke of above were still as flagrant as ever. The income of the benefices went to absentee clergy who often held several of these benefices. Even worse, the clergy were often appointed to these benefices by secular patrons. These patrons ranged from the queen on down the political ladder to local squires who controlled the appointment of the parson to the parish church or the chapel of a manorial estate.

---

5. Trinterud, *Elizabethan Puritanism*, p. 136.

Alas, these patrons were not above appointing someone on the condition that the patron be allowed to keep a certain portion of the money from the benefice. In fact, royal patrons were often the worst offenders in this matter. Those concerned for establishing a learned and regular ministry of the Word were beginning to realize that the sort of Protestantism which England had gotten was not much better than the old Catholicism. The queen of England was perpetuating the same abuses as the Roman pope. Those who wanted reform had waited patiently for a generation, and the "dumb dogs" were still lolling in the manger.

Dering was not the only sincere Protestant who by 1570 was beginning to lose patience with the Elizabethan settlement. It was about this time that Thomas Cartwright, the new Lady Margaret Professor of Divinity at Cambridge, began to lecture on the Acts of the Apostles.[6] These lectures made a point of showing that the organizational structure of the New Testament Church was much looser than the kind of monarchical episcopacy which at that time held sway in the Church of England. The bishops of Christian Europe had been feudal lords for centuries, and in England the Reformation had done nothing to change this. It was this problem to which Cambridge presbyterianism addressed itself. Cartwright's interpretation of the government of the New Testament Church had learned much from the attempts of Bucer and Calvin to recapture the polity of an earlier form of Christianity. Cartwright's lectures on Acts showed that the monarchical episcopate was a development of later centuries and was unknown in the earliest Christian Church. Cartwright rejected the hierarchical principle and called for a parity of ministers. He emphasized the primary importance of the ministry of preaching and teaching in the Church. It did not take long for the supporters of the Elizabethan settlement to sound the alarm. Cartwright was soon silenced and finally driven into exile.

It was about this time that the Admonitions to Parliament were drawn up.[7] At first they were published anonymously, but later John Field and Thomas Wilcox admitted to writing them. Once again the "dumb dogs" were the primary grievance. Certain features of the prayer book service were criticized, as well as the hierarchical form of church

6. For a very thorough study of Cartwright, see A. F. Scott Pearson, *Thomas Cartwright and Elizabethan Puritanism, 1535-1603* (Cambridge: University Press, 1925).

7. For the text of the Admonitions, see Walter H. Frere and Charles E. Douglas, eds., *Puritan Manifestoes* (London: Published for the Church Historical Society, SPCK, 1954).

government. The Admonitions stirred up quite a controversy. The queen showed no signs of allowing any further reforms in the Church of England. Things became more and more polarized between the Anglican party, that is, those who were satisfied with the way the queen was running the Church of England, and the Puritans, those who pressed for a more profound reform of the Church.

Slowly but effectively the government silenced all opposition, and the Puritans were driven into either conformity or exile. The tragedy is that the great preachers of Elizabethan England, like Edward Dering, never came to full bloom. Thomas Cartwright would probably have been a great preacher had he been allowed a significant pulpit in his native land. His lectures on Acts at Cambridge certainly left their mark. Toward the end of his life he is known to have preached through the wisdom books of the Old Testament at Warwick. In some ways those who were forced into exile were blessed. As Trinterud puts it, "A majority of the parochial clergy were in a paralysis of demoralization. Only a few of the Protestant clergy were able to break out of this stasis to reach the people in new ways."[8]

One way out of this predicament was exile. Some sought refuge in the Netherlands, including several prominent Puritans such as Cartwright and William Ames, but that was not a very promising solution. Much more promising, as it turned out, was emigration to America. For us Americans the flight of our ancestors to the New World meant the birth of our nation. As the seventeenth century progressed, the genius of this solution became ever clearer. To emigrate to America was to have the opportunity to shape a truly Christian nation. One could leave the king and his bishops behind and worship God according to Scripture. But that story we will leave to another time. At this point, what is more important is that this government opposition forced the Puritans to turn their attention to developing the inward, more subjective, and devotional aspects of the faith.

If Edward Dering and Thomas Cartwright heralded seventeenth-century Puritanism in a more general sense, another Elizabethan divine, William Perkins, is regarded as the preceptor of the Puritan School of preaching. We must now turn our attention to him.

---

8. Trinterud, *Elizabethan Puritanism*, p. 134.

II. William Perkins (1558-1602)

Although William Perkins left us little in the way of sermons, he did leave us a manual of preaching which is usually regarded as the handbook of Protestant plain style preaching.[9] It is a short work, and much about the important Puritan School is not expressed in it. Nonetheless, we need at this point to look at Perkins's work, *The Art of Prophesying*.[10]

Perkins's education and background were similar to that of many English ministers.[11] He studied at Christ College, Cambridge. Showing outstanding aptitude as a student, he was made fellow of his college in 1578. His preaching ability was recognized by his appointment to the pulpit of Saint Andrew's Church in Cambridge in 1585, where he had a lasting influence on the younger generation. Being careful not to antagonize the establishment on the issues of polity and liturgy, he devoted his attention to matters of the heart. He steered clear of the Admonitions Controversy as well as the controversy over vestments. This was fairly easy because the most intense phase of the discussion was already past before he was of sufficient age to become involved. Yet his inclination toward Puritanism was obvious. Although he died at the age of forty-four, three volumes of his works were published between 1616 and 1618.

It is important to see Perkins's handbook on preaching in the context of his whole theological work. Perkins was one of the few theologians

9. No doubt Perkins's commentary on Galatians is based on a series of *lectio continua* sermons on that book. It is, however, published as a commentary rather than as a series of sermons. See William Perkins, *A Commentary on Galatians*, ed. Gerald T. Sheppard, introductory essays by Brevard S. Childs, Gerald T. Sheppard, and John H. Augustine (New York: Pilgrim Press, ca. 1989).

10. William Perkins, *The Art of Prophesying or a Treatise Concerning the Sacred and only Manner and Method of Preaching*, in *The Workes of the Famous and Worthy Minister of Christ . . . William Perkins*, 3 vols. (London: John Legate and Cantrell Legge, 1616-18), 2:640-73; the page references in the text refer to vol. 2 of this work. The original Latin edition appeared in Cambridge in 1592. The English translation first appeared in 1607. A modern edition is available: William Perkins, *The Art of Prophesying*, rev. ed. (Edinburgh and Carlisle, Pa.: Banner of Truth Trust, 1996).

11. For biographical material on Perkins, see *The Works of William Perkins*, introduction and edited by Ian Breward (Appleford, Abingdon, Berkshire: Sutton Courtenay Press, 1970). Note especially pp. 3-131. For bibliography and notes, see pp. 327-49. See also Donald K. McKim, *Ramism in William Perkins' Theology*, American University Studies VII: Theology and Religion, vol. 15 (New York: Peter Lang Publishing, 1987); and Young Jae Timothy Song, *Theology and Piety in the Reformed Federal Thought of William Perkins and John Preston* (Lewiston, N.Y.: Edwin Mellen Press, 1998).

in England during the reign of Queen Elizabeth who achieved any kind of international reputation. In those days, when English theology was divided into "Calvinist" and "Arminian" parties, Perkins was one of those who defined what was "Calvinist." He tacked down his understanding of Calvinism in a very formal and precise way. His most popular work was a diagram or chart which put down on paper the whole process of salvation from God's eternal decree to the Last Judgment and the eternal glory of the elect. This "Golden Chain" was a sort of popular catechism that enjoyed a wide circulation, but it made things a bit too clear. As we look at his theological work four hundred years later, it is easy to see it as an example of Protestant scholasticism, and yet he presents a clear antithesis to baroque homiletics in his approach to preaching.

The Art of Prophesying was originally published in Latin and then translated into English. The first English edition was published in 1592, and it was frequently reprinted. Several Latin editions appeared on the Continent, one in Basel in 1602 and another in Hannover in the same year. A Dutch translation appeared in 1606, and it was sufficiently popular to demand a reprint three years later. Perkins's handbook on preaching was obviously very popular over a wide area.

One of the most unusual and significant features of this work is its title, *The Art of Prophesying*. This title immediately evokes the image of the Old Testament prophets and suggests that preaching is following in the prophetic tradition. Certainly that is an important element of Puritan preaching. But those thoroughly versed in Scripture will even more readily recognize the reference to I Corinthians 14, where Paul discusses at length the nature of Christian preaching and speaks of preaching as prophecy. Surely it is to this passage of Scripture that the title alludes. In I Corinthians the Spirit-filled dimension of Christian worship is under discussion. For the Puritan understanding of preaching, nothing is quite so important as seeing it as the continuing work of the Holy Spirit in the Church. Preaching is God at work in the Church through his Spirit. It is the Holy Spirit who through the means of preaching gathers the Church, sanctifies the Church, and vivifies the Church. Preaching is through and through a divine work. By using this word "prophesying" in his title, then, Perkins gives a deep resonance to the concept of preaching.

The definition which begins the work tells us, "Prophecy . . . is a public and solemn speech of the prophet pertaining to the worship of God and the salvation of our neighbour" (p. 646). Perkins obviously finds both doxological and evangelistic dimensions to preaching. That preaching is worship is supported by a reference to Romans 1:9, in which the apostle speaks of serving God through the preaching of the gospel. According to this definition, preaching has two aims: the worship of God and the salvation of the neighbor. It is through preaching that the glory of God is revealed, especially when the preaching leads to the salvation of human beings. Preaching is part of God's saving work, and this saving work reveals his glory. God called the Church to maintain a preaching ministry in order that his Word bring salvation to his people. When we serve him in this ministry, we worship him as he has called us to worship him. Preaching is worship because it serves the glory of God.

Adding yet another dimension, Perkins puts on the title page, without comment, the well-known passage from Nehemiah 8 which describes the prototype of synagogue preaching: "And Ezra the scribe stood upon a pulpit of wood which he had made for the preaching. And Ezra opened the book before all the people: for he was above all the people: and when he opened it all the people stood up. Moreover Ezra praised the Lord the great God and all the people answered, Amen, Amen. . . . And they read in the book of the law of God distinctly, and gave the sense and caused them to understand the reading" (Neh. 8:4-6 and 8) (p. 640).[12] This was one of the key passages of Scripture on which the Puritans based their service of worship. It tells us how the books of the Law were read through and systematically expounded so that the congregation understood the reading. This was the way the Puritans understood preaching. It was a matter of reading Scripture and then making its meaning clear. It was this which they understood as "biblical" preaching.

Still another dimension of the preaching ministry implied by the use of the word "prophecy" is the intellectual. A study of Paul's use of the word "prophesying" in I Corinthians 14 shows that he would have the Christian preacher address the understanding of the worshiping assembly. He insists, "He who prophesies edifies the church" (14:4).[13] Then again, "In church I would rather speak five words with my mind, in order to instruct others, than ten thousand words in a tongue" (14:19). Worship is not merely an emotional experience; it is not a matter of the heart over

12. For the most part this quotation reflects the Geneva Bible, although not completely. This was typical of the Puritans, who used the Geneva Bible long after 1611 when the King James Version appeared.

13. Perkins often only cites the passages of Scripture he discusses. In order to make it easier to follow his thoughts, we quote the passages he cites. When we do this we quote the RSV.

against the head, as the Pietists of later times would say. Perkins recognized that even in New Testament times preaching had an intellectual component.

While "prophecy" suggests the continuity of Christian preaching with the ministry of the Old Testament prophets, Perkins goes on to point out that Christian preaching must be specifically Christian. "Preaching of the Word is prophesying in the name and room of Christ" (p. 646). We understand that to mean that Christian preaching is a continuation of the teaching ministry of Jesus. This, of course, was the reason preaching was so important to the Puritans, and it is why they so resented the disparaging of preaching by the established church. Jesus himself had been a preacher, and the responsibility to continue that preaching ministry he passed on to the apostles (Matt. 28:18-20 and Mark 16:15). This is clear from the Great Commission. Jesus sent the apostles out to preach. The Puritans did not invent the idea. The Franciscans and Dominicans had made the same point when they led their great revival in the thirteenth century. Preaching is the work of the Holy Spirit, the Spirit of Christ, fulfilling the work of Christ among his people. It is Christ's work performed by his ministers through the Holy Spirit to the glory of the Father. The Puritans had a thoroughly trinitarian understanding of preaching.

The fact that Perkins uses the word "prophesying" in the title of his manual of preaching makes it clear that he is very purposely trying to use the vocabulary of the New Testament. Far from being a senseless biblicism, this was an attempt to rediscover the liturgical concepts of the earliest Christians. All these biblical references which flowed from his pen so rapidly show the complexity and the depth of the Puritan understanding of preaching.

An interesting feature of this work is the way Perkins pairs the ministry of the Word and the ministry of prayer. The proclamation of the Word of God and the conceiving of the prayers of the people are both alike the calling of the prophet, as Perkins shows from a number of passages of Scripture (pp. 672-73). In this concern we see once again how naturally preaching is thought of in the context of worship. Certainly in this Perkins is very close to Calvin.

Fundamental to Perkins's work is his strong sense of Scripture being the Word of God. Perkins, as the Puritans in general, had a strong sense of the authority of Scripture. When he tells us that the object of preaching is to set forth the Word of God, he intends us to understand that the purpose of preaching is not to present one's own ideas about religion, but rather to expound the teachings of Scripture. The sermon has as its purpose the proclamation of God's Word. The authority of this Word is beyond and above the authority of the preacher, as is made clear by Luke 16:29 and Matthew 23:2-3. Jesus heard even in the preaching of the rabbis the authoritative Word of God. Certainly it was not because the rabbis taught the Word that it had authority. It has authority because it is God's Word. It was as simple as that. The Word of God had transcendent authority far above any human authority. The Puritans were not about to confuse the personal authority of the preacher with the authority of the Word of God. If Catholic theology, either in the sixteenth century or in our own century, made the authority of Scripture depend on the authority of the Church, Reformed theology insists that it is the other way around. The authority of the Church as well as the authority of her ministers depend on the authority of Scripture. Scripture is first and foremost the Word of God; only secondarily is it the teaching of the Church.

Perkins finds the transcendent nature of the Word of God affirmed in the Epistle of James (James 3:17), which speaks of the Word as the wisdom that is from above (p. 646). Perkins's understanding of the concept is obviously influenced by the Wisdom theology. This is as it should be, to be sure, because the Wisdom theology is an important component of New Testament teaching. Again, Perkins finds the understanding of the Word developed by the Wisdom school in Titus 1:1-3, where the apostle Paul describes himself as "a servant of God and an apostle of Jesus Christ, to further the faith of God's elect and their knowledge of the truth which accords with godliness, in hope of eternal life which God . . . promised ages ago and at the proper time manifested in his word through the preaching with which I have been entrusted by command of God our Savior." The Word of God is transcendent truth which accords with and tends to godliness. That the worship of the one transcendent God should take the form of instruction in righteousness was as important to the Puritans as it had been to the Wisdom writers of biblical times.

Perkins further elaborates his concept of the Word of God in a passage about the excellence and perfection of that Word. The modern reader recognizes the concerns of Protestant scholasticism here. Not long after Perkins wrote his manual on preaching, Reformed dogmatics formalized this discussion by establishing a traditional terminology for these ideas, but in Perkins's day the terminology apparently was still fluid. First we hear of the sufficiency of the Word of God. It is sufficient for teaching us the Christian way of life and bringing us to salvation. Then we hear of the purity of the Word of God. It is pure in that it does not lead us astray. In Reformed dogmatics it is at this point that one usually uses the term "inerrancy," but that is not the term Perkins uses here. By using the term "purity," Perkins avoids the term "infallibility," but in the discussion it is clear that he is trying to speak of infallibility or, perhaps better, inerrancy. Apparently he does not want to use either of these words; one wonders why. Next Perkins speaks of the eternity of the Word of God (p. 646). It is eternal in that its promises are sure for all eternity. Finally Perkins speaks of the vitality of the Word of God (p. 647). It is endowed with virtue in its operation. This means that the Word has a vitality, a power to convince the hearers of its truth and to bring about that which it promises. We notice that others in the history of preaching have spoken of this virtue or vitality of God's Word. It is a fundamental concept for understanding the Puritan School of preaching, because it is on this insight that the confidence of the preacher is built. He does not have to rely on the arts of oratory, although he may use them, because the power of preaching is not in the preacher but in the Word itself. This affirmation comes out several times in the course of Perkins's essay.

After taking up the proofs which show that Scripture is the Word of God, and briefly enumerating and elaborating on this very traditional theme, Perkins tells us that in the last analysis the sheep recognize the voice of the shepherd. That is why we recognize the authority of Scripture (p. 650). The Church may bear witness to the truth of Scripture, but ultimately it is not the Church which persuades us of the truth but the Holy Spirit (p. 649). This principle is a complement to the classic idea that the Word itself bears its own authority. If what is preached is God's Word, that fact alone gives it authority. The traditional ten proofs only testify to the veracity of Scripture; they do not in the end convince us. The ten proofs make very good sense if we already believe.

There is good reason why Perkins gives so much attention to showing that Scripture is the Word of God. This is fundamental to the Puritan approach to the reading and preaching of Scripture in the worship of the Church. Preaching is worship because it is the setting forth of God's Word. The minister of the Word serves God in devoutly expounding God's Word. The congregation serves God by listening to and living by God's Word. When the Church so serves God's Word, then God is worshiped. If Scripture were not God's Word, preaching would hardly be worship, but since indeed it is God's Word, preaching is worship.

Having spoken at length on the sermon as the Word of God,

Perkins turns to how one is to prepare for the preaching ministry (p. 650). For Perkins as well as the other leading Puritans, the preparation of a sermon is supposed to employ all the scholarly disciplines of the arts as well as formal studies in divinity. A theological education must be diligently imprinted on the mind and memory of the preacher. With this preparation, then, one should begin the systematic study of the whole of Scripture, beginning at the center with the Epistle to the Romans and the Gospel of John. From here one should work out to the other New Testament books and then to the books of the Old Testament. As Perkins apparently sees it, this is a lifetime work of weekly sermon preparation. While the actual study of Scripture itself is central to the preparation of the sermon, one must at the same time study the orthodox theological writers and biblical commentators. Those of the ancient Church as well as more recent writers should come equally under review. One does well to keep a notebook of quotations and reflections from this reading, so that one can incorporate them when appropriate in one's preaching. It is obvious that for Perkins the preacher is not only supposed to have a degree in arts and divinity, but he is also supposed to maintain a continual discipline of theological studies throughout his ministry. The preaching of the Word should be the fruit of a life of study as well as a life of constant prayer. The preacher must constantly seek God's guidance and illumination as he studies the Scriptures.

"Rightly dividing the word of truth" (II Tim. 2:15 KJV) is one of Perkins's major concerns (p. 662). He speaks of it several times. By this he apparently means portioning it out. Dividing up the message of Scripture so that it can be applied to the congregation is fundamental to interpretation. By this Perkins has in mind not only how one is to organize one's preaching Sunday by Sunday, but also how one is to divide up a particular text. Not every congregation needs to hear the same doctrines or be taught the same moral precepts. The needs of the times can change greatly from year to year, and the wise interpreter of Scripture must be sensitive to these changes. Again and again every congregation needs to be brought back to the fundamentals of the gospel as found in Romans and John, but there are also times when one may need to preach on special problems.

Again Perkins comes back to the doctrine of the Holy Spirit. It is the Holy Spirit, he tells us, who is the principal interpreter of Scripture (p. 651). The Bible itself is very clear: "No prophecy of scripture is a matter of one's own interpretation" (II Pet. 1:20). Perkins knows nothing of any right of private interpretation. Quite to the contrary, he tells us, "He that makes the law is the best interpreter of the law" (p. 651). It is God himself who interprets his Word. Augustine's maxim, therefore, makes very good sense. Scripture is to be interpreted by Scripture. Perkins does mention three means of interpretation which are consistent with this principle. First, the interpreter of Scripture must be guided by the analogy of faith. What Perkins apparently means is that one's interpretation must square with the whole of biblical teaching as found in the Apostles' Creed and the Ten Commandments (p. 652). These are short summaries of the basic tenets of the Christian faith as they are found in Scripture. The Apostles' Creed, obviously, is not a canonical text, but evidently Perkins considers it a sufficiently accurate summary of biblical teaching to serve the function he gives it. Second, one must always interpret one's text in the context of the passage of Scripture in which it is found. Third, one must draw in parallel passages of Scripture to make clear the meaning of any particular text. As Perkins sees it, it is sufficient to establish doctrine from Scripture. "Any point of doctrine collected by just consequence is simply of itself to be believed" (p. 663). Human testimonies, whether of the philosophers or of the Fathers, are not really needed. Sometimes they can be helpful, and we certainly have an example of the apostle Paul quoting a Greek philosopher in his sermon on the Areopagus (p. 663). Perkins himself quotes both the Greek and Latin authors as well as the Fathers of the ancient Church, and even quotes a number of such authorities in this essay on preaching. In preaching, however, this should not be done frequently. A few testimonies of Scripture are more to the point. One cannot help observing that there is a tremendous difference here between what Perkins says and what the preachers of the Counter-Reformation had to say on the subject. To support biblical truth by the tradition of the Church and the sayings of the philosophers was obviously very important to baroque Catholic preaching. It helped make the mighty impression which would win the hearer. The mighty impression and the dazzling display were of the essence of the baroque style. Perkins plainly has little interest in making an impressive display. This is quite typical of the Protestant plain style.

Having established the doctrine or teaching of the passage of Scripture, the minister should then think of how this should be applied to the congregation. Application is defined as "That whereby the doctrine rightly collected is diversely fitted according as place, time, and person do require" (p. 664). Perkins gives much time to the subject of application.

This, of course, was typical of the Puritans. One of the first topics he discusses under this heading is the distinction between law and gospel. The preaching of the gospel is the first concern of the Christian preacher, but there are legitimate uses of the law and appropriate times for preaching the law. The gospel should follow the law, however, and one should take care never to leave out speaking of Christ and his benefits. One should never be so concerned with getting across the requirements of the law that the law overshadows the gospel.

Following in the tradition of Gregory the Great, Perkins speaks of the importance of suiting one's message to all sorts and conditions of people. To this subject he gives several pages. As more modern homileticians have put it, the interpretation of the congregation has to figure in preaching just as the interpretation of the Scriptures does. Another topic under this heading is the distinction between mental application and practical application. Again typical of the Puritans, Perkins was concerned that the mind be properly informed, otherwise one could not make right decisions about doctrine or morals. The mental application was just as important as the practical application. Practical application has to do with the living of the Christian life. It is to prepare men, women, children, and servants to live well in the family, commonwealth, and Church. One dimension of the practical application is consolation; another is exhortation. What is interesting here is that the mental application is thought of as being, in fact, very practical.

Having spoken of how the sermon is to be prepared, Perkins finally turns to its delivery. He seems to have in mind that the preacher should speak to the congregation in a free, flowing, and spontaneous way. This spontaneous character should not be hindered by a manuscript either read off the page or out of the memory. But, on the other hand, the sermon should be carefully prepared. Perkins uses the word "premeditated" (p. 670). This, as we remember, was the method of the orators of classical antiquity. They thought through very carefully what they wanted to say, but it was not until they were in front of the congregation that they actually put it all together. This is of the essence of classical oratory, and it made oratory an art distinctly different from the strictly literary arts, which have to do primarily with written texts. Perkins assures us that if the sermon is well thought out and the thoughts well organized, the preacher will be able to pour out his message freely and spontaneously before the congregation. As Perkins sees it, writing a sermon out and memorizing it should be avoided because it hampers the spontaneity.

One finds the greatest distinction between Puritan preaching and baroque preaching in Chapter X. This distinction has to do with the nature of art. That preaching is an art is, again, clear from the title of the work, *The Art of Prophesying*. As Perkins sees it, preaching is indeed an art, and the preacher should be a master of the art, but the greatest art of art is to conceal one's art. This, of course, was a principle of the arts well known to classical antiquity, and Perkins duly quotes from Horace the well-known and famous formulation of the principle, "Artis etiam celare artem" (p. 670). We might put this principle something like this: "By all means use all the art you can, but don't let it appear to be art." The Puritans abhorred the "artificial." On the other hand, they deeply valued solid craftsmanship. Their philosophy of art was very different from that of the baroque. For the baroque artist it was important to amaze people with the virtuosity of the artist. The artistry was of interest in itself because of its ability to impress. The Puritan was not interested in artistic virtuosity. The less the virtuosity was noticeable, the less it distracted one from the message. The art of the preacher was to impress the congregation not with great preaching but with the majesty of the Word of God revealed in Christ. The congregation, in the Puritan view, is not edified by a display of human wisdom. What moves the congregation is the demonstration of the Spirit. When the people of God discern that in the preaching of the minister the Holy Spirit is at work, then they are moved. When the minister is simple, serious, and sincere, and when his personal life is consistent with his message, then there is a demonstration of the Spirit (p. 671). This is far more effective than any kind of artistic eloquence. Once again Perkins brings forward the central affirmation of his work, that the Word of God, in and of itself, has the power to plant the Church, to edify the Church, to vivify the Church, and when necessary, to reform the Church. As the apostle Paul put it, the gospel itself is "the power of God for salvation" (Rom. 1:16).

III. Richard Sibbes (1577-1635)

The "Heavenly Dr. Sibbes" was regarded with uncommon reverence by his contemporaries because of his learned preaching of the love of Christ.[14] Although he came from a humble family, he was able to study in

---

14. For biographical material on Richard Sibbes, see the "Memoire of Richard

Cambridge and there was inspired by the preaching of William Perkins. As a rather young man, he was recognized as a gifted preacher and received a call to preach at Trinity Church in Cambridge. Here Sibbes's "plain style" sermons attracted the most devout minds of Cambridge. His personal humility, his integrity of character, and the simplicity of his homiletical style only made the gems of his biblical interpretation sparkle more brilliantly. In 1616 he was called to be preacher at the chapel of Gray's Inn, the famous law school in London. There he drew large congregations from the most influential elements of society. In 1625 he became master of Saint Catherine's Hall in Cambridge, preaching daily at the college chapel. At Trinity Church in Cambridge John Preston was preaching daily at the same time, and the two friends had a strong influence on the university town. For the history of American preaching, it is significant that among their hearers were a considerable number of the founders of New England: Thomas Shepard, John Davenport, and Nathaniel Ward. Cotton Mather tells us how influential Sibbes's preaching was on the serious students of Cambridge. Between terms Dr. Sibbes continued to preach in London at Gray's Inn, where the leading legal minds of England welcomed him as the advocate of holy law.

A. The Bruised Reed and the Smoking Flax

Richard Sibbes was a preacher of holiness, but he inspired holiness by preaching hope and encouragement to those who yearned for holiness but found it hard to attain. His most famous series of sermons was *The Bruised Reed and the Smoking Flax*.[15] We do not know when these sermons were preached, but the first edition of them was published in 1630. In the preface the author tells us that they had been "long since preached" (p. 37). Neither is it known whether they were preached at Gray's Inn, at the chapel of Saint Catherine's Hall, or at Saint Mary's in Cambridge. The whole series was preached on a single text from the Gospel of Mat-

---

Sibbes, D.D.," by Alexander Grosart, in the first volume of *The Works of Richard Sibbes,* ed. Alexander Grosart, photolithographic reproduction of the edition of 1862-64, 7 vols. (Edinburgh and Carlisle, Pa.: Banner of Truth Trust, 1979). Grosart gave great care to the editing of the seven volumes of Sibbes's works. While this work was done well over a hundred years ago, apparently it has not been surpassed.

15. The basis of this study is vol. 1 of *The Works of Richard Sibbes*. The page numbers in the text refer to this volume.

thew: "A bruised reed shall he not break, and smoking flax shall he not quench, till he send forth judgment unto victory" (Matt. 12:20 KJV). In fact, the published series is presented as though it were one very long sermon. Dr. Sibbes begins by explaining that the words really come from the prophet Isaiah. With the eyes of faith and the spirit of prophecy Isaiah has given us a profound statement of the ministry of the Messiah. It was to be a ministry of comforting the poor, strengthening the weak, and encouraging the slow of heart. Matthew recognized that indeed Jesus had fulfilled this ministry, and so he gives us in these words first a description of the office of Christ and secondly an assurance of his execution of it.

Our preacher divides the text into three parts. First he handles "A bruised reed shall he not break." God's people, Sibbes tells us, are a bruised people. Scripture compares the Church to things that are by nature weak, a dove among the fowls, a vine among plants, sheep among beasts. God's people are the poor in spirit who, according to the teaching of Jesus, are nevertheless blessed. The bruised are those who, suffering from some kind of misery, turn to Christ for help (p. 43). The ministry of Christ is toward those who are bruised. He will not break the bruised reed because, as Isaiah tells us, he himself was bruised for our transgressions (Isa. 53:5). The ministry of Christ was a gentle ministry, for Christ was the Lamb of God. At the beginning of his ministry, when he was baptized, he was anointed by the descent of a gentle dove. He called the weak and heavy laden to him that he might give them rest (Matt. 11:28). Christ was a physician, we are told, that he might bind up the brokenhearted (p. 45). Having given this exposition of Christ's ministry to the weak, Sibbes, in the usual Puritan way, gives us the "use" or application of this teaching. If indeed Christ has come to perform this kind of ministry, then we should be encouraged to come to Christ in our bruised and wounded state. Sibbes sums it up in one of his magnificent one-liners: "There is more mercy in Christ than sin in us" (p. 47).

Our preacher proceeds to the second division of his text, "and smoking flax shall he not quench." Not only will God not quench the smoking flax, but even more, he will blow on it until it breaks into flame. Sibbes explains the smoking flax to mean the wick of a candle. A smoking wick gives little light and the smoke is offensive. This figure speaks to us of Christians who in the beginning of their Christian life have only a small portion of grace, and even that is often mingled with corruption (p. 49). Even the purest actions of the purest men need Christ to perfume them. They need the sweet savor of Christ's sacrifice. Most of us when we

271

are in great distress do not know what to pray, but the Holy Spirit, with sighs too deep for words, makes our requests to God (Rom. 8:26). Sibbes sums it up with another of his brilliant aphorisms: "Broken hearts can yield but broken prayers" (p. 50). This is followed by a host of biblical examples of the same principles. Jonah cries that he is cast out of God's sight and then prays his hope that again he will look on God's holy Temple (Jon. 2:4). Paul confesses before God, "Wretched man that I am! Who will deliver me from this body of death?" and yet breaks into thanks to God for his redemption in Christ (Rom. 7:24 RSV). The seven candlesticks in the Revelation which stand for the seven churches of Asia had much smoke mixed with their light (Rev. 2 and 3) (p. 50). Christ will not snuff out the small sparks of faint beginnings because they have been struck by his Spirit. Christ was patient with Thomas in his doubting, just as he bore with the discouragement of the disciples on the road to Emmaus (p. 51).

Having made the point that in Christ God is most merciful and gentle in his dealings with us, Sibbes then turns to cautioning his congregation. God deals harshly with hardened sinners and with hypocrites. Sibbes takes up a text from the Epistle of Jude to show that God's mercy to some is strict in order that they be snatched forcibly out of the fire (Jude 23). In the end they will bless God for it. It is another matter with those who are aware of their weaknesses and repentant of their sin (pp. 52-53).

Our preacher goes on to say that ministers should be tender toward beginners (p. 53). They should follow the example of the apostle Paul, who understood himself to be a nursemaid to the weaker brethren (I Thess. 2:7). As we see in the cases of both Saint Peter and Saint Paul, Christ chose those to preach mercy who had felt most his mercy, that they might be examples of what they taught. Ministers must strive to use the keys rightly, not loosing what God has bound and not binding what God has loosed. Only God can give the minister the wise judgment to distinguish stinking firebrands from smoking flax. Sibbes, who is not one to decorate his sermons with quotations from others, appeals to the advice of Martin Bucer, who upon long experience resolved to refuse no one in whom he found something of Christ (p. 57).

Sibbes now turns to a discussion of some of the problems raised by this teaching. How are we to know whether we are firebrands or smoking wicks? Can one be said to have saving faith even if one does not have the assurance of salvation? Should we offer worship or perform charitable deeds even when our service is not entirely pure? How is the weak Christian to deal with discouragement in spiritual matters (pp. 57-77)? To each of these questions our preacher brings passages of Scripture to show the gentleness of Christ with imperfect human beings who are nevertheless his disciples. It becomes very clear from all this that for Sibbes, being a Puritan is not the same thing as being a rigorist.

Finally Sibbes comes to his third division of the text, "till he send forth judgment unto victory." The text, he explains, tells us of God's establishing his judgment in us, that is, the rulership of grace in us whereby Christ sets up his throne in our hearts. Christ cherishes the beginnings of his grace in us until it has the victory (p. 78).

Sibbes develops at some length the doctrine of the Holy Spirit. Christ's judgment in us is accomplished when his will becomes our will. This is done by the Holy Spirit, who writes his law in our hearts. The Holy Spirit, who is the Spirit of Christ, will work in us what he worked in Christ. He joins us to Christ through faith. We are united to Christ in both his humiliation and his exaltation so that we both die with Christ and rise with Christ (p. 85). Sibbes gives considerable attention to the means at our disposal to make grace victorious in our lives. The Christian should give attention to acquiring knowledge of the will of God and should cultivate affection for the things of God. The Christian should develop a clear recognition of human weakness. It is important to be careful in the use of the means of grace, and to exercise grace in the doing of good works (p. 89).

Having spoken of means, he concludes the sermon by making clear that we must look to Christ for the victory (p. 94), for his Spirit within us preserves our faith, nourishes our hope, and cherishes our love. He quotes Luther to the effect that faith is the means whereby Christ has his victory both in the Church and in individual Christians (p. 100). It would seem from this sermon that if Luther taught justification by faith, the Puritans were encouraged by him to add that sanctification is by faith as well.

B. Sermons on II Corinthians

A sizable amount of Sibbes's preaching was the continuous preaching of single chapters or major portions of various books of the Bible. Only a selection of these series has been published. We have series on the second and third chapter of Philippians; Sibbes may well have preached through

the whole book. There is a series on Hosea 14 and two series on II Corinthians (chaps. 1 and 4). We are tempted to suppose that he preached on
other chapters of II Corinthians but that, for one reason or another, these
series have never come down to us.

The series on II Corinthians 1 was edited and published twenty
years after Sibbes's death by Dr. Thomas Manton, one of the greatest of
the Puritan preachers. The title he gives is *A Learned Commentary or Exposition upon the First Chapter of the Second Epistle of S. Paul to the Corinthians, being the Substance of Many Sermons Formerly Preached at Grayes-
Inne, London.* The series takes up the whole of the third volume of
Grosart's edition numbering 528 pages. The sermons were finished up as
a commentary. It is not clear whether this was done by Sibbes himself or
by Manton. Manton does tell us that this work, unlike others, was gone
over by Sibbes during his lifetime and corrected by his own hand.

Manton in his preface gives us some feeling for the way the preaching ministry of the Heavenly Dr. Sibbes was received by his contemporaries. He tells us of Beza's remarks about the three preachers of Geneva:
none thundered more loudly than Farel, none piped more sweetly than
Viret, none taught more learnedly than Calvin. So variously doth the
Lord dispense his gifts! The gift of Dr. Sibbes, Manton continues, was to
unfold the mysteries of the gospel in a sweet and mellifluous way. It was
therefore that his hearers styled him "the Sweet Dropper." From him
came "sweet and heavenly distillations with such a native elegance as is
not easily to be imitated."[16] The adjective "mellifluous," traditionally reserved for Bernard of Clairvaux, makes it as clear as could be that for
Manton, who knew the medieval doctors so well, England had heard in
the mellifluous doctor of Cambridge what the Middle Ages had heard in
the mellifluous doctor of Clairvaux.

C. Sermons on the Song of Solomon

Nowhere was the epithet "mellifluous" more appropriate than in Sibbes's
series of twenty sermons on the fourth, fifth, and sixth chapters of the
Song of Solomon.[17] As we have seen, series of sermons on this book were

---

16. Sibbes, *Works,* 3:4.

17. The title of the series is *Bowels Opened.* In the English of the seventeenth century "bowels" meant the inward parts of the human body where the seat of the affections

very popular during the Middle Ages because they gave the preacher an opportunity to engage in the most imaginative sort of allegorical exegesis. Such series became almost a special genre of preaching in which the doctrines of mystical theology were unfolded. The most famous was undoubtedly that of Bernard of Clairvaux. It is interesting that Bernard's series never got beyond the third chapter. One wonders if Sibbes purposely avoided the chapters the great Bernard had treated. None of the major Continental Reformers has left us a series of sermons or a commentary on the Song. First, they were not interested in allegorical exegesis, and second, they had very negative feelings about what passed for mysticism in the Middle Ages. In spite of all this, the Song was recognized as something of a special case. Calvin defended the spiritual sense of the book. Against Sebastian Castellio, the Spanish humanist scholar, he insisted that the Song spoke of the mutual love between Christ and the Church. If Calvin would have wanted to avoid an allegorical interpretation, he was willing to recognize a typological interpretation. Although he never worked out his interpretation in a series of sermons or in a commentary, he did recognize that the Song had a very distinctive Christian interpretation. The notes of the Geneva Bible transmitted to English-speaking Protestants the outlines of this Christian interpretation, and surely it was the Geneva Bible which was in the hands of the greater part of Sibbes's congregation. What is interesting about this series is that it is a serious attempt by a Protestant preacher to interpret this difficult book using the canons of exegesis which had by this time become traditional within Protestantism.

The uniqueness of Sibbes's interpretation is set forth in his introduction to the first sermon. He tells his congregation that the Holy Spirit condescends to our human understanding that he might lift us up to heavenly things. He speaks of the sweetest experience of life, marriage, and the most delightful affection, love, and the sweetest manner of expression, a song, in order that he might carry up the soul to things of a heavenly nature (p. 6). For Sibbes the Song of Solomon is poetry, and as poetry it uses poetic means of expression. All through Scripture marriage

---

or, as we would say, the emotions was to be found. The series more accurately treats Song of Sol. 4:16–6:3; the preacher recognized that the passage he wanted to interpret begins at the end of the fourth chapter and continues through to the first three verses of the sixth chapter. The work was edited posthumously by Thomas Goodwin and Philip Nye in London in 1639. The basis of this study is the text found in vol. 2 of *The Works of Richard Sibbes*. The page numbers in the text refer to this volume.

is a metaphor for communion with God. This is seen with particular clarity in the book of Hosea, but it is also found in numerous passages of the New Testament (p. 201). In Ephesians 5 the apostle Paul speaks of marriage as a great mystery which reflects the love between Christ and the Church. "For here the greatest things, the 'mystery of mysteries,' the communion betwixt Christ and his church, is set out in the familiar comparison of marriage, so that we might better see it in the glass of comparison" (p. 6). Again it is Paul who tells us that the knowledge of the love of Christ for the Church is above all knowledge (Eph. 3:19). The poetic language is the means the Holy Spirit has used to communicate these profound truths to us. For Sibbes the Song is not to be approached as allegory or even as typology so much as it is to be approached as metaphor.

A principle of exegesis used again and again by the Puritans is that the Scriptures must be interpreted out of Christian experience. It is the devout who best understand what Scripture has to say. Sibbes puts this very clearly in the introduction to the sermon. "As none entered into the holy of holies but the high priest, . . . so none can enter into the mystery of this Song of Songs, but such as have more near communion with Christ" (p. 5). To be sure, Sibbes would never have dreamed of spinning an interpretation of Scripture out of pure introspection. He was as committed to grammatical-historical exegesis as Calvin had been. Yet Sibbes, as the Puritans in general, saw a legitimate place for introspection in the interpretation of the Scriptures. The gospel was, after all, revealed from faith to faith. Calvin's approach to the interpretation of Scripture was classical and objective. The Puritans, on the other hand, were eager to maintain the disciplines of grammar and history in their interpretation of Scripture, but they were more subjective. The seventeenth century was beginning to have a concern for the experiential. Descartes was, after all, Sibbes's contemporary. For Sibbes Christian experience not only explains Scripture, it also proves the truth of Scripture.

For Sibbes the Song of Solomon is an opportunity to rhapsodize on the love of Christ for the Church. If, to be sure, the book speaks of Christ's love for the Church, it also speaks of Christ's love for each member of the Church. But Sibbes's exposition takes as its framework the overall theme of Christ's love for the Church; it works into that framework the theme of Christ's love for each individual Christian.

Let us look briefly at how Sibbes develops his exposition. We take portions of his second and third sermons, based on this text:

276

I am come to my garden, my sister, my spouse:
   I have gathered my myrrh with my spice;
   I have gathered my honeycomb with my honey;
   I have drunk my wine with my milk:
Eat, O friends;
   drink, yea, drink abundantly, O beloved.

(Song of Sol. 5:1)

In the previous sermon he began the exposition of this verse by observing that here we learn of Christ's answer to the invitation of the Church to enter her garden. In this sermon he begins by speaking of the two words by which he addresses the Church. The Church is the sister of Christ and the bride of Christ. Christ is our brother, Sibbes assures his congregation, and the Church, just as every member, is his sister. At the resurrection Jesus told Mary Magdalene that he was ascending to his Father and her Father, to his God and her God, and then he told her to go tell his brethren (John 20:17). Christ is our brother by the incarnation. That is our first union with him, for in his becoming bone of our bone and flesh of our flesh he became our blood relative. But the Church is also united to Christ in marriage. The Church is the spouse of Christ (pp. 22 and 23). It springs out of the pierced side of Christ even as Eve was taken out of Adam's side. When Christ's side was pierced, the Church came forth out of his death. Christ must redeem us before he weds us. We are united to him first by his incarnation, and second by redemption. The two are very different relationships. The first is not sufficient without the second. The second is infinitely more profound than the first. Our redemptive relationship to Christ is at the heart of the gospel. Because we were in bondage to sin, we had to be redeemed so that Christ might marry us (p. 24).

The redemptive relationship is essential for a true communion with Christ. Only the redeemed are free to love Christ. The Church is the bride of Christ through her consent. This is an important point for Sibbes. The consent, however, comes through the working of the Holy Spirit in our hearts (pp. 24-26). Christ is present with the Church in the garden. He is in the garden as both brother and bridegroom, for all those relationships which as creatures we know in different and separate experiences are brought together and fulfilled in our union with Christ (p. 23).

Our preacher now turns his attention to Christ's delight in the offerings of the Church. "I have gathered my myrrh with my spice; I have gath-

277

ered my honeycomb with my honey; I have drunk my wine with my milk."
The Church has prepared this feast for her spouse from what Christ himself
had graciously provided. Still, Christ delights in what the Church has prepared and hopes that in his return he will bring an even greater abundance
of spiritual treasures for her enjoyment (p. 27). Sibbes admonishes his congregation, "Therefore, let us be stirred up to have communion with Christ,
but this motive, that thus we shall have an increase of a further measure of
grace. Let us labour to be such as Christ may delight in, for our graces are
honey and spices to him, and where he tastes sweetness he will bring more
with him" (p. 28). Sibbes then asks what exactly is meant by myrrh, spice,
honey, wine, and milk. He tells us that to give a specific meaning to each of
these foods would press beyond the meaning that the Holy Spirit intended.
They are all delightful foods which give pleasure to those who eat them.
Taken together they speak of the joy of the covenant of grace which is a
pleasure both to us and to God himself. This bit of exegetical good sense
shows how fresh the interpretation of our preacher really is.

Then, to make his point even clearer that Christ gives grace that he
might give more grace, he brings out a most sparkling biblical image. As
Isaac sent Rebecca before their marriage jewels and ornaments to wear
that she might be more lovely when they met, so our blessed Savior sends
to his spouse jewels and ornaments from heaven that he might delight in
her ever more and more till at last the marriage be consummated (p. 29).
This is not, of course, exegesis according to the strictest school. It is poetry. And our preacher has the good sense to realize that just as one explains Scripture by Scripture, one explains poetry by poetry.

A bit further on in the third sermon, Sibbes draws from this same text
a beautiful passage on the variety of good things with which Christ feasts
his bride (p. 33). The grace Christ bestows on the Church has variety and
abundance. The Gospel of John teaches that Christ is full of grace and
truth. As he multiplied the loaves and the fish for the multitude, so he multiplies grace for the soul. If he gives life, he gives it that we might have it
abundantly. If he gives the water of life, he gives it not as a simple cup but as
a fountain of living water welling up within us. If he gives wine, he gives it
as he did at Cana, a great quantity which never fails. The gifts of God are
far more abundant than all that we ever ask or think (Eph. 3:20).

Here, as so often in this series of sermons, we find the same dazzling
use of biblical imagery that we found in Gregory of Nazianzus. Yet these
sermons come from the Puritan "plain style" of preaching. Apparently the
texts we have are the notes the preacher wrote out in preparation for the

actual preaching of the sermon. This one gathers from the concentrated style in which they were written down. The sermons themselves were preached much more spontaneously. The notes do not seem to have been finished up after their preaching. They were not published as examples of great oratory but as examples of great exposition; nevertheless, they probably were, as they were preached, great oratory. True to the intention of the Puritan School, their greatness was in the depth of their insight into the meaning of the text. They abound in beautiful similes, metaphors, and aphorisms, but all this is quite secondary, and they are never studied or artificial. They flow naturally from a gentle scholar who lovingly meditated on the Word of God. These sermons are the fruit of a profound spiritual love for Christ. They are the work of a preacher who found the highest poetry in the truths of God and the greatest rationality in the ways of God. Bernard of Clairvaux could hardly have found a better preacher to continue where he left off.

IV. John Preston (1587-1628)

John Preston was very much like his friend Richard Sibbes.[18] Both were brought up in rural England and sent off to study at Cambridge. Neither studied abroad, nor were they particularly inspired by current trends of thought popular in foreign parts. They absorbed the faith and life of the Reformed Church of England very much as they received it. They meditated deeply on the traditions of English Protestantism as they had been shaped during the long reign of Queen Elizabeth. They deepened those traditions and enlarged them, lived them and preached them. Both were Calvinists in the sense that most ministers of the Church of England were Calvinists at the time. It was Calvinism with a distinctive English twist, but Calvinism nevertheless. As Arminianism began to appear in the early decades of the seventeenth century, Sibbes and Preston sided with Calvinist orthodoxy. Preston particularly was a vigorous supporter of Calvinism as represented by such men as William Perkins in the generation before him. Both Sibbes and Preston stayed away from any kind of separatism. Neither did they want to get involved in controversies over matters of lit-

18. For biographical material on Preston, see Irvonwy Morgan, *Prince Charles's Puritan Chaplain* (London: George Allen and Unwin, 1957), and Thomas Ball, *The Life of the Renowned Doctor Preston* (Oxford: Parker, 1885).

urgy or church polity. They were much more concerned with matters of the heart. They both knew that Archbishop Laud and his party would have liked to silence them, but they were not going to give him any grounds for doing so.

There was one way that Preston was quite different from Sibbes. We sense in Preston a definite continuity with the piety of the late Middle Ages. One finds traces of a sort of Protestant scholasticism in his preaching, both in his message and his homiletical method. One cannot help but wonder if his Protestantism is not as much the heritage of John Wycliffe as it is of Luther and Calvin.

Preston succeeded Sibbes as preacher at Trinity Church in Cambridge. He was for some time preacher at Lincoln's Inn, London's other prestigious school of law. In 1622 he became master of Emmanuel College in Cambridge. About the same time, Sibbes returned to Cambridge as master of Saint Catherine's Hall, and the two preachers provided the university town with outstanding preaching. Both exemplified the Protestant plain style of preaching, and they practiced it in a place where it would influence English preaching for several generations.

Although Preston was only forty-one years old when he died, he has left us several collections of sermons. *The Saints Daily Exercise* is a fine collection of sermons on prayer showing the Puritan concern to deepen the devotional life.[19] Preston left us several collections of sermons on the subject of piety: *The Saints Qualifications, The Doctrine of the Saints Infirmities,* and *Riches of Mercy to Men in Misery.*[20] Of a more theological nature was his *Life Eternal; or, A Treatise of the Divine Essence and Attributes Delivered in 18 Sermons.*[21]

The Breast-plate of Faith and Love is commonly regarded as one of the classics of Puritan spirituality.[22] The work is made up of three series

---

19. John Preston, *The Saints Daily Exercise,* photolithographic reproduction of the edition of London, 1629 (Amsterdam and Norwood, N.J.: Walter J. Johnson, 1976).

20. John Preston, *The Saints Qualifications,* 3rd ed. (London: Printed by R.B. for N. Bourne, 1637); John Preston, *The Doctrine of the Saints Infirmities* (London: Imprinted by I. Oakes for Taunton, 1638); and John Preston, *Riches of Mercy to Men in Misery* (London: F. Eglesfield, 1658).

21. John Preston, *Life Eternal; or, A Treatise of the Divine Essence and Attributes Delivered in 18 Sermons,* 2nd ed. (London: Imprinted by R.E., 1631).

22. John Preston, *The Breast-plate of Faith and Love,* photolithographic reproduction of the edition of 1634 (Edinburgh and Carlisle, Pa.: Banner of Truth Trust, 1979); page numbers in the text are to this work. The Banner of Truth Trust has also reissued this work in a 1991 edition.

of sermons. The first is a series of four sermons on faith; the second, six sermons on effectual faith; the third, eight sermons on love. Series of this sort had been popular in the late Middle Ages; we saw examples in the preaching of Johann Geiler von Kaysersburg. Again and again we find the English preachers being rather slow to follow the Continental Reformers, especially in matters of homiletical form. At this point the Puritanism of Preston is cast in the homiletical form of the late Middle Ages.

These sermons may properly be regarded as evangelistic sermons. Their aim is the conversion of those to whom they are addressed. Preston is fully aware that he is preaching to baptized Christians, but he is concerned that his congregation enter into the full reality of which their baptism is a sign and a promise. One hears in these sermons certain concerns and insights that are not present in Luther and Calvin. The seventeenth century was a new age, and it had new concerns. Puritanism, just as the Protestant orthodoxy of the Continent, had its own distinct preoccupations. Surely one of its great concerns was the conversion of those who were only nominally Christian to full Christian faith. The evangelism of so many of the Puritans aimed at explicit commitment and full discipleship. In these sermons we see a classic example of how they went about preaching conversion.

The four sermons of the series on faith all have the same text and might well be regarded as one long sermon. It is the classic text of the Reformation, Romans 1:16 and 17, "For I am not ashamed of the gospel of Christ: for it is the power of God unto salvation to every one that believeth; to the Jew first, and also to the Greek. For therein is the righteousness of God revealed from faith to faith: as it is written, The just shall live by faith" (KJV). Let us look in considerable depth at the first of these sermons, because it exemplifies quite completely Preston's approach to evangelistic preaching. The sermon unfolds according to the principles of William Perkins. First the text is read; then in a few very brief words the sense of the text is brought out. There is no elaborate exordium or introduction. This was the sort of thing the Puritan plain style was trying to get away from.

As Preston explains the text, some people found Paul's gospel embarrassing because of both his plainness of speech and the persecutions and imprisonments he endured, but the apostle is not ashamed of the gospel because it is that which, being received, will bring us to heaven (p. 1). The text, Preston tells his congregation, tells us why the gospel is the power of God. In it the righteousness of God, that is, the righteousness which is of God, is revealed, which only God accepts, and by which alone men can be saved. But why is it revealed? our preacher asks. It is revealed to us so that we can do something about it, so that we can receive it by faith. Something is to be done on our part. God manifests it, and lays it open so we can receive it by faith. The text then, Preston concludes, teaches us this point of doctrine, that righteousness, by which alone we can be saved, is revealed and offered to all who will take it (p. 2). This is the teaching that is found in the text.

Preston then makes a few remarks, of the sort found in the typical Scholastic *prothema,* about the text's importance. This revelation is an exceedingly great thing to see, he tells his congregation. It is the great glorious mystery of the gospel. It is so glorious that it swallows up our thoughts. Now, in this last age, Christ has revealed through us the unsearchable riches of his grace. It is therefore that the apostle Paul prays that God would open our eyes that we might comprehend with all the saints the height, the length, and the breadth of that redemption which Christ has wrought for us (Eph. 3:18). It is necessary that this be revealed because it had not previously been revealed and is not written in our hearts by nature. The apostle prays that our eyes might be opened so that we might know the hope of our calling (Eph. 1:18). For what point is there in having a light if our eyes be shut (p. 4)?

Preston now begins to develop his point. He proposes to open up the teaching he finds in the text by asking six questions (p. 4). The first is, How does the righteousness of God save us? Preston answers that it saves us in the same way that the unrighteousness of Adam condemns us. He explains his point by explaining Romans 5:14 and then II Corinthians 5:21. We are saved by the vicarious death of Christ (pp. 5-6). The second question is, How shall we come by it? It is offered to us as a gift, Preston explains. This he supports with several passages of Scripture such as Isaiah 9:6, John 3:16, and Romans 5:17, and then he gives three reasons why it is a gift (p. 7). Our preacher's third question is, To whom is this gift offered? It is offered to all, as we find throughout the Bible. He mentions particularly Revelation 22:17, "And let him who is thirsty come, let him who desires take the water of life without price" (RSV). Preston treats several objections to this at some length. He concludes that the gate is open to all, but only those will enter whom God enables to enter. Those who do not understand this do not understand the doctrine of our divines, Preston maintains. In substance we propound nothing other than they, even if in method we differ somewhat (p. 10). The point for each of us is that the offer is made to all of us, and on this promise we can build. Were the promise made only to the elect, then we would have to ask if we are the elect. This is not the method. They who take hold of the promise and build on it are pardoned, but they who do not take hold of it are excluded (p. 10).

Preston proceeds to his fourth question. What qualifications are expected of those to whom this offer is given? He answers that the offer is given to all, and no qualification is required in terms of either a degree of righteousness or tears of humiliation. It is only required to come with the hand of faith and receive it in the midst of all our unworthiness (p. 11). Our preacher turns to the fifth question: How is the righteousness of Christ made ours? We take it, Preston says, and we take it by faith. Faith is not only an act of the intellect but also an act of the will. For the righteousness of God is both revealed to the mind and offered to the will (p. 13). Preston begins to define faith at considerable length, showing that faith is not only assenting to a truth but embracing it as well. This is explained by an example. If a physician prepares a medicine for one who is sick, the patient must take the medicine. If he does not, the work of the physician will do no good. Preston defines very carefully how faith is taking Christ. This taking of Christ is the main point which makes Christ ours. Three things must concur (p. 15). First, it is Christ and Christ alone who must be taken. Second, we must understand what this taking is. Taking Christ means turning away from the world and being subject to him alone. Third, Christ must be taken with a complete, deliberate, and free will (p. 19). Preston now takes up his sixth and final question: What is required of us when we have it? He answers that we must love Christ, we must repent of our sins, we must leave all other things behind, we must be willing to suffer for him, and we must serve him (p. 20).

Having opened up the teaching of this text, Preston proceeds to make applications of it. This is once more typical of the homiletical forms of Protestant scholasticism. His application is developed in two uses. First, we should be aware of the danger of refusing to take this righteousness which is revealed in the gospel. Rejecting Christ is the greatest sin (p. 23). Second, we should be aware of the danger of putting off the taking of Christ until some future time. Preston develops his application by retelling the parable of the invitation to the wedding feast (p. 27). He then makes an appeal to his congregation to consider whether they will take Christ or refuse him (p. 29). The invitation to the wedding feast is now open, but the time will soon come when the Bridegroom will enter in and the doors will be shut (p. 30).

Reading the sermons of John Preston, one very quickly notices that they are quite different from those of Luther, Calvin, and the other Continental Reformers we have studied. In the first place, their homiletical form is not so much expository as it is scholastic, or thematic. The text is studied briefly in order to draw out of it a specific teaching or theme, and then this theme is developed in a number of points which are then supported by various arguments, drawn mostly from Scripture. They are illustrated by examples or illuminated by similes. Then, finally, they are applied to the lives of those in the congregation. In this respect Preston's sermons resemble those of medieval Scholasticism. As we have seen, this approach to homiletical form became popular with the Protestant scholasticism of the Continent. One does not find in these sermons the verse-by-verse commentary of a longer portion of Scripture which characterized the expository preaching of Luther, Oecolampadius, Brenz, and Calvin. Preston usually takes one verse and develops from it a theme or a number of themes. In fact, he often develops a whole series of sermons from a particular verse.

One also notices a far greater concern to systematize Christian doctrine than one finds in the Reformers of the sixteenth century. One does not find in Preston anything like the simple and straightforward enthusiasm to dig out of the text what is to be found. It was this concern which made the older generation of Reformers happy to preach the *lectio continua*. Preston has a theme on which he wants to preach, and he finds the appropriate text. One misses in Preston the concern for biblical philology, for the rhetoric of Scripture, and for the original languages that one finds in the older Reformers. No doubt Preston could use the original languages, but one never gets the impression he has spent much time finding out what a particular word or phrase means in the context in which it is found.

His definition of faith, for example, which we find in the second sermon, is much more systematic than it is expository (pp. 40ff.). Rather than going over some of the classic passages on faith one by one to show how the word is used, he first distinguishes between different kinds of faith. There is faith in general, then there is justifying faith. Justifying faith Preston defines as "A grace or habit infused into the soul by the Holy Ghost, whereby we are enabled to believe, not only that the Messias is offered to us, but also to take and receive him as Lord and Saviour" (p. 42). Having given us a definition of faith packed with the terminology of medieval Scholasticism, he continues by defining faith according to its object, its subject, its manner of working, and its effects (pp. 44ff.). To be sure, he supports his points with quotations from Scripture, but the whole tenor of the discussion breathes the air of a very scholastic approach to Scripture. It is not an expository approach. It is systematic theology rather than biblical theology.

What one notices immediately in this series of sermons is the way Preston explains faith as an act of the will. We have seen how faith is defined as a taking or embracing of Christ in the first sermon. It is an act of both the mind and the will. In the second sermon he develops this even more clearly. Faith must be consent as well as assent, he tells us (p. 47). He is aware that not everyone is in agreement with this, but he insists that if the righteousness of God is offered it must be received, and receiving is an act of the will. "It must needs be that the will must come into this worke as well as the understanding" (p. 48). Preston's definition of faith introduces a voluntarism one does not find in the Reformers of the sixteenth century. They would never define faith as an act, much less as a work! They understood it as a gift. They never tired of quoting Ephesians 2:8, "For by grace you have been saved through faith; and this is not your own doing, it is the gift of God" (RSV). Preston figures that he has covered himself by going on to say, "So then we see that faith in an action both of the mind and the will, wrought by God, enlightening the mind, and changing the will" (p. 50). Be that as it may, Preston's understanding of faith is thoroughly voluntarist, and as we shall see, this has a tremendous effect on his approach to preaching, particularly evangelistic preaching.

In Preston's series of sermons on love he gives us several insights into his understanding of preaching. At one point he tells us, "The word that wee deliver to you should be like nailes, driven to the head, . . . that they may stick and abide in the Soule . . . that they may not easily fall out again. Therefore the maine businesse that wee have to doe in preaching the Word, is to fasten these words thus upon your hearts" (pp. 109ff.). At another point he tells his congregation that simply coming to church and hearing the sermon is not enough. The hearing of the true Word includes the practicing of the Word. It is the same way as with those who study music. It is not enough to take the lesson if one does not practice. To have the affections inflamed to the Lord is true hearing. Until that has been done, the Word has not been truly heard (pp. 80ff.). In both the preaching of the sermon and the hearing of the sermon, the important thing is the moving of the will, the inflaming of the heart. This is, to be sure, something God himself must do through the inner working of the Holy Spirit, as Preston makes clear at the end of the second sermon on love (pp. 53ff.). God works through preaching that the word be nailed into our souls, and that our hearts be inflamed, but in the end it is clear that for Preston the aim of the sermon is to move the human heart.

With this understanding of preaching, it is easy to see why Preston's sermons are above all evangelistic sermons. Preston preaches for conversion. The way he does it is to map out the plan of salvation and then urge his hearers to follow it through. He tells us that faith is an act of the mind and of the will, and then he urges us to perform this act. He makes it very clear that faith is an embracing of Christ, and that if it is that, it is also a turning away from the world, and so he inevitably concludes by urging us to turn away from the world and embrace Christ. Here we find a very distinct approach to evangelistic preaching, an approach which will reappear frequently in the centuries which follow.

V. Thomas Goodwin (1600-1680)

Thomas Goodwin was one of those preachers who inspired in Protestantism a profound sense of personal devotion. It would have been easy for Protestantism, especially in England, to become a sort of civil religion. Elizabeth I, the head of state, had made herself the head of the Church as well. The Church of England had by the end of the sixteenth century become a state-controlled religion. Yet Goodwin, as the Puritans generally, insisted on the spiritual dimensions of worship. We noticed this tendency in Goodwin's teacher, Richard Sibbes. The Puritans regarded worship as first of all communion with God. The Christian faith, as they saw it, was a matter not so much of the correct performance of the rites prescribed by the government as it was of entering into the fellowship of the saints. It was a matter of abiding in the presence of God. The transcendent experience of worship was Goodwin's primary concern.

While Goodwin's deep piety was his most noteworthy characteristic, he is remembered for several other reasons as well. One of the architects of Congregationalism and one of the most influential theologians of the Commonwealth, Goodwin was highly respected as a preacher in his day. Although his literary legacy is primarily made up of theological treatises, enough of his sermons have been preserved to show that his reputation as a preacher was well deserved.

Thomas Goodwin was born in Norfolk.[23] He was educated at Christ College, Cambridge, and then at Saint Catherine's Hall, where he became a fellow. While in Cambridge he came under the influence of both Richard Sibbes and John Preston, then at the height of their preaching careers. While he was a student at Cambridge, the Synod of Dort was held (1618-19). Goodwin studied Calvin's *Institutes* with enthusiasm and found himself less and less inclined toward Arminianism. He developed his Calvinism in a supralapsarian direction, in much the same fashion as William Ames. From 1625 to 1634 he preached in Cambridge, and served the last two of these years as vicar of Trinity Church. His Puritan views brought him into conflict with the bishop, who was of distinctly Laudian tendency. Finally he resigned and moved to London. In 1639 he went to Holland as pastor of the English congregation at Arnhem, returning to London only after Laud's impeachment. For the next several years he served as pastor of an independent church in London. Being chosen as a member of the Westminster Assembly, he developed into one of the most influential advocates of Congregationalism. In 1650 he was named president of Magdalen College in Oxford. More and more he became one of Oliver Cromwell's most trusted advisers. When Cromwell died in 1658, it was Goodwin who attended him. With the restoration of the Stuart monarchy, Goodwin was quite predictably removed from his position at Oxford. By this time he was sixty years old, and given the efforts of the Restoration episcopacy to silence the Puritans, it is not surprising that he retired from public ministry, devoting himself more and more to his writing and the devotional life in which he found such peace.

The chief example we have of Goodwin's homiletical work is a magnificent series of thirty-six sermons on Ephesians 1,[24] a chapter that gives

23. For biographical information on Goodwin, see the memoir of Robert Halley in *The Works of Thomas Goodwin, D.D.,* 8 vols. (Edinburgh: James Nichol, 1864); Erik Routley, *Thomas Goodwin (1600-1680)* (London: Independent Press, 1961); Harry Lee Poe, "Evangelistic Fervency among the Puritans in Stuart England (1603-1688)" (Ph.D. diss., Southern Baptist Theological Seminary, 1982); and Barker, *Puritan Profiles,* pp. 70-77.

24. The basis of this study has been *The Works of Thomas Goodwin sometime President of Magdalene College in Oxford, First Volume, containing an Exposition on the First, and part of the Second Chapter, of the First Epistle to the Ephesians* (London: J.D. and S.R., 1681); page references in the text are to this work. This first volume is bound together with two other volumes bearing different titles. See n. 27 below. For a more recent edition, see *The Works of Thomas Goodwin,* photolithographic reproduction of the edition of James Nichol published in Edinburgh in 1864, 9 vols. (Edinburgh and Carlisle, Pa.: Banner of Truth Trust, 1985).

the preacher an opportunity to treat at length the eternal purposes of God in our redemption. This chapter reveals Christ's saving work as the essential mystery of the cosmos. Goodwin's sermons are a hymn of praise to the love of God as it is manifested in Christ. They set forth the wonder of God's redemptive purposes. It is in this context that Goodwin sets the doctrine of predestination and develops it in doxological terms. As Goodwin presents it, God's love to his people is not some recent new-found invention but is as old as eternity. It is like the love of childhood sweethearts who are finally married after many years. Goodwin preaches to the elect, confident that they will hear with joy that God's electing love is from all eternity and will in the end overcome all obstacles and win the victory that will last unto all eternity. This series of sermons is a great theological statement and deserves to be recognized as one of the most profound doctrinal statements of the Christian pulpit.

Goodwin is a marvelous exegete. His sermons are filled with tightly stitched expositions of the Greek text. One suspects that they were carefully edited for publication and that the exact exegesis of the published sermons is more detailed than the exegesis in the sermons that were preached. Even at that, careful study of the text must have stood behind the preached sermons. One imagines that the intensity of the preacher's engagement with the text was what fascinated his congregation. Goodwin obviously studied a wide variety of theologians ranging from Augustine and Thomas Aquinas to Girolamo Zanchi and William Ames. The fact that such sermons could be preached to a Puritan congregation is a tribute to the high level of theological discussion of the day.

The editors' preface tells us that these sermons had been preached some forty years before, and that in his retirement Goodwin revised them for publication. This suggests that they were preached during his pastorate in Cambridge. This seems more than likely, because these sermons seem to assume a congregation accustomed to thinking through their sermons on a more advanced level.

A. Worship as Benediction

The first couple sermons treat us to a magnificent meditation on the blessing of God. The text our preacher wants to open up is Ephesians 1:3, "Blessed be the God and Father of our Lord Jesus Christ, who hath blessed us with all spiritual blessings in heavenly places in Christ." Two things are involved in this text as Goodwin interprets it: our blessing God and God's blessing us. To bless God is worship at its highest. To receive the blessings of God is our greatest happiness.

Sermon 2 begins by pointing out that these words from the apostle Paul represent the outpouring of a heart richly blessed. "The holy heart of this blessed Apostle was so full in his own person of being blessed by God, that he falls a *blessing* him as soon as he begins to speak. 'Tis his first word he begins the body of this epistle with, and continues the same course and the way of blessing God through the first half of the Chapter" (p. 18). Goodwin intends to show us that blessing God is a distinct approach to the serving of God's glory. It is a sort of praise or thanksgiving, and yet it has its distinct characteristics.

It is particularly appropriate that this epistle begin with blessing God, because nowhere had Paul experienced such blessings as in his ministry in Ephesus, and not only that, the Ephesians themselves had been so richly blessed by the apostle's ministry among them. The epistle begins with blessing God for the blessings God has poured out not only on the author of the epistle but on the recipients as well. This is part of the unique character of blessing. It is reflexive. To bless God is to acknowledge God's blessings. It is to reflect back to God the goodwill he has shown to us (p. 20).

For Paul, Goodwin tells us, this enumeration of gospel blessing is in itself a kind of preaching of the gospel. He shows how this is particularly the case in the blessing at the beginning of the apostle's epistle to the Romans. Whenever the gospel is preached, the goodness of God is shown forth. And that is the reason the preaching of the gospel is worship, no matter where that preaching is done, no matter by whom or to whom the gospel is preached. The proclamation of the gospel reveals the wondrous grace of God. Preaching publishes the glory of God in opening up to the world his redemptive love. Goodwin has summed up one of the basic principles of Protestant worship. This insight is expressed in a beautiful line: "The Gospel is made up of blessings, is nothing but blessings, and the fulness of blessings" (p. 21).

Having begun his sermon with these remarks, he divides his text into three points. First he wants to discuss what it is to bless God, second he wants to speak about the different titles by which the apostle blesses God, and third he wants to elaborate on the blessings with which God has blessed us (p. 21).

Goodwin tells us that to bless God is to wish God well or to speak well of God. To be sure, God is "blessed for ever," as we find in Romans 1:25. He is full of blessing in such a way that we cannot add anything but our "Amen" to his blessedness. When the glory of God is revealed, we can respond with the acclamation "Worthy is he" (p. 23). This is a sort of joyful congratulation, an expression of our delight in his power and wisdom (p. 21). This definition is followed by a succession of biblical illustrations of how the saints of the Old and New Testaments have blessed God. In fact, the most beautiful thing about this whole sermon is the skill with which the preacher conducts what might be called a biblical word study of this weighty theological word. One might call Goodwin a seventeenth-century Gerhard Kittel. Goodwin has studied his Hebrew Old Testament and his Greek New Testament. He has made diligent use of his commentaries and other lexical aids. By the middle of the seventeenth century there was a sizable collection of such material, and Goodwin was known to have had a large, well-stocked personal library. Most of all, however, he knew how to use this material so as to give us fresh insights into the biblical vocabulary.

Next, our preacher turns to the significance of the phrase "the God and Father of our Lord Jesus Christ" (p. 23). Goodwin speaks at length of the theology of the Trinity and the significance of his text for that theology. What he is aiming at, however, is showing the christocentric nature of our worship. We bless God in Christ because God has blessed us in Christ. It is the relationship between the Father and the Son that makes possible our communion with God. This relationship is the foundation of Christian worship. It was because of the covenant that God made with Abraham that God was the God of Abraham, Isaac, and Jacob. In the same way, it was because God made a covenant with David that David was able to call God his God. It is the same way with Christ, the Son of David (Ps. 22:1 and Matt. 27:46) (p. 25). In both the covenant with Abraham and the covenant with David, the covenant was the basis of fellowship with God. So it is now with the new covenant. It is on the basis of the new and eternal covenant established in the death and resurrection of Christ that in our worship we can enter into fellowship with God the Father.

But to understand Christian worship we must understand what it means to bless not only the God of our Lord Jesus Christ but also the Father of our Lord Jesus Christ. That God is the Father of our Lord Jesus Christ shows us that "God becomes our Father by being his Father." That God is the Father of our Lord Jesus Christ makes it possible for God to be our Father. Goodwin continues, "and then in the next verse he answerably proceeds to shew, how all other blessings do flow from this relation, first of God to Christ, then this of Christ to us" (p. 28).

The third sermon is devoted to elaborating on the blessings with which God has blessed us. This is the third of the three points Goodwin wanted to make in the previous sermon. Most of us will no doubt consider this a bit untidy. We would rather have all three points in one sermon. Such a concern never seems to have crossed our preacher's mind. It is perhaps inevitable that such depth of study often issues in prolixity. What our preacher has to say, however, makes it all worthwhile. Sermon 3 takes up the phrase "Who hath blessed us with all blessings" (p. 33). The point our preacher wants to make is, "God blesseth us under the relation of our Father" (p. 34). He points out that when we first begin to hear about blessings or about blessings being given or received, it is always part of the father-son relationship. The patriarchs blessed their sons. Abraham blessed Isaac and Isaac blessed Jacob and Jacob blessed his sons and grandsons. These blessings were an expression of the goodwill and great love of the father for his children (pp. 34-35). So it is when God blesses us. That God is our Father entails the bestowing of blessings. That is the nature of the relationship.

Again our preacher takes up the covenantal nature of blessing. Blessing is a particularly covenantal concept (p. 35). Covenant theology was highly developed during the lifetime of Goodwin. Johannes Cocceius (1603-69) was a contemporary of Goodwin. The famous theologian of Leyden had done much to try to produce a more biblical theology. His theology is often called "covenant theology." As a matter of fact, the biblical doctrine of covenant does help us understand what Scripture means by blessing. It shows us that the covenantal relationship is the basis of God's blessing. This is made clear particularly in Psalm 89, which speaks of God's covenant with David and how in that covenant God promised to be a father to David and David would be a son to God.[25] From the very beginning, when God made this covenant with Abraham, we read, "I will bless thee . . . and in thee all the families of the Earth shall be blessed" (Gen. 12:2-3). Goodwin goes on to comment, "Now that in God's intendment the whole total of the Gospel was expressed to Abraham, and wrapped up in that term blessing" (p. 36). It is for this reason, according

25. The significance of Ps. 89 to the development of Goodwin's thought is clear from the previous sermon (p. 25).

to our preacher, that in the New Testament the apostles put such an emphasis on God's covenant with Abraham. It was to be fulfilled by their preaching the blessings of the covenant to the Gentiles (Acts 3:25 and Gal. 3:8). Jesus himself, in his Sermon on the Mount, had preached the blessings of the covenant to Israel, and after the ascension the apostles preached these same blessings to the Gentiles (p. 36). Goodwin's understanding of worship is based on his understanding of covenant. In the covenant God promises us his blessing and calls us into the covenant community that we might participate in his blessings. Then, having participated in his blessings, we reflect his blessings by living according to the terms of the covenant, and in so doing reflect his blessing by blessing God.

B. The Gospel of Predestination

Following the text of Ephesians, Goodwin comes to verses 4 and 5: "According as he hath chosen us in him before the foundation of the world, that we should be holy and without blame before him in love: having predestinated us unto the adoption of children by Jesus Christ to himself, according to the good pleasure of his will" (KJV). This gives our preacher the occasion to preach at length on the doctrines of election and predestination, doctrines which were widely discussed at the time. While Goodwin was a student at Cambridge, the Synod of Dort (1618-19) was held, bringing these matters into the most vigorous discussion. If nothing else, Goodwin knows he must address himself to one of the urgent intellectual issues of the day.

Our preacher tells us that these words, "according as he hath chosen us in him before the foundation of the world," are among the most controverted in Scripture (p. 54). Clearly this text teaches some kind of doctrine of election. The text says, "God hath chosen us." As Goodwin sees it, this text can be understood in several ways. Some figure it means that God chose those who he foreknew would have faith in Christ (pp. 54-55). This is the Arminian position. What this opinion really means is that election is based on "Faith foreseen: For (say they) no man is in Christ till such time as he believeth: and God chooseth us in Christ; therefore he chooseth only foreseeing them to be Believers in Christ" (p. 54). This is not, however, what the text is saying, as Goodwin proceeds to demonstrate from a grammatical analysis of the text (p. 55).

Another approach to the text is particularly popular among the "Popish Divines."[26] According to this position, it is really Christ who is the elect. He is chosen because of the merit he won through his death and resurrection (pp. 55-56).

A third interpretation puts a strong emphasis on the future. According to this position, "We are not elected as being in Christ when elected, or by election put into Christ; but elected to be in Christ in the fullness of time" (p. 56). There is a certain truth to this position, according to Goodwin, but it does not fully cover what the text says.

Having set aside these interpretations, Goodwin offers his own. As he sees it, God, before all time, chose us to live in holiness. God chose us to live in communion with himself. To this end he has blessed us with the gifts of faith, hope, and love, that we might live the life of the children of God. This choosing, or "election," as theologians use the term, is based on the good pleasure of God's will; that is, it is not on the basis of any principle or rule, but purely on the basis of his love. Having chosen us, he predestined us. That is, he set up the means by which we should fulfill our destiny. He determined that we would fulfill the destiny for which we were created. He set in motion the process of adoption (pp. 58-64).

The sermon as it was published goes on for several big folio pages, advancing different passages of Scripture to support his position. One easily imagines that all this argumentation was never included in the sermon as it was preached. And yet, if these sermons were preached in a university pulpit to people who had been very much involved in the current discussion, we can well imagine that this sermon did include some very technical argumentation. One cannot help but notice a certain similarity in these sermons to the ones Gregory of Nazianzus preached in Constantinople to defend the orthodox doctrine of the Trinity. The detailed argumentation was possible because the subject was so widely discussed.

What is surprising is the way Goodwin takes these rather abstract doctrines and shows their significance for Christian spirituality. First of all, he draws from this passage that the Christian should "learn to give Christ his full honor" (p. 64). He is the cause of all the grace and glory that we have or ever shall have. God the Father gave him glory before the world began, and so now we should glorify him in our hearts. The devo-

---

26. Parenthetically, Goodwin assures us that there are exceptions; the best of the Catholic theologians suggest it only tentatively, as is the case with the Spanish Jesuit theologian Francisco de Suárez.

tion to Jesus, so characteristic of Protestant worship, has strong doctrinal foundations in the doctrine of election. We have been chosen in Christ to live in fellowship with God.

Still further, we can draw from this doctrine the assurance that if God loved us from all eternity, then God's love is everlasting. How highly we should value the love of God! It is an eternal reality. It is far above all the treasures of this world. "Let God's love have the same valuation with you, that the love of God himself has of you." Paraphrasing Matthew 6:33, our preacher exhorts us to seek first the kingdom of God, and all these other things will be added unto us. "Value God and his love more than all the world, though there were millions of them. He valued you before the world, and therefore is beforehand with you in love. He not only loved you from everlasting (whereas your love is but of yesterday;) but in the valuation of it, he loved you before all worlds, and preferred you to all worlds: though you loved the world first, before you loved him." When we fully understand this, it is clear "Why all things in this world do further God's decree of election. All things work together for good to them that love God" (p. 66).

Even more, once we understand the biblical doctrine of election, we can understand why the apostle Paul is able to assure us that nothing shall be able to separate us from the love of God, neither angels nor principalities nor powers (cf. Rom. 8:31-39). As Goodwin sees it, this world can run to ruin, heaven and earth can cease to keep their laws, and yet God's covenant will stand forever. Our preacher becomes quite eloquent as he paraphrases passages from Psalm 19, Isaiah 45, and Proverbs 8, all showing that God's eternal decrees are prior even to creation itself (p. 67). These must have been eloquent words when they were preached. Goodwin's sermons are filled with stirring applications like these. For him great doctrine is inspiring.

Sermon 6 focuses on the doctrine of predestination. One would expect this from the text, for our preacher has come to the words "Having predestinated us unto adoption by Jesus Christ. . . ." The sermon opens by pointing out that while the previous sermon had focused on election, this one now must focus on predestination. The two can be distinguished as follows: election, or choosing, "is to single out and call out from others, or out of a common lump: And to Predestinate, is (in English) to fore-ordain, or fore-appoint to some end" (p. 70). A bit further on he tells us that election is that act of God's will which calls us out from the mass of humanity, while predestination is the divine setting of our destiny. Predestination blesses us with all the privileges which we have through Christ. It confirms to us our destiny of adoption into the family of God's people and a life of holiness in communion with God (p. 71).

Goodwin, typical of so many Puritans, begins his sermon with a thorough grammatical and philological study of his text. He analyzes both the vocabulary and the syntax. He mentions the insights of the leading theologians of the day, and even some of the leading Schoolmen of the Middle Ages. Thomas Aquinas, for example, is frequently quoted. Goodwin obviously held him in high esteem. He ends his analysis of the text with a quotation from the Italian Reformed theologian Girolamo Zanchi: "That God should choose us in Christ to be perfectly holy, there was grace; but that he should add Glory and Heaven and Son-ship unto it too this is to the glory of his grace as we have it in the sixth verse; and so he makes a heightening of his love. That he not only chose us to be Holy, but also predestinated us unto Adoption and Glory" (p. 74).

Having gone through all this, however, Goodwin always gets down to what it all has to do with living the Christian life. From the doctrine of predestination the Christian should learn the purpose of life. God has made us for himself. As we have it in Isaiah 43:21, "This people have I formed for myself; they shall shew forth my praise" (KJV). The purpose of life is to live to the praise of God's glory (p. 77). At the very center of the Christian life is worship. This, of course, is made abundantly clear by the catechism of the Westminster Assembly: "Man's chief end is to glorify God and enjoy him forever."

A second implication for the Christian life is the importance of holiness. God has chosen us to be "holy before him." This choice consecrates us to his service and worship (p. 78). It is the worship of a holy people which glorifies God. It is the same with the Church today as it was in the time of Elijah: God has called out a remnant to worship him in purity and truth, while he allowed the rest to worship Baal in the hardness of their hearts (Rom. 11:4). The elect, however, have a different destiny. "These I have reserved to cleave unto, and worship me in purity and in truth." This we do, however imperfectly, here in our services of worship on earth, and yet the time will come when we will worship him perfectly in heaven, for, Goodwin assures us, heaven is nothing other than a perpetual worship of God (p. 79).

For Goodwin, all this is a marvelous assurance that our destiny is in Christ. His doctrine of predestination is thoroughly christocentric. "And therefore God hath predestinated us to Adoption of Sons, and *through* him, so *for* him, that he might have company in Heaven. . . . He is God's Fellow; we are his Fellows" (p. 83). Again Goodwin becomes eloquent. If Christ is God's Son, we are his sons and daughters because we are in him. If Christ is holy before his Father, so are we, because we are in him. If Christ is blessed with all heavenly blessings, so are we, for we are heirs and fellow heirs with him. If Christ is beloved of the Father, so are we, for we have been joined to him from all eternity. For Goodwin the doctrines of election and predestination are good news.

C. The Word of God on a Day of Fasting

While still in Cambridge, in 1628, Goodwin was called on to preach two sermons for the observance of a fast day, probably called by King Charles I because of the assassination of the duke of Buckingham, his prime minister. Charles had been on the throne three years by then, and had begun to push for High Church ceremonial and Arminian theology. He made himself even more unpopular with the committed Protestants of his realm by appointing William Laud, the leader of the High Church party, as the bishop of London, and making him his chief adviser in religious matters. Laud was determined to make the altar the center of worship, and to relegate the pulpit to the side as much as possible. Preaching was generally suppressed, but especially Puritan preaching. In ecclesiastical appointments the Puritans were regularly discriminated against. Largely influenced by his Catholic wife, Henrietta Maria of France, Charles wanted the Church of England to be a compromise between Protestantism and Catholicism. In matters of worship he was determined to reestablish Catholic ceremonial. By 1628 those of firm Protestant conviction were fully aware that he was trying his best to compromise their faith.

Goodwin was by this time one of the more popular young preachers in Cambridge. He chose to preach on a text from Zephaniah on this occasion. Zephaniah had seen the danger of syncretism to the faith of Israel at the end of the seventh century before Christ. He had preached against the attempted revival of idolatry, the secret operations of the priests of Baal, and idolatrous rites celebrated under the cover of night. Too many Israelites were worshiping the Lord in public and Baal in private. This was certainly an appropriate passage of Scripture on which to preach in the reign of Charles I.

If one were unaware of the historical situation in which they were preached, one would never suspect the very practical implication of these most prophetic sermons. The first sermon begins with a dispassionate division of the text. While Goodwin chose to preach on the first three verses of chapter 2, the sermon really treats all three chapters of this brief prophetic book.[27] He tells us that while the first chapter gives a "fearful denunciation" of the judgment God will send on Judah and an explicit enumeration of the causes of God's wrath toward the nation, the second chapter gives a "gracious Exhortation to Repentance to prevent that Decree." Two points are to be found in the text: first, the whole nation is called to repentance, and second, the duties of repentance are defined (p. 147).

This sermon is especially interesting for the history of Protestant worship because it shows us the biblical sources of public fast days. These fast days were a significant feature of seventeenth-century Protestant worship. To see this, one only needs to turn to the *Westminster Directory for Worship,* which has a chapter on both public fast days and public thanksgiving days. Here in America one of these public thanksgiving days has become our traditional Thanksgiving Day. Days of public fasting and humiliation seem to have disappeared from our national calendar, though they were observed until just a few generations ago. Goodwin goes into detail showing how national days of fasting are found in Scripture. The long prayers of confession of both Daniel and Ezra are offered as corporate prayers of repentance. Even more specifically, an example of a public day of fasting is found in the prophetic book of Joel (p. 148). From these examples it is clear that a national day of repentance has as its purpose the searching out of the sins of the nation. To be sure, there are the outward sins, the objective transgressions of the Law, the sins of greed and lust, but Goodwin is more concerned with the spiritual sins of faithlessness, idolatry, and superstition. Very diplomatically our preacher assures his congregation that it is not their responsibility to search out the distempers of the heads of the state, but rather the nation as a whole (p. 149).

With this disclaimer Goodwin attacks quite openly the drift of the nation toward idolatry. As Goodwin sees it, the state of religion in Judah

27. By a misprint the title claims that this text is taken from Zeph. 1:1-3, whereas the text is found in Zeph. 2:1-3. Thomas Goodwin, "A Sermon on Zephaniah 1:1-3," found in Thomas Goodwin, *Thirteen Sermons Preached on Diverse Texts of Scripture,* part III of *The Works of Thomas Goodwin,* three volumes bound as one (London: Jonathan Robinson, 1681). Page numbers in the text refer to this volume.

which Zephaniah describes helps us reflect on the state of religion in our own nation. Zephaniah had spoken of the "relicks of Baal," the idolatrous images and altars of the old Canaanite religion. Zephaniah had spoken of the danger of the priests of Baal who were so zealously going about the land trying to revive the old superstitions. You all know in your own consciences, Goodwin charges his congregation, that this same thing is happening in England today (p. 150). How many people still hold on to their crucifixes, their idols of Mary and the saints, their rosaries? How many Jesuit priests are maintained as chaplains in the private houses of our nobility? Goodwin is careful not to be too specific here, but everyone in his congregation knew that the queen, Henrietta Maria, was the worst offender. Her court was the center of Jesuit operations. Under the guise of being chaplains to the queen, Jesuit priests were saying Mass all over England, trying their best to seduce the aristocracy to embrace Catholicism. With this audacious charge we can be sure our preacher had the ears of the congregation.

As the sermon unfolds, we find a thoroughgoing critique of the state of religion in England during the reign of Charles I. As the more devout Protestants saw it, the ministry was a major problem. There were still too many "reading priests" and not enough "teaching priests" (p. 151). The complaint against the "dumb dogs" was still the major Protestant criticism against the state religion. Goodwin's lament is simple: throughout the whole of England, in village after village, there is no preaching ministry. The prayer book is read but no sermon is preached. Even worse, the ministers of the established church all too often do not give a good personal witness by living a truly Christian life (p. 152).

As important as Goodwin finds the reform of the national religion, the reform of the heart is his first priority. Civil religion was not enough for the Puritans. They wanted to get down to more personal concerns. Quite naturally, then, Goodwin turns to the question of how personally we should observe a day of fasting and humiliation. He exhorts every man and woman in his congregation to go home and commune with his or her own heart (p. 153). This is followed by a vivid description of what the Puritans meant by meditation (p. 154). As Goodwin presents it, a day of fasting should above all be a day of self-examination, a day of vigorous wrestling with God as Jacob wrestled with the angel that he might in the end be blessed (p. 156).

The second sermon addresses the duties of those who are truly repentant. Goodwin points out that the passage gives us three duties: to seek the

Lord, to seek righteousness, and to seek meekness (p. 161). The parable of the wise and foolish virgins is brought in to make the point that the wise prepare themselves for the coming of the Lord, that they might share in the joy of his blessings (p. 162). Our preacher does not stick very closely to his outline. The heart of the sermon centers on how we are to seek the Lord in those times when God's displeasure is upon us. Goodwin suggests a number of things. Even in such times we are to reaffirm our faith and take God as our portion and refuge. This is supported by a number of biblical illustrations (p. 164). He assures us that, especially in such times, we must trust perfectly in God (p. 165). Alluding to the apostle Paul, he exhorts us to be zealous in good works (Titus 2:14) (p. 170). This point is expanded at length. The giving of alms and the supporting of worthy causes is especially commended. Finally he gets down to explaining what the text means by seeking meekness (p. 173). He suggests there are two ways of doing this: by being completely realistic about our sins, shortcomings, and failures, and by having a lively hope of mercy (p. 174). When we have these two dispositions of soul, then we can have a genuine contentedness even in the midst of tribulation. Alluding to Romans 8, Goodwin ends the sermon on a note of victory. For those of us in Christ, nothing can separate us from the love of God (p. 175).

Given the times in which it was preached, this was a most prophetic sermon. It took courage to preach it. Far from being politically correct, it was politically very dangerous. One can well understand why an absolutist monarch like Charles I wanted to discredit the Puritans.

VI. Dr. Thomas Manton (1620-77)

One of London's most popular and highly respected preachers during the tumultuous days of the Revolution, the Commonwealth, and the Restoration, Thomas Manton exercised an irenic and reverent ministry.[28] He was one of the most mature biblical scholars of his day, producing expository sermons of the highest quality. They are, to be sure, sermons of high intensity, and yet he drew large congregations even after he was denied

28. For biographical material, see the memoir written by William Harris in the first volume of *The Complete Works of Thomas Manton, D.D.,* reprint of the Edinburgh edition, 23 vols. (Worthington, Pa.: Maranatha Publications, 1978), and Charlotte Fell-Smith, "Manton, Thomas," in *Dictionary of National Biography,* 22 vols. (London and New York: Oxford University Press, 1973), 12:986-89.

the pulpit during the Restoration. We are told that he was a good-looking man and had an attractive presence in the pulpit. From the records we have of what he preached, we are encouraged to imagine that his sermons were delivered with the same vigor and precision with which they are written. Manton preached a practical holiness. He preached it simply and directly within the bounds of the Protestant plain style, and yet his sermons are charged with a magnificent rational holiness, a sparkling sanctified intellect.

Manton was a son of the manse. His father was curate of Lawrence-Lydiat in Somerset, and both his grandfathers had been ministers. He was still quite young when he was sent off to Oxford, where he received his bachelor of arts degree in 1639. He was ordained by Joseph Hall, the bishop of Exeter, before he was twenty years of age. The hostilities of the Civil War had broken out by this time, and Manton lectured and preached where he was able to for several years.

In 1644 Colonel Popham, who remained his patron for many years, presented him with the living of Stoke-Newington, just outside of London. During the meetings of the Westminster Assembly, he served as scribe and was given the honor of writing the preface to the Westminster Confession of Faith. When Cromwell assumed the protectorate, Manton was summoned to Whitehall and was pressed by Cromwell to lead in prayer on the occasion. Not approving of the execution of Charles I, as was typical for Puritans of Presbyterian leaning, he discharged this duty with reluctance. Nonetheless, he was held in high respect by leaders of the Commonwealth, being asked on a number of occasions to preach before Parliament.

In 1656 he succeeded the famous Obadiah Sedgwick as pastor of Saint Paul's Covent Garden, one of the leading Puritan pulpits in London. He continued to occupy that famous pulpit until the ejection of the Puritans in 1662. Charles II tried to win his support for episcopacy by offering him the position of dean of Rochester, but Manton could not deny his scruples against *The Book of Common Prayer*. He participated in the Savoy Conference, which tried to work out a compromise with the Episcopalians, but when it became clear that no compromise was acceptable to the king and his bishops, he could not conscientiously subscribe to the new constitution of the Church of England and was therefore denied the pulpit. He was replaced at Saint Paul's Covent Garden by Dr. Patrick, and on Sunday mornings he regularly attended the services conducted by his successor.

On Sunday afternoons, however, he preached in his own home to a large congregation. His sermons and particularly his prayers were greatly admired. This clandestine congregation included a number of very devout and prominent members of London society, such as Lord and Lady Wharton, the duke of Bedford, and the countess of Manchester. This daring infraction of the law was diplomatically ignored by the authorities for several years until Manton was finally arrested and imprisoned in 1670. Even in prison he managed to preach. In 1672, after his release, the merchants of London established a lectureship at Pinners' Hall. There prominent Puritans were allowed to preach unmolested, and Manton was chosen to inaugurate this lectureship. He continued to preach regularly at Pinners' Hall until his health began to fail in 1675.

Manton's preaching was admired by other prominent preachers of the day, and it is to a large extent due to their efforts that so many of his sermons have been preserved. Dr. Bates, who saw many of Manton's sermons to the publishers, said he had heard the greatest preachers preach poor sermons, but he had never heard Manton preach a sermon that was not of the highest quality. Unlike the sermons of Luther and Calvin, Manton's published sermons were not taken down by a stenographer. What we apparently have in most cases is his own manuscript written out in preparation for his preaching. At certain points in his career he seems to have had the services of a secretary who finished up his manuscripts. He himself finished up some of his sermons, such as those on the Epistle of James, in the form of commentaries. This may explain why his sermons are almost totally devoid of illustrative material. Most were published after his death and show very little evidence of having been prepared by the preacher for publication. It may well be that when they were preached, they had considerably more oratorical polish than they have in their published form. For most of these sermons there is no indication of the date and place of their preaching.

Although almost six hundred of his sermons have been preserved, we know he usually preached three times a week for almost thirty-five years. We have therefore only a small portion of his sermons. Be that as it may, we do have a far richer selection of Manton's sermons than we have for any other leading Puritan preacher. Regrettably, Richard Baxter (1615-91) and Edmund Calamy (1600-1666), who are usually named with Manton as the three most prominent Puritan preachers, have not left us any appreciable collections of sermons. Manton, therefore, probably gives us the best sustained impression of Puritan preaching which is available.

Among his more important published series we find the following:

27 sermons on Matthew 25
45 sermons on John 17
24 sermons on Romans 6
47 sermons on Romans 8
40 sermons on II Corinthians 5
32 sermons on Ephesians 5
16 sermons on II Thessalonians 1
18 sermons on II Thessalonians 2
190 sermons on Psalm 119
65 sermons on Hebrews 11

In addition to this, we know he did series of expository sermons on Matthew 6, the temptations of Christ and the transfiguration from Matthew, the Epistle of James, the Epistle of Jude, and Isaiah 53. He also preached a number of sermons at weddings and funerals, before Parliament or the mayor of London, and in preparation for the celebration of the Lord's Supper. Even this limited selection shows a considerable variety in the types of biblical books treated. Manton had obviously intended in his ministry to reflect the whole range and breadth of the biblical witness, even if he concentrated on certain passages in the most minute detail. He selected the most crucial passages of the apostle Paul and balanced them with James on the one hand and Matthew on the other. As for the Old Testament, we have his intense sermons on Psalm 119, but we know he did series from the Pentateuch as well as the Prophets. The series on Isaiah 53 deals with a profoundly different type of Old Testament literature.

A. Sermons on James

Early in his ministry, while pastor of the church at Stoke-Newington, a village in the outskirts of London, Manton preached a remarkable series of sermons on the Epistle of James. The sermons were finished up as a commentary which even today is regarded as the classic work on this controversial book of Holy Scripture.[29] Although we have not often studied sermons which have been worked up as treatises or commentaries, we

29. Thomas Manton, *A Practical Commentary, or an Exposition, with Notes, on the Epistle of James*, in *The Complete Works of Thomas Manton, D.D.*, vol. 4. References that follow in the text are from this volume of his *Works*.

make an exception in this case because the commentary shows the preacher at work in his study in a way that the sermons do not. Besides that, the commentary is clearly very close to Manton's preaching style as we find it in his published sermons.

In the dedicatory epistle to his benefactor Alexander Popham, member of Parliament from the area, Manton further remarks that he was thankful while at Stoke-Newington to have had the quiet leisure to dig deeply into the Epistle of James. This commentary is clearly the result of careful and disciplined study of the whole history of the interpretation of the book of James. Because the work has come down to us as a commentary rather than as sermons, our preacher has felt freer to speak of the commentaries and other sources he has used. He obviously used his famous personal library to good advantage. We find his commentary filled with apt quotations from the literature of the ancient Church, the Schoolmen of the Middle Ages, the Protestant Reformers, and the most learned theologians of his own day.

In the prolegomena to his commentary, Manton discusses the reservations certain writers of the ancient Church had about the canonicity of James. He goes over the well-known passages in Eusebius and Jerome (p. 9). On the other hand, he quotes a number of sources to show that it was regarded by the ancient Church as canonical. He tells us that neither Cajetan nor Erasmus had a very high opinion of the book (p. 10). He then turns to the remark of Luther that James is an epistle of straw. He finds Luther's remark unfortunate and notes that among the learned Lutheran scholars of his own day, the book is received as canonical (p. 11). As Manton makes clear at the proper place in his commentary, he does not find the teaching of James in regard to the relation of faith and works contradictory with the rest of the New Testament. The epistle is to be treated as inspired by the Holy Spirit, just as any other canonical book is.

For Manton it is irreverent to imagine that James and Paul, who were both inspired by the same Holy Spirit, should have taught contradictory doctrines. To deny the authority of either is to cut the knot rather than untie it. A more reverent approach to Scripture seeks to reconcile them rather than discredit one or the other (p. 261). Manton investigates the attempt of Cardinal Bellarmine to explain the difficulty. Finally he turns to the explanations of the Arminians and Socinians (pp. 261-62). As Manton sees it, Paul and James are reconciled when one recognizes that Paul is talking about the cause of justification while James is speaking about its effects (p. 264). For James the point at issue is who has the right faith. This is clear when one studies the scope of the whole passage. Is it those who merely hold proper doctrine or those whose faith produces the works of charity and mercy who are saved? The point James wants to make is that faith which produces no works of mercy is dead, that is, it is no faith at all. Dead faith justifies no one (cf. pp. 232 and 238ff.). When the text is understood this way, there is no contradiction between James and Paul (p. 232). Manton's resolution of the seeming contradiction is as sound as it is clear.

What is impressive about this series is not so much the harmonizing of Paul and James on the question of justification by faith as the way our preacher opens up the spiritual treasures of the book as a whole. Manton shows that the epistle has rich teachings on patience, on resisting temptations and enduring trials, on good works, on humility, on true wisdom, on providence, and on prayer. Luther was not the first preacher to neglect the book. The lectionary of the Western Church as it took form from the fifth to the ninth centuries had neglected it as well.[30] That Manton preached through this book so carefully and recorded the fruit of his preaching in his commentary was a great service to the Church. It is somewhat analogous to the service of Basil the Great in the fourth century, who in his sermons on the Hexaemeron discovered for the Church of his day the riches of the creation story. Manton opened up through his careful and scholarly study of James a rich treasure for the Church. The Puritans were specially concerned for the enrichment of Christian piety. It was one of the main burdens of their preaching, and these sermons offer us a particularly fine example of this homiletical concern.

Manton saw preaching as the continuing work of the Church: listening to the Scriptures, carefully studying them, and applying them to the life of God's people. The preaching of the Word is based on the study of the Word. The ministry of the Word for Manton is just as much listening and studying as it is reading and preaching. If Manton takes up the Epistle of James and makes it the object of a profound study to discover what it has to say to the Church, he is doing it as a service of worship. This concern that the whole of Scripture be faithfully heard and truly understood is at the center of expository preaching.

30. The Anglican Sunday lectionary gives a reading from the first chapter of James on the fourth Sunday after Easter, followed by another passage from the first chapter on the fifth Sunday after Easter.

B. Sermons on Romans 8

Let us turn now to a series of sermons with a very different sort of message.[31] James and Paul had contrasting concerns, as the Church has long recognized. To select the eighth chapter of Romans for a major series of sermons is to devote oneself to preaching the heart of the gospel as it was proclaimed by the apostle Paul. This chapter speaks of God's saving grace in Christ with consummate majesty, and any preaching of it is of necessity evangelistic preaching. Let us look at the final seven sermons of the series to see how Manton preached the heart of the gospel.

Sermon 41 takes up with the text, "What then shall we say to these things? If God be for us, who can be against us?" (Rom. 8:31).[32] In terms of homiletical form the sermon is scholastic; in terms of style it is Protestant plain style at its most clear and direct. The exordium is brief. Manton simply announces that at this point in the chapter the apostle turns to the triumph of believers over sin (12:319). The first point he draws from his text is that when we hear divine truth, it is good to think with our own hearts about these things with serious consideration and close application. "Faith will not be settled without serious thoughts" (12:321). As Luke encourages us, we should search the Scriptures to know the certainty of that in which we have been instructed (cf. Luke 1:4 and Acts 17:11-12). As Manton understands this text, it insists on the importance of thinking about our faith (12:322).

Manton then moves on to his second point. The apostle asks, "If God be for us, who shall be against us?"[33] Pointing to the grammar of the text, our preacher explains that the question is not one of doubting but one of reasoning. God is indeed for us, and therefore we can be comforted. There is a warfare in this world between Christ's kingdom and Satan's kingdom. In our baptism we were enlisted as soldiers of Christ, and in the Lord's Supper our oath of allegiance is renewed. This does not

---

31. These sermons were not published until 1684. The first edition appeared under the title *Several Sermons upon the Eighth Chapter of Romans.* . . . This study is based on the text found in vols. 11 and 12 of *The Complete Works of Thomas Manton, D.D.* References cited in the text are from these volumes, with the volume number followed by the page reference.

32. The text is quoted according to the King James Version, but Manton often makes his own translation. We quote according to the text of Manton before us.

33. Here Manton is not quoting from the King James Version. Manton's knowledge of the original languages was such that he could make his own translation.

mean that we will not have to fight against the legions of Satan, but rather that our victory is assured (12:325). There are very clear reasons why we can have confidence in the face of those who are against us. First, we can have confidence because of the infinite power and sovereignty of God. Our preacher develops this from a number of passages of Scripture, such as Psalm 103:19, "His kingdom ruleth over all," and I Chronicles 29:11b, "Thine is the kingdom, O LORD, and thou art exalted as head above all." Second, we can have confidence because of God's love for his people (12:328). This, too, is developed by numerous passages of Scripture. Third, we can have confidence because of the incarnation of Christ (12:329). Here we have the greatest foundation of our confidence. This is expanded into a magnificent discussion of several key texts on the incarnation. Jesus Christ is Emmanuel, God with us (Matt. 1:23). In Christ we have access to God in a new and living way (Heb. 10:20). Not only do we have access to God, but we have reconciliation with him. "God was in Christ, reconciling the world to himself . . ." (II Cor. 5:19). When God is willing to come among us and take our nature and die for a sinful world, there is a foundation laid for his being with us, to help us and bless us upon all occasions. The incarnate Christ has taken on the office of high priest and continually makes intercession for us (Heb. 8:1 and 2).

In good scholastic form our preacher now raises an objection (12:330). If God be so sovereign and so loving and has given us such a mediator, why then do Christians experience such struggles? To his question he proposes an answer. The Christian must go through trials in order that faith be strengthened. In these trials, however, God is with us to comfort us and bless us, and in the end we will overcome all afflictions (12:330-32).

Finally, Manton begins to apply his teaching to the congregation. Here the homiletical form resorts to a more Puritan cast. This passage teaches the Christian not to have an inordinate fear of merely human powers in this world, nor to attach an inordinate respect to worldly happiness. Our highest happiness is in the coming of God's kingdom. When we are confident in the victory of that kingdom, a foundation is laid for true religion (12:332-36). Faith in the victory of Christ over sin gives us confidence to live a truly Christian life. Manton is preaching to Christians. They are baptized and they receive the Lord's Supper (12:325). He explicitly tells them that he supposes them to be Christians (12:330). For Manton, evangelistic preaching is proclaiming Christ's victory to his people, that they might live in that victory.

The forty-second sermon takes the text "He that spared not his own Son, but delivered him up for us all, how shall he not with him also freely give us all things?" (Rom. 8:32). Manton again opens his sermon with a succinct statement of the meaning of the verse on which he intends to preach. The apostle, he tells us, has in the previous verse spoken of God's eternal decree, which is his hidden love; now he speaks of redemption by Christ, which is his declared love. In predestination God's love was conceived in his own heart; in redemption it is manifested and communicated to us (12:336). In the former verse we learned of the cause of our redemption; in this verse we learn of the sign of our redemption, that is, the gifts of grace which he has so abundantly poured out on us. Our preacher gives a brief grammatical analysis of the text and then formulates its teaching. In the death of Christ God has laid a broad foundation for a large superstructure of grace to be freely dispensed to his people (12:337).

Commenting on the words "but gave him up for us all," Manton makes three points. Here again we see our preacher's scholastic methods. His first point, made with very striking words, is that God himself has given us this sign. To be sure, Judas delivered Jesus to the soldiers, Pilate delivered him to be crucified, the high priest delivered him to Pilate, the people of Israel delivered him to be scourged and crucified by the Gentiles. All this we find explicitly stated in the Gospels. We even read that Jesus delivered himself up, but in this passage we read that God delivered him up. If God had not delivered him up, if Jesus had delivered himself up in obedience to God, the delivering of Judas, of Pilate, of the high priest, and of the people would have done nothing for our salvation. Christ died not by mere human wickedness, but by the righteous and wise ordination of a gracious God. What a great proof this is of God's love (12:338)! The Father sacrificed his only Son because he so loved us (cf. John 3:16)! One can well imagine that words such as these, from the pulpit of a very gifted preacher, must have been extremely moving.

Second, Manton speaks of how our salvation is based on an act of God himself. It was God himself who became incarnate and went to the cross and suffered there for our salvation (12:339). Third, Manton makes the point that God did this for us all. God himself in the person of his Son did all this "for the cursed race of fallen Adam, who had no strength to do anything for themselves; who cast away the mercies of our creation, and were senseless of our misery and careless of our remedy; had abused the goodness of his bounty and patience, and were utterly lost to God and

307

themselves" (12:340). What a serious sentence this must have been from Manton's pulpit!

Manton goes on to develop at length the theme of how the Father's sacrifice of his beloved Son reveals God's love, and then he makes his application. This text should bring us to a holy admiration of God's love for us. It should give us every reason to obey God and to glorify him (12:343ff.). It should give us great boldness in prayer (12:345ff.). In the life of prayer particularly, we discern God's special love for us as his children. When we believe that God dearly loves us and has taken us for his children, that God delights in our prosperity, how cheerfully we come into his presence (12:346). Manton makes his point by developing John 16:27, "For the Father himself loves you, because you have loved me and have believed that I came from the Father." What a master Manton is at explaining a text of the Bible by another text of the Bible! We know that we are heard in prayer not only because of Christ's intercession, but also because of the Father's special love for us as his children. The indwelling Holy Spirit works faith in our hearts. Faith produces love toward God, and when we begin to perceive the tokens of God's love in our lives, then we know we are his children. Manton hammers home his point with a rapid fire of rhetorical questions. Does God love me? Has he given me his Holy Spirit? How shall we know this? We know it by its effects. We know it when we discover in ourselves the sort of sincere love which seeks after God and delights in him (12:347). Once we have gotten this straight, then the life of prayer becomes the means of experiencing again and again the love of God.

Having said that these are in the truest sense evangelistic sermons, we would point out that Manton evangelizes not by bringing his congregation to question their salvation, but by assuring them of their salvation. Manton's work is to evangelize the baptized. His strong Calvinistic theology leads him to assume that he is preaching to the elect, and therefore he proclaims to them the salvation that is theirs.

We turn now to the forty-fourth sermon in the series, particularly its last half, where our preacher develops the theme of Christ's resurrection and ascension. His text is Romans 8:34, "It is Christ that died, yea rather, that is risen again, who is even at the right hand of God, who also maketh intercession for us." He begins by treating very briefly Christ's death as a ransom for sinners, then as a mediatorial sacrifice, and then as a propitiation for our sins (12:366-68). With a few deft phrases Manton reminds his congregation of these classic doctrines. As he understands it,

Christ's death is expiation; that is, it puts away sin. His death is sufficient to put away all sin for all time. Then our preacher takes up Christ's resurrection. The text implies that there is something even more significant for our salvation in Christ's resurrection than in his sacrificial death. This he finds in the text before him, "Yea, rather, that is risen again" (12:368). Was not Christ's death in every way sufficient to free us from sin? Yes, it was, but that death would not have been any use to us if it had not been swallowed up by his resurrection (12:369).

Manton then develops the resurrection as first a sign, the visible evidence of the sufficiency of Christ's sacrifice. He brings out a number of Scripture passages which show that the resurrection was the proof that Christ had fulfilled his mediatorial office. I Peter 1:21 tells us that "God raised him from the dead, that our faith and hope may be in God." Romans 1:4 tells us that Christ was "mightily declared to be the Son of God by his resurrection from the dead." Jesus himself told the Jews that the only sign he would give them was the sign of Jonah (Matt. 12:39), that is, the sign of his resurrection. Manton in the most beautiful way develops a number of different facets of the imagery of the resurrection. Christ as our ransom was imprisoned by death. His release from that prison proves that the price was paid in full (12:370). But even beyond that, Christ is our Savior because of his capacity to convey life to us. If he had remained in the state of death he could not do that, but being risen from the dead he becomes a source of life for all who believe in him. As we find it in the Gospel of John, "Because I live, ye shall live also" (John 14:19b). In Romans 5:10 the apostle tells us that "much more, being reconciled, we shall be saved by his life." His death was for the expiation of sin, but the effectual application of it to us depends on his life, that is, his resurrection life. Finally Manton speaks of Christ's resurrection as victory over death. If Christ is risen, then sin is conquered, and the resurrection declares plainly that sin has been overcome (12:370).

This profound section on the resurrection leads naturally to an even more profound section on the ascension. Our preacher proceeds to the next phrase, "Who is at the right hand of God." The exaltation of Christ in heavenly glory is the sign that the sacrifice made on earth has been received in heaven. Taking David as the type of Christ, Manton tells us that while David was anointed as king by Samuel, he was not actually crowned until he had overcome his enemies. Then being crowned at Hebron, he began to administer his kingdom and to reward his servants. So it is that Christ in his heavenly glory conveys life to the faithful. Manton alludes to

Ephesians 4:8-11, which tells us how Christ ascended into heaven that he might fill all things and bestow spiritual gifts to the faithful (12:370). Referring to Psalm 2 and Hebrews 10:13, our preacher assures us that it is the ascended Christ, who rules in heaven, who will have all his enemies as a footstool for his feet. Then our preacher develops John 14:2, "I go to prepare a place for you," to show that in his ascension Christ has opened for us a way into heaven, that where he is there we might be also. For us the sign that Christ is indeed seated upon the throne of heaven is the pouring out of his Spirit on the Day of Pentecost. The events of Pentecost are a pledge to us of what Christ continually dispenses to the Church. Christ is still enthroned and still pours out his Spirit to convince the unbelieving world, to conquer the opposing wisdom and power of the flesh, and to supply life to his people (12:372).

We have seen in these sermons how Manton makes a detailed presentation of Christ's redemptive acts, his incarnation, his crucifixion, his resurrection, his ascension, and the pouring out of his Spirit. This is for him the heart of evangelistic preaching. It is both careful exposition of the text and solid theology. Manton does not preach these sermons merely in order to develop astute theologians or brilliant biblical scholars, but far more to develop mature Christians. Christian learning serves Christian piety. It is the wisdom of God which converts our souls.

The next sermon, number 45, gives us further insight into the evangelistic ministry of Thomas Manton. Having spoken of our triumph over sin, our preacher begins, we must now speak of our triumph over afflictions (12:374). His text is, "Who shall separate us from the love of Christ? Shall tribulation, or distress, or persecution, or famine, or nakedness, or peril, or sword?" (Rom. 8:35). Our preacher begins with his usual analysis of the text. He points out that it is the love of Christ which is the cause of our love for him. We love because he first loved us. The stability of our love depends on the stability of his love. Seven kinds of afflictions are enumerated. Again we notice the homiletical habits of Scholasticism. All these afflictions can be overcome through our union with Christ (12:375). The Christian must be prepared for trials. If Christ our head endured trials, we his body must endure them too (12:376). It is through tribulation and affliction that our faith grows and matures. It is in this way that the bond of love between Christ and the Christian is strengthened. Justifying faith leads to sanctifying faith. It is not that there are two kinds of faith, but that we go from faith to faith. In this sermon we become very much aware that Manton's evangelistic ministry is directed not to those who have never heard the gospel, but rather to those who have heard and received it but have not yet experienced its full power. His aim is to bring his congregation to an ever more faithful profession of Christianity (12:378). Manton never divides Christians into two kinds, those who are merely justified and those who are sanctified. Saving faith is a growing grace and sanctification is a lifelong process. Our first profession is a beginning and leads us on to ever more faithful professions.

In a particularly fine passage, Manton speaks at length of the bond of love between Christ and the Christian. The bond is made on our part by faith and on Christ's part by the gift of his Spirit. Once Christ in his love has given us his Spirit and we love him in return, nothing can unclasp these mutual embraces by which Christ loves us and we love him (12:380). Our preacher then calls on Song of Solomon 8:6-7 to show us the eternal strength of the bond of love: "Love is strong as death, . . . the coals thereof are the coals of fire, which hath a most vehement flame. Many waters cannot quench love, neither can floods drown it." Christ's love for us was not quenched by the waters of affliction (12:382). This love which now is within us by his Spirit, being of such a vehement nature, can no more be resisted than death or the grave. This love we first apprehend by faith and then prove by patience in affliction and fruitfulness in obedience (12:383). Manton concludes this sermon with a moving invitation to enter into an ever more faithful profession of the Christian faith.

In the forty-sixth and forty-seventh sermons, Manton has more to say of the victory of Christ's love in us. In several places his words are almost hymnic. In Sermon 46 there is a beautiful passage on the properties of Christ's love. He develops the following themes: its transcendence, its tenderness, its immutability, and its efficacy. Although the form of his presentation is quite scholastic, if not academic, the content is doxological.

In Sermon 47, the final sermon in the series, we find another hymn to the love of Christ. The text is Romans 8:38 and 39, "For I am persuaded, that neither death, nor life, nor angels, nor principalities, nor powers, nor things present, nor things to come, nor height, nor depth, nor any other creature, shall be able to separate us from the love of God, which is in Christ Jesus our Lord." Our preacher tells us that first he wants to speak of what the love of God in Christ is. It is one of the divine perfections. In Christ God's love flows out of himself to bless his people (12:413). It is God's nature flowing out of himself for our happiness (12:414). It is the source of an abundant fruitfulness in human life. It is a bond which unites us to himself (12:415).

Having once again rhapsodized on the subject of God's love, Manton now speaks of the second subject he wants to address, how we are persuaded of this love. This is particularly interesting for our purposes, because in the course of his development we find some of his thoughts on the purpose of preaching, particularly evangelistic preaching. Our preacher begins by telling us that we are persuaded by the Word of the gospel. The Word itself persuades us of God's love. The preaching of the gospel unveils to us the whole mystery of our redemption in Christ, and presents to us all its benefits. God's plan for our justification, sanctification, and glorification is set forth to be the matter of our faith. The purpose of the gospel ministry is to persuade us of all things concerning God's kingdom, as we are taught in Acts 19:8. It should persuade us to come out of the kingdom of Satan and enter into the kingdom of Christ. Again with references to Acts (28:23 and 13:43), he tells us that this is to be done on the one hand by testifying and assuring us of Christ's willingness and power to save us, and on the other hand by warning us of the dangers of remaining in the kingdom of darkness (12:416). Our preacher continues by telling us of the role of the Holy Spirit in persuading us, then the role of faith, and finally the role of experience.

This reference to experience is particularly interesting. What Manton means is that while at first faith comes by hearing and while it must constantly be nourished by hearing again and again, faith builds on faith. As Christians mature, we discover that by our having had faith in the promises of the gospel, this faith has borne fruit in our own lives. Our initial faith is now a much stronger faith. Our initial faith has begun to produce the bond of love; it is now rooted and grounded. Manton admits there is an initial faith which may wither, but there is also a rooted faith which will flourish and stand fast. Therefore it is not enough to assent to the truth of the gospel in our understanding or embrace the good things offered to us by our will and affections; we must be rooted and grounded in the faith. It is the same with love. We must be rooted and grounded in love as well. Rooting and grounding in faith and love gives us the kind of experience which can persuade us of God's love. At the beginning of the Christian life we do not have this kind of experience, but as we grow we do.

One of the things one notices in Manton's preaching is that he preaches to this experience. Even today one reads his sermons and says, yes, that is true. That is what I have experienced as well. For Manton the preaching of the Word is a witness to the power of the Word to give us life, the sort of abundant life which reflects the holiness of God. To witness to this life-giving Word, we as preachers must first experience it ourselves, as Manton so obviously had. Of the very essence of preaching is that it is witness; it is telling to all what one has experienced oneself.

For many of us the sermons of Thomas Manton constitute one of the classics of Christian theology. Twenty-two volumes of his sermons, edited by James McCosh, president of Princeton University about the time of the Civil War, were to be found in the library of my double-great-grandfather. They are, like the works of Matthew Henry, among the foundation stones of American Christianity.

VII. Thomas Watson (ca. 1620-87)

Although Thomas Watson's sermons and devotional writings have been highly prized by generations of devout and serious Christians, a good number of the basic facts of his life are obscure.[34] As with many of the Puritan preachers of the period, there has been no thorough study of either his life or his writings. Nevertheless, he has bequeathed to us a sizable literary legacy. While in the nineteenth century there were those who collected and edited the works of the leading Puritan preachers, these editions showed little interest in the critical and historical questions which concern us today. Unfortunately the editors of that era also "improved" the text. Be that as it may, we do have a considerable corpus of Watson's homiletical work. Of particular interest to us is his series of 176 sermons on the *Shorter Catechism* of the Westminster Assembly, *A Body of Practical Divinity*, published a few years after his death in 1692.[35]

We do know that Watson studied at Emmanuel College in Cam-

---

34. For biographical material on Thomas Watson, see "Brief Memoir of Thomas Watson," compiled by C. H. Spurgeon in *A Body of Divinity Contained in Sermons upon the Westminster Assembly's Catechism by Thomas Watson,* photolithographic reproduction (Edinburgh and Carlisle, Pa.: Banner of Truth Trust, 1974), hereafter Watson, *A Body of Divinity;* and Edward Irving Carlyle, "Watson, Thomas," in *Dictionary of National Biography,* 20:948-49.

35. This study is based on Watson, *A Body of Divinity.* Page references in the text are to this work. For an older edition, see Thomas Watson, *A Body of Practical Divinity: Consisting of Sermons on the Lesser Catechism* (London: Printed for Thomas Parkhurst, 1692). For other collections of Watson's sermons, see Thomas Watson, *The Beatitudes* (Edinburgh and Carlisle, Pa.: Banner of Truth Trust, 1975), and *The Sermons of Thomas Watson* (Ligonier, Pa.: Soli Deo Gloria Publications, 1990).

bridge. During the Commonwealth he was pastor of Saint Stephen's Walbrook in London. He soon became one of London's most popular preachers. As was often the case with those of Presbyterian tendency, he was loyal to the House of Stuart. He even went so far as to reprimand Cromwell for the execution of Charles I. He was a supporter of Christopher Love's attempt to return Charles II to England, and as a consequence he was imprisoned for a short time. After his imprisonment he resumed his ministry at Saint Stephen's and devoted himself to his preaching ministry until the restoration of the monarchy.

With the restoration of Charles II, Watson was turned out of his church, in spite of his loyalty to the House of Stuart. The Act of Uniformity was designed to rid the Church of England of the Puritans who had objections to either episcopacy or the *Book of Common Prayer,* and Watson had objections to both. Furthermore, Watson's ordination was presbyterial rather than episcopal, which the determined Episcopalianism of the Restoration would not accept. For the next ten years he preached secretly wherever he could. In 1672, under the Indulgence, he began to preach in the great hall of Crosby House. Apparently a congregation was organized, and a few years later Stephen Charnock came to share his pastorate. Charles Haddon Spurgeon remarks, "Men of such most extraordinary gifts and graces were seldom if ever united in one pastorate" (p. x). After a few years Watson's health made it necessary for him to retire to Essex, where he died in 1687.

Watson had a reputation for being a popular preacher, and also for being particularly endowed with the gift of leading public prayer. Spurgeon, in his memoir of Watson, tells us that one time Bishop Richardson attended one of his midweek services (p. viii). The bishop was favorably impressed by the sermon, but even more by the prayer which followed. After the service he called on Watson to thank him for his ministration and asked him if he might have a copy of the prayer. That, Watson explained, he did not have, for it was his practice to pray out of the fullness of his heart. It is not surprising that Watson's public prayers were so well received, because the most beautiful sermons in this series of catechetical sermons are those on the Lord's Prayer. The Puritans often devoted as much effort to leading prayer as they did to preaching. Even their midweek "lectures" often gave almost as much time to prayer as to preaching.

Watson opens his series with a preliminary discourse on catechizing. He begins with a text from the apostle Paul, "provided that you continue in the faith, stable and steadfast" (Col. 1:23 RSV). It is his hope, he tells his congregation, to begin the work of catechizing at the afternoon service on the following Lord's Day, and he wants therefore to say something about the needfulness of being well instructed in the fundamentals of the Christian faith (p. 1). He alludes to a number of biblical images for those who are doctrinally unstable. They are like wandering stars (Jude 13) and unstable as water (Gen. 49:4). Then he quotes a letter Theodore Beza wrote to a man whose religion changes like the phases of the moon. Christians, Watson tells us, need to be taught solid doctrine so they are not led astray by heresies. He obviously intends to address these sermons to adults, for he tells us that he undertakes this task to bring Christians to a mature faith. Christians should not be as children tossed to and fro by every wind of doctrine (Eph. 4:14). The way they are to be settled and grounded in their faith is by a knowledge of the fundamentals. The Epistle to the Hebrews speaks of "the first principles of God's word" (Heb. 5:12). It is this that is to be taught in the catechetical instruction (p. 4). Calling on Hebrews 6:1, Watson tells us that catechizing lays the foundation for preaching; to preach and not to catechize is to build without a foundation (p. 5). Finally he tells his congregation something of the catechetical ministry of the ancient Church. The admonition of Paul to Timothy that he maintain the form of sound words "which he had delivered to him" is, Watson proposes, a reference to the catechetical teaching Paul had given his disciple.[36] Erasmus and Grotius both tell us of how the early Church instructed catechumens. Fulgentius, Augustine, Theodoret, and Lactantius have all left us writings for the instruction of catechumens. God has blessed the catechetical ministry in the past, and Watson hopes God will bless his attempt to perform this same ministry.

Watson's catechetical preaching is thought out entirely in terms of teaching adults the fundamental doctrines of the Christian faith. Here we see a distinction from Luther, Bucer, Zwingli, and the first generation of Continental Reformers. Nothing is said about the relation of catechetical preaching to baptism. The text from the last chapter of Matthew on teaching those that have been baptized is not quoted. On the other hand, Watson finds his scriptural basis for catechetical preaching in a number of New Testament texts which even today many scholars think do in fact refer to catechetical preaching in the New Testament Church. This is par-

---

36. Many New Testament scholars would agree with Watson on this point. See vol. 1 of this work on the catechetical ministry in New Testament times.

ticularly the case with Hebrews 5:12–6:2. To put it very briefly, Watson interpreted catechetical preaching to be not so much introductory instruction as fundamental instruction. Catechetical preaching has become doctrinal preaching. This is quite consistent with the Puritan concern to deepen the Reformation. The catechizing of children was already institutionalized in the Church of England. Children learned the catechism, and yet all too many adult members of the Church were not rooted and grounded in sound Christian doctrine. The Puritan approach to catechetical preaching was much the same as the approach to evangelistic preaching. Evangelism was not winning a first commitment. That had already been done. The problem was one of reviving and deepening the faith of those who had made that commitment. Evangelistic preaching had to be continually experienced in the Christian life. It could not be left as a once-and-for-all conversion experience. So it was with catechetical preaching. It was not sufficient to go through communicants' class as a child and pass the course by reciting the catechism to the minister and the elders. These things had to be deepened through the whole of life. Baptism itself was not a once-and-for-all act so much as a sign performed at the beginning of life which presided over the whole unfolding of life. That was why the Puritans were always speaking of improving their baptism. In the same way, catechetical instruction needed to be a continual experience of the Christian. It was all quite consistent with that cardinal concern of the Puritans to deepen the institutional reality.

Watson's approach to catechetical preaching is to go through the *Westminster Shorter Catechism* question by question and explain the material in it. Watson does not feel obliged to treat all questions, and he occasionally introduces other material as well. For example, he gives us ten sermons on the attributes of God mentioned in question 4, and his list does not completely correspond to the one in the catechism. Instead of treating the goodness of God, he treats the mercy of God. He also inserts a sermon on the knowledge of God. A large part of the catechism is devoted to explaining the Lord's Prayer and the Christian interpretation of the Ten Commandments. Here, of course, the preacher interprets the text of Scripture much as one would in an expository sermon. The rest of the catechism presents another problem. Watson explains the text of the catechism rather than a particular text of Scripture. To be sure, he offers plenty of passages of Scripture to support the doctrine presented in the catechism, but essentially the sermons are expositions of the catechism itself. Frequently he speaks of the history of the particular doctrines involved. He brings up the historic difficulties and doctrinal controversies of the past and tells us how these problems have been resolved, particularly by the Church Fathers and the Continental Reformers. For Watson catechetical preaching is obviously doctrinal preaching. For many generations his work *A Body of Practical Divinity* served as a popular exposition of the *Westminster Shorter Catechism.* Even today it is a good document to show how that catechism was understood by a Puritan pastor who lived in London at the time it was written. It shows us how catechetical preaching was done by the typical Reformed preacher of the seventeenth century.

VIII. John Flavel (1627-91)

John Flavel, the seamen's preacher, was minister in Dartmouth, a port city in the south of England.[37] He ministered to the sea captains and sailors who in those days were beginning to build the mercantile empire that for the next three centuries would spread over all the seas and oceans of the world. He had the vision to see the importance of preaching the gospel to those seamen, who were destined to exercise such an important role in history. He understood well the peculiar sins and vices of mariners, their fears, their ambitions, and their spiritual needs. He had the sensitivity to preach a very practical sort of Christianity to that maritime congregation, even though for the greater part of his ministry he was hampered by the political and ecclesiastical climate of the Restoration.

Flavel was the son of a minister, and as a young man was sent to Oxford to be trained to follow his father's profession. By the time young Flavel was ready to begin his ministry, the Church of England had set aside episcopacy and had adopted a presbyterian polity. In 1650, being only twenty-three years old, he was sent to Diptford to assist the elderly minister there, and shortly afterward was examined and ordained by a presbytery meeting at Salisbury. In 1656 he was elected by the church of

---

37. For biographical material on Flavel, see *The Works of John Flavel*, 6 vols. (Edinburgh and Carlisle, Pa.: Banner of Truth Trust, 1982), hereafter Flavel, *Works*. The complete works of Flavel were first published in London by W. Baynes and Son in 1820. This study is based on the photolithographic reproduction of this edition by the Banner of Truth Trust listed above. See as well Michael Boland's biographical introduction to the Banner of Truth Trust's edition of John Flavel, *The Mystery of Providence*, photolithographic reproduction (Edinburgh and Carlisle, Pa.: Banner of Truth Trust, 1976), pp. 7-14, and Thomas Hamilton, "Flavel, John," in *Dictionary of National Biography*, 7:253-54.

Dartmouth, and his election was approved by the commissioners for approbation of public preachers. Both his ordination and call had been according to the order of the Church of England during the Commonwealth. Five years later Charles II was restored to the throne and episcopacy was reestablished. Flavel could not conscientiously support episcopacy, nor could he deny his dissatisfaction with *The Book of Common Prayer,* and so, in accordance with the Act of Uniformity, he was officially removed from his pulpit, but he continued to minister to the faithful of Dartmouth as best he could for almost thirty years. His ministry began to take on dangers not unlike those faced by his beloved seamen. Sometimes he preached in woods and private homes. Often he preached from a rock in the harbor of Dartmouth. It is this picture of Flavel in his black preaching gown, proclaiming the gospel on that rock in the harbor at Dartmouth, which has been remembered for centuries. Finally in 1688, when nonconforming Puritans were allowed greater liberty, his supporters built a large meetinghouse for him at Dartmouth, and there he was able to carry out his ministry unmolested. In 1691 he served as moderator of an assembly of Presbyterian and Congregational ministers trying to unite the two groups. This was a project to which he was particularly committed, and the meeting reached a consensus. Flavel concluded the meeting with great joy. A few hours later he died, and his body was taken back to Dartmouth and interred in Saint Savior's Church.

The main weight of Flavel's preaching was, in all probability, the regular exposition of various chapters of Scripture, which he went through one verse at a time. That was the standard procedure for the Puritan preacher. The scanty biographical information we have tells us of a series of this sort which he preached on John 3. Unfortunately no series of this sort ever reached publication. The sermons which have been preserved are of a more catechetical or doctrinal nature. A particularly fine series which he did see through to publication was *The Fountain of Life.*[38] This series of forty-two sermons has as its subtitle, *A Display of Christ in His Essential and Mediatorial Glory.* What we find in this series is a very thorough Christology worked out in a most original and pictorial way. One might say it is not so much a systematic Christology as an expository Christology. It is not a speculative Christology; it is both practical and profound. In many ways it is a companion to that masterpiece of Puritan theology, Stephen Charnock's *The Nature and Attributes of God.* That

---

38. For the text of this series, see Flavel, *Works,* 1:21-561.

such solid theology was preached to clandestine congregations gathered in the middle of the night or from a rock in the harbor of Dartmouth says something about the passion of the Puritans for solid theology.

Flavel's delight in catechetical preaching is further evidenced by *An Exposition of the Assembly's Shorter Catechism*.[39] While this document does not give us a series of sermons, it does show us what was preached at the regular Sunday catechetical exercises once Flavel had an organized congregation and a meetinghouse. Apparently, beginning in 1688, Flavel took one question of the *Westminster Shorter Catechism* each Lord's Day, and at the time of his death he had gotten through all but the last few of the 107 questions. For Americans it is of particular interest that the famous New England divine, Increase Mather, visited Dartmouth a few months after Flavel's death and, being shown the manuscript, wrote a preface for its publication. Mather's remarks testify to the renown which Flavel had already attained in "both Englands." They also indicate that he was even then recognized as one who had been blessed with a particularly strong awareness of the presence of God in his life. He had had what some call mystical experiences. He was a man of profound and powerful prayer and intense awareness of God's providence in his life. As Mather put it, Dartmouth knew a prophet had been in her midst.[40]

The sacrament of the Lord's Supper as most Reformed ministers of the period understood it required special preaching. We are told that Flavel preached at preparatory services on Thursdays before the celebration of Communion. Among his published sermons we find a collection of twelve *Sacramental Meditations*.[41] Possibly these sermons were preached at these preparatory services. They may, on the other hand, have been preached at the actual celebration of the Lord's Supper on the Lord's Day as a second sermon, after the regular sermon and before the sharing of the bread and wine. These sermons are considerably shorter than most of Flavel's published sermons. They show us the great reverence with which the Puritans approached the celebration of Communion.

One of the best examples of Flavel's preaching is found in the *Seaman's Companion*.[42] This is a series of six sermons "Wherein the Mysteries of Providence, relating to Seamen, are opened; their Sins and Dangers

39. For the text of this series, see Flavel, *Works*, 6:138-317.

40. This preface is found in the 1820 edition of Flavel, *Works*, 6:139-40.

41. Flavel, *Works*, 6:378-469.

42. Flavel, *Works*, 5:343-416. The page references that follow in the text are to vol. 5 of Flavel, *Works*.

discovered; their Duties pressed, and their several Troubles and Burdens relieved," as we find it on the title page. Flavel published these sermons so that sea captains might read them to their crews on the Lord's Day or so sailors deprived of the regular ministry of the Word during their voyages might be nourished by the Scriptures nevertheless. One gets the impression that they are the substance of what our preacher must have preached regularly to his seafaring congregation before they set sail. Herman Melville's marvelous chapter on sailors going to the seamen's chapel before a voyage no doubt gives us the setting in which these sermons must have been preached. Englishmen may have been Anglican at court and cathedral, but once they went off to sea they were Puritan through and through. Once out of port, the king's religion was not quite enough.

The first sermon, "The Seaman's Farewell," is on a text from Acts: "And we kneeled down on the shore, and prayed. And when we had taken our leave one of another, we took ship; and they returned home again" (21:5b-6 KJV). The preacher gives us the setting of the text. The apostle Paul was embarking at Tyre on his journey to Jerusalem. Everywhere along the way he was warned that dangers awaited him in Jerusalem, but at Tyre, particularly, certain disciples warned him in the Spirit of what was ahead. Paul resolved that, in spite of the difficulties, he was to go. He therefore engaged the prayers of his fellow Christians. This, Flavel tells us, has been the practice of Christians for centuries. Tertullian reports that Christians engaged in it in his day. He calls them *orationes littorales,* "shore prayers" (p. 345). Although the scope of the prayers is not mentioned, we can assume from the place and occasion that they were prayers for a prosperous voyage and for divine protection. Paul knew the hazards of life to which mariners are hourly exposed. He would never have committed himself to the sea until first he had solemnly committed himself to God, whose voice the winds and seas obey. Nor was he willing to take leave of his friends until he had poured out his heart to God with them, and for them whose faces he might never see again (p. 345). Having opened up the text in the way it was typically done in those days, our preacher deduces the principle that those who undertake sea voyages should not only pray earnestly for themselves, but should also engage the prayers of other Christians for them.

Flavel develops his principle by enumerating the divine mercies for which seamen are to pray. First, the seaman should pray for pardon of sin. It was because of Jonah's guilt that his ship was pursued by wind and storm. "Woe to him that finds at once a raging sea and a roaring conscience; trouble without, and terror within; ship and hope sinking together" (p. 347). What a line! Flavel clearly had a grasp for the arts of rhetoric.

With this our preacher goes on to his second point: the seaman should pray that the presence of God go with him. Flavel has in mind not the general presence of God that is with us whether we pray for it or not, but rather his gracious special presence, the presence Moses prayed for when he made the supplication, "If thy presence go not with me, carry us not up hence" (Exod. 33:15 KJV). For Moses it was better to be in a wilderness with God than in a Canaan without him. It is about this special presence that we read in Psalm 91:4: "He shall cover thee with his feathers, and under his wings shalt thou trust" (KJV). It is this special presence of God which, as a hen gathers her young under her wings, both cherishes and protects us. In the same psalm we read, "He shall give his angels charge over thee, to keep thee in all thy ways" (v. 11 KJV). Luther tells us that the angels have two offices — *superius canere, et inferius vigilare* — to sing above and watch below. The angels are a lifeguard to those on whom God's special presence rests. Psalm 91 also promises this to those who enjoy the special presence of God: "He shall call upon me, and I will answer him; I will be with him in trouble; I will rescue him, and honor him" (v. 15 KJV) (p. 348).

Third, the seaman should pray to be delivered from temptations. Fourth, he should pray for protection from the jeopardies to life and estate so common to those who live from the sea. Tonight, Flavel tells his congregation, you may be sleeping safely in your cabin, tomorrow tugging at the pump, and the next night taking up your lodging on a cold rock. How wisely the apostle James advises those who trade abroad: "Go to now, ye that say, To-day or to-morrow we will go into such a city, and continue there a year, and buy and sell, and get gain: Whereas you know not what shall be on the morrow" (James 4:13-14a KJV). Fifth, the seaman should pray for counsel and direction. In developing this point, our preacher brings out a nice quotation from Thomas Manton and a number of appropriate passages of Scripture which support his point. Sixth, the seaman should pray for success in his lawful employments and credit that success to God. Flavel calls on the example of Abraham's servant, who asked God's blessing on his mission before setting out on his journey (Gen. 24:12). In so doing we acknowledge providence and submit to his sovereignty.

Flavel now turns to developing two other points, namely, that our prayers do have influence on our receiving the mercies which we have asked and that the prayers and intercessions of others are effective as well. One notices that Flavel, as the Puritans in general, has a very deep faith in God's providence, but at the same time calls us to an intense discipline of prayer. It is here, of course, that we see the difference between the Christian doctrine of providence and both the fatalism of antiquity and the mechanistic determinism of the Enlightenment.

Flavel's application is as specific as his exposition is vivid. Let this text reproach those who set out to sea minding every kind of preparation but prayer. Even more, let this reproach be on those who instead of going on board praying as the apostle Paul did, go to sea cursing, swearing, and blaspheming God's name; not going from their bended knees, but drunken from their ale benches, to the ship (p. 354). How can the sailor who has profaned the name of God day after day with the language of hell call out in time of extremity, Mercy, mercy (p. 355)? Let seamen be men of prayer, Flavel admonishes his congregation. This point he enlarges at length, giving his congregation the promises of Scripture that assure us that God hears our prayers (pp. 355-59).

The second sermon, "The Seaman in a Storm," is taken from Psalm 107:23-28. "They that go down to the sea in ships, that do business in great waters; These see the works of the LORD, and his wonders in the deep. For he commandeth, and raiseth the stormy wind, which lifteth up the waves thereof. They mount up to the heaven, they go down again to the depths: their soul is melted because of trouble. They reel to and fro, and stagger like a drunken man, and are at their wit's end. Then they cry unto the LORD in their trouble, and he bringeth them out of their distresses" (KJV). This psalm as a whole treats the mysterious and admirable effects of providence, and these verses in particular tell us of divine providence to seamen, a sort of men more immediately dependent upon the favor of providence than any men in the world (p. 359). In these verses we find a description first of the persons: "They that go down to the sea in ships, that do business in great waters" (v. 23). Second, they describe the dangers, the stormy wind and the turbulent waves. Our preacher observes at some length that our text tells us that it is God who commands the winds and the waves. He distinguishes the principal cause, which is God, and the instrumental causes of nature. Third, the text tells of the deliverance of the seamen: "Then they cry unto the LORD in their trouble, and he bringeth them out of their distresses" (v. 28).

Flavel's theme is that the preservation of seamen in the dreadful storms and tempests at sea is the wonderful work of divine providence (p. 362). He develops this theme by speaking of the marvelous providence of God that we should be able to navigate the ocean at all. He quotes at length a number of authors of the day to make his point. One gets the impression that Flavel was a well-read parson. Then our preacher turns to more specific instances of God's providence in delivering seamen from the perils of the sea. Again he relates some remarkable stories of deliverance either from his reading or from accounts which members of his congregation had perhaps given him. This whole presentation is enlivened by his familiarity with ships and seamen. We know that Flavel himself once experienced a deliverance at sea. All this helps make this exposition vivid and interesting.

The application of the sermon exhorts the seamen to be thankful to God for his providential care. "Oh that men would praise the LORD for his goodness, and for his wonderful works to the children of men!" (Ps. 107:8 KJV). He knows that many in his congregation have similar stories to tell. These experiences should increase our ardor in the praise of God and encourage us to reform our lives. If God has brought us these tribulations to make us more aware of his power and mercy, we would be foolish to ignore it. He quotes Bernard of Clairvaux to make his point (p. 365). Then he suggests that if God's providence has so wonderfully saved us from the perils of the sea, God must have had a particular purpose in sparing us and we should be careful to seek out his purpose for us and fulfill it (p. 369). This is particularly so for any who at the time of this mercy were without Christ. They should from this experience be encouraged to repentance and conversion, that in Christ they find the fulfillment of even richer promises (p. 370).

The fourth sermon, "The Successful Seaman," takes as its text Deuteronomy 8:17-18, "And thou say in thine heart, My power and the might of mine hand hath gotten me this wealth. But thou shalt remember the LORD thy God: for it is he that giveth thee power to get wealth" (KJV). He begins the sermon by placing the verse in its context. The principle he draws from the text is that the prosperity and success of our affairs are not to be ascribed to our own abilities, but to the blessing of God on our lawful endeavors (p. 386). Our preacher discusses two verses from the tenth chapter of Proverbs, "The hand of the diligent maketh rich" (v. 4 KJV) and "The blessing of the LORD, it maketh rich" (v. 22 KJV). He concedes that both are true, but the first is subordinate to the second. It is wise to conjoin the two and understand that a diligent hand cannot make rich without God's blessing; and God's blessing does not ordinarily make rich without a diligent hand. "Faith must not stifle industry, nor industry blind faith" (p. 387).

In developing this point Flavel tells us that very often the providence of God disposes things quite contrary to the way reason would expect. He discusses the passage in Ecclesiastes where we read, "The race is not to the swift, nor the battle to the strong, neither yet bread to the wise, nor yet riches to men of understanding" (9:11 KJV). Our preacher produces several examples from history of men of great wisdom who lived in poverty. He mentions both Aristides and Socrates. On the other hand, foolish men often come to great wealth. Of Pope Clement V it was said, "None more rich, none more foolish." He quotes a Latin proverb, *Fortuna favet fatiis,* "Fortune favors fools" (p. 388). If God allows such things to happen, it is because we need to know that wealth is not purely the work of our own hands. Having said this, however, Flavel goes on to enumerate five ordinary causes for success in business, and shows that each depends on a kindly disposition of providence. One notices that Flavel draws heavily on the Wisdom literature to develop his points (pp. 389-90).

Our preacher then applies his teaching. First he cautions his congregation not to take prosperity as an evidence of God's favor (p. 393). Then he warns them not to become proud in their prosperity, for providences in these things are often very changeable. God often pulls down the proud heart. He recounts the story of Hezekiah proudly showing his treasures to the emissaries of the king of Babylon. Even the heathen understand this principle, and to make his point he quotes a couple lines from Ovid. If indeed success in business is from the Lord, Flavel says, then certainly the best way to prosperity is to commend our affairs to God in prayer. He quotes Psalm 37:5, "Commit thy way unto the LORD; trust also in him; and he shall bring it to pass" (KJV). In the same way, if our prosperity depends upon God, then it should be faithfully employed to his glory. To the faithful God gives wealth that they might have the means of doing his work. The prosperous Christian has the means of honoring God by relieving the poor and by supporting the proclamation of the gospel (p. 394). In fact, it is the duty of Christians to perform these services in proportion to the success God grants in one's trade. Finally he warns his congregation against being satisfied with worldly prosperity and negligent in the cultivation of spiritual prosperity. To make this point he recounts a story about Luther, who once was offered a very handsome present and earnestly protested that God should not put him off with such things (p. 395).

This sermon is particularly interesting because it shows what the Puritans really did preach on the relation of piety and prosperity. The series of six sermons as a whole is an admirable attempt to teach a very practical kind of holiness to people who were engaged in the affairs of the world. It was sermons such as these which molded a race of devout merchant seamen who built an empire. To be sure, not all the sea captains and sailors of England and New England heard or heeded these sermons, but many did. It was they who were the leaven in the lump.

One of the most engaging features of Flavel's sermons is what one might call the personal mysticism of his doctrine of providence. This theme is most fully worked out in his essay *Meditation on the Mystery of Providence,* one of the classics of Puritan spirituality.[43] We have noted in these sermons how Flavel balances his strong doctrine of providence with an equally strong discipline of prayer. Here we find no "inhuman Calvinistic determinism," as some have termed it. Here we see the way a devout Calvinist personally appropriated his faith in the sovereignty of God. For Calvin himself the doctrine of predestination was a way of getting beyond the elaborate network of secondary causes and finding oneself immediately in the hands of God. Flavel develops in his preaching something that was implicit in Calvinism from the beginning. Yet it is something that is classically Christian. It is only since the Enlightenment that Christians have begun to forget the doctrine of providence and neglect the disciplines of prayer.

Another thing we should notice about these sermons is that Flavel may have been an evangelist to sailors, but he was nonetheless a most learned minister. His sermons evidence his wide reading. He loved to develop his points with illustrations from ancient history, to quote Latin proverbs, and to cite writers of his own day. It never occurred to him that learning was only for the leisure class. Sailors needed a learned preacher as much as did the students and professors of Oxford.

His sermons did differ from most of those we have studied in this chapter on one point, however. They are filled with rich illustrative material. Flavel follows the Protestant plain style in many respects, but he also

43. This was originally published as John Flavel, *Divine Conduct or the Mystery of Providence* (London, 1678). It was included in the edition of his works published in 1820 in London by W. Baynes and Son. A recent edition is available under the title *The Mystery of Providence,* photolithographic reproduction (Edinburgh and Carlisle, Pa.: Banner of Truth Trust, 1976).

divided the text in characteristic scholastic fashion. On the other hand, he did not employ the elaborate introductions and conclusions that had been so cultivated by the medieval schools. While there is no obvious attempt at literary polish, there is nevertheless a profusion of examples drawn from history, from literature, and from personal experiences. In Flavel's hands the Protestant plain style is not quite so plain.

IX. Conclusion

What we have observed up to this point should make it clear that Puritanism indeed built on much that it inherited from Luther, Bucer, Vermigli, and Calvin, and yet the Puritans had their own concerns. Their theology of worship is still built on covenant theology. The covenant theology of William Perkins and William Ames had developed considerably from that of Oecolampadius, Zwingli, and Bullinger, and throughout the Puritan period it continued to develop, but it was there that the rich soil was found in which Puritan preaching was rooted. Yet, as we have seen in Perkins's *Art of Prophesying,* the Puritans had some of their own thoughts on preaching. Perkins especially shows us that they had a profound understanding of preaching as worship.

As we have noticed, the Puritans made a number of departures from the homiletical practice of the sixteenth century. They did not always follow the Reformers in using the form of the patristic homily, that is, a running commentary on a number of verses of Scripture. They did intend to do expository preaching — Manton and Goodwin are examples — but they used much of the scholastic method as well. In England the break between medieval homiletics and Reformation homiletics was not nearly as clear as it was on the Continent. The Puritans most frequently used the scholastic, analytical form. This is a most suggestive detail! English Puritanism is an expression of Protestant scholasticism. The theologians of Oxford and Cambridge never had the strong reaction against Scholasticism which the Christian humanists of the Continent had. Many of the Puritans we have studied had read with great profit the Scholastic theologians, particularly Bernard of Clairvaux, Bonaventure, and Thomas Aquinas. On the other hand, England never had anything like the patristic revival to which Rhenish Protestantism was heir.[44] If the Continental

---

44. Henry Savil's edition of John Chrysostom did not begin to appear until 1610.

Reformers wanted to model their sermons after the patristic homilies, the English Puritans were often content to maintain the medieval scholastic sermon form.

Given this form, they tried to make the best they could of the *lectio continua*. The scholastic sermon form slowed down the *lectio continua*. Rarely could one cover in one sermon more than a single verse of Scripture using this form; in fact, it often took several sermons to treat but one verse, if the method was used to its full rigor. Consequently, the Puritans got to the place where they preached through chapters rather than whole books. There were a few exceptions. Thomas Manton was able to get through the whole book of James, and perhaps the whole of Colossians and Philippians, but most often the Puritans preached on chapters. These chapters were chosen carefully, of course. The choosing of the right chapter for the right congregation at the right time was the responsibility of a qualified interpreter of Scripture. Preaching on chapters, however, had its limitations. What this ultimately meant was the finishing off of the *lectio continua* and the gradual development of thematic preaching. When John Preston preached six sermons on Romans 1:17-18, he was preaching on a theme more than a text, in spite of his best intentions.

The charge is often made that the Puritans separated preaching from worship. There are certain justifications to this charge, but in the end it is misleading. Indeed, much of their preaching often took place at "lectures." These lectures often had to be held after the completion of the prayer book service or at some time other than the ordinary services. Sunday afternoon or weekday mornings were the favorite times. This meant that the preaching was outside the liturgy. This was a situation forced on the Puritans by their parish ministers, who for one reason or another did not preach. The Franciscans and Dominicans faced the same problem in the Middle Ages. Established authority has a way of resisting earnest piety. Alas, the story is often repeated in the history of the Church. But a considerable amount of medieval preaching stood outside the liturgy as well. Bernard of Clairvaux normally preached to his monks in the chapter house rather than in the chapel, and Bernardino da Siena, during his Florentine revival, preached daily in the square in front of Santa Croce after Mass was over. Many of the endowed preachers of the Rhineland preached completely outside the context of either Mass or office. If the preaching of the Puritans tended to get separated from the liturgy, it was not altogether unprecedented. Preaching does not, after all, have to be enclosed in the liturgy in order to be worship.

A more serious problem we begin to encounter in the seventeenth century is the drifting apart of the reading of the Word from the preaching of the Word. Both Puritans and Anglicans were guilty of the same tendency. In Anglican churches the office of morning prayer was read from the prayer book, then a sermon was preached. Presbyterian and Congregational churches, unfortunately, began to follow this pattern, and put the sermon at the end of the service, thus separating the lesson from the sermon. Anglican preachers did not feel constrained to preach on the passage appointed by the lectionary. Even on feast days they selected texts appropriate to the feast that had not been drawn from the Gospel or Epistle of the day. There was no doubt a very practical reason for this. Protestants had the Bible in their own language, and by the seventeenth century most homes had a family Bible. For the Puritans particularly, the daily reading of the Bible at family prayers was vigorously cultivated. The public reading of the Scriptures was therefore not as crucial as it once had been. The invention of the printing press had its effect on public worship.

There was another reason which was probably not unrelated to this. The Puritans became more and more critical of "dumb reading," of the simple reading of a Gospel or Epistle from the lectionary without comment. They no doubt felt they could do that at home. When the Puritans were able to shape the service of worship, the practice grew up of reading a chapter of the Old Testament and a chapter of the New Testament and commenting on the readings as they were read. Later in the service there was a sermon on a text drawn from still another portion of Scripture. It was not that the Puritans saw little value in simply reading the Scriptures. This was one of the distinctions between family worship and the worship of the congregation. At family worship the reading of the Scripture lesson was not supposed to be explained or commented upon. That was the responsibility of the minister of the Word. When the congregation was assembled and a minister of the Word was available, then they expected more than the simple reading of the lesson.

As we have had occasion to remark, the Puritans did build a very strong relationship between the ministry of the Word and the ministry of prayer. This they no doubt inherited from Calvin, but they built on Calvin appreciably. William Perkins had taught that the two ministries were very closely connected. He pointed out the prophetic aspect of both preaching and prayer. One notices how often the Puritans preached on prayer. In the same way, they built a strong unity between Word and sacrament. Here, too, they built on covenant theology. Preaching was the proclamation of the covenant and the sacraments were the sealing of the covenant. The Puritans had an intense sacramental devotion. If the English Puritans had a ministry of the Word outside the regular worship of the Church, it was not because that was implicit in their understanding of worship or because they lost interest in prayer or in the sacraments, but because of the historical situation in which they found themselves.

Finally, we must say something about how the Puritans found preaching to be worship. As we have already indicated, William Perkins's *Art of Prophesying* gives us about as good an insight into Puritan preaching and its place in Christian worship as we can find. It was a very popular work which in many ways expresses the central thrust of the Puritan pulpit. At the center of Puritan preaching was a profound sense that Scripture is the Word of God. Christian piety therefore gave high priority to the reading and preaching of that Word with the utmost devotion. As Luther himself had put it, the first duty of the disciple is to learn from the master. Listening to the Word of God was at the center of true Christian worship. But there is more to be said.

In the sermons of Richard Sibbes, Thomas Manton, and Thomas Goodwin, we find beautiful examples of preaching at its most doxological. In Sibbes's sermons we hear the glory of God's mercy and the majesty of his love. His sermons on the Song of Solomon are lyrical hymns to the heavenly Bridegroom. Manton preached the glory of God's grace. His sermons on Romans 8 delight in the wonder of God's faithfulness to his people. Such preaching could not be more doxological. Goodwin preached the splendor of God's eternal purposes as they are revealed in Christ. If the Westminster divines taught that man's chief end is to glorify God and enjoy him forever, the preaching of the Puritan worship service had exactly that same end. It led the congregation in the glorifying and enjoying of God.

CHAPTER IV

Anglican Preaching

The progress of Protestantism in England was slow, but it was persistent. We have spoken, although only briefly, of John Wycliffe, the Lollards, and the uniquely English sources of the Reformation. Wycliffe died in 1384, a century before Luther was born, so Protestantism was in the English soil long before Luther began to preach against indulgences. King Henry VIII allowed Protestantism to reestablish itself in his kingdom for the most questionable of motives. He rejected papal authority and made himself the head of the Church of England, but that was a long way from making the English church truly Protestant. By all odds, the Reformation should never have been able to strike root in England, because there were only a very few preachers of ability. Two of these, Hugh Latimer and John Hooper, we treated in detail. Much more important for the development of English Protestantism was the production of an English Bible and a system for its regular public reading in the service of daily morning and evening prayer. Even at that, when the first generation of Reformers met their martyrdom, their work seemed to have only the weakest kind of support. Yet the fires which consumed Latimer, Ridley, Tyndale, Hooper, Rogers, and Cranmer did indeed become a light which finally shone through the whole of England. It happened just as Cranmer had prayed it would. Protestantism, quite surprisingly, survived the reestablishment of Catholicism during the reign of Queen Mary. Only the providence of God can explain it.

During the forty-year reign of Elizabeth I, English Protestantism grew and matured. And yet the age of Elizabeth was not an age of great preaching. There was no master of the Elizabethan pulpit. One assumes that the saintly George Herbert was a conscientious preacher, but his sermons have not come down to us. The sermons of John Jewel were effective enough, but by no means outstanding. Anglicanism would produce some marvelous preachers, but not during the reign of Elizabeth I. Not until the beginning of the seventeenth century do we find a distinctly Anglican school of preaching. William Perkins and the Puritans of Cambridge began to develop a distinctly English school of preaching, but its greatest preachers did not begin to appear until the end of Elizabeth's reign.[1] It took England most of the sixteenth century to develop enough preachers to allow for truly Protestant worship throughout the whole land.

With the beginning of the seventeenth century and the accession to the English throne of James Stuart, the son of Mary, Queen of Scots, the Church of England began to divide into opposing camps. There was Puritanism, which sought to deepen classical Protestantism with its emphasis on piety, and Anglicanism, which sought to develop a national religion by making loyalty to the monarchy one of the foundations of faith. It is about Anglicanism that we must now speak.[2] For the rest of the century, the Church of England was torn between these two opposing tendencies. The great majority, as in many other things like this, wavered between the two positions, sometimes going with the Puritans, sometimes with the Anglicans. While one must recognize this quite clearly, we want in this chapter to look at how several of the leading supporters of the Anglican

---

1. Horton Davies dates the golden age of English preaching as 1588-1645, while William Fraser Mitchell would situate it between Andrewes and Tillotson. The difference of approach is found in the titles of these two masterful studies: Horton Davies, *Like Angels from a Cloud: The English Metaphysical Preachers, 1588-1645* (San Marino, Calif.: Huntington Library, 1986), and William Fraser Mitchell, *English Pulpit Oratory from Andrewes to Tillotson: A Study of Its Literary Aspects* (London: SPCK, 1932).

2. On Anglicanism in general, see the following: Paul Avis, *Anglicanism and the Christian Church: Theological Resources in Historical Perspective* (Minneapolis: Fortress Press, 1989); John E. Booty, "Anglicanism," in *Oxford Encyclopedia of the Reformation*, 4 vols. (New York and Oxford: Oxford University Press, 1996), 1:38-44; Urban T. Holmes III, *What Is Anglicanism?* (Wilton, Conn.: Morehouse-Barlow Co., 1982); Henry Robert McAdoo, *The Spirit of Anglicanism* (London: A. & C. Black, 1965); Stephen Neill, *Anglicanism*, 3rd rev. ed. (London: Mowbrays, 1977); John F. H. New, *Anglican and Puritan* (Stanford: Stanford University Press, 1964); H. C. Porter, *Reformation and Reaction in Tudor Cambridge* (Cambridge: At the University Press, 1958); and Stephen W. Sykes, *The Integrity of Anglicanism* (New York: Seabury Press, 1978).

position understood the ministry of the Word and its place in Christian worship.

To understand Anglicanism, one must see it in the context of baroque culture. Far from merely an English phenomenon, Anglicanism was, like Gallicanism, an expression of a very particular zeitgeist which was appearing all over western Europe at about the same time. Fundamental to this spirit of the age was the political philosophy of absolutism. Whether in the Papal States, the Kingdom of France, the Duchy of Florence, or England, the key to the culture was the monarch. The monarch ruled by divine right. God had put all that was in the monarch's territory under the monarch's feet. The function of the Church was to provide divine sanction for the state. The baroque understanding of absolutism was a logical development of the political philosophy of Machiavelli, but how the Church could fit into this kind of governmental structure was largely the contribution of the Jesuits. The Jesuits were at work in every court of Europe to show how Catholicism fit so well into this political philosophy. James I, on the other hand, was determined to impose the political-religious ideology of the baroque age on his Protestant subjects. To do this, however, he had to counteract the influence of the Puritans, who insisted the Church be independent of the state. Polity was not the only matter at issue. There was a deeper theological problem. Even more, James I had to overrule the Calvinists, who in their doctrine of predestination insisted on the sovereignty of God. That was the deep theological issue of the seventeenth century.

The influence of baroque culture was very strong at the Stuart court. The queens of all three major Stuart kings were Roman Catholics. The fact that the queen of James I, Anne of Denmark, was converted to Catholicism after her marriage should by itself indicate how strong Counter-Reformation propaganda was at the Stuart court. Charles I had married Henrietta Maria, the sister of Louis XIII of France, who was the daughter of Marie de' Medici. Henrietta Maria was a vigorous promoter of both political and religious absolutism. From 1628 until she finally fled England in 1644, she exercised a considerable influence on her husband. She even went so far as to maintain a personal ambassador at the papal court.

The queen of Charles II, Catherine of Braganza, was a Portuguese princess who definitely stayed in the background, but she was one more member of the court who supported Catholicism. When Charles II returned from his exile at the palace of Vincennes on the outskirts of Paris, many of his courtiers returned deeply influenced by both the religious and political outlook of baroque Catholicism. They may very well have remained members of the Church of England, but they had begun to look at English Protestantism as French Catholics looked at their religion. It was the culture of the French court which really set the taste of cultivated Englishmen. This concern for French culture brought with it a wide familiarity with the baroque spirit. Every cultivated Englishman could read French, and consequently a great deal of French literature was read in England. The literary and artistic taste of England enjoyed the flavors of France.

This was important for the development of the Anglican School of preaching. One of the reasons the baroque spirit appreciated art was its usefulness in propaganda. The Counter-Reformation patronized art because of its ability to attract. Art can make things attractive. It has a persuasive power. For the Counter-Reformation, art was supposed to convey the awe in which the common people were to behold both temporal and spiritual authorities. It was with magnificence and glory that the artist should concern himself. One of the classic expressions of this was the cycle of paintings which Rubens painted on the life of Marie de' Medici. Sir Anthony Van Dyke, the student of Rubens, became court painter to Charles I and helped the Cavaliers see themselves as the divinely established aristocracy. How noble Van Dyke's courtiers appear! The preacher was to do much the same thing as the painter: to make virtue appear noble, intelligent, and valiant. He was to amaze his hearers with the glory of godliness. In chapter 2 we spoke of this in relation to the preachers of the Counter-Reformation; in this chapter we will show how the Anglican School of preaching used this same approach to art. We will notice with particular interest how preaching becomes important as an art form. Preachers will give increasing care to publishing their sermons. Here we will see preaching becoming literature. The preachers of the Anglican School will make of sermons what their *Book of Common Prayer* had made of their prayers — very refined literature.

Not all of English Protestantism followed the Anglican approach. Puritan preaching had a tendency to run counter to the prevailing baroque culture of the seventeenth century. Horton Davies has pointed out that a good number of Puritans, including Thomas Adams, Henry Smith, and John Prideaux, used a more elaborate style but remained thoroughly Puritan in theological outlook.[3] Surely one could find Anglicans who

3. Davies, *Like Angels,* pp. 7-31.

tended to maintain a Protestant plain style even in the age of the baroque, but there was a distinct philosophical affinity between Anglicanism and the baroque spirit. The characteristics of baroque preaching we noticed in chapter 2 were almost identical to what we find among the Anglican preachers of the seventeenth century.[4] They loved to demonstrate their wit, to quote patristic and classical authors, to illustrate their points from natural history, and to use elaborate rhetorical forms, riddles, puns, paradoxes, and emblems. They were very much concerned that their preaching appear learned.

Again it is in the context of baroque culture that one must see the Anglican rejection of the more Augustinian theology of grace and the revival of Pelagianism. Toward the end of the seventeenth century, the Jesuits had pushed very hard for a liberalizing of the doctrine of grace. Luis de Molina (1535-1600), a Spanish Jesuit, had tried to show that Thomas Aquinas had not taught predestination. The conservative Spanish Dominican Báñez argued that he did. The matter was brought to Rome, with the Jesuit position being championed by Cardinal Bellarmine, but the pope finally decided not to make a pronouncement on this issue. Even at that, the Jesuits continued to make attacks on predestination part of their polemic against Protestantism.

In the Netherlands Jacobus Arminius began to follow in a similar vein. Arminius (1560-1609) studied theology in a wide variety of places: Marburg, Geneva, Padua, and even Rome. He began to develop a very different approach to the theology of grace than the standard Calvinists of his day. While surely he never intended it, his denial of predestination was a significant support to absolutist views of political authority. His ideas were very popular at the court of both James I and Charles I. Archbishop Laud was thoroughly Arminian. The issue continued to be debated throughout the seventeenth century. In France, during the reign of Louis XIV, the Jansenists once again made the doctrine of grace a primary subject of debate. No one fooled Louis XIV, to be sure. He realized the Jansenists had made a subtle theological attack on his absolutism.

These theological issues had, as one would expect, their effect on the way one approached the ministry of the Word. In the preachers we have chosen to study, we will see this being worked out in several directions.

4. Davies, *Like Angels,* pp. 45-88.

I. Lancelot Andrewes (1555-1626)

With Lancelot Andrewes we begin to see the emergence of a distinctly Anglican School of preaching. It was very different from the Puritan School of preaching William Perkins had defined in his 1592 preaching manual.

For almost twenty years Andrewes was preacher at the court of King James I.[5] His wit, his scholarship, and his eloquence delighted the court. Shortly after his death a collection of ninety-six of his sermons was published by command of Charles I, the son and successor of James I, as testimony to the esteem in which Andrewes was held by his father. Not only had Andrewes pleased the Stuart monarchy with his preaching, but even more he had won the gratitude of the Stuarts by helping to shape for them the sort of church they wanted for their kingdom. Andrewes was one of the fathers of Anglicanism. A devout churchman, he helped bring into focus the *via media* and showed the way to a courtly piety. His greatest contribution, one for which all English-speaking Protestants must indeed be grateful, was his work on the King James Version of the Bible. It is he who is largely responsible for the beautiful language of the historical books of the Old Testament. Andrewes, as the poet T. S. Eliot has testified, was above all a master of language.

Brought up in comfortable circumstances in London, he was prepared for the university at Merchant Taylor's school. He studied at Pembroke Hall in Cambridge, becoming a fellow in 1576. While he was at Cambridge, Thomas Cartwright held his famous lectures on the Acts of the Apostles and the Admonitions Controversy occupied the attention of the Cambridge Puritans. In fact, it was the master of Andrewes's own college, John Whitgift, who led the attack on Cartwright. Andrewes was from his earliest student days a stout supporter of the Elizabethan settlement and had no sympathy for the reforms advocated by the Puritans. Ordained in 1580, he soon became chaplain to Archbishop Whitgift, the Cambridge professor who had been rewarded by Elizabeth for his support of her ecclesiastical settlement with the see of Canterbury. Andrewes's service to Whitgift was rewarded by a succession of prestigious appointments. During Elizabeth's reign he was appointed canon of Saint Paul's Cathedral and then dean of Westminster. At the accession of James I, a conference was

---

5. For biographical information on Lancelot Andrewes, see the following: Florence Higham, *Lancelot Andrewes* (London: SCM Press, 1952), and Paul A. Welsby, *Lancelot Andrewes, 1555-1626* (London: SPCK, 1958).

called at Hampton Court to deal with the concerns of the Puritans who had presented the Millenary Petition. Andrewes distinguished himself by his opposition to the Puritan proposal. His unhesitating support of the Church of England as it was then constituted led to his preferment in the Anglican hierarchy as well as at the court of James I. He was appointed king's almoner, bishop of Chichester in 1605, bishop of Ely in 1609, privy councillor in 1616, and finally bishop of Winchester in 1618.

The sermons Bishop Andrewes has left us are those he preached at court.[6] We have no record of sermons he might have preached in the cathedrals of Chichester, Ely, or Winchester. His responsibilities at court required him to spend most of his time in London. From the sermons that have been preserved we gather that he did not preach on ordinary Sundays, but rather on the feast days and fast days of the Anglican liturgical calendar. This is no doubt to be explained partly by a reaction against the Puritans, whose strongest demand was for preaching every Sunday in every parish, but the strong emphasis on the church year is typically Anglican. We have in the collection of his sermons the following:

> seventeen sermons for Christmas Day
> eight sermons for Ash Wednesday
> six sermons for Lent
> three sermons for Good Friday
> eighteen sermons for Easter
> fifteen sermons for Whitsunday
> eight sermons for the commemoration of the Gowrie Conspiracy
> ten sermons for the commemoration of the Gunpowder Plot
> (Guy Fawkes Day)

This list suggests that for the major feasts of Christmas, Easter, and Whitsunday, Bishop Andrewes was the most popular preacher at the court of James I. Records for the period indicate that his preaching drew great crowds to the palace chapel at Whitehall and that the king often spoke most approvingly of his preaching. A good sermon from the lord bishop was evidently considered a natural part of the festivities. Most of the sermons are on the traditional Gospels and Epistles of the day, but there are

---

6. Lancelot Andrewes, *Ninety-Six Sermons,* 5 vols. (Oxford: J. H. Parker, 1841-45); the references in the text are to this work, with the volume number followed by the page reference.

some exceptions. The eight sermons in commemoration of the Gowrie Conspiracy and the ten sermons for Guy Fawkes Day may seem a bit discordant, but they claim an important place in Andrewes's preaching, as we will have occasion to remark a little further on.

Andrewes was much admired in his day as an orator. His published sermons would indicate that he deserved the reputation. His sermons were carefully written out beforehand, and it would appear that the sermon he preached was very close to his prepared text. What is most pleasing in his sermons is the rhythm of his prose. His sentence structure has great variety and sparkle. His vocabulary is varied and interesting. He is capable of very clever plays on words, and he has a pleasing use of alliteration. All this must have made his sermons very easy to hear. He was indeed an orator of ability.

Part of his appeal as a preacher was due to his scholarship. His congregations loved his obvious display of learning. He mastered the art of scholarly showmanship. His sermons are filled not only with Latin quotations, but with whole sentences in Greek and even occasional words and phrases of Hebrew. The bishop of Winchester was reported to have known fifteen languages! Interestingly enough, his quotations are almost always from sacred literature. He does not seem particularly concerned to demonstrate his mastery of secular literature. He loves to quote the Latin text of Scripture; in fact, he carries it to the point where one gets the impression that he is really preaching on the Latin text rather than the English text. This seems a bit strange for one of the principal draftsmen of the King James Version of the Bible, but even stranger is the fact that long after 1611 he still used the Geneva Bible. This can no doubt be explained by his great facility with language. As a child he must have already known great portions of the Geneva Bible by heart, and as a student he studied theology in Latin and the Scripture in their Greek and Hebrew texts. But there is another explanation. The lord bishop was preaching to a king who liked to think of himself as a scholar and theologian. The king liked sermons with all the theological trappings. As a boy in Scotland, James I had been educated by George Buchanan, one of Scotland's best biblical scholars, and he had a taste for theology in the original languages. Andrewes understood the court. If the king was pleased with his pulpit erudition, the court would be pleased as well.

Andrewes had an amazing ability to bring edifying thoughts out of the most minute details of his text. He put his mastery of grammar and lexicography to good use, and he communicated to his congregation his fascination with the very wording of the text. One of the best examples of this is the sermon he preached at Whitehall on the Day of Pentecost 1606. In it he explains in the most imaginative way the imagery of the sound of the mighty wind that came from heaven and the descent of the cloven tongues of fire (3:107-29). Surely his congregation must have taken away from that sermon a vivid impression of the biblical narrative. Andrewes always makes a conscientious attempt to explain the text of Scripture. He was convinced that this was the preacher's sacred responsibility, a point he makes very clear in the sermon he preached on Pentecost at Holyrood House in 1617. He took as his text Luke 4:18-19, which tells of Christ's sermon at Nazareth. He points to the fact that Jesus took the book of the prophet Isaiah and selected a text from it. "There was no fear that Christ would have ranged from His matter, if He had taken none; yet He took a text, to teach us thereby to do the like. To keep us within not to fly out, or preach much, either without, or beside the book. And he took His text for the day, as is plain by His application, 'This day is this Scripture fulfilled in your ears.' 'This day this Scripture.' Our Master's Scripture was for the day; so would ours be" (3:280ff.).

Unfortunately his great concern to interpret the text for the day prevented him from producing anything like the magisterial interpretations of Scripture which many of his contemporaries produced. He interpreted the traditional texts for Christmas, Easter, and Whitsunday, but we have no great exposition of major books, or even major chapters, of the Bible. He is not a great biblical preacher, even though his sermons are quite biblical. What one does not see is the big picture. He produced fascinating miniatures, but never a great canvas.

One of the chief burdens of his ministry was the cultivation of private piety. His masterpiece was his *Preces privatae,* a collection of prayers in Greek and Latin which he had written for his own devotions. His preaching had a close connection to these prayers. He preached sermons designed to inspire the private devotion of the members of the court. He had about himself an air of personal sanctity which gave integrity to his message. He was regarded in his day as a man of serenity who moved undisturbed, unruffled, and untainted through a world of intrigue.

The other burden of his ministry was to establish for England a national church under the authority of a divinely anointed king. It was his practice in his sermons commemorating the Gowrie Conspiracy and the Gunpowder Plot to preach his doctrine of the divine right of kings. In his first sermon for Guy Fawkes Day, he chose to preach on Psalm 118, which celebrates a deliverance of King David (4:203ff.). In this sermon he established the typological relation between the king of Israel and the king of England that he would develop through the years. As he saw it, the king of England was divinely anointed in the same way David had been. Just as David had divinely given authority over Israel, so James I had the same authority and the same rights over England. He was entitled to the same obedience and submission to which David was. Even the Church must be submissive to the king. His person was sacred, and any treason or conspiracy against him was a crime against God. In his sermon for Guy Fawkes Day in 1613, Andrewes preached on the text "By me kings reign" (Prov. 8:15). In his exposition he discusses at length the divine appointment of both David and Solomon and shows how those who rebelled against their rule were resisting divine authority. Even the high priest Abiathar had no right to resist David's rule (4:281). If the Stuart dynasty developed a rather extreme theory of the divine right of kings, they were obviously encouraged to do so by their favorite court preacher. Unfortunately Andrewes had a higher doctrine of royal authority than he did of divine sovereignty. He claimed that he never preached predestination. In fact, he seems to have had an abhorrence for Calvinism. That is easy enough to believe. The sort of royal absolution which he preached on Guy Fawkes Day is rather hard to reconcile with a high doctrine of the sovereignty of God.

II. John Donne (1571-1631)

John Donne has the distinction of being as well known as a poet as he is as a preacher. His preaching is greatly admired for its literary excellence, for the poetic character of its language, and for the artistic expression of its concepts. Donne is beloved for his ability to express heavenly ideas in the imagery of this world. It is this which distinguishes him both as a poet and as a preacher. He is the first of the metaphysical poets. Here is a preacher who made an art of preaching, a poet who brought to the pulpit an exquisite linguistic refinement.

Donne was a man who went through much spiritual anguish during his life.[7] It was not the heroic struggles of saintliness which beset him, but

---

7. For biographical material on Donne, see the following: Robert Cecil Bald, *John Donne: A Life* (New York: Oxford University Press, 1970); William R. Mueller, *John Donne: Preacher* (Princeton: Princeton University Press, 1962); and Isaak Walton, *Life of*

the tribulations of a very worldly man who was embarrassed by a secret marriage, who endured the loss of five of his twelve children, who was frustrated in his attempts to seek preferment at court, and who had to struggle again and again with both poverty and illness. Somehow all his anguished personal struggles gave a note of authority and conviction to his proclamation of grace. He was born into a Roman Catholic family. In fact, he was the great-grandnephew of Sir Thomas More, who was martyred for his resistance to Henry VIII's assumption of supremacy over the Church of England. The motives of his conversion from Catholicism to Protestantism have never been too clear, but by the time he began to appear in public life he was a strong supporter of the Anglican establishment. Donne was much more explicitly Protestant than Andrewes. This one observes especially in his strong doctrine of grace. Urged by his friends to seek ordination in the Church of England, he resisted the suggestion, hoping that eventually he would achieve a position at court. His doubts about the genuineness of his vocation and his hesitation to take up the ministry bothered him for years. Finally in 1615, when even the king had made it clear that the only preferment he would get would be in the service of the Church, Donne accepted ordination, being forty-four years of age at the time. He evidently took the words of the king as the voice of providence. Donne began his preaching career at the chapel of Lincoln's Inn. This was one of the most prominent pulpits in London, and to fill that pulpit was to be chaplain to the legal profession of the capital. The king was faithful to his implied promise, and in 1621 Donne was made dean of Saint Paul's Cathedral, where for the remaining years of his life he performed a distinguished preaching ministry.

A. Festal Sermons

Donne is known above all as a preacher of the great feasts of the liturgical calendar.[8] As dean of Saint Paul's, he was responsible for preaching at

John Donne, Dr. in Divinity, and late Dean of Saint Pauls Church, London (London: Printed by J.G. for R. Marriot, 1658).

8. For his sermons, see *The Sermons of John Donne,* ed. Evelyn M. Simpson and George R. Potter, 10 vols. (Berkeley and Los Angeles: University of California Press, 1956-58); references in the text are to this work, with volume number followed by page reference. It will be noticed that this edition retains the peculiarities of spelling and capitalization found in the original edition.

Christmas, Easter, Whitsunday, and at the feast of the conversion of Saint Paul. On such red-letter days of the church year he preached at Saint Paul's, but he often preached before both James I and Charles I at White-hall. He had other preaching responsibilities as well. As any clergyman favored by the king, he had a number of livings, that is, endowed pulpits. The most prominent of these was Saint Dunstan in the West. Donne's biographer Isaak Walton tells us that if he was in good health, Donne preached at least once a week. William R. Mueller says Donne himself was responsible for the preservation of his sermons, and he chose chiefly his festal sermons to be preserved. This is, of course, quite understandable in light of the peculiar importance given to feast days by Anglicans.

A sermon of particular interest for our study is Donne's inaugural sermon at Saint Dunstan in the West, preached on Trinity Sunday in 1627. His text is Revelation 4:8, "And the foure beasts had each of them sixe wings about him, and they were full of eyes within; and they rest not day and night, saying, holy, holy, holy, Lord God Almighty, which was, and is, and is to come." He begins by putting Trinity Sunday in relation to the major feasts of Christmas, Easter, and Whitsunday and defending its observance in the Church of England (8:34-38). The text, Donne tells us, comes from the lesson appointed by the Church of England for the feast of Trinity. Trinity Sunday is not an ancient feast; the Church, in its wisdom, established in the liturgy a distinct commemoration of the Trinity as a defense against the increase of Arianism. This feast was retained by the Church of England at the time of the Reformation because it seemed wise to continue such a celebration. After all, the Church of England was not in her reformation so concerned to depart from Rome as to come to the truth (8:38).

Donne begins his division of the text by telling us that since the Church has appointed this lesson to be read on Trinity Sunday, we can be sure that the Church understands these words to apply to the Trinity. First, our preacher draws our attention to the four creatures mentioned in the text, the lion, the ox, the eagle, and the man (8:39). Second, he notes what these creatures did, that is, they sang the hymn "Holy, Holy, Holy." Obviously for Donne the placing of the text in the lectionary of the church year is to guide us in the interpretation of the text.

In developing his first point he asks who these four creatures might be. He tells us there is a great variety in interpretation here, but he prefers that of Ambrose, who understands them to be the doctors of the Church. They stand for all the ministers of the gospel. Each minister should have the qualities of a lion, an ox, an eagle, and a man. Since this sermon is Donne's inaugural sermon at Saint Dunstan in the West, he takes this opportunity to speak of the qualities of a true minister. This he does with considerable imagination, showing that a minister must have the courage of a lion in standing against temptation and persecution, the methodical hard work of an ox in plowing the soil by his preaching, the sharp-sightedness of an eagle in discerning the truth in his study of Scripture, and the rationality and gentleness of a man in applying that truth to his congregation (8:41-42). One notices here how concerned Donne is to interpret his text as one of the great preachers of the patristic age had interpreted it. He is aware that for this text the Fathers offered many different approaches. He has chosen and developed just one possible interpretation, but the fact that he has patristic precedent for the line he follows is important to him.

Over the course of his life Donne had thought deeply over the nature of the ministry, and particularly over the nature of his own calling into it. He obviously sees the ministry as above all the gospel ministry. For Donne, a minister is minister of the Word; the word he habitually uses for his office is not "priest" or even "pastor," but "minister." Donne, as John Chrysostom before him, understood the pastoral office to be performed through teaching and preaching.

Coming to the second part of his sermon, Donne points to the fact that the four beasts, the ministers of the gospel, praise God by their proclamation, that is, by saying, and declaring, publishing, and manifesting, their devotion (8:51). To make his point he presents an appropriate biblical illustration: the story of three young men in the fiery furnace found in the book of Daniel. Even in the fiery furnace they praised God. The point he wants to make is that while they exemplified the ministry of preaching by praising God in the fiery furnace, the hymn they sang is a summons to all creatures to praise God. Here we have a perfect example of a poetic use of a biblical example. So much more is evoked by the image than is in fact said. The voice of the preacher is a voice out of the fiery furnace. It is a witness which comes out of tribulation. The sermon he preaches is a hymn of praise. Preaching is doxological. The word of the preacher is an invitation to the whole house of Israel to praise God, but the invitation to join in this praise through preaching is far broader than that; it is extended to all peoples, to all creatures, animate and inanimate, to fire and rain, to moon and sun. It never occurred to Donne to think of true preaching as the expression of the individual creativity of the minister. It is the ministry of the whole Church, for the whole Church envelops the preaching with her hymns of praise, that so clothed it might be presented in its true form. It begins with the ministry of the four Evangelists, then comes the ministry of the ministers of the gospel, and finally the whole Church praises God in the song "Holy, Holy, Holy." When this happens, the full trinitarian faith is confessed. Donne speaks of the doctrine of the Trinity at length and concludes the sermon with a powerful appeal to stand fast in that profession.

Let us look at another festal sermon, one he preached for Whitsunday in 1629. Donne chose as his text Genesis 1:2, "And the Spirit of God was moving over the face of the waters." The sermon begins with a magnificent piece of prose poetry based on the Gospel of the day, John 14:15-31, which speaks of the Holy Spirit as the Comforter.

> The Church of God celebrates this day the third Person of the Holy, Blessed, and Glorious Trinity, The Holy Ghost. The Holy Ghost is the God, the Spirit of Comfort; A Comforter; not one amoungst others, but the Comforter; not the principall, but the intire, the onely Comforter; and more than all that, the Comfort it selfe. That is an attribute of the Holy Ghost, Comfort; And then the office of the Holy Ghost is to gather, to establish, to illumine, to govern that Church which the Son of God, from whom together with the Father the Holy Ghost proceeds, hath purchesed with his blood. So that as the Holy Ghost is the Comforter, so is this Comfort exhibited by him to us, and exercised by him upon us, in this especially, that he has gathered us, established us, illumined us, and does govern us, as members of that body, of which Christ Jesus is the Head; that he hath brought us, and bred us, and fed us with the means of salvation, in his application of the merits of Christ to our souls, in the Ordinances of the Church. (9:92)

One can well imagine how a great orator would deliver these words: slowly, deliberately, stressing that marvelous word "Comforter" and using it to accentuate the rhythm of his prose. These carefully worked out cadences are designed to inscribe in the minds of his hearers this great teaching of Jesus that his Spirit is their comfort. The whole point of the sermon is that the Christian, set adrift on uncertain seas of tribulation, the water of the great deep, the primeval sea of creation, is comforted by the presence of God's Spirit.

The sea was a very real experience for Donne, who, as a young man, had spent time at sea with the earl of Essex and Sir Walter Raleigh in their expedition to Cádiz and then to the Azores. The sea is an image which constantly returns to our preacher, and as this sermon unfolds we will notice how significantly he uses it.

Donne proposes to develop his text in two parts. First he will speak of the literal meaning of the text as found in the beginning of the book of Genesis. He asks what the Holy Spirit did in the first creation. Then he will develop the spiritual meaning, what the Holy Spirit does in the second creation, the new creation. Donne tells us that his sermon treats the meaning of the text first for the macrocosm and then for the microcosm. This is a typical bit of baroque oratory, providing an image for the division of the text. This technique has the advantage of pictorializing the division of the text, so that his sermon outline becomes more than an abstract analysis.

Aware, as Donne was, how much speculation preachers have spun around the opening lines of the creation story, he begins his exposition of the literal sense of his text by speaking of Augustine's concern not to pry into the hidden things of God which might be found in the words of Moses. Donne, as Augustine, wishes Moses had said more, but he didn't, and so he must be content to understand what Moses did say. Yet the words can be taken in many senses which can equally be true. Augustine gives four elements which must belong to a true interpretation: it must glorify God, it must be true to the articles of faith, it must promote devotion, and it must further the peace and unity of the Church. Donne is apparently not willing to claim that the senses of Scripture are infinite, that anything goes in interpreting it. On the other hand, he does want to allow at least for a multiplicity of senses. Donne is aware, as were the Continental Reformers of the sixteenth century, that to multiply the senses of Scripture too much is to dissipate the authority of Scripture, but that, on the other hand, even the literal sense must allow for the metaphors and other rhetorical forms already in Scripture. Donne is concerned, even in seeking out the literal meaning of the text, not to be hindered from going along with the historic Christian understanding of the text. The Jews and even some Christians have insisted that the text does not speak of the Holy Spirit moving upon the face of the waters, but rather of wind blowing over the water (9:96). As Donne sees it, this is an unnecessarily literalistic interpretation of the text. He defends the idea that it is the Holy Spirit who is mentioned in the text with several passages of Scripture such as Psalm 104:30 and Job 26:13, which make it clear that the spirit of creation is God's Spirit (9:98). A number of

Church Fathers such as Basil, Augustine, and Jerome have understood the text this way as well.[9]

Donne now takes up the action of the Holy Spirit. The Holy Spirit moved upon the face of the waters. The Hebrew word signifies both motion and rest. Saint Jerome expresses the idea by saying the Holy Spirit brooded over the waters. Not only does God create by his Spirit, but he remains with his creation by his Spirit. Providence is a work of the Spirit, too (9:98-99). Having made his exegetical point, our preacher sums it all up with his image of the sea: "The waters enwrapped all the whole substance, the whole matter, of which all things were to be created, all was surrounded with the waters, all was embowelled, and enwombed by the waters; And so the holy Ghost moving, and resting upon the face of the waters, moved and rested, did his office upon the whole Mass of the world, and so produced all that was produced" (9:99). One notices the gentle alliteration, the preponderance of deep vowels, and the series of verbs, "enwrapped," "embowelled," and "enwombed." The very sound of the preacher's words evoke the mystery of creation.

Next our preacher turns to the spiritual sense of the text (9:100). Literally it speaks of how the Holy Spirit brought life to the creation. Spiritually it speaks of the new life in the Christian Church and how the Holy Spirit moves upon the waters for our regeneration. When it comes to the spiritual sense of this text, Donne does not have the parallel texts of Scripture on which to base his meaning as he did for the literal sense. He launches out on his interpretation with the Church Fathers as his compass. The Holy Spirit first moves on the water of baptism, then the water of sin, then the water of tribulation, and finally the waters of death. From an artistic point of view this is the most ingenious part of the sermon, as Donne explores the various spiritual meanings which water can have for the Christian. To understand an analogy between the waters of baptism and the waters of creation is a very old idea. With a clever play on words he tells us, "The water of Baptisme, is the water that runs through all the Fathers. All the Fathers that had occasion to dive, or dip in these waters . . . make these first waters, in the Creation, the figure of baptisme" (9:104). He presents ideas from Tertullian, Jerome, John of Damascus, Basil, and Augustine. The Spirit broods on the waters of baptism. These

9. Donne does not mention the fact, but Calvin and Luther also understood the text to speak of the Holy Spirit. Luther and Calvin, on the other hand, find texts such as Pss. 104:30 and 33:6 sufficient to establish the Christian understanding.

waters become thereby the womb of the Church, the mother of Christians. But the Scriptures also use water as a figure of sin. The Whore of Babylon sits upon many waters and hatches a brood of venomous creatures. Water can be the means of our destruction! Let us praise God that the Holy Spirit has moved upon these waters and has delivered us from sin (9:106). Scripture also presents water as a figure of tribulation, as we find in Isaiah 43:2, "When you pass through the waters I will be with you; and through the rivers, they will not overwhelm you." When God's Spirit moves upon the waters of tribulation, they can be a means of our salvation (9:107). The same is true of death. Water is also a figure of death, but when God's Spirit moves upon these waters there is resurrection (9:108).

As a poet, Donne understands the power of metaphor. In this sermon he takes a powerful biblical metaphor, the creative, providential, and redemptive moving of the Spirit upon the waters, and shows how it is developed through the whole of Scripture. The power the metaphor has is to suggest to our minds infinitely more than it says. It invites us to draw from our own experience the appropriate meaning and to bring to our own experience the most significant application. The metaphor engages us in the interpretation of Scripture. Jesus himself understood this, as we see so clearly in his parables. The Scriptures are a treasure-house of metaphor, and whenever a preacher presents these metaphors vividly to his congregation to meditate on and apply their meaning to their own experience, he has been a faithful minister of the Word.

B. Prebend Sermons

The greatest of Donne's sermons were preached on great occasions. He was indeed a master of the festal sermon. Each of these is a separate and self-contained statement. Like his sonnets, each sermon stands on its own. Just as Donne produced no great epic poem, so he has left us very little in the way of sermon cycles; he was not a master of the big canvas. He left us no cycle of festal sermons, nor do we have series on a single book of the Bible or on the articles of faith. The best we have is two short series on the Psalms. One of these, eight sermons on Psalm 32, one of the penitential psalms, was perhaps preached during Lent, but the sermons are not dated. The other is a series of five sermons on five psalms he was required to say each day as prebendary of Saint Paul's Cathedral, namely,

Psalms 62, 63, 64, 65, and 66.[10] As Donne explains it, the thirty canons of the cathedral prayed the whole 150 psalms each day, each canon being responsible for saying five of them that were allotted to him. While the five psalms themselves have no literary unity, the very fact that Donne had prayed them every day over a period of years had made them points on which his thoughts had crystallized. According to Janel Mueller, the series gives us a balanced picture of Donne's preaching. It shows us the whole sweep of his thought. It is particularly interesting for our study because it often touches on the subject of worship and the relation of preaching to worship.

The first sermon begins with several remarks on the dignity of the book of Psalms. He quotes Saint Basil as saying that if all other books of Scripture should perish, there remains in the Psalms enough spiritual nourishment to fully supply the Church (p. 72). No book of the Old Testament speaks more fully of Christ. Jesus himself had a special love for the Psalms, as did many of the Church Fathers. Donne tells us of Athanasius's introduction to the praying of the Psalms, in which he says Psalm 62 is a good prayer for standing fast in the face of tribulation and temptation. It is in that sense, then, that Donne intends to interpret the psalm. The psalm tells us that in times of trouble we must put our hope in God.

The text Donne chooses from this psalm is the ninth verse: "Surely men of low degree are vanity, and men of high degree are a lie; To bee laid in the balance, they are altogether lighter then vanity." Dividing up the text, Donne tells us that first he wants to speak of the manner in which it is said and then the matter about which it speaks. The vanity of man is not spoken of absolutely but comparatively (p. 75). The text does not say that man can be of no help to man, but that God's help outweighs man's help. The verse immediately preceding our text tells us, "Trust in God at all times, for hee is a refuge for us." It is not that man is of no value, but that, put in the balance with God's help, man's help is outweighed. Throughout the whole sermon, although in most subtle ways, this figure of the balance, weighing out things in the scales, considering this on one side and that on the other, recurs again and again.

When seen in the context of the age of the baroque, Donne appears as a baroque Christian humanist, not a Renaissance Christian humanist.

---

10. For the text of these sermons, see John Donne, *Donne's Prebend Sermons,* ed. Janel M. Mueller (Cambridge: Harvard University Press, 1971). Page references in the text are to this work.

During the Renaissance one would never have tried so hard to reconcile oneself to medieval Scholasticism. Donne had lost the exegetical vision of the Renaissance Christian humanists which sought to free the text from the accretions of Scholasticism. It was that exegetical vision which shaped Protestantism. Yet Donne's Christian humanism is thoroughly Protestant. In this sermon he addresses himself to Christian anthropology. He takes his text as an occasion to develop his thought on the dignity of man, an important theme for the Christian humanist. One has to admit that the text does not particularly invite such a development; in fact, the theme of the sermon is more an objection to the text than an exposition of it. When the text tells us that man, be he rich or be he poor, is vanity, we are not to lose all hope in man but rather to put that hope in the right thing. When man becomes an instrument of God, man can be trusted. When we trust in godly men, we are in reality trusting in God. Donne proceeds to lay the ground for his baroque Christian humanism. To be sure, he finds a basis for the dignity of man in the doctrine of creation as well as in the doctrine of the incarnation. These were the ideas on which older forms of Christian humanism were built. But what is of special interest here is that Donne finds a basis for believing in the value of man in the doctrine of redemption. This is where one would expect a Protestant to construct his doctrine of the dignity of man. "When man was at his worst, he was at a high price; man being fallen, yet then, in that under-value, he cost God his own and onely Son" (p. 76). God's redemptive love for man is also a basis for finding dignity in man. God has called man to serve him, and with the gifts of his Spirit God has anointed man to a holy priesthood. God has called some men to be priests and some to be princes. As Donne sees it, God has communicated his power to every sanctified man (p. 77). The dignity of man is to be found in both his justification and his sanctification. The Protestant doctrine of vocation also suggests a basis for a doctrine of human dignity. In all our vocations we are necessary and useful to each other as merchant, artisan, soldier, or physician. Here we have a clear statement of a Protestant humanism which finds human dignity in God's redemptive love for man and the vocation of every man to serve God in ministering to the needs of others, "that all that man needs might be communicated to man by man" (p. 79).

Now Donne proceeds to the matter of the text. He puts in balance wealth and poverty. It can be debated whether men of high degree or low are worse, whether prosperity or adversity occasions most sins (p. 82). What is interesting here is that one finds not a trace of the sort of medieval piety which embraced Dame Poverty. At considerable length Donne enumerates the spiritual dangers of poverty just as he does the spiritual dangers of wealth. He even points out the dangers of mediocrity. The point of the text, he concludes, is that man's help, at its best or at its worst, when weighed in the balance with God's help, is as nothing. In times of trouble it is God who is our refuge. To conclude the sermon Donne meditates on the titles of God which are used in this psalm. God is our refuge, our defense, our glory, and our salvation.

The second prebend sermon, preached on Donne's return to London after the devastating plague of 1625, is on the text "Because thou hast been my helpe, therefore in the shadow of thy wings will I rejoyce" (Ps. 63:7). He begins by speaking of the psalm title, which he, as Saint Jerome before him, considers the key to the interpretation of the whole psalm. The title tells us that this was a prayer uttered by David while he endured the afflictions of the wilderness. During his affliction he remembered how in times past God had been his help. Remembering God's help sustains him in the present by giving him confidence in the future. This is, to be sure, a profound principle of Christian worship. It is in remembering God's help in the past that we invoke his help for the future, and throughout the sermon Donne reiterates this principle in a variety of ways. The schema for the sermon, then, will be one of past, present, and future. Here again we find one of Donne's figures for the division of the text, much like we found in his sermon for Pentecost, where he gave the figure of macrocosm and microcosm to his schema for developing the text. In the first prebend sermon the obvious figure used for the division was the balance suggested by the text, but in this sermon he proposes the schema of past, present, and future (p. 92). It is as Scripture elsewhere puts it: "Jesus Christ is the same yesterday and today and for ever" (Heb. 13:8 RSV).

Donne begins with a consideration of the afflictions of the present. David's affliction in the wilderness was one of banishment. There were temporal afflictions in his exile, but also the spiritual affliction of being banished from the sanctuary. Affliction is a universal and inevitable part of human experience. We could not bear it except that God balances it with the eternal weight of glory (II Cor. 4:17). What a blessed metaphor the Holy Ghost put in the mouth of the apostle Paul (p. 93)! We could not bear our afflictions if it were not for that exceeding and eternal weight of glory. Donne evokes the weight of affliction with a series of afflictions mentioned in Scripture. There was the weight of the plagues which grew heavy on the land of Egypt. Job's sufferings were a heavy burden to him.

There were the fetters and chains that bore down the captives taken off to Babylon, and the heat and burden of day of the laborers in the harvest. How many suffer under affliction, "fall under some one stone, some grinding stone, some millstone, some one insupportable crosse that ruins them? . . . And how many children, and servants, and wives suffer under the anger, the morosity, and peevishness, and jealousie of foolish Masters, and Parents, and Husbands, though they must not say so? David and Solomon have cried out, That all this world is vanity, and levity; And (God knows) all is waight, and burden, and heavinesse, and oppression; And if there were not a waight of future glory to counterpoyse it, we should all sink into nothing" (p. 94). The sound of Donne's words evokes the weight of affliction. This is baroque oratory at its best! Here again we hear the poet in the pulpit. But he uses another poetic device here: he brings the image of the balance once more into play. We notice, then, a series of interlocking images which binds the series of sermons together.

Our preacher now addresses himself to the second part of his sermon, a consideration of God's help in the past, "Because thou hast been my helpe" (p. 100). Again he enunciates the principle that a consideration of God's ways in the past helps us to see God's plans for the future. Here Donne takes off against the Puritans and their extemporary forms of worship. For Donne the time-tested forms of the Catholic Church have far greater promise (p. 101). The ways God has gone in the past are the ways he will go in the future.

In the third part of the sermon, Donne begins to develop the image of wings found in his text, "In the shadow of thy wings will I rejoyce" (p. 105). Donne goes through an inspiring list of scriptural metaphors for God's power, and then comes to this metaphor of God's wings, which emphasizes the refreshing aspect of God's power. It is under the shadow of God's wings that we rejoice. He goes through a number of biblical allusions to wings to make his point: the classic passage where God tells Moses how he brought Israel out of Egypt on eagles' wings (Exod. 19:4), the wings above the mercy seat in the Tabernacle (Exod. 25:20), and the words of Jesus as he wept over Jerusalem, "'How often would I have gathered your children together as a hen gathers her brood under her wings'" (Matt. 23:37 RSV).

Donne's beautiful elaboration of this biblical image of rejoicing under the shadow of God's wings inspires him to mount up even higher in his praise of God's faithfulness. The shadow of the wings is but a relief from the afflictions of this life, but the text speaks of rejoicing, and for the

350

Christian there is far more to rejoice about than the refreshment God gives us in the midst of our afflictions. Donne gives us a figure for the relation of present joys to future joys. It is as with a map of the world (p. 109). It is pictured as two hemispheres. The Eastern Hemisphere is the world we all know, and those who sail about it find a measure of joy. Recently, Donne tells us, we have begun to discover the Western Hemisphere, and there is a far greater wealth to be discovered. So the Christian, who has known some joy in this life, will with the resurrection sail into a new world of far greater joy. Donne goes over some of the great Gospel promises of eternal joy and then issues a peroration on the joy of heaven. The joy we begin in this life is the beginning of an eternal joy.

> This joy shall not be put out in death, and a new joy kindled in me in Heaven; But as my soule, as soone as it is out of my body, is in Heaven, and does not stay for the possession of Heaven, nor for the fruition of the sight of God, till it be ascended through ayre, and fire, and Moone, and Sun, and Planets, and Firmament, to that place which we conceive to be Heaven, but without the thousandth part of a minutes stop, as soone as it issues, is a glorious light, which is Heaven, (for all the way to Heaven is Heaven; And as those Angels, which came from Heaven hither, bring Heaven with them, and are in Heaven here, So that soule that goes to Heaven, meets Heaven here; and as those Angels doe not devest Heaven by comming, so these soules invest heaven, in their going.) As my soule shall not goe towards Heaven, but goe by Heaven to Heaven, to the Heaven of Heavens, So the true joy of a good soule in this world is the very joy of Heaven. (pp. 110-11)

For the third of the prebend sermons Donne takes a text from Psalm 64. This is a psalm of lamentation which complains of the persecution of the godly by the wicked. It ends with the assurance, "Let all the upright in heart glory!" (v. 10). Donne chooses this last verse as his text, from which he develops a sermon which extols the glory of the godly life. He begins by taking up the metaphor with which he closed the previous sermon. Just as there are two hemispheres of joy, so there are two hemispheres of glory. The godly life has its glory in this life, but it is only the beginning of a far greater glory to be discovered in the world to come (pp. 113ff.).

Donne first speaks of "the upright in heart." He wants to make it clear that the upright are rewarded with glory, and they are rewarded on the basis of their being upright. They are not rewarded on the basis of God's eternal decree, but on the basis of their actions. Donne denies that this is Pelagianism (pp. 116-17). To say that God created some men for damnation would imply that he created man after the image of the devil. Moses tells us that God created heaven first and tells of no hell made at creation. At this point Donne takes off on the doctrine of purgatory (p. 118). God was loath and late in making places of torment. Forgetting the psalm before him, he goes so far as to say that God is loath to speak of judgments. The whole book of Psalms, he tells us, is filled with words of blessing. Again and again we hear the word "blessed," and never do we hear the word "woe" (p. 119).

As Donne sees it, man is by both nature and grace to be upright, to look upward toward heaven and to contemplate God. Man is not to bend downward, to lick the dust as the serpent. Donne castigates the ascetic approach to life as religious melancholy, whether it be in its Catholic form or its Puritan form. This kind of religious rigorism is "a Diversion, a Deviation, a Deflection, a Defection from this rectitude, this uprightness" (p. 120). How powerfully this alliteration accentuates our preacher's rejection of gloomy-minded religion!

In order to distance himself from seventeenth-century Calvinism on one hand and Catholic asceticism on the other, Donne proposes a doctrine of rewards to the upright in heart. It is not a doctrine of rewards to the perfect, but to those who from the heart are as upright as is humanly possible. "He that comes as neere to uprightnesse, as infirmities admit, is an upright man" (p. 121). God is not rigorous in his demand for doctrinal orthodoxy or harsh in the penance he requires. All he asks is a humble and repentant spirit. God is all-merciful, just as he is all-powerful and all-knowing (p. 124). One hardly needs to comment that Donne has not only distanced himself from seventeenth-century Calvinism, but from Calvin himself, and Luther as well. Here at least he sounds more like Gabriel Biel than any of the Reformers.

The sermon moves to its second concern, the glory of the upright. Various English translations are discussed. The oldest English translation, based on Saint Jerome, reads, "All men of up right heart shall be praised." This is the proper sense of the Hebrew, our preacher tells us. The text speaks not of a praise they shall give to God, but of a praise they shall receive for having served God. It is not that they shall praise God in having done so, but that godly men shall praise them for having done so (p. 124). Donne dwells at some length on the value of praising upright men. He quotes Aristotle to the effect that to praise good men is to encourage them (p. 125). He quotes Proverbs 22:1, "A good name is to be chosen rather than great riches" (RSV). Then he adds appropriate quotations from Bernard, Jerome, and Augustine. Surely our text also includes the praising of ourselves. It is appropriate that the upright have the comfort of a good conscience. It is concerning such things that the apostle Paul speaks when he tells us that if there be anything that is true, honest, just, pure, and lovely, if there be anything virtuous or worthy of praise, we are to think on these things (Phil. 4:8) (p. 128).

The praise of good men is not limited to this life. Donne points to the fact that the Hebrew verb is in the future tense. Once again he recalls his figure of the two hemispheres. Indeed we experience some praise in this life, but there is far greater praise to be experienced in the life to come (p. 130). With this Donne begins his conclusion. He tells of how the Church militant will commend us to the Church triumphant with this praise, this recommendation: he had lived in the obedience of the Church of God, he died in the faith of the Son of God, and he departed himself in the company and conduct of the Spirit of God. All these things that I have done for God's glory shall follow me, Donne says. Donne's baroque eloquence mounts as he rejoices in the service of God which he has been able to perform in this life. This will be his praise to heaven, his recommendation thither. Then the angels who rejoiced at his conversion shall praise his perseverance in the profession of faith and admit him to a part in their hymns, and hosannas, and hallelujahs (p. 131). Donne's words glow with the assurance of salvation as he expresses his confidence that at last he will hear that ultimate praise of the Savior: well done, thou good and faithful servant.

The next sermon in the series is an admonition to approach the worship of God with reverential awe. It takes as its text Psalm 65:5 (RSV):

> By dread deeds thou dost answer us with deliverance,
>   O God of our salvation,
> who art the hope of all the ends of the earth,
>   and of the farthest seas.

Appropriate to the theme of the sermon, Donne begins with a series of surprising statements designed to evoke amazement. Here, too, we see his baroque eloquence. The baroque age loved the startling, the dramatic, the *trompe l'oeil.* "God makes nothing out of nothing now. God eased himselfe of that incomprehensible worke, and ended it on the Sab-

353

bath. But God makes things of little still; and in that kinde hee works most upon the Sabbath; when by the foolishness of preaching hee infatuates the wisdome of the world, and by the word in the mouth of the weake man, he enfeebles the power of sinne and Satan in the world . . ." (p. 134). By these paradoxical thoughts one is engaged; by their smooth alliteration and assonance one slips into the spell of the sermon. He has more surprising things to say about preaching. "And this work of his, to make much of little, is most properly a miracle. For the Creation, (which was a production of all out of nothing) was not properly a miracle: A miracle is a thing done against nature; when something in the course of nature resists that worke it is a miracle; But in Creation, there was no reluctation, no resistance, no nature, nothing to resist. But to do great works by small means, to bring men to heaven by Preaching in the Church, this is a miracle" (pp. 134-35). Here is a fascinating statement on the nature of preaching, but one wonders how far one should press the obvious rhetoric. He goes on to compare preaching to the miracle of feeding the five thousand with merely five loaves. He hopes that by Christ's blessing, his preaching of these five psalms will be multiplied to the salvation of his congregation.

After this brilliant introduction, he divides up his text. He intends to preach on the knowledge of God's saving works which we have first in nature, then in the law, and finally in the gospel. Again Donne gives his divisions of the text a clever figure. Since the sermon is a miraculous feeding of the multitude, he proposes that his first point is a breakfast, his second a dinner, and his third a supper. For all three meals the text itself serves as a grace (pp. 135-36). He belabors the relation of his three points to his text, but one senses that what interests him in the text is that God's saving ordinances are called terrible, that is, they demand our reverence.

The most interesting part of the sermon for our purposes is his third point, in which he speaks of the gospel ordinances, Word, prayer, and sacraments. Even the Gentiles, Donne tells us, had set prayers. With only the light of nature they knew enough to have a common form of prayer in their temples. Surely we should do the same. If God is to speak to us in the sermon, we must come to prayer beforehand. The prayers prepare us for the sermon. Faith comes through preaching, but the Holy Spirit prepares us to hear by means of the prayers. One should perhaps remark at this point that in the Anglican Church, most sermons followed the order of morning or evening prayer. The sermon was not an integral part of the order but an addition to it. This perhaps explains why Donne has nothing to say about prayers which follow the sermon (pp. 145-47).

At this point our preacher focuses in on the word "terrible." These terrible acts of God in Word, prayer, and sacrament are stupendous, reverent, and mysterious things. We should not therefore make religion too homely, but come to every exercise of religion with reverence, with fear, and with trembling (p. 148). In all religions, even in the pagan religions and in the Jewish religion, priests and rabbis have been mysterious in their teachings. Even Jesus taught in parables (p. 149). He astonished the people with his authority, so that a majesty and reverential fear be maintained for that teaching. The love of God should be seasoned with a fear of God. One should not approach the church service as though it were some form of recreation. One should not be overly familiar or "fellowly" with God, nor overhomely with places of worship or acts of religion (p. 151).

Donne has a few things to say about being reverent toward preaching. He castigates those who take preaching lightly and think it something beneath them. He criticizes those who take great liberty in criticizing preachers and in comparing preacher to preacher. Here Donne makes an interesting distinction. "All the Sermon is not God's word, but all the Sermon is God's Ordinance, and the Text is certainly his word." The dignity of the sermon is far greater than most people realize. There is no salvation but by faith, and there is no faith but by hearing, and there is no hearing but by preaching. It is by preaching that the power of the keys is exercised and the promises of the gospel are proposed. Then, in a magnificent line, Donne tells us that the dignity of preaching swells in every chapter, blows in every verse, and thunders in every line of every book of the Bible (p. 154).

After speaking of the reverence with which we should approach the sacrament of Communion, our preacher turns to the subject of death. This, too, we should approach with awe and fear. Finally he concludes the sermon with a somber admonition to work out our salvation with fear and trembling (p. 158).

The last of the five prebend sermons is devoted to Psalm 66, a psalm of thanksgiving for deliverance from afflictions. Verse 3 is taken as the text:

> Say to God, "How terrible are thy deeds!
> So great is thy power that thy enemies cringe before thee." (RSV)

The sermon opens with an affirmation of the patristic principle that the title of the psalm is the key to its understanding. The fact that Donne was still affirming this principle almost a century after the Reformers had brought biblical Hebrew back into the theological curriculum and had demonstrated the problematical nature of the psalm titles shows that Donne was definitely behind the times in matters of exegesis. Nevertheless, after affirming this principle, he uses the title very conservatively. He understands the title to indicate that the psalm is prophetic of God's raising up his people from the tribulations and afflictions which they endure in this world. This particular text, Donne tells us, speaks of God's saving acts in history, which we can therefore expect to occur in the future. The text has its historical part and its prophetic part.

In opening up the first part, the historical part, Donne calls the attention of his congregation to the fact that it is David, the king of Israel, who calls the people of Israel, and to be sure, all other peoples of the world, to worship God. As king, he institutes those orders which the Church is to observe in the public service of God (p. 165). This is the foundation stone of Anglicanism, that the king has the divine right to order the public worship of the Church, and Donne defends this doctrine with considerable vigor. Not only is it the duty of a Christian king to settle religion in his own land, he is to promote true religion in foreign parts and propagate it to the ends of the earth. David calls even the Gentiles to worship God. The emperor Constantine set a good example for the Christian prince. He supported the Church over the whole of his vast empire and protected the Church by banishing the Arians from his realm (p. 168).

Having made the point that the king is to establish religion, Donne speaks of the function of that religion. It is to celebrate God's works (p. 169). This is done in true prayer and faithful preaching. Here Donne spends some time attacking those who in their prayer and preaching spend too much time meditating on the hidden mysteries and counsels of God. This is a double-edged sword intended to fell the Puritans on the left, with their discussions of infralapsarian and supralapsarian predestination, and Catholic mystics on the right, with their disciplines of contemplative mysticism. Donne would promote a much more utilitarian sort of religion which turns its attention to celebrating the works of God (pp. 171-76).

Once again Donne focuses in on the terribleness of God. Here we see our preacher at his most paradoxical, at his most baroque. We quote at length a passage of great literary beauty.

> When I look upon God, as I am bid to doe in this Text, in those terrible Judgements, which he hath executed upon some men, and see that there is nothing between mee and the same Judgment, (for I have sinned the same sinnes, and God is the same God) I am not able of my selfe to dye that glasse, that spectacle, thorow which I looke upon this God, in what colour I will; whether this glasse shall be black, through my despaire, and so I shall see God in the cloud of my sinnes, or red in the blood of Christ Jesus, and I shall see God in a Bath of the blood of his Sonne, whether I shall see God as a Dove with an Olive branch, (peace to my soule) or as an Eagle, a vulture to prey, and to prey everlastingly upon mee, whether in the deepe floods of Tribulation, spirituall or temporall, I shall see God as an Arke to take mee in, or as a Whale to swallow mee; and if his Whale doe swallow mee, (the Tribulation devour me) whether his purpose bee to restore mee, or to consume me, I, I of my selfe cannot tell. I cannot look upon God, in what line I will, nor take hold of God, by what handle I will; Hee is a terrible God, I take him so; And then I cannot discontinue, I cannot breake off this terriblenesse, and say, Hee hath beene terrible to that man, and there is an end of his terror; it reaches not to me. Why not to me? In me there is no merit, nor shadow of merit; In God there is no change, nor shadow of change. I am the same sinner, he is the same God; still the same desperate sinner, still the same terrible God. (pp. 173-74)

These lines evoke the pictures of the Spanish painter Zurbarán, who loved to paint monks in contemplation. Part of Donne's appeal as a preacher is that he knows the anguish of mortal life. He knows terror. He knows how frightening human frailty can be, and yet he knows that the fear of the Lord is the beginning of wisdom. But Donne's point is that the fear of the Lord does not need to turn to jealousy or suspicion of God. There is all this terribleness; he is a consuming fire to his enemies, but we are not his enemies. God is our God, and God is love (p. 175).

The second part of the sermon is not nearly as thoroughly developed as the first. The second point is the prophetical point that God will bring about the submission of his enemies. This should be a great comfort to us because our enemies are his enemies as well (pp. 177-79). Donne finds in the text, "Thy enemies shall submit themselves to thee," an indication that the submission is not only forced but feigned. For

Donne that is all right as long as they submit. Clearly for Donne the state has the right to insist on religious conformity, even if he paradoxically claims that he is not speaking of public policy (p. 179). The sermon concludes with a justification of the established Church. "So hast thou reason too to call it Peace in the Church, and peace in the State, when Gods enemies, though they be not rooted out, though they be not disposed to a hearty Allegeance, and just Obedience, yet they must be subject, they must submit themselves whether they wil or no, and though they will wish no good, yet they shall be able to doe no harme. For, the Holy Ghost declares this to be an exercise of power, of Gods power, of the greatnesse of Gods power, that his enemies submit themselves, though with a fained obedience" (p. 179).

John Donne's great contribution was to show the value of literary skill in the Christian pulpit. Donne was not the first to demonstrate this. Saints Basil, Gregory of Nyssa, and Gregory of Nazianzus had done much the same thing. (Donne is often compared to John Chrysostom as the greatest of Christian orators. But in actual fact, he is not nearly as comparable to Chrysostom as to Gregory of Nazianzus, and even more to Gregory of Nyssa.) But of those who have preached in the English language, Donne is the supreme example of great rhetoric. He was not a profound theologian nor a great expositor of Scripture, but he understood something very important about biblical preaching: the power of the metaphor. He knew how to clothe his thought with imagery. His mastery of poetry gave him an unparalleled ability to develop the imagery he found in the Bible so that his congregation sensed its full power. Scripture is rich in imagery, and Donne was inspired by this imagery to find in all of life images of the eternal. He developed the biblical imagery, but he also developed his own. As he understood it, the biblical imagery, which comes by revelation, is the key to a natural imagery which the Christian poet finds in all that is about him.

Unlike Calvin, who used his literary ability primarily to understand Scripture, Donne used his to engage the hearts and minds of his hearers. He saw great value in expressing the truths of religion in the cultivated rhythms and cadences of the language. For Calvin it was enough to present the Word of God simply and clearly, for that Word, being the Word of God, had authority. For Donne the preacher needed to court human hearts and affections for the ways of God. The beauty of language was a means of doing this. Baroque art aimed at impressing the viewer. It saw its function as buttressing the truth. Whether Caravaggio or Rubens or

Bernini, the baroque artist aimed at amazing the spectator with the glories of the faith. In this sense Donne's art is thoroughly baroque. Preaching is a miracle which by the blessing of Christ multiplies the bread of God for the salvation of men. Preaching magnifies the Word of God so that the pious are quickened to devotion. If the Puritans reacted against the cultivated oratory of the Anglicans and fashioned their own "plain style," there was far more to their resistance than lack of culture. It was a very different vision of what culture was supposed to be. For Donne grace was not irresistible. It needed to be supported by eloquence. The text of the sermon was the Word of God, and the sermon was the ordinance of God. The faithful needed the miraculous power of preaching to buttress the Scriptures, just as the Church needed the authority of the king to support her and bring her enemies to subjection. Donne's preaching did just that: it presented the Word of God to the faithful with all the enhancements of Christian culture. Given the task he set himself to perform, he accomplished it about as well as any preacher in the English language.

III. Jeremy Taylor (1613-67)

Early in life Jeremy Taylor was recognized as a potential supporter of the Stuart establishment.[11] He was a nimble-witted, attractive, handsome young preacher, and even as a young man, had a facility with words. From a literary point of view he was refined, learned, and ingenious. Quickly he came to the attention of Archbishop Laud, who was looking for just this sort of man to support his vision of a national religion. Taylor's origins were humble. His father was a barber in Cambridge, but that held him back in no way. More important for him was the support of prelates and courtiers who saw to it that he was advanced from one position to another. Laud provided him with a fellowship at Oxford, and then when he was not more than twenty-five, gave him the parish of Uppingham. Five years later Charles I presented him with a parish in Northamptonshire. He was obviously headed for a promising career in the Anglican establishment and was advancing rapidly, when suddenly the establishment fell

11. For biographical information, see "Taylor, Jeremy," in *Encyclopedia Britannica*, 11th ed., 29 vols. (New York: Encyclopedia Britannica, 1910-11), 26:469-71; Henry Trevor Hughes, *The Piety of Jeremy Taylor* (London: Macmillan, 1960); and Charles James Stranks, *Life and Writings of Jeremy Taylor* (London: Published for the Church Historical Society by SPCK, 1952).

from power. Taylor was loyal to his patrons even when they had fallen on hard days. As a royalist, he was imprisoned several times during the Commonwealth, but with the restoration of Charles II and the Anglican establishment, he was made bishop of Down and Connor in Ireland. There he waged war against Catholics on one side and Presbyterians on the other.

As a preacher, Taylor is interesting for several reasons.[12] First we mention his cultivated prose. He did write beautifully; even granting that his art is baroque through and through, one reads it with pleasure. One makes the allowances one has to make in our age for the florid and sometimes pompous taste of the baroque, but when one has gotten beyond that, one finds real art in his work. He is a writer of prose who is recognized for his prose, and in this he is quite different from John Donne, whom we recognize for his poetry. He, as everyone else who went to the English schools of his day, had been thoroughly trained in the classical literary arts. He knew how to write long sermons which were nevertheless fascinating because of their rich vocabulary, their varied syntax, and their copious rhetorical flourishes. Taylor is never at a loss to illustrate a point with an epigram from Juvenal, a phrase from Sophocles, or a maxim from Lucan. While so many of the metaphysical preachers liked to use a Senecan style, Taylor is much more Ciceronian. He loves long, flowing, periodic sentences.

A rather surprising thing about Taylor is that his preaching plan seems to be guided by neither the order of the Anglican calendar nor the Scriptures themselves. His series of fifty-two sermons is intended to be a year's course of sermons, but apparently it touches the traditional calendar only at Advent and Whitsuntide. He obviously likes to preach edifying moral discourses, but he never seems to finish them in a single sermon. He takes two or three sermons to make his point. Supposedly there are fifty-two sermons for the year, but it appears that these are really only twenty-one sermons stretched out over fifty-two weeks.

By far the most interesting thing about these sermons is that they are an example of Arminian preaching as it was patronized by the Stuart establishment. The religion Taylor preached was concerned with making people good. It exhorted Christians to be virtuous, honest, hardworking

12. For Taylor's sermons, see *Works of Jeremy Taylor: With Some Account of His Life, Summary of Each Discourse, Notes, etc.,* ed. T. S. Hughes, 5 vols. (London: A. J. Valpy, 1831). Citations in the text come from these volumes, with volume number preceding page reference.

subjects. A life of wisdom and virtue had its rewards, and God was, to be sure, merciful and generous in dispensing the blessings of life, but the greatest reward of the good life was virtue itself. One notices again and again in Taylor's sermons that the life of virtue as understood by the philosophers of ancient Greece and Rome and the righteousness as taught by the prophets and apostles of Scripture are not too far apart. Classical literature teaches Christian virtue almost as well as Scripture, if we take his quotations and illustrations seriously. Scholastic moral theology is not very far away from Jeremy Taylor. Much of the preaching we find here is a warning against the seven deadly sins of the Schoolmen.

The first three sermons are intended for Advent (1:1-169). In terms of literary form, these three are one complete sermon. The text is taken from II Corinthians 5:10, "For we must all appear before the judgment seat of Christ; that every one may receive the things done in his body, according to that he hath done, whether it be good or bad" (KJV). From this text Taylor develops a long warning to his congregation of the severity of the Last Judgment. All are to stand before the judgment seat of Christ as both their public and secret sins are revealed. The first part of this long, vivid sermon ends with the medieval funeral dirge *Dies irae* (1:24). There is, throughout the entire sermon, no suggestion of vicarious atonement, only the assertion of the righteousness of Christ, who lived a human life without sin and therefore is entitled to be our judge. It is only in works of obedience, repentance, prayer, and almsgiving that we can hope to escape. Conversion is the best preparation for doomsday (1:28). This simple, straightforward preaching of commonsense Arminianism seems theologically naive. There is no attack on the doctrine of justification by faith, nor are any aspersions cast on Calvinism. It is a simple reversion to the Pelagianism of the late Middle Ages. Taylor's message is clear: be good or suffer the consequences.

Taylor's sermon "Of the Spirit of Grace" is of particular interest because it points up another dimension of the popular Arminianism favored by the Anglican establishment (2:141-86). One gets the impression that receiving the Holy Spirit is a matter of entering into a state of Christian perfection. The text is Romans 8:9-10, "But ye are not in the flesh, but in the Spirit, if so be that the Spirit of God dwell in you. Now if any man have not the Spirit of Christ, he is none of his. And if Christ be in you, the body is dead because of sin; but the Spirit is life because of righteousness" (KJV). The sermon has a beautiful passage on being captive to the Spirit and the law of Christ and free from sin, but as it progresses, one more and more gets the impression that the preacher thinks of receiving the Holy Spirit as entering into a state of moral perfection. Again, we have to say, the sermon seems theologically naive, and one is not too sure how Taylor would explain this theologically. One thing is clear: Taylor interprets Paul's complaint about his inability to do what is right, found at the end of Romans 7, as belonging to his pre-Christian experience. The interpretation of this passage is one of the traditional watersheds between Arminians and Calvinists. Calvinists, as Lutherans, see the Christian as both justified and at the same time a sinner, *simul justus et peccator.* This is one of those classic points of interpretation which has again and again led Arminianism to perfectionism.

Further on in the collection we find a group of four sermons which show us again how the popular Anglican Arminianism of the early seventeenth century was preached. Sermons XXXIX and XL have the title "Growth in Grace, with Its Proper Instruments and Signs" (2:395-431). The sermon intends to stir up the Christian to grow in grace. To do that he must make religion the business of life. The way is long and hard, but as one advances devotion increases. One must mortify one's passions, and as one does grace grows. In fact, growth in grace consists in the lessening of our passions. One who is grown in grace pursues virtue for its own sake. One dwells on serving God for the joy of delighting God. The cultivation of devotional disciplines is something to which Taylor obviously gives much attention. They are holy delights. We remember that his classic book on the devotional life has the title *The Art of Holy Living.*[13] For Taylor, as for every good Arminian, the secret of being a good Christian is working very hard at it.

There is an interesting correlation between the Arminian approach to the ministry of preaching and the baroque approach to the art of preaching. For the Arminian the preacher's ministry was to persuade, or even more, to stir up the Christian to live a Christian moral life. The preacher's job was to motivate his congregation to live a good moral life. The art of doing this was eloquence. The artist had an important place in baroque society. As we have said before, it was the job of the artist to im-

---

13. Originally published in 1650 under the title *The Rule and Exercise of Holy Living.* A modern edition of this work was published in 1970: Jeremy Taylor, *The Rule and Exercise of Holy Living,* abridged with a preface by Anne Lamb, foreword by Henry Chadwick (New York: Harper & Row, 1970). For a complete edition, see Jeremy Taylor, *The Rule and Exercises of Holy Living* (London: J. M. Dent, 1900).

press the masses with the grandeur of the institutional structure of society, whether that society was political or religious.

IV. Robert South (1634-1716)

Robert South was the very model of the Restoration divine.[14] He was a student in Oxford during the Protectorate of Cromwell, and although he tried to curry the favor of the Puritans by preaching the merits of Calvinism against Socinianism, he never was anything other than a convinced Cavalier, dedicated to both monarchy and episcopacy. In 1658 he sought out a bishop of the Scottish Episcopal Church and had himself ordained. As the Restoration approached, things began to go very well for him. In 1660 he was appointed public orator of the University of Oxford, and the following year chaplain to Lord Clarendon. This brought South into intimate contact with the life of the court. He soon became the favorite preacher of Charles II. South's devastating wit amused the courtiers and entertained His Majesty. Profound he was not. Neither as a moralist nor as a theologian was he ever much more than a proponent of the conventional. He did have wit, and he was able to present his case with a nimble sort of cleverness. Sad to say, sincerity was not exactly in vogue at the court of Charles II. But if South was the most polished sycophant of the Restoration establishment, he was also the most annoying scourge of the Puritans. It was they who were most often the butt of his stunning invective.

From the standpoint of English literature, South has a certain importance. He is a good example of how preaching had become a literary art among the Anglicans.[15] His sermons were carefully written out beforehand and then either memorized or read from the manuscript. After being preached, they were often carefully edited for publication. Evidently many people bought and read sermons during this period. What had happened to prayer had now happened to preaching. South's sermon

14. For biographical information, see "South, Robert," in *Encyclopedia Britannica,* 11th ed., 25:463, and Irène Simon, *Three Restoration Divines, Barrow, South, Tillotson,* 2 vols. (Paris: Société d'Edition "Belles Lettres," 1967).

15. South's sermons were frequently published as separate sermons. An edition of his collected sermons appeared as early as 1692 in six volumes. A second edition appeared in 1715. Other editions have appeared in 1823, 1842, and 1845. The edition on which this study is based is Robert South, *Sermons Preached upon Several Occasions,* 4 vols. (Philadelphia: Sorin and Ball, 1844).

against extemporary prayer certainly fits well into the pattern of worship which had evolved in England since the publishing of *The Book of Common Prayer* in 1549. For the good conforming Anglican, sermons came more and more to be read just as the prayers of the liturgy were read. Liturgy had become literature. It was superb literature, to be sure, but for those who came to church, that is, to the average sort of parish church Sunday by Sunday, it had a way of getting a bit dull. Read sermons, however interesting when read in a book, rarely come off as well when they are preached.

South himself was evidently quite exciting in the pulpit. In fact, it is often said that he was a rather racy preacher. The sermons that have come down to us have been carefully edited, however. He spent his last years, for he lived long past his contemporaries, carefully editing his sermons. The 1715 edition of his sermons was a revised edition of the collection he had published more then twenty years before. These sermons may have been oratory when they were preached, but they were a sort of oratory strongly under the influence of literary concerns and literary intentions. By the time they were revised for final publication, they were far removed from living oratory.

While some Anglicans believed in a broad-based Church of England, South pressed the most exclusive claims of Anglicanism. South was very much the opposite of Archbishop Tillotson, the classic latitudinarian; South was the model High Churchman. His preaching was constantly setting forth the positions of the Anglican establishment. And it was largely topical: he left us no series of sermons on the creed, or even on the catechism,[16] and not even a cycle of sermons on the lectionary. He chose rather to preach on the issues of the day, more likely than not those that had become matters of public controversy. In this way he hoped to recapture the flagging interest of the typical Restoration congregation. Typical of topical preaching, which was to become increasingly popular in the centuries ahead, his sermons had titles, and these titles are a fair index of what he preached:

"The Ways of Wisdom Are Ways of Pleasantness"
"Ecclesiastical Policy the Best Policy"
"The Duties of the Episcopal Function"
"God's Peculiar Regard to Places Set Apart for Divine Worship"

16. I have looked only at the first of four volumes printed in Philadelphia in 1844.

"All Contingencies under the Direction of God's Providence"
"The Wisdom of This World"
"Good Intentions No Excuse for Bad Actions"
"The Practice of Religion Enforced by Reason"
"Of the Superlative Love of Christ to His Disciples"
"Against Long Extemporary Prayers"
"Of the Light within Us"
"Jesus of Nazareth Proved the True and Only Messiah"

South preached much the same sort of conventional morality that we find in the typical Arminian pulpit of the day. In his view, preaching seems to serve the purpose of improving public morals. He evidently felt this would bring salvation to the kingdom of England.

V. John Tillotson (1630-94)

Our study of the Anglican approach to the ministry of the Word logically ends with John Tillotson.[17] He died as archbishop of Canterbury in 1694 and provides a sort of symmetrical finish to the struggles which had so engrossed the Church of England during the whole of the seventeenth century. Although Robert South survived Tillotson for more than twenty years, he expressed the spirit of the Restoration, an earlier and different age from that of Tillotson.

Tillotson might best be described as a man who caught the spirit of the new age. He was among those Puritans who were disappointed with Cromwell's commonwealth. There were plenty of Puritans like him. What Cromwell provided was not at all what most Puritans had in mind. With the restoration of the monarchy, Tillotson was willing to conform to the establishment. Figuring that the Puritan cause was lost, he was willing to move on to other things. In time he became an apostle of moderation in a day when many people had tired of the religious intensity of the older generation. He preached a reasonable religion and a practical, virtuous life. He was the apostle of civil religion. For him the Anglican tradition of the *via media* meant moderation in all things. As he saw it, the Church of England should be as broad as possible, allowing all shades of

17. For studies of Tillotson, see Simon, *Three Restoration Divines, Barrow, South, Tillotson;* and "Tillotson, John," in *Encyclopedia Britannica,* 11th ed., 26:976.

Protestant opinion. He would exclude only Roman Catholics and Unitarians. He had strong personal friendships with people of diverse religious inclinations. A man of calm reasonableness, he never succumbed to the bitter polemics of High Church Anglicanism. The nonconformity of many of the heirs of the Puritan tradition did not unduly offend him.

During the last two decades of the seventeenth century, the heirs of Puritanism were recovering. Nonconformity was showing a surprising vitality, and Anglicanism was finally embarrassed by the deathbed conversion of Charles II to Catholicism. It was becoming clearer and clearer that he had been a Catholic all along. On the other hand, with the events of 1688 it was equally clear that England was staunchly Protestant, and that no longer could a Catholic monarch expect the people to submit to an undoing of the Reformation. It was not at all surprising that a man of such broad sympathies as Tillotson's was chosen by William and Mary to be archbishop of Canterbury.

There is no doubt that Tillotson was the most popular Anglican preacher at the end of the seventeenth century. He was widely read, and well into the eighteenth century was considered the model of literate preaching. Numerous volumes of his sermons were published at the end of the seventeenth century and throughout the eighteenth century.[18] Numerous other editions were printed and reprinted for several generations. Alas, Tillotson was the most conspicuous example of what the Evangelical revival reacted against in the middle of the eighteenth century. He is one more example of the dictum that he who marries the spirit of one age finds himself a widower in the age that follows. John Wesley about summed it up when he edited a volume of Tillotson for his Christian Classics. He did so, Wesley tells us, in order that one might see the limits of Tillotson's appeal on one hand, and on the other to show that he did have some value.

There is no doubt about it: Tillotson wrote in a very fine English

---

18. Some representative editions of his works include John Tillotson, *Sermons,* 14 vols. (London: Printed for R. Chiswell, 1700); *The Works of the Most Reverend Dr. John Tillotson* (London: Printed for T. Goodwin, 1714); *The Works of the Most Reverend Dr. John Tillotson,* 2 vols. (London: Printed for Timothy Goodwin, 1717); *The Works of the Most Reverend Dr. John Tillotson* (London: Printed for T. Goodwin, 1720); *The Works of the Most Reverend Dr. John Tillotson,* 3 vols. (London: Printed for J. and R. Tonson, 1752); *The Works of the Most Reverend Dr. John Tillotson,* 10 vols. (Edinburgh: Printed by Wal. Ruddiman & Co., 1772); and *The Works of Dr. John Tillotson, late Archbishop of Canterbury,* 10 vols. (London: Printed by J. F. Dove for Richard Priestley, 1820).

style. He is often regarded as having led an important reform of the literary quality of English preaching. His pulpit idiom was sober and reasoned. From the standpoint of style, he was the antithesis of the baroque prose of the Anglican preachers who preceded him. His preaching had neither the flashes of transcendence found in Donne nor the glow of devotion found in Andrewes or Taylor. Those who study him for his contribution to English style, such as Irène Simon, tell us that he was a master of English prose. His prose, nevertheless, tended to the prosaic. It had little to fire the imagination or warm the heart. The conscious attempt at wit is completely absent, and yet one often finds the claim to erudition, the quotation of classical poets in Latin, or the appeal to philosophers. This was not necessarily out of place when one considers that much of his preaching was at Lincoln's Inn, the chapel of the law school in London. His appeal, quite in the spirit of the Enlightenment, was to reason and reasonableness, to fairness and justice.

Tillotson has often been regarded as one of the harbingers of Deism, but he resolutely defended trinitarian orthodoxy and published a series of sermons to make that clear. All things considered, however, he must be regarded as a preacher who pointed the way to an enlightened, common-sense sort of religion, strong on conventional morality but showing little interest in the things of eternity or the matters of the heart. It is little wonder that after half a century of his influence, Wesley and Whitefield would be a welcome relief.

In looking over the whole mass of Tillotson's sermons, one is impressed by the strong moralistic flavor of his preaching.[19] To be a Christian was to live a good moral life. Tillotson was a pragmatic sort of Arminian. He believed in grace, to be sure, but the important thing was whether the Christian lived a good life. This would certainly seem to be the point of a series of sermons he preached on the subject "Of the Nature of Regeneration, and Its Necessity, in Order to Justification and Salvation." The position he clearly holds is that while God is merciful and forgives our sins, he does expect us to have some sort of success in living the Christian life in order to achieve salvation. In another one of his most popular sermons, "The Wisdom of Being Religious," he tells us that reason makes it clear that the best life is the religious life.

Tillotson cannot be called a biblical preacher. Although he consci-

---

19. Among the numerous editions of Tillotson's sermons, the edition on which this study has been based is Tillotson, *Sermons*.

entiously begins his sermons with an explication of his text, and although his interpretations are often thoughtful, one never senses a profound grasp of Scripture. There are no sustained interpretations of major passages of Scripture, nor are there cycles of sermons based on the Anglican lectionary. His sermons tend to be isolated essays on religious subjects. Emblematic of this is that they have titles. Something in one of the lectionary selections may suggest the topic of the sermon, but the intellectual authority does not appear to be the biblical text so much as the reasons which support what he finds in the text.

One has to admit that his preaching has had a long and continuing influence on the pulpits of the English-speaking world. Tillotson made a virtue of necessity. He realized he was preaching to people who were not passionately concerned with the Word of God. The English Civil War and the Restoration which followed it had exhausted the passion for the Word of God. There were still those who were passionately Christian, some Protestant and some Catholic, but the majority wanted something less intense. They wanted to get on with other things. Tillotson understood this and provided for them a civil sort of Christian faith. He became for his age the paragon of polite preaching.

CHAPTER V

The Flowering of Protestant Orthodoxy in Germany

The age of Protestant orthodoxy was a great age, a far greater age than her children have realized.[1] It was from the preaching of Protestant orthodoxy that the Psalm settings of Heinrich Schütz grew. It was from the very orthodox grammatical-historical expositions of the Dutch Calvinists that Rembrandt's biblical illustrations developed. Without the passion sermons of Heinrich Müller, it is hard to imagine the *Saint Matthew Passion* of Johann Sebastian Bach. Johann Gerhard, the most Lutheran of Lutherans, could write the most orthodox theology and still produce popular devotional writings. Paul Gerhardt, the greatest hymn writer of all, was meticulously orthodox in his theology. As Hans Ruckert used to point out, Protestant orthodoxy, in the age of its flowering, was anything but dry, anything but dead, anything but boring. German Protestants took a delight in theological speculation which overflowed into a profound devotional intensity. In turn, this profound theological reflection produced the doxological classics of Protestant hymnody and liturgical music. When one looks at the Huguenot preachers of France, one finds a marvel-

---

1. For works on German orthodoxy, see Alfred Niebergall, "Die Predigt in der Zeit der Orthodoxie," in *Leiturgia, Handbuch des evangelischen Gottesdienstes,* ed. Karl Ferdinand Müller and Walter Blankenburg, 5 vols. (Kassel: Johannes Stauda Verlag, 1955), 2:288-93; Martin Schian, *Orthodoxie und Pietismus im Kampf um die Predigt* (Giessen: Töpelmann, 1912); Werner Welzig, *Predigten der Barockzeit, Texte und Kommentar* (Vienna: Österreichischen Akademie der Wissenschaften, 1995).

ous vitality, an intelligent classical simplicity in noble contrast to the baroque power of Louis XIV.

Historians of our day have had little appreciation for the age of Protestant orthodoxy. The attempt of Johann Gerhard to develop a Protestant scholasticism, as brilliant as it was, has hardly been regarded with any excitement by theologians of the twentieth and twenty-first centuries. The Synod of Dort's definition of Calvinism, to the point of insisting on limited atonement and reprobation, is regarded with embarrassment by the up-to-date theologian of today, and the squabbles between Lutheran and Reformed over the Lord's Supper are regretted by ecumenically minded churchmen. It has been easy to dismiss the age of Protestant orthodoxy as a period of mannerism and to imagine that Gerhard betrayed Luther and that the Synod of Dort embalmed Calvin. One can hardly deny that the century and a half or more which followed the Reformers sometimes lost sight of their brilliant insights, but the age had its own insights, its own needs, and its own brilliance. The age of Protestant orthodoxy was an age of deepening. From the classical objectivity of Luther and Calvin, Protestantism moved to a far greater subjectivity. It developed its own religious interiority. Continental Protestantism became just as Puritan as Anglo-Saxon Protestantism did. It began to put the emphasis on the inward transformation of life which must follow the initial hearing and believing. Having been completely convinced that Luther was right about justification by faith, the Protestants of the Continent began to feel the need to emphasize sanctification. In the covenant theology of Johannes Cocceius (1603-69), four steps to salvation were elaborated: election, justification, sanctification, and glorification. The new emphasis on sanctification was hardly a compromise of the doctrine of justification by faith, because sanctification was by faith, just as justification was. This new concern for holiness was supported by an equally great interest in glorification. The hope of heaven became more and more acute for Protestants. Philipp Nicolai's *Freudenspiegel* was only one of a whole series of meditations on the Christian hope of the life to come. This, too, was part of the deepening, part of the growing interiority of Protestantism.

The century and a half which followed the Reformation was a period of tribulation for the Protestants of Europe. The Huguenots of France had the Wars of Religion and then the long struggle to maintain their identity against the absolutism of Louis XIV. In the Netherlands there was the struggle to gain independence from Spain. In Germany there were the constant outbreaks of plague and the deprivations of the

Thirty Years' War. All this brought Protestants to a greater inwardness in their religious life. The inwardness of this orthodoxy has yet to be fully appreciated, even though the outward evidences of it are clearly recognized in the hymnody and the devotional writings of the period. We shall find in the preaching of this age an equally eloquent testimony to the same inner life of Protestant orthodoxy.

The age of Protestant orthodoxy produced several homiletical manuals, the first of which was by Andreas Hyperius.[2] Hyperius was professor at the Protestant University of Marburg and is claimed by both Lutherans and Reformed as the first Protestant homiletician. He brought to Protestant preachers an appreciation of the classical discipline of public speaking, and yet he was fully aware of the difference between the classical forms of oratory and the biblical concern for the proclamation of the gospel. He understood the main purposes of Reformation preaching as developed by the Reformers and gave it expression in a homiletical system. Although he published his work during the lifetime of the Reformers, the spirit of his undertaking may be regarded as more properly belonging to the age of Protestant scholasticism. That is, it is an attempt at the codification and systematization of the work of the Reformers.

As Hyperius understood it, the sermon was above all the exposition of Scripture. Its purpose was the proclamation of the gospel for our salvation. The sermon should teach, inspire devotion, and change lives. Drawing on II Timothy 3:16 and Romans 15:4, he proposed five dimensions of Christian preaching: teaching, reproof, correction, training in righteousness, and encouragement. Sometimes one of these dimensions should be stressed, while most often a sermon would follow a combination of these concerns. Hyperius taught that in the preaching of a sermon seven things should take place: the reading of the lesson, the invocation of God's blessing, the exordium or introduction, the division of the text, the confirmation of the message, the confutation of objections, and finally the conclusion. Certainly we find no radical departure from the *ars predicandi* produced by the preaching orders of the Middle Ages. One notices that the sermon is tightly bound to the reading of the Scripture lesson and the prayer for God's blessing.

Hyperius's fundamental work was developed in a number of differ-

---

2. Andreas Hyperius, *De formandis concionibus sacris: seu de interpretatione scripturarum populari* (Marburg: n.p., 1553). An English translation appeared early in the reign of Elizabeth I.

ent directions in the next century and a half, especially in Germany, where a whole constellation of preaching manuals appeared. Among the best known of these were the works of Aegidius Hunnius (ca. 1596), Lukas Osiander (1534-1604), Johann Förster (d. 1613), and I. J. Carpzov (d. 1699). An array of different methods and variations of these methods developed. Sometimes these more formal approaches to homiletics were followed fairly closely, but in actual practice the example of the major Reformers held sway. Preachers generally went through the passage of Scripture on which they were to preach, commenting on it phrase by phrase. The Reformers had learned to do this from the collections of patristic sermons the Christian humanists had published, and they had found it an effective method of teaching their congregations the Scriptures.

Let us turn now to some of the preachers of the period to see how they went about fulfilling the ministry of the Word. We begin with several German preachers. In the following chapter we will treat some of the Huguenot preachers, and finally in chapter VII we will look at some of the Dutch preachers.

I. Philipp Nicolai (1556-1608): Serving during Tribulation

Philipp Nicolai is best remembered today as a hymn writer.[3] Even modern American hymnbooks contain such masterpieces as "O Morning Star, How Bright and Fair" and "Sleepers, Wake, a Voice Astounds Us." Even if we don't know them as hymns, we surely know their cantata versions by Bach and Buxtehude. What we are surprised to learn is that, in his own day, Nicolai was widely heralded as Hamburg's Chrysostom. He was one of the most exacting theological controversialists of his day. Being the son of a Lutheran pastor in Westphalia, he was sent off to the Universities of Erfurt and Wittenberg to study theology at an early age. Soon after ordination he appeared to be a young man of promise, and was appointed court preacher of the princess of Waldeck. He soon became involved in the theological controversies which so embroiled Westphalia. He took on Calvinists and Roman Catholics alike, both in

3. On the life of Nicolai, see Victor Schutze, "Nicolai, Philipp," in *Realencyklopädie für protestantische Theologie und Kirche,* ed. Johann Jakob Herzog, 24 vols. (Leipzig: J. C. Hinrichs, 1896-1913), 14:28-32.

his preaching and in written works. Then in his early forties the plague brought his whole family to an untimely end. In his depression he turned away from theological controversies and devoted himself entirely to prayer. Because the Evangelical ministry is so devoted to the disciplines of Christian marriage and family, its ministers inescapably bear the anxieties of family life. Protestant ministers, for better or worse, are often distracted from their ministry by the sufferings of their families, but among many ministers this has led to a spiritual refinement. The fruit of Nicolai's tribulation was his devotional classic, *Freudenspiegel des ewigen Lebens,* published in Frankfurt in 1599.

Eventually Nicolai married the widow of one of his colleagues, and in 1601 he was called to become senior pastor of Saint Catherine's Church in Hamburg. It was there that he gained his greatest reputation as a preacher. Hamburg had always had a solid reputation as a center of Lutheran orthodoxy, and Nicolai fit well into the tradition.

Not a great number of Nicolai's sermons have been preserved. What has been preserved shows him to be a preacher rich in ideas and imagery; these sermons provide a good example of the devotional passion and intensity so characteristic of Protestant orthodoxy. We mention Nicolai first because his name is so well known. He is greatly admired as a good example of Protestant orthodoxy at its best. For a better picture of the preaching of the period, however, we turn to Valerius Herberger, who has left us a much larger collection of sermons. Herberger's published sermons were widely distributed at the time, and for a long time were regarded as classics of German homiletical literature.

II. Valerius Herberger (1562-1627): Contemplative Preaching

Several of the Reformers were still alive when Valerius Herberger was born.[4] His father was a pious carpenter in the Silesian city of Fraustadt. Before he was nine years old he was orphaned. His mother's sister and her husband, a shoemaker, took him into their home. The schoolmaster Ar-

---

4. For biographical material, see the study in the introduction to Valerius Herberger, *Valerius Herberger. Ausgewählte Predigten. Mit einer einleitenden Monographie,* ed. Dr. Orphal (Leipzig: Fr. Richter, 1892), and Ferdinand Cohrs, "Herberger, Valerius," in *Realencyklopädie für protestantische Theologie und Kirche,* 7:695-97.

nold, who providentially was his godfather, saw to it that the precocious boy was prepared for the ministry as his father had hoped. After Herberger had studied at Frankfort on the Oder and then at Leipzig, the schoolmaster died and Herberger was called back home to take his place. Herberger's loyalty to the small city which had so fondly raised him was evidently an important principle of his life. In the course of time he was chosen pastor of the Protestant church of the city. Although often invited to fill more prominent pulpits, he exercised his whole ministry in his native town.

In 1604 the changing winds of politics and religion demanded that the Protestants of Fraustadt turn over their church building to the Catholics. Fraustadt was at the time a German Protestant city within the borders of the Kingdom of Poland. Happily, they were allowed to transform another building in the city into a place of worship. Since this move from their old church to new, makeshift accommodations occurred on Christmas Eve, they called it the Church of Christ's Crib. When the Thirty Years' War began, Herberger's congregation was in a most precarious position, but that was not the only tribulation through which our preacher guided his congregation. Several times the city experienced severe epidemics. The plague of 1613 took more than two thousand people in Fraustadt. Herberger faithfully visited the sick and heroically attended the dying.

A. Sermons for the Heart

Because Herberger did not preach in one of the famous pulpits of Germany, but in a small and remote city, his fame as a preacher spread because of his published sermons. He published *postils* on the Gospels and Epistles of the Lutheran lectionary. His most famous work was *Magnalia Dei de Jesu scripturae nucleo et medulla*. This collection of meditations and prayers appeared in twelve volumes over a period of seven years, from 1611 to 1618. These meditations are based on his *lectio continua* sermons on the Old Testament historical books from Genesis to Ruth which he preached on weekdays. His works went through many editions, becoming one of the devotional classics of the age.

Herberger's sermons aimed at developing the devotional life. One notices, for instance, that even his *postils* on the Gospels and Epistles are called *Hertz Postille*. We might freely translate this as "Sermons for the

Heart." It was often said that Herberger's sermons came from the heart, and therefore went to the heart. In addition to these collections of sermons on the traditional Lutheran lectionary, there were collections for Easter, *Osterschatz*, or "Easter Treasure"; on the passion of Christ, *Passionszeiger*, or "Passion Guides"; and on the Psalms, *Psalterparadise*, or "Paradise of Psalms." Here we have contemplative preaching at its most devotional. His *Evangelische Hertzpostille* and his *Epistolische Hertzpostille* give a strongly christocentric interpretation of Scripture.

In the same way, his *Magnalia Dei* aims at a thoroughly Christian interpretation of the Old Testament. He finds Christ the marrow and nucleus of the Old Testament, and, as so many other Christian preachers over the centuries, he is convinced that the Christian interpretation of the Old Testament edifies the Church. This is not simply the allegory of the Alexandrian School. It is much more typological in spirit than it is allegorical. The apostle Paul himself gave a strong typological interpretation to the tribulations in the wilderness in I Corinthians 10. It was the Alexandrian allegory that the Reformers of the sixteenth century had rejected. Typology they did not reject. To be sure, they never imbued typology with anything near the lushness that Herberger did, but to charge him with a lapse from Protestant canons of interpretation is a mistake. Christians had for centuries taken comfort from the heroic faith of the Old Testament saints, and in these sermons Herberger once more brings out this rich tradition of interpretation.

B. Sermons on the Joseph Cycle

Let us take a closer look at some individual sermons from Herberger's *Magnalia Dei*.[5] A particularly rich portion of this series contains the sermons devoted to the story of Joseph. We will look at three sermons which give something of the flavor of this classic of Protestant spirituality. Herberger devotes about fifty sermons to the Joseph cycle, which means

5. Originally published as Valerius Herberger, *Magnalia Dei de Jesu scripturae nucleo et medulla,* 12 vols. (Leipzig: Thomas Shürer, 1600-1611). This study is based on an edition from the middle of the nineteenth century kindly made available to me by the library of the Lutheran Theological Seminary in Philadelphia: Valerius Herberger, *Magnalia Dei. Die grossen Thaten Gottes. 1-4 Theil: Das erste Buch Mose ausgelegt und erklärt,* new ed. (Halle: Julius Fricke, 1854). The page references in the text are to this work.

he proceeded through the last dozen or so chapters of Genesis at the rate of four sermons per chapter.

First, let us look at the sermon on the coat of many colors (Sermon XIII). Our preacher begins by recounting the story. He explains that Joseph was the most beloved of all Jacob's children. One wonders why he was the favorite. Surely it was not because he was the strongest or the shrewdest. To some extent it was because he was the firstborn of his mother Rachel, who was the woman Jacob really wanted to marry. His father-in-law Laban had tricked him into marrying Leah first. She bore Jacob many sons. Jacob also married Rachel, but she remained barren for some time. Herberger says nothing about all these strained circumstances and how they may have affected the relation between Joseph and his brothers. What he emphasizes is that Joseph was the most truly pious. Joseph was honest, humble, and law-abiding. He was a truly good man to whom one could not help but be attracted. People were drawn to him naturally, like iron to a magnet (p. 509). Joseph had the same sort of attractive goodness that Jesus had, and this is surely one of the ways that he is an intimation of Christ. Joseph was beloved of his father because he was a good man. The same was true of Jesus as well, for we read that both at his baptism and at the transfiguration the voice of the Father came from heaven, saying, "This is my beloved Son in whom I am well pleased." The Father was pleased with the Son because he was a good man (p. 510).

Something else about Joseph reminds us of Jesus, and that is that Joseph was the child of Jacob's older years. Jesus was the Son of God, but God is eternal, without years or days. It would not be proper to speak of Jesus as the Son of God's old age. In fact, in the Psalms we read of the Messiah being conceived from all eternity (Pss. 2:7 and 110:3). Yet, from the standpoint of the history of the world, Christ is the Son of the Father in this later age (p. 511). For we read in Hebrews that at many times and in many ways God spoke to the fathers through the prophets, but he has in these last times spoken to us through the Son (Heb. 1:1-2). Our preacher comments on this text by addressing Christ in prayer.[6] We will have more to say about this devotional technique, but for the moment it

---

6. One of the features of Herberger's preaching is these prayers which punctuate his sermons. In order to help the reader get the feel of this, I have put these little homiletical prayers in quotation marks; it does not seem necessary to give the German text in the footnotes.

is the commentary which catches our attention. "Oh, dear Lord Jesus, history is beginning to wind down, and at last as Son of the Father you have been born in these last days; help us to be ready for the last Day, the day of judgment." For many of us this may sound a bit contrived. To speak of Jesus as the Son of God's old age is not exactly a statement of systematic theology, as poetic as it may be. Herberger's typology, if typology it be, is stretched beyond its proper limit. Here, at least, that is the way it seems to me.

Our preacher takes up another point. Joseph had a marvelous robe, a coat of many colors. It was given to him by his father as an expression of his special favor. Herberger at one point tells us that this robe symbolized the threefold office of prophet, priest, and king (p. 510). For Herberger, Joseph's robe is an intimation of the robe of Christ in its most profound sense. Our preacher takes the biblical imagery and develops it to the fullest. Jesus had a robe, he tells us, a wonderful robe. In the incarnation he put on the robe of human flesh. The heavenly Father gave it to him out of love. This robe was knit together by the Holy Spirit in the womb of the virgin Mary. Philipp Melanchthon said, "O Miracle of miracles! That fallible human flesh has been taken on by God himself" (p. 511). It is this which Psalm 93 finds so glorious: "The Lord is clothed in majesty." Our preacher finishes his point by addressing Jesus, "O Lord Jesus Christ, when I think of you the well-beloved Son of the Father, incarnate in human flesh like mine, then my love goes out to you. Love for you springs forth in everlasting joy." Again we have one of Herberger's homiletical prayers. These little devotional thoughts addressed to Jesus are characteristic of this very devotional approach to preaching. We find them in many German preachers of the seventeenth century. So often preaching becomes a loving meditation on the Word of God, a pious conversation with the Savior.

The coat of many colors reminds us as well that Jesus is the "fairest of the sons of men," as we find it in the Forty-fifth Psalm. This has always been a favorite psalm for those who like to think of Christ as the Bridegroom. Herberger develops this nuptial imagery. The Bridegroom is filled with all the gifts of the Holy Spirit. He is anointed with the oil of gladness more than all his companions (Ps. 45:8). To this our preacher brings the imagery of Isaiah 11:2. The Spirit of the Lord rests upon him, the spirit of wisdom and understanding, the spirit of counsel and might, the spirit of knowledge and the fear of the Lord (p. 512). Christ was clothed in the robe of human flesh, but Christ was also clothed in a spiritual robe through his anointing with the manifold gifts of the Spirit.

It is this spiritual robe which the faithful Christian seeks. Once again our preacher turns to Christ in devout meditation: "O Lord Jesus Christ, the soldiers at the foot of the cross divided among themselves your clothes, but for your robe they cast lots. The children of this world seek material goods from you, but I would have spiritual treasures from you. I would have your robe of innocence. I would clothe myself in true faith. I would have that robe of purity which you gave me at my baptism" (p. 513). For Herberger the line between praying and preaching is not always distinct. Prayer, meditation, and preaching meld into each other.

Another passage on the spiritual clothing of the faithful comes to mind. Isaiah speaks of being clothed in the garments of salvation, being covered with the robe of righteousness, decking oneself as a bridegroom with a crown of flowers or as a bride adorning herself with her jewels (Isa. 61:10). This intimation of heavenly glory inspires yet another prayer from Herberger: "O clothe me, Lord Jesus, with the robe of your mercy and righteousness, that I might in the last day be clothed with honor and glory" (p. 513). In the end, Joseph's coat of many colors is an intimation of the festal garments of those who gather for the wedding feast of the Lamb.

The second sermon that comes to our attention concerns Joseph's imprisonment in Egypt (Sermon XXII). The sermon begins with a bit of irony. Innocent Joseph must go to prison, but the promiscuous wife of Potiphar retains her position of honor (p. 546). "O dear God," our preacher prays. "Give innocent Christians patience that they might endure the trials they have to go through." Joseph was trustworthy in his service, and what did he get for his reward? Ingratitude and nothing more. Alas, power has a way of getting the advantage over justice. It seemed for a long time that Joseph's piety would generate the worst for him, but because he patiently held out, he experienced a wondrous work of God. This is what we find in Scripture: "But God is faithful, he will not let you be tempted above what you are able to endure, and will bring the temptation to an end, that you might overcome it" (I Cor. 10:13). Joseph is a good example of a faithful man who was true to the ways of God not only in temptation but in tribulation as well. His patience in prison, especially when he was there unjustly, shows tremendous faith in the providence of God.

It is this innocent suffering of Joseph which inspires Herberger to think of Jesus as a type and pattern of all righteousness. Again our preacher addresses the Savior: "Lord Jesus, such a judgment was given to you that I might go free. You suffered that no condemnation might fall on those who love you." Our preacher continues to meditate on the suffering of the Savior: "Lord Jesus, you were bound as a captive in Gethsemane, accused in the court of Pilate, you were tied to the bloody pillar and flogged, and hammered to the cross with iron nails. The snares of death encompassed you (Psalm 116:3). It is I, O precious Lord, who should have been enclosed in the prison, but it was you who were bound and imprisoned and nailed to the cross. You suffered the cross that all sinners might be redeemed." Through your bonds I am unbound, Herberger prays. I am freed from all my sins and all their punishment (p. 547).

To be sure, this is all very orthodox theology which Herberger spins out of the story of Joseph, but not infrequently one has the feeling that it is a bit overplayed. That Joseph's imprisonment was a burial one can follow, but Herberger goes on to develop a whole meditation on the "all holy burial of Jesus." Jesus had a chance to rest in the tomb, we are told. We, too, will have a chance to rest in the grave. Through Christ's burial the ground in which we will rest has been made holy. We have no need, Herberger assures us, to fear the cold of the grave, for Christ by his burial has warmed our beds (p. 548). Some will find all this a bit too maudlin, but apparently it was part of the intellectual atmosphere of the age.

Herberger goes on, noticing from his text that the Lord was with Joseph. This suggests to him the text from the apostle Paul which tells us that in Christ the whole fullness of deity dwells bodily (Col. 2:9), or the text which tells us that God was in Christ reconciling the world unto himself (II Cor. 5:19) (p. 548). It was Jesus, the Son of God, true God and true man, who came into the world, just as Joseph, the beloved of his father, came into Egypt. It was Jesus, the divinely appointed Savior of all peoples, who descended into hell to do battle with the powers of evil, just as Joseph descended into the pit and then into Egypt and then into prison, that he might do battle with the devil by patiently enduring the trials Providence had laid upon him. Just as Joseph was released from prison and given honor and power over the whole land of Egypt, so Christ, triumphing over all the powers of the underworld, rose triumphantly to reign over heaven and earth, and is even now seated at the right hand of the Father.

While the imagery of Joseph's enslavement and imprisonment in Egypt is undeniably suggestive of Christ's works of humiliation, the Joseph cycle is not quite as suggestive when it comes to imagery for the resurrection. Joseph is simply released from prison. But this does not restrain

Herberger in the least. He meditates on the victory of the resurrection by speaking of how Christ crushed the head of the serpent, how he destroyed the works of the devil and then put him to flight (p. 549). The themes of *Christus Victor* come through very clearly. The story of Samson is related as an intimation of the resurrection. Strangely enough, this story, like the story of Joseph itself, is not really a New Testament type, even though it was frequently treated as one by late patristic and medieval sources. Still, we have to recognize some sound theological instincts in Herberger even if he often overplays his typology. As far as it may be removed from the imagery of the Joseph cycle, our preacher recognized the need to lead his congregation beyond a meditation on the suffering of Christ to a meditation on the victory of Christ.

What is interesting in these sermons is how all this is made so thoroughly subjective. Whether it is the story of Joseph's victory or of Christ's victory, it is an intimation of the resurrection of the Christian. Herberger, of course, believed in the objective historical account, but he wants to go beyond this to a subjective appropriation of these *Magnalia Dei,* these saving acts of God for our salvation. This concern for the subjective dimension of faith we have already recognized in John Tauler, Thomas à Kempis, and Johann Geiler von Kaysersberg. As he concludes his sermon, Herberger prays, "You and you alone, Lord Jesus, have overcome the power of Satan and the fires of Hell. . . . Lord Jesus, you have done all this in my heart" (p. 549). We notice that once again the sermon has become a prayer; at the same time, the objective, historic victory of Christ in his resurrection has become a subjective victory in the heart. This sort of mysticism is typical of classical German Protestantism. It is really very hard to separate the orthodoxy and the mysticism. As much as the romanticism of the early nineteenth century liked to cast orthodoxy as cold and unfeeling, one has to ask if this was really the case.

Let us look at another of Herberger's sermons, Sermon XXVIII. This sermon takes as its text the story of Joseph revealing his true identity to his brothers, found in Genesis 45:4-14. The blood relationship is strong, Herberger tells us. In spite of all that has happened, in spite of all the cruelty of his brothers, Joseph finds that his love still goes out to them. They are still his brothers. Joseph can no longer hide his identity from them (p. 586). He is overcome with love for them as he sees them humbled by famine and frightened before the future. He cannot even bring himself to scold them, much less take the revenge he could so easily have taken. He could only forgive them. That was just the kind of man Joseph was. As we find it in Scripture, "Love bears all things, believes all things, hopes all things, suffers all things" (cf. I Cor. 13:7).[7] Surely this picture of Joseph as a man of generous love does have a reflection of Jesus in it. This is the sort of thing we find all through these sermons on the Joseph narrative. For Herberger Christ is always the type, the heavenly pattern incarnate in human flesh. Christ is the type of the patriarchs, the prophets, and the saints of the Old Testament as well as of the apostles and disciples who came after him. Jesus was, simply put, the pattern of the Christian life.

More specifically, this story suggests to our preacher the story of Jesus talking to the two disciples on the road to Emmaus. The two disciples did not recognize Jesus, just as the brothers did not recognize Joseph (p. 587). Joseph had all the Egyptians leave his audience chamber so he could be alone with his brothers. Then he said to them, "I am Joseph; is my father still alive?" The brothers were speechless. He told them to come closer to him and reiterated that he was their brother: "I am your brother Joseph, whom you sold into Egypt" (Gen. 45:4). Joseph assured his brothers that they had nothing to fear. He was not angry with them, for he recognized the hand of Providence in it all. "For God sent me before you to preserve life" (Gen. 45:5). With this Joseph assured his brothers that he would provide for them.

Herberger seems a bit quick to draw his conclusions here. What interests him at this point in the story is that just as Joseph has comforting words for his brothers in their embarrassment, so God has comforting words for us. Again he crosses the line from sermon to prayer. "O Lord Jesus, when I am in doubt and tribulation give me a word of comfort. Say to me that you have removed my trespasses and that you remember my transgressions no more" (cf. Isa. 43:25). The preacher goes through a whole catalogue of the comforting words of Scripture and applies them to the congregation. Very specifically, it is to "the hearts" of his congregation that this application is made. Again we recognize the strong subjectivity of this preaching. The concerns of medieval pietism, about which we spoke in the previous volume, have obviously not been forgotten. The concerns of pietism here, however, are not simply nominalistic. There is both an appreciation for the objective events of salvation history, preeminently manifested in the *Magnalia Dei,* the mighty works of God for our salvation, and also an appreciation of the personal engagement of the

---

7. Here again we find our preacher giving us a loose paraphrase of Scripture rather than an exact quotation.

Christian with the transcendent Christ in the experiences of the Christian life. It would appear that the biblical realism of classical Protestantism has significantly moderated the nominalism of the late Middle Ages.

The Christian needs to hear the comforting words of Christ, just as Joseph's brothers needed to be assured by the words of Joseph. Again our preacher centers his attention on repeating the comforting words of Scripture. Joseph very specifically said, "I AM Joseph your brother." Herberger sees in this an intimation of the I AM sayings of Jesus: I am the good shepherd, I am the bread of life, I am the resurrection and the life, and so forth (p. 588).

Another intimation of Christ which Herberger finds in this episode of the Joseph cycle is the embarrassment of the brothers. This suggests to our preacher the embarrassment of the disciples who hid themselves at the time of Christ's passion. The brothers were embarrassed because they thought that in selling their brother into slavery in Egypt he would come to an ignominious end, but instead he had been promoted to a position of high honor. Herberger sees in this an intimation of the embarrassment of the disciples in the Upper Room when the risen Jesus appeared to them. They had for the most part deserted the suffering Jesus. Peter had even denied him. Joseph rose above the hesitations of his brethren just as Jesus rose above the doubts of his disciples and removed their remorse. Our preacher says this should encourage every Christian soul to trust Christ for one's salvation (p. 590).

Most of us will find that this most devout and beloved preacher has taken typology much too far. One must ask if this is really typology. As we have already indicated, the Joseph typology is not one of the canonical typologies; that is, it is not a type we find in the New Testament. Strictly speaking, a true typology must be based on an interpretation of a passage of the Old Testament suggested in the New Testament. Furthermore, even if it had been a typology commended to us by the New Testament, we find some of the resemblances Herberger points out a bit artificial. Much too much is read into the story of Joseph which is not there. The Joseph cycle is one of the richest portions of the Bible. There is plenty which can be legitimately brought out of the text.

Having said this, however, we must say that these sermons show an admirable devotional intensity. Here we have an example of a contemplative reading of Scripture. The Scriptures are read and preached to give guidance to the members of the congregation. It is a very personal approach to Scripture which surely has a place in the Christian life.

III. Johann Gerhard (1582-1637): Preaching the Passion of Christ

Johann Gerhard was without a doubt the outstanding theologian of Lutheran orthodoxy.[8] He was born in Quedlinburg; studied in the Universities of Wittenberg, Jena, and Marburg; and after serving several years in administrative positions in the various state churches in Saxony, was called to the University of Jena as professor of theology.

One of the most attractive features of Gerhard as a theologian is the variety of his theological works. His first important work to appear was his *Meditationes sacrae*. This collection of devotional meditations published in 1606 achieved considerable attention, and as early as 1631 an English translation appeared, which went through numerous editions. Today it is regarded as a classic of German devotional literature. It seems to have been particularly popular among pastors. What interests us about this work is what it tells us about the devotional depth of Protestant orthodoxy. Under the towers and behind the ramparts of their theological fortresses was a boiler room of devotional fire which provided heat and power for the whole culture.

His dogmatics began to appear in 1610, four years after his *Meditationes sacrae*. For the next twelve years this classic of scholastic Protestantism, *Loci theologicae,* came out volume by volume. What is characteristic about this work is its attempt to explain the basic doctrines of Protestant Christianity in terms of medieval Aristotelian metaphysics. It was not until the end of Gerhard's life that his polemical work *Confessio catolica* appeared. In the meantime, he produced several commentaries on various books of both the Old and the New Testament, the most important of which was his *Harmonia evangelistum,* in which he did a careful study of the passion and resurrection narratives of the Gospels.

A collection of his sermons has come down to us, *Sacrum homiliarum in pericopas evangeliorum dominicalium et praecipuorum totius anni festorum.*[9] A study of this volume would suggest that it is not so

8. For biographical material on Gerhard, see Bengt Hägglund, *Die heilige Schrift und ihre Deutung in der Theologie Johann Gerhards* (Lund: CWK Gleerup, 1951), and Johannes Kunze, "Gerhard, Johann," in *Realencyklopädie für protestantische Theologie und Kirche,* 6:554-61.

9. Johann Gerhard, *Sacrum homiliarum in pericopas evangeliorum dominicalium et praecipuorum totius anni festorum* (Jena: Blasi Lobensteini Bibliopolae, 1647), hereafter

much a collection of sermons to be read by the faithful as a collection of sermon notes to be used by other ministers in the preparation of their sermons. These sermon notes are written in Latin and are filled with Greek and Hebrew phrases. In general, the work is written in a lapidary style which only someone who had a formal theological education could follow. We find no attempt at literary refinement. There are no exempla, no similes or metaphors, nor are there any traces of rhetorical devices of even the simplest sort. On the other hand, the notes are rich in the way they suggest parallel passages which throw light on the text. The patristic citations are very full as well. In a sermon for Good Friday, for example, Gerhard takes up the story of Abraham's sacrifice. He knows Origen's sermon on the subject as well as John Chrysostom's. He even speaks of a sermon on Abraham and Isaac by Ephrem of Syria.[10] He has studied Bernard of Clairvaux's sermons carefully, and refers to them frequently.[11] Bernard's sermons were often taken as models among Counter-Reformation preachers, a phenomenon we saw particularly in the sermons of Luis of Granada. It is clear that admiration for this classic was in no way limited to Catholics.

One of the interesting features of Gerhard's *Homiliarum* is the ample treatment of the passion of Christ. Bernard left us only one sermon on this topic, and many medieval collections of sermons on the liturgical Gospels and Epistles had no sermons on it, but Gerhard left us twelve. The pendulum swung in the opposite direction with Jean Gerson, who is supposed to have preached twelve sermons on the passion between the hours of twelve and three on Good Friday, followed by another twelve in the evening. That is what the record tells us, at least. As we saw in the previous volume, Bernardino da Siena was equally thorough in his preaching on the passion. So, when set against the Good Friday preaching of Gerson and Bernardino, Gerhard's preaching twelve sermons on Good Friday is not quite so incredible.

Let us look at the schema of this Good Friday series of sermons:

Sermon 1, Genesis 22:1-19
    Sermon on the sacrifice of Abraham

Gerhard, *Homiliarum*. Again I am in the debt of the library of the Lutheran Theological Seminary in Philadelphia for their loan of this precious volume.

10. Gerhard, *Homiliarum*, pp. 726ff.

11. Gerhard, *Homiliarum*, p. 758 and passim.

Sermon 2, Genesis 22:1-19
Second sermon on the sacrifice of Abraham
Sermon 3, Leviticus 16:1-34
Sermon on the typology of the Day of Atonement
Sermon 4, Numbers 21:1-10
Sermon on the typology of the brazen serpent
Sermon 5, Matthew 27:45-46
Sermon on the meaning of the darkness while Christ was on the cross
Sermon 6, Luke 22:44
Sermon on Christ sweating blood in the Garden of Gethsemane
Sermon 7, John 19:17
Sermon on the significance of Golgotha
Sermon 8, I Corinthians 2:2
"For I decided to know nothing among you except Jesus Christ and him crucified."
Sermon 9, Galatians 2:20
". . . it is no longer I who live, but Christ who lives in me; and the life I now live in the flesh I live by faith in the Son of God, who loved me and gave himself for me."
Sermon 10, Galatians 3:1
"O foolish Galatians! Who has bewitched you, before whose eyes Jesus Christ was publicly portrayed as crucified?"
Sermon 11, Galatians 6:14
"But far be it from me to glory except in the cross of our Lord Jesus Christ."
Sermon 12, Revelation 1:5-6
"To him who has freed us from our sins by his blood and made us a kingdom, priests to his God and Father, to him be glory and dominion for ever and ever. Amen."

One particularly striking thing about this series of sermons is its strong use of typology. It is not allegory that is used, but the classic typology of the New Testament. One notices particularly the importance of the Abraham typology as found in John 3:16 and the brazen serpent typology as found in John 3:15. The typology of the Day of Atonement as found in the Epistle to the Hebrews is also very important to this series. On the other hand, the Passover typology does not play a central role in this series. We can well imagine that in other years it might be dwelt upon at greater length. This series of sermons for Good Friday does not seem to be based on an established series of pericopes.

Another striking characteristic is the strong emphasis on the vicarious atonement as it is clearly stated in the Nicene Creed. Christ died for us and for our salvation. Luther had made a strong point of this doctrine, and he was followed very closely in this by the other Reformers. How often Gerhard brings in the fifty-third chapter of Isaiah to explain his texts! The doctrine of the vicarious atonement which the New Testament found so frequently in Isaiah was at the very heart of classical Protestant preaching. To preach Christ and him crucified was to preach the gospel.

What seems to be at play in these sermons is the centrality of the biblical imagery. Gerhard recognizes that the beauty of typology is that it is the biblical imagery. He is not only preaching biblical concepts, but he is preaching in the biblical imagery as well. Gerhard preached the message of Scripture in the language of Scripture.

IV. Christian Scriver (1629-93)

Catechetical preaching became a characteristic of the Protestant religious experience early in the Reformation. In the seventeenth century, from the Lutheran city-states along the shores of the Baltic Sea to the Puritan colonies of New England, the preaching of the catechism had a fixed place in Protestant devotional life. A number of series of catechetical sermons have come down to us. We spoke in chapter III of the sermons Thomas Watson preached on the *Westminster Shorter Catechism* in London. In the next chapter we will speak of Jean Daillé's sermons on the Huguenot catechism preached outside the walls of Paris. Certainly among these classics should be numbered the sermons on Luther's catechism preached by Christian Scriver in 1658, in Stendal, in the eastern part of Germany.[12]

12. Christian Scriver, *Chrysologia Catechetica oder Goldpredigten über die Hauptstücke des Luther'schen Katechismus,* new and revised ed. (Stuttgart: J. S. Steinkopf'schen Buchhandlung, 1848); page references in the text are to this volume. Special appreciation is expressed to the Library of the Lutheran Theological Seminary in Philadelphia for allowing me to study this work in their rare book collection.

A. Preaching Luther's Catechism

Scriver's introduction to these sermons tells us more about their liturgical setting than we usually learn from series of sermons preached so long ago. Apparently it was a custom of long standing in Stendal that four times a year the catechism was preached through each day of the week from Sunday to Sunday. Each of the four series was held at one of the four parish churches in the city: the week following the first Sunday in Advent at Saint Nicholas', the week following Estomihi Sunday at Saint Mary's, the week following Trinity Sunday at Saint James', and the first week in September at Saint Peter's. The purpose of these catechetical sermons was to prepare the congregation for the celebration of Communion, and especially young people for their first celebration of the Sacrament. There is no suggestion, however, that they were primarily for young people. By 1658 confirmation had not yet become an established means of receiving young people into the Church in Protestant Germany, but young people were expected to receive catechetical teaching before their first Communion.[13] These sermons are of special interest to students of the history of Christian worship because they show us that catechetical preaching was increasingly recognized as a significant dimension of the preaching ministry. In Stendal, as no doubt in many other north German cities, there was, in the middle of the seventeenth century, regular catechetical preaching for adults.

Protestant orthodoxy developed a deep love for serious theological reflection in the pulpit. The preaching of the catechism on Sunday afternoon often attained an amazing penetration into formal theology. A congregation in Leipzig, or Leiden, or London, was capable of following the finest points of theological discussion. A thorough doctrinal sermon would be discussed all the rest of the week in a good Protestant home in Bremen, Lübeck, or Hamburg. Congregations loved solid theology. They loved to think about it and talk about it. They wanted to hear sermons that would stimulate their minds.

Scriver was still a young man when he preached these sermons.[14]

---

13. On the introduction of confirmation into Protestant worship, see my *The Shaping of the Reformed Baptismal Rite in the Sixteenth Century* (Grand Rapids: Wm. B. Eerdmans Publishing Co., 1992), pp. 209-16.

14. For biographical information on Scriver, see Hermann Beck, "Scriver, Christian," in *Realencyklopädie für protestantische Theologie und Kirche*, 18:102-3; Martin Schmidt, "Christian Scrivers 'Seelenschatz' als Beispiel vorpietistische Predigtweise," *Kirche in der Zeit* 17 (1962); and Martin Schmidt, "Scriver, Christian," in *Die Religion in*

He had done his theological studies in Rostock, one of the Hanseatic cities on the shores of the Baltic. The University of Rostock had been established well before the end of the Middle Ages and had done much to shape the intellectual life of northern Germany and Scandinavia in the years following the Reformation. Scriver had begun his ministry in Stendal in 1653 as *Archidikonus*. We assume this means that he, along with other young pastors, served as an assistant to the pastoral staff of Stendal. Scriver mentions that he came to preach these sermons because his senior colleague, Petrus Belkovius, the pastor of Saint James', had taken ill and he took over the responsibility. The series of eight sermons was very well received, and the young pastor was urged to publish it. In 1667 Scriver was called to the Saxon city of Magdeburg. Today he is recognized as one who did much to deepen the pastoral ministry in his day.

B. Biblical Foundations of Protestant Worship

Scriver's catechetical sermons show a maturing of the devotional life of German Protestantism. In many ways the maturing was similar to what was happening in England among the Puritans of the early seventeenth century. In studying these catechetical sermons, let us focus in on that part of the series which studies the Ten Commandments, one of the basic catechetical pieces along with the creed and the Lord's Prayer. Then, focusing in even more precisely, let us look at Scriver's sermons on the first group of commandments, that is, the first tablet of the Law, where we find an especially perceptive statement on the nature of Christian worship.

As Scriver interprets it, the first commandment is the commandment to love God (p. 34). Jesus himself had interpreted it the same way: the first and greatest commandment is, "You shall love the Lord your God with all your soul, with all your feelings and with all your power" (Matt. 22:37).[15] To love God is to put God before all things, Scriver tells us. It is to put him before all things in heaven and earth, it is to exalt him, to lift him up. That is what Jesus meant when he said we are to love God with all our soul, with all our feelings, and with all our power. We are to love God not only with

Geschichte und Gegenwart, ed. Hans von Campenhausen et al., 3rd ed., 6 vols. (Tübingen: J. C. B. Mohr [Paul Siebeck], 1957-62), 5:1628.

15. Following our usual procedure in these volumes, we are translating the text of the sermon before us rather than quoting one of the established English versions of the Bible.

the words of our mouths but from the bottom of our hearts. The virgin Mary set a good example of the wholehearted exaltation of God as we find in Luke 1:46ff., "My soul magnifies the Lord, and my spirit exalts in God my Savior" (p. 34). With considerable eloquence our preacher draws out the meaning of this commandment. He emphasizes that the love for God must be faithful and constant, in both good days and bad. Scriver is a preacher who often brings personal reminiscences into his sermons, and here he tells of a young man he knew who had a fatal accident. In his dying agony he could only say, "O loving God, O loving God" (p. 37). In his last breath he poured out his constant love for God. That was worship at its most profound, an expression of our love for God.

Our preacher takes up the question of the relation between the love of God and the fear of God. In many places in the Bible, worship, the faithful living of the Christian life, and a devout relation to God seem to be expressed by the term "the fear of the Lord." Should we think of worship as the fear of God? As we read in I John 4:18, there is no fear in love, but a full love comes from fear. There is a difference between the fear of a slave and the fear of a child, Scriver tells us. Perfect love casts out fear. The stronger our love for God, the more afraid we are to do something inconsistent with that love (p. 39).

True love of God overcomes fear and in its place becomes trust. Trust is a noble and treasured virtue, best observed in the natural trust children have for their parents. There is a childlike simplicity in this trust. It is this same sort of trust that Christians should have toward God (p. 42). Saving faith is trusting faith. It is because we trust God that we follow his Word. There is no dichotomy between faith and love here. The sort of anti-Protestant polemic which was so popular at the time is hardly justified by these catechetical sermons. Faith loves God just as love for God has faith in God. God is our Father, and therefore we should go to him in all our needs and in all our sorrows. Because he is our Father, we know that he cares about our troubles, and because he is God above all gods, we know that he can care for us (p. 43).

That the foundation of Christian worship should be based on Jesus' interpretation of the first commandment is basic to a Protestant understanding of worship. It is the heart of what we have elsewhere called a covenantal theology of worship.[16] We find it important to underline that

---

16. Cf. Hughes Oliphant Old, *Themes and Variations for a Christian Doxology* (Grand Rapids: Wm. B. Eerdmans Publishing Co., 1992), pp. 111-37.

this approach to the theology of worship is to be found among the most orthodox of seventeenth-century Lutherans. We discover it among the Puritans of both England and America. It is a fairly general approach to worship in seventeenth-century Protestantism. There is nothing surprising about this; it seems implicit in a theology that recognizes in Scripture our sole authority.

Commenting on the second commandment, Scriver takes up the subject of hallowing God's name.[17] Here his insights are particularly rich. The primary way God's name is to be used is in blessings (p. 46). We use it in vain in curses, in magical incantations, and in superstitious rites (p. 60). Scriver reminds us of the Aaronic blessing which was given to the priestly clan (Num. 6:22ff.). It is in this way that the name of God is especially to be used. When used this way, God's name is not used in vain. But there are other ways in which we properly use God's name as well. First, we are to use God's name in blessing him (p. 46). Jesus taught us to hallow God's name by praying to him. This is a fundamental insight which we find in the Lord's Prayer. In our prayers we should hallow God's name. Psalm 72 tells us to bless the Lord, the God of Israel, to bless the God who does wonderful things, and to bless his glorious name forever and ever (vv. 18-19). First of all, we are to use God's name by blessing his name. We are to hallow God's name when we address him with the honorific titles found in Scripture: God Almighty; God Most High; O merciful God; O faithful God; O God full of loving-kindness and mercy; and Lord God, from whom come all good and perfect gifts (p. 47).

Second, we use the name of God aright in blessing ourselves. We should devote ourselves to prayer. When awakening in the morning, one should rise and pray for protection. When beginning work, one should ask God's help and guidance. When sitting down to a meal, one should give thanks to God for the nourishment he has provided. When going to bed in the evening, one should bless God, calling on his name in prayer. To do all this in sincerity of heart is not to use God's name in vain, the sin against which Moses warned us, but rather it is to do what Jesus taught us, to hallow God's name (p. 48).

Third, we use the name of God aright when we bless our neighbors. To obey this commandment positively is to intercede regularly for others. In biblical times it was customary to greet each other in the name of the

17. Scriver, of course, follows Luther's catechism in using the numbering of the commandments found in the Septuagint rather than in the Hebrew Bible.

Lord; "The Lord be with you" was their common greeting (p. 51). Even more, however, it was the practice of Christians to intercede for their rulers, for the church, and for the ministry. Jesus went so far as to teach us to pray for our enemies (p. 52). As Scriver interprets it, the second commandment teaches us to maintain the disciplines of Christian prayer.

Next our preacher takes up the third commandment, which in Luther's catechism treats remembering the Sabbath day to keep it holy. Our preacher reminds us of the story of Mary and Martha (Luke 10:38-42) (p. 52). Martha was occupied with all kinds of serving, which is certainly appropriate for the Christian, but Mary sat at the feet of Jesus and listened to his teaching. That is even more important. We remember that this was a key text for Luther in defending the centrality of the reading and preaching of Scripture in worship. Scriver uses it somewhat differently here, saying the story supports spending one day each week in the study of God's Word. There is, of course, the public ministry of the Word which we should all attend, but there is also the private ministry of meditating on the Word, teaching it to one's family, and praying over what one learns from the Word. One is amazed here, again and again, at how similar Scriver is to the teaching of the Puritans of England and America at this point. Much classical piety was recovered by seventeenth-century Protestantism.

When talking about the sanctification of the Sabbath, Scriver is careful to emphasize that God is always with us, even in the midst of all our work. At all times God speaks to us through his Word, by his Spirit, and in our conscience. God is in no way limited to the public reading and preaching of Scripture at church on Sunday. Yet he has appointed one day in seven for us to devote to him. On that day we are to lay aside our usual tasks so that we might come before God to receive his blessing. It is to be a time to listen to his Word as it is preached to us by his servants (p. 53). It is a day to rest from our work, that God might do his work in us.

Scriver is very specific about the devotional practices of seventeenth-century Protestantism. One cannot help but admire the careful sincerity of the religious practice he describes. One is not careless in sacred matters, but rather one is meticulous, preparing for them in the same way one dresses oneself for a spiritual feast. On Saturday evening one should close the barn, shut down the shop, and put away the ledgers. One should begin the feast day by getting out the Bible, books of Bible study helps, and commentaries. One should study the Scripture passage the pastor will treat in his Lord's Day sermon, so that one is prepared to listen carefully to the sermon.

In a Protestant city in northern Europe during the seventeenth century, and in some places in Germany even today, the bells of the churches
were rung on Saturday evening to mark the beginning of the Christian
Sabbath. For Scriver this was a sacred practice which reminded the Christian of the spiritual feast which was to begin. One began with the study of
the Scriptures and continued with the singing of the hymns appointed for
the following day (p. 55). By this time the hymnal had come to have a
prominent place in Protestant spirituality. Everyone had his or her own
hymnal, and hymns were sung in the home as part of morning and evening prayer. The hymnal was the backbone of the daily prayer of the
faithful.

On arriving at church, one should enter, Scriver tells his congregation, leaving all one's cares at the door (p. 57). One should pray for the
preaching, that through it God might speak to one's deepest needs. One
should not find what is said applicable to others but to oneself. No spiritual busybodying here! This is a time for honest self-evaluation. On leaving the church, one should thank God for his rich supply of grace, for his
promises, his words of comfort, and his assurances of salvation.

Returning home, the Christian should enter into conversation with
friends and family about the sermon. At Sunday dinner this should be the
subject of the table talk, as the father rehearses the children and the servants on the significance of the pastor's words (p. 58). Good works and
the giving of alms are likewise appropriate, as is visiting the sick. One is
struck by the fact that much more is said about what one should do on
Sunday than about what one should not do. All in all, this sermon is very
similar to what John Willison, pastor in Dundee, Scotland, had to say on
the sanctification of the Lord's Day, or again Thomas Shepard in Cambridge, Massachusetts. We will have more to say about these preachers in
volume V. For the moment, however, we want only to make one point.
This careful observance of the Lord's Day is apparently the common good
of seventeenth-century Protestant piety. From Danzig to New Haven,
from Nîmes to Glasgow, the Lord's Day was a day of spiritual feasting.

V. Heinrich Müller (1631-75)

Among the leading German preachers of the seventeenth century, Heinrich Müller has always been held in particular honor. He was, as were the
great English Puritans, a preacher of practical piety and heartfelt devo-

tion, and yet he was also a scholar of considerable attainment. As were the Huguenots and the Puritans, he was a plain-style preacher who was content to preach the Scriptures in a simple and direct manner. He was above all concerned to lead his congregation to an inward experience of God and a sincere faith which expressed itself in a simple and holy life. For myself, Heinrich Müller is about as fine a preacher as ever mounted a pulpit.

Müller was the son of a respected merchant of Rostock, one of the more important Hanseatic cities on the Baltic Sea.[18] During the Thirty Years' War, his parents were forced to flee Rostock and take refuge in Lübeck, where the future preacher was born. The family was soon able to return to Rostock, and it was there that their precocious son began his education. Heinrich's father, Peter Müller, was a leader in church affairs of this independent mercantile city and was able to provide the best education for his son, whom he directed very early toward the ministry. After a solid foundation in the Greek and Latin classics, young Heinrich, only thirteen years of age, began to study theology at the University of Rostock. He received the master's degree before he was twenty years old and was sent on a tour of the universities of northern Germany to hear the leading theologians of the day. In Leipzig he was particularly drawn by the distinguished theologian J. B. Carpzov. He was also influenced by Georg Calixtos. In 1653 he was granted a doctorate in theology by the University of Helmstedt. Returning to Rostock, he began to earn a reputation as an able preacher and was soon named professor of Greek and, in 1662, professor of theology. In 1671 he was named superintendent of the Church of Rostock.

A. Preaching as Worship

Let us look at a number of Müller's sermons.[19] First we take a sermon preached on the Gospel for Christmas Day, Luke 2:1-14. This sermon is of

---

18. Hermann Beck, "Müller, Heinrich," in *Realencyklopädie für protestantische Theologie und Kirche*, 13:521-23.

19. Regrettably, we do not have a modern edition of Müller's sermons. The sermons at which we will look are taken from a volume printed over a hundred years ago: Heinrich Müller, *Ausgewählte Predigten*, edited and introduction by Gustav Leonhardi (Leipzig: Friedrich Richter, 1891); page references in the text are to this volume. Müller's sermons were frequently reprinted. The following editions are among many: Heinrich Müller, *Evangelischer Herzensspiegel: oder geistreiche Erklärung und Betrachtung der Sonn-*

particular interest to us because it is introduced by a fine statement on preaching as worship. It begins by reminding us of a saying of Moses. That man of God, remembering the divine acts of deliverance which brought Israel out of Egypt, exclaimed, "Oh, how loving God has been to his people." When we think of this today, how much more we as Christians must marvel at the love of God in the incarnation of Christ. We can only wonder at the love of God, that he himself became a man and took on our humanity. Were God not our friend, even our lover, he would never have become man. It is of the very nature of love that it willingly gives. God gives us today his child, his only begotten Son. What more precious gift could he give us? God so loved the world that he gave his only begotten Son. It is the nature of love that the lover seeks to be united to the beloved. That God does even today. God became man that he might fill us with all his blessings. This love therefore moves us to love God in return, to rejoice in the Lord and sing hymns of praise to him (p. 1). At this point the congregation is asked to sing the Christmas carol "Ein kindlein so löbelich."

After the hymn the preacher reminds us of the first verses of Psalm 105, which call on us to speak of the wonders of God. That, to be sure, is one of the classic passages of the Bible on the nature of worship. It speaks of worship as recounting the mighty acts of God, and that is what our preacher intends to do in this sermon. He alludes to the text of the apostle Paul, "Great is the divine mystery, God is revealed in the flesh" (I Tim. 3:16).[20] Here in our text we find three marvelous wonders of God: a wondrous mother, a wondrous child, and a wondrous birth (p. 2). In remembering these wonders, the congregation worships God.

We will not take the time to report this whole sermon, but we would like to draw attention to the fine statement of the purpose of preaching in its introduction. Müller tells us that in his preaching he wants to recount the mighty acts of God for our salvation. He wants to remember the story of the incarnation of the Son of God. He wants to meditate on the mystery of God's revelation in human flesh. Surely when that is done by the Christian Church, then God is worshiped.

---

und festtäglichen Evangelien, wie auch beigelegten Passionspredigten (Lüneburg: Stern'schen Buchdrucherei, 1752), and Heinrich Müller, *Apostolische Schlusskette und Kraftkern: oder gründliche Auslegung der gewöhnlichen Sonn- und Fest-tags-Episteln* (Frankfurt am Main: Benjamin Andreä und Heinrich Hort, 1734). Regrettably, neither of these editions has been available to me.

20. Here, as elsewhere in these volumes, we translate the German text as the preacher gives it.

B. The Struggles of the Soul

This sermon is on Matthew 4:1-11, the Gospel the Lutheran lectionary appoints for the beginning of Lent. This follows an old and widespread tradition. We have in previous volumes seen a number of sermons for the beginning of Lent, but this sermon is especially noteworthy because it says nothing of Lent at all. The preacher does not seem at all interested in exhorting the congregation to submit to the spiritual disciplines usually associated with the season. What he is primarily interested in doing is expounding the text as it is found in Scripture. Understanding the text in the context of the liturgical calendar never seems to cross his mind.

For Müller the story of the temptation speaks to us about the living of the Christian life. The Christian life is filled with temptations, and the story of Christ being tempted by the devil assures us that we can face temptations and resist them. We, as Christ, can have the victory.

The first part of the sermon recalls the situation. Jesus had been baptized in the river Jordan, and in that event he was consecrated to his preaching ministry. But no sooner had he been ordained to this sacred task than the Spirit led him into the wilderness to be tempted. Those who are given positions of leadership can expect to be tempted. Our preacher puts it in an epigram, "Ein Lehrer, ein Leider." To be a teacher is to be a sufferer (p. 84). No question about it, Müller had a way with words. As soon as he began his ministry, Jesus had to suffer temptation. There is reason to this, of course. It is through temptation that our faith is tested and strengthened. For the godly, being alone is a spiritual school, a school of the Holy Spirit. It is a time for us to learn about ourselves.

But if the Spirit leads us into temptation, we can be well assured that the Spirit will arm us so that we can resist. The Spirit led Jesus into the wilderness so that he might be tempted and overcome that temptation. He armed Jesus for that victory (p. 85). It is often that way with us. God brings us into temptation that our faith be strengthened. The devil, on the other hand, tempts us so that our faith might be weakened.

Jesus allowed himself to be tempted so that we might know that he has overcome the devil. It proved his complete sanctity. His temptation made it possible for him to have sympathy with us when we are tempted. The Epistle to the Hebrews tells us that he was tempted as we, and yet he was without sin (Heb. 4:15). Müller goes on to point out that having been tempted as we are tempted, he has given us an example of how we can meet temptation and overcome it (p. 86).

395

Müller quotes I John 2:16 to show that basically there are three forms of temptation: the lust of the flesh, the lust of the eye, and the pride of life. Then he elaborates these three famous phrases. Temptation comes in many ways, he says, using one of his striking metaphors: the devil has a quiver full of arrows. Now he uses one; now he uses another; all aim at the same target, getting us to forget that we are children of God (p. 88).

Having spoken of temptation in general, our preacher turns to the first of the three temptations, turning stones into bread. He asks the congregation to imagine the situation. At his baptism a voice from heaven had said to Jesus that he was God's Son, but then for the next forty days he was without food. How is this? we ask. If Jesus was really God's Son, would he have hungered? In the same way the devil tempts us. We do not have enough food in the house to feed our families, so we doubt that God is taking care of us. We notice here Müller's very chaste use of the rhetorical question. How is this? our preacher asks once again. Müller knows how important it is to get his congregation to think with him. He asks them to consider a hypothetical situation, one that was very real to many who were listening to him.

But the temptation was in vain. Jesus was not fooled by his tempter. He had no interest in the devil's stony bread (p. 89). In the original German this is a great line. Müller knew how to use his German. Every language has its basic strengths and structures, and a good preacher knows how to use them. Notice the next line. We should be careful, our preacher warns his congregation, not to want what the devil wants us to want. If we make Satan's will our will, then Satan becomes our lord.

Jesus then answered his adversary. As Müller points out, he answered him by quoting Scripture. Man shall not live by bread alone but by every word that comes from the mouth of God. God will feed us, our preacher assures his congregation, but not with Satan's kind of bread. He has heavenly bread for us like the manna he gave his people in the wilderness. Be well assured, the God who loved us in the past will continue to love us. He who sustained Israel without bread can sustain us without bread. God's heart has not changed. To make his point Müller formulates it as a statement of faith. God's heart never changes. His hand is not shortened. He has helped, he still helps, he is our ever faithful God. In German this formulation is pungent: "Gottes Herz wird nicht verändert, seine Hand wird nicht verkürzt. Er hat geholfen, er hilft auch noch, der alte fromme Gott." Here is simple, powerful language.

Our preacher again picks up his text: "It is written." Jesus resisted the tempter by quoting the Scriptures he had memorized so well and understood so thoroughly. The Spirit had armed Jesus from childhood as he had learned his Bible in the synagogue school. God arms us for the hour of temptation by giving us his Word as a sword. If we would do battle, we must have a good sword. Alluding to the text of the apostle Paul, Müller tells us that here is the sword of the Spirit, the Word of God (Eph. 6:17) (p. 90). Again we find Müller developing the biblical imagery. He comments, This is the sword Christ used; this is the sword we must use, too. But we must be careful to use the sword of the Word as God has given it. When the serpent tempted Eve, he twisted the meaning of God's Word and made it say something it did not say. If we allow Satan to twist God's Word, then the battle is lost (pp. 90ff.). We must learn to hold the Word firm and tight and we will slay the old serpent, as we find it in Luther's hymn, "One little word will fell him."

Returning to his text, our preacher points out that the Scripture Jesus quoted says that while we shall not live by bread alone, God has other food for us: the food which comes from God's very mouth, that is, his Word (p. 91). So it is, Müller says: God is our life, and we live from him over and above the bread of this world. Otherwise the rich would never die. If we live from God, then the bread of this world will nourish us, but if we do not, no bread will be enough. God provides us with what we need, be it much or little, but it is in God that we must put our hope, not in bread. To hammer down his point Müller quotes a line from the Psalms: "I have been young, and now am old; yet I have not seen the righteous forsaken or his children begging bread" (Ps. 37:25).

Going on to the second temptation, Müller grabs our attention with another of his striking metaphors. Beelzebub, he reminds us, is the lord of the flies. It is the very nature of flies that when they are shooed away from one place, they light on another. Restless spirits never rest (p. 92). So the devil tries again. This time the tempter leads Jesus to the Holy City and stands him on a pinnacle of the Temple. Our preacher elaborates the words of the tempter — "So you are a rabbi; I hear that you know your Bible well; why don't you demonstrate your belief in God's providence by throwing yourself off the pinnacle of the Temple and landing on your feet unharmed? Does not the Bible say, 'He will give his angels charge over you'?" Our preacher points out that again Satan twisted the meaning of Scripture and again Jesus took up the Scriptures to defend himself. Jesus quoted the Bible, Deuteronomy 6:16: "You shall not tempt the Lord your God." We tempt God when we go off and make our own way, leaving behind us the way on which God has called us to follow him. Whoever departs from righteousness departs from the protection of God (p. 95). At some length our preacher expounds the meaning of Psalm 91 as well as the passage Jesus used to counter the devil's foolish suggestion (pp. 96-97). What it all tells us is that instead of dreaming up our own plans for furthering the kingdom, we should stick to God's plans.

The third temptation follows. Satan takes Jesus up on a mountain and shows him all the kingdoms of the earth. This is Satan's favorite temptation, the promise of the mountain of gold, the mountain of fame and glory. It is the attempt to awaken in Jesus pride, the deepest root of sin (p. 99). Müller again develops the biblical imagery by recalling Psalm 121: "I will lift my eyes to the mountains from whence comes my help. My help comes from the Lord who made heaven and earth." It is not to the mountains of gold or the mountains of praise and glory that we should direct our gaze, but to the mountain of God. Satan thinks he can stimulate the Savior's taste for power and glory with this fantasy. All this, Satan suggests to Jesus, can be yours if only you will fall down and worship me. Müller retorts with a powerful series of exclamatory sentences. What foolishness, Müller says; this picture the tempter paints is only a devilish dream! The devil is a liar and has always been a liar! He makes promises to us he cannot fulfill! He makes dreams of things that will never come about (p. 100)!

To worship the devil would be to break the first of the Ten Commandments, and it is pride that leads to this. The first temptation seemed innocent enough, to make bread out of stones. It seemed so reasonable. The second temptation seemed little worse, although it was certainly foolish. But the third temptation was to break the Law in the most obvious way possible. That is the way the devil works: he leads us ever deeper into sin. We must not let him even begin his evil progression.

Once more Jesus takes the sword of the Spirit, the Word of God, to defend himself from demonic attack. He quotes the Bible: "You shall worship the Lord your God and him only shall you serve" (Deut. 6:13). We belong to God and not to the devil, and therefore only him should we worship (p. 101). We should worship neither angels nor saints, but God alone. Not only that, we should be careful to worship God as he has revealed himself in Scripture. This is the responsibility of every human being, both my responsibility and your responsibility, Müller says (p. 102). The very essence of sin is to worship the devil rather than God. Therefore

398

protect yourself from every satanic temptation and in no way give yourself up to his will. Resist him and he will flee from you.

Jesus resisted his tempter at every point, and so that is just what Satan did: he fled. Jesus did not believe his lies; he saw through his crooked fantasies; he played around with none of his tricks. The hour of temptation came to an end and Christ had won the victory. So it is with our temptations: their time comes to its end (p. 103). So the angels came and ministered to Jesus. To help the godly the angels ever stand in service. Therefore, beloved Christian people, be steadfast in the ways of God. Be well assured of the Father's constant care and protection. His protective hand remains with you always, even to that day when we are received into heaven (p. 104). What a conclusion!

C. The Inner Experience of Easter

Müller's sermon for Easter Monday takes up the story of Christ's appearance to the two disciples on the road to Emmaus in Luke 24:13-35. The introduction makes clear the preacher's hermeneutical strategy. He intends to show us what the passage has to say about living the Christian life. As Müller reads it, this passage speaks to the problem so many Christians experience, that of a dormant faith. Jesus is still dead in the hearts of many. Many are spiritually sad because they do not sense the presence of Christ; they do not experience his support and blessing. They do not have the sort of faith that takes hold of Christ nor the sort of love that reaches out to Christ; neither do they have the sort of hope that is grounded in him. And yet, as soon as Jesus blows the breath of Pentecost on their hearts, the little spark of faith that was still there revives. Faith takes hold of the Savior, love begins to stir the heart, and faith regains its firm foundation. This is what we see happening in the story of Christ's appearance to the two disciples on the road to Emmaus (p. 105).

Having delivered this classic *prothema,* our preacher announces the hymn, "Christ ist erstanden," one of the classics of the German Protestant hymnal. We might point out that the tradition in the late Middle Ages was to conclude the *prothema* by having the congregation repeat the Pater Noster or the Ave Maria. This was especially the case when the sermon was held on Sunday afternoon or at some time other than the celebration of Mass on Sunday morning.

Resuming his sermon, Müller reminds his congregation of the words of Jesus in the Gospel of John, that to those who loved him, he would reveal himself (John 14:23). To make his point he gives an example, like the exempla the medieval preaching orders so loved to use. To sinners God is always hidden, like the sun on a cloudy day. God is always there, just as the sun is always there behind the clouds. Even for the godly God is sometimes hidden. The clouds of the cross hide Christ from us time and again, but Christ does not always remain hidden, especially when we seek him earnestly with sighs and tears. In this story we read of two disciples who mourned the death of Christ. Jesus came to them in their sorrow, and yet he came in a hidden form so that they did not recognize him (p. 106).

Müller's sermons are not always divided up into neat headings, but this one is. He announces that he intends to address four points: (1) the friendly companionship of the Lord with his two disciples, (2) his conversation with them, (3) his revelation of himself to them, and (4) the outreach of this revelation (p. 107).

It was now the third day after the sad events of the crucifixion. When Jesus had been with his disciples they had real faith in him, but now they doubted and were leaving all their fond hopes behind. Perhaps they were fleeing Jerusalem for fear of what the authorities might do to those who had been the disciples of Jesus. Perhaps they were simply going back home to take up life where they had left it when they took off to be Jesus' disciples. Müller's sermons are always filled with his intense investigation of the text. He thinks about every detail of the sacred Word. One thing was clear, Müller concludes: their faith had all but died out. Yet we must recognize that although their faith at that moment was very weak, it was nevertheless true faith. This we know because they were still talking about Jesus even if they were discouraged. True faith, even when it is very weak, still holds on to Jesus.

Here, superb artist in the use of words that he was, Müller gives us a beautiful series of short definitions of faith. Faith is the tongue that tastes the sweetness of the Savior. Faith is the ear that hears the song of the Lord. Faith is the hand that reaches out to the priceless treasures of God. Faith is the sense that delights in the incense of holiness (p. 109).

Christ loved these two disciples who were so discouraged, whose faith had dimmed so low. Christ is a spiritual physician who cares for those whose faith is sick. He has a passion that it become well and strong. We can be well assured, Müller insists, that when we are weak in faith we are especially dear to God, just as the sickly child is especially dear to the mother.

Next our preacher directs his attention to the conversation these two disciples had with Jesus. Jesus asks them why they are so disturbed. This should tell us that our Lord indeed wants to hear about our sorrows and anxieties. He indeed is willing to listen to us, for he suffers our pains even as we do (p. 111). Cleopas answers Jesus' question, expressing surprise that he does not know about what had happened in Jerusalem in the last few days. They tell him the whole story about Jesus of Nazareth, who they had hoped was the Messiah. The problem with all the disciples was that they could not completely get beyond a materialistic understanding of the kingdom of God. They somehow imagined that they would be the princes and prelates of an earthly kingdom, but they imagined in vain. They put their hope in the wrong kind of salvation. Oh, dear Christian brothers and sisters, Müller tolls from his pulpit, if you would seek goods from Christ, seek true and eternal goods (p. 114).

The sermon follows every turn of the conversation, commenting on it phrase by phrase, and yet in such a way that the story line is maintained and the dramatic intensity is supported. More and more we become aware of the despair of the disciples. Three days they waited for God to step in and change things, but nothing had happened and they lost their faith. So it often is, Müller comments, that God takes a long time to do things. Three days, three weeks, three years. Yes, God often takes a long time, but the Christian must wait upon the Lord (p. 115).

Cleopas goes on telling his unrecognized Lord that there had been reports of a resurrection from some of the women. This had frightened the disciples. Some had gone to the tomb. It was empty, but they did not find Jesus. Perhaps they thought the women had seen a ghost, Müller suggests. How strange! What should have encouraged the disciples had frightened them. What irony! Did they think they had to have reasonable proof? our preacher asks. But listen: reasonable proof is not what faith needs. Faith needs only the promises of God. Müller sums up his point in a sound theological affirmation. Faith is not based on seeing, nor on feeling, but on God's Word and promise.

Müller begins his third point with a simile. Now that Cleopas had shown his wounds, Christ as a physician begins his treatment (p. 116). Building his simile from the vocabulary of the parable of the Good Samaritan, he tells his congregation that the Great Physician poured into the wound the wine of the prophets and the oil of the gospel. That is the best spiritual medicine. How ingenious Müller is at developing the biblical imagery. But notice, Müller continues: the text says that beginning with Moses and all the prophets, Jesus interpreted to them in all the Scriptures the things concerning himself. Christ opened to his two discouraged disciples the Scriptures of the Old Testament. He told them how it was necessary for Christ to suffer before entering into the kingdom. Müller pounds his pulpit: Listen, fellow Christians, you must not build your faith on any other foundation than the prophetic promises of Scripture. Neither reason, nor experience, nor the opinion of learned teachers can be the basis of faith, but only the prophetic Scriptures. What God says must be true.

Now Christ applies the gentle oil of the gospel. It was necessary for Jesus to suffer and then to enter into his glory. There is a necessity for us to go through suffering, but we are supported in this suffering because we know that Christ has gone before us. We have his counsel and his word. We are supported by Christ's example. Christ's love for us made it necessary for him to suffer for us, so now our love for Christ makes it necessary for us to suffer for him. Paraphrasing Romans 8, Müller repeats the apostle's question. Shall tribulation, or fear, or persecution, or danger, or sword, or anything else separate us from the love of Christ? Certainly not! In all these things we will be supported by the assurance that he first loved us and suffered for us. Finally we are supported by the hope of eternity, knowing that in the end our faith will wear the crown of glory (p. 118).

As they continued speaking, they arrived at Emmaus. Jesus, still unrecognized, appeared to be going farther, but the two disciples urged him to stay with them. Müller comments that all of us come at last to the end of our pilgrimage. We come to the heavenly Emmaus, to the mighty fortress of our God. Here we notice that Müller spiritualizes the text, or perhaps better, devotionalizes it. Emmaus becomes a symbol of heaven. Müller's application is very personal. This is surprising because the division of the text at the beginning of the sermon had announced that his fourth and last point would concern the outreach of Christ's revelation to his two disciples. But in applying this so personally, so devotionally, Müller seems to be bringing out something that really is in the text. This is already a long sermon. Apparently the preacher decided to leave the last part of the text to another time.

It is this devotional application of the text that he wants to develop here. Müller comments, Just as the two disciples urged Jesus to stay with them, so we should urge Jesus to stay with us. Be well assured, our preacher and astute theologian says, that Christ allows our prayers to constrain him just as a father allows the tears of his children to constrain him.

The Son is the very image of the Father. The disciples plead with Jesus and Jesus complies with their prayer. Indeed, the kingdom can be taken by storm. The day is far spent and the night comes on. Our preacher quotes a stanza of a hymn that speaks of the coming of old age and death. Oh, Jesus, stay with us, Müller intercedes for his congregation. The pastor prays the prayer that we all should pray. If it seems that Jesus is starting to leave us, we must hold on to him with our prayers, enter the inn, sit down at the table and break bread together, share whatever we have with whoever is there, and thank God for the grace he has given us in Christ (p. 119).

D. The Outpouring of the Holy Spirit

Müller's sermon for Pentecost interprets the opening verses of Acts 2. The preacher announces a six-point sermon, but, as we observed above, his division of the text is often rather perfunctory. Müller follows the homiletical forms that were popular in his day, but he is hardly a slave to convention. He is much more apt simply to follow the text, commenting as he goes along.

Taking up the opening words of the passage, "When the fifty days of Pentecost had been fulfilled," Müller comments that the Holy Spirit was not given immediately after the ascension, but only when the fifty days had been fulfilled. The time which God appointed must come before he fulfills his promises. The time God had appointed was very significant. It was the feast of Pentecost, the memorial of God's gift of the Law. That was the significant time for the giving of the Spirit (p. 120).

Our preacher goes on to the next phrase, "They came together in one house." The Holy Spirit was given to them not while each Christian was off somewhere alone, but when they were assembled together. Müller comes up with another group of similes. When a father gives food to his children, he gathers them around his table. He does not go around taking the food to each one in his own room (p. 121). So should the reading and preaching of the Word be in public worship. Preaching should take place in the assembly of the faithful. In the preaching of grace God sets the table. Whoever wants to hear the Word sits down at the table. If there is bitterness in our hearts, however, then the bond of fellowship is broken. We cannot have Christian worship if there is no love between the members of the congregation. We, then, become wedding guests inappropriately dressed and are ushered out, just as in the parable of the wedding feast. Those who would receive the Holy Spirit must be careful to respect the bond of peace. Pride, envy, and bitterness are all the work of the devil trying the work of the Spirit. The Spirit comes to the humble soul, not to those who are proud. It is the lowly heart in which the Holy Spirit wishes to dwell.

The passage continues, telling us that the apostles were gathered in expectation. They did not idly come together just to while away the hours. They came together waiting on the Lord to fulfill his promises. They devoted themselves to prayer and supplication. It is through God's Word that the Spirit comes. On that we have often insisted, but it is also through prayer. We find in the Gospel that Jesus promised that the Father would give the Holy Spirit to those who ask him (Luke 11:13). As one inhales air, so supplication inhales the Spirit. As a breath of fresh air refreshes us body and soul, so breathing in the Spirit opens our hearts to heaven (p. 122).

Next, the Bible tells us that the Spirit came with the sound of a gust of wind. Here again Müller elaborates on the biblical imagery. The Holy Spirit, he tells us, is like the powerful wind that drives the chariots of God, as we find it in Psalm 104. To Nicodemus Jesus spoke of the Holy Spirit as wind. The wind blows where it wills and indeed you hear the sound of it, but you do not know where it comes from or where it goes (John 3:8). The Spirit works free, Müller insists. No one can forbid him; no one can restrain him. When the Spirit moves, the Spirit moves, but when it does not move, we can only wait. Like sailors who often must wait weeks in port for a favorable wind to set their sails, so Christians must wait for the moving of the Spirit. As the crippled waited by the pool of Bethesda for an angel to move the waters, so you, my heart, must wait for a little hour. But the Christian waits in patience, for only God knows what hour is best (p. 123).

But as the Spirit is free, our preacher continues, so is the Spirit sensitive. The Spirit is compassionate and gentle. The mighty wind hears our gentlest sighs. The presence of the Holy Spirit is very real in the Christian even if we do not recognize his work, even if we do not realize that it is he who is at work within us. We sigh for the Spirit, wishing that we might have certainty and victory in the Christian life, not realizing that the sigh for the Spirit is also a sigh of the Spirit. The apostle Paul tells us that it is the Spirit himself who cries out within us, Abba, Father (Rom. 8:15). The quickening of the Spirit is a life-giving power. The Spirit is a comforter enlivening our spirits even though we be filled with fear. Again a masterful simile makes his meaning vivid. As the wind drives away the storm clouds, making the heavens clear and bright, so the Holy Spirit drives away the storms of sin and suffering in our hearts and reveals the Sun of righteousness, our Lord Jesus Christ, who again begins to shine in our hearts (p. 124).

The other sign of the outpouring of the Spirit on the apostles on the Day of Pentecost is fire. We remember that the Pentecost of the Old Testament was accompanied by the same sign. Although the Law was given to Moses on Mount Sinai with frightening fire, the fire that accompanied the giving of the Spirit was a loving flame, flickering above the heads of the apostles. For we find in Romans that the love of God is poured out upon our hearts through the Holy Spirit which has been given to us (Rom. 5:5). While the Law proclaims anger, the gospel proclaims grace. The one frightens and bowls over, the other encourages and lifts up. Furthermore, we notice that the means by which the Spirit works is the Word of God. Is the Word of God not a fire? Where it is preached in the Spirit, there it enters into the heart. So then we say, like the two disciples at Emmaus, did not our hearts burn within us when the risen Christ spoke to us?

Müller sees the work of the Holy Spirit as a sort of irresistible grace. No one, he tells us, can resist the fire of the Holy Spirit; no one dare try to keep it from burning. To do so would be to attempt to quench the Spirit. No one dare hinder the effect of the Spirit in himself, lest he dampen the spark of the Spirit and destroy the work of God. The fire of the Spirit brings to ashes everything that would stand against his sanctifying inspiration, for what he has established he will not let fall. Fire rages against the outrages of sin. Fire is a fighter, fighting against the flesh. It destroys the works of the flesh. Fighting against the world, the Spirit overcomes the world. Fighting against the devil, he puts the devil to flight. Where he is, there is always a struggle, for he keeps the enemy heartily at bay (p. 125).

No translation can do justice to Müller's magnificent use of words. The variety of his vocabulary, his alliterations, his rhythms, and his balanced phrases all reveal him to be a master of the use of his native language. How often we find great preachers to be great linguists! The linguistic genius of this preacher is used to develop the biblical imagery, to sharpen the biblical vocabulary, and to define the biblical concepts. In its essence it helps us to understand Scripture by means of Scripture.

405

He has more to say on how fire is a sign of the Spirit. Fire is a sign of the Spirit because it converts whatever it touches. When we put iron into the fire, what was by nature cold, hard, dark, and heavy becomes soft, glowing, and warm. The Spirit changes us through the Word and makes us like the Spirit himself. He gives our lives a new sense and a new disposition, a new way of life. If we were carnal he makes us spiritual; if we were unholy he makes us holy. Out of the lion he makes a lamb; out of the snake he makes a dove. Those who in the beginning were hard and brittle like iron, he warms so that they are warm and soft like wax (p. 125). Our hearts are hard by nature; they are like stone. They are not good for very much when they are like that. They are so resistant and insensitive. But when God's Spirit warms our heart through his Word, then the image of God, the very form of Christ, is impressed upon us and we are sealed by the Spirit (p. 126).

Our preacher has given a good part of his sermon to developing the idea of the Holy Spirit. This is an important biblical concept. It was much misunderstood in the seventeenth century, even as it was in the ancient world of Greek and Roman philosophy in which the apostles first began to minister in the Spirit. The Christian preacher has the same problem today. It is hard to talk about the Holy Spirit in a world where "spirit" means so many things. That is why Müller is so careful to develop the biblical vocabulary and define the biblical concept.

Having spent so long drawing out the meaning of the signs of wind and fire that were given at Pentecost, our preacher picks up his text again where the disciples began to preach. It was as though the preaching were a trumpet blast which called together an assembly. The amazing thing was that all who came together heard the preaching each in his native language. Our preacher develops this at length, again speaking of the irresistibility of the work of the Holy Spirit (p. 129). The miracle of tongues astounded the crowd, but it did not convert them. Only when Peter preached to them were they converted. Amazement may be a step to conversion, but it is not in itself enough. Some heard with joy but others ridiculed it all, saying they were all filled with wine. The preacher of the gospel must be patient, our preacher advises. The children of this world will always ridicule the Word of God. Not everyone is going to accept the gospel. This should not disturb us. When we are filled with the Spirit the world may well mistake it for drunkenness, but the truth is, we are filled with the Spirit.

With this the sermon comes to its conclusion. Müller gives us an

406

audacious simile. Those who are filled with the wine of this world sing and dance; those who are filled with the wine of the Spirit sing and dance as well, but it is a heavenly dancing and a heavenly singing. It is because, although we are on earth, we drink the wine of heaven.[21] The Spirit as a wine steward has taken us into the wine cellar and given us here below a taste of what in heaven we will drink to the full (p. 130).

We conclude with a few remarks on these sermons as a whole. First is an observation on the beauty of their Protestant plain style. They were preached in the age of the baroque, and yet they are hardly baroque. These sermons were preached when Rembrandt was painting his simple, profound portraits with all their brooding shadows and all their sparkling lights. Dietrich Buxtehude was at the keyboard of his ponderous organ at the Marienkirche in Lübeck, joyously thundering out his preludes and fugues. What we have here is no less profound, no less majestic, no less joyful. They are superb works of art, the art of sacred oratory. The rhetoric is plain and simple. It is not the high oratory of Bossuet, Müller's contemporary, who preached before Louis XIV. It is a much more direct oratory which seeks no glory in itself but only the glory of the Word of God. Protestant plain style is art, too, in its simple, unassuming way. In the sermons of Müller, as in so many of the sermons of Protestant orthodoxy, it is superb art.

We cannot help but recognize in Müller's sermons true classics of Christian preaching. When he preached these sermons, Protestantism had shaped the devotion of a good part of Germany for a century and a half. It had elaborated its theology; it had deepened its devotional life. It had trained its pastors to study the Scriptures with an astounding thoroughness and depth, but it had also trained its congregations to read the Bible carefully and thoughtfully. Sermons like these can be preached only by a preacher who has lived with his Bible for long years, but it is just as true that they can be heard only by a congregation which knows the Bible almost as well. It takes a mature piety to listen to sermons like these. It is a tribute to orthodox Lutheranism that it had produced congregations like these. Today we can all profit from these sermons of classic Protestant orthodoxy. Somehow we are going to have to learn to preach like this

21. The eucharistic theme would have been particularly important for a Pentecost sermon, because more than likely it was followed by the Pentecost Communion service. Interestingly enough, we find the same eucharistic imagery in a Communion sermon by the Dutch preacher who was Müller's contemporary, Jodocus van Lodenstein, as we will see in a subsequent chapter.

again. Somehow we have to learn to listen to the Word of God with the same devotion. These sermons are as rich today as they were in the seventeenth century. They are even worth the eyestrain of reading them in that old-fashioned German Gothic print. These sermons are true classics. They will mean as much in San Juan Capistrano, California, as they did in the Hanseatic port of Rostock when Bach was a baby.

CHAPTER VI

The Flowering of Protestant Orthodoxy in France

French-speaking Protestantism has always had a character all its own.[1] It sprang from its own sources and developed through its own struggles. The same was true of English-speaking Protestantism. It, too, had its own wellsprings. Protestantism has never been essentially German any more than it is essentially English or American. To be sure, Luther played a fundamental role, but Protestantism was much bigger than the work of a single star Reformer. Luther was a theological genius. He was a Christian leader of amazing insight and balance, but he was not the founder of Protestantism. Protestantism also has some very deep French roots. It was a movement that welled up from the foundations of Christian faith. It was a movement of international proportions. Protestantism has never seen itself as being monolithic; it is neither Greek nor Roman, black nor white, Mediterranean nor Nordic, Anglo nor Latino. Protestantism delights in the variety of its expressions. If the great French Catholic polemicist Jacques-Bénigne Bossuet reproached Protestantism with his famous *Histoire des variations des églises protestantes,* Protestantism itself delights in its variations.

---

1. On French Protestantism in general, see the following: Janet Glenn Gray, *The French Huguenots: Anatomy of Courage* (Grand Rapids: Baker Book House, 1981); Émile G. Leonard, *Histoire générale du protestantisme,* 3 vols. (Paris: Presses universitaires de France, 1961-64); Jacques Pannier, *L'Église réformée de Paris sous Henri IV* (Paris: H. Champion, 1911); and George A. Rothrock, *The Huguenots: A Biography of a Minority* (Chicago: Nelson-Hall, 1979).

From the time of the promulgation of the Edict of Nantes in 1598 until its revocation in 1685, almost a century, French Protestantism enjoyed a measure of toleration. It flourished even if it was a minority. Large congregations were established, especially in the south, where such cities as Nîmes, Montpellier, Uzès, and Montauban took on a distinctly Protestant character.

Protestantism became the faith of the rising French middle class. It was especially strong in the growing textile, chemical, and printing industries. Many professional people embraced it. There was a strong Protestant contingent in the military. When the Edict of Nantes was revoked, hundreds of thousands of these people went into exile, taking their industrial skills and professional training with them. This decimated the French middle class, yet for most of the seventeenth century the Protestants of France were a vigorous, disciplined, and cultured people supported by a well-trained and vigorous ministry. French Protestant preaching achieved a high level of excellence during the seventeenth century.[2]

The Reformed Church of France had its own theological schools. The most important were the academy of Saumur in the west of France and Sedan in the north. In the south there were academies at Montauban and Nîmes.[3] These seminaries provided the training in the biblical languages, in the interpretation of Scripture, and in systematic theology which classical Protestantism considered essential to learned preaching. Ministers were expected to live godly, moral lives, but they were also expected to be men of learning. To be a minister of the Word presupposed a rigorous, disciplined study of the Word.

There was a depth to French Protestantism which was very rational and very moral. French Protestants demanded serious, well-thought-out preaching. Being a minority in a frequently hostile society gave them maturity. Their faith was deep and sincere; it was not taken lightly. Preaching was an earnest matter, a matter which might cost one one's life.

Protestant orthodoxy as it flourished in France in the seventeenth century was a profoundly held orthodoxy. It was solid, and yet it was neither conformist nor absolutist. It was classic.[4] Seventeenth-century French

2. Françoise Chevalier, *Prêcher sous l'Édit de Nantes, la prédication réformée au XVIIe siècle en France* (Geneva: Labor et Fides, 1994).

3. Chevalier, *Prêcher sous l'Édit de Nantes*, p. 39.

4. The title of the study of Pierre du Moulin given us by Lucien Rimbault suggests the whole air of French Protestantism: Lucien Rimbault, *Pierre du Moulin, 1568-1658, un pasteur classique à l'âge classique* (Paris: J. Vrin, 1966).

Protestantism had a witness to give. Far from being a merely negative critique of medieval Christianity, it had a very positive message. It preached the grace of God in Jesus Christ and offered a new life to those who would receive that grace. One senses the balance between the moral, the devotional, and the intellectual dimensions of Christian experience as one reads the sermons of the Huguenots. The beauty of their witness was its earnestness, its simplicity, and its clarity. It left Montaigne and Molière far behind.

I. Pierre du Moulin (1568-1658)

Pierre du Moulin was born at the height of the Wars of Religion.[5] His father, Joachim, was one of those courageous young Protestant pastors who preached the gospel where he could, but apparently at that time, at least, had no settled charge. Pierre was born at Sedan, which in those early days served as a center of Protestant missionary activity. When he was four years old the Massacre of Saint Bartholomew's Day chased the du Moulin family from their lodgings. Little Pierre barely escaped with his life, although he lost his mother due to the rigors of the event. After things settled down, Sedan was a fairly safe place for Protestants. Even at that early date it had a Protestant school, and it was there that du Moulin received his education.

At the age of twenty he became the tutor of the young earl of Rutland and accompanied him to the University of Cambridge in England; this gave du Moulin the opportunity to study in that thoroughly Protestant university. William Perkins was at the height of his career when he studied there, as was William Whitaker; both professors were strongly Calvinist in their theology. Over time an opportunity to teach Greek at Leiden opened up, and du Moulin got his foot on the academic ladder, teaching not only Greek but logic as well. Leiden was also a center of Calvinist teaching at the time, and it was there, apparently, that he became a firm opponent of Arminianism. By the time he was thirty, he had received a thoroughly cosmopolitan education.

At the threshold of the seventeenth century he received a call to join the pastoral staff of the Reformed Church of Paris. On returning to France he spent a few days with his sister, whose husband was pastor at

---

5. On Pierre du Moulin, see Brian G. Armstrong, *Pierre du Moulin (1568-1658)* (Geneva: Droz, 1997), and Rimbault, *Pierre du Moulin, 1568-1658, un pasteur classique à l'âge classique.*

Rouen, and a somewhat longer time at Orléans with his father, who by this time was a settled pastor. According to the terms of the Edict of Nantes, which had just been granted by Henry IV, the Protestants were allowed churches in a number of cities throughout the kingdom, but not within the walls of the city of Paris. A Protestant church was built at Charenton, up the Seine from the city. When I was a student in Paris, Charenton was at the end of the subway line. In the seventeenth century it must have been a good five miles out of town. There was an important exception to the proscription against Protestant churches inside Paris, however, and that was the private chapel of Catherine de Bourbon, the sister of the king. Sometimes as many as fifteen hundred people would join the royal princess for Protestant worship at the Louvre. Maintaining pastoral services for Catherine was a major ministry of the Reformed Church of Paris, and recognizing du Moulin's extraordinary gifts, the other pastors gave him particular responsibility for that ministry.

Du Moulin's preaching ministry, by the very nature of the religious situation of the day, often involved a disproportionate amount of polemic. It could hardly be otherwise. Catherine was under heavy pressure to convert to Catholicism, and at one point was manipulated into hearing a sermon by Père Coton, one of the leading Jesuit polemicists of the day.[6] The royal lady had a mind of her own, however. She had du Moulin, her Protestant chaplain, seated in the next room so that he could hear the sermon unobserved. Coton's sermon that morning was on the Good Samaritan. As Coton interpreted it, the parable made clear the errors of Protestantism. That afternoon, then, du Moulin was invited to preach on the same passage of Scripture. Neither sermon has come down to us, but the story gives a candid picture of at least one aspect of the ministry of the Word as exercised in Paris by Pierre du Moulin.[7]

Responding to the attacks of the Catholic pulpit had to have its place. When another Jesuit, Père Jean Arnoux, in the course of preaching before the court, attacked Calvin, the leading French Protestant theologian, claiming he made God the author of sin, it was on du Moulin's shoulders to respond to this attack. He took to the pen, producing his famous work, *Bouclier de la foy*,[8] but we can also be sure he took to the pul-

---

6. On the preaching ministry of Father Coton, see chap. II above.
7. Rimbault, *Pierre du Moulin*, pp. 31ff.
8. Pierre du Moulin, *Bouclier de la foy, ou défense de la confession de la foi des églises réformées de France contre les objections du Sr. Jehan Arnoux* (Charenton, 1618).

pit as well.[9] What amazes us is that Huguenot preaching did not get completely mired down in controversy. It seems in fact to have been amazingly free from theological argumentation.[10]

For twenty years du Moulin provided the Protestants of Paris with quality leadership, both in his literary output and in his preaching. While Henry IV was sincerely tolerant, his successor, Louis XIII, was not. Supported by his prime minister, the famous Cardinal Richelieu, Louis became more and more determined to rid France of Protestantism. Slowly he began to erode the provisions of the Edict of Nantes and harass the Huguenots. Part of this harassment was to chase du Moulin from Paris. At the age of fifty-five, du Moulin returned to Sedan, his native city, where he became director of the theological academy and preacher in the church of Sedan. Today Sedan is nine miles south of the Belgian border, but at that time it was just outside the borders of the kingdom of France, although clearly in French-speaking territory. It was French country even if it was not under the control of Louis XIII. Du Moulin lived to a great age, continuing his ministry in Sedan for some thirty-seven years.

A large collection of his sermons has come down to us. They were published in Geneva between 1645 and 1654.[11] The nature of the collection does not permit us to determine when they were preached or in what context. The evidence does not suggest that they were taken either from different *lectio continua* series or from the lectionary. They are simply separate, individual sermons. On the other hand, we do have special sermons for fast days and series of preparatory sermons.[12]

The sermons we have take a single verse of Scripture and, after expounding the text, use it as the basis of an exhortation to the living of the Christian life. Scripture is to be explained in terms of the biblical revelation. It does not need to be understood in terms of classical philosophy or the intellectual theories that might be currently popular. All of this was much the same as the typical Protestant plain-style preaching of the day.

Lucien Rimbault, in his study of du Moulin's pastoral ministry, tells us that his goal was the proclamation of the truth in all its power and

9. Rimbault, *Pierre du Moulin*, pp. 80-85.

10. Chevalier, *Prêcher sous l'Édit de Nantes*, pp. 193-211.

11. Pierre du Moulin, *Première à dixième décade*, 10 vols. (Geneva, 1641-54).

12. Pierre du Moulin, *Préparation à la Sainte Cène* and *Prière et méditation de l'âme fidèle, sur l'affliction présente de l'Église ensemble les prières du matin et du soir,* in Pierre du Moulin, *Saintes prières plus divers traittez* (Geneva: Chouët, 1622).

beauty. Du Moulin gives us a model of the preaching of Protestant orthodoxy. There is nothing dogmatic or proud about it. There is no pretentious display of learning. Du Moulin had no interest in copying the high rhetoric so popular in the Catholic pulpit of his time. Rimbault quotes a passage from one of his sermons which well sums up our preacher's purpose. Preaching, du Moulin tells us, should present the truth with simplicity, without any kind of affectation. What we have been commissioned by God to do is preach his Word for the salvation of souls. God is honored in the preaching of the gospel with soundness and simplicity, and with a profound clarity. True preaching is food for the soul which not only tastes good but is easily digested as well.[13] Preaching is worship because it honors God, it performs a service he has called us to perform, and it nourishes God's people to his honor and glory.

Pierre du Moulin was the most famous French Protestant preacher of his day, but it is one of his successors, Jean Daillé, who gives us the clearest picture of seventeenth-century Huguenot preaching. Let us turn now to the preaching ministry of Jean Daillé.

II. Jean Daillé (1594-1670)

For almost fifty years Jean Daillé served the Protestants of Paris as minister of the Word. His life spanned the great age of French Protestantism.[14] He was born just four years before Henry IV brought an end to the devastating Wars of Religion by embracing Roman Catholicism and granting religious toleration to the Huguenots in the famous Edict of Nantes. He died only fifteen years before that great age came to an end with Louis XIV's infamous revocation of the same edict in 1685. Daillé was born in Châtellerault. He studied at the University of Poitiers and then at the Reformed Theological College at Saumur. For several years he was tutor to the grandchildren of Philippe du Plessis-Mornay, traveling with

---

13. Rimbault, *Pierre du Moulin*, p. 142.

14. For biographical material on Daillé, see the following: Jean Daillé (Son), *Abrégé de la vie de Mr. Daillé,* which appeared with Jean Daillé (Father), *Les deux derniers sermons de Mr. Daillé* (Geneva: Iean Ant. & Samuel de Tournes, 1671); Eugène Haag, *La France protestante,* 9 vols. (Geneva: J. Cherbuliez, 1846-59), 4:180-86; Eugène Haag and Émile Haag, *La France protestante,* 6 vols. (Paris: Sandoz et Fischbacher, 1877-88), 5:23-38; and Alexandre Vinet, *Histoire de la prédication parmi les réformés de France au dix-septième siècle* (Paris: Chez les éditeurs, rue de Rivoli, 1860).

them both in Italy and in England. When he was called to be pastor of the Reformed Church of Paris in 1626, the church was required, according to the Edict of Nantes, to hold its services outside the walls of Paris. The congregation that gathered at Charenton was large, and required the services of as many as five or six ministers. Daillé shared his ministry with such eminent preachers as Michel Le Faucheur, Jean Mestrezat, and Jean Claude.

The congregation Daillé served was a tolerated minority. The toleration, however, was not stable. Particularly under the reign of Louis XIV, it was neither gladly given nor wholeheartedly observed. Theological apologetic was a constant necessity. It is hardly surprising, then, that Daillé's preaching often treats the points of controversy between Catholics and Protestants, and yet, considering the situation, such matters do not claim a disproportionate amount of his attention.[15] One is in fact impressed by his moderation. His sermons lack bitterness and contain very little that might be called invective. The Protestant orthodoxy of Daillé is solid but not heavy. It is clear and precise but not pedantic. It is simple and straightforward rather than complex, intricate, or exhaustive. Daillé belongs to the period of Protestant scholasticism, and yet his sermons are fresh. They are free from any kind of dry, abstract intellectualism which, unhappily, one associates with the term "Protestant scholasticism."

Although Daillé lived in the century of the baroque, his sermons bear the marks of the classical. One finds in them the beauty of the Protestant plain style. His language is simple and clear. He knows how to use good imagery. He uses a variety of rhetorical devices, but he uses them with an admirable restraint. There is no straining after effect, no pompous use of learning or pretentious display of culture.[16]

Daillé has left us a considerable legacy of sermons. Some twenty volumes of his sermons have been published. Several of these have gone through a number of editions, indicating that they were quite popular among French-speaking Protestants of the period. We find, for example, series of *lectio continua* sermons on Philippians, Colossians, and I and II Timothy and Titus. We find a volume of his sermons for the feasts of Christmas, Good Friday, Easter, Ascension, and Pentecost. There is a volume for the celebration of Communion and series of sermons on Hebrews 12, I Corinthians 10, and John 3. We have a number of his occa-

15. Chevalier, *Prêcher sous l'Édit de Nantes*, pp. 193-211.
16. Chevalier, *Prêcher sous l'Édit de Nantes*, pp. 47-64.

sional sermons and a series of his catechetical sermons. The large number of sermons he published gives us an opportunity to get a much broader picture of his preaching ministry than we can get from any of his contemporaries who were equally well received as preachers but far better known as theologians or church leaders. His sermons have been preserved in their original context, unlike those of du Moulin. We will give considerable attention to Daillé, not only because of the quality of his preaching ministry, but also because he gives about as broad a picture of how a minister in the age of Protestant orthodoxy did actually preach as we have been able to find.[17] The picture he gives us is indeed very attractive.

A. Evangelistic Preaching

Daillé's approach to evangelistic preaching was very simple. He preached expository sermons on passages of Scripture which had to do with repentance, conversion, and growth in the Christian life. He deserves to be recognized as an evangelistic preacher, and we have three series of sermons in which his evangelistic concern is particularly obvious. One is on I Corinthians 10, in which the apostle Paul calls the Corinthians to repentance for becoming involved in pagan idolatry. The series makes a point of the completeness of the conversion which is demanded of us. Another series is on Hebrews 12. This chapter is also a call to repentance, but it is addressed to those who have grown weary in their witness. It is a call to rededicate one's life to Christ.

In the third of these evangelistic series, ten sermons on the discourse of Jesus with Nicodemus in John 3, where Jesus insists that Nicodemus must be born from above, we see Daillé very clearly performing the work of an evangelist.[18] He uses the story of Nicodemus, as so many evangelists have, to show us how one experiences conversion. As he presents it, Jesus opened up to Nicodemus the revelation of God's redemptive love in his being sent into the world by his Father and his sacrifice on the cross. Jesus

17. Happily, Speer Library at Princeton Theological Seminary preserves a very rich collection of Daillé's works, giving me the opportunity to study his preaching much more thoroughly than any of the other preachers of Protestant orthodoxy, either in France, the Netherlands, or Germany.

18. The series was preached when Daillé was over seventy years old, which perhaps explains why he took more than a year to complete it. It may well have been a series he had often preached before.

came not to condemn Nicodemus but as light into the world, so that Nicodemus might believe in him and thereby inherit eternal life. Jesus taught Nicodemus the mystery of redemption. Nicodemus did not have a conversion experience at that point. Jesus, as the sower in his parable, had sown the Word and the Word would take a while to germinate, take root, grow up, and finally produce fruit. It would only be after Jesus had been lifted up on the cross, as the brazen serpent had been lifted up in the wilderness, that Nicodemus would come to claim the body of Christ. That is the way it goes with the sowing of seed. One does not have to be anxious about how long it takes for the seed to grow; one just has to sow it, and then water it, and God does the rest. Daillé's approach to evangelism is characterized by his confidence that the Word of God has power to convert those who hear it, because it is the Word of God. The simple exposition of Scripture is in itself evangelistic.

The first sermon in the series begins with a well-conceived exordium introducing the three verses Daillé intends to treat.[19] He recalls the words of Jesus on how difficult it is for the rich to enter the kingdom of heaven. But it is just as difficult, he continues, for those who have attained high positions in society and enjoy the approval of the world. They, too, have a hard time entering the kingdom. The first three verses of John 3 provide a good example of a man who was hindered from entering the kingdom because of his position of high respect in Jewish society. Nicodemus was a doctor of the Law, one of the leaders of the Jewish community. Yet Jesus had just the right word for him. And although Nicodemus returned home that night in the same state as he had come, interested but perplexed, the word of Jesus did have its effect and finally bore its fruit at just the time when the offense of the cross was most obvious. As we read later in the Gospel, Nicodemus finally came out into the light and claimed the body of Jesus. Having given us this introduction, Daillé divides the text into two parts. First he wants to look at the portrait John's Gospel gives of Nicodemus, then he wants to listen to the word Jesus has for him (p. 4).

The text tells us that Nicodemus was a Pharisee. Drawing on other passages of the New Testament, Daillé explains what a Pharisee was in the time of Jesus. Our preacher relates what Josephus has to say about the various Jewish sects and parties of the time (p. 5). He also relates these par-

---

19. Jean Daillé, *Explication du chapitre troisième de l'evangile selon saint Jean* (Geneva: J. Ant. et S. de Tornes, 1686). Page references in the text are to this volume.

ties to various developments in the Jewish culture of his own day in Germany, Constantinople, and Cairo (p. 7). Then he explains what the text means when it tells us Nicodemus was a ruler of the Jews. Continuing his study of the text, our preacher interprets the fact that Nicodemus comes to Jesus at night. This was no doubt because, although he had been attracted to Jesus by the signs he had performed, he was afraid of offending his colleagues. This is put in the context of other New Testament passages which tell us of leading Jews who had come to believe in Jesus but hesitated to become his disciples (pp. 12ff.). Nicodemus was not willing to admit to his tentative faith in public. He had only the first beginnings of faith. He recognized that Jesus was sent from God but did not yet understand that he was the Son of God. At this point Daillé quotes John Chrysostom's sermon on this passage to the same effect (p. 18).

Daillé is fully aware that some of his listeners were in much the same situation as Nicodemus. They sensed the rightness of the claims of the Reformation but hesitated to embrace it openly. We notice how gently our preacher deals with the problem. He addresses Nicodemus, "Are you embarrassed to speak with a prophet sent from God? Are you afraid to speak the truth in public?" (p. 19). Our preacher makes the point that Jesus in his infinite love will not break the bruised reed (Matt. 12:20) (p. 20). Here we see an example of Daillé's restraint and pastoral sensitivity.

Our sermon now comes to its second point, the exposition of the word Jesus spoke to Nicodemus, "Truly, truly, I say to you, unless one is born anew, he cannot see the kingdom of God" (John 3:3). As Daillé understands it, this is a word of healing spoken by Jesus to heal the weakness of his disciple's faith. Grotius, the Dutch Arminian New Testament scholar, suggested that Nicodemus must have asked Jesus how he might be saved. Otherwise Jesus' words are not appropriate. Daillé does not think this suggestion is justified, even if from an Arminian point of view it is understandable. As he sees it, Jesus has responded not so much to the words of Nicodemus as to the need of Nicodemus (p. 21). Our preacher goes on to explain the words of Jesus phrase by phrase. To see the kingdom of God means to become a part of the Church of Christ (pp. 25-27). It is to enjoy the benefits of new life in Christ and to inherit eternal life (pp. 28ff.). To explain the phrase "born anew," Daillé speaks of various rites of regeneration in the paganism of antiquity as well as in the Jewish traditions of that period. Even more clearly the new birth is explained from a number of passages of the apostle Paul. To be reborn is to die to sin and be born into the life of the new creation. For Nicodemus, being a well-instructed Jew, it was important to understand that he could not be saved simply because he was born a son of Abraham. He needed to be reborn and reformed into a new man. This sermon, as the other sermons in the series, is clearly an expository sermon.

With this Daillé begins his application. It is not enough simply to recognize the errors of the Jews or even of those who trust in their allegiance to the Roman Church. Every human being, regardless of his birth, his quality, or his condition, is addressed here by the Savior (p. 38). One cannot remain in sin and enter the kingdom (p. 39). One must be born anew. Let us therefore put aside the works of the flesh and devote ourselves to innocence and purity of life, Daillé says. Let us truly repent by applying ourselves to prayer, to good works, and to the study of Scripture. If we do this, God will not be slow in reaching out to us and renewing us in the image of his Son. We shall see the blessed kingdom and enjoy his grace in this life and his glory in the life to come (p. 42). Here we have the first in a series of evangelistic sermons. It is begun with a call to repentance.

The second sermon takes up verses 4 and 5: "Nicodemus said to him, 'How can a man be born when he is old? Can he enter a second time into his mother's womb and be born?' Jesus answered, 'Truly, truly, I say to you, unless one is born of water and the Spirit, he cannot enter the kingdom of God.'" The sermon begins with a marvelous simile for Nicodemus's confusion about Jesus' demand that he repent. Just as the earth before the rising sun sends up mists to protect itself from the heat of the sun, so now Nicodemus beclouds the issue by taking Jesus literally that he must enter a second time into his mother's womb (p. 43). But for Daillé, orthodox as he was, grace is irresistible. Just as the sun keeps on shining until the mists of morning are cleared away, so Jesus keeps on opening up the Word of life to Nicodemus (p. 45). Having with this simile put the two verses he wants to treat so clearly in light, Daillé speaks at length of the folly of taking things literally which are meant to be taken spiritually. This is particularly the case when we come to speak of the sacraments. It is the spiritual reality behind the outward signs of the sacraments which is essential to our salvation. In this particular passage, Jesus makes clear to Nicodemus the importance of the cleansing and vivifying work of the Holy Spirit in our hearts (p. 70). The Holy Spirit, working within us, purifies our hearts and enlivens us by nourishing us so that we grow in grace and develop the gifts of the Spirit (p. 80). Baptism is the sign of this washing away of sin and this watering which enlivens us; the inner working of the Holy Spirit signified by the sign of baptism saves us. Baptism, as Daillé evidently understands it, is the outward sign of what happens to us in evangelism.

The third sermon develops at even greater length the doctrine of the Holy Spirit. Daillé believes such emphasis on this doctrine is necessary because the Holy Spirit is the true evangelist. The fourth sermon treats the incredulity of Nicodemus. In spite of the advantages of being a teacher in Israel, Nicodemus was still a man of the flesh, and without turning to Christ in humility, he could not understand the things of God (p. 136). What God teaches, whether it be in the person of Jesus or in Scripture, is spiritual. It must be understood spiritually. We must not be surprised therefore if the world does not understand it. All of us as Christians must guard against the same sort of incredulity Nicodemus had (p. 170). We must all devote ourselves to the truth, Daillé admonishes his congregation; even today we are taught from God's own mouth. We hear the reading and preaching of his Word. God indeed speaks to us today. His Word, enthroned in the Scriptures, even now presides over our lives. There in Scripture he is seated, and from there, even in our own day, he speaks to his disciples (p. 170). What we need if we are to be disciples of Jesus is to approach his Word in humility, and to hear it with a simple and sincere faith (p. 172).

The fifth sermon takes as its text, "If I have told you earthly things and you do not believe, how can you believe if I tell you heavenly things? No one has ascended into heaven but he who descended from heaven, the Son of man" (John 3:12-13).[20] Daillé begins his sermon by telling us that our Lord Jesus Christ is not only the teacher of wisdom, but the wisdom itself. Our preacher knows how to put this in a few pithy and well-pointed sentences. Jesus is himself what he teaches; he is the subject of his magisterial discourse; he is the new life he proclaims. In Christ is the way, the truth, and the life (p. 173). Following his usual pattern, Daillé ends his introduction with a division of the text. Two thoughts are to be found in the text: the distinction between earthly wisdom and heavenly wisdom, and a clear teaching about the heavenly origin and eternal subsistence of Christ (p. 176). That Daillé, as other *lectio continua* preachers, should take up two, three, or even four subjects in the course of his exposition is, we have often seen, quite normal.

Even if Nicodemus has not understood everything immediately,

20. An RSV marginal note adds "who is in heaven" to the end of the quotation.

Daillé points out, Jesus nevertheless speaks to him of heavenly things. Jesus does this that the faith of Nicodemus might blossom (p. 184). Here we see something very significant about the evangelistic technique. If Jesus expounds the essential mysteries of the Christian faith to a puzzled Nicodemus so that his faith might blossom, Daillé begins to explain the cardinal doctrines of the Christian faith to his congregation so that their faith might blossom. First Daillé takes up the doctrine of the incarnation. Jesus explains to Nicodemus that the Messiah teaches heavenly wisdom because of his heavenly origin. None of the prophets who had gone before had ascended to heaven; the Son of man, on the other hand, speaks with authority of heavenly things because he is heavenly. Daillé treats at length the expression "Son of man." It is both a title for the Messiah and a claim that the Messiah is true man (pp. 188ff.). Then he takes up the phrase "who has descended from heaven." This refers to the birth of Christ by the Blessed Virgin Mary. The Messiah is true man and true God; he is of the seed of David, born of woman, and yet descended from heaven (p. 190). There have been those who find difficulties with the interpretation of this verse. Some have read out of it two ascensions. At this point Daillé attacks the interpretation of Hugo Grotius, who thinks this passage is to be taken figuratively and that it says nothing of Christ's heavenly origins, but rather tells us only that Christ acquired knowledge of divine things. Daillé much prefers the interpretation of the Spanish Jesuit New Testament scholar Juan Maldonado, who understood this verse to mean that at the time of the incarnation there was an ascension of human nature parallel to the descent of the divine nature. This interpretation, Daillé tells his congregation, is perfectly orthodox, but it is unnecessarily elaborate. The difficulty, as he sees it, is explained by the style of biblical writers. They often double up meanings on a single verb. The point the text is trying to make is that none of the prophets could claim heavenly origin. The Messiah, on the other hand, could. What is interesting is that Daillé gives so much time in his sermon to the discussion of what we today would consider an obscure point. It shows us that congregations expected their ministers to know both the classical commentaries of the Fathers of the ancient Church and the more recent commentaries, and to be able to weigh their interpretations. As we see here, a Jesuit commentator was not necessarily dismissed simply because he was a Jesuit. In fact, as is clear elsewhere, Juan Maldonado seems to be a favorite of Daillé's.

Next Daillé takes up the question of the eternity of the Son of God. The Son is begotten from eternity and remains forever true man and true

God. The eternal subsistence of the Son is made clear by the fact that the text tells us that he has not only descended from heaven but is also he "who is in heaven." (Daillé does not tackle the problems of textual criticism here. In fact, he seems unaware of them.) It was of course Servetus who had denied that Jesus was eternally the Son of God. His errors were as detestable to Protestant theologians in the seventeenth century as they were in the sixteenth century. Daillé explains at length the traditional teachings of Nicaea and Chalcedon which Servetus had denied (pp. 202ff.). For this evangelist, at least, a careful explanation of doctrine is obviously not out of place.

The conclusion of the sermon is an appeal to receive Jesus Christ, Son of man, Son of God. Let us confess the unity of his person, for it is for our salvation that the Son of God became man (p. 214). It is of his great love for us that he descended from heaven to earth, that he joined his almighty power to our mortal fallibility, his glory to our misery. Here we find one of those passages, not by any means infrequent in Daillé, where his simple but moving oratory is indeed eloquent. He goes on urging his congregation to consider what love we owe to Christ (p. 215)! The divine wisdom of his teaching, the sovereign perfection of his holiness, and the incomprehensible glory of his miracles all move us to believe that he is indeed who he claimed to be. Let us therefore embrace Christ with faith. Let us leave behind us the doubts of Nicodemus. Why should we be charmed by the eloquence of this world, its philosophy, its pomposity, and its ceremonial (p. 216)? In Christ and in no other is the purest source of heavenly wisdom. It is far more profound than the traditions of all those other teachers who have gone before. In the end it is the teacher descended from heaven who shows us the way of salvation (p. 217).

Sermons 6 and 7 are perhaps best understood as a single sermon. They both take as their text John 3:14-15, "And as Moses lifted up the serpent in the wilderness, so must the Son of man be lifted up, that whoever believes in him may have eternal life." Our preacher divides his text into three points, but then takes two sermons to complete them. The sermon begins with one weighty sentence telling us that the death of our Lord is the foundation of our salvation (p. 219). He develops this theme as his introduction to both sermons. It is now appropriate, having unfolded the doctrine of the incarnation, Daillé explains, that Jesus present to Nicodemus the essence of his message, that is, the mystery of his saving death (p. 223). This Jesus does by developing the story of the brazen serpent as the type of his own death.

Daillé dwells on this story at great length. In the first place, he wants to make clear that it gives us no excuse to rely on magic, talismans, charms, the veneration of images, or any other superstition for our salvation (p. 242). Those of the Israelites who believed God's promise and looked on the serpent were saved by faith. Daillé points out that eventually the brazen serpent became an object of idolatry and had to be destroyed (II Kings 18:4) (p. 250). When it was used as it was instituted, the serpent was one of the Old Testament sacraments. Even the sacraments of the New Testament can be abused and used idolatrously, as when the bread and wine of the Lord's Supper are worshiped. This may appear to us as a needlessly long diversion from the subject. One immediately recognizes the polemic against the Roman Catholic use of images in worship. It is, however, more than polemic. Daillé's treatment brings out the nature of true faith. It explains the biblical objection to idolatry. Idolatry is wrong, as Daillé understands it, because it short-circuits the direct personal relation which the believer has with Christ. Saving faith is faith in the person of Christ, not in the means of grace, no matter how helpful means of grace might be when used as God intends them to be used. Even the Christian sacraments can be misused when we put our faith in them rather than in the God who gave them as a means of uniting us to himself (pp. 256ff.). The Scriptures forbid the use of images because through faith the believer has a direct relationship to God. God wants us to relate to him by hearing his Word and believing it.

The seventh sermon begins with an explanation of how prophetic types function in Scripture. This is one of the unique features of Christianity, Daillé tells us. The Bible moves from prophecy to fulfillment. God gives shadows of the future in order that he might lead us by faith from the shadows to the fulfillment of his promises (pp. 265ff.). We must not rest with the shadows but move on to the fulfillment. Many aspects of the story of the brazen serpent might mislead us, and our preacher gives several examples. The essential thing to notice in this type is the lifting up of the serpent, which speaks to us of the cross (p. 271). The rich meaning given to this "lift up" in the Gospel of John is explored. The phrase is also found in John 8:28 and 12:32-34. For the Gospel of John, this lifting up makes clear that the death of Christ was both a sacrifice made necessary for our sin and a substitute for the sacrifice we cannot make (pp. 292ff.). The death of Christ was a vicarious sacrifice. God has provided for us in the death of Christ a means of being healed from our sins, and if we embrace the crucified Christ by faith, we will inherit eternal life (p. 298).

The eighth sermon takes as its text John 3:16. Daillé sees in this text, as so many Christians from John Chrysostom to Billy Graham, the perfect summary of the essential mystery of the gospel. Dividing up the text, he announces that he wants to treat three subjects: the love of the Father, the gift of his Son, and the blessing of the believer (p. 307).

If Nicodemus was surprised to learn that the Messiah must die on the cross, Jesus was quick to explain that the cause of that death was the love of the Father. It was not the failure of Jesus, or the blindness of the Jews, or the power of the Romans which would bring Jesus to the cross, but the love of God for the world (pp. 308ff.). Following his usual expository method, Daillé proceeds to explain the sense in which Jesus spoke of the world (pp. 311ff.). God's love is for the great mass of sinners who have rebelled against his majesty, who are guilty of a thousand sins and vices, and who are worthy of eternal death. Daillé shows that the apostle Paul taught the same thing in several of his epistles. God's love is not just for good people, for the better part of humanity, or for just the Jews, but for the whole of humanity.

Our preacher moves to his second point. The depth of God's love for the world is shown by the gift of his Son. The text, Daillé tells us, makes it very clear that the Son whom the Father gave was his only begotten Son, the Son who was uniquely God's Son, the special delight of the Father (pp. 321ff.). Again the point is made that Paul teaches the same thing, for we read in Romans 8:32 that God did not spare his own Son but gave him up for us all (p. 335).

Daillé's third point is that we receive the gift of the Son by faith, and that the fruits of this gift are produced in our lives (p. 330). Daillé is always clear that true faith leads to the living of a holy life. Faith makes it possible for us to participate in the new life which Christ won through the victory of the cross (p. 334). Faith is the vase or vessel in which the grace of God is transported from the Savior to us.

The sermon ends with an appeal to admire the love of God in all its breadth and all its depth, and to build our faith on the foundation of God's love (p. 339). Believe vigorously in Christ, Daillé exhorts us, and be assured that we will not perish but have eternal life. Have no fear! You know that God loves you, that he has forgiven your sins. You have already begun to experience the fruit of eternal life, even here in this world. Don't let the devil frighten you! Follow along in the ways of God, for as Paul puts it, "If God is for us, who is against us?" (Rom. 8:31) (p. 340). For my money, whether in Jerusalem, or Paris, or Los Angeles, never was the gospel set forth more directly! This is evangelism, pure and simple.

We turn now to the ninth sermon in this series. It takes up John 3:17-18, "For God sent the Son into the world, not to condemn the world, but that the world might be saved through him. He who believes in him is not condemned; he who does not believe is condemned already, because he has not believed in the name of the only Son of God" (RSV). The text teaches us two things, our preacher tells us: God's purpose in sending the Son and the effect of that sending. It is only natural, he explains, that those who have a sense of guilt fear the coming of Christ. They are convinced that God sent his Son to punish them. The text makes it clear that this fear is groundless. This is developed at length by our preacher, who brings in a number of passages of Scripture to show God's redemptive intention (pp. 361ff.). We have every reason to find comfort in these words, for again and again God's grace to us is promised throughout the whole of Scripture. It is this grace of God which is the ultimate cause of salvation.

Following his text, Daillé returns to the theme of faith. Faith is the means by which God accomplishes his redemptive purposes in us. Our faith does not merit our salvation, but rather produces it (pp. 368ff.). In view of this text, it is clear that the doctrine of purgatory is misleading (pp. 373ff.). To be sure, a faith that does not produce love for God, love for the neighbor, and works of charity is not real faith, but real faith produces this kind of love (p. 379).

The sermon ends with an exhortation against simulated faith. It is true that some profess faith and yet do not have a genuine faith. One can easily tell the difference between real faith and simulated faith. At a distance, the eye can be deceived. One can think one sees a flame in the distance when it is really only a reflection of the sun or something else which has the shape and color of a flame, but coming close, one can reach out and touch that object and find whether it has any heat. Simple as this simile is, Daillé develops it with a master's touch. He challenges his hearers to reach out and touch their faith to discover if it has any heat, whether it has a burning love for Christ, and whether it has ardent works of charity. If it does not, then one is lost, but yet one is not irredeemably lost. One does indeed still have the possibility of repentance. One may, as the prodigal son in the Gospel, return to the Father with the assurance that he willingly receives his children (p. 383).

The final sermon in the series treats two subjects: the effects of incredulity and the resistance of the unfaithful to the light of the gospel (p. 391). Our preacher insists that no one is forced to reject the gospel as though some invisible force prevented him from believing (p. 404). The wicked do not come to the light because, as the text makes clear, they love the darkness. Nicodemus, as we discover later in the Gospel, came to claim the body of Christ, as he saw those things taking place which Jesus had taught him must take place (p. 425). God wants for all of us to hear the gospel and to receive it. Let us pray that these teachings Jesus gave to Nicodemus be the seed of the gospel sown in our hearts as well, that they be sown not on rocky ground or thorny ground but on good ground, and that the seed grow and produce fruit in our lives. Be well assured that it is God himself who wishes to give us the faith to believe these things, the courage to do them, and the steadfastness to persevere in them. It is in the end our salvation which serves his glory (p. 426).

B. Festal Preaching

The Reformed Church of France had thought out very carefully its approach to the observance of Christian feasts. Daillé's collection of festal sermons serves as a beautiful example of how this was worked out.[21] Clearly following the example of Bucer and Calvin, the emphasis is on the five evangelical feasts — Christmas, Good Friday, Easter, Ascension, and Pentecost.[22] Reformed Protestantism, and especially the Reformed Church of Strasbourg, had made a major effort to reestablish the dignity of the Lord's Day. The recovery of the observance of the Lord's Day had become a major feature of the piety of Protestantism by the middle of the seventeenth century, but there was also a very hearty observance of the five evangelical feast days. On the continent of Europe, at least, that too had become characteristic of Protestantism.

The fact that there were so few of these feast days made them specially important. One of the problems with the medieval liturgical calendar was that there were so many feast days, it was hard to keep track of them. The more elaborate liturgical calendar followed during the Middle

21. Jean Daillé, *Sermons de la naissance, de la mort, resurrection, et ascension de notre Seigneur et de la descente du saint Esprit sur les Apôtres* (Charenton: Samuel Perier, 1651). Page references in the text of this section are to this volume.

22. "The evangelical feasts" was the term which seems to have been accepted. The problem with the term is that Good Friday could hardly be called a feast day. They might better have chosen the term "the five evangelical holy days," but they probably felt the term had certain implications they did not like.

Ages may have been appropriate for a monastic community, but it was too complicated for the usual congregation of men and women who were engaged in ordinary affairs of life. The Reformers had pruned the liturgical calendar down in order to accentuate the importance of the central events in the history of salvation. We notice this especially in the collection of festal sermons before us. Easter is the primary feast day. It is prepared for by two sermons on Good Friday and then celebrated by the service on Easter morning and followed by five services during Easter week. There are an observance of the ascension and then three sermons for Pentecost. Christmas is celebrated with a special sermon for the Lord's Day before Christmas as well as for Christmas Day. Then on the Lord's Day after Christmas, there is a celebration of Communion.

Surely one of the features of these festal observances was their particular linkage with the observance of the sacrament of the Lord's Supper. Generally the Sacrament was celebrated on Christmas, Easter, and Pentecost, and then on the first Sunday in October. That meant three of the four celebrations each year were linked with one of the feasts. The impression which inevitably prevailed was that Communion days were feast days. This gave special solemnity to the celebration of the feasts, lending high honor to the Sacrament in return.

Of special interest in this series of festal sermons is the prominence given to the preaching of Easter. The year these sermons were preached, Daillé chose to present a series on the story of Christ's appearance to two disciples on the road to Emmaus and the subsequent appearance in the Upper Room as found in the conclusion of the Gospel of Luke.[23] Doubtless in other years he would have done similar series on such passages as the resurrection appearances recorded in the Gospel of John, or perhaps Paul's teaching on the resurrection in I Corinthians 15. In Geneva it had been the practice to preach on the passion narrative each day during the week before Easter, as we noticed above. Quite clearly, in the course of a century the emphasis had shifted. We know that a number of the Church Fathers had celebrated the resurrection by preaching special sermons during Easter week. Augustine comes first to mind.[24] Whatever may have been the usual practice, it is clear that for French Protestantism in the seventeenth century, the feast of the resurrection was the primary feast of the year.

---

23. At the conclusion of the series there is a sermon on John 21:24.

24. Cf. Augustine, *Sermons pour la Pâque,* ed. Suzanne Poque, Sources chrétiennes, vol. 116 (Paris: Éditions du Cerf, 1966).

Almost as interesting is what this series shows us about the celebration of Christmas. Christmas Communion was celebrated on the Lord's Day following Christmas rather than on 25 December, that is, unless the twenty-fifth happened to fall on the Lord's Day. Early in the Reformation there was a certain amount of opposition to the observance of Christmas. This was because it was a perfect example of a pagan feast which had been taken up into the worship of the Church.[25] One did not have to be a particularly sharp theologian to pick this information up from the source documents that were available at the time.[26] John Chrysostom at one point tells us that the church of Antioch had only begun to celebrate Christmas in his lifetime. If one was going to rid the church of pagan accretions, then the celebration of Christmas would be a logical one to eliminate. Popular piety, on the other hand, just could not give it up. A compromise was reached by celebrating the feast on the Sunday following 25 December. The compromise is obviously modeled on that passage in the *Ecclesiastical History* of Eusebius which tells how the church of the second century insisted that the Christian Passover not be celebrated on the fourteenth of Nisan with the Jews but rather on the Lord's Day following the fourteenth of Nisan.[27] In both cases the Lord's Day remained the principal feast, and yet allowance was made for a Christian interpretation of a preexisting feast.

The introduction to the first of Daillé's three Christmas sermons provides us with some valuable insights into how French Protestants understood their observance of Christmas. At the beginning of this sermon he gives us a brief justification for the observance of a feast celebrating the birth of Christ. There is no suggestion that the feast be of divine appointment. It is a rather common custom to celebrate the birth of kings and others of importance. Centuries ago Christians considered it appropriate, and for Daillé that is sufficient reason to observe the feast (p. 1).

The problem is that the manner in which we have celebrated this feast has degenerated over time. Now it scarcely honors the Savior it is supposed to honor. The purpose of this sermon, then, is to recover the

25. On the origins of Christmas, see, in preceding volumes of this work, 1:345-50 and 2:99ff. Source documents are noted in the footnotes.

26. The Reformers knew a good number of patristic passages. On the origins of the liturgical calendar, see above in the section on Oecolampadius and the festal sermons of Gregory of Nazianzus, and the section on Calvin's sermons for Holy Week.

27. On the Quartodeciman controversy in the second century, see 1:290ff. of this work. For the literature on the subject, see 1:290 n. 89.

central theme of the celebration (p. 2). For the Protestants of France, the observance of the Christian feasts called for a solemn and holy celebration. Profane revelry, as they understood it, was out of place at a sacred feast. Overeating and overdrinking was hardly the way to celebrate the birth of Christ. The three sermons which follow are marked by a simple and sober sort of joy, springing from a profound understanding of the gospel of the incarnation.

There is, however, another consideration which bothered many about the observance of the feast days. Like Origen, French Protestants had doubts about the value of singling out one particular day for celebrating Christmas or Easter (pp. 3ff.).[28] All our days should be lived out in a conscious celebration of the incarnation and the resurrection. Had not Paul warned us against making too much over the observance of days and the holding of festivals (Col. 2:16)?

These three Christmas sermons are rich in theological insights. One gets the impression that Daillé saw the feast days as a time to meditate on the cardinal doctrines of the Christian faith. The third sermon can well serve us as an example. It takes as its text Luke 2:13-20, which recounts the story of the appearance of the angels to the shepherds and their going to Bethlehem to present their homage to the Christ child.[29]

The sermon has a magnificent introduction which points to the doxological nature of preaching (pp. 72-75). As Daillé understands it, the purpose of preaching is so to proclaim the Word of God that God is praised. Indeed, this sermon does just that. It opens by observing that while our Savior Jesus Christ lived here below hiding the marvels of his divinity under the veil of feeble flesh, nevertheless the divine majesty from time to time allowed certain flashes of glory to shine forth upon that humble form of a servant which he had assumed. Observed with pure eyes, these flashes reveal the glory of the Son of God. Daillé gives us a simile here. The glory of the incarnate Son of God is like the glory of the sun behind thick cloud cover, but from time to time there is a break in the clouds and the full radiance of the sun shines forth. That is what we have here in the story of the appearance of the angels to the shepherds. One often notices this in the story of the ministry of our Lord. In the course of

---

28. On Origen's view of the observance of feast days, see 1:345-50 of this work.

29. While this sermon follows on a sermon on Luke 2:1-7 and, before that, one on Gal. 4:4, apparently the three sermons do not fit together as a series. In this they differ from the Easter sermons which treat the story of Christ's appearance to the two disciples on the road to Emmaus.

his humble life there are these miraculous happenings which shine forth as rays of divine light on the shadows of human infirmity (p. 73). Miracles have a way of accompanying suffering, and heaven has a way of mixing with earth. That was always the case with the life of our Lord. Especially now we find it in the story of Christ's birth; that miserable stable, that embarrassing manger — all were glorified by such heavenly signs.

Every word of this three-page introduction is marvelous! It concludes by telling us that it is the purpose of God to touch our hearts with his Spirit, that we glorify him just as the shepherds did. The purpose of preaching is doxological. It is the will of God that we receive the Christ as the shepherds did, that we, too, adore him as the Son of God, not being offended by his lowliness and infirmity but recognizing the beatitude and grace which dwell in him.

Our preacher divides the text in two parts. Our text tells us first about the song of the angels, and second about the homage of the shepherds (p. 75). Daillé follows the familiar pattern of the expository sermon as he inherited it from Origen, Chrysostom, Augustine, Luther, Zwingli, and Calvin. He takes up the text, explaining it phrase by phrase. Taking the phrase "And suddenly there was with the angel a multitude of the heavenly host . . ." (Luke 2:13 RSV), he explains that the Scriptures often speak of the heavenly host. Sometimes one has the impression that the stars are meant, at other times that some sort of angelic ministers are indicated. Our preacher reminds us of Psalm 103, which speaks of the heavenly host as ministers of God, appointed to execute the divine decrees (p. 77). To be sure, they are not divinities as the pagans so often imagine. This whole passage evokes the vitality of the heavens and the vastness of the creation (pp. 75-80). Our preacher sums it all up with a simile: the heavenly host which suddenly the shepherds saw served as an honor guard of the Son of God as he came to assume his service among men.

Next our preacher takes up the phrase "praising God" (p. 81). He comments that in their praising God the heavenly hosts give us a lesson in how we too are to fulfill our destiny. The heavenly hosts begin the song that we too are to take up. Our worship should take up and continue the heavenly worship. Right here the application of the sermon is obvious, and our preacher quickly tacks it down. Let us in our worship join our voices to the song of the heavenly hosts (p. 83).

After these remarks, the actual text of the song of the angels claims the attention of our preacher. He divides it into three phrases: (1) glory to God, (2) peace on earth, and (3) the goodwill of God toward men. The meaning of this hymn has been discussed for centuries. Daillé goes over some of the philological problems found in the text. He was, after all, well trained in the arts of Christian humanism. By the middle of the seventeenth century, classical Protestantism had produced an abundance of preachers who were well trained in the literary arts. They knew how to bring all the insights of grammar and rhetoric, the original languages, textual criticism, and historical research to bear on the interpretation of a text of Scripture. Whether in Huguenot France, Lutheran Germany, or Puritan England, Protestant congregations expected this kind of erudition from their preachers.

The song of the angels may be rather short, but it is filled with profound insights. Although Daillé draws out many ideas from the text of this song, we will focus on only one. Rich ideas are the treasure of Daillé's preaching. Especially notable are his remarks on the nature of God's glory. He speaks of the meaning of the Hebrew word for glory. Then he tells us that the glory of God signifies two things as we find it in Scripture: it signifies the virtues of God in themselves, that is, his power, his wisdom, and his goodness, in a word, all his exalted qualities (p. 86); and it is understood as the *éclat,* or splendor, of his admirable virtues. As Daillé puts it, the luster and luminosity of these excellent virtues radiate abroad. The French word *éclat* is a bit hard to translate into English; it signifies a sudden burst of light or power. This radiating of the divine virtues is God's glory. But then our preacher says that just as the different stars vary in the magnitude of their radiance, so it is with the multitude of God's virtues. The divine virtues are numerous, but some surpass others. Surely God's highest virtue is the depth of his mercy in sending his Son to endure the miseries of human life. None of the other wondrous works of God manifest such profound mercy (p. 87). So it is that the angels sing the glory of God in the highest, that on earth he has brought peace. What a marvelous rhapsody on the praises of God Daillé has played for us on his scholarly harp!

Daillé points out that as long as the shepherds heard the heavenly music, they stood there in amazement, never thinking of budging from their place. But when the angels departed, they began to reflect on what the meaning of all this might be and what they therefore must do (p. 98). We are taught an important lesson by this, Daillé insists. Surely we should learn from this to listen carefully to the Word of God and consider attentively what its meaning is for us. Although it is not angels who preach to us today, but rather ministers, we should listen just as carefully to them (p. 99).

The second half of the sermon has to do with the witness of the shepherds. The text tells us that they went with great haste and found Mary and Joseph, and the baby lying in a manger. The shepherds could have found all kinds of excuses for staying where they were. After all, who was going to take care of the sheep were they suddenly to go off to Bethlehem? But they made no such excuses. They went right away. The application is obvious; the preacher hardly needs to belabor it.

Once they got there, what they saw was so surprising! They saw an old man and a young woman and a newborn child in such simple circumstances. They were poor. They were alone. What they expected to see was a royal baby wrapped in silk and purple, but this child whom the angels so cherished was lying in a manger. Here was a prince so unlike the princes of this world. Our preacher did not need to say that the child was so different from the princes of the House of Bourbon. How great the contrast was! He needed only to insist on the simplicity of Christ's birth. The irony of this sermon, which had to be preached outside the walls of Paris, the city where the grand court of Louis XIV was, is so beautifully understated. The Jews, Daillé tells us, had looked forward to a superb monarch, flourishing in worldly glory and conquering the whole world with the force of arms (p. 101). Yet the glory of God is something quite other. It is infinite power and eternal wisdom. The shepherds, of course, might have been scandalized at the lowliness and humility of the child. They might have quite understandably dismissed it all as a dream; however, the Scriptures tell us that they told everyone about the child. By their faith the shepherds had become witnesses, and with their witness they ministered to the very Son of God. Yes, they became preachers, or perhaps better said, they became angels (p. 102).

Again Daillé moves along with his text. In verse 20 he reads that the shepherds told everyone of what they had heard and seen concerning the child. God saw to it that this was recorded in Scripture to show us how God uses the witness of simple people. We naturally expect to hear about the things of God from people of high station, but God has a way of humiliating us by using the simplest of witnesses. The text goes on to say that everyone who heard the witness of the shepherds marveled at what was said to them. What is said here is as much for the faithful as for those just being introduced to the sacred story. The witness of the shepherds strengthened the faith of Mary and Joseph as much as it amazed the townspeople of Bethlehem. However, just because people are amazed does not mean they are going to accept the gospel and live in faith

(p. 104). The text tells us that Mary heard all these things and pondered them in her heart. The witness of the shepherds was important to her. They were a sign to her, just as she was a sign to them. She received their word and treasured it in her heart. She meditated on it all, and as she meditated her faith was strengthened. She had such an important ministry to perform, but her faith needed support just as our faith needs support. It needs to be strengthened and encouraged if we are to do what God has called us to do (p. 105).

The body of this sermon has made two points. It has spoken about both the praise of the angels and the homage of the shepherds. Both give us an example. The angels lead the way in presenting their praises to God. We should follow them, joining in their praises. The shepherds lead us as well. They gave their witness to everything they had seen and heard. For us the giving of our witness is a sacred service well pleasing to God.

Here is a preacher who makes a running commentary on his text as the preachers of the synagogue and ancient Church so often did, and yet he comes up with beautiful introductions and conclusions as well. Perorations were more characteristic of Greek and Latin oratory than of the more biblical preaching forms of the ancient synagogue and the early Church. Here we have a beautiful conclusion; our preacher exhorts his congregation to embrace Christ as the Savior, to imitate the zeal of the angels and the faith of the shepherds. No matter what your station of life, great or small, wise or simple, come to Bethlehem, our preacher urges us, and adore the Prince of Peace! Surely here is a good example of a very biblical preacher using the arts of classical oratory effectively.

One more thing needs to be said about this conclusion, and that is the way it recalls the teaching of Isaiah 53, which speaks so eloquently of the Messiah's works of humiliation. The lowliness of the true Servant of the Lord is something on which we must constantly meditate, Daillé tells us. One wonders how that congregation would have understood this conclusion, whether this might have been an opportune word for the Protestants of Paris in 1651. Daillé looks out on his congregation so despised at that magnificent court of the Sun King. He reminds them of the words from the apostle Paul (I Cor. 1:26-27), that there were not many noble, not many wise, not many great in their assembly. Then he comments that it might well be that their witness, like the witness of the shepherds, is well pleasing in God's sight. There in the stable of Bethlehem God was truly praised and rightly honored, whereas among the great of this world God too often is blasphemed. It is for us to let loose of these worldly attachments and honors. Let us rather direct our gaze on heaven and mount up to the things of God. Let us be caught up with angels and glorify God in the highest (p. 109).

The beautiful thing about this sermon is the transparency of its exposition. The application here is not self-conscious. It is more implicit than explicit. One immediately sees the application without the preacher having to explain it. These transparent expositions one finds again and again in the course of Daillé's sermons, and here too, perhaps the most important application in this sermon was merely implied — the contrast between the simplicity of the birth of the King of Kings and the court of Louis XIV. The preacher never really made it too explicit. It is often that way when one does profound exposition. Applications spring up in the hearts of the faithful that had never been expressly suggested by the preacher. The exposition becomes so transparent that the application is inevitable. The most important application may have been no more than a sort of realization in the back of Daillé's mind. God may not have given the Huguenots worldly importance, but they had been divinely called to deliver a witness that was precious in God's sight. To give such a witness is worship in the highest.

C. Catechetical Preaching

Jean Daillé was like John Chrysostom, one of those exceptional preachers who treated all the major genres of preaching with exceptional ability. He was above all an expository preacher, but he was also an evangelist and a prophet. We have just spoken of his festal sermons. Now we must turn to his catechetical sermons.[30] The collection of catechetical sermons which has come down to us is very extensive. It is published in three volumes. We will look at only a portion of it, namely, the portion on prayer.

How Christians are to pray was one of the most profound concerns of the Reformation. The intercession of the saints, prayers for the dead, prayers of repentance, and the nature of confession are only the most explicit points of concern. On a deeper level were the question of mental prayer, the function of meditation, and the whole Neoplatonic approach to prayer. Monasticism had led prayer a long way in the Neoplatonic di-

---

30. Jean Daillé, *Sermons sur le catechisme des églises réformées,* 3 vols. (Geneva: La Société des libraires, 1701). Page references in the text are to vol. 3 of this work.

rection. It radically separated prayer from the common concerns of life in an attempt to achieve a mystical experience of transcendence. For Protestantism the teaching of the Lord's Prayer was a powerful means of bringing Christians back to a more biblical prayer discipline.

To be sure, the explanation of the Lord's Prayer had been a fundamental component of catechetical preaching from very early times. We have many patristic sermons on the Lord's Prayer, which apparently were preached to the catechumens shortly before their baptism. One thinks of those of Augustine and Theodore of Mopsuestia. Tertullian's essay on prayer as well as Cyprian's *On the Lord's Prayer* were probably originally sermons addressed to catechumens. In fact, New Testament scholars have often suggested that the Lord's Prayer as found in Matthew 6 is part of an early collection of catechetical material.

The sermons to which we now turn are found in a comprehensive collection of fifty-four catechetical sermons published in three volumes in Geneva in 1701, sixteen years after the revocation of the Edict of Nantes. Apparently the collection represents a year's worth of catechetical preaching. Furthermore, we notice that these sermons are obviously addressed to adults. No doubt they were preached in the afternoon of the Lord's Day. More and more, catechetical preaching had risen in importance from the teaching of children in preparation for their first Communion to a regular part of the worship of the Lord's Day. In fact, the evidence seems to suggest that doctrinal preaching was widely appreciated. For the Protestants of Paris who gathered at Charenton, outside the walls of the city, it must have been important to hear very exact and precise sermons on the points of doctrine for which they so willingly suffered such hardships.

One notices this throughout orthodox Protestantism. Much attention is given to serious doctrinal preaching. The orthodox Lutheran preachers gave a marvelous example of very earnest interpretations of classical Christian doctrine. The English Puritans John Howe and Thomas Watson did the same thing in London. Even in the Massachusetts Bay Colony Thomas Shepard was interpreting the catechism of Geneva while founding Harvard University.

The title of this collection, *Sermons sur le catechisme des églises réformées,* makes it clear that these sermons are based on the *Catechism of Geneva,* the one John Calvin had drawn up in 1541. This catechism of 373 questions was divided into four sections, namely, (1) the articles of faith, that is, the Apostles' Creed; (2) the Law, that is, the Ten Commandments; (3) the Lord's Prayer; and (4) the sacraments. Calvin's catechism was put together rather hastily and has never been considered one of his better works. It has never been regarded as a classic in the same way that the *Heidelberg Catechism* has. Be that as it may, it was available, and it was in French.

One notices that these sermons are an exposition not so much of the text of the catechism per se as of the text of the actual catechetical pieces themselves: the creed, the Ten Commandments, and in this case, the Lord's Prayer. In fact, these sermons are commentary on the traditional catechetical pieces to which a commentary on the sacraments has been added.

Let us look at several sermons very briefly: the introductory sermon, Sermon XXXVII; the sermon which interprets "Our Father in heaven," Sermon XXXVIII; the sermon on "Hallowed be your name," Sermon XXXIX; the sermon on "Give us this day our daily bread," Sermon XLI; and the sermon on thanksgiving, Sermon XLIV.

Sermon XXXVII introduces the subject of the Lord's Prayer. The great attention given to the Lord's Prayer in this catechism points to the fact that the Reformation brought in a prayer revival. The Reformation was a reformation of prayer as much as of preaching or of sacramental doctrine and practice. Our preacher begins by making the point that one finds teaching on prayer throughout the whole Bible. All through the Scriptures we find the texts of prayers and examples of prayers offered by the faithful in a variety of situations. Here, however, in the Lord's Prayer, the prayer Jesus taught his disciples, we have the summary and culmination of all this wealth of teaching (pp. 2-3). The Lord's Prayer is not simply one prayer of many found in Scripture. It is the exemplary prayer, the pattern to which all our prayers should aspire.

In this prayer our best and truest desires are most admirably expressed (p. 4). First are the desires of a spiritual nature, and second are desires of a temporal and material nature. Here Jesus himself teaches us to seek first the kingdom of God and his righteousness, and all these things will be added unto us. The first three petitions, "Hallowed be thy name," "Thy kingdom come," and "Thy will be done on earth as it is in heaven," have to do with our spiritual desires. The second three, "Give us this day our daily bread," "Forgive our debts," and "Lead us not into temptation, but deliver us from evil," have to do with our more temporal needs (pp. 6-7). We notice, however, that the petitions for spiritual blessings come first while prayer for the material goods comes second (p. 8). The first petitions express our desire for faith, for holiness, and for immortality.

Above all other holy desires should be an ardent zeal for God's glory. It is a passion for holiness. Far beyond a concern for our own happiness, and even for the welfare of our neighbor, is a love for the holiness of God, that our Lord reign, that he be known and adored, obeyed and loved by all (p. 11). To pray that God's name be hallowed is to express the highest and holiest of desires. It is, Jesus teaches us, the driving force of Christian prayer.

Sermon XXXVIII takes up the invocation of the Lord's Prayer, namely, "Our Father in heaven." In very traditional homiletical form, the text is divided into three points: that our prayer should be addressed to the Father, that the Father is our Father, and that he is a heavenly Father. That Jesus taught us to pray to God as our Father was a fundamental insight for the Protestant prayer revival. In it they found the clearest possible refutation of the hierarchical interpretation of prayer fostered by Neoplatonism. For a thousand years Christians had been taught to think of prayer in terms of both an ecclesiastical and a celestial hierarchy. In prayer one had to ascend to God through a system of mediators. The clergy, the saints, the angels — all in proper order mediated our communion with God. But Daillé, typical of Protestant teaching, insisted that when it comes to prayer, we are related to God as children to a father. Because God is our Father, we can count on his kindliness and generosity (p. 33). After a long discussion of the doctrine of the Trinity, and of how knowing the Son we come to know God as Father, our preacher tells us that invoking God as Father should engender in us an assurance of God's kindly disposition toward us. In the most profound sense God is the Father only of those who are disciples of Christ and in faith pray "Our Father" (p. 41). It is God alone who makes us Christians and gives us a new being and a new form. As Christians we are to be a new creation, born not of blood or the will of man but of God (John 1:13). The faithful should not think of God as clothed in fire and flame, too majestic for us to approach. He is our Father and we should approach him in confidence (p. 47). Jesus himself made this very clear when he taught that just as human fathers know how to give good gifts to their children, how much more our heavenly Father gives good gifts to those who ask him (Matt. 7:11).

Here the polemic becomes explicit. Our preacher charges the Roman Church with teaching that the faithful dare not present themselves to God except by the hand of a saint. One imagines that approaching God is like approaching a king at his royal court. One must be presented by an officer of the court or by a royal favorite. Not at all! our preacher insists. The very fact that Jesus teaches us to pray to God as our Father refutes this whole approach to prayer (p. 49).

Public prayer in the Huguenot church made a point of invoking God as Father. In fact, this is most clear from reading the prayers in the *Genevan Psalter* of 1542, which normally invoke God as Father. This is in marked contrast to the prayers of the Roman missal, which consistently invoked God as Lord Eternal, Omnipotent God, Heavenly Sovereign, Ruler of All, and other titles of a distinctly hierarchal tone. The Reformation brought a revolution in the way Christians prayed, and this is very clear in these catechetical sermons.

One of the places where this prayer revolution always became most explicit was in the teaching on the nature of the petition for daily bread. Those heavily influenced by Neoplatonic thought had very early in the history of the Church tried to avoid the idea that we should pray for material goods. We find this especially in the essay on prayer written by Origen at the beginning of the third century. All the early Protestant catechisms from Luther on taught quite differently. Sermon XLI takes up the petition "Give us this day our daily bread."

The sermon opens by recalling the creation of Adam and Eve in the Garden of Eden. As idyllic as that existence must have been, it should always remind us that as much as we may be destined to a heavenly fellowship with God, we are, after all, as long as we are on this earth, human creatures made of the dust of the earth. We have earthly needs (pp. 139ff.). It is for this reason that our Lord Jesus taught us to pray for our daily bread.

Daillé recognizes that from very early times there was a tendency among the Church Fathers to allegorize this petition of the Lord's Prayer (p. 142). But as Daillé sees it, there is no reason to allegorize the Lord's Prayer. The swipe at Origen is obvious if not explicit. There is every reason to believe that we are intended to understand this petition in the most literal and straightforward sense. All through Scripture we find God promising his people a good supply of the material goods of this life. God promised at Bethel to preserve the patriarch Jacob during his pilgrimage with bread to eat and clothing to wear until at last he returned in peace to the house of his father (Gen. 28:20) (p. 143). Solomon in his admirable prayer of dedication recognized that one of the functions of the Temple was to be a place to pray to God in times of drought and famine (I Kings 8:35 and 37). Jesus himself taught us to pray for our material needs in other passages of the Gospels besides the Lord's Prayer. In Matthew 6:33

we read that while we are first of all to seek the kingdom of God and his righteousness, we are nevertheless to be assured that God will provide all these other things as well (p. 144). The important thing is that we seek the spiritual gifts first, and only secondly the material gifts.

Daillé is well aware of the problems involved in translating the original Greek text, and even quotes the Greek in the footnotes. He discusses the opinion of Saint Jerome, finally coming to the conclusion that it is indeed our daily bread for which we are to pray (p. 149). The main thing is that we are to put ourselves in the hands of providence, having confidence in the graciousness of our heavenly Father toward us in all things.

This does not mean, however, that we are to neglect our daily work. Adam and Eve had to earn their daily bread by the sweat of their brow. The doctrine of vocation was indeed very important to Protestant spirituality. God has called each one of us to some form of work, the artisan in his shop, the soldier in his camp, the peasant in his field, and the scholar in his study (p. 155). We all have our work, but work alone is not enough. We must have God's blessing on the work of our hands. That is why we pray for our daily bread. We ask God to bless our work. We should be careful to keep a balance between relying on God's providence and maintaining a vigorous industry (p. 163). One must avoid being obsessed with working hard to provide an excess of luxuries, just as one must avoid laziness.

From the very beginning of the Reformation Protestants had attacked the mendicant orders. They saw no value in monks begging in the streets. They were very critical of the artificial poverty of monasticism. The monastic orders were rich, and yet they sent their members out to beg. This sort of spirituality may have made sense in a Neoplatonic worldview, but Protestantism did not find asceticism in Scripture. This sermon quite naturally launches a polemic against monasticism. The monks spent a life in idleness. They prayed instead of working. Prayer should never be in place of work. The true Christian should both pray and work (pp. 165ff.). This polemic against monasticism is not some sort of Protestant extremism. The Reformers had made a radical departure from the spirituality of the Middle Ages. This is what the Protestant work ethic was all about. At the heart of Protestant civilization was a whole new approach to prayer, and they found that new approach in the Lord's Prayer.

Let us look at one more of these catechetical sermons on prayer. Sermon XLIV has to do with prayers of thanksgiving. Daillé introduces it by telling us that the Reformed catechism gives special attention to thanksgiving, one of the principal components of the honor and service that we owe to God (p. 149). Our catechist defines thanksgiving as recognizing with heart and lips the Author of all good things, and rendering to him that glory which is his due. As we read in the Epistle of James, he is the Father of lights from whom comes down every good and perfect gift (James 1:17). It is only good and right that all praise should be offered to him (pp. 258ff.).

Our preacher begins a catalogue of all the good gifts of creation. God has indeed endowed nature with a cornucopia of marvels and treasures (p. 260). But then, even more admirable are the good gifts of grace which God has granted to the elect. Psalm 104 gives us a wonderful sense of the sheer glory of God's providential care for all his creatures (p. 262). If God's providence toward the beasts of the field and the birds of the air amazes us, how much more we should admire the marvelous construction of the human body and the capacities of the human spirit (p. 263).

The Bible is filled with hymns of thanksgiving. We find them in the Psalms, the stories of the patriarchs, the Song of the Sea, and the songs of Deborah and Hannah; in the epistles of Paul we find prayers of thanksgiving as well. To offer such prayers for all the benefits of creation, providence, and redemption is an obligation we owe to the Author of all good things (p. 266). We notice that Daillé hones in heavily on the recognition of providence. Those who have been misled into imagining that all these good things come to us by mere chance may understandably neglect this sacred duty, but for those of us who confess a strong doctrine of providence, it is only logical that we should be constant in our thanksgiving to God (p. 268).

Daillé finds great importance in prayers of thanksgiving said at the table in the course of family meals as well as in the short prayers said on rising in the morning and retiring at night (p. 274). Such private prayers are every bit as important as the ministry of public praise. The singing of the psalms in public worship is essential to our service of God, but so is the private devotion. While the outward forms of praise and thanksgiving are more obvious in public prayer, and while they have particular value as a profession of faith before others, private prayer makes more obvious the lifting up of the heart toward God. Earlier in the sermon Daillé had spoken of this dimension of prayer (p. 251). He had made the point that we need not be tied to the exact wording of the Lord's Prayer. In fact, we should vary the words of our prayers from time to time so that our prayers are appropriate to the time and the situation (p. 257). In the last analysis prayer is not a reciting of formulas but an attitude of the heart.

Again we find another of Daillé's marvelous conclusions. Oh, that the whole of our lives might be a thanksgiving to God for his goodness, that the living of life might be a continual singing of praise for the blessings of God. Nothing could be more beautiful, nothing more holy, than to employ the Creator's good gifts in his service. How wonderful it is to employ the understanding he has given us to meditate on him, the emotions he has given us to seek him out, the wills he has given us to love him, the tongues he has given us to praise him, the bodies he has given us to glorify him in all purity, and finally to use the goods he has poured out on us to relieve the poor. This is a great piece of oratory, very simple and yet very profound.

Above all, Jean Daillé was a true preacher of the gospel. Although in the providence of God he had been called to a pulpit where he constantly had to defend the Protestant faith against misleading caricatures of Protestant teaching, he had a genius for making clear the fundamentals of the faith. Daillé was not a controversialist; he was a pastor. His purpose was to present the gospel as it is found in Scripture to the people of God so that it nourished their faith, inspired their hope, and demanded their love. To be sure, controversial issues were often treated in his sermons. Given the historical situation, it had to be that way. But Daillé, as in fact so many of the Huguenot preachers, went way beyond controversy. They preached with directness and simplicity the truth itself.

III. Jean Mestrezat (1592-1657)

Succeeding Pierre du Moulin in the pastorate of the Reformed Church of Paris, Jean Mestrezat offered a ministry of solid biblical teaching.

Mestrezat was born in Geneva. He pursued his theological studies at Saumur,[31] where he was a brilliant student, presenting a thesis that so impressed his professors that he was offered immediately a chair of philosophy. Preferring to enter the pastorate, he turned down the offer and accepted a position on the pastoral staff of the Reformed Church of Paris at Charenton. There he joined that distinguished group of preachers in that very dangerous and precarious ministry.

31. For biographical material, see the article of C. Schmidt, "Mestrezat, Johann," in *Realencyklopädie für protestantische Theologie und Kirche,* ed. Johann Jakob Herzog, 24 vols. (Leipzig: J. C. Hinrichs, 1896-1913), 12:739.

As a Reformed pastor in Paris, he was often called upon to defend Protestantism in public debates staged by the Jesuits. In these hopeless trials he acquitted himself with modesty and patience, winning much respect, especially at court. Mestrezat took an active part in the affairs of the national synod of the Reformed Church of France, being elected moderator at the Synod of Charenton in 1631. Aside from his published sermons, he was particularly well known for a work on the Lord's Supper, *Communion with Jesus Christ in the Sacrament of the Eucharist.*[32] It was so well received that it was translated into German, English, and Italian.

His published sermons were widely read in the seventeenth century. One of the pastors of the Protestant church of Paris, for many years he was naturally in a conspicuous position, and his sermons would have been taken as models for French-speaking Protestantism. We find the following collections:

1. *Trois sermons faits pour le jeusne à Charenton le 19 Novembre 1637* (Charenton: N. Bourdin and L. Perier?, 1638).
2. *Trois sermons sur la venue et la Naissance de Jésus-Christ au mond* (treating Ephesians 2:5-10) (Geneva: n.p., 1654). These sermons were first published in Charenton in 1638.
3. *Sermons sur les chapitres troisieme, quatriesme, cinquiesme, et sixieme de l'épistre aux Hébreux* (Geneva: Samuel Chouët, 1653).
4. *De la sacrificature de Jésus-Christ notre Seigneur ou sermons sur les chapitres VII, VIII, IX, et partie de X de l'épistre aux Hébreux* (Geneva: Samuel Chouët, 1653).
5. *Des fruits de la foy en vertus chrestiennes, ou sermons sur les chapitres XII et XIII de l'épitre aux Hébreux* (Geneva: Samuel Chouët, 1653).
6. *Vingt sermons sur divers textes de l'Écriture sainte* (Geneva: n.p., 1658).
7. *Sermons sur le chapitre huitième de l'épitre de Saint Paul aux Romains* (Amsterdam: François Changuions, 1726).
8. Catechetical sermons. (Seven of the sermons in Daillé's *Sermons sur le catechisme des églises réformées* are by Mestrezat.)
9. *Expositions de la premiere epistre de l'Apostle S. Iean en sermons,* 2 vols. (Geneva: Pierre Chouët, 1651).

---

32. Jean Mestrezat, *La communion à Jesus Christ au sacrament de l'Eucharistie* (Sedan, 1624).

From this list we see that the bulk of his preaching was the regular and systematic exposition of one book of the Bible after another. There were also sermons for feast days and fast days. There would have been sermons for Good Friday, Easter, Ascension, and Pentecost as well as the set of Christmas sermons we have just mentioned. Mestrezat had a long ministry, and the list of published sermons we have is surely but a small sample of what he actually preached.

The sermons on the First Epistle of John are a particularly fine example of the preaching of Protestant orthodoxy in the seventeenth century. Even if there is no show of erudition in them, they are very learned and obviously come from long hours in the study. They have behind them all the arts and sciences of biblical study so elaborately developed by the Christian humanists of the previous century. By the time young Mestrezat began his theological studies, the Protestants had established good schools for training their ministers. One did not have to go to Germany, Switzerland, the Netherlands, or England to get a good theological education.

It is particularly obvious in these sermons that the pulpit oratory of French Protestantism was anything but baroque. It was solidly Protestant plain style. In fact, these sermons are examples of Protestant plain style at its purist. What is fascinating about them is their interpretation of Scripture. This is what must have captured the attention of those who went through the ordeal of going out to Charenton to listen to them. One listens to these sermons because they present us with the Word of God, and that is sufficient to make them interesting. The sermons do have a simple, straightforward sort of rhetoric. The sermon outlines are clear and easy to follow. The points are carefully delineated. The introductions lead us into the subject simply and with dispatch. One is never distracted by their cleverness. One is never amused by homiletical jokes or ravished by dramatic flourishes. The syntax is masterful. Here is a preacher who knows how to compose a sentence. He uses a variety of sentence structures but in such a way that one's attention is never caught by his artistry.

True to the most fundamental traditions of expository preaching, Mestrezat relies on the old principle that Scripture is the best interpreter of Scripture. He is forever explaining the text in these sermons by bringing to it texts from the rest of the Johannine literature. Again and again he calls on the Synoptic Gospels and the epistles of Paul to explain his text. His illustrations from the Old Testament are a delight. Nothing convinces a Protestant congregation of the truth of a preacher's interpretation quite so much as an apt citation of a parallel passage or an appeal to a biblical illustration. Here Mestrezat is at his strongest.

The conclusions of his sermons show a good knowledge of classical oratory. He applies his text, he draws out the doctrinal points he has developed, he consoles, exhorts, and admonishes, but always with directness and dignity. There is nothing showy about these sermons. Rather, one finds in them an admirable modesty. Here again we notice that Huguenot preaching tended to shy away from anything that might appear pretentious. It consciously moved away from the baroque art of oratory so popular in the Counter-Reformation pulpit.

Perhaps the most important thing to notice about his preaching is its double emphasis on orthodox teaching and the sanctity of life. Here is a classical Protestant preacher who is as interested in sanctification as in justification. As we have noticed before, this is characteristic of seventeenth-century Protestantism. One notices this simply in the titles of his sermons on Hebrews. While one volume treats the priestly work of Christ, the other treats Christian virtues. We find also that while there is a volume of sermons on Romans 8, which teaches at length the grace of God in the redemptive work of Christ, there is also a thorough treatment of the evangelical commandment to love one another as found in I John. The sermons on I John make very clear the emphasis on sanctification which we find so typical of seventeenth-century Protestant preaching, whether in France, Germany, the Netherlands, or England.

IV. Jean Claude (1619-87)

Although Jean Claude was the most well known of the French Huguenot preachers of the generation immediately before the revocation of the Edict of Nantes, less than a dozen of his sermons have been preserved. In his day he was the leading defender of Protestantism in France, and his able defense of the Reformation is found in several apologetic writings. A native of southern France, he began his ministry in the small town of Sainte Afrique. In 1654 he was called to Nîmes, where he served as pastor until 1661 when he was refused the right of the pulpit because of his vigorous opposition to the attempt of the government to force a "reunion" of Protestantism and Catholicism. For several years he devoted himself to writing, and in 1666 was called to become one of the pastors of the Reformed Church of Paris at Charenton. From that time until the revocation of the Edict of Nantes in 1685, almost twenty years, he was the leading voice of French Protestantism. It was during this period that he held his famous debate with Bossuet, the most renowned French Catholic preacher of the day. The revocation of the Edict of Nantes recognized Claude's effectiveness as a defender of Protestantism by specifying that he must leave the country within twenty-four hours while other Protestant pastors were allowed fifteen days. Claude took refuge in the Netherlands, where he died less than two years later.

Although Claude left us very few actual sermons, he did leave us a manual for the composition of sermons. It is a presentation of the Protestant plain style of preaching. Most of what he advocates in this essay had been exemplified by Jean Daillé, who was his older colleague in the pastorate of the congregation at Charenton. Seen against its environment, the essay might be called an apology for the simple approach of biblical exposition which normally took place in the worship services of French Protestantism. Claude argues for an approach to preaching markedly different from the famous French Catholic pulpit orators such as Bossuet and Fénelon. He assumes that a sermon should be an exposition of a text of Scripture and argues that it be simple, serious, and devout, that it avoid both oratorical display and theological speculation. He assumes that the preacher has carefully studied the text in the original languages, and that he has consulted the commentaries, both ancient and modern. This erudition is not, however, to be displayed in the sermon. It is for the purpose of giving the minister a thorough understanding of the text. The typical baroque preacher was all too often guilty of buttressing his sermons with profuse quotations from impressive authorities. It is this which Claude criticizes. An occasional quotation from the Jewish rabbis, the Fathers of the ancient Church, more recent theologians, or even secular authors can be effective, but it should be done sparingly. The important thing is that one not try to impress the congregation with one's learning. The Word of God has sufficient authority in itself, and the minister's task is to present that Word with clarity. For Claude, simplicity is still the greatest eloquence. Reading the sermons of the French Huguenots, one finds in them a compelling power which comes from their complete sincerity and utter seriousness. The message these sermons present is clear, reasonable, and earnest. The method of composition Claude presents in his essay is designed to help sermons attain that clarity and simple sincerity which was the heritage of classical French Protestantism.

Not everything in Claude's essay follows the tradition of French

Protestant homiletics. He advocates one very significant modification of the tradition. While Claude still assumes expository preaching, he becomes the advocate of preaching on texts rather than passages. Whereas the expository preaching of the sixteenth century tended to treat paragraphs, much Protestant preaching in the seventeenth century tended to preach on single sentences. This tendency, and it was a tendency, not a rule, is particularly marked in England, as we have seen. Claude makes a point of telling us that a sermon should treat a text in which one complete thought is expressed. Alexandre Vinet, the great French Protestant preacher of the nineteenth century, tells us that from the time of Claude on, the preacher treated a subject rather than a text. This is not borne out by a study of the few sermons of Claude's which have survived. Claude is evidently concerned that each sermon make one point, and that a sermon have a unity of thought. This is a good principle of composition in the classical tradition, but the older tradition of expository preaching did not feel particularly obliged to follow it. The passage of Scripture took the lead and the preacher followed, going over as many subjects as time allowed. To be sure, a sensitive preacher would be aware of the overall unity of a longer passage of Scripture and would often be able to make the unity of the whole passage clear in his sermon. The effect of Claude's approach was to make the amount of Scripture covered in a single sermon rather small. More and more sermons treated single verses of Scripture rather than pericopes or paragraphs. The one series we have from Claude is five sermons on the parable of the wedding feast. What he treated in five sermons the sixteenth-century Reformers, as well as the Church Fathers, would more than likely have treated in a single sermon. If one followed Claude's approach, one could hardly expect to preach through a whole book of the Bible in any reasonable amount of time.

Jean Claude hardly fits the usual generalizations made about the preaching of Protestant orthodoxy. He was a popular preacher who attracted a large congregation in spite of the attempts of the government to suppress Protestantism. The time finally came, however, when his voice was silenced.

V. Conclusion — Witness as Worship

For the Christian historian, the question of providence is always present. The secular historian may insist on avoiding the question, but the Chris-

446

tian, even one who in no way thinks of himself as a historian, cannot help but wonder what meaning there is in the way things have unfolded.

What is the significance of the Huguenot witness, especially since it was to a large extent suppressed? Here was great preaching which did not change the world. It nourished a remnant, but a remnant that would soon be dispersed. To be sure, there are heroic stories to be told of clandestine congregations in the mountains of Languedoc. All the way through the eighteenth century there was the Church in the desert. Once again God called his people into the wilderness. In the nineteenth century there was a significant revival. Again the Protestant witness in France was a creative voice, but it was still a minority, even as it is today.

Especially in our own time, when ecumenical feelings have run so high, we cannot help but ask whether there is a place for a minority witness. When I was a student in France in the late sixties, it seemed as though Catholics were finally recognizing the legitimacy of Protestant Christianity and were beginning to come up with some of their own reforms. A Christianity both Catholic and Reformed seemed just around the corner. The visions that so many of us had in those days have, sad to say, somewhat paled, and yet one can never forget them.

The long view of Church history would seem to suggest that God often does call some of his people to bear a minority witness. Rarely does God give all his gifts to one person, or even to one group of people. Even the best of us bear but a partial witness. God in his providence has so arranged it that the most effective witness is made by a fellowship of witnesses. In the same way, God seems to be glorified by a variety of witnesses, even if the witnesses do not always completely agree. It would, to be sure, be so much better if all the witnesses were in complete concord, but then again, that may be an ideal impossible to realize in this life. Perhaps only in the eschaton will the Jesuit and the Calvinist lie down together.

Certainly we don't want to say that there was something partial, or marginal, or eccentric about the Protestant witness; it was so obviously a witness to the centralities of the Christian faith. This becomes so clear as one reads these sermons even today. It was a mature witness, a well-balanced witness.

Even in the worship of ancient Israel, the giving of a witness was understood to play a very special role in worship. The sacrifice of thanksgiving made in the Temple witnessed to the faithfulness of God. As we find it in the Law of Moses and even more in the Psalms, that witness was worship at its highest. In the same way, the witness of the martyrs in the ancient Church was understood to serve God's glory as nothing else. Witness is essential to worship, especially witnessing in difficult places.

It was a witness which God himself had called the Huguenots to make, and in the end that is the essential mark of a true service of worship. That is the mark of the worship that is well pleasing to God. We serve God's glory best when we do what he calls us to do. For some reason God called those courageous Christian people to make the witness they did outside the walls of Paris. Inside the walls something else was going on. About that we will have occasion to speak further on. The point we want to make here is that the witness of a minority is often very precious in God's sight. Such a witness is worship indeed; it glorifies God in the highest.

CHAPTER VII

The Flowering of Protestant Orthodoxy in the Netherlands

Those who lived in the Dutch Republic during the age of Frans Hals, Jan Vermeer, and Rembrandt van Rijn were indeed blessed. It was one of the bright clear days of human civilization. The United Provinces had won their independence from their Spanish overlords. In religious matters the Reformation had been widely accepted and was beginning to shape the character of the people. A very distinct Protestant culture was developing, for the most part middle-class. Dutch artisans were producing wares of high quality. Textiles, lacework, metalwork, ceramics, scientific instruments, and lenses were being manufactured and marketed throughout the land. The shipbuilding industry prospered, and Dutch merchants were trading their goods for exotic wares from as far away as the islands of Japan, Brazil, Curaçao, and lest we forget, the port of New Amsterdam. The Netherlands was open to the world. For its day, it was a tolerant society. It was a prosperous, hardworking land. Creative people found it a good place to live and work. In fact, our own Pilgrim Fathers found refuge in the Netherlands when they were driven out of their native England. For the French philosopher René Descartes, it was an intellectual haven. The Dutch Republic was a good place to be, as we see it painted by the seventeenth-century Dutch Masters.

The Netherlands was a good place to preach as well.[1] The Dutch

1. For the context of seventeenth-century Dutch preaching in general, see the fol-

449

have always loved solid preaching.[2] What a pity it is locked away in leather-bound volumes only Dutchmen can read. Thus is Dutch preaching rather inaccessible, although I am assured that Dutch is fairly easy to learn. Not only is the problem that few of us can read Dutch; apparently few Dutch preachers committed their sermons to writing! This chapter is one I have wanted to write for years, but I have put it off in hope that I could spend some time in the Netherlands, make a stab at learning Dutch, and see if I could unearth some firsthand information.[3] But the time has come for this volume to be finished up, so I will do the best I can with what I have. Hopefully my fragmentary, secondhand observations will inspire some learned Hollander to bring this secret treasure into better view.[4]

Traditionally, Dutch preaching is divided into several schools. It was recognized that in addition to the usual preaching of the Dutch Reformed Church, there was Lutheran, Mennonite, Walloon, and Remonstrant preaching. The Lutherans, in the port cities and in several cities in the north, followed the usual Lutheran pattern of lectionary preaching.[5]

---

lowing: Heinrich Heppe, *Geschichte des Pietismus und der Mystik in der reformirten Kirche, namentlich der Niederlande* (Leiden: E. J. Brill, 1879); Albrecht Ritschl, *Geschichte des Pietismus in der reformirten Kirche* (Bonn: A. Marcus, 1880), reprinted in Albrecht Ritschl, *Geschichte des Pietismus,* 3 vols. (Berlin: de Gruyter, 1966); and F. Ernest Stoeffler, *The Rise of Evangelical Pietism* (Leiden: E. J. Brill, 1965).

2. On the history of Dutch preaching, see the following: Izaak Boot, *De allegorische Uitlegging van het Hooglied, voornamelijk in Nederland* (Woerden: Zuiderduijn, 1971); T. Brienen, K. Exalto, et al., *De Nadere Reformatie. Beschrijving van haar voornaamste vertegenwoordigers* (The Hague: Uitgeverij Boekencentrum B.V., 1986); T. Brienen, *De Predeking van de Nadere Reformatie. Een Onderzoek naar het gebruik van de klassifikatiemethode binnen de predeking van de Nadere Reformatie* (Amsterdam: Uitgeverij Ton Bolland, 1974); T. Brienen, K. Exalto, et al., *Theologische Aspecten van de Nadere Reformatie* (Zoetermeer: Uitgewerij Boekencentrum, 1993); Jan Hartog, *Geschiedenis van de Predikkunde in de Protestantsche Kerk van Nederland* (Utrecht: Kemink & Zoon, 1887); and Klaas Runia, *Het hoge Woord en de Lage Landen: hoe er door de Eeuwen heen in Nederland gepreekt is* (Kampen: J. H. Kok, 1985).

3. Appreciation is hereby expressed to the Reverend Dr. Iain Stewart Maclean, who, in addition to supplying me with a translation of sermons by Teellinck and van Lodenstein, has supplied me with generous amounts of information on seventeenth-century Dutch preaching.

4. One particularly helpful work which is available to the English reading public is Stoeffler, *The Rise of Evangelical Pietism.*

5. A few years ago Howard Hageman found a collection of sermons on the Sunday Gospels published in Groningen sometime in the seventeenth century which he offered as evidence that Dutch Reformed preachers saw nothing wrong with following the lectionary. It would seem that such a conclusion was a bit hasty in view of the fact that

Apparently there were several very prominent Mennonite preachers. One remembers Rembrandt's portrait of the famous Mennonite preacher Cornelius Anslo, about whom the jest was made that not even Rembrandt could paint his magnificent voice. The Walloon preachers were those Protestants who preached in French to French-speaking congregations. Jacques Saurin, a French Huguenot who preached in the Hague, would be the best-known example, but another prominent Walloon preacher was Jean d'Outrein (1662-1722).

More important were the Remonstrant preachers. The Remonstrance was a group of Dutch ministers who, influenced by Jacobus Arminius, opposed the teachings of the Synod of Dort. The Remonstrance challenged what it perceived to be the Calvinist doctrines of predestination, human depravity, and irresistible grace, but also opposed the Calvinist insistence on the independence of the church from state control. Hugo Grotius was a strong supporter of the Remonstrance. The Remonstrance was very important intellectually, but it did not win a popular following. It was civic religion at its most obvious.

In addition to these schools, there was the usual preaching of the Dutch Reformed Church. Traditionally that preaching took one of two directions: it followed after either Gisbertus Voetius or Johannes Cocceius. We will speak of the preaching of these men in a moment, but first we must treat a very important figure for the history of Dutch preaching, namely, Willem Teellinck.

I. Willem Teellinck (1579-1629)

The mainstream of Dutch Protestant preaching as it developed in the seventeenth century owes much to Willem Teellinck. He was one of the first to emphasize the concerns of piety which became so important in Dutch preaching for the following century.

Bringing together the typical strands of Dutch spirituality which for generations had been brewing in that most devout land, Teellinck preached a very serious Christian piety.[6] He has often been regarded as a

---

there was a certain amount of Lutheran preaching in the Netherlands. Hageman failed to show that the lectionary sermons he discovered were preached from a Reformed pulpit, even if they were in Dutch.

6. For further information on Teellinck, see W. J. M. Engelberts, *Willem Teellinck* (Amsterdam, 1898).

Protestant Thomas à Kempis. He was intent on deepening the theological insights of the Protestant Reformation so that they bore fruit in the Christian life. One might say that he was concerned not so much with theological Protestantism as with devotional Protestantism.

Teellinck received the blessings of a thoroughly cosmopolitan education. As a young man he studied law at the University of Saint Andrews in Scotland and then went to France, where he studied at the University of Poitiers. From Poitiers he went to England, where he was attracted by William Perkins and the early Puritans. Moving in these circles, he underwent a conversion experience and dedicated his life to the service of the gospel. Then, returning to the Netherlands, he took up theological studies, studying under both Gomarus, the famous proponent of orthodox Calvinism, and Arminius, Calvin's equally famous detractor. In 1606 Teellinck was called to be minister at Hamstede en Berg, and finally in 1613 he was called to Middelburg, a major city in Zeeland in the far southwest of the Netherlands.

Teellinck wrote a considerable amount of material. Particularly important was his work on conversion, *Noodwendigh vertoogh aengaende den tegenwoordigen bedroefden staet van God's volck* (Necessary protest against the present sorrowful state of God's people), published in 1627. This work was so highly valued at the time that Voetius, the champion of Dutch orthodoxy, made it required reading for his students. In 1620 he published a book on simplicity of dress, a concern generally shared by Protestants at the time, as any admirer of Dutch seventeenth-century portraits will recognize. The lavish styles promoted by the French court were offensive to the Protestants of the day. Protestant plain style had wide repercussions. Yet another typical concern of seventeenth-century Protestantism that Teellinck wrote on was the observance of the Sabbath. His work *De rustijd, ofte tractaet van d'onderhoudinge des christelijcken rustsdachs* (Concerning the time of rest; or, a tractate on the keeping of the Christian days of rest) develops the role of the observance of the fourth commandment in the Christian life. Still another theme he developed was the missionary imperative. The Dutch East India Company and the Dutch West India Company were coming into increasing contact with people to whom the gospel had not yet been taken, and Teellinck pressed the demands of the Great Commission in both his writing and his preaching. Toward the end of his life he wrote several other devotional guides which had a wide circulation in the Netherlands. Particularly to be noticed are his *Het Nieuwe Jerusalem* (The new Jerusalem) and *Sleuetel der devotie* (Key of devotion).

452

Alongside the observance of Sunday as the Christian Sabbath and a commitment to simplicity of both public worship and lifestyle, Dutch Protestantism gave a high priority to the solemn observance of the Lord's Supper. As simply and directly as this celebration was done, it was a high point of the devotional life. This is very clear from a collection of four sermons Teellinck preached on preparation for Communion. *The Spiritual Adornment of Christ's Wedding Guests; or, The Practice of the Holy Supper* was published in Middelburg in 1620.[7] In this series of sermons he directs his congregation in the devotional participation in the Sacrament. In the first sermon he takes the imagery of the parable of the guests invited to the wedding feast as a figure for our spiritual approach to the Sacrament. The parable, of course, makes a point of the fact that one guest was thrown out of the feast because he had not come suitably dressed. We learn from this that we should not approach the Holy Supper carelessly prepared. In the second sermon he speaks at length of the preparation one should make in one's prayer closet during the week before the Sacrament is celebrated. More and more as the seventeenth century unfolded, this devotional preparation for the Sacrament became a central feature of Protestant spirituality.

The third sermon treats the devotional exercises which are appropriate for the communicant during the actual celebration of the Sacrament. For Teellinck the presence of Christ at this feast is the key to the spiritual appreciation of the Sacrament. Christ is surely present, seated with us at the table. He may indeed be present in a different manner than he was at the Last Supper in the Upper Room, but he is, to be sure, present. Indeed, he presides at the meal. It is because the congregation senses the presence of Christ at this celebration that so many hundreds of people in the church sit in solemn silence. All in turn come to the table, seat themselves, and then return to their places without making a sound. Is any other meal eaten with such reverence and solemnity (p. 98)? The vivid picture Teellinck draws of a celebration of Communion in a seventeenth-century Dutch Reformed church is moving. One cannot help but be reminded of the Dutch Masters' many paintings of their majestic churches, all whitewashed inside, filled with light and resounding with the thought-

---

7. Willem Teellinck, *Het Geestelyk Cierat van Christi Brutlofts-Kinderen, ofte de Oractijke des Heylighen Avondtmaels Daer inne* (Middelburg, 1620). The following study is based on a twentieth-century edition, Willem Teellinck, *Het Geestelyk Cierat van Christi Brutlofts-Kinderen, ofte de Oractijke des Heylighen Avondtmaels Daer inne*, 20th ed. (Franeker: T. Wever, 1969). Page references in the text are to this latter volume.

ful teaching of the Word. The poetry of these paintings tells us so much about the interiority of the worship which took place in these churches.

This vivid word picture of what must have been the regular experience of his congregation is used to introduce a favorite text for the Protestant Communion service: ""Behold, I stand at the door and knock; if any one hears my voice and opens the door, I will come in to him and eat with him, and he with me""" (Rev. 3:20 RSV) (p. 99). This text was commonly used to bring out the eschatological dimension of the celebration of Holy Communion. The Sacrament was regarded as a foretaste of the heavenly banquet, the wedding feast of the Lamb. In this text one discovers that in the Lord's Supper it is both true that Christ is present in our celebration of the Sacrament here on earth and that we, by means of this Sacrament, enter into the heavenly celebration of the wedding feast of the heavenly Bridegroom before the throne of God.

It is this vivid sense of Christ's presence at the Supper which inspires us to be careful to conduct ourselves appropriately. The sermon suggests several things which would define an appropriate celebration of the Lord's Supper. First, we should have a deep sense of awe before the divine majesty (p. 100). To make his point Teellinck marshals a series of rhetorical questions based on Old Testament texts. Solomon teaches us to conduct ourselves wisely when we sit down at the feasts of the rulers of this world; how much more should we be careful of our deportment at this banquet in the presence of God (cf. Prov. 23:1)? Isaiah tells us that even the angels approach the divine presence with covered faces; should we not show our most profound deference at the celebration of this Holy Sacrament (Isa. 6:2)? Even Moses teaches us that God will be glorified in all those who approach him; how much more should the Christian approach God in holiness (Lev. 10:3)? The Gospels tell us that the woman who secretly touched the hem of Christ's robe fell down before Jesus with fear and trembling when he spoke to her; so should we approach this sacred table with deep reverence, not to touch his garment but to be fed with his flesh and blood, that we be refreshed to eternal life (Mark 5:33) (p. 101).

It is because Christ is truly present at this sacred meal that we must partake of the feast in awe and wonder. Here at this feast we are seated next to him. We must open the eyes of faith and observe the presence of the Lord Christ (p. 102). It is with us as it was with the patriarch Jacob, who in his flight to Haran came to Bethel and was given a dream in which the Lord appeared to him. On awakening from that dream Jacob spoke with wonderment and deep reverence. He exclaimed that certainly the

Lord was in that place but he did not know it. Jacob was afraid and said: How fearful is this place! Is this not the house of God and the door to heaven (Gen. 28:16ff.) (p. 103)? So, when we approach the Lord's Supper, let us regard everything with the eyes of faith and be filled with awe and wonder, for indeed we are entering through the gates of heaven itself.

The second point Teellinck wants to make in this sermon is that we must approach the table with meekness and humility (p. 103). The previous sermon had spoken at length of the self-examination and confession of sin that was appropriate before coming to the Supper. We sit at the table conscious of all this, but even more, we should sit with a sense of thanksgiving. Thanksgiving is a key concept for Teellinck's eucharistic doctrine. It should be a heartfelt thanksgiving that fills us as we sit at the table of the Lord, a thanksgiving that recognizes the friendliness or openness of God toward us. As we remember the story of Christ's passion and resurrection, our hearts should overflow with thanksgiving (pp. 111-17). It is all this which makes us hunger and thirst for this sacred food and drink (pp. 118-23).

Next we should think of the all-sufficiency of the Lord Jesus Christ whose benefits are offered us in this supper (p. 133). He can forgive all our sins and heal all our wounds, for his blood is powerful. It is able to cleanse us from all our sin. Our preacher goes through some of the key New Testament passages which speak of the power of Christ's redemptive sacrifice (Rom. 3:24-26; I Pet. 2:24; and Heb. 9:14) to assure his congregation of the sufficiency of Christ's sacrifice to save us from all our sins and deliver us from our tribulations.

Our preacher has much to say on the nature of the Lord's Supper as a sign of the covenant. For Teellinck there is no suggestion that these signs are "mere signs" or "empty signs." They were instituted by Christ to seal his covenant promises (p. 134). With this he goes on to speak of the assurance we can have that the promises of God, set forth in these signs, will at last be fulfilled. This assurance, which comes so richly to those who devote themselves to seeking it, is the source of an amazing joy (p. 143).

Finally Teellinck comes to the subject of fellowship with other Christians who participate with us in the Sacrament. The Supper is not only communion with God; it is communion with fellow Christians as well. "Cast now your eyes upon those who are seated with you; . . . look at them with eyes full of Christ-like love" (p. 144). At the Supper the Christian should meditate on the wonder of God's redemption of these brothers and sisters. We should think to ourselves that they are dear and valuable, beloved and pleasant. What a glorious and attractive people true Christians are!

For Protestant piety the meditation inspired by the celebration of the Lord's Supper was a fundamental spiritual discipline. The liturgical service itself was simple, and that simplicity enhanced its solemnity. In fact, as seventeenth-century Protestants understood it, the high solemnity demanded the utmost simplicity. The meditation required from the communicant was essential to a true celebration. It was all part of the interiority demanded by Protestant worship. The preparatory sermons, which by this time were becoming such an important part of Protestant sacramental piety, led the communicant in this meditation.

II. Gisbertus Voetius (1589-1676)

Considered at its simplest, there were two major schools of preaching in the Dutch Reformed Church, the school of Gisbertus Voetius and the school of Johannes Cocceius. While the original sermons of these preachers have not been available for this study, a few remarks about them need to be made in order to put in context the sermons which have been available.

Often unfairly portrayed as an example of the extremes of Protestant scholasticism, Voetius was a church leader of remarkable balance. He occupied himself with both the most abstract sort of systematic theology and the practical concerns of building up the local congregation. He gave much attention to speculative theology on the one hand and to an intense devotional life on the other. In many ways he set the tone for Dutch Protestantism ever since. He preached a profoundly devotional Christian way of life informed by the insights of classical Christian theology.

Voetius was born in Heusden, where his family was well known for its strong commitment to the Reformation. In fact, his grandfather had been a martyr to the cause of Protestantism.[8] At the age of fifteen, young Gisbertus went off to Leiden to begin his theological studies. He spent

---

8. For further information on Voetius, see Jürgen Moltmann, "Voetius, Gisbert," in *Die Religion in Geschichte und Gegenwart*, ed. Hans von Campenhausen et al., 3rd ed., 6 vols. (Tübingen: J. C. B. Mohr [Paul Siebeck], 1957-62), 6:1432-33; G. D. van Been, "Voetius, Gisbertus," in *Realencyklopädie für protestantische Theologie und Kirche*, ed. Johann Jakob Herzog, 24 vols. (Leipzig: J. C. Hinrichs, 1896-1913), 20:717-25; and Arnoldus Cornelius Duker, *Gisbertus Voetius* (Leiden: J. J. Groen en Zoon, 1989).

seven years in that exciting new university, studying under both Arminius and Franciscus Gomarus, the champion of the Calvinist cause. In 1617 the young Voetius was called to be pastor of his native town, Heusden. In the following year he was delegated to the Synod of Dort. For the rest of his life he defended the canons of the synod and maintained a high respect for the polity of the Reformed faith. He was a Protestant canon lawyer through and through.

Ten years later Voetius came in contact with Cornelius Jansen, a Roman Catholic theologian at the University of Louvain. Louvain had been the intellectual center of the Counter-Reformation in the Netherlands from the very beginning. Jansen (1585-1638) became famous for his attacks on the Jesuits and his attempt to recover a more Augustinian theology for the post-Tridentine Catholic Church. The two theologians, Voetius and Jansen, had much in common. They were both supporters of a more Augustinian theology. While Jansen was dedicated to developing a thoroughly Catholic interpretation of Augustine, Voetius saw Augustinianism in terms of the Reformation. This theological engagement won Voetius name recognition throughout the Netherlands.

In 1634 Voetius was called to be professor of theology and Oriental languages at the Academy of Utrecht. Utrecht had been a major ecclesiastical center during the Middle Ages. The prince-bishop of Utrecht was regarded as the primate of the Netherlands. The city had experienced a long struggle between the ecclesiastical authority and the civil authority. With the Reformation the bishop's authority was repudiated and the city became the center of Dutch Protestantism. Voetius found himself in a position of leadership as professor in the city's major academic institution. His duties included not only teaching in the academy but also regular preaching in the major churches of the city.[9]

9. While we have not been able to locate a collection of the regular sermons of Voetius, a few of his occasional sermons were published during his lifetime. Among these are the following: Gisbertus Voetius, *Meditatie van de Ware Practijcke der Godtsalicheydt of der goeder Wercken* . . . (Amsterdam: Cornelis Hendricksz., 1628); Gisbertus Voetius, *Afscheydt Predicatie uyt Philipp I vers 27. Ghedaen in de Ghemeynte tot Heusden, den 20 Augusti 1634* (Utrecht: Aegidius ende Petrus Roman, 1636); Gisbertus Voetius, *Sermoen van de Nutticheydt der Academien* (Utrecht, 1636); Gisbertus Voetius, *Inaugurele rede over Godzaligheid te verbinden met de wetenschap,* ed. A. de Groot (Kampen, 1978); Gisbertus Voetius, *Eerste Predikatie in de Dom-Kercke tot Utrecht te negen uren den 16 Novembris 1673 Gedaen door Gisbertius Voetius na dat de Fransche macht de stadt, ende die van het Pausdom de dom-Kercke op den 13 November voor den Middagh verlaten hadden* (Utrecht, 1674).

Voetius, as one of the more important examples of Protestant scholasticism, had a high respect for Christian philosophy. He was of the opinion that before one studied theology one should study philosophy for at least two years. He was also a firm believer in the value of natural theology. The light of reason was sufficient, as Voetius saw it, to establish the existence of God and show the need for justice and morality. To establish the doctrines of the Trinity, the divinity of Christ, and the plan of redemption, however, one must turn to God's revelation as it is recorded in Scripture. He gave a much larger place to natural theology than did William Ames, the English Puritan who taught theology at Franeker and enjoyed much favor in the Netherlands at the time. On the other hand, Voetius took pains to refute the French philosopher René Descartes, who was spending his exile in Amsterdam. As Voetius saw it, Descartes was entirely too subjective. Voetius regarded his attempt to discredit natural theology with horror. In the end Descartes did not really establish a rational system, as Voetius saw it, but subverted the rational endeavor with his extreme subjectivity. Descartes's famous dictum *cogito ergo sum,* "I think, therefore I am," starts with the self and ends with the self. As Voetius saw it, this was the sort of subjectivism which destroyed all rationality.[10]

Voetius gave as much attention to questions of personal piety and devotion as he did to systematic theology. His work *Ascetika sive exercitia pietatis,* published in 1664, is fundamental for understanding the deepening of Protestant piety which was so central to the spirituality of the seventeenth century. Building on the work of the English Puritans, especially that of William Perkins and William Ames, and ultimately on Calvin himself, Voetius attempted to spell out the practical piety of the Protestant Reformation. These ideas, as Voetius understood it, were implied by the Reformers, but they had not been explicitly worked out, and that he saw as his vocation. He ran into much opposition. He set himself to refuting the charges that his work was a novelty, that it was precisionism, or pharisaism. His response was that theology is properly understood only when it becomes practical theology. Questions of ethics, devotion, and church polity should be among the most fundamental concerns of theology. If nothing else, the practical bent of twenty-first-century American Christianity should find in Voetius an unsuspected precursor.

10. Voetius's major work on systematic theology is his *Disputationes theologiae selectae,* which appeared in installments between 1648 and 1669.

III. Johannes Cocceius (1603-69)

Although Cocceius lived most of his life in the Netherlands, he was born and raised in Bremen, the renowned Hanseatic port city of north Germany.[11] At a relatively early age he distinguished himself in the study of Greek and Hebrew. In 1626 he went to the Frisian university at Franeker, a city well known at the time for its leading theologians, especially Muscovius and Ames. Eventually he was appointed professor of Oriental languages at Franeker, and then in 1650 he was invited to Leiden as professor of theology, where he taught until he succumbed to the plague in 1669.

The brilliance of seventeenth-century Dutch theology was to a large extent fueled by the dialectic between Cocceius and Voetius. Whereas Voetius was the proponent of Protestant scholasticism, Cocceius pressed the claims of a more biblical theology. He advocated a theology which kept closely to biblical concepts rather than the concepts of classical philosophy. His theology is usually referred to as federal theology or covenant theology. Insisting on the disciplines of grammatical-historical exegesis so dear to the Reformers, he developed Protestant theology in a direction very similar to that of Zwingli's successor in Zürich, Heinrich Bullinger. He emphasized salvation history and the personal covenant of each Christian with God.

It is quite possible, as we noticed with the preachers of the patristic age, that we have his sermons in commentary form. Cocceius has left us volume upon volume of commentaries on the books of both the Old Testament and the New. Quite possibly these commentaries are the fruit of years of *lectio continua* preaching on these books. Such a practice would certainly be consistent with his whole theological endeavor.

The biblical theology of Cocceius had, to be sure, strong implications for the preaching ministry. Those influenced by him tended to fill their sermons with detailed discussions of exegesis, and might discuss the derivation of Hebrew words and the fine points of Greek grammar at

11. For further information on Cocceius, see the biographical study in his collected works, Johannes Cocceius, *Opera omnia,* 12 vols. (Amsterdam: [P. & J. Blaev], 1706), and Johannes Cocceius, *Omnia opera,* 7 vols. (Frankfurt am Main: Balthasar Christopher Wustius, 1702). See also Gottlob Schrenk, *Gottesreich und Bund im älteren Protestantismus, vornehmlich bei Johannes Coccejus* (Giessen: Brunnen-Verlag, 1985); Ritschl, *Geschichte des Pietismus in der reformierten Kirche,* pp. 130-52; and E. F. Karl Müller, "Cocceius und seine Schule," in *Realencyklopädie für protestantische Theologie und Kirche,* 4:186-94.

length. Some preachers were able to make all this quite interesting and relevant, but others made it dry and gave the appearance of trying to make themselves appear erudite. Philosophical terminology, on the other hand, was avoided by Cocceius and his followers. Sometimes so much time was given to the exposition that little attention was given to application. However, the followers of Cocceius could become very interested in the practical application of the text and make all their studies of the text quite applicable to the Christian life, so the overall effect of Cocceius was to give good biblical foundations to the Dutch concern for piety. As we will see further on, the preaching of van Lodenstein was a good example of this. In actual fact, most preachers in the Netherlands were influenced by both Voetius and Cocceius. Friedrich Adolph Lampe, a generation later, synthesized the insights of both in his very influential *Institutionum Homileticarum Breviarum,* the classic of Dutch homiletics.

As we have said, neither of these premier theologians has left us an appreciable example of his regular preaching, although each is known to have been well received as a preacher. On the other hand, we are able to look at the sermons of one very influential Dutch preacher, namely, Jodocus van Lodenstein. Van Lodenstein, the friend and disciple of both Voetius and Cocceius, was one of those who brought together the insights of both, and helped make Dutch preaching so remarkable for its concern for both sound theology and earnest piety.

IV. Jodocus van Lodenstein (1620-77)

While Teellinck opened the seventeenth century, van Lodenstein lived during the middle of those golden years of the Dutch Republic.[12] His ministry took place when that glorious age was in full bloom. He was born in Delft and studied at Franeker, where he not only studied under Cocceius but lived in his house for two years as well. After two shorter pastorates in Zoetemeer and Sluis, he began his twenty-four-year pastorate in Utrecht, where he was the younger colleague of Voetius.

Van Lodenstein is chiefly remembered as one of the leading spirits

---

12. For further information on van Lodenstein, see J. Proost, "Jodocus van Lodensteyn," *Academic Proefschrift* (Amsterdam, 1880); M. Goebel and S. D. van Been, "Lodenstein, Jodocus van," in *Realencyklopädie für protestantische Theologie und Kirche,* 11:572-74; and Marinus Johannes Antoinie de Vrijer, *Lodenstein (Uren met Lodenstein)* (Baarn, 1947).

of the movement to deepen the Reformation, the "Nadere Reformatie." This movement was characteristic of Dutch seventeenth-century Protestantism. It was not some marginal splinter group but the central thrust of the most devout members of the Dutch Protestant church and similar to Puritanism in England. It pressed for a deepening of the Reformation, but it never resulted in a schism. As van Lodenstein understood it, the Reformation only began the reform that needed to be made. It was too concerned with correct doctrine and too quickly lost sight of the practical applications of the doctrines. Van Lodenstein's criticisms of the Reformation were not at all theological. He and the "Nadere Reformatie" were quite firm in their insistence that the theological insights of the Reformers were all quite sound, especially the strong doctrine of grace taught by Luther and Calvin. At this point van Lodenstein appeals to Teellinck's *Noodwendigh Vertoogh,* making the point that external reform requires a corresponding internal reform.

There was nothing schismatic about van Lodenstein. He was on friendly terms with his colleagues. Cocceius had been his teacher and continued throughout his ministry to exercise a strong influence on him. In Utrecht, Voetius, as pastor of Saint Catherine Church, was a colleague, and apparently the two got along quite well. Deepening the Reformation was the common concern of seventeenth-century Protestantism.

There were certainly those who criticized van Lodenstein. Some opposed his mysticism, others his asceticism. To some this seemed to return to medieval spirituality. We regret that we have not been able to study a Dutch preacher who opposed the "Nadere Reformatie." Had we been able to find two or three less intense preachers, van Lodenstein might appear as a marginal figure, but we have not found them. It is Teellinck and van Lodenstein whose sermons have come down to us. Even more, as we have observed again and again, this deepening of piety seems to be characteristic of seventeenth-century Protestantism.

A. Eucharistic Sermons

Again a series of preparatory sermons enables us to get a look at this major emphasis of the preaching of orthodox Protestantism in the seventeenth century.[13] The series originally contained at least four sermons, only three

13. Several years ago Iain Maclean, at that time a graduate student at Harvard Di-

of which have come down to us.[14] The series at one time included a preparatory sermon on Song of Solomon 2:4, "He led me into his wine-cellar, and love is his banner over me." This earlier sermon is mentioned in the last of the published sermons but is not found in the standard collection of van Lodenstein's sermons. There are sermons on Song of Solomon 5:3, "I had taken off my garment, how could I put it on again?" and 5:8, "I adjure you, you daughters of Jerusalem, that if you find my beloved that you say to him that I am sick with love." These two sermons are clearly preparatory sermons preached before a Communion service, but the sermon for the actual service does not seem to be included.[15] Finally, there is a thanksgiving sermon on Song of Solomon 1:4, "The king brought me into his inner-room,"[16] which was preached at a service following the Communion service. Series of eucharistic sermons such as these played an important role in the piety of Protestantism in the seventeenth century, as is clear from the number of series of such sermons which were published.

For twenty-first-century tastes a series of sermons on the Song of Solomon may seem a bit capricious. Serious exegesis seems so difficult on this text for the contemporary preacher, but seventeenth-century preachers did not look at it that way. They figured that the key to the interpretation of the Song is given to us in the parables of the wedding feast and the wise and foolish virgins, the story of the marriage at Cana, and the vision of the wedding feast of the Lamb in the Revelation of John. The exegesis

---

vinity School, read a paper at the Calvin Colloquium at Davidson College on these preparatory sermons. Immediately the importance of these sermons for the history of Christian worship became evident to me. Very graciously Dr. Maclean has provided me with an English translation of the complete series of these sermons.

14. The three sermons available to this study are found in a collection of van Lodenstein's sermons: Jodocus van Lodenstein, *Geestelyke Opweker voor het Onverloochende, Doode en Geestelose Christendom* (Amsterdam: Andr. Douci, 1732).

15. This seems to be the convention for a series of preparatory sermons. I am at a loss to explain this.

16. It is this final sermon which Prof. Maclean published in *Calvin Studies VI*: Iain S. Maclean, "The First Pietist: An Introduction and Translation of a Communion Sermon by Jodocus van Lodenstein," in *Calvin Studies VI*, ed. John Leith (Davidson, N.C.: Calvin Colloquium, 1992), pp. 15-34. References to the sermon on Song of Sol. 5:3 as well as references to the sermon on Song of Sol. 5:8 will appear as *Eucharistic Sermons* 2 and 3 respectively, followed by the page number of the Amsterdam edition, translations of which Prof. Maclean has provided me. References to the sermon Prof. Maclean published in *Calvin Studies VI* are given under the title *Eucharistic Sermons* 4, followed by the page number in *Calvin Studies VI*.

of this difficult book found in the ancient Church was well grounded, as seventeenth-century preachers understood it. Calvin had defended the traditional Christian interpretation, and orthodox Protestantism continued in train.

These sermons contain a number of remarkable features which help us understand this concern to deepen the Reformation. To begin with, they show us the tremendous importance which the celebration of the Lord's Supper occupied in Protestant piety. All too many have imagined that the frequency with which the Sacrament was celebrated is the index to its evaluation — those churches which celebrate it daily treasuring it most dearly, those celebrating it but quarterly valuing it least. Nothing could be more misleading. One need only read the preparatory sermons of the English Puritan John Preston or the American Presbyterian Gilbert Tennent to realize that the celebration of the Lord's Supper was the high feast of the Christian life. These preparatory sermons of van Lodenstein show us the same thing. They are symptomatic of the deepening of the devotional life which was being experienced throughout Protestantism during the seventeenth century.

One notices in these sermons an intensified sense of the presence of Christ. Christ is understood to preside at this feast. Granted, he is present in a different way than he was present at the Last Supper, but he is present nevertheless.[17] This presence is, to be sure, not so much a matter of his body being on the plate or his blood in the cup, but rather his being present as the bridegroom at the wedding feast.[18] The presence of Christ is intensified because it is a transcendent presence. One notices how often the seventeenth-century Protestant Communion sermons chose texts from the Song of Solomon or from Revelation, or how often they are preached on Jesus' parable of the wedding feast. The reason would appear to be that this imagery well expressed a sense of the transcendent presence of Christ in the celebration of the Sacrament.

17. Van Lodenstein, *Eucharistic Sermons,* 4:23.

18. No doubt van Lodenstein could also have preached on the Sacrament in terms of the Passover imagery. At the Supper we feast upon the Lamb of God, offered up as a sacrifice to atone for our sins. Christ is present at the Supper both as the Lamb who was sacrificed and as the High Priest who once and for all made the sacrifice and who now, as often as we keep the feast, presides over it. The sermons before us emphasize the wedding feast imagery rather than the Passover imagery, but the two are by no means incompatible with each other. Calvin's preparatory sermons which we studied above are more inclined toward the Passover imagery.

A particularly important text for van Lodenstein was Revelation 3:20, "'"Behold, I stand at the door and knock; if any one hears my voice and opens the door, I will come in and eat with him, and he with me"'" (RSV).[19] This had been an important text for Teellinck as well; it evoked for both men the imagery of the Supper in terms of both Christ's presence at our Supper here on earth and our presence at his Supper in heaven. There are both our eating with him and his eating with us.[20] As we have already pointed out, this text evokes as well the eschatological dimension of the Supper. The Lord's Supper is a foretaste of the wedding feast of the Lamb to be celebrated at the consummation of existence. Such an emphasis had long been characteristic of the Reformed understanding of the Supper. We find it already in Calvin's interpretation of the *sursum corda* which concluded the Communion Exhortation found in the eucharistic liturgy of the *Genevan Psalter* of 1542. Calvin exhorts his congregation not to dwell upon these earthly and corruptible elements which they see present with their eyes and feel with their hands, but to lift up their hearts and minds on high, where Jesus Christ abides in the glory of his Father and whence they expect his coming at their redemption. To come to the Lord's Supper is to enter into the heavenly reality while still living in this life.[21]

Again van Lodenstein follows the lead of Teellinck in his interpretation of Jacob's dream at Bethel. Jacob saw heaven open up before him with a staircase leading up to the divine presence. On it were angels ascending and descending, and Jacob awoke, saying, "'How awesome is this place! This is none other than the house of God, and this is the gate of heaven'" (Gen. 28:17 RSV). These words are for van Lodenstein a confession of Christ's presence in the celebration of the Supper. It is not through the outward senses that one becomes aware of this presence. It is rather a deeper, spiritual realization. "'Surely the LORD is in this place; and I did not know it'" (Gen. 28:16 RSV).[22]

For van Lodenstein the celebration of the Lord's Supper is an experience of communion. The text chosen for the final sermon, "The king brought me into his inner-room," naturally suggests this subject of com-

19. Van Lodenstein, *Eucharistic Sermons,* 2:266.

20. Van Lodenstein, *Eucharistic Sermons,* 4:19.

21. Interestingly enough, we find this same eucharistic theme in a Pentecost sermon by the German Lutheran pastor Heinrich Müller, who preached at just about this time in Rostock. See above.

22. Van Lodenstein, *Eucharistic Sermons,* 4:26.

munion with Christ.[23] The New Testament word *koinonia* is the word most aptly used here, and our preacher, who obviously has given himself to a careful study of the original languages, is fully aware of this.[24] *Koinonia* is an important word for his understanding of the Sacrament. Our preacher does a beautiful piece of exegesis to show that the king mentioned in the text is none other than Jesus the royal bridegroom. He supports this with texts from Daniel, Zechariah, and the Psalms, each being among the classic messianic texts of the Old Testament.[25] Then van Lodenstein turns his attention to the inner room and again gives us a beautiful piece of exegesis.

For those who knew their Bibles well, as so many everyday Dutchmen did, the exciting thing about these sermons was the wealth of parallel passages which were brought out to elucidate the text. To explain the "inner-room," several Old Testament passages are brought out, but even more interesting are the two references from the Gospel. Jesus at one point tells us that when we pray we are to go into our inner room or closet. Then in the Gospel of John we read that in our Father's house are many rooms. These are for the Christian what the Holy of Holies was in the Temple. By this inner room our preacher understands the tender love of Christ and the inner communion of the soul with her Lord.[26] What a magnificent unfolding of the biblical imagery van Lodenstein has laid before us!

In the sermon on Song of Solomon 5:8, "I adjure you, you daughters of Jerusalem," our preacher brings out the idea that in the Lord's Supper there is communion with fellow Christians. The *koinonia* goes in two directions. It is fellowship with Christ and it is fellowship with the congregation. Again we notice the resourcefulness of his exegesis in showing that the daughters of Jerusalem are fellow Christians. In her plight the bride, who is estranged from the bridegroom, cries out to the daughters of Jerusalem to ask their help.[27] This is what the Church is all about, according to our preacher. The daughters of Jerusalem are the true professors of the faith, who have God as their Father and the Church as their Mother. Quite naturally they exercise love toward one another as best they can. It is particularly the duty of Christians to comfort and exhort

23. Van Lodenstein, *Eucharistic Sermons,* 4:21.
24. Van Lodenstein, *Eucharistic Sermons,* 4:22.
25. Van Lodenstein, *Eucharistic Sermons,* 4:20.
26. Van Lodenstein, *Eucharistic Sermons,* 4:21.
27. Van Lodenstein, *Eucharistic Sermons,* 3:234.

one another, as we find in I Thessalonians 2:11 and 4:18.[28] This is elaborated at some length, and finally the point is made that there is nothing the Lord blesses so abundantly as our sharing our blessings one with another.[29] This is why the prayer of intercession is so important in public worship. Nehemiah is a good example of a godly man who exercised a ministry of intercessory prayer. So should all of us as Christians exercise a ministry in easing the burdens of one another.[30]

Perhaps one of the most striking features of this series is its strong sense of the primacy of grace. There is nothing here of the Pelagianism which was so common to late medieval pietism. There may be similarities to Thomas à Kempis in the emphasis on piety, but the strong Reformed doctrine of grace is most evident. Van Lodenstein's Protestantism is completely orthodox. This comes out particularly in the sermon on Song of Solomon 5:3, "I had taken off my garment; how could I put it on again?" These words, in van Lodenstein's interpretation, speak of the Bride of Christ having lost her first love.[31] This is often the case with Christians: they lose their first love and become worldly, as had the church of Ephesus. We read about this in Revelation.[32] The sermon develops this theme at length, speaking of the spiritual condition of worldly Christians who have lost their initial devotion. Apparently this was the way our preacher regarded many in his congregation; they were Christians who had lost their first love. Even at that, van Lodenstein insists on both the irresistible nature of grace and the perseverance of the saints. Christ remains steadfast in his eternal love, van Lodenstein insists. He does not change his goodness nor revoke his covenant of peace. He still remains the sworn comforter of his bride.[33] Here is the orthodoxy of the Synod of Dort in all its mysterious beauty.

These sermons make it very clear that the concern to deepen the piety of the faithful was in no way at the expense of Protestant orthodoxy. It is not as though orthodoxy and pietism were in some sort of Hegelian dialectic. They were quite complementary. We notice here an enrichment of classical Protestantism. In the seventeenth century the sacramental life, the prayer life, and the moral life intensified. The intensity of devotion in

---

28. Van Lodenstein, *Eucharistic Sermons,* 3:235.
29. Van Lodenstein, *Eucharistic Sermons,* 3:237.
30. Van Lodenstein, *Eucharistic Sermons,* 3:239.
31. Van Lodenstein, *Eucharistic Sermons,* 2:207.
32. Van Lodenstein, *Eucharistic Sermons,* 2:214.
33. Van Lodenstein, *Eucharistic Sermons,* 2:222.

the celebration of the Lord's Supper is most obvious from these sermons. These sermons were well received. According to Professor Maclean, over thirty editions were published.

What got these sermons across was not magnificent oratory. They were Protestant plain style from beginning to end. From time to time one finds a metaphor, a few simple exempla, but for the most part their beauty is in their exegesis. They offer a rich supply of parallel passages and biblical examples. There is such wisdom in the applications, such insight into the human condition.

What got these sermons across was their interiority. That is not quite the same thing as subjectivity. These sermons have a tremendous sense of interiority in that they bring us into the inner room, just as the Sacrament itself does. We find in these seventeenth-century Dutch sermons the same thing we find in the seventeenth-century Dutch paintings. The Dutch Masters had a marvelous ability to intimate the interiority of our existence. The interiors of seventeenth-century Dutch homes as painted by Pieter de Hooch, Gerard Terborch, and Jan Vermeer tell us much about life and what it meant to these people. One looks at an interior of de Hooch and marvels at the eloquence of its simplicity and order. Or again, one looks at an interior by Vermeer and senses the quiet of the room. Perhaps it is a woman reading a letter or doing a simple household task. Perhaps it is a man contemplating the vanities of life. It all had to do with the mystery of the inner room, that Holy of Holies, the Song of Songs. That is what Protestantism is all about. It is not about baroque power and authority but interiority, the secret communion with God. That is what justification by faith is all about and that is what sanctification by faith is all about as well.

B. Sermon for a Day of Prayer and Fasting

As we have seen, the preaching of days of prayer and fasting played an important role in the ministry of seventeenth-century preachers. These days were called at times of public sorrow or special emergency. A plague, a drought, a military disaster, the death of a revered public leader, or threatened invasion could lead either a civil or ecclesiastical authority to call for a day of public humiliation and prayer. The *Westminster Directory* gives us a concise description of these days of prayer and fasting. We have already spoken of the fast-day sermons Thomas Goodwin preached in England at about this time, and we will speak again of similar sermons when we come to preaching in New England.

One of van Lodenstein's fast-day sermons appears in his collected sermons.[34] This sermon is particularly interesting because it gives us a few glimpses of how a devout Protestant would observe a day of prayer and fasting. One prepared for the day in one's prayers and spiritual meditations (p. 183). This was done both in private prayer and in family prayer, and consisted in examining one's own conscience as well as the collective social conscience of the community. Examples of this are found in the prayers of Daniel 9 as well as Nehemiah 9. On the day of fasting a service would be held at the church — perhaps both in the morning and the evening — at which the minister would preach an appropriate sermon and lead the congregation in appropriate prayers. Psalms would be sung. Many of the biblical psalms were intended to be public prayers of confession and lamentation, and the minister would easily find psalms that fit the occasion. Then, again, at the end of the day in both family and private prayers, one would meditate on the sermon and appropriate its message in one's prayers (p. 203). In fact, the conclusion of this sermon urges the congregation to go home, pray about these matters, and thereby wait upon the Lord (p. 204).

The text of the sermon before us is II Corinthians 4:6, "For God, who has declared that the light should shine out of the darkness, is the one that has shone in our hearts, in order to give enlightenment of knowledge of the glory of God in the presence of Jesus Christ."[35] The preacher explains that since this was a fast day, he has chosen this text because he wants to preach about conversion. That is supposed to be what fast days are all about: repentance, turning oneself around (p. 183). Strangely enough, although fast days were usually called because of some specific public sorrow or danger, one gets not a hint from the sermon as to the occasion of this fast day, as to what might have been the reason for calling for a day of humility and repentance. All our preacher seems to be interested in is repentance, or conversion, itself.

34. Van Lodenstein, *Geestelyke Opweker voor het Onverloochende, Doode en Geestelose Christendom;* the page numbers in the text are from the Amsterdam edition. Again I am indebted to Prof. Maclean for his English translation.

35. This is an attempt at a literal translation of the Dutch as it appears in van Lodenstein's sermon. The RSV reads, "For it is the God who said, 'Let light shine out of darkness,' who has shone in our hearts to give the light of the knowledge of the glory of God in the face of Christ."

This emphasis on conversion is something we should notice very carefully. In the middle of the seventeenth century, it was a growing emphasis in Protestantism. More and more Protestants were becoming interested in the experience of conversion. This was not nearly so important a sermon topic in the classical Protestantism of Luther and Calvin, which was not especially interested in the subject. It had a much more objective understanding of salvation. With the English Puritans and the Dutch Pietists in the seventeenth century, things began to change. It was not the objective act of Christ's atonement which captured the attention of the preacher so much as the subjective experience of conversion. Perhaps this helps explain why this sermon does not focus objectively on some troubling event which took place, a devastating fire or an outbreak of the plague, but rather quite subjectively on the experience of conversion.

There is a common misunderstanding about conversion, van Lodenstein insists. One imagines that it is simply to turn away from evil (p. 184). There is much more: a divinely given enlightenment which fills us with spiritual joy and happiness. After one has grieved over one's sin, then there are the living of the Christian life and the performing of good works. Beyond that, conversion is not so much coming to the good life from evil as it is turning from oneself to God (p. 185). In conversion we need to put the emphasis on this turning to God.

Our preacher takes up his text and elaborates on the idea of the enlightening knowledge of the glory of God (p. 186). Here is the genius of the sermon — its magnificent exegesis of the converting power of God's glory. God's glory in itself enlightens us. This spiritual enlightenment enables true conversion. It concerns God's perfection, deals with the most glorious mysteries through which the Lord is glorified, and deals in particular with the counsels of God on account of human salvation and glorification so that the soul sees God's glory and realizes his sufficiency. The more the soul reflects this glory, the more it loses itself. That eternal view of God's all-sufficiency and endless glory shall be our blessedness (p. 187). This awareness of the glory of God, his sufficiency, and his worthiness transforms us so that we have true knowledge of God. It is not the knowledge that comes from hearing about God, but the personal, experiential knowledge of knowing God in himself. This personal knowledge is the love of God that the apostle Paul speaks about in I Corinthians 13, whereby we are no longer noisy gongs and clashing cymbals (p. 188). This is the enlightening of the glory of Christ about which our text speaks.

But now we must speak of where this light comes from, our preacher continues. God has shone in our hearts, our text tells us (p. 189). Here van Lodenstein develops his strong doctrine of grace. It is God who takes the initiative, who in the person of his Spirit transforms us from the inside out (p. 191). When God does this, we become partakers of the divine nature as we find it in II Peter 1:4. We are conformed to the image of God and move from glory unto glory, and as we find it in II Corinthians 3:18, this transformation is the work of God's Holy Spirit. It is the sanctification which leads to glorification. As anyone in van Lodenstein's congregation recognized, here is the classical *ordo salutis* of seventeenth-century Reformed orthodoxy: election, justification, sanctification, and glorification. These are the steps which lead to the fulfilled life.

Much of the sermon, so typical of seventeenth-century preaching, is devoted to application. The preacher's obvious concern is that each member of his congregation have the experience of conversion. He asks why so few have genuinely been converted (p. 195). He answers in the words of his text: it is because so few know the glory of God in the presence of Jesus Christ. Christ himself is not known. Our Savior is among us as an unknown god. The problem is that we have put the emphasis on reconciliation with God rather than regeneration (p. 196). We have sought the forgiveness of sins rather than entering into a loving relationship with Christ and our fellow Christians. It is in order that we might have this kind of life that Jesus came (p. 197). Our preacher now develops this in terms of knowing Christ first as prophet, then as priest, and finally as king. When we know Christ fully, then we have the real basis for the assurance of salvation (p. 198). Then we walk in the light as he is in the light.

We notice here a special feature from this time: the application is offered differently to different segments of the congregation. This approach was outlined long before the seventeenth and eighteenth centuries and has enjoyed special popularity from time to time. Gregory the Great suggested it in his *Regula pastoralis;* it was also a prominent feature of the preaching of George Whitefield during the Great Awakening. Van Lodenstein divides up the members of his congregation in terms of their spiritual need. There are those who still await conversion (p. 201). He urges these members to constantly seek to widen their knowledge of Christ. Interestingly enough, he gives them no program to follow. He seems completely confident that God will act in their lives and that he will take the initiative to convert them. He assures them very simply. Be well assured, God is at work within you! Others in the congregation are troubled that God does not seem to be at work. To these he would offer encouragement. Be constant in prayer and meditation on God's Word. God will do far more than all that we ask or think, as we find it in Ephesians 3:20. It is the Lord who converts us; our part is to wait upon the Lord. Let us be content with the measure of grace which God is pleased to grant us (p. 204).

One hardly needs to say that for the typical American Protestant of our day, this sermon is less than helpful. It hardly meets our activist expectations, and yet it does speak to the deepest realities of our Christian experience. Somehow what gets communicated is that here is a preacher who knows well the struggles of the soul and is able to witness from the midst of these struggles to the faithfulness of God. This kind of spiritual inwardness had long been characteristic of Dutch Christianity. This was the overwhelming strength of the *Devotio Moderna* before the Reformation, and even after the Reformation it continued. This interiority took on a very different nature once the Reformers were able to move it beyond the Pelagian tendencies we noticed in Thomas à Kempis. No doubt it was in reaction to the excesses of nominalist pietism that the Synod of Dort came out so strongly for the sovereignty of grace.

C. Conversion, Interiority, and Worship

It somehow belonged to the very nature of Dutch Christianity that the inward experience of worship was taken to be of the greatest possible importance. It was the natural heritage of the *Devotio Moderna*. But between Thomas à Kempis and the preachers we have looked at in this chapter, there was a major development. The Dutch Reformed theologians had developed a very strong doctrine of grace. They knew better than to put the emphasis on devotional techniques or liturgical formulations. It was not that sort of thing which glorified God. To be sure, there were those who tried to make piety a matter of strict Sabbath observance, abstinence from card games, and avoidance of the tavern and the dance hall. But that was all very external. Such things had to do with the outward appearance of piety. The mature Dutch Christian understood this very well, whether that Christian was in the pulpit or in the pew.

Conversion had to do with the inward experience of the Christian life. It was the transforming of the human life so that it reflected the glory of God. When that happened God was truly worshiped.

One often looks at the worship of Dutch Protestantism and gets the impression that nothing is going on. One looks in vain for a prayer book filled with profound prayers expressed in poetic language. One looks for cantatas or intricate musical settings of the services. The Dutch Reformed Church just never produced such things. One can't even find tome upon tome of pulpit oratory; at least it never reached such a level of artistic elegance that it was translated into English. It always remained Protestant plain style through and through. On the other hand, we know that everyday Dutchmen went to church frequently. They listened to sermons for hours. They may not have been interested in pulpit eloquence, but they loved a careful exposition of the text. As far as they were concerned, that was the art of the sermon. They were regular in their disciplines of prayer both in church and at home. Their celebrations of the Sacrament were occasions of intense devotion. How is it that such a devout people had such simple worship?

The answer may be found in the canvasses of the Dutch Masters. The portraits of Frans Hals, the interiors of Jan Vermeer and Pieter de Hooch, the landscapes of Ruisdael and Hobbema, and the Bible stories of Rembrandt all speak in different ways to the interiority of life. They all speak of the inner life of that very Christian people who lived out their lives on the shifting sandbars between the North Sea and the delta of the Rhine. Scratching out a livelihood on that unpromising strip of real estate was a battle, but the people of the Netherlands were sustained by a lively faith in God. God was a constant reality on whom they daily depended.

One looks at the paintings which Saenredam and de Witte did of the interiors of Dutch churches, so plain with their whitewashed walls and clear glass windows, and one gets a sense of how dear those churches were to those who worshiped in them. One looks at the landscapes of van Goyen and senses that the heavens are alive with the presence of God. One only has to catch sight of van der Velde's skies to realize that God presides over the busy port of Amsterdam with its worldwide commerce. God presides over the cornfields and pastures with their flocks and windmills. Dutch seventeenth-century painting is an eloquent testimony to the sovereignty of God.

But it is the faces of everyday Dutchmen which tell us the most. It is the interiority of a Rembrandt portrait which so clearly witnesses to the depths of the soul. It is the spiritual potential that one reads in the faces of a Frans Hals portrait of an old wife, dressed up in Sunday best, holding her Bible in her lap. But still Rembrandt surpasses them all when he paints an old man meditating on the meaning of life. And then there were the Bible illustrations. No one could illustrate the Bible quite like Rembrandt. He saw his whole life played out in the stories of Jesus. If there was ever a picture of the glory of preaching, it is Rembrandt's hundred-guilder print showing Jesus surrounded by the common people of his day, pouring out the light of eternal truth. For Dutch art it is the light, the true light, which converts everything.

CHAPTER VIII

The Age of Louis XIV

Pulpit eloquence reached an unparalleled height during the reign of the most splendid of French kings. When one thinks about it, what else would one expect? It was only appropriate that an age of such culture should produce preachers of renown. It was during the reign of Louis XIV that Molière wrote his witty masterpieces of theater, and that Racine created his dramatic tragedies. Surrounding the French court was a galaxy of brilliant, clever people who appreciated all kinds of artists and writers. Madame de Sévigné described in her letters and journals the intellectual life of Paris in the middle of the seventeenth century. It was dedicated to good taste, to refinement and excellence. It was the age in which Mansart built baroque palaces for the aristocracy and equally glorious churches for the state religion. Today one marvels at his masterpieces, such as the chapel he built for Anne d'Autrice at the Hôpital de Val de Grace and the church built for the retired soldiers of Louis' military campaigns, the glorious Les Invalides. One admires Lenôtre's Vaux le Vicomte, the château he designed for Le Fouquet, the finance minister of Louis, with its symmetrical formal gardens and the light-filled salons with their parqueted floors. And finally there was Versailles, which summed up the spirit of the age. Such elegance demanded eloquence. How could one preach in the chapel at Versailles without responding to the royal demand for magnificence!

In fact, Louis XIV was a patron of good preaching. All things considered, he was a good Catholic, or at least the established Church of his day was willing to consider him a good Catholic. As the most absolute of absolute monarchs, he was devoted to the Catholic Church. He understood the Catholic principle of authority. In the same way God had given absolute spiritual authority to the pope, so he had given to the king of France absolute temporal authority. At the height of the controversy over the rights of the Gallican church, Pope Innocent XI could worry as to whether Louis was going to go the way of Henry VIII, but he did not have to. Louis had a high respect for papal authority. It was the spiritual analogy to his absolute temporal authority and sanctioned his whole political philosophy. To be sure, he could carefully distinguish between spiritual and temporal authority, and once those distinctions had been made he could be quite insistent that the spiritual authority not invade the temporal, but he very firmly believed in the authority of the Church in its own sector. Louis had respect for his preachers. They had their sphere of authority as well. He even allowed them considerable liberty as long as they respected court etiquette. Preachers were supposed to preach against sin. That was their responsibility. Even if they occasionally came rather close to reprimanding the king for his adulterous affairs and his extravagant luxury, he recognized that that was what preachers were supposed to do. Fortunately, for the sake of their consciences, it never occurred to them that military aggression was a sin against which they should be preaching. They never batted an eye at the exorbitant taxes demanded by the government. Much less did it ever occur to them that they should be preaching against the kind of religious politics that was involved in the revocation of the Edict of Nantes. In the seventeenth century that was politics, not sin. Yet Louis knew he was a sinner, and when he got old he would repent. He was sure God would understand. In the meantime, he wanted brilliant preaching that would assure him that the glory of his reign was a reflection of the divine glory.

The history of preaching has enshrined the names of three consummate orators who satisfied the taste of that age: Jacques-Bénigne Bossuet, Louis Bourdaloue, and Jean-Baptiste Massillon. Their sermons have an undisputed place among the classics of French literature. They preached the Word of God in such polished eloquence that even the most cultured despisers of the Christian faith listened with admiration. The Age of Louis XIV was the golden age of French literature. And what was admired at the court of the Sun King was admired throughout Europe. Even down to our own day the sermons of Bossuet, Bourdaloue, and Massillon have been regarded as the paradigms of pulpit eloquence.

Their sermons came as the fruition of a tradition of preaching solidly based in the Counter-Reformation. We have already spoken of the preaching of Saint Francis de Sales, who realized that serious and competent Catholic preaching was an important defense against Protestantism. He saw that Catholic preaching needed to be cultured and learned in order to appeal to the intellectuals of the day, who had been attracted to the obviously learned sermons of the Reformers. The Jesuits, too, realized the importance of cultured and learned preachers. Vigorously they cultivated the arts of sacred oratory, just as they cultivated all the arts, that they might enthrall the world with the glories of Holy Mother Church. They were particularly vigorous in their appeal to the upper classes.

There was another dimension to French Catholic preaching in the seventeenth century. Saint Vincent de Paul extended this concern to the poor. He convinced French Catholics of the need to provide even the poor parishes of the city as well as the countryside with preachers who could articulate the Catholic faith. While his sermons have not come down to us, he must have been one of the most effective preachers of the seventeenth century.

The Catholic Reformation made a serious attempt to counter the Protestant Reformation with effective preaching. The sermons of Bossuet, Bourdaloue, and Massillon were the flowering of this attempt.

To complete this chapter we will look briefly at a fourth preacher, François de Salignac de la Mothe Fénelon, the archbishop of Cambrai. Fénelon represented a different tendency in French Catholicism. Although an aristocrat by birth, he was one of those who had reservations about the absolutism of Louis XIV. He saw its spiritual dangers much more clearly than did Bossuet. He, too, was a master of the French language, but he was not completely charmed by the baroque spirit. It would be a mistake to speak of Bossuet without speaking of Fénelon. While few of Fénelon's sermons have come down to us, they are of particular interest because they show us the first tentative moves toward pietism. They show us the beginning of a move away from the absolutism of the baroque.

I. Jacques Bossuet (1627-1704)

Today celebrated as the greatest of French orators, Jacques-Bénigne Bossuet was more widely known in his own day as the leading theologian of France.[1] Bossuet was court theologian to the Most Christian King,

1. For biographical material on Bossuet, see the following: Jean Calvet, *Bossuet:*

Louis XIV of France. "The Most Christian King" was the unique title the pope granted to the kings of France to express the unique relation these kings had had with the papacy ever since Charlemagne, the king of the Franks, had become the political sponsor of a specifically Roman Catholicism. The alliance between Charlemagne and Hadrian brought the final victory of Roman Catholicism over the Western Church and made the Roman popes the supreme ecclesiastical authority in the West. Louis XIV did understand himself as the heir to Charlemagne, and in fact, even to Constantine and Theodosius, the primary princes of the Church. And that was the way Bossuet saw Louis XIV. His admiration for his king was genuine and complete. He was Louis' theologian, the voice not so much of Roman Catholicism as of French Catholicism. He earned his doctorate of theology from the Sorbonne and wrote many volumes of learned theology which were read throughout Europe. His *Exposition de la doctrine catholique sur les matières de controverse* (1671) and *Histoire des variations des églises protestantes* (1688) were regarded by many as the most important theological works of the century.

Bossuet was a forceful apologist who engaged many Protestants in a reevaluation of their position. His attempt to win Protestants to his vision of the integral and timeless unity of the one true Catholic faith was often kind and imbued with the sort of patience which comes from being absolutely convinced that one is right. He never for a moment understood what the Protestants were talking about. He was completely self-assured and therefore genteel and courteous. He firmly believed that his attempts to convert the Protestant minority of France were born of a benevolent concern for their spiritual welfare. His high-mindedness must be recognized even if he did provide the theological foundations of the revocation of the Edict of Nantes.

Some have claimed that he had an ecumenical concern, but his ecumenical approach is illustrated by his famous debate with the Huguenot pastor Jean Claude. Unfortunately, Bossuet would allow a discussion only

---

L'Homme et l'oeuvre (Paris, 1939); Augustin Largent, "Bossuet," in *Dictionnaire de théologie catholique,* 18 vols. (Paris: Letouzey & Ane, 1903-50), 2:1049-89; Jacques Bossuet, *La Prédication au XVIIe Siècle,* Actes du Colloque tenu à Dijon les 2, 3 et 4 décembre 1977 pour la trois cinquantième anniversaire de la naissance de Bossuet (Paris: Librairie A.-G. Nizet, 1980); Ella Katharine Sanders, *Jacques Bénigne Bossuet: A Study* (London: SPCK; New York: Macmillan, 1921); William John Sparrow Simpson, *A Study of Bossuet* (London: SPCK, 1937); and Jacques Truchet, *La prédication de Bossuet,* vols. 1 and 3 (Paris: Éditions du Cerf, 1960).

of the points Bossuet proposed. Could Protestantism provide the authority necessary for a Christian society? How could the free inquiry allowed by Protestantism do anything but degenerate into individualism? The two theologians debated in the most civil and polite terms, but Claude was forced to fight with one hand tied behind him. Today one would hardly call this ecumenism. One may fault Bossuet's vision of Christianity for its absolutism. He was, sad to say, a complete integralist. Be that as it may, it was a typical position for a man of his day. He may have been the theologian of absolutism, but, sad to say, many have been attracted to his vision of an authoritative Church ever since.

Bossuet was a statesman of the Church. He was a diplomat who knew how to still the often troubled waters between church and state. Even though he was the bishop of a relatively unimportant see, and never received the cardinal's red hat, he did have tremendous influence in the Church. It was Bossuet who kept the Gallicanism of the French Catholic hierarchy from becoming a movement for the independence of the church of France. On the one hand he curbed the strongly Gallican archbishop of Paris, François de Harlay, but on the other hand he won the disapproval of Pope Innocent XI because of his conciliarist views.

Part of the secret of Bossuet's influence was his ability to sense what the king wanted even before the king himself had figured it out. Louis XIV had no intention, as we have said, of going the way of Henry VIII. He wanted to remain a loyal son of the Roman Catholic Church, but he wanted to have the same relation to the Church that Constantine and Charlemagne had had before him. If Lancelot Andrewes understood the divine rights of James I in terms of King David, Bossuet saw his sovereign in terms of Constantine, the patron and protector of the Church. Bossuet, in fact, saw the role of Louis XIV in much more universal terms than the Anglicans saw the role of their king. The Catholic Church was fortunate to have Louis, the most powerful king in Europe, as her sponsor. It was only natural, as Bossuet saw it, that the Gallican church had special rights and privileges. More than eight hundred years before, Charlemagne had enjoyed many special privileges in ordering the affairs of the Church, and as Bossuet and other French Catholic churchmen understood it, Louis XIV was heir to these privileges.

In the Middle Ages the French church felt called to protect the pope at Avignon. It was always a strong supporter of the conciliarist position, which had never died out in France. The Pragmatic Sanction of Bourges, issued in 1438, had upheld the right of the French church to administer its temporal property and appoint its own hierarchy. The Concordat of Bologna, issued in 1516, had allowed the king of France to appoint bishops in his realm. Louis XIV, as the most powerful Christian monarch of his day, saw himself as having unique privileges in the Catholic Church, and Bossuet was sympathetic to the vision of his king. Bossuet looked to the king of France to lead the Catholic Church to greater triumphs and greater glory than she had known even in the days of Constantine. It was the king of France who would end the schisms of the Reformation and bring the Protestants back to the unity of the Catholic Church. Bossuet saw himself as a diplomat of the Catholic Church, but it must be said that he was a diplomat not so much in the service of the Roman Catholic Church as of the French Catholic Church.

As all the great men of letters in the Age of Louis XIV, Bossuet was inspired by the culture of classical antiquity. As a boy in the College of Navarre in Paris, he had been trained in the Greek and Latin classics. He, too, as many before him, shared the ideal that a great statesman must be a great orator. Just as Racine modeled his dramas on Sophocles, Bossuet molded his sermons on Demosthenes. He saw himself as an orator, a Christian orator at the court of the Most Christian King. It is only natural, therefore, that his sermons take the literary form of a discourse on a religious theme rather than an exposition of Scripture as developed in the synagogue and the early Church. His sermons have not much in common with those of Origen or John Chrysostom. He had a passion for Saint Augustine, and yet his sermons remind us more of the orations of Gregory of Nazianzus, "the Christian Demosthenes," than they do of the sermons of Augustine. Perhaps the sermons he delivered in Meaux, if they had been recorded, would have resembled more his beloved Augustine. We can only guess. We know that he preached frequently at his cathedral in Meaux in the last twenty years of his life. When he made his visitations of the parish churches, he would preach several times a day in the course of a single visit. All that has been preserved, however, are the orations he delivered on great occasions. It is these, therefore, that we will have to study.[2]

The Lenten sermons of Saint Germain were to be preached before Louis XIV at the chapel of the Louvre, but because of the death of the queen mother, Anne d'Autrice, shortly before the beginning of Lent, the

---

2. For editions of Bossuet's sermons, see Jacques Bossuet, *Oeuvres oratoires de Bossuet,* ed. J. Lebarq, 7 vols. (Paris and Lille: Desclée de Brouwer et Cie, 1890-97). The page references in the text are to vol. 5 of this work.

court left Paris and the series was held at Saint Germain-en-Laye. This was the second series of Lenten sermons Bossuet preached before the king, and unfortunately it is incomplete. A number of the sermons have been lost while others are preserved only in fragment. Few of Bossuet's sermons were published during his lifetime, and all we have for most of his sermons are the manuscripts of the preacher, who did not always write his sermons out in full. Only the introduction of the Easter sermon, for example, has been preserved. We have only twelve sermons or parts of sermons from a series that must have included almost twice as many. One wonders why a writer as conscientious about his literary work as Bossuet never finished up his sermons for publication. Perhaps he thought of himself primarily as a theologian, or perhaps he felt that sermons were meant to be heard rather than read. But we should also remember how much he admired Augustine, who did not give much attention to the publication of his sermons either. Whatever the reason, we are grateful for what we have. Let us look at five sermons from the series to get a picture of Bossuet's preaching ministry.

A. A Sermon for the Feast of the Purification of the Virgin

The series begins with a sermon for the feast of the purification of the Virgin. The text is taken from the Gospel of the day, "And when the time came for their purification according to the law of Moses, they brought him up to Jerusalem to present him to the Lord" (Luke 2:22 RSV). The introduction to the sermon is magnificent! Referring to the Christian emperor Theodosius, our preacher says, "A great emperor once declared that there is nothing more royal, nothing more majestic, than a prince who himself submits to the law; to do this in fact is to submit to reason itself; and certainly humanity may see nothing more beautiful than justice on the throne; and one can not think of anything more grand, nor more august than the noble alliance of power and reason which brings together both authority and example through an observance of law" (p. 2).[3] Our

3. "Un grand empereur a prononcé qu'il n'y a rien de plus royal ni de plus majestueux qu'un prince qui se reconnaît soumis aux lois, c'est-à-dire, à la raison même: et certes le genre humain ne peut rien voir de plus beau que la justice dans le trône; et on ne peut rien penser de plus grand ni de plus auguste que cette noble alliance de la puissance et de la raison, qui fait concourir heureusement à l'observance des lois et l'autorité et l'exemple."

preacher goes on to observe that the text tells us of the example the holy family set of submission to the law. For our Lord, although he came to abolish the Law of Moses by a law more perfect, nevertheless fulfilled the Law of Moses when he was taken to the Temple. Nothing could be more appropriate to the feast we celebrate today, Bossuet says, than for your preacher to speak of dependence on God and on the order he has established. The Virgin has given us an example of the necessity of obedience; let us therefore call upon her for help. With this the preacher and his congregation, in good Catholic tradition, recite the Ave Maria (p. 3).

Having introduced his theme, Bossuet now divides up his text. There are three kinds of law, he tells us. There is the law that directs us, the law that constrains us, and the law that entices us. One notices the studied parallelism in this threefold division. It is for this kind of literary finesse that homileticians have admired Bossuet for centuries. Our preacher points out that the text tells us how the faithful are to respond to each of these kinds of law. Jesus and his holy mother submitted to the law which directed them to present themselves at the Temple. Simeon submitted himself to the constraining law of death without anxiety, and Anna, the faithful widow, in her penance and mortification of the flesh, overcame the enticements of the law of sin. That Anna should be brought so prominently into the sermon was a genial bit of court diplomacy. Anne d'Autrice, the queen mother, had died less than two weeks before. She, too, had lived many years as a widow. She was a devout lady, sincere and generous in her charitable works. Her son, Louis XIV, was devoted to her even if he did not yield to her pleas that he respect his marriage vows. Bossuet himself had enjoyed her patronage. It was probably through her influence that he was first invited to preach at court. This brief homage to Anna, the prophetess, was a subtle and tasteful homage to the queen mother which the whole congregation would have deeply appreciated, above all the king himself.

Our preacher now sets out to develop his first point. He begins with a few words on liberty. The word "liberty" is surely the most agreeable and delightful of words, but the way it is used is often quite deceptive. It is often used as though it were the opposite of law, and is called on to excuse all kinds of lawlessness and sedition (v. 4). Bossuet's target is clear. The intellectuals of the court, the rich and fashionable of French society liked to think of themselves as libertines, as above the law. The sophisticated flatterers who surrounded the king liked to tell him he was above the law; whether regarding the laws of marriage or the laws of international diplomacy, he was king, and could do whatever he wished. It was obviously against such an attitude that Bossuet intends to preach. True liberty, Bossuet tells us, comes from submission to the law. In the Gospel of John we read that if the Savior makes us free, then we really are free (John 8:36). There is a freedom which is genuine, but there is also a freedom which is only apparent (p. 5). Animals, to all appearances, are quite free. They know neither law nor reason, nor in the end do they know genuine freedom. Tertullian tells us that God has given laws to man, not to deprive him of liberty but to show his respect to man. In giving us law God recognizes man's intelligence and rationality. When, on the other hand, we live as lawless animals, we despise our reasonable nature (p. 6). It is the glory of man to live a regulated life, Bossuet claims (p. 8). True liberty is to depend on God. To refuse our obedience to his authority is not liberty but rebellion (p. 9). The rebellious are foolish to think they have true liberty. Quite the opposite from being free, they are driven by their pleasures and passions. In the empire of God regulated so absolutely by his authority, the time will come when such rebels will lose their liberty and enter into an eternal servitude (p. 11). Our orator brings his first point to a stirring conclusion by addressing the Virgin and her divine Son. "Appear to us, O most holy Virgin, Appear to us, O divine Jesus, that your example might pierce our hearts. What pretext can we find for excusing ourselves from the law when we find your example of obedience!" (p. 13).[4] The point we can be sure our preacher hopes that even the king will draw, is that not even the king is excused from obedience to the law. To make that point in the king's presence takes considerable courage.

Our preacher now turns to his second point, a consideration of the law that constrains and Simeon's example of how the Christian is to accept the constraining counsels of God with patience. Bossuet tells us that one must distinguish among the things God wants of us between those about which we must make a choice and those we must do even if it is not our choice (p. 14). God wants us to be just, moderate in all our desires, sincere in all our words, equitable in all our actions, prompt to pardon all our injuries, and incapable of injuring others. But in such things God does not force our liberty. On the other hand, there are things in our life

---

4. "Paraissez, ô très sainte Vierge! paraissez, ô divin Jésus! et fléchissez par votre exemple nos coeurs indomptables. Qui peut être exempt d'obéir, puisqu'un Dieu même se soumet?"

which God determines by the secret disposition of his providence, which go beyond our abilities to determine or even discern. It is about this that Isaiah spoke: ""My counsel shall stand, / and I will accomplish all my purpose"" (Isa. 46:10 RSV). Bossuet begins a long and most interesting discussion of why there is this difference (pp. 15ff.). He concludes the discussion by observing that many things come our way in life about which we can do nothing except put our faith in God and be confident in the guidance of his providential hand. Simeon himself was one who lived by the providence of God.

The third point becomes, in fact, the peroration. Bossuet wanted to make the point that Anna, the prophetess, had overcome the law of sin by living a long life of sexual abstinence, fasting, and prayer. The death of Anne d'Autrice gave the preacher an opportunity to eulogize one of the grand dowagers of Catholic piety. For such an occasion he brings out his most effusive eloquence: "It is her faith, it is her piety, it is her abandon to the established order of God, who himself inspired her courage; and it is that same faith and that same abandon toward Providence, which always supported her despite the cruel sufferings even to the point of entering the arms of death" (pp. 23-24).[5] Perhaps the modern reader finds this tribute a bit florid, but the ladies and gentlemen of the court found it quite fitting. Anne d'Autrice was the kind of royal personage one would expect the clergy to admire. The sermon could well have ended here and everyone gone away quite happily — including the preacher.

Suddenly the sermon takes an unexpected turn. The framework of the three-point sermon is completely broken. Bossuet quotes the Second Psalm,

> Now therefore, O kings, be wise;
> be warned, O rulers of the earth.

> (v. 10 RSV)

The God who determines the span of life determines the events of history. It is not the stars that shape history, but the providence of God (p. 25). With this Bossuet attacks the astrologers who had such influence at the court of the Sun King. They had divined the death of the queen,

---

5. "C'est sa foi, c'est sa piété, c'est son abandon aux ordres de Dieu, qui animait son courage; et c'est celle même foi et ce même abandon à la Providence, qui la soutenant toujours malgré ses douleurs cruelles jusques entre les bras de la mort."

which was in itself not in the least surprising, but they were also confidently predicting war with England, which was having a disastrous effect on French foreign policy. If we really are concerned about war, Bossuet intones, let us repent of our sins, live a godly life, and trust in the help of God (p. 26). Unfortunately, Bossuet ends his sermon with a shameless bit of Pelagianism. "Let us do the will of God and afterward he will do ours." The effusiveness of the remarks about the queen mother and the Pelagianism notwithstanding, this was a courageous sermon. Bossuet was not as blunt as Amos, or John Chrysostom, or John Knox, but he had a prophetic word for a political regime that claimed Christian faith. He preached that word with an eloquence and a diplomacy we must admire.

B. A Sermon on the Virtue of Honor

We now look at a sermon on the virtue of honor. The text is taken from Matthew 23:5, "'They do all their deeds to be seen by men . . .'" (RSV). Our preacher begins by saying how surprised he is that those who take such pride in the wisdom of their own judgments are so dependent on the approval of others (p. 41). The Pharisees in the Scripture lesson were so shamefully captive to winning the honor of the world. Let us not follow their example, Bossuet says. We far too often also seek honor in such vain things as ceremonial, jewelry, and fine clothing (p. 42). True honor is something quite different.

Bossuet begins to develop his first point by quoting the apostle Paul: "Brethren, do not be children in your thinking; be babes in evil, but in thinking be mature" (I Cor. 14:20 RSV). There is nothing more childish, our preacher comments, than seeking honor in external ornamentation rather than in the moral beauty of a good life (p. 44). Bossuet quotes John Chrysostom, one of his favorite authorities, to the effect that foolish men think they can render themselves illustrious by external brilliance even if they lose the inner beauty of a good conscience (p. 45). Indeed, all men are born for grandeur, Bossuet assures his congregation, but the grandeur for which they have been born is to have communion with God. When, through sin, man loses this communion with God, he tries to recapture his faded glory by grabbing the vain shadows of that glory. He imagines himself being glorified by sumptuous clothing and costly jewels, by a retinue of servants, and by finely decorated apartments and vast estates. Bossuet fascinates his hearers by his word pictures. He speaks of the

484

women of the court who have the wealth of a whole patrimony in pearls strung around their necks (p. 46). He speaks of men who multiply their titles and honors and make of their persons spectacles to dazzle others as foolish as themselves (p. 47). This remarkable series of word pictures is concluded by the figure of Nebuchadnezzar, king of Babylon, whom Bossuet styles the very model of vanity itself (p. 48). To this our preacher adds a series of impressive quotations. He quotes Psalm 4:2, "O men, how long . . . / How long will you love vain words, and seek after lies?" (RSV). Outward vanities, Chrysostom tells us, are the clearest evidence of inward poverty. It would appear, then, that the first point of this sermon is an attack on vanity, the antithesis of honor.

In the second point we also find an attack. This time it is against the display of an outward honor for the purpose of concealing an inward evil. Classical rhetoric, as anyone who has read Cicero's orations against Catiline in high school Latin will remember, loved to cultivate invective, and here we find the orator's love of invective given full expression. Bossuet attacks mixing honor and shame and then crowning it with the honors of this world, the giving of honorable pretexts for evil actions, and the claim of good intention when one has been motivated by selfishness all along (pp. 50-54).

Finally, for his third point our orator speaks of the honor which accompanies virtuous actions. True honor does not need to be praised. In fact, those who would be truly virtuous must learn to overcome the love of praise (p. 54). There is a certain integrity of soul which feels itself violated by too many praises (p. 55). Bossuet speaks at some length of John Chrysostom's comparison of virtue to a beautiful young woman born and educated in the privacy of the family home. She is never to be seen in the theater or other public places. Her time is spent in devout prayer and pious works (p. 56). Again, Bossuet serves his hearers with a quotation from the eloquent patriarch of Constantinople. Vainglory, Chrysostom tells us, corrupts a good education and prostitutes the modesty of virtue. The Christian does good works that God be glorified. As Christians, we should not seek our own glory. Glory belongs to God, and to claim it for ourselves is to rob God of his due. God reproaches the proud as he reproached the king of Tyre (Ezek. 28:2), who claimed divine honors for himself (p. 57).

Bossuet concludes his sermon by addressing the king. He desires for him more than the glory which men give. He wishes for him the increase of his reputation for his arms and councils throughout the world, but even more he wishes him the splendor appropriate to a Christian king, eternity with God (p. 59).

One wonders how King Louis XIV and his court reacted to this sermon. Was there ever a Christian king more concerned for his glory or a court more devoted to vanities? One wonders if the preacher himself was aware that stupendous luxury was a conscious political tactic of the king. Did this sermon have any effect at all? Did it fall on such stony ground that it bore no fruit? Preached to the court of France at the end of the seventeenth century, this was a prophetic sermon. One has to admit that it was courageous, but was it so diplomatic that it lost its effect? Bossuet quotes John Chrysostom often in the sermon, but one cannot help comparing it to the sermons the patriarch of Constantinople preached against luxury at the Byzantine court. Is it better to be forthright and lose one's pulpit or diplomatic and lose one's point? This is a question the preacher often has to face.

C. A Sermon on the Prodigal Son

Bossuet's sermon on the prodigal son was no less audacious than his sermon on honor. The sermon was intended for the third Sunday in Lent, when the parable of the prodigal son was the appointed lesson. He was unable to preach it then, for reasons we do not know, and therefore preached it the following Wednesday. Bossuet was determined to preach this sermon because this text provided him an opportunity to bring to repentance both the king, who engaged in openly adulterous affairs, making no attempt to cover them up, and his court, which countenanced his behavior.

The introduction is a masterpiece. In a few words Bossuet brings us to identify ourselves with the prodigal son. He inspires us to desire the same merciful acceptance from God which the prodigal received from his father on his return home (p. 63). He quotes Proverbs 14:13 (RSV),

> Even in laughter the heart is sad,
>> and the end of joy is grief.

Our preacher comments that it is a thorough familiarity with the ways of this world which speaks in this way of worldly pleasures. Pleasures are never pure, but are always mixed with one sort of sadness or another.

Pleasures pass away very quickly and are all too soon followed by suffering (p. 64). The delights of the world are so many parts and pieces of which one or more are always missing. Suffering, in the end, seems to preside over mortal life in such a way that we rarely enjoy peace and comfort for very long. Bossuet is a master of French vocabulary! His very choice of words brings us all into the story as he speaks of the sufferings of the prodigal son, then of his repentance, and finally of his joy in the house of the father. The prodigal's story becomes our story. The succession of his failures brought the prodigal to himself, and to return repentant at last to his father. In regret and in tears he found again the tranquil joy of his father's house. Such is the miracle of penance. The sermon, our preacher announces, is to have two points. First, he will speak of worldly pleasures, the source of suffering, and second, of suffering, the source of more enduring pleasures (p. 65). Again we notice Bossuet's genius for a symmetrical sermon outline.

Bossuet begins the exposition of his first point with one of those verbal surprises which so delighted the baroque age. He tells us how the Church was persecuted from its earliest days. Then he makes an amazing statement. Each child of the Church is himself her persecutor. Taking full advantage of this element of surprise, he explains how each Christian must put to death in himself the love of sinful pleasure (pp. 65ff.). Bossuet confesses that Christians often murmur against the severity of the gospel. We should not be surprised, however, if Christ commands us to persecute in ourselves the love of pleasure. Pleasures claim to be our friends, but they are our worst enemies. Bossuet makes an adroit thrust against the pleasures of the flesh, comparing them to flatterers at court. Are flatterers not the worst enemy one can have? Bossuet draws out his figure at length, describing the dishonesty and artificiality of flatterers and how they bring ruin to those who flatter the pleasures of the flesh (pp. 67 and 68). In the end, these flattering pleasures brought the prodigal into servitude. Indeed, sin is a servitude. There is nothing noble about sin. With oratorical flourish our preacher says of the prodigal son, "Weep, weep, O Prodigal, for what could be more miserable than to discover that one is forced to love those pleasures which only too soon are lost for eternity!" (p. 74).[6]

Bossuet turns to his second point: the pain of repentance is filled

---

6. "Pleurez, pleurez, ô Prodigue! car qu'y a-t-il de plus misérable que de se sentir comme forcé par ses habitudes vicieuses d'aimer les plaisirs, et de se voir sitôt après forcé, par une nécessité fatale, de les perdre sans retour et sans espérance?"

with joy. He tells how the Jews after the Babylonian exile witnessed the restoration of the Temple. They both rejoiced in the grace of God and wept at the memory of their sins. This is a figure of the joy of repentance (p. 75). Then he quotes his beloved Augustine: "How joyful is he who knows such sorrow" (p. 76). God rejoices in a contrite heart, Bossuet continues, and God united the repentant to Jesus and the mystery of his cross. But to have within ourselves the invisible consolation of the Holy Spirit, it is necessary that the conscience be purified. No water can do this other than the tears of repentance. Again Bossuet uses apostrophe to dramatize his point. "Pour out, then, O tears of repentance; pour out as a torrent, blessed waters; cleanse the soiled conscience, wash the profane heart, and restore me to the joy of thy salvation" (p. 79).[7]

The sermon ends with a dazzling conclusion. The preacher promises his congregation that the time when the fruit of repentance will taste sweetest is at the hour of death (p. 81). Then, in another lively apostrophe, he addresses the dreaded enemy: "O Death, you can do me no evil, you can take nothing away from me which is dear. You shall separate me from this mortal body and for that I will be thankful. I have labored all my life to do just that. You do nothing more than put the final touch to what I have begun. You destroy nothing for which I have labored, but rather establish it. Do your work, then, O Death, and present me soon to him whom I love" (p. 83).[8]

D. A Sermon for Palm Sunday

The sermon for Palm Sunday is another courageous attempt to introduce the leaven of Christian teaching into the dough of court life. It is a dis-

---

7. "Coulez donc, larmes de la pénitence; coulez comme un torrent, ondes bienheureuses; nettoyez cette conscience souillée; lavez ce coeur profané, et {{rendez-moi cette joie divine}} qui est le fruit de la justice et de l'innocence: *Redde mihi laetitiam salutaris tui.*"

8. "O mort, lui dit-il d'un visage ferme, tu ne me feras aucun mal, tu ne m'ôteras rien de ce qui m'est cher. Tu me sépareras de ce corps mortel; ô mort, je t'en remercie: j'ai travaillé toute ma vie à m'en détacher. J'ai tâché durant tout son cours de mortifier mes appétits sensuels; ton secours, ô mort, m'était nécessaire pour en arracher jusqu'à la racine: ainsi, bien loin d'interrompre le cours de mes desseins, tu ne fais que mettre la dernière main à l'ouvrage que j'ai commencé. Tu ne détruis pas ce que je prétends; mais tu l'achèves. Achève donc, ô mort favorable, et rends-moi bientôt à Celui que j'aime!"

course on the ideal of royal justice originally planned for the previous Sunday, the Gospel for which was taken from John 8. The original draft of the sermon had taken the text of John 8:16, "'Yet even if I do judge, my judgment is true . . .'" (RSV). Again, because of the complications of the court calendar or something of the sort, Bossuet's preaching plans had to be changed, and he revised his sermon to fit the Gospel for the following Sunday. Our prophet was confident he already had a word from the Lord, and the new text, with a certain amount of juggling, served that word almost as well. The Gospel for Palm Sunday included a quotation from Zechariah 9:9 (RSV):

> Rejoice greatly, O daughter of Zion!
>   Shout aloud, O daughter of Jerusalem!
> Lo, your king comes to you;
>   triumphant and victorious is he,
> humble and riding on an ass. . . .

The Vulgate of the text from Zechariah reads, "Ecce Rex tuus venit tibi justus et Salvator." This provided Bossuet with the necessary reference to justice, which allowed him to preach the sermon he felt called to deliver.

In the introduction Bossuet tells us that the lines from Zechariah speak of the triumphal entry of the Savior into Jerusalem. In celebration of the triumph of the King of Glory, the prophet acclaims the Christ as a king of justice and as the Savior. That is, he unites those two qualities which bring eternal happiness to humanity, justice and mercy. (Bossuet has a hard time getting the word "mercy" out of the text. *Salvator* does not reduce very well into one of the classical virtues. Here *justus et Salvator* is translated by *justice et bonté*. The awkwardness of the translation derives from the difficulty of finding a biblical text for the four moral virtues of classical philosophy.) Bossuet tells his congregation that these acclamations invite him to preach on justice and how justice is to be tempered by generosity and mercy. The subject is of such importance, he continues, that he feels himself weighed down by the responsibility (p. 159). He addresses the king directly, telling him that his presence encourages him to speak of the subject because his reputation for justice is known throughout Europe. Our preacher confesses that he would rather preach a panegyric than give the impression of offering instruction to the king, but the Holy Spirit opens his mouth not to speak his own ideas but rather the oracles of God (p. 160). Here we find a remarkably clear statement of the biblical concept of the burden of prophetic preaching and the grace of the divine inspiration of preaching.

Bossuet plans his discourse around the traditional four virtues of classical moral philosophy. Scholastic theology had distinguished the moral virtues of justice, fortitude, wisdom, and temperance from the theological virtues of faith, hope, and love. While the theological virtues were taken from Scripture, the moral virtues were taken from Greek and Roman philosophy. It is following the tradition of Scholastic theology, then, that Bossuet divides up his subject. He tells us that justice is the queen of the virtues and is supported by the other three virtues of fortitude, wisdom, and temperance (p. 161). First he will speak of how justice must be constant, second of how it must be wise, and third of how it must be generous.

Bossuet develops his first point by telling us that it is above all in God that we find justice. This source of justice is heavenly, and from that heavenly source it descends to man. God governs the world in general and humanity in particular by eternal justice (p. 162). This divine source gives justice its uniformity. Bossuet, still working in the framework of classical philosophy, defines justice as a firm and perpetual intention to give to each one that which belongs to him (p. 163). In this definition the echo of Plato and Aristotle is clearly heard. This continual firmness or constancy belongs by definition to justice. Justice must have fortitude so that it be not swayed by the self-interest of individuals (p. 164). Self-interest is the enemy of justice (p. 166). Humanity is divided, Bossuet tells us, into two kinds of persons, public persons and private persons (p. 167). Public persons have a responsibility to maintain justice, but private persons have a responsibility to be just in their demands on others. In this we must be guided by the Golden Rule. Let us do to others as we would have them do to us (p. 169). Let us maintain equity to one another that the poor receive their due and the rich their proper rewards (p. 170). With this Bossuet addresses an eloquent invective against self-interest. Self-interest is the god of the world and the god of the court, the deceiver from its beginning (p. 171). It is because of the deceptiveness of self-interest, and because of its power and universality, that God has so wisely endowed kings, and particularly the most wise king of France, with the power to resist those who press their own claims (pp. 173-74). Bossuet quotes a passage from Gregory the Great to make his point. Then, after several compliments to the king, he affirms that the power to maintain justice is a gift from God. Of this we see a great example in Solomon (p. 175).

The reference to Solomon brings Bossuet to his second point. Justice must be exercised with wisdom (p. 176). Here we see an example of one of Bossuet's masterful transitions. Having introduced the biblical prototype of the wise king, he brings up a rather curious subject: the story of Sodom and Gomorrah and how God descended to see if the charges made against these cities were true (pp. 176-78). From this story he draws the principle that one must not judge by the reports of others, but must search out for oneself to see if the things one hears are true. Then our preacher returns to the subject of Solomon's wisdom. Solomon prayed for a docile heart, submissive to the truth. There is no weakness, Bossuet assures his congregation, in being submissive to the truth (p. 181). Now his curious train of thought begins to approach its goal. He warns the courtiers before him: at court one must be very careful what one says, for nothing pollutes the common good more than to give false information to those responsible for public affairs (pp. 181-83). One gets the impression that the preacher was touching on something everyone in his congregation knew about but which we who read this sermon three hundred years later cannot quite decipher. It sounds as though Bossuet is suggesting to the king that some of his advisers are not giving him the straight story!

For his third point, Bossuet takes up the subject of how justice must be tempered with mercy. He quotes the apostle Paul to the effect that Christians must support one another in love. When this principle is followed by the Christian prince, then justice is applied with mercy (p. 184). Quoting Proverbs 16:15, "In the light of the king's face there is life, and his favor is like the clouds that bring the spring rain," Bossuet makes a marvelously imaginative comment. Taken literally, this tells us that a good king is as agreeable to men as the evening rain which tempers the heat of the day. But one might be permitted to add that as the morning speaks to us of virtue, which alone can illumine human life, the evening speaks to us of our fallen state, for it is then that the day declines and reason illumines us no longer. The dew of the morning is the reward of virtue, just as the rain of the evening is the pardoning of our faults. Thus Solomon would teach us that to bring gladness to the earth and to produce the fruits of public prosperity, the prince must see that there are both dew in the morning and showers in the evening, ever rewarding those who do good and from time to time pardoning those in need (pp. 185-86). Bossuet's French puts this so delicately that one must admit that he has succeeded in gilding even Solomon's lily.[9]

9. "A la lettre, il faut entendre que la clémence est autant agréable aux hommes,

The sermon is concluded with the brilliance we have come to expect from Bossuet. We are convinced, our preacher says, that neither scepters nor crowns are the greatest glory of a Christian king. Look at the splendid empires of the Orient. They have all the perishable glories that one could imagine. Look at the greatest enemy of Christendom, enthroned in the palace of Constantine. God has far greater gifts for a Christian king. What I desire for you, Bossuet says to his king, is to be on earth the image of God's majesty, imitating his justice and generosity, that the whole universe admire in your sacred person a just king, a royal savior of the example of Jesus Christ, a royal savior who relieves the sufferings of his people. It is that which I wish for your majesty, with the grace of the Father, and the Son, and the Holy Spirit. Amen.

This sermon raises a great number of questions. It obviously intends to be a prophetic sermon. If there were ever a court where repentance needed to be preached, it was the court of Louis XIV. It was the absolute disregard of justice, the mad pursuit of luxury and vainglory, that brought the fall of the French monarchy a century later. The court had so closed itself into the artificial life of Versailles that it did not realize the sufferings of the poor. All this Bossuet preached against, and yet he did it in such a way that court etiquette was never offended. Every year some preacher was asked to preach a Lenten series, and of course, an appropriate Lenten series was a series on repentance. Repentance was built into the system. Every year it was repentance all over again. The preaching of repentance was so institutionalized that in spite of the best intentions and consummate art of a great orator such as Bossuet, the seed he sowed never so much as hit the ground; it was blown away by the winds of vacuity. Preaching became part of the perpetual theater that was the court of Louis XIV.

---

qu'une pluie qui vient sur le soir tempérer la chaleur du jour et rafraîchir la terre que l'ardeur du soleil avait desséchée. Mais ne me sera-t-il pas permis d'ajouter que comme le matin nous désigne la vertu, qui seule peut illuminer la vie humaine, le soir nous représente au contraire l'état où nous tombons par nos fautes, puisque c'est là en effet que le jour décline et que la raison n'éclaire plus? Selon cette explication, le rosée du matin ce serait la récompense de la vertu, de même que la pluie du soir serait le pardon accordé réjouir la terre et pour produire les fruits agréables de la bienveillance publique, le prince doit faire tomber sur le genre humain et l'une et l'autre rosée, en récompensant toujours ceux qui font bien et pardonnant quelquefois généreusement à ceux qui manquent, pourvu que le bien public et la sainte autorité des lois n'y soient point trop intéressés."

E. A Sermon for Good Friday

Bossuet chooses for the sermon for Good Friday a text which serves as a motto for the sermon:

> The righteous man perishes,
>   and no one lays it to heart. . . .

(Isa. 57:1 RSV)

This sermon is a meditation on the mystery of the cross rather than an exposition of Scripture. It is a panegyric for the central Christian mystery.

The sermon begins with a broad and sweeping statement appropriate to a panegyric. The whole of the knowledge of the Christian, Bossuet tells us, is enclosed within the cross. Paul, who ascended to the third heaven and therefore knew the highest of divine secrets, proclaimed to the world that he would know nothing but Jesus Christ and him crucified (p. 191). To those who have the eyes of faith, the wisdom of God is nowhere discovered more clearly than in the mystery of the cross. Utilizing his vivid imagery, our preacher then tells us that it is there that Christ, stretching out his arms, opens to us the blood-stained book in which we can learn the whole plan of the counsels of God, the whole economy of salvation, the fixed and invariable rule for forming all our judgments, the sure and infallible direction for leading us in right conduct, and in the end a mysterious summary of all the teachings of the gospel and all of Christian theology (pp. 191-92). The dramatic effect of these opening lines is heightened by the carefully worked parallel structures of his syntax. Having begun so dramatically, our preacher adds an apostrophe, one of his favorite rhetorical devices: "Therefore, O cross, who bring before our eyes today the greatest of all miracles in the greatest of all scandals; O cross, dying agony of justice, refuge of criminals, who lift up Jesus Christ and yet present him to us, who make him our victim and our monarch, receive our adoration and make us part of your graces and illuminations. I give to you, O cross of Jesus, that religious adoration which the Church teaches us; and for the love of him whose agony honors you, whose blood consecrates you, whose indignities render you worthy of eternal worship, I say with that same Church, Hail, O Cross" (pp. 192-93).[10] With this

---

10. "Donc, ô croix qui nous fais voir aujourd'hui le plus grand de tous les miracles dans le plus grand de tous les scandales; ô croix, supplice du juste, et asile des criminels,

the preacher and his congregation recite, rather than the Hail Mary, the Good Friday salutation, *"O Crux, ave."* This is, to be sure, magnificent prose in the original French, the height of baroque oratory! His congregation must have quivered at its splendor. It reminds one of the painting of the exaltation of the cross in the ceiling of the Church of the Gesu in Rome, where with the glory of illusionistic painting the roof is pierced and one gazes into the heavens as the cross is borne triumphantly into heaven.

The first point Bossuet makes is that our crimes persecute Christ. The Christian faith teaches us that Christ was delivered up to death for our sins. He quotes Saint Bernard as saying that we are all authors of Christ's agony, more than Judas who betrayed him, more than the Jews who accused him, more than Pilate who condemned him, and more than the soldiers who crucified him (p. 195). All kinds of human sin and faithlessness conspired together in the death of Christ. To make his point, our preacher speaks at length of the betrayal of Judas, the denial of Peter, and the compliance of Pilate. Each of them sinned against Christ in a different way; so, too, each of us, in a different way, brings Christ to the cross (pp. 197-204).

The second point of the sermon is that Christ's obedience on the cross is our example. Bossuet quotes Saint Augustine that three sorts of persons brought Christ to his passion: his Father, his enemies, and himself (p. 205). Appropriate Scripture quotations are given for each of the three points. At considerable length we hear of the mystery of God's providence. What Christ's enemies were doing out of their ill will was being done by the good will of God (pp. 206-9). Again Bossuet calls on Augustine to make his point: God presides even over the councils of the wicked. Finally our preacher puts it all in another of his dramatic flourishes and addresses the enemies of Christ: "Dare all, therefore, O evil spirits; attack, press, overrun, sharpen your malign tongues, sink in your venomous teeth . . . for you can undertake nothing, nor can you bring anything to pass other than what God wills" (p. 210). It is because Jesus recognized that those who persecuted him could do nothing but what God permit-

---

qui nous ôtes JÉSUS-CHRIST, et qui nous le donnes; qui le fais notre victime et notre monarque, et enfermes dans le mystère de même écriteau la cause de sa mort et le titre de sa royauté! reçois nos adorations, et fais-nous part de tes grâces et de tes lumières. Je te rends, ô croix de JÉSUS, cette religieuse adoration que l'Église nous enseigne; et pour l'amour de celui dont le supplice t'honore, dont le sang te consacre, dont les opprobres te rendent digne d'un culte éternel, je te dis avec cette même Église: *O crux, ave."*

ted that he had no feeling of revenge against his enemies, but rather sought their pardon. We, too, must have patience in tribulation and forgive those who persecute us. In doing this we follow the example of Jesus (p. 211).

The third point this sermon makes is that we find grace and hope in the forgiveness of sin which on the cross Christ granted to all. On the cross Christ prayed, Father forgive them. Our preacher hastens to make his application. Let not this day pass until we have responded to Christ's passion by forgiving our enemies (p. 213). Without this pardon there is no Easter for us. How well aware I am, says Bossuet, that this evangelical precept is hardly ever honored at court. But be assured that without this forgiveness of others, there is no communion with Christ. Surely, brethren, you are not unaware that we have all been included in the prayer of Jesus (p. 214). He was lifted up on the cross so high that he could discover all the mockery of men, not only of the Jews, but of each of us as well. With tears he implored the Father that we be forgiven (p. 215). Not only did he pray for us; he sacrificed for us. Bossuet quotes Paul: "In Christ God was reconciling the world to himself . . ." (II Cor. 5:19 RSV). Here Bossuet introduces a masterful simile. As a storm comes over the earth and pours out its fury and then recedes and becomes calm, so now the divine justice pours out all its indignation on the Son of God as he bears the sin of the world, and having discharged all of its force, begins to relent. God now begins to open to the children of Adam his kindly and radiant face. The storm passed, the mystery of salvation shines forth, and the Father tenderly embraces all men for the love of his innocent Son (p. 217).

Having seen this salvation, we preachers implore you to be reconciled to God. Let each of us examine himself and approach the mystery of the Eucharist, the sacred memorial of the passion of Christ. There he is again on Calvary, there he pours out again the blood of the New Testament, there he renews, there he represents, there he perpetuates his holy sacrifice (p. 218). Therefore, at the sight of this holy altar, let each one examine himself. At this point Bossuet's manuscript becomes tentative and indistinct, but we can be sure that in the pulpit he concluded the sermon as eloquently as he began it.

If for us this sermon seems much too melodramatic and if we find some of Bossuet's theatrical effects inappropriate for Good Friday, we would do well to remember that Bossuet was sensitive to the taste of his day. His congregation, no doubt, thrilled to every word.

Let us conclude our study of Bossuet with a few words of evaluation. Bossuet has been regarded for more than three hundred years now as one of the greatest of the great. His place in the history of French literature is undisputed. Those of us who admire great French prose read him with enjoyment. One delights in hearing sacred thoughts expressed with such artistry. This has been said many times before, and we leave further discussion of the literary merits of our preacher to those whose competence is in that field.

From the standpoint of the history of Christian worship, we find Bossuet particularly interesting as an evangelistic preacher. He was not a great expositor. Apparently he had a fascination for Scripture and even a fairly good knowledge of the Bible. He seems to have had a better understanding and appreciation of the Old Testament prophets than did most preachers of his age. He uses biblical quotations and illustrations with considerable insight and imagination. On the other hand, he often uses his text as a mere motto. A number of his sermons are discourses on a religious theme rather than an exposition of either the text or the lesson appointed for the day. Bossuet is concerned not so much with the exposition of God's Word as with winning people for the faith. Whether it is a question of winning Protestants to the Catholic faith or winning the libertines of the court to a Christian way of life, Bossuet is an evangelist or, perhaps even better, an apologist.

The question one inevitably asks when reading Bossuet is whether his polemics really serve the true evangelistic ministry. His zeal for winning converts is evident, but one has the feeling that this is not quite the same thing as preaching the gospel. Perhaps the problem was that Bossuet saw himself as an evangelist not so much of the individual soul as of the social order as a whole. He figured that his primary job was to convert French society to complete, consistent Catholicism. He was a thorough integralist, a perfect absolutist.

What makes him so fascinating is that he carried out this task as court preacher to an absolute monarch who was not very profoundly Christian. Bossuet had a very different task as preacher to Louis XIV than Bonaventure had with Louis IX, who was deeply Christian. Bossuet understood himself to bear the burden of the prophet, but unlike Amos, he was part of the establishment. He preached against the luxury of the court, but without messing up the lace collars of the courtiers. In the end the court to which he preached fell before the French Revolution because of the very vices about which he had warned them. Yet Bossuet, unlike

Jeremiah, never spent as much as a night in a cistern. If Bossuet saw Louis XIV as the Theodosius of his day, he never followed the example of Ambrose and confronted the Sun King with his all too public sins. In the end he was more the courtier than the prophet. And yet he was a great orator, perhaps not a great preacher, but at least a great orator.

II. Louis Bourdaloue (1632-1704)

Bourdaloue's understanding of evangelism was more profound than Bossuet's. The conversion of souls was the main burden of his ministry. He certainly approved of Bossuet's vision of a French Catholic monarchy. His sermons at court, like those of Bossuet, hail Louis XIV as the hero of the Church, but his overriding concern is much more personal than social. Bourdaloue, as Bossuet, was a great orator and a master of French prose, and yet with Bourdaloue one is much less conscious of hearing great literature. He is so intent at getting through to the hearts of his hearers that one becomes oblivious to the outward form of his message. Perhaps this alone makes him a greater preacher. With Bossuet one is always aware that one is hearing great and profound ideas, but with Bourdaloue one is much more aware of an intense concern for the spiritual renewal of his hearers. It is this concern for conversion of the heart that draws our attention even today.

Bourdaloue was born in Bourges, a town which boasts one of the most inspiring Gothic cathedrals; the rich farming country surrounding it also is the site of some of the most pleasant châteaux of France.[11] He came from a respected family and received a good education in the Jesuit college of Bourges. Joining the Society of Jesus at the age of sixteen, he soon was given teaching responsibilities in various colleges of his order. His ability as a preacher was recognized, and in 1669 he was sent to Paris to preach at the Church of Saint Louis. He arrived in Paris at about the same time Bossuet took up his duties as bishop of Meaux, and so Bourdaloue fell heir to Bossuet as court preacher. He frequently preached the Advent and Lenten sermons at court. After the revocation of the Edict of Nantes, he was sent to Languedoc to confirm the conversion of Protes-

11. For biographical material on Bourdaloue, see the following: H. Chérot, *Bourdaloue inconnu* (Paris, 1898); H. Chérot, "Bourdaloue," in *Dictionnaire de théologie catholique,* 2/1:1095-99; Richard Byrne Meager, "Bourdaloue, Louis," in *New Catholic Encyclopedia,* 17 vols. (Washington, D.C.: Catholic University of America Press, 1967), 2:732-33; and A. A. L. Pauthe, *Bourdaloue, d'après des documents nouveaux* (Paris, 1900).

tants. This was a difficult task. Those who had been won to Catholicism for political reasons tended to be less than sincere about their new faith. The cynicism of the new Catholics was all too often a scandal. His Lenten sermons at Montpellier, a center of Protestant resistance, were regarded as a triumph of Catholic preaching.

A large part of the preserved sermons of Bourdaloue is made up of his different Lenten and Advent series. This is not surprising because from the Middle Ages Lent and Advent were regarded as the preaching seasons of the year. Even if there was little preaching the rest of the year, the faithful expected frequent, often daily, preaching during Advent and Lent. Larger churches invited the most famous preachers of the day to do an Advent or Lenten series, and preachers gave their best efforts on such occasions. These Lenten and Advent series were traditionally devoted to penitential themes. That was the way the lectionary was set up. That was the time when evangelism was supposed to be done.

Let us look at the first series of Advent sermons which Bourdaloue preached before the king to see how he approached evangelistic preaching.[12]

Bourdaloue addressed his evangelistic message to the ladies and gentlemen of the court. For this series of sermons that was appropriate. He knew he had before him a congregation of baptized Christians, but for the most part they were very worldly Christians. There were, of course, exceptions. Some exceptional individuals, in spite of the atmosphere of the court, practiced their religion faithfully and remained untainted from the world. They were truly good Catholics. On the other hand were the libertines. Ever since Montaigne wrote his essays, a segment of French society had taken pride in being above the superstitious practices of the common people. They saw themselves as being liberated from the restraints of Christian morality, and maintained the outward forms of religion only to the extent that a prudent self-interest demanded. The court was filled with such libertines, and Bourdaloue knew many in his congregation were present only because the king was in attendance and they wanted to make a good appearance. To the libertines Bourdaloue often addressed himself, but for the most part he preached to those who were somewhere in between.

---

12. For the text of these sermons, see Louis Bourdaloue, *Oeuvres complètes de Bourdaloue, de la compagnie de Jésus,* 16 vols. (Versailles: J. A. Lebel, 1812). The page numbers in the text are from vol. 1 of this work.

The court was far from devout. The king openly maintained a mistress, and the adulterous affairs of those who surrounded him were the subject of constant gossip. A dashing lover or a beautiful coquette had every advantage at court. All he or she had learned in Jesuit colleges and convent schools was soon forgotten in the round of glittering banquets and theater parties that were a part of court life. The standard of conspicuous luxury which the king quite intentionally set demanded a whole-hearted devotion to haute couture and haute cuisine, which left the courtesan little time to think of anything else. That was the way the king intended it. He wanted the energies of the aristocracy to be absorbed in hunting parties and masked balls so that he would be free to run the country. The court was made up of people who had been enticed by his strategy. The very fact that they were spending their time at court, at the kind of court Louis XIV had developed, implied that they had left behind them the kind of piety traditional Catholic Christianity had taught. Even at that there was a commitment to being a good Catholic. This, too, as we have said, Louis XIV quite consciously furthered. Duplicity was built into the system. Bourdaloue had as tough a job as any evangelist ever had: he was to preach sincerity to a people who had cultivated insincerity. His own sincerity, it seems, was the greatest spiritual gift with which he approached his ministry.

Perhaps the strongest characteristic of these sermons is a straightforward accusation of sin. Bourdaloue confronted his congregation with their sins. In his sermon for the second Sunday in Advent, he takes up the subject of scandals, or stumbling blocks, which keep us from true faith. He warns his congregation against being a stumbling block to others. He pictures the worldly women of the court constantly engaged in their visiting and their risqué conversations. They imagine that it is all quite innocent. Yet to satisfy their vanity they delight in inflaming the sensual desires of young men. They think they have been quite virtuous because they have not yielded to the passions they have inflamed, but in reality they have tempted these young men to engage in the immorality by which they have lost their souls. In the opinion of the world, their immodest fashions, their luxurious coiffures, their indecent nudities all pass for such light things, and yet they are the work of the devil (pp. 77-78). A bit later in the sermon Bourdaloue draws another of his engaging character sketches. Here his accusation is aimed at the worldly father who betrays his Christian faith by giving his children a poor example. He should as a father train them in the practices of the Christian faith, but instead he ridicules the rites of the Church and makes light of the disciplines of piety. He himself would never think of being a libertine, but his children grow up libertines (p. 87). In his sermon for the third Sunday of Advent, in which he takes as his subject the false conscience, Bourdaloue confronts his congregation with their refusal to consult their consciences in deciding the weighty matters of state. He grants that these matters are often difficult to decide, but then he asks them how often God is consulted. Not very often, he imagines. They are decided more often than not purely on a basis of politics (p. 112). Bourdaloue's accusations are frequent and repeated. Through his insightful character sketches he brings his congregation into court again and again. As Isaiah before him, he proclaims that God has a controversy with Israel.

As Bourdaloue sees it, this accusation is an appeal to the conscience, intended to awaken the conscience, and he devotes a whole sermon to it. With Thomas Aquinas, he defines the conscience as that by which each one applies to himself the law of God (p. 102). Our preacher reminds us of the saying of Jesus, that the eye is the light of the body, and if the eye is pure then the whole body will be enlightened (Luke 11:34), and then tells us that Jesus is speaking about the conscience (p. 116). It is through the conscience that God's call finally reaches us, that he presses his demands on us, and if one may put it this way, that he forces us back into order and makes us submissive and obedient to his will. To make his point, Bourdaloue adduces an example from the history of the Church. It was in the conscience that the grace of Jesus Christ won its victory in the heart of Augustine. Augustine's conscience declared itself for God in spite of his best efforts to deny God entry (p. 122). We notice here that, once again, Augustine's conversion experience has become one of the paradigms for the evangelistic ministry of the Church. Bourdaloue finds that even the pagan Romans of antiquity were guided by their consciences to maintain strict laws against oppressive usury. Moslem women are even today guided by their consciences to maintain modest dress (pp. 129ff.). God can speak to the conscience even of those who are not Christians at all. If there is to be effective evangelism, then, the conscience must be awakened. This is what Bourdaloue tries to do by his forthright accusation of the sins of his congregation.

Another characteristic of Bourdaloue's evangelism is his appeal to the reasonableness of Christian devotion. The libertine is foolish. He is acting against reason. It is the pious Christian, on the other hand, who is truly rational. In the second sermon of the series, Bourdaloue takes up the subject of the Last Judgment. He makes two points: God judges us on the basis of our faith and on the basis of our reason. In regard to this second point, Bourdaloue insists that even after the fall, and independently of faith, man has enough reason to know that there is a God who requires certain duties of him. Natural human reason alone tells us God has decreed to us certain laws and expects us to submit to his order. To be sure, reason alone is not enough to save us from our sins, our preacher insists. Without grace and without faith this reason is insufficient for salvation, but it is sufficient for our damnation. This reason, as much as it may be darkened by the clouds of sin, is never completely extinguished (p. 52). Again Bourdaloue appeals to Augustine, who makes it clear that even in his error his reason testified to the justice of God. Augustine's reason finally led him to his conversion (p. 54). As much as the passions might entice one to find reasons for rejecting God's ways, those reasons are never completely convincing (pp. 57ff.). As Bourdaloue understands it, the evangelist has good reason to appeal to the reason of the sinner. The reason, even the reason of hardened sinners, plays its part in their conversion.

In the first sermon of the series our preacher takes as his theme the rewards of godliness. He uses as his text Matthew 5:12, "'Rejoice and be glad, for your reward is great in heaven . . .'" (RSV). Bourdaloue points out that one can depend on God to reward those who serve him and that those who serve the world are often disappointed (p. 4). It stands to reason that those who devote themselves to the service of perishable riches will find that their rewards perish with their enjoyment. On the other hand, God is eternal. He perishes not. God is dependable, and one can depend on the rewards he promises. As the apostle Paul put it, "I know whom I have believed" (II Tim. 1:12 RSV). One can be sure of God's goodness and his fidelity. That is the nature of God (p. 5). Furthermore, God proves himself trustworthy. Our preacher argues from personal experience that again and again he has put his hopes in fellow men and has been let down. But he can say that God has never let him down (p. 11). Particularly at court he has found David to be right:

> It is better to take refuge in the LORD
>   than to put confidence in princes.

> (Psalm 118:9 RSV)

David was a king himself, and he knew about the fidelity of princes (p. 12). God is by his very nature unchangeable, and therefore we can have confidence in him. Here we find Bourdaloue again trying to convince his congregation of the reasonableness of Christian faith.

As we have pointed out before, evangelistic preaching is particularly related to the sacrament of baptism. In the earliest days of the Church the evangelistic sermon typically reached its climax with an offer of baptism. In the Middle Ages, as more and more of the people who needed to be evangelized had already been baptized, evangelistic preaching was based on the sacrament of penance. The typical Lenten or Advent evangelistic mission was aimed at getting the congregation into the confessional booth. Bossuet's Lenten sermons made a special point of encouraging his congregation to go to confession, do the penance prescribed, and receive Communion at Easter. Bourdaloue is even more specific. The whole purpose of this series of Advent evangelistic sermons is to get each member of his congregation to do penance.

The introduction to the sermon for the fourth Sunday in Advent is most interesting in regard to the relationship between evangelistic preaching and the sacrament of penance. Bourdaloue tells us that it is not by virtue of the baptism of Saint John that our sins are remitted, but his baptism was a necessary preparation for arriving at the remission of sins, without which one cannot participate in the redemption of Christ nor profit from that inestimable blessing. It is through penance that one is disposed toward receiving it. Penance, ever since the establishment of the Christian law, has commonly been called a second baptism, just as baptism, following the teaching of the Fathers, was in those days called the first penance (p. 133). This is an extremely interesting statement about which much could be said. It would be far afield our concern to discuss it at any length, but it does show how Bourdaloue understands his evangelistic ministry in relation to the sacraments.

One is sometimes tempted to make a strong distinction between evangelistic preaching and penitential preaching. One could well argue that the former is aimed at baptism while the latter is aimed at those who have been baptized but need a second repentance. This is particularly the case if one makes a strong distinction between the sacrament of baptism and the sacrament of penance. If, on the other hand, one sees baptism as a sign of repentance, a repentance which the Christian must experience through the whole of Christian life, then penitential preaching becomes an important aspect of evangelistic preaching. Evangelistic preachers have often perceived this relationship quite differently, and consequently they have had very different approaches to their work. Bourdaloue has not lost sight of the relation of evangelistic preaching to baptism, but his theology of baptism is such that the relation is only indirect. The thrust of his evangelistic ministry is determined by his theology of penance.

The sermon on the severity of penance makes two points: first, that penance must be strenuous, and second, that there is a sweetness and joy which comes from truly genuine penance (p. 136). If we are strict with ourselves, we can be sure God will be gentle with us (p. 140). True repentance mortifies the spirit, crucifies the flesh, combats the passions, and renounces the self (p. 154). True penance appeases God and disarms his anger (p. 156). The sermon ends with John the Baptist's call, "'Repent, for the kingdom of heaven is at hand'" (Matt. 3:2 RSV). For Bourdaloue this means: Do penance now, set your conscience in order, for you may not have another chance. You may die tomorrow (p. 166).

Bourdaloue clearly understands his ministry as a continuation of the ministry of John the Baptist, a point he makes quite explicitly in this sermon. The Precursor, our evangelist insists, even today preaches the baptism of penance with uncommon zeal. Being at the eve of that great solemnity where we are to celebrate the birth of the Savior whom John announced to the Jews, it seems appropriate to preach the same sermon he preached (p. 133). Different evangelists have taken different biblical figures as models for their ministry, and Bourdaloue obviously develops his approach on the ministry of John the Baptist. It is perhaps inevitable that Bourdaloue should do this because John figures so prominently in the lectionary for Advent. One wonders, however, if the Christian evangelist, preaching to baptized Christians, does not have a mission essentially different from that of John the Baptist. Is there not something more to evangelism than a call to repentance?

Even in Bourdaloue's sermon for the feast of Christ's nativity, the call to repentance is heard loud and clear. The sermon invites the Christian to be united to Christ in the humility of Christ's birth. In this way we will have peace with God, peace with ourselves, and peace with our neighbors. Peace among nations is something else; it is the work of God's general providence. But to reestablish peace between humanity and God, to conserve peace with oneself, and to give to the human race a sure and infallible means to find eternal peace with one's neighbor is a special work of God. It is the miraculous effect of the wisdom of God incarnate, the birth of Jesus Christ and his entry into the world (p. 171). Peace with God comes through the penance Jesus has already done for us in the stable of Bethlehem. This penance of the incarnate Jesus is the model of the penance we should do (p. 177). If we have performed this penance, then we are worthy to approach the mysteries we celebrate this day to our consolation (p. 179). Do penance, and in doing it conform your penance to the penance of the infant Jesus. This is the grace you are offered (p. 180).

Louis Bourdaloue surely deserves to be recognized as an important evangelistic preacher. His approach to his ministry was, as one would expect, very much shaped by the life and thought of French Catholicism in the seventeenth century. We must admire him for the courage and sincerity with which he preached repentance to the court of Louis XIV. One is amazed that such a worldly group of Christians sat there and listened to him at all, but they did. One is also amazed that such brilliant preaching seemed to have so little effect on the life of that glittering congregation. There were undoubtedly those who were converted, but the court as a whole continued to devote itself to the vanities which finally destroyed it. God sent them great preachers, and they admired their greatness but did not repent.

III. Jean-Baptiste Massillon (1663-1742)

Massillon was the Jeremiah of the Age of Louis XIV, the prophet who foresaw the doom of that decadent age.[13] A man of personal purity, respected for his exemplary life, he called the court of Versailles to repentance, a call which was largely ignored. Yet the court realized that he was a great orator: far more perceptive than Bossuet, far more realistic than Bourdaloue, far more consequent than Fénelon. Massillon was not, however, a theologian or political theorist like Bossuet. His theological insights were often exaggerated. He was not the moral philosopher that Bourdaloue was. He had none of the mystical flair of Fénelon. He was, quite simply, an outstanding Christian orator.

Massillon was born in Hyères, a small Provençal city on the Mediterranean coast. He was educated in a local school run by the Oratory, a religious order inspired by the Counter-Reformation, and later was sent to another Oratorian school in Marseilles. He joined the order and even-

13. For a brief, sympathetic treatment of Massillon, see Clyde F. Fant, *Twenty Centuries of Great Preaching*, 13 vols. (Waco, Tex.: Word Books, 1971), 2:385-93. For further biographical material, see Sylvia Juanita Washington, "Massillon, Jean Baptiste," in *New Catholic Encyclopedia*, 9:435-36.

tually found himself in Paris with responsibility for the Oratorian school in the capital.

The Oratory gave particular attention to preaching. Inspired by the example of Philip Neri, who in the late sixteenth century had earned a good reputation for preaching to the poor of Rome, the Oratorians cultivated their preachers. Massillon went through the chairs of advancement so typical for the preaching profession in Catholic France. In 1699 he was called to preach Advent before Louis XIV at Versailles. The series was a great success, and he was invited back several times, notably for Lent both in 1701 and 1704. By the time he was forty years old he had reached the pinnacle of the preaching profession.

No one had ever done such an effective job of calling the court to repentance. Massillon's sermon "The Small Number of the Elect" is one of the most daring calls for repentance ever preached. Only Savonarola or Jonathan Edwards could begin to rival it.[14]

For the Catholic pulpit in the centuries following the Council of Trent, the annual series of sermons for Advent and Lent were the heart of the preaching ministry. We have spoken of this several times. Massillon, like so many Catholic preachers of his day, was famous for a particular series of Lenten sermons, usually referred to as his *Petit Carême*.[15] These sermons were preached before Louis XV and his court. At the time the king was only a boy. His regent was the duke of Orléans, and the duke and duchess of Orléans were favorably inclined toward Massillon. This series was obviously intended for the members of the court. The sermon for the first Sunday of Lent has the title "The Temptations of the Great." For the second Sunday his title was "The Respect Which the Great Ought to Have for Religion." This was followed by "The Sorrows of the Great Who Abandon God," then "On the Generosity of the Great for the People." The sermon for the fifth Sunday in Lent is entitled "The Vanity of Human Glory." On Palm Sunday he once again directs his remarks to "the Great," preaching "The Stumbling Blocks to the Piety of the Great." Finally on Good Friday he preached "The Obstacles Which Truth Finds in the Hearts of the Great." Easter takes up the theme "The Triumph of Religion." For many of us these sermons reveal a rather shallow under-

---

14. For the English translation, see Fant, *Twenty Centuries*, 2:294-410. For the French original, see Jean-Baptiste Massillon, *Oeuvres Choisies de Massillon*, 6 vols. (Paris: Delestre-Boulage, 1823-25), 1:1-267.

15. For the French text, see Massillon, *Oeuvres Choisies de Massillon*, 1:1-267.

standing of sin and forgiveness. They show little grasp of God's redemptive work in the death and resurrection of Christ, but they do confront the leaders of French society with their sins. This they do magnificently.

Such honesty was not long tolerated at the French court. Massillon had insisted that if this was going to be the court of the Most Christian King, the title the popes had traditionally granted the kings of France, then some changes had to be made. The court, however, had no intentions of making any changes. The courtiers were all titillated by the preacher's condemnation of their luxuries, their insensitivity to the problems of the poor, their lascivious fashions, their adulterous affairs, their intemperate feasts, and their indecent theater parties. Massillon's sermons brought them to tears on several occasions, but enough was enough. Massillon was sometimes in favor and sometimes out of favor. Rumors were circulated as to his Jansenist sympathies. Then there were stories about the compromising relationships he had with certain prominent families. Alas, slander has long been a favorite weapon of the wicked.

Wise servant of Christ that he was, he withdrew to Claremont, the bishopric which had been conferred upon him when he was in favor, and there, as a godly prophet in exile, he exercised his ministry in a most exemplary way. He tired of being preacher to the court and devoted himself to the pastoral care of his flock in the mountains of central France. The court continued in its infamous debauchery until at last the guillotine brought it all to a timely end. Massillon had warned them, but they had paid no attention.

IV. François de Salignac de la Mothe Fénelon (1651-1715)

The proud name itself tells us worlds about one of the most fascinating figures of the Age of Louis XIV.[16] Born in the family château, a younger son of a large family which had for a generation struggled under reduced circumstances, young François was educated at home. He was of delicate health, the second son of his father's second marriage. Even if the family was short of financial resources, he had been provided with a good tutor

16. For biographical material on Fénelon, see the following: Michael de la Bedoyere, *The Archbishop and the Lady* (London: Collins, 1956); Ely Carcassonne, *Fénelon, l'homme et l'oeuvre* (Paris: Boivin, 1946); James Herbert Davis, Jr., *Fénelon* (Boston: Twayne Publishers, 1979); and Henk Hillenaar, *Fénelon et les Jésuits* (The Hague: Martinus Nijhoff, 1967).

who gave him a solid grounding in the classical languages. The future archbishop was a sensitive, intelligent boy, the sort of son who would quite naturally be designated for the priesthood.

At twelve years old he was sent to the Jesuit college in Cahors, not too far from home. There he received the typical Counter-Reformation education, studying the humanities and philosophy in such a way that it made Catholic orthodoxy inevitable. While he was at Cahors his father died and his uncle, the marquis de Fénelon, took the young man under care, bringing him to Paris and placing him in the College Le Plessis, a very devout institution which fostered a disciplined Catholic piety. The uncle had in his more mature years given up the ways of the world and turned to religion. He was a supporter of the established religion and strong on civic piety. Not surprisingly, he had good connections and was able to open the doors of opportunity to his talented nephew. It was through his uncle that he was given a place at the seminary of Saint-Sulpice, an institution greatly in favor with the French Catholic establishment.

Fénelon did well at the seminary and in time was given pastoral responsibilities in the parish of Saint-Sulpice. By 1675 he was preaching regularly and, already at that young age, was attracting the attention of the archbishop, François de Harlay. Possibly through the influence of his uncle, in a short time he received his first important position. In 1678 he was named superior of the Congregation des Nouvelles Catholiques, an institution dedicated to the conversion and indoctrination of young women of Protestant background.

In December 1685, a few months after the revocation of the Edict of Nantes, Fénelon was sent to the west of France on a preaching mission to convert Protestants. Protestantism was now officially banned from the kingdom of France, but in the area of La Rochelle in the west, as in the south of France, there were distinct areas of Protestant resistance. The military was doing what it could, but preachers were needed to convince those who had been forcefully converted. Fénelon spent something more than two years trying to make good Catholics of the Huguenots. His mission was hardly a raving success, but he did convince such members of the Catholic establishment as Bossuet that he had done his best to wear down the intransigence of the Huguenots.

Returning to his work at the Congregation des Nouvelles Catholiques, he continued to win the respect of influential people, especially those who moved in the circles of his uncle. At one point the young

Fénelon wrote an essay for the duchesse de Beauvillier on the education of young women. From his work with the Nouvelles Catholiques he could claim practical experience in the matter. The work was really quite remarkable considering the times, and when the duc de Beauvillier was given the responsibility of supervising the education of the grandsons of Louis XIV, he signed up Fénelon to be the actual preceptor of the young princes. One step led to another, and Fénelon soon became one of the inner circle of the French Catholic establishment. In 1693 he was elected to the French Academy, and in 1695 was named archbishop of Cambrai.

The absolutism of the French Catholic establishment inevitably began to provoke resistance, even from the staunchest of Catholics. One of the manifestations of this resistance was the popularity of a Catholic mystic, Madame Guyon. Her quietism scandalized the more militant supporters of the establishment. Bossuet, the famous apologist for Catholic absolutism, was one of those most offended by Madame Guyon.

Only slowly did Fénelon succumb to the spiritual charm of that saintly lady. He found her mysticism attractive because it transcended the absolutism of the Catholic establishment which, as he grew more mature, apparently had begun to weary the young aristocrat. The ensuing controversy brought out a pietist strain in Fénelon's nature, and he almost unwittingly began to defend Madame Guyon over against Madame de Maintenon, the former mistress of Louis XIV who, on the death of the queen, had become the king's morganatic wife. Eventually Fénelon found himself at odds with Bossuet as the controversy became more heated, and finally he was banished from the court and exiled to his archepiscopal duties in Cambrai.

In Cambrai he maintained an admirable preaching ministry, not only in his cathedral but in all the villages and parish churches of his archdiocese. It is this, above all, which captures our attention. He was a popular preacher who spoke freely in the pulpit without the aid of a manuscript. He does not seem to have written out his sermons beforehand, although a few preliminary sketches of sermons have survived, notably the outline for a series of Lenten sermons.[17] Besides these sketches, a limited number of his sermons were published during his lifetime.

17. On the textual survival of Fénelon's sermons, see Marguerite Haillant, *Fénelon et la prédication* (Paris: Éditions Klincksieck, 1969), pp. 11ff.

A. *Fénelon as Evangelist*

Fénelon first became prominent as a preacher in the service of the Catholic establishment, serving primarily as an evangelist for the Catholic cause. We have already mentioned his work with the girls' school as well as his preaching mission to the strongly Protestant regions of western France around La Rochelle.

Two sermons have survived which reflect Fénelon's evangelistic concerns. The first was preached on the feast of the Epiphany,[18] and is really a remarkable sermon when seen in the context of the long tradition of the preaching of that feast. It brings out a dimension of the text which others had all too often neglected. Treating the theme of the revelation of Christ to the Gentiles, Fénelon makes the sermon an appeal for the evangelization of the heathen. The freshness of his exegesis is remarkable. Here, already, we begin to notice one of the dimensions of Christian preaching which will become increasingly important under the influence of pietism. Count Zinzendorf, one of the leaders of German pietism, would only a few years later send missionaries to Greenland, the West Indies, North America, and India. Evangelism was destined to be revived by pietism, and already in Fénelon we see a few tentative steps in that direction.

Another sermon which shows Fénelon as evangelist is his "Sermon for the Profession of a New Convert."[19] This new convert was Mlle. de Peray, a member of the Protestant aristocracy who, after the revocation of the Edict of Nantes, sought out the counsel of Bossuet, the chief spokesman of Louis XIV's new religious settlement.[20] A Protestant of Mlle. de Peray's social standing did not have many options after the Edict of Nantes: she could either convert or leave all behind and flee the country. It must have been relatively easy for Bossuet to convince the woman of the errors of Protestantism. Having dispatched her Protestant faith, he handed her over to Fénelon and his school for "New Catholics." It was for

---

18. For the French text, see François Fénelon, *Oeuvres de Fénelon, Archevêque de Cambrai,* 3 vols. (Paris: Firmin Didot Frères, 1838), 3:656-92. For an English translation, see François Fénelon, *Dialogues on Eloquence,* translated with introduction and notes by Wilbur Samuel Howell (Princeton: Princeton University Press, 1951). This reference is to Fénelon, *Oeuvres,* 3:366-74.

19. Fénelon, *Oeuvres,* 3:402-10. The page references to this sermon placed in the text are to Fénelon's *Oeuvres,* vol. 3.

20. Haillant, *Fénelon et la prédication,* p. 17.

just this sort of thing that the school had been founded. Apparently Fénelon did his job very well, and before too long Mlle. de Peray was a thoroughly convinced Catholic and determined to join a convent, the very strictest of convents, the Grandes Carmelites in the Foubourg Saint-Jacques. It was on the occasion of her entering this convent that Fénelon was asked to preach.

The sermon is interesting because it gives us a good look at a sort of triumphalist approach to evangelism which the Christian Church should be careful to avoid. The introduction is a dazzling piece of baroque oratory. Fénelon exhorts his convert to set her vision on the heavenly Bridegroom who awaits her in eternity (p. 402). "O Christian daughter, cry out to all peoples and even to the angels themselves, who gather around to observe this spectacle of grace." Alluding to Mary's prayer, the Magnificat, he urges her in all humility to be the handmaid of the Lord and to give her witness that he who is mighty has done great things for her (p. 403), for such a conversion glorifies not her so much as Christ himself.

Then, becoming ever more dramatic, our preacher summons the Holy Spirit, the heavenly flame, to embrace the sacrifice to be made in the preaching of the sermon. He prays that in his mouth the tongues of flame might be kindled, that all his words be as fiery arrows in the hearts of his listeners, that in the end the grace of the Lord be praised, and with this he leads the congregation in reciting the Ave Maria. Here is a rhetorical masterpiece, as flamboyant as any.

For Fénelon, at least in his early years, the first step to evangelizing the Protestants was to destroy their faith.[21] Consequently, this sermon expends much energy combating the teachings of Protestantism. The Protestants appeal to Scripture; Scripture, Scripture, Scripture, they cry. It is in just this way that the priests of the Temple back in the days of Jeremiah cried out, "The Temple of the Lord, the Temple of the Lord, the Temple of the Lord." The Protestants have no idea what Scripture says. Their besetting sin is pride. Arrogantly they insist that for centuries the Catholic interpretation has been wrong. The real problem with Protestantism is that it resents any kind of authority. Only they, the Protestants would have us believe, know how to understand Scripture. Their private interpretations have no foundation. They simply lack the humility needed to understand the Bible (p. 404). If they would just dare to call into ques-

21. Haillant, *Fénelon et la prédication,* pp. 127ff.

tion their own peculiar interpretation, they would easily discover the authority of the Church, for only the Church has the authority to interpret Scripture (p. 405).

This is followed by an attack on the Protestant understanding of the Eucharist (p. 406). Here most obviously the Protestants twist Scripture. Scripture says, "This is my body." Why don't Protestants believe it? They believe Scripture only if it suits their purposes. From this Fénelon goes on to the Protestant view of prayers for the dead and penance (p. 407). The conclusion of the sermon is another masterpiece of baroque prose. Fénelon lifts his eyes to heaven praying the good Lord that his voice be the hammer that would smash the stony hearts of the Huguenots, that at last these proud spirits who pretend to be reformed would come with tears of repentance in their eyes and recognize that in the Catholic Church indeed are the fruits of Zion. Grant to them, O Lord, the multitude of your mercies, our preacher intones. Alas, how long, O Lord, will they continue to persecute your church? After all, more than a century of night has passed already. How long must this time of spiritual blindness continue? O Good Shepherd, have mercy on the Protestants, lost and erring in the wilderness. Bring back to the true flock all those who truly love you (p. 410).

None of this is particularly edifying reading for an American Protestant with a good dash of Huguenot blood. The chances are, however, that this was the sort of preaching Fénelon had done on his preaching missions in the Protestant areas of western France. No doubt it was no more convincing then than it is today, but for the congregation of good French Catholics gathered to witness Mlle. de Peray's entrance into the convent, it must have been regarded very favorably. It proved beyond reasonable doubt that anyone of pure heart and good will, properly instructed, would ultimately embrace the Catholic Church.

Ironically enough, Fénelon himself seems to have tired of this kind of evangelism. More and more he turned away from absolutism, both politically and theologically.

B. Aristocrat of Eloquence

Fénelon is of most interest to the history of preaching because of his famous work on homiletics, *Dialogues sur l'éloquence*.[22] There are also his

22. For the French text, see Fénelon, *Oeuvres*, 3:656-92.

letters to the French Academy, which often give us the more mature reflection of later years. All together they were pivotal works summing up the preaching theory of the Counter-Reformation and yet turning the corner to a more pietist approach to preaching.

Fénelon was still very much concerned with using the pulpit to defend Catholicism from the claims of the Reformation. He makes a point of the difference between *convaincre,* that is, to conquer or win the debate, and *persuader,* to win the heart. One gathers that he was somewhat frustrated that, while he was able to show that the Protestant positions were quite unreasonable, the Protestants still would not convert. He could show that they were wrong, but that did not win their affections for Catholicism. Even in his girls' school he learned that he had to win the affections of the girls for Catholic ways. These girls or their parents had for one reason or another decided to conform to the established religion, but in their hearts they were still Protestants. How could one move from winning the argument to winning the heart?

The spirituality of the Jesuits as well as that of Francis de Sales is evident throughout Fénelon. It is not enough to engage the ears of the listeners. The preacher must appeal to the eyes as well. All the arts should be drawn into the pulpit — the dramatic, the poetic, the oratorical.[23] In fact, that is the justification of the arts. The whole baroque school of art was developed to support the claims of the Counter-Reformation. Bernini, Caravaggio, and Poussin all lent themselves to bolstering the authority of the Catholic Church. The arts make the truth attractive so that one is moved to embrace the truth they portray. The arts make the faith attractive, and therefore, as Fénelon sees it, the preacher should cultivate the arts of rhetoric. In short, eloquence should be cultivated for the sake of effectiveness.

Another aspect of Counter-Reformation homiletics which comes through very clearly in Fénelon is the idea that bishops have the chief responsibility in preaching. Fénelon, at least after he fell from favor at court, was one bishop who conscientiously fulfilled this ideal. Despite the teaching of the Council of Trent, few Catholic bishops in the sixteenth and seventeenth centuries did much in the pulpit. At the end of the seventeenth century in France, preaching was left to those who had a special gift for it.[24] It was not done at Mass on Sunday morning by the one who

---

23. Fénelon, *Oeuvres,* 3:668-77.
24. Haillant, *Fénelon et la prédication,* p. 57.

presided at the liturgy, but by professional preachers on Sunday afternoon or during the week at the annual Lenten or Advent preaching missions. Fénelon, true to the Council of Trent, made a point of preaching regularly in his cathedral, throughout the parishes and chapels of his diocese, even in the small towns and villages. In this he was the ideal Counter-Reformation prelate, like Carlo Borromeo, Thomas of Villanova, or Francis de Sales.

Inspired by the spirit of the baroque, Fénelon studied the classics of antiquity side by side with Scripture and tradition. The Council of Trent built on Christian humanism very differently than the Reformation had; it put a much stronger emphasis on learning from the Greek and Roman pagan literature. Fénelon carefully studied the rhetoric of Cicero and the poetry of Virgil. Demosthenes, Isocrates, and Plato are his constant guides. His preaching uses all the rhetorical devices of the Greeks and Romans, and consequently his type of eloquence is florid and dramatic. It is thoroughly baroque.

Fénelon took up all that the tradition of the Counter-Reformation passed on to him, but he saw beyond it. As he read Augustine, he got a very different picture of the preaching of the bishop of Hippo. Rather than seeing him as the Christian Cicero conquering heresy by the force of his eloquence, he began to see him as the pastor of the flock. To be sure, one can look at Augustine as the Christian Cicero, but Fénelon saw a much more pastoral aspect of Augustine's preaching.[25] He was, to be sure, a great orator, but he was more profoundly the father of his spiritual children.

In older years, as Fénelon turned away from the Catholic establishment and became more and more pietistic, it was this vision of the preaching of the ancient Church which motivated him. In his last years as archbishop of Cambrai he took Augustine's example to heart. He preached in his own cathedral frequently, as well as in parish churches all over his diocese.

Fénelon notes in his *Dialogues sur l'éloquence* that the Fathers of the ancient Church made an attempt to explain Scripture in terms of the context of each passage in the Scriptures themselves.[26] In other words, he was beginning to get an insight into the nature of expository preaching as it had been understood in the early Church.[27] He also notes that it was for-

---

25. Haillant, *Fénelon et la prédication,* p. 60.
26. Fénelon, *Oeuvres,* 3:679ff.
27. Haillant, *Fénelon et la prédication,* p. 44.

merly the practice to preach following the lessons ordinarily read during the liturgy, rather than on Sunday afternoon at a special preaching service.[28] As archbishop of Cambrai, he began to revive this practice, preaching informally to his congregation. He did not write out his sermons but spoke freely out of the fullness of his heart. These sermons were much more intimate, treating the matters of personal faith and life. Sad to say, little of this preaching has survived.[29] What has survived suggests that he was pointing the way to an entirely new approach to preaching, an approach much more in accord with the pietism which was beginning to develop in the late seventeenth century. The concern for holiness that we found among the Puritans in the earlier part of the century, which became yet stronger among the orthodox Protestants in Germany and the Netherlands, was now manifesting itself in French Catholicism.

As much as Fénelon may awaken our resentment for all kinds of ecclesiastical absolutism, he does at least give us some intimations of a Catholicism more profound than ever the court of Louis XIV dreamed.

28. Fénelon, *Oeuvres,* 3:690ff.

29. Traditionally, a limited number of discourses have been published as representing the sort of preaching Fénelon did in later years. Cf. Haillant, *Fénelon et la prédication,* pp. 5-20.

Bibliography

Bibliography for Chapter I

Abray, Lorna Jane. *The People's Reformation: Magistrates, Clergy, and Commons in Strasbourg, 1500-1598.* Ithaca, N.Y.: Cornell University Press, 1985.

Adam, Johann. *Evangelische Kirchengeschichte der Stadt Strasbourg bis zur französische Revolution.* Strasbourg: Heitz, 1922.

Althaus, Paul. *Die Theologie Martin Luthers.* 2nd ed. Gütersloh: Gerd Mohn, 1963.

Atkinson, James. *Martin Luther and the Birth of Protestantism.* Harmondsworth: Penguin Books, 1968.

Bainton, Roland H. *Here I Stand: A Life of Martin Luther.* New York: New American Library, 1955.

Barth, Hans-Martin. "Luthers Predigt von der Predigt." *Pastoraltheologie* 56 (1967): 481ff.

Bizer, Ernst. *Fides ex auditu.* 3rd ed. Neukirchen-Vluyn: Neukirchener Verlag, 1966.

Booty, John E. "The First and Second Prayer Books of King Edward VI." In *Oxford Encyclopedia of the Reformation,* 1:189-93. 4 vols. New York: Oxford University Press, 1996.

―――. *The Godly Kingdom of Tudor England.* Wilton, Conn.: Morehouse-Barlow, 1981.

Bornert, René. *La réforme protestante du culte à Strasbourg au XVIe siècle (1523-1598).* Leiden: E. J. Brill, 1981.

Bornkamm, Heinrich. *Luther's World of Thought.* Translated by Martin H. Bertram. St. Louis: Concordia Publishing House, 1958.

―――. *Martin Bucers Bedeutung*. Gütersloh: C. Bertelsmann, 1952.

―――. *Martin Luther in der Mitte seines Lebens*. Göttingen: Vandenhoeck und Ruprecht, 1979.

―――. "Das Wort Gottes bei Luther." *Luthergeselleschaft*, 7:37.

Bouwsma. William J. *John Calvin: A Sixteenth-Century Portrait*. New York: Oxford University Press, 1988.

Brecht, Martin. *Johannes Brenz, Neugestalter von Kirche, Staat und Gesellschaft*. Stuttgart: Calwer Verlag, 1971.

―――. *Martin Luther*. 3 vols. Minneapolis: Fortress Press, 1985-93.

Brendler, Gerhard. *Martin Luther, Theology and Revolution*. Translated by Claude R. Foster, Jr. New York and Oxford: Oxford University Press, 1991.

Brenz, Johann. *Homiliae vel Sermones nonnulli in Prophetam Danielem*. Edited by Martin Brecht, W. Willy Göltenboth, and Gerhard Schäfer. Tübingen: J. C. B. Mohr, 1972.

Brightman, Frank Edward, ed. *The English Rite*. 2 vols. London: Rivingtons, 1915.

Bring, Ragnar. *Luthers Anschauung von der Bibel*. Berlin: Lutherisches Verlaghaus, 1951.

Bromiley, Geoffrey W. *Thomas Cranmer, Archbishop and Martyr*. London: Church Book Room Press, 1956.

―――. *Thomas Cranmer, Theologian*. New York: Oxford University Press, 1956.

Bucer, Martin. *Grund und ursach auss gottlicher schrift der neüwerungen an dem nachtmal des herren, so man die Mess nennet, Tauf, Feyrtagen, bildern und gesang in der gemein Christi, wann die zusamenkompt, durch und auf das wort gottes zu Strassburg fürgenomen*. In Martin Bucer, *Martin Bucers Deutsche Schriften*, edited by Robert Stupperich. Vol. 1, *Frühschriften 1520-1524*. Gütersloh: Gerd Mohn, 1960.

―――. *Martin Bucers deutsche Schriften*. Edited by Robert Stupperich. 7 vols. Gütersloh: Gerd Mohn, 1960-78.

―――. *Psalmen und geystliche Lieder, die man zu Strassburg, und auch die man inn anderen Kirchen pflegt zu singen. Form und gebett zum eynsegen de Ee, den heiligen Tauff, Abentmal, besuchung der Krancken, und begrebnüss der abgestorbnen. Alles gemert und gebessert. Auch mit seinem Register*. Strasbourg: Hans Preüssen, 1537.

Butterworth, Charles C. *The Literary Lineage of the King James Bible, 1340-1611*. Philadelphia: University of Pennsylvania Press, 1941.

Cadier, Jean. *Calvin: L'homme que Dieu a dompté*. Geneva: Labor et Fides, 1958.

Calvin, John. *Institutes of the Christian Religion*. Edited by John T. McNeill. Translated by Ford Lewis Battles. 2 vols. Library of Christian Classics, vols. 20 and 21. Philadelphia: Westminster Press, 1960.

————. *Joannis Calvini, Opera Selecta,* vols. 3-5. Edited by Petrus Barth and Guilelmus Niesel. Munich: Christoph Kaiser, 1957.

————. *Joannis Calvini Opera Quae Supersunt Omnia.* Edited by William Baum, Eduard Cunitz, and Eduard Reuss. 59 vols. Corpus Reformatorum 29-87. Brunswick and Berlin, 1863-1900.

————. *Sermons sur le Livre de Michée.* Edited by Jean Daniel Benoît. Supplementa Calviniana, vol. 5. Neukirchen-Vluyn: Verlag des Erziehungsvereins, 1964.

Chester, Allan G. *Hugh Latimer, Apostle to the English.* Philadelphia: University of Pennsylvania Press, 1954.

Chrisman, Miriam Usher. *Lay Culture, Learned Culture: Books and Social Change in Strasbourg, 1480-1599.* New Haven: Yale University Press, 1982.

————. *Strasbourg and the Reform.* New Haven: Yale University Press, 1967.

Clarke, William Kemp Lowther, and C. Harris, eds. *Liturgy and Worship: A Companion to the Prayer Books of the Anglican Communion.* New York: Macmillan, 1932.

Cottret, Bernard. *Calvin, Biographie.* Paris: Éditions Jean-Claude Lattès, 1995.

Cruel, Rudolf. *Geschichte der deutschen Predigt im Mittelalter.* Detmold: Meyer'sche Hofbuchhandlung, 1879.

Davies, Horton. *Worship and Theology in England, from Cranmer to Hooper, 1534-1603.* Princeton: Princeton University Press, 1970.

Demaus, Robert. *Hugh Latimer, a Biography.* London and Dallas: Lamar & Barton, n.d.

Diwald, Helmut. *Luther, Eine Biographie.* Bergisch Gladbach: Gustav Lübbe Verlag, 1982.

Dix, Gregory. *The Shape of the Liturgy.* 2nd ed. Westminster, Eng.: Dacre Press, 1949.

Douglass, Jane Dempsey. *Justification in Late Medieval Preaching: A Study of John Geiler of Keisersberg.* Leiden: E. J. Brill, 1966.

Ebeling, Gerhard. *Evangelische Evangelienauslegung: Eine Untersuchung zu Luthers Hermeneutik.* 3rd ed. Tübingen: J. C. B. Mohr (Paul Siebeck), 1991.

————. *Luther: An Introduction to His Thought.* Translated by R. A. Wilson. Philadelphia: Fortress Press, 1970.

Edwards, Mark U. *Luther and the False Brethren.* Stanford: Stanford University Press, 1975.

Eells, Hastings. *Martin Bucer.* New Haven: Yale University Press, 1931.

Eire, Carlos M. N. *War against the Idols: The Reformation of Worship from Erasmus to Calvin.* Cambridge: Cambridge University Press, 1986.

Erichson, A. *Matthäus Zell.* 1879.

Farner, Oskar. *Hüldrych Zwingli.* 4 vols. Zürich: Zwingli Verlag, 1943-60.

Fider, Johannes. "Matthäus Zell." In *Realencyklopädie für protestantische Theologie und Kirche,* edited by Johann Jakob Herzog, 21:650-52. 3rd ed. 22 vols. Leipzig: J. C. Hinrichs'sche Buchhandlung, 1896-1906.

Forstman, H. Jackson. *Word and Spirit: Calvin's Doctrine of Biblical Authority.* Stanford: Stanford University Press, 1962.

Frick, Robert. "Luther als Prediger, dargestellt auf Grund der Predigten über 1. Kor. 15 (1532/33)." *Lutherjahrbuch* 21 (1939): 28ff.

Gairdner, James. *The English Church in the Sixteenth Century from the Accession of Henry VIII to the Death of Mary.* London and New York: Macmillan, 1902.

―――. *Lollardy and the Reformation in England: An Historical Survey.* 3 vols. London: Macmillan, 1908-11.

Gasquet, Francis A., and E. Bishop. *Edward VI and the Book of Common Prayer.* London: John Hodges, 1890.

George, Charles H., and Katherine George. *The Protestant Mind of the English Reformation, 1570-1640.* Princeton: Princeton University Press, 1961.

Gerrish, Brian A. *Grace and Reason: A Study in the Theology of Luther.* Oxford: Clarendon Press, 1962.

Greenslade, Stanley L. *The Works of William Tyndale.* London: Blackie and Son, 1938.

Hagenbach, Karl Rudolf. *Johann Oekolampad und Oswald Myconius, die Reformatoren Basels, Leben und ausgewählte Schriften.* Elberfeld: R. L. Friderichs, 1859.

Hartmann, Julius. *Johannes Brenz, Leben und ausgewählte Schriften.* Elberfeld: R. L. Friderichs, 1862.

Herding, Otto. "Probleme des frühen Humanismus in Deutschland." *Archiv für Kulturgeschichte* 38 (1956): 344-89.

Higman, Francis. *The Style of John Calvin in His French Polemical Treatises.* Oxford: Oxford University Press, 1967.

Hirsch, Emanuel. *Lutherstudien.* 2 vols. Gütersloh: C. Bertelsmann, 1954.

Holl, Karl. *Gesammelte Aufsätze zur Kirchengeschichte.* 6th ed. 3 vols. Tübingen: J. C. B. Mohr (Paul Siebeck), 1932.

Hooper, John. *Early Writings.* Edited by Samuel Carr. Parker Society edition. 2 vols. Cambridge: University Press, 1843.

―――. *Later Writings of Bishop Hooper.* Edited by C. Nevinson. Cambridge: University Press, 1852.

―――. *An oversight and deliberacion uppon the holy prophet Jonas.* London: John Tisdale, 1550.

Hopf, Constantin. *Martin Bucer and the English Reformation.* Oxford: B. Blackwell, 1946.

Hubert, Friedrich. *Die Strassburger liturgischen Ordnungen im Zeitalter der Reformation.* Göttingen: Vandenhoeck und Ruprecht, 1900.

Hughes, Philip. *The Reformation in England.* 2 vols. London: Hollis & Carter, 1950-54.

Hunt, E. W. *The Life and Times of John Hooper (c. 1500-1555), Bishop of Gloucester.* Lewiston, N.Y.: E. Mellen Press, ca. 1992.

Jenny, Markus. *Die Einheit des Abendmahls gottesdienstes bei den Elsässischen und Schweizerischen Reformatoren.* Zürich and Stuttgart: Zwingli Verlag, 1968.

Jung, Andreas. *Geschichte der Reformation der Kirche im Strassburg und der Ausbreitung derselben in den Gemeinden des Elsasses.* Strasbourg: F. G. Leyrault, 1830.

Ketley, Joseph, ed. *The Two Liturgies, A.D. 1549 and A.D. 1552 with Other Documents Set Forth by Authority in the Reign of King Edward VI.* Parker Society edition. Cambridge: At the University Press, 1846.

Kittelson, James M. *Wolfgang Capito, from Humanist to Reformer.* Leiden: E. J. Brill, 1975.

Klaustermeyer, William H. "The Role of Matthew and Catherine Zell in the Strassburg Reformation." Ph.D. diss., Stanford University, 1965.

Köhler, Walther. *Huldrych Zwinglis Bibliothek.* Zürich: Kommissionsverlag Beer, 1921.

————. *Zwingli und Luther. Ihr Streit über das Abendmahl nach seinen politischen und religiösen Beziehungen.* 2 vols. Leipzig: M. Heinsius Nachfolger, 1924.

Krüger, Friedhelm. *Bucer und Erasmus, Eine Untersuchung zum Einfluss des Erasmus auf die Theologie Martin Bucers.* Wiesbaden: Steiner Verlag, 1970.

Lang, August. *Der Evangelienkommentar Martin Butzers und dis Grundzüge seiner Theologie.* Leipzig: Dietrich, 1900.

Latimer, Hugh. *Selected Sermons.* Edited by Allan G. Chester. Charlottesville: University Press of Virginia, 1968.

————. *Sermons.* Parker Society edition. 2 vols. Cambridge: University Press, 1844.

Legg, J. Wickham, ed. *A Second Recension of the Quignon Breviary.* 2 vols. London: Henry Bradshaw Society, 1908-12.

Leith, John H. "Calvin's Doctrine of the Proclamation of the Word and Its Significance for Today." In *John Calvin and the Church, a Prism of Reform,* edited by Timothy George, pp. 206-29. Louisville: Westminster/John Knox Press, 1990.

Lenhart, J. M. "Quinones' Breviary." *Franciscan Studies,* n.s., 6 (1946): 468.

Locher, Gottfried W. *Im Geist und in der Wahrheit. Die reformatorische Wendung im Gottesdienst in Zurich.* Neukirchen, 1957.

————. *Die Zwinglische Reformation in Rahmen der europäische Kirchengeschichte.* Göttingen: Vandenhoeck und Ruprecht, 1979.

————. *Zwingli's Thought: New Perspectives.* Leiden: E. J. Brill, 1981.

Luther, Martin. *Ausgewählte Werke.* Edited by H. H. Borcherdt and Georg Merz. 3rd ed. 7 vols. Munich: Chr. Kaiser Verlag, 1953-63.

————. *D. Martin Luthers Werke kritische Gesamtausgabe.* Edited by J. C. F. Knaakel et al. 67 vols. Weimar: Hermann Bohlaus, 1883ff.

————. *Luther's Works.* Edited by Jaroslav Pelikan and Helmut T. Lehmann. 55 vols. St. Louis: Concordia Publishing House; Philadelphia: Fortress Press, 1955-76.

————. *Sermons.* Edited and translated by John W. Doberstein. *Luther's Works,* vol. 51. Philadelphia: Muhlenberg Press, 1959.

————. *Sermons.* Edited by Hans J. Hillerbrand. *Luther's Works,* vol. 52. Philadelphia: Muhlenberg Press, 1974.

————. *Sermons on the Gospel of St. John, Chapters 1–4.* Edited by Jaroslav Pelikan. *Luther's Works,* vol. 22. St. Louis: Concordia, 1957.

McGrath, Alister. *A Life of John Calvin.* Oxford: Blackwell, 1990.

Marcel, Pierre. "Jean Calvin: Les Béatitudes, quatre prédications." *La Revue Réformée* 120 (1979).

————. "L'Actualité de la prédication." *La Revue Réformée* 7 (1951).

————. "Une lecture non-Calviniste de Calvin." *Supplément à la Revue Réformée* 4 (1979).

Millet, Olivier. *Calvin et la dynamique de la Parole. Essai de rhétorique réformée.* Paris: H. Champion, 1992.

Moeller, Bernd. "Die deutschen Humanisten und die Anfänge der Reformation." *Zeitschrift für Kirchengeschichte* 70 (1959).

————. *Reichsstadt und Reformation.* Gütersloh: Verlaghaus Gerd Mohn, 1962.

Moorman, John R. H. *A History of the Church in England.* 3rd ed. 1973. Reprint, London: A. & C. Black, 1980.

Mozley, James Frederic. *William Tyndale.* New York: Macmillan, 1937.

Müller, Johannes. *Martin Bucers Hermeneutik.* Gütersloh: Gerd Mohn, 1965.

Neill, Stephen C. *Anglicanism.* Rev. ed. London: Mowbrays, 1977.

Nembach, Ulrich. *Predigt des Evangeliums, Luther als Prediger, Pädagoge und Rhetor.* Neukirchen-Vluyn: Neukirchener Verlag, 1972.

Niebergall, Alfred. "Die Geschichte der christlichen Predigt." In *Leiturgia, Handbuch des Evangelischen Gottesdienstes,* edited by Karl Ferdinand Müller and Walter Blankenburg. 5 vols. Kassel: Johannes Stauda Verlag, 1954-70.

Oberman, Heiko A. *Luther: Man between God and the Devil.* New Haven: Yale University Press, 1989.

————. *Die Reformation von Wittenberg nach Genf.* Göttingen: Vandenhoeck und Ruprecht, 1986.

Oecolampadius, John. *De amandis pauperibus Gregorii Nazanzeni episcopi et theologi sermo, eiusdem ad virginem admonitorius, eiusdem laudes Maccabaeorum, interprete Joanne Oecolampadio, concionatore Augustensi.* Augsburg: Grimm und Wirsung, 1519.

————. *De risu paschali Oecolampadii ad V. Capitonem theologum epistola apologetica.* Basel: J. Froben, 1518.

————. *Divi Gregorii Nazanzeni eruditi aliquot et mirae frugis sermones: In Pas-*

cha; In dictum Mattaei . . . , cap. XIX; Laudes Cypriani Martyris, Oecolampadio interprete. . . . Augsburg: Grimm und Wirsung, 1519.

—. *Divi Ioannis Chrysostomi, Archiepiscopi Constantinopolitani, in totum Geneseos librum Homiliae sexaginta sex, a Ioanne Oecolampadio hoc anno uersae. . . .* Basel: Cratander, 1523.

—. *Enarratio in evangelium Matthaei d. Jo. Oecolampadio auctore et alia nonnulla, quae sequens pagella indicabit.* Edited by Oswald Myconius. Basel: Cratander, 1536.

—. *In epistolam d. Pauli ad Colossenses conciones aliquot piae ac doctae, ad tempora nostra valde accomodae, nunc primum in lucem editae, authore Joanne Oecolampadio.* Bern: Mathias Apiarius, 1546.

—. *In epistolam Joannis apostoli catholicam primam Joannis Oecolampadii demegoriae, hoc est: homiliae una et XX.* Basel: Cratander, 1524.

—. *Inn die clag Hieremie, des heligen propheten, eine schöne uszlegung durch Johanem Oecolampadium in der Kirchen zu Basel geprediget, vorhin nie im truck uszangen.* Basel: Ruprecht Winter, 1545.

Old, Hughes Oliphant. "The Homiletics of John Oecolampadius and the Sermons of the Greek Fathers." In *Communio Sanctorum: Mélanges offerts à Jean-Jacques von Allmen.* Geneva: Labor et Fides, 1982.

—. *The Patristic Roots of Reformed Worship.* Zürich: Theologischer Verlag Zürich, 1975.

—. *The Shaping of the Reformed Baptismal Rite in the Sixteenth Century.* Grand Rapids: William B. Eerdmans Publishing Co., 1992.

—. *Themes and Variations for a Christian Doxology.* Grand Rapids: William B. Eerdmans Publishing Co., 1992.

O'Malley, John. "Lutheran Preachers." *Michigan Germanic Studies* 10 (1984): 3-16.

—. *Religious Culture in the Sixteenth Century: Preaching, Rhetoric, Spirituality, and Reform.* Brookfield, Vt.: Variorum, 1993.

Ozment, Steven. *The Age of Reform (1250-1550): An Intellectual and Religious History of Late Medieval and Reformation Europe.* New Haven and London: Yale University Press, 1980.

—. *The Reformation in the Cities.* New Haven: Yale University Press, 1975.

Parker, T. H. L. *Calvin's Preaching.* Edinburgh: T. & T. Clark, 1992.

—. *John Calvin: A Biography.* London: J. M. Dent & Sons, 1975.

—. *The Oracles of God: An Introduction to the Preaching of John Calvin.* London and Redhill: Lutterworth Press, 1947.

Payne, John. *Erasmus: His Theology of the Sacraments.* Richmond: John Knox Press, 1970.

Peter, Rodolphe. "Jean Calvin Prédicateur." *Revue d'histoire et de philosophie religieuses* 52 (1972): 111-17.

————. "Rhétorique et prédication selon Calvin." *Revue d'histoire et de philosophie religieuses* 55 (1975): 249-72.

Pollard, Albert F. *Thomas Cranmer and the English Reformation, 1489-1556.* London: G. P. Putnam's Sons, 1905.

Porter, Harry C. *Reformation and Reaction in Tudor Cambridge.* Cambridge: At the University Press, 1958.

Potter, George R. *Zwingli.* Cambridge and New York: Cambridge University Press, 1976.

Procter, Francis, and W. H. Frere. *A History of the Book of Commmon Prayer.* London: Macmillan, 1949.

Ratcliff, Edward C. "The Liturgical Work of Archbishop Cranmer." *Journal of Ecclesiastical History* 7 (1956): 189-203.

Richter, Aemilius Ludwig, ed. *Die evangelischen Kirchenordnungen des sechzehnten Jahrhunderts.* 2 vols. Weimar: Landes-Industriecomptoirs, 1846.

Ridley, Jasper G. *Thomas Cranmer.* Oxford: Clarendon Press, 1962.

Röhrich, Timotheus W. "Matthäus und Katherina Zell." In *Mitteilungen aus der Geschichte der evangelischen Kirche des Elsasses,* 3:84-179. 3 vols. Paris: Treuttel und Wurtz, 1855.

Roth, Dorothea. *Die Mittelalterliche Predigttheorie und das Manuale curatorum des Johannes Ulrich Surgant.* Basel, 1956.

Ryle, John Charles. "Life of John Hooper." In *Five English Reformers.* London: Banner of Truth Trust, 1965.

Schwiebert, Ernest G. *The Reformation.* 2 vols. Minneapolis: Fortress Press, 1993.

Smend, Julius. *Die evangelischen deutschen Messen bis zu Luthers Deutsche Messe.* Göttingen: Vandenhoeck und Ruprecht, 1896.

Spitz, Lewis W. *The Religious Renaissance of the German Humanists.* Cambridge: Harvard University Press, 1963.

Staehelin, Ernst. *Briefe und Akten zum Leben Oecolampads.* Quellen und Forschungen zur Reformationsgeschichte, vols. 10 and 19. Leipzig: M. Heinsius Nachfolger, 1927 and 1934.

————. *Das Buch der Basler Reformation.* Basel: Helbing und Lichtenhahn, 1929.

————. *Oekolampad-Bibliographie, Verseichnis der im 16. Jahrhundert erschienenen Oekolampaddrucke.* Basel: Verlag der historischen und antiquarischen Gesellschaft, 1917.

————. *Das theologische Lebenswerk Johannes Oekolampads.* Quellen und Forschungen zur Reformationsgeschichte, vol. 21. Leipzig: M. Heinsius Nachfolger, 1939.

Stauffer, Richard. "Un Calvin méconnu; la prédicateur de Genève." *Bulletin de la Société de l'histoire du Protestantisme français* 123 (1977): 184-203.

————. *Dieu, la création et la providence dans la prédication de Calvin.* Bern: P. Lang, 1978.

————. *L'humanité de Calvin.* Neuchâtel: Delachaux et Niestlé, 1964.

Steinmetz, David C. *Luther and Staupitz: An Essay in the Intellectual Origins of the Protestant Reformation.* Durham, N.C.: Duke University Press, 1980.

Stephens, Peter. *The Holy Spirit in the Theology of Martin Bucer.* Cambridge: University Press, 1970.

Stierle, Beate. *Capito als Humanist.* Quellen und Forschungen zur Reformationsgeschichte, vol. 42. Gütersloh: Gerd Mohn, 1974.

Strasser, Otto Erich. *La pensée théologique de Wolfgang Capiton.* Neuchâtel: Secrétariat de l'Université, 1938.

Stupperich, Robert. "Zell, Matthäus." In *Religion in Gegenwart und Geschichte,* 6:1891ff. 3rd ed. 7 vols. Tübingen: J. C. B. Mohr (Paul Siebeck), 1957.

Surgant, Johann Ulrich. *Manuale curatorum predicandi prebens modum; tam latino quam vulgari sermone; practice illuminatum: cum certis aliis ad curam animarum pertinentibus: omnibus curatis tam conducibilis quam salubris.* Basel: Michael Furter, 1503.

Thompson, Bard. *Liturgies of the Western Church.* Cleveland and New York: World Publishing Co., 1961.

Trinterud, Leonard J. *Elizabethan Puritanism.* New York: Oxford University Press, 1971.

Tyndale, William. *The Work of William Tyndale.* Edited by G. E. Duffield. Courtenay Library of Reformation Classics, vol. 1. Appleford, Eng.: Sutton-Courtenay Press, 1964.

Vajta, Vilmos. *Luther on Worship.* Philadelphia: Muhlenberg Press, 1958.

————. *Die Theologie des Gottesdienstes bei Luther.* Göttingen: Vandenhoeck und Ruprecht, 1952.

Van de Poll, G. J. *Martin Bucer's Liturgical Ideas.* Assen: Van Gorcum, 1954.

Warren, Frederick Edward. "Prayer, Book of Common." In *Encyclopedia Britannica,* 22:258-62. 11th ed. 32 vols. New York: Encyclopedia Britannica, 1910.

Whitaker, Edward Charles. *Martin Bucer and the Book of Common Prayer.* Alcuin Club Collection, vol. 55. Great Wakering: Mayhew-McCrimmon, 1974.

Williams, Charles Harold. *William Tyndale.* London: Nelson, 1969.

Zwingli, Ulrich. *Huldreich Zwingli's sämtliche Werke.* 3 vols. Corpus Reformatorum 88-90. Berlin: Verlag von C. A. Schwetschke und Sohn, 1905.

————. "Of the Clarity and Certainty of the Word of God." In *Zwingli and Bullinger,* edited by G. W. Bromiley. Library of Christian Classics, vol. 24. Philadelphia: Westminster Press, 1953.

523

Bibliography for Chapter II

Albergio, Giuseppe. "Carlo Borromeo come modello di vescovo nella chiesa post-tridentina." *Revista Storica Italiana* 79 (1967): 1031-52.

Arnold, Franz Xaver. *Die Staatslehre des Kardinals Bellarmin.* Munich: M. Heuber, 1934.

Bangert, William V. *A History of the Society of Jesus.* St. Louis: Institute of Jesuit Sources, 1972.

Bayley, Peter. *French Pulpit Oratory, 1598-1650.* Cambridge and New York: Cambridge University Press, 1980.

Bellarmine, Robert. *Opera oratoria postuma.* Edited by Sebastian Tromp. 9 vols. Rome: Gregorian University Press, 1945.

Blackwell, Richard J. *Galileo, Bellarmine, and the Bible.* Notre Dame, Ind.: University of Notre Dame Press, 1991.

Borromeo, Charles. *Homiliae nunc primum e mss. Codicibus Bibliotecae Ambrosianae in lucem productae.* Edited by Giuseppe Antonio Sassi. Milan: Bibliotheca Ambrosiana, 1747-48.

Broderick, John Francis. "Jesuits." In *New Catholic Encyclopedia,* 7:898-909. 17 vols. Washington, D.C.: Catholic University of America Press, 1968.

Brodrick, James, S.J. *Robert Bellarmine, Saint and Scholar.* Westminster, Md.: Newman Press, 1961.

————. *Saint Francis Xavier (1506-1552).* New York: Wicklow Press, 1952.

————. *St. Ignatius of Loyola: The Pilgrim Years.* New York: Farrer, Stans and Cudahy, 1956.

————. *Saint Peter Canisius.* Chicago: Loyola University Press, 1962.

Canisius, Peter. *S. Petri Canisii doctoris Ecclesiae Meditationes seu notae in evangeliae lectiones.* 3 vols. Freiburg and Munich, 1939-61.

Carney, Edward John. "Francis de Sales, St." In *New Catholic Encyclopedia,* 6:34-36. 17 vols. Washington, D.C.: Catholic University of America Press, 1968.

Cochrane, Eric W. "Counter-Reformation or Tridentine Reformation? Italy in the Age of Carlo Borromeo." In *San Carlo Borromeo: Catholic Reform and Ecclesiastical Politics in the Second Half of the Sixteenth Century,* edited by John M. Headley and John B. Tomaro. Washington, D.C.: Folger Books, 1988.

Coleccion de Incunables Americanos, Siglo XVI. Prologo Don Ramon Menendez Pidal. Madrid: Ediciones cultura Hispanica, 1944.

Dalmases, Cándido de. "Ignatius of Loyola, St." In *New Catholic Encyclopedia,* 7:354-56. 17 vols. Washington, D.C.: Catholic University of America Press, 1968.

Deroo, André. *Saint Charles Borromée: Cardinal réformateur, docteur de la pastoral.* Paris: Éditions Saint-Paul, 1963.

Diaz del Castillo, Bernal. *The Discovery and Conquest of Mexico*. Translated by A. P. Maudslay. Introduction to the American edition by Irving A. Leonard. New York: Noonday Press, 1956.

Diez, Felipe. *Conciones quadruplices in Evangelia*. Salamanca, 1682.

Donnelly, John Patrick. "Bellarmino, Roberto." In *Oxford Encyclopedia of the Reformation*, 1:139ff. 4 vols. New York and Oxford: Oxford University Press, 1996.

———. "Canisius, Peter." In *Oxford Encyclopedia of the Reformation*, 1:253. 4 vols. New York and Oxford: Oxford University Press, 1996.

Dudon, Paul. *St. Ignatius of Loyola*. Translated by W. J. Young. Milwaukee: Bruce Publishing, 1949.

Dupré, Louis, and Don Saliers, eds. *Christian Spirituality: Post-Reformation and Modern*. New York: Crossroad Publishing, 1982.

Friske, Joseph Peter. "Bellarmine, Robert, St." In *New Catholic Encyclopedia* 2:250-52. 17 vols. Washington, D.C.: Catholic University of America Press, 1968.

Fumaroti, Marc. *L'âge de l'éloquence: Rhetoric et "res literaria" de la Renaissance au seuil de l'époque classique*. Geneva: Droz, 1980.

Galeota, Gustavo, ed. *Roberto Bellarmino: Archivescovo de Capua, teologo e pastore della Riforma Cattolica*. Capua, Italy: Archidiocesi de Capua, Istituto superiore di scienze religiose, 1990.

Guibert, Joseph de. *The Jesuits: Their Spiritual Doctrine and Practice*. Translated by William J. Young. Chicago: Loyola University Press, 1964.

Hamon, André Jean Marie. *Life of St. Francis de Sales*. Translated by Harold Burton. 2 vols. London: Burns, Oates & Washbourne, 1925-29.

Harney, Martin Patrick. *The Jesuits in History: The Society of Jesus through Four Centuries*. New York: American Press, 1941.

Headley, John M., and John B. Tomaro, eds. *San Carlo Borromeo: Catholic Reform and Ecclesiastical Politics in the Second Half of the Sixteenth Century*. Washington, D.C.: Folger Books, 1988.

Hens, N. *Die Augustinusinterpretation des heiligen Robert Bellarmine*. Rome, 1939.

Jayne, Kingsley Garland. "Xavier, Francisco de." In *Encyclopedia Britannica*, 28:882-83. 11th ed. 32 vols. New York: Encyclopedia Britannica, 1910.

Jedin, Hubert. *A History of the Council of Trent*. 2 vols. London: Thomas Nelson and Sons, 1957-61.

———. *Katholische Reformation oder Gegen-reformation?* Lucerne: Stocker, 1946.

Jobit, Pierre. *L'évêque des pauvres, saint Thomas de Villeneuve*. Bibliothèque Ecclesia, vol. 63. Paris: Montréal, 1961.

Juan of Ávila. *Obras completas del B. Mtro. Juan de Ávila: Edición crítica*. Edited and introduction by Luis Sala Balust. 2 vols. Madrid: La Editorial Católica, 1953.

525

Kaegi, Werner. *Humanische Kontinuität im konfessionellen Zeitalter.* Schriften der "Freunde der Universität Basel," vol. 8. Basel, 1954.

Kleinman, Ruth. *Saint François de Sales and the Protestants.* Travaux d'Humanisme et Renaissance, vol. 52. Geneva: Droz, 1962.

Lajeunie, Etienne-Jean, O.P. *Saint François de Sales, l'homme, la pensée, l'action.* 2 vols. Paris: Éditions Guy Victor, 1967.

Lampe, Elmer Lewis. "Counter-Reformation." In *New Catholic Encyclopedia,* 4:384-89. 17 vols. Washington, D.C.: Catholic University of America Press, 1968.

Larios, A. "La reforma de la predicatión en Trento." *Communio* 6 (1973): 223-83.

Lezat, Arien. *De la prédication sous Henry IV.* Geneva: Slatkin Reprints, 1970.

Littledale, Richard, and Ethelred Taunton. "Jesuits." In *Encyclopedia Britannica,* 15:337-47. 11th ed. 32 vols. New York: Encyclopedia Britannica, 1910.

Luis of Granada. *Conciones de tempore.* 4 vols. Lisbon, 1573-76.

———. *Ecclesiastica rhetoricae, sive De Ratione Concionandi.* Lisbon: A. Riberius, 1576.

———. *Obras.* Edited by Justo Cuervo. 14 vols. Madrid: viuda e hija de G. Fuentenebro, 1906-8.

———. *Obras.* Vol. 3. Biblioteca de Autores Españoles, vol. 11. Madrid: Ediciones Atlas, 1945.

———. *Los seis Libros de la Retórica Eclesiastica, o De la Manera de Predicar.* In Biblioteca de Autores Españoles, vol. 11. Madrid: Ediciones Atlas, 1945.

McGinness, Frederick J. *Right Thinking and Sacred Oratory in Counter-Reformation Rome.* Princeton: Princeton University Press, 1995.

Mackey, H. B. "Francis of Sales." In *Encyclopedia Britannica,* 10:940ff. 11th ed. 32 vols. New York: Encyclopedia Britannica, 1910.

Maynard, Theodore. *St. Ignatius and the Jesuits.* New York: P. J. Kennedy, 1956.

Moore, John A. *Fray Luis de Granada.* Boston: Twayne Publishers, 1977.

Murray, J. C. "St. Robert Bellarmine on the Indirect Power." *Theological Studies* 9 (1948): 491-535.

O'Malley, John W. "Early Jesuit Spirituality." In *Christian Spirituality: Post-Reformation and Modern,* edited by Louis Dupré and Don Saliers. New York: Crossroad Publishing, 1982.

———. *Praise and Blame in Renaissance Rome: Rhetoric, Doctrine, and Reform in the Sacred Orators of the Papal Courts, c. 1450-1521.* Durham, N.C.: Duke University Press, 1979.

———. *Religious Culture in the Sixteenth Century: Preaching, Rhetoric, Spirituality, and Reform.* Brookfield, Vt.: Variorum, 1993.

———. "Saint Charles Borromeo and His Preaching." In *San Carlo Borromeo: Catholic Reform and Ecclesiastical Politics in the Second Half of the Sixteenth*

Century, edited by John M. Headley and John B. Tomaro. Washington, D.C.: Folger Books, 1988.

————. "Saint Charles Borromeo and the *Praecipuum Episcoporum Munus:* His Place in the History of Preaching." In *San Carlo Borromeo: Catholic Reform and Ecclesiastical Politics in the Second Half of the Sixteenth Century,* edited by John M. Headley and John B. Tomaro. Washington, D.C.: Folger Books, 1988.

Orsenigo, Cesare. *Life of St. Charles Borromeo.* English translation by Rudolph Kraus. St. Louis and London: B. Herder Book Co., 1943.

————. *Vita di S. Carlo Borromeo.* 2 vols. Milan: Casa Editrice s. Lega Eucaristica, 1929.

Oswald, Julius, and Peter Rummel, eds. *Petrus Canisius — Reformer der Kirche, Festschrift zum 400. Todestag des zweiten Apostels Deutschlands.* Augsburg: Sankt Ulrich Verlag, 1996.

Parkes, Henry Bamford. *A History of Mexico.* Boston: Houghton Mifflin, 1969.

Rahner, Hugo. *The Spirituality of St. Ignatius Loyola.* Translated by F. J. Smith. Chicago: Loyola University Press, 1953.

Sales, Francis de. *Oeuvres de Saint François de Sales, évêque et prince de Génève et docteur de l'église. Édition complète d'après les autographes et les éditions originales enrichie de nombreuses pièces inédites . . . publiée par les soins des Religieuses de la Visitation du 1er Monastère d'Annecy.* 26 vols. Annecy: Impr. J. Nierat, 1892-1932.

————. *On the Preacher and Preaching.* Translation of a letter to André Frémont. Introduction and notes by John K. Ryan. Chicago: Henry Regnery, 1964.

————. *The Spiritual Conferences of St. Francis de Sales.* Translated by H. B. Mackey. Westminster, Md.: Newman Bookshop, 1943.

Schurhammer, Georg. *Francis Xavier: His Life, His Times.* Translated by Joseph Costellac. 4 vols. Rome: Jesuit Historical Institutes, 1973-82.

Seguiran, Gaspar de. *Sermons doctes et admirables sur le Evangilles des Dimanches et Fests de l'année.* Paris: Nicolas de Fossé, 1612.

————. *Sermons doctes et admirables sur tous les jours de Caresme.* Paris: Nicolas de Fossé, 1613.

————. *Sermons sur la parabole de l'enfant prodigue.* Paris: Nicolas de Fossé, 1612.

Servière, Joseph de la. *La théologie de Bellarmin.* Paris: Beauchesne, 1909.

Smith, Hilary Dansey. *Preaching in the Spanish Golden Age: A Study of Some Preachers of the Reign of Philip III.* Oxford: University Press, 1978.

Taunton, Ethelred. "Loyola, St. Ignatius of." In *Encyclopedia Britannica,* 17:80-84. 11th ed. 32 vols. New York: Encyclopedia Britannica, 1910.

Thomas of Villanova. *The Works of Saint Thomas of Villanova: Sermons, Part 2: Christmas.* Translated by Maria Boulding. Edited by John E. Rotelle. Augustinian Series, vol. 20. Villanova, Pa.: Augustinian Press, 1994.

Überbacher, Philipp. "Petrus Canisius als Hofprediger." In *Petrus Canisius-Reformer der Kirche, Festschrift zum 400. Todestag des zweiten Apostels Deutschlands,* edited by Julius Oswald and Peter Rummel. Augsburg: Sankt Ulrich Verlag, 1996.

Valiero, Agostino. *Vita Caroli Borromaei.* Verona: apud Hieronymum Discipulum, 1586.

Wicki, Josef. "Xavier, Francis, St." In *New Catholic Encyclopedia,* 14:1059-60. 17 vols. Washington, D.C.: Catholic University of America Press, 1968.

Willey, Gordon R., William T. Sanders, and John V. Murra. "Pre-Columbian Civilizations." In *The New Encyclopedia Britannica,* 26:1-44. 15th ed. 32 vols. Chicago: Encyclopedia Britannica, 1994.

Bibliography for Chapter III

Ball, Thomas. *The Life of the Renowned Doctor Preston.* Oxford: Parker, 1885.

Barker, William. *Puritan Profiles, Fifty-four Puritans: Personalities Drawn Together by the Westminster Assembly.* Fearn, Ross-shire, Scotland: Christian Focus Publications, 1996.

Carlyle, Edward Irving. "Watson, Thomas." In *Dictionary of National Biography,* 20:948-49. 22 vols. London and New York: Oxford University Press, 1973.

Collinson, Patrick. *The Elizabethan Puritan Movement.* Berkeley: University of California Press, 1967.

———. *English Puritanism.* London: Historical Association, 1983.

———. *The Religion of Protestants: The Church in English Society, 1559-1625.* Oxford, 1982.

Coolidge, J. S. *The Pauline Renaissance in England: Puritanism and the Bible.* Oxford, 1970.

Cragg, Gerald Robertson. *Puritanism in the Period of the Great Persecution, 1660-1688.* Cambridge: University Press, 1957.

Davies, Horton. *Like Angels from a Cloud: The English Metaphysical Preachers, 1588-1645.* San Marino, Calif.: Huntington Library, 1986.

———. *Worship and Theology in England.* 6 vols. Princeton: Princeton University Press, 1961-75.

———. *Worship of the English Puritans.* 2nd ed. Morgan, Pa.: Soli Deo Gloria Publications, 1997.

Emerson, Everett H. *English Puritanism from John Hooper to John Milton.* Durham, N.C.: Duke University Press, 1968.

Fell-Smith, Charlotte. "Manton, Thomas." In *Dictionary of National Biography,* 12:986-89. 22 vols. London and New York: Oxford University Press, 1973.

Fincham, Kenneth, ed. *The Early Stuart Church, 1603-1642.* Stanford: Stanford University Press, 1993.

Finlayson, Michael George. *Historians, Puritanism, and the English Revolution.* Toronto and Buffalo: University of Toronto Press, 1983.

Flavel, John. *Divine Conduct or the Mystery of Providence.* London, 1678.

————. *The Mystery of Providence.* Photolithographic reproduction. Edinburgh and Carlisle, Pa.: Banner of Truth Trust, 1976.

————. *Works.* London: W. Baynes and Son, 1820.

————. *The Works of John Flavel.* Photolithographic reproduction of the edition of 1820 published by W. Baynes and Son in London. 6 vols. Edinburgh and Carlisle, Pa.: Banner of Truth Trust, 1982.

Frere, Walter H., and Charles E. Douglas, eds. *Puritan Manifestoes.* London: Published for the Church Historical Society, SPCK, 1954.

Goodwin, Thomas. *The Works of Thomas Goodwin, D.D.* 8 vols. Edinburgh: James Nichol, 1864.

————. *The Works of Thomas Goodwin.* Photolithographic reproduction of the edition of James Nichol published in Edinburgh in 1864. 9 vols. Edinburgh and Carlisle, Pa.: Banner of Truth Trust, 1985.

————. *The Works of Thomas Goodwin.* Three volumes bound as one. London: Jonathan Robinson, 1681.

Haller, William. *The Rise of Puritanism; or, The Way to the New Jerusalem as Set Forth in Pulpit and Press from Thomas Cartwright to John Lilburne and John Milton, 1570-1643.* New York: Columbia University Press, 1938.

Hamilton, Thomas. "Flavel, John." In *Dictionary of National Biography,* 7:253-54. 22 vols. London and New York: Oxford University Press, 1973.

Knappen, Marshall M. *Tudor Puritanism: A Chapter in the History of Idealism.* Chicago and London: University of Chicago Press, 1939.

Lake, Peter. *Anglicans and Puritans? Presbyterian and English Conformist Thought from Whitgift to Hooker.* London, 1988.

Lamont, William M. *Puritanism and the English Revolution.* Aldershot, Hampshire, Eng.: Gregg Revivals; Brookfield, Vt.: Distributed by Ashgate Publishing, 1991.

Lloyd-Jones, David Martyn. *From Puritanism to Nonconformity.* 2nd ed. Bridgend: Evangelical Press of Wales, 1991.

Manton, Thomas. *The Complete Works of Thomas Manton, D.D.* Reprint of the Edinburgh edition. 23 vols. Worthington, Pa.: Maranatha Publications, 1978.

McKim, Donald K. *Ramism in William Perkins' Theology.* American University Studies VII: Theology and Religion, vol. 15. New York: Peter Lang Publishing, 1987.

Morgan, Irvonwy. *The Godly Preachers of the Elizabethan Church.* London: Epworth Press, 1965.

————. *Prince Charles's Puritan Chaplain*. London: George Allen and Unwin, 1957.

Neal, Daniel. *History of the Puritans*. 2 vols. New York: Harper, 1848-49.

New, John F. H. *Anglican and Puritan: The Basis of Their Opposition, 1558-1640*. Stanford: Stanford University Press, 1964.

Pearson, A. F. Scott. *Thomas Cartwright and Elizabethan Puritanism, 1535-1603*. Cambridge: University Press, 1925.

Perkins, William. *The Art of Prophesying or a Treatise Concerning the Sacred and only Manner and Method of Preaching*. In William Perkins, *The Workes of the Famous and Worthy Minister of Christ . . . William Perkins*, 2:640-73. 3 vols. London: John Legate and Cantrell Legge, 1616-18.

————. *The Art of Prophesying*. Rev. ed. Edinburgh and Carlisle, Pa.: Banner of Truth Trust, 1996.

————. *A Commentary on Galatians*. Edited by Gerald T. Sheppard. Introductory essays by Brevard S. Childs, Gerald T. Sheppard, and John H. Augustine. New York: Pilgrim Press, ca. 1989.

————. *The Workes of the Famous and Worthy Minister of Christ . . . William Perkins*. 3 vols. London: John Legate and Cantrell Legge, 1616-18.

————. *The Works of William Perkins*. Introduction and edited by Ian Breward. Appleford, Abingdon, Berkshire: Sutton Courtenay Press, 1970.

Poe, Harry Lee. "Evangelistic Fervency among the Puritans in Stuart England (1603-1688)." Ph.D. diss., Southern Baptist Theological Seminary, 1982.

Preston, John. *The Doctrine of the Saints Infirmities*. London: Imprinted by I. Oakes for Taunton, 1638.

————. *Life Eternal; or, A Treatise of the Divine Essence and Attributes Delivered in 18 Sermons*. 2nd ed. London: Imprinted by R.E., 1631.

————. *Riches of Mercy to Men in Misery*. London: F. Eglesfield, 1658.

————. *The Saints Daily Exercise*. Photolithographic reproduction of the edition of London, 1629. Amsterdam and Norwood, N.J.: Walter J. Johnson, 1976.

————. *The Saints Qualifications*. 3rd ed. London: Printed by R.B. for N. Bourne, 1637.

Routley, Erik. *Thomas Goodwin (1600-1680)*. London: Independent Press, 1961.

Seaver, Paul S. *Puritan Lectureships: The Politics of Religious Dissent, 1560-1662*. Stanford: Stanford University Press, 1970.

Sibbes, Richard. *The Works of Richard Sibbes*. Edited by Alexander Grosart. Photolithographic reproduction of the edition of 1862-64. 7 vols. Edinburgh and Carlisle, Pa.: Banner of Truth Trust, 1979.

Song, Young Jae Timothy. *Theology and Piety in the Reformed Federal Thought of William Perkins and John Preston*. Lewiston, N.Y.: Edwin Mellen Press, 1999.

Sykes, Norman. *Old Priest and New Presbyter.* Cambridge: At the University Press, 1956.

Trinterud, Leonard J. *Elizabethan Puritanism.* New York: Oxford University Press, 1971.

Wallace, Dewey D., Jr. *The Spirituality of the Later English Puritanism.* Macon, Ga.: Mercer University Press, 1987.

Watkins, Owen C. *The Puritan Experience.* New York: Schocken Books, 1972.

Watson, Thomas. *The Beatitudes.* Edinburgh and Carlisle, Pa.: Banner of Truth Trust, 1975.

————. *A Body of Divinity Contained in Sermons upon the Westminster Assembly's Catechism by Thomas Watson.* Photolithographic reproduction. Edinburgh and Carlisle, Pa.: Banner of Truth Trust, 1974.

————. *A Body of Practical Divinity: Consisting of Sermons on the Lesser Catechism.* London: Printed for Thomas Parkhurst, 1692.

————. *The Sermons of Thomas Watson.* Ligonier, Pa.: Soli Deo Gloria Publications, 1990.

Bibliography for Chapter IV

Andrewes, Lancelot. *Ninety-six Sermons.* 5 vols. Oxford: J. H. Parker, 1841-45.

Avis, Paul. *Anglicanism and the Christian Church: Theological Resources in Historical Perspective.* Minneapolis: Fortress Press, 1989.

Bald, Robert Cecil. *John Donne: A Life.* New York: Oxford University Press, 1970.

Booty, John E. "Anglicanism." In *Oxford Encyclopedia of the Reformation,* 1:38-44. 4 vols. New York and Oxford: Oxford University Press, 1996.

Davies, Horton. *Like Angels from a Cloud: The English Metaphysical Preachers, 1588-1645.* San Marino, Calif.: Huntington Library, 1986.

————. *Worship and Theology in England.* 5 vols. Princeton: Princeton University Press, 1961-75.

Donne, John. *Donne's Prebend Sermons.* Edited by Janel M. Mueller. Cambridge: Harvard University Press, 1971.

————. *The Sermons of John Donne.* Edited by Evelyn M. Simpson and George R. Potter. 10 vols. Berkeley and Los Angeles: University of California Press, 1956-58.

Eliot, T. S. *For Lancelot Andrewes, Essays on Style and Order.* Garden City, N.Y.: Doubleday & Doran, 1929.

George, Charles H., and Katherine George. *The Protestant Mind of the English Reformation, 1570-1640.* Princeton: Princeton University Press, 1961.

Higham, Florence. *Lancelot Andrewes.* London: SCM Press, 1952.

Holmes, Urban T., III. *What Is Anglicanism?* Wilton, Conn.: Morehouse-Barlow, 1982.

Hughes, Henry Trevor. *The Piety of Jeremy Taylor.* London: Macmillan, 1960.

Hughes, Phillip. *The Reformation in England.* 2 vols. London: Hollis & Carter, 1952.

McAdoo, Henry Robert. *The Spirit of Anglicanism.* London: A. & C. Black, 1965.

Mitchell, William Fraser. *English Pulpit Oratory from Andrewes to Tillotson: A Study of Its Literary Aspects.* London: SPCK, 1932.

Moorman, John R. H. *A History of the Church of England.* 3rd ed. 1973. Reprint, London: A. & C. Black, 1980.

Mueller, William R. *John Donne: Preacher.* Princeton: Princeton University Press, 1962.

Neill, Stephen. *Anglicanism.* 3rd rev. ed. London: Mowbrays, 1977.

New, John F. H. *Anglican and Puritan.* Stanford: Stanford University Press, 1964.

Porter, H. C. *Reformation and Reaction in Tudor Cambridge.* Cambridge: At the University Press, 1958.

Procter, Francis, and W. H. Frere. *A History of the Book of Common Prayer.* London: Macmillan, 1949.

Schleiner, Winfried. *The Imagery of John Donne's Sermons.* Providence, R.I.: Brown University Press, 1970.

Simon, Irène. *Three Restoration Divines, Barrow, South, Tillotson.* 2 vols. Paris: Société d'Edition "Belles Lettres," 1967.

"South, Robert." In *Encyclopedia Britannica*, 25:463. 11th ed. 29 vols. New York: Encyclopedia Britannica, 1910-11.

South, Robert. *Sermons Preached upon Several Occasions.* 4 vols. Philadelphia: Sorin and Ball, 1844.

Spurr, John. *The Restoration Church of England, 1646-1689.* New Haven: Yale University Press, 1991.

Stranks, Charles James. *Life and Writings of Jeremy Taylor.* London: Published for the Church Historical Society by SPCK, 1952.

Sykes, Stephen W. *The Integrity of Anglicanism.* New York: Seabury Press, 1978.

"Taylor, Jeremy." In *Encyclopedia Britannica*, 26:469-71. 11th ed. 29 vols. New York: Encyclopedia Britannica, 1910-11.

Taylor, Jeremy. *The Rule and Exercises of Holy Living.* London: J. M. Dent, 1900.

———. *The Rule and Exercise of Holy Living.* Abridged with a preface by Anne Lamb. Foreword by Henry Chadwick. New York: Harper & Row, 1970.

———. *Works of Jeremy Taylor: With Some Account of His Life, Summary of Each Discourse, Notes, etc.* Edited by T. S. Hughes. 5 vols. London: A. J. Valpy, 1831.

"Tillotson, John." In *Encyclopedia Britannica*, 26:976. 11th ed. 29 vols. New York: Encyclopedia Britannica, 1910-11.

Tillotson, John. *Sermons.* 14 vols. London: Printed for R. Chiswell, 1700.

————. *The Works of the Most Reverend Dr. John Tillotson.* London: Printed for T. Goodwin, 1714.

————. *The Works of the Most Reverend Dr. John Tillotson.* 2 vols. London: Printed for Timothy Goodwin, 1717.

————. *The Works of the Most Reverend Dr. John Tillotson.* London: Printed for T. Goodwin, 1720.

————. *The Works of the Most Reverend Dr. John Tillotson.* 3 vols. London: Printed for J. and R. Tonson, 1752.

————. *The Works of the Most Reverend Dr. John Tillotson.* 10 vols. Edinburgh: Printed by Wal. Ruddiman & Co., 1772.

————. *The Works of Dr. John Tillotson, late Archbishop of Canterbury.* 10 vols. London: Printed by J. F. Dove for Richard Priestley, 1820.

Walton, Isaak. *Life of John Donne, Dr. in Divinity, and late Dean of Saint Pauls Church, London.* London: Printed by J.G. for R. Marriot, 1658.

Warren, Frederick Edward. "Prayer, Book of Common." In *Encyclopedia Britannica,* 22:258-62. 11th ed. 29 vols. New York: Encyclopedia Britannica, 1910-11.

Welsby, Paul A. *Lancelot Andrewes, 1555-1626.* London: SPCK, 1958.

Bibliography for Chapter V

Beck, Hermann. "Müller, Heinrich." In *Realencyklopädie für protestantische Theologie und Kirche,* edited by Johann Jakob Herzog, 13:521-23. 24 vols. Leipzig: J. C. Hinrichs, 1896-1913.

————. "Scriver, Christian." In *Realencyklopädie für protestantische Theologie und Kirche,* edited by Johann Jakob Herzog, 18:102-3. 24 vols. Leipzig: J. C. Hinrichs, 1896-1913.

Campenhausen, Hans von, et al., eds. *Die Religion in Geschichte und Gegenwart.* 3rd ed. 6 vols. Tübingen: J. C. B. Mohr (Paul Siebeck), 1957-62.

Cohrs, Ferdinand. "Herberger, Valerius." In *Realencyklopädie für protestantische Theologie und Kirche,* edited by Johann Jakob Herzog, 7:695-97. 24 vols. Leipzig: J. C. Hinrichs, 1896-1913.

Gerhard, Johann. *Sacrum homiliarum in pericopas evangeliorum dominicalium et praecipuorum totius anni festorum.* Jena: Blasi Lobensteini Bibliopolae, 1647.

Hägglund, Bengt. *Die heilige Schrift und ihre Deutung in der Theologie Johann Gerhards.* Lund: CWK Gleerup, 1951.

Herberger, Valerius. *Magnalia Dei de Jesu scripturae nucleo et medulla.* 12 vols. Leipzig: Thomas Shürer, 1600-1611.

————. *Magnalia Dei. Die grossen Thaten Gottes. 1-4 Theil: Das erste Buch Mose ausgelegt und erklärt.* New ed. Halle: Julius Fricke, 1854.

————. *Valerius Herberger. Ausgewählte Predigten. Mit einer einleitenden Monographie.* Edited by Dr. Orphal. Leipzig: Fr. Richter, 1892.

Herzog, Johann Jakob, ed. *Realencyklopädie für protestantische Theologie und Kirche.* 24 vols. Leipzig: J. C. Hinrichs, 1896-1913.

Hyperius, Andreas. *De formandis concionibus sacris: seu de interpretatione scripturarum populari.* Marburg: n.p., 1553.

————. *De formandis concionibus sacris, seu de interpretatione s. s. populari.* Edited by H. B. Wagnitz. Halle: Impensis orphanothrophei, 1781.

Kunze, Johannes. "Gerhard, Johann." In *Realencyklopädie für protestantische Theologie und Kirche,* edited by Johann Jakob Herzog, 6:554-61. 24 vols. Leipzig: J. C. Hinrichs, 1896-1913.

Müller, Heinrich. *Apostolische Schlusskette und Kraftkern: oder gründliche Auslegung der gewöhnlichen Sonn- und Fest-tags-Episteln.* Frankfurt am Main: Benjamin Andreä und Heinrich Hort, 1734.

————. *Ausgewählte Predigten.* Edited and introduction by Gustav Leonhardi. Leipzig: Friedrich Richter, 1891.

————. *Evangelischer Herzensspiegel: oder geistreiche Erklärung und Betrachtung der Sonn- und festtäglichen Evangelien, wie auch beigelegten Passionspredigten.* Lüneburg: Stern'schen Buchdrucherei, 1752.

Müller, Karl Ferdinand, and Walter Blankenburg, eds. *Leiturgia, Handbuch des evangelischen Gottesdienstes.* 5 vols. Kassel: Johannes Stauda Verlag, 1955.

Niebergall, Alfred. "Die Predigt in der Zeit der Orthodoxie." In *Leiturgia, Handbuch des evangelischen Gottesdienstes,* edited by Karl Ferdinand Müller and Walter Blankenburg, 2:288-93. 5 vols. Kassel: Johannes Stauda Verlag, 1955.

Schian, Martin. *Orthodoxie und Pietismus im Kampf um die Predigt.* Giessen: Töpelmann, 1912.

Schmidt, Martin. "Christian Scrivers 'Seelenschatz' als Beispiel vorpietistische Predigtweise." *Kirche in der Zeit* 17 (1962).

————. "Scriver, Christian." In *Die Religion in Geschichte und Gegenwart,* edited by Hans von Campenhausen et al., 5:1628. 3rd ed. 6 vols. Tübingen: J. C. B. Mohr (Paul Siebeck), 1957-62.

Schutze, Victor. "Nicolai, Philipp." In *Realencyklopädie für protestantische Theologie und Kirche,* edited by Johann Jakob Herzog, 14:28-32. 24 vols. Leipzig: J. C. Hinrichs, 1896-1913.

Scriver, Christian. *Chrysologia Catechetica oder Goldpredigten über die Hauptstücke des Luther'schen Katechismus.* New and revised ed. Stuttgart: J. S. Steinkopf'schen Buchhandlung, 1848.

Welzig, Werner. *Predigten der Barockzeit, Texte und Kommentar.* Vienna: Österreichischen Akademie der Wissenschaften, 1995.

Bibliography for Chapter VI

Armstrong, Brian G. *Pierre du Moulin (1568-1658)*. Geneva: Droz, 1997.

Chevalier, Françoise. *Prêcher sous l'Édit de Nantes, la prédication réformée au XVIIe siècle en France*. Geneva: Labor et Fides, 1994.

Claude, Jean. *Cinq sermons sur la parabole des noces*. Geneva: Samuel de Tournes, 1677.

Daillé, Jean. *Les deux derniers sermons de Mr. Daillé*. Geneva: Iean Ant. & Samuel de Tournes, 1671.

————. *Explication du chapitre troisième de l'evangile selon saint Jean*. Geneva: J. Ant. et S. de Tornes, 1686.

————. *Sermons de la naissance, de la mort, resurrection, et ascension de nôtre Seigneur, et de la descente du saint Esprit sur les Apôtres*. Charenton: Samuel Perier, 1651.

————. *Sermons sur le catechisme des églises réformées*. 3 vols. Geneva: La Société des libraires, 1701.

Daillé, Jean (Son). *Abrégé de la vie de Mr. Daillé*. Which appeared with Jean Daillé (Father), *Les deux derniers sermons de Mr. Daillé*. Geneva: Iean Ant. & Samuel de Tournes, 1671.

Du Moulin, Pierre. *Bouclier de la foy, ou défense de la confession de la foi des églises réformées de France contre les objections du Sr. Jehan Arnoux*. Charenton, 1618.

————. *Première à dixième décade*. 10 vols. Geneva, 1641-54.

————. *Préparation à la Sainte Cène*. In Pierre du Moulin, *Saintes prières plus divers traittez*. Geneva: Chouët, 1622.

————. *Prière et méditation de l'âme fidèle, sur l'affliction présente de l'Église ensemble les prières du matin et du soir*. In Pierre du Moulin, *Saintes prières plus divers traittez*. Geneva: Chouët, 1622.

————. *Saintes prières plus divers traittez*. Geneva: Chouët, 1622.

————. *Sermons sur quelques texts de l'ecriture Sancte*. Geneva: P. Aubert, 1636.

Gray, Janet Glenn. *The French Huguenots: Anatomy of Courage*. Grand Rapids: Baker Book House, 1981.

Haag, Eugène. *La France protestante*. 9 vols. Geneva: J. Cherbuliez, 1846-59.

Haag, Eugène, and Émile Haag. *La France protestante*. 6 vols. Paris: Sandoz et Fischbacher, 1877-88.

Le Faucheur, Michel. *Sermons sur les onze premiers chapitres des Actes des Apostres*. Geneva: Pour Pierre Chouët, 1663.

Leonard, Émile G. *Histoire générale du protestantisme*. 3 vols. Paris: Presses universitaires de France, 1961-64.

Mestrezat, Jean. Catechetical sermons. (Seven of the sermons in Daillé's *Sermons sur le catechisme des églises réformées* are by Mestrezat.)

————. *La communion à Jesus Christ au sacrament de l'Eucharistie*. Sedan, 1624.

————. *De la sacrificature de Jésus-Christ notre Seigneur ou sermons sur les chapitres VII, VIII, IX, et partie de X de l'épistre aux Hébreux.* Geneva: Samuel Chouët, 1653.

————. *Des fruits de la foy en vertus chrestiennes, ou sermons sur les chapitres XII et XIII de l'épitre aux Hébreux.* Geneva: Samuel Chouët, 1653.

————. *Exposition de la premiere epistre de l'apostre S. Jean.* Geneva: P. Chouët, 1651.

————. *Expositions de la premiere epistre de l'Apostle S. Iean en sermons.* 2 vols. Geneva: Pierre Chouët, 1651.

————. *Sermons sur le chapitre huitième de l'épitre de Saint Paul aux Romains.* Amsterdam: François Changuions, 1726.

————. *Sermons sur l'Epistre aux Hebreux.* Geneva: S. Chouët, 1653-55.

————. *Sermons sur les chapitres troisieme, quatriesme, cinquiesme, et sixieme de l'épistre aux Hébreux.* Geneva: Samuel Chouët, 1653.

————. *Trois sermons faits pour le jeusne à Charenton le 19 Novembre 1637.* Charenton: [N. Bourdin and L. Perier?], 1638.

————. *Trois sermons sur la venue et la Naissance de Jésus-Christ au mond* [treating Ephesians 2:5-10]. Geneva: n.p., 1654. These sermons were first published in Charenton in 1638.

————. *Vingt sermons sur divers textes de l'Écriture sainte.* Geneva: n.p., 1658.

Pannier, Jacques. *L'Église réformée de Paris sous Henri IV.* Paris: H. Champion, 1911.

Rimbault, Lucien. *Pierre du Moulin, 1568-1658, un pasteur classique à l'âge classique.* Paris: J. Vrin, 1966.

Rothrock, George A. *The Huguenots: A Biography of a Minority.* Chicago: Nelson-Hall, 1979.

Schmidt, C. "Mestrezat, Johann." In *Realencyklopädie für protestantische Theologie und Kirche,* edited by Johann Jakob Herzog, 12:739. 24 vols. Leipzig: J. C. Hinrichs, 1896-1913.

Vinet, Alexandre. *Histoire de la prédication parmi les réformés de France au dix-septième siècle.* Paris: Chez les éditeurs, rue de Rivoli, 1860.

Bibliography for Chapter VII (the bibliography for this chapter owes much to the research of Dr. Iain Stewart Maclean)

Been, G. D. van. "Voetius, Gisbertus." In *Realencyklopädie für protestantische Theologie und Kirche,* edited by Johann Jakob Herzog, 20:717-25. 24 vols. Leipzig: J. C. Hinrichs, 1896-1913.

Boot, Izaak. *De allegorische Uitlegging van het Hooglied, voornamelijk in Nederland.* Woerden: Zuiderduijn, 1971.

Brienen, T. *De Predeking van de Nadere Reformatie. Een Onderzoek naar het gebruik van de klassifikatiemethode binnen de predeking van de Nadere Reformatie.* Amsterdam: Uitgeverij Ton Bolland, 1974.

Brienen, T., K. Exalto, et al. *De Nadere Reformatie. Beschrijving van haar voornaamste vertegenwoordigers.* The Hague: Uitgeverij Boekencentrum B.V., 1986.

————. *Theologische Aspecten van de Nadere Reformatie.* Zoetermeer: Uitgewerij Boekencentrum, 1993.

Cocceius, Johannes. *Omnia opera.* 7 vols. Frankfurt am Main: Balthasar Christopher Wustius, 1702.

————. *Opera omnia.* 12 vols. Amsterdam: [P. & J. Blaev], 1706.

Duker, Arnoldus Cornelius. *Gisbertus Voetius.* Leiden: J. J. Groen en Zoon, 1989.

Engelberts, W. J. M. *Willem Teellinck.* Amsterdam, 1898.

Goebel, M., and S. D. van Been. "Lodenstein, Jodocus van." In *Realencyklopädie für protestantische Theologie und Kirche,* edited by Johann Jakob Herzog, 11:572-74. 24 vols. Leipzig: J. C. Hinrichs, 1896-1913.

Hartog, Jan. *Geschiedenis van de Predikkunde in de Protestantsche Kerk van Nederland.* Utrecht: Kemink & Zoon, 1887.

Heppe, Heinrich. *Geschichte des Pietismus und der Mystik in der reformirten Kirche, namentlich der Niederlande.* Leiden: E. J. Brill, 1879.

Herzog, Johann Jakob, ed. *Realencyklopädie für protestantische Theologie und Kirche.* 24 vols. Leipzig: J. C. Hinrichs, 1896-1913.

Lodenstein, Jodocus van. *Geestelyke Opweker voor het Onverloochende, Doode en Geestelose Christendom.* Amsterdam: Andr. Douci, 1732.

Maclean, Iain S. "The First Pietist: An Introduction and Translation of a Communion Sermon by Jodocus van Lodenstein." In *Calvin Studies VI,* edited by John Leith, pp. 15-34. Davidson, N.C.: Calvin Colloquium, 1992.

Moltmann, Jürgen. "Voetius, Gisbert." In *Die Religion in Geschichte und Gegenwart,* edited by Hans von Campenhausen et al., 6:1432-33. 3rd ed. 6 vols. Tübingen: J. C. B. Mohr (Paul Siebeck), 1957-62.

Müller, E. F. Karl. "Cocceius und seine Schule." In *Realencyklopädie für protestantische Theologie und Kirche,* edited by Johann Jakob Herzog, 4:186-94. 24 vols. Leipzig: J. C. Hinrichs, 1896-1913.

Proost, J. "Jodocus van Lodensteyn." In *Academic Proefschrift.* Amsterdam, 1880.

Ritschl, Albrecht. *Geschichte des Pietismus.* 3 vols. Reprint, Berlin: de Gruyter, 1966.

————. *Geschichte des Pietismus in der reformirten Kirche.* Bonn: A. Marcus, 1880.

Runia, Klaas. *Het hoge Woord en de Lage Landen: hoe er door de Eeuwen heen in Nederland gepreekt is.* Kampen: J. H. Kok, 1985.

Schrenk, Gottlob. *Gottesreich und Bund im älteren Protestantismus, vornehmlich bei Johannes Coccejus.* Giessen: Brunnen-Verlag, 1985.

Stoeffler, F. Ernest. *The Rise of Evangelical Pietism.* Leiden: E. J. Brill, 1965.

Teellinck, Willem. *Het Geestelyk Cierat van Christi Brutlofts-Kinderen, ofte de Oractijke des Heylighen Avondtmaels Daer inne.* Middelburg, 1620.

————. *Het Geestelyk Cierat van Christi Brutlofts-Kinderen, ofte de Oractijke des Heylighen Avondtmaels Daer inne.* 20th ed. Franeker: T. Wever, 1969.

Voetius, Gisbertus. *Afscheydt Predicatie uyt Philipp I vers 27. Ghedaen in de Ghemeynte tot Heusden, den 20 Augusti 1634.* Utrecht: Aegidius ende Petrus Roman, 1636.

————. *Eerste Predikatie in de Dom-Kercke tot Utrecht te negen uren den 16 Novembris 1673 Gedaen door Gisbertius Voetius na dat de Fransche macht de stadt, ende die van het Pausdom de dom-Kercke op den 13 November voor den Middagh verlaten hadden.* Utrecht, 1674.

————. *Inaugurele rede over Godzaligheid te verbinden met de wetenschap.* Edited by A. de Groot. Kampen, 1978.

————. *Meditatie van de Ware Practijcke der Godtsalicheydt of der goeder Wercken. . . .* Amsterdam: Cornelis Hendricksz., 1628.

————. *Sermoen van de Nutticheydt der Academien.* Utrecht, 1636.

Vrijer, Marinus Johannes Antoinie de. *Lodenstein (Uren met Lodenstein).* Baarn, 1947.

Bibliography for Chapter VIII

Bedoyere, Michael de la. *The Archbishop and the Lady.* London: Collins, 1956.

Bossuet, Jacques. *Oeuvres oratoires de Bossuet.* Edited by J. Lebarq. 7 vols. Paris and Lille: Desclée de Brouwer et Cie, 1890-97.

————. *La Prédication au XVIIe Siècle.* Actes du Colloque tenu à Dijon les 2, 3 et 4 décembre 1977 pour la trois cinquantième anniversaire de la naissance de Bossuet. Paris: Librairie A.-G. Nizet, 1980.

————. *Trois sermons du carême des minimes.* Ouvrage publié avec le concours du Centre National de la Recherche Scientifique. Nancy, 1965.

Bourdaloue, Louis. *Oeuvres complètes de Bourdaloue, de la compagnie de Jésus.* 16 vols. Versailles: J. A. Lebel, 1812.

Calvet, Jean. *Bossuet: L'Homme et l'oeuvre.* Paris, 1939.

Carcassonne, Ely. *Fénelon, l'homme et l'oeuvre.* Paris: Boivin, 1946.

Chérot, H. "Bourdaloue." In *Dictionnaire de théologie catholique,* 2/1:1095-99. 18 vols. Paris: Letouzey & Ane, 1903-50.

————. *Bourdaloue inconnu.* Paris, 1898.

Davis, James Herbert, Jr. *Fénelon.* Boston: Twayne Publishers, 1979.

Fant, Clyde F. *Twenty Centuries of Great Preaching.* 13 vols. Waco, Tex.: Word Books, 1971.

Fénelon, François. *Dialogues on Eloquence.* Translated with introduction and notes by Wilbur Samuel Howell. Princeton: Princeton University Press, 1951. (A must!)

―――. *Oeuvres de Fénelon, Archevêque de Cambrai.* 3 vols. Paris: Firmin Didot Frères, 1838.

Haillant, Marguerite. *Fénelon et la prédication.* Paris: Éditions Klincksieck, 1969.

Hillenaar, Henk. *Fénelon et les Jésuits.* The Hague: Martinus Nijhoff, 1967.

Largent, Augustin. "Bossuet." In *Dictionnaire de théologie catholique,* 2:1049-89. 18 vols. Paris: Letouzey & Ane, 1903-50.

Massillon, Jean-Baptiste. *Oeuvres Choisies de Massillon.* 6 vols. Paris: Delestre-Boulage, 1823-25.

Meager, Richard Byrne. "Bourdaloue, Louis." In *New Catholic Encyclopedia,* 2:732-33. 17 vols. Washington, D.C.: Catholic University of America Press, 1967.

Pauthe, A. A. L. *Bourdaloue, d'après des documents nouveaux.* Paris, 1900.

Reynolds, E. E. *Bossuet.* Garden City, N.J.: Doubleday, 1963.

Sanders, Ella Katharine. *Jacques Bénigne Bossuet: A Study.* London: SPCK; New York: Macmillan, 1921.

Simpson, William John Sparrow. *A Study of Bossuet.* London: SPCK, 1937.

Truchet, Jacques. *La prédication de Bossuet.* Vols. 1 and 3. Paris: Éditions du Cerf, 1960.

Washington, Sylvia Juanita. "Massillon, Jean Baptiste." In *New Catholic Encyclopedia,* 9:435-36. 17 vols. Washington, D.C.: Catholic University of America Press, 1967.

Index